Understanding Organizational Behavior

Second Edition

Stuart M. Klein
Cleveland State University

R. Richard Ritti
Pennsylvania State University

Kent Publishing Company
A Division of Wadsworth, Inc.
Boston, Massachusetts

Senior Editor: John B. McHugh
Production Editor: Michael Paladini
Interior Designer: DeNee Reiton Skipper
Cover Designer: Glenna Lang
Production Coordinator: Linda Siegrist

Kent Publishing Company

A Division of Wadsworth, Inc.

© 1984 by Wadsworth, Inc., 10 Davis Drive, Belmont, California 94002. All rights reserved. No part of this book may be reproduced, stored in a retrieval system, or transcribed, in any form or by any means, electronic, mechanical, photocopying, recording, or otherwise, without the prior written permission of the publisher, Kent Publishing Company, 20 Park Plaza, Boston, Massachusetts 02116.

Printed in the United States of America

1 2 3 4 5 6 7 8 9 — 88 87 86 85 84

Library of Congress Cataloging in Publication Data

Klein, Stuart M., 1932–
    Understanding organizational behavior.

    Includes bibliographical references and index.
    1. Organizational behavior. I. Ritti, R. Richard.
II. Title.
HD58.7.K56 1984   658.4   83-18715
ISBN 0–534–03119–6

Preface

This text differs in some significant ways from others we have seen. That is primarily the case, we suppose, because we undertook the writing with a point of view shaped by our own considerable experience as professionals and managers in several large corporations.

We do not pretend that this gives us special license to proclaim what works and what does not, but we do believe that this experience has developed in us an appreciation of the complex, the "political," internal workings of human organizations. We think we have a pretty good understanding of the kinds of problems you will be facing in your first few positions as professionals and managers in such organizations. This perspective has shaped our approach in several ways. Let us take a minute or two to outline just how.

Who Is This Text For?

We envision the reader as someone who will go first to a professional and then to a managerial career in a corporate organization. This is someone who is first a participant in the ongoing process of organizing, either an undergraduate or an MBA. It is someone who looks to courses in organizational behavior to help him or her understand the process and structure of human organization from the point of view of the *participant*. This approach rests on our observation that most managers start their careers in professional or staff positions, and only later, after they have developed a better understanding of organizations, gain management responsibility. Therefore, we will first address the task of understanding. We have not stressed "how to do it" for the practicing manager, although it is clear to us that a task of major importance to the practicing manager is just that — understanding organizational behavior.

Presentation of Material

Our presentation of the material is influenced by our experience in several ways. Since we assume our readers will shortly become participants in the process of organizing and are not going to be organizational researchers, we stress the organizational consequences or principles derived from research studies rather than the studies themselves. A comprehensive list of references follows each chapter and provides a guide to these studies and their authors. We understand that not everyone will agree with this approach, but it is the best way we know to prepare future professionals and managers for participation in the real world of organizations.

A Systems Approach

We continually emphasize the linkages among different aspects of organizational process and function. To convey this idea better, we present the different functional aspects of human organization within a framework of systems building blocks: a *systems structure* of formal relationships of authority and compliance, of roles and norms, of mutual networks of behavioral expectations, and of communications; a *motivation system* of personal goals and contingencies of reinforcement; a *mobility system* of the structure of opportunity for success and failure; an *interaction system* of group process and leadership; and finally, a system of *information feedback and control,* of organizational goals, of the behavioral consequences of the measurement process, of the consequences of the depersonalization of control systems, and of intergroup conflict.

Several fundamental assumptions are embodied in this strategy. First, changes taking place in one system are likely to affect other systems. Because systems are constrained, the outcomes of these changes are, to some extent, predictable. Second, each formally described system or systems structure has both consequences that are intended and those that are *emergent* — that is, neither intended nor necessarily unintended, but simply emerging from social processes. Third, organizational behavior is shaped in part as a series of in-process responses to organizational constraints. Some of these constraints are created by the organization itself: the formal task structure, the feedback and control system, and material incentives. Other constraints derive from the informal network of relationships, or from individuals seeking rewards of status and esteem contingent on "proper behavior." We believe that organizational behavior, to a large extent, is the study of behavior shaped by constraints.

Fourth, there is a dilemma in gaining compliance from participants while still allowing sufficient incentive for them to exercise discretion. If compliance is required for organizational purposes, so too is latitude of action. One provides predictability and control; the other adaptability to new conditions. The inevitable tension between these two requirements may well be largely responsible for the development of the field of organizational behavior. If people were only obedient puppets, behaving according to organizational rules and requirements, there would be little to explain beyond the rationalist prescriptions provided by classical management theories. We could design an organization according to the organizational purposes desired and achieve these outcomes directly. Since this rarely happens, we have directed much of our attention to understanding how people respond to organizational structures and policies that are intended to produce one kind of consequence, but that result both in intended *and* emergent consequences. The field of organizational behavior, then, accounts for intended behavior stemming from formal system requirements, and also informs us of the likely consequences of emergent behavior.

To be complete, this systems framework requires several topics not included in the usual text. For example, the systems context requires that we understand how information becomes distorted in measurement and feedback to the motivation system, how group process and subunit goal formation also affect the motivation system, and how these processes may affect structures of authority and compliance.

Our Cases, Slices of Corporate Life

With this in mind, we have tried to make these principles live, to help people with perhaps little experience in corporate organizations to feel what corporate life might be like. We have done this primarily through vignettes or cases that illustrate incidents that occurred in real organizations, and that illustrate key points in our understanding of organizational behavior. These incidents have been fictionalized and involve a group of characters who reappear throughout the text. The vignettes will be especially useful in helping you get the flavor of organizational life.

As you read through these stories you will note that the actors continually struggle to respond appropriately to the forces they encounter in organizations and to shape these forces to their own purposes. It is usually Stanley who tries to understand, whereas the others — because of their greater experience and understanding — do their best to manage the situation. In each vignette several things happen simultaneously, although each vignette emphasizes specific points. Also, none has a particular beginning or end; each is only a slice from an ongoing process.

We feel our approach is entirely realistic, for this is the way organizations are. For example, the case introducing our section on groups deals with the causes and consequences of group cohesion, yet it might just as well serve as a case in leadership. It is Kerry's (the leader's) behavior and his relationship to the group that "causes" the group cohesion that results in the feeling of elitism and the exceptionally high performance. Because each vignette illustrates several attributes of behavior, you should keep them all in mind throughout.

How This Edition Differs from the First One

Reorganization

We have reorganized the text according to the preference of many of our users. The motivation chapters have been moved up and can now be found in Part III. Many people felt that we placed too much early emphasis on the macro aspects of organizational behavior, and that an earlier treatment of motivation would remedy that problem. Group processes come next as we build toward additional constraints on individual behavior. However, the chapter on conflict is placed just before the last part, which concerns organizational change. It seemed logical that conflict should be moved in this way since so much of the literature on change and organizational development deals with conflict management. Finally, we combined the two chapters from the first edition, "Changing Motivation Systems" and "Changing Control Systems," into one chapter and moved most of the material on job enrichment to the section on motivation. A new section "Careers: The Mobility System" has also been added.

Chapter Changes

We have attempted, through rewriting, to make the chapters on organizations as social systems, organizational goals, and measurement and control, less difficult for students. The chapters "Technology and Environment: Constraints as Organizational Form," and "Intergroup Relations: Conflict and Cooperation," have been overhauled to reflect more current theories. "Motivation in Organizations: The Process of Directed Behavior" has been expanded to include a heavier emphasis on the cognitive elements of motivation. The chapter on "The Structure of Opportunity" has been substantially revised. All chapters have been updated.

New Chapters

Three new chapters have been added: "The Research Foundations of Organizational Change," "Communications in Organizations," and "Maintaining Motivation: The Consequences of Blocked Opportunity." Each was considered necessary by more than one user, and each generally follows the themes and orientations of the book.

Acknowledgements

We are grateful to many people. Some serve as models — either completely or partially — for the characters in our vignettes. Others have made more specific contributions. We would especially like to thank Bill Whyte for his inspiration to us as graduate students. Bill's emphasis on understanding what was actually going on in a situation, on looking "under the skin" of organizational behavior, has shaped our approach to this day.

Colleagues who have carefully reviewed chapters and who offered constructive criticisms include Harry Martin, Jan Muczyk, Joe Miller, Yoash Wiener, John Solcum, and Randy Schuler. To Alyce Ritti we express our appreciation for much of the research and writing of Chapter 7.

Of those who reviewed the manuscript, we would particularly like to thank the following, who gave a great deal of their time and attention to the book: Harold Carrier of the State University of New York at Albany; Walter W. Smock of Rutgers; Malcolm Walker of San José State University; Allen J. Schuh of California State University at Hayward; Leslie J. Berkes of Ohio State University; Francine S. Hall of Northwestern University; and Craig Lundberg of the University of Southern California.

In addition, we are grateful to the following for many helpful comments and suggestions: Carl R. Anderson of the University of North Carolina; Mark Hammer of Washington State University; Robert T. Keller of the University of Houston; Stephen R. Michael of the University of Massachusetts; Leonard Sayles of Columbia University; George Strauss of the University of California at Berkeley; Robert Swinth of the University of Kansas; Kenneth Wheeler of California State University at Fresno; and Stanley Young of the University of Massachusetts. Others who have provided substantial insights (usually unknowingly) include Dick Dunnington, Fred Goldner, Dave Sirota, Allen Kraut, Bill Alper, Andy Grimes, Jim Gibson, and John Douglas. At one time or another each has been a colleague, and each has helped shape our thinking. Graduate student Amy Fried also made contributions. And Cathy Thomas's patience with a seemingly endless flow of illegible script proves that the work ethic still lives.

Foreword

A key feature of this text is the stories that appear here and there in each chapter. Some of you have not had much experience in real corporate organizations, so we've included these vignettes, these slices of corporate life, to help you get a better feel for how people act and how things are done.

There is no real continuity to the stories, no plot as such. The events are based on real incidents and real people from a number of different organizations. However, we have constructed a set cast of characters, each of whom represents a major character type in organizations, for the vignettes. They are composites of real people we have known. Most of the events occur in *The Company*, a fictional representative of the type of large, complex organization in which most of you will have some experience sooner or later.

Our hero (if that is an appropriate term for him) is *Stanley*. In the personnel nomenclature of The Company, Stanley is a "professional employee." That means he has a college degree, that he works mostly with paper, and that he can hope someday to become part of management. Stanley is Everyman, both the sinew and the fat of The Company, destined to neither meteoric success nor abysmal failure. Most of you already have some inkling of who he is — and you will get to know him better shortly. Much of what you see of The Company will be seen through Stanley's eyes. You also will see something of the rest of the organizational world from his personal experiences in the military and from his relationship to *Dr. Faust*, professor at The University and consultant to The Company.

Stanley was one of Dr. Faust's favored students at The University (although it is not quite clear why) and he uses Stanley occasionally in his consulting work with The Company. As for Faust himself, words such as *respected, clever, stuffy, pedantic,* and *well-to-do,* all describe aspects of his image, though they miss the essence of his person. For again, that can be conveyed only through our stories. Yet one thing is certain, though his field of endeavor is industrial administration, Dr. Faust understands organizational behavior well.

The same can be said of *Ben Franklyn,* though in a different way. As Dr. Faust likes to put it, Ben knows more about running a mill than he understands. Which is not so unfathomable. At the age of 16, Ben Franklyn went to work for The Company in their first expandrium rolling mill. Now, 40 years later, Ben has been a mill superintendent and a plant manager. He hasn't changed much, though. Honest to the core, intractable, "sympathetic to the men," intensely loyal to The Company and the "Old Man" (Marsh, Sr.), Ben believes that someone who has not come up through the working ranks cannot possibly understand how to run a company.

And this, of course, applies doubly to *Edward Wilson Shelby IV.* Ted Shelby knows that all the enemies of corporate enlightenment are incarnate in Ben Franklyn. Ted cannot understand how anyone without a MBA could have the necessary grasp of modern management tools so essential for success in the "highly competitive business environment of today." Just as Ben Franklyn is our prototypical manufacturing man, Ted Shelby is our exemplar staff person. Ted has made his career by moving up through the ranks of the staff "assistants to" (although some suspect that being the son of Edward W. Shelby III, The Company's first chief engineer, may have had something to do with it).

Kerry Drake, like Ben Franklyn, is part of The Company's middle management. Kerry has the appropriate university degrees, yet in many ways he and Ben are much alike. Neither tolerates nonsense from staff "smart alecks," and both use rather expressive language. Kerry has been down and up in The Company, usually in the management of professional functions in engineering and the like. Kerry — again like Ben — is intensely loyal to The Company and likes to appear the tough manager. When things go wrong in the ranks he likes to comment, "I don't have time to separate the unfortunate from the incompetent." Yet, in fact, he takes great pains to do so.

Rounding out the list of our major characters is *Pat Jones,* Ph.D., Psychology, The University. Pat came with The Company a number of years ago when it was smaller and less diversified. She was the first "doctor" The Company hired in the personnel function. Her early responsibilities were to develop effective personnel testing and selection programs within The Company, and because of this function she came to know many of the younger management people very well. As a result, Pat now has many good friends and confidantes in the middle and upper management ranks of The Company. Consequently, her job has gone beyond the nuts and bolts of applied psychology, and she is now a consultant to The Company management. She can't imagine a more interesting or exciting career, and because of her no-nonsense, honest competence, her advice is widely sought. In fact, some don't understand why she has never moved her career beyond the confines of The Company.

From time to time we also employ some special characters or characters that are primarily symbolic. One of these is *Penny Scribner,* from corporate communications, who, in some ways, is Stanley's counterpart. But unlike Stanley, Penny well understands what is going on in the organization about her, amazingly so for someone with relatively little experience. Perhaps this is because she is a "company brat" — that is, she is the daughter of a widely travelled executive in Another Company. However, like Stanley, Penny is not particularly happy in her job, but neither is she unhappy — it doesn't seem to be the way she wants to spend her life, but there is no clear alternative.

From time to time you will see a reference to *M. M. Marsh* or Mr. Marsh, president and chairman of the board of The Company. Mr. Marsh is one of those people everyone in The Company *knows of,* but whom nobody *knows.* He is always referred to by Ted as *Mr.* Marsh, and by Kerry, somewhat irreverently, as Marsh. Maybe his wife knows him by his first name — but only maybe.

Claude Gilliam is black. Ted Shelby thinks of Claude as an "equal opportunity employee." And this means to Ted that Claude was recruited, regardless of his qualifications, because he is black. This is an odd thing for Ted to believe, for Ted usually takes the time and trouble to know exactly what The Company is doing and why. Had he taken the trouble or had the interest, he would have known that The Company took great pains to ensure that all its professional employees were potential management material. However, it is readily apparent that Claude is not from a middle class background. Claude struggled his way to a high-quality technical degree from The University, working part-time and on an educational opportunity scholarship. Perhaps it would be best just to say that to Ted, Claude seems very different.

Finally, we have our "lower organizational participants." *Jimmy Szekely* is our exemplary "worker." He operates The Company's machines, or works in the mailroom or in any of dozens of places The Company's engineers felt it either too expensive or not otherwise practical to replace a man with a machine. Jimmy doesn't have much formal education and he knows that the job he has is as good as he will ever have. But you don't want to make the mistake of thinking that Jimmy doesn't have a practical understanding of his immediate mechanical surroundings that doesn't rival that of the engineers. As Jimmy once put it to Stanley in a flash of insight, "For a long time I confused ignorance with stupidity."

So there you are, our people in The Company. From time to time we shuffle characters around in different jobs and different contexts. This is unavoidable if we are to keep the list of characters at a minimum. So at one time Stanley will appear in a technical function, then in personnel, in Company headquarters, and then in the mill. But his essential role remains the same. So do those of others. They all illustrate a *role* in The Company and its affairs, rather than play true individuals pursuing careers. In spite of this, however, we have done our best to endow each with a personality and an identity.

Brief Contents

PART I PERSPECTIVE 1

Chapter 1 Introduction: Perspectives on the Understanding of Organizational Behavior 3

Chapter 2 Organizations As Social Systems 22

PART II THE BASIS FOR ORGANIZATIONAL ACTION 45

Section 1 The Formal Organization — Systems Structure (I) 47

Chapter 3 The Social Structure of Organizations 50

Chapter 4 The Bases for Compliance: Authority, Power, and Persuasion 69

Chapter 5 Technology and Environment: Constraints on Organizational Form 96

Section 2 Patterns of Social Behavior — Systems Structure (II) 123

Chapter 6 Socialization: The Assumption of Roles 126

Chapter 7 Impression Management in Organizational Life 156

Chapter 8 Communications in Organizations 179

PART III THE PROCESS OF GOAL ATTAINMENT 205

Section 1   Meeting Personal Goals: The Motivation System   207

Chapter 9   Motivation in Organizations: The Process of Directed Behavior   208

Chapter 10 Motivation: Need Theories, Incentives, and Reinforcements   247

Section 2   Careers: The Mobility System   287

Chapter 11 The Structure of Opportunity   289

Chapter 12 Maintaining Motivation: The Consequences of Blocked Opportunity   323

Section 3   Modifying Personal Goals: The Interaction System   359

Chapter 13 Groups and Their Dynamics   362

Chapter 14 Leadership   396

PART IV ACHIEVING MANAGEMENT GOALS: ORGANIZATIONS IN ACTION   437

Introduction   Achieving Management Goals — The Feedback and Control System   439

Chapter 15 What Is an Organizational Goal?   446

Chapter 16 Measuring Performance: Consequences of the Process   476

Chapter 17 Systems for Feedback and Control: The Depersonalization of Management   503

Chapter 18 Intergroup Relations: Conflict and Cooperation   534

PART V PROCESSES FOR ORGANIZATIONAL IMPROVEMENT   559

Chapter 19 Understanding Organizational Change   563

Chapter 20 The Research Foundations of Organizational Change   588

Chapter 21 Changing Interaction Patterns for Organizational Improvement   610

Chapter 22 Changing Motivation and Control Systems   640

Contents

PART I PERSPECTIVE 1

Chapter 1 Introduction: Perspectives on the Understanding of Organizational Behavior 3

Case: Do Unto Others 3
Rationality in Human Behavior: A First Perspective 5
  Reinforcement Theory 5
  Complexity in Human Behavior 6
  Utility 7
  Emotionality 7
Collective Versus Individual Behavior: A Second Perspective 8
The Effect of Social Structure: A Third Perspective 11
Focus on Problems and Process: The Final Perspective 12
A Brief History of the Study of Organizational Behavior 13
  Work, Fatigue, and Effort: Individual Productivity as the Problem 14
  The Industrial Work Group: Social Relations as the Problem 15
  The Systems Approach: Our Contemporary Era 17
Summary 19
Notes 19
References 20
Discussion Questions 21

Chapter 2 **Organizations As Social Systems** 22

Case: Unfortunate or Incompetent? 22
Organizational Actions and Organizational Outcomes: A Systems Perspective 24
   The Hawthorne Lighting Experiments 24
   Improving Industrial Relations Through Training 25
   Understanding Process 26
   Classical Management Theory 27
Some Systems Concepts Applied to Organizations 28
   Organizations Are Interrelated 29
   Organizational Systems Are Open to the Environment 30
   Organizational Systems Are Purposeful 30
   Organizational Systems Are Adaptive 30
   Organizational Systems Are Constrained 31
   Organizational Systems Need Feedback 31
The Organizational System 32
   The Formal Organization — Systems Structure (I) 32
   Patterns of Social Behavior — Systems Structure (II) 34
   The Motivation System 35
   The Mobility System 36
   The Interaction System 38
   The Feedback and Control System 39
   Processes for Organizational Improvement 41
Summary 41
Notes 42
References 43
Discussion Questions 43

PART II   THE BASIS FOR ORGANIZATIONAL ACTION 45

Section 1   The Formal Organization — Systems Structure (I) 47

Chapter 3   **The Social Structure of Organizations** 50

Case: Welcome Aboard 50
Specialization and the Division of Labor 53
The Organization Chart 53
   The Company 54
   The Church 57
   The Department of Public Welfare 58
   Position and Status 58
   Box 1: Power, Status, and Organizational Function 60

Expected Behavior as Social Structure   61
   Position and Role   62
   Norms and Rules   64

Summary   65
Notes   67
References   67
Discussion Questions   68

Chapter 4   The Bases for Compliance: Authority, Power, and Persuasion   69

Case: Peeping Tom   69
Compliance and the Problem of Coordination   72
Power   74
Authority as Justified Power   75
   Bureaucracy: The Legal Justification   76
   The Traditional Justification   77
   The Charismatic Justification   78
   Power and Authority — One More Time   78
   Box 2: The Bases of Social Power   79
   The Zone of Indifference   80
   Authoritylike Relationships   82

Human Behavior and the Formal Organization   83
   The Real Versus the Ideal   83
   Box 3: Promotion Criteria in Public Bureaucracies   85
   Lateral and Diagonal Relationships   87
   Bureaupathology   89

Summary   90
Notes   92
References   93
Discussion Questions   94

Chapter 5   Technology and Environment: Constraints on Organizational Form   96

Case: The Long and Short of It   96
Work Technology, Organizational Structure, and Organizational Behavior   99
   What Do We Mean by Technology?   100
   Technology and Structure   101
   Technology as a Leading Factor   102

Characterizing Core Technology   103
   Box 4: Technology, Structure, and Success   104
   Complexity   107
   Interdependence   108

Routineness 108
Predictability 109

Organizational Environment, Organizational Structure, and Organizational Behavior 111
Characterizing Environments 112
Adapting to Environmental Uncertainty 112
Adaptation in Organizational Process 113
Box 5: Organizational Adaptation to Institutional Environments 114
Perception and the Social Construction of Environments 116

Summary 117
Notes 118
References 119
Discussion Questions 121

Section 2 Patterns of Social Behavior — Systems Structure (II) 123

Chapter 6 Socialization: The Assumption of Roles 126

Case: You're in the Army Now 126

Socialization: An Overview of the Process 127
Career Stages in the Socialization Process 128
Characteristics Affecting Recruitment and Socialization 131

Welcome Aboard! — Patterns of Recruitment 133
When Does Recruiting Begin? 133
Recruiting Traps: Systems Consequences of Selection 135
Environment and Organizational Adaptation 137
The Giants of Wall Street 138

Socialization: The Way We Do It Here 140
Socialization into the First Position 140
Box 6: Socialization as Surprise and Sense Making 143
Key Characteristics of Socialization Settings 144

Building Commitment 146
Case: Let's Have a Song 146
Controlling Threats to Commitment 148
Consequences of the Loss of Commitment 149

Summary 150
The Socialization Process 150
Notes 152
References 153
Discussion Questions 155

Contents

Chapter 7 Impression Management in Organizational Life   156

Case: Clothes Make the Man   156
What Is Impression Management?   158
   The Importance of Impression Management   158
   Impression Management: An Overview   160
   Perceiving and Organizing Impressions of People   161
Principles of Dramaturgy   163
   Box 7: Managing the Impression of Competence in an Environment of Uncertainty   165
   Elements of Dramaturgical Performances   166
   Symbols and Symbolic Acts   167
Case: Dr. Faust Visits the Agency   169
Four Key Roles: Superior, Subordinate, Lower Participant, and Specialist   169
   Dramaturgy of the Superior   170
   Dramaturgy of the Subordinate   171
   Dramaturgy of the Lower Participant   172
   Dramaturgy of the Specialist   173
Summary   174
Notes   175
References   176
Discussion Questions   178

Chapter 8 Communications in Organizations   179

Case: His Master's Voice   179
Communications in Organizations: Some General Comments   182
Elements of the Process of Communication   182
   The Source   182
   The Message   183
   The Receiver   186
   The Social Context   187
   Feedback   188
Attitudes and Communication   189
   Attitudes and Behavior   190
   Attitude Change   191
   Box 8: Confidence in Your Belief   194
Case: . . . Not Harder?   195
Communications Programs and Their Problems   196
   Building a Communications Program   196
Summary   199
References   200
Discussion Questions   203

PART III THE PROCESS OF GOAL ATTAINMENT 205

Section 1 Meeting Personal Goals: The Motivation System 207

Chapter 9 Motivation in Organizations: The Process of Directed Behavior 208

Case: Who Could Have Known? 208
Definitions of Key Terms 211
    Reinforcement and Punishment 211
    Incentives 213
    Generalization 213
    Extinction 214
    Quantity and Quality of Rewards 214
    Frequency of Reinforcement 216
    Schedules of Reinforcement 217
    Box 9: Incentives and Behavior 220
Motivation Systems for Directed Behavior: Enter Cognition 221
    Expectancies as Part of the Cognitive Process 223
    Money as a Generalized Reinforcer 225
The Expectancy Framework 228
Managing Cognitions 229
    The Effort-Performance Expectancy 229
    The Instrumentality of Performance for Desired Outcomes 230
    The Performance-Reward Expectancy 230
    Value of the Reward 230
The Lincoln Electric Experience 232
Goal Setting and Performance 234
    Work Goals as Personal Goals 234
    Goal Setting 235
    Variations in Work Performance 237
    Box 10: Valued Goals Seem Best 238
Summary 239
References 240
Discussion Questions 246

Chapter 10 Motivation: Need Theories, Incentives, and Reinforcements 247

Case: Virtue Is Its Own Reward 247
Need Theories 251
    The Need Hierarchy 251
    The Herzberg Motivation-Hygiene Theory (M-H Theory) 253
    Special Cases of Higher Order Needs 256
    Role Motivation Theory 258

  Box 11: Role Motivation and Executive Success 260
   Need Arousal in Organizations: A Perspective 260
 Cognitive Balance Theory 261
 The Lordstown Plant Case and the Notion of Equity 265
 Job Satisfaction and Motivation 268
  Job Satisfaction and Performance 268
  Box 12: Do Well, Feel Good 270
 Job Enrichment as a Part of a Motivation System 271
 Summary 277
 Notes 280
 References 280
 Discussion Questions 285

Section 2 **Careers: The Mobility System** 287

Chapter 11 **The Structure of Opportunity** 289

 Case: Nothing Succeeds Like Success 289
 The Structure of Opportunity 293
  Box 13: Careers as Tournaments 294
 Definitions of Success and Failure 296
  Terminology of Success and Failure 297
  Perception of Success 298
 Success: Consequences and Structures 303
  Organizational Factors 304
  Situational Factors 305
  Personal Factors 306
  Box 14: Motivation Chickens or Advancement Eggs? 307
 Case: Misfits and Malcontents 308
 Failure: Consequences and Adaptations 310
  Motivational Consequences of Failure 311
  Individual and Organizational Adaptations to Failure 314
 Summary 317
 Notes 319
 References 319
 Discussion Questions 321

Chapter 12 **Maintaining Motivation: The Consequences of Blocked Opportunity** 323

 Case: Mac's Shop 323
 Types of Blocked Opportunity 326
 Plateaued Careers 327

Motivational Consequences   329
Individual and Organizational Adaptations   330
Box 15: The Dual Management Hierarchy: How Well Does It Work?   333

Completed Careers   334

Deadend Careers: The Motivations of "Lower Participants"   337
Sources of Power of Lower Participants   338
Some Organizational Adaptations to Deadend Careers   340

Ascribed Careers: Roles for Women and Minorities   341
Ascribed Careers and Attribution   343
The Social Roots of Ascribed Careers   345
Barriers to Opportunity in the Social Structure   347
Box 16: Sex and Power in the Office   349
Individual and Organizational Adaptations   351

Summary   353
Plateaus   353
Ascription and Attribution   354
Things Are Changing   354

Notes   355
References   355
Discussion Questions   357

Section 3   Modifying Personal Goals: The Interaction System   359

Chapter 13   Groups and Their Dynamics   362

Case: In Unity, Strength   362
What Is a Group?   365
How Groups Get Started   365
Stages of Group Development   367
Group Structure and Role Behavior   369
Importance of Group Structure   370
Box 17: The Leader-Group Match: Does It Make a Difference?   372

Group Norms: A Force Toward Behavioral Regularities   372
Group Cohesion: A Force Toward Behavioral Uniformity   374
Group Cohesion Defined   374
Group Functions and Group Instrumentality   375
Leader Behavior as an Influence on Group Cohesion   378
Organizational Consequences of Group Cohesion   378
Group Goal Setting   381
Group Cohesiveness and Productivity   382
Box 18: Different Groups, Different Leaders   384

Consensual Validation, Group Illusion, and Irrationality 384
  Groupthink: A Perspective 386
Summary 387
Notes 388
References 388
Discussion Questions 394

Chapter 14 Leadership 396

Case: Rank Has Its Privilege 396
Leadership Defined 399
Leadership Traits and Charisma 400
  Box 19: On the Road to Understanding Leadership 401
Organizational Supports for Leader Behavior 404
  Symbols of Rank 404
  Allocation of Power 405
Power, Influence, and Leadership: Some Nonobvious Implications 406
  Reward Equity 406
  The Authority of Expertise 407
Leader Behavior: Building a Power Base in the Group 408
  Leader-Follower Dyad 410
  Leader-Group Relations 410
  Participative Leadership: Increasing the Link Pin Quality 412
The Vroom-Yetton Normative Model of Participative Leadership 414
  The Leader as Instrumental to Group Goal Attainment 417
  Box 20: When Leaders Are Viewed as Instrumental 420
Political Behavior as Leadership 422
  Lateral Relations as Leader Behavior 423
  Relations Upward 425
Summary 426
Notes 428
References 429
Discussion Questions 434

PART IV ACHIEVING MANAGEMENT GOALS: ORGANIZATIONS IN ACTION 437

Introduction Achieving Management Goals — The Feedback and Control System 439
  Organizational Behavior and Organizational Effectiveness: A Point of View 441

Organizational Effectiveness as a Concept   442
Approaches to Measuring Effectiveness   443
Goal Achievement as Effectiveness   444

Notes   445
References   445

Chapter 15   What Is an Organizational Goal?   446

Case: Plan, Organize . . . (Part 1)   446
Organizational Goals and Organizational Behavior   450
Products of Conflict, Compromise, and Negotiation   450
Goals Embody Resource Allocation Decisions   451
What Is an Organizational Goal?   452
Goals Have Different Time Horizons   452
Goals Sets   453
Opportunities and Constraints   454
Horizontal and Vertical Goal Differentiation   457
Differentiation by Function   458
Case: Plan, Organize . . . (Part 2)   460
Organizational Goals and Personal Goals   463
Resource Allocation: One More Time   463
Box 21: The Role of Idea Champions in Organizational Growth   466
Goals, Decisions, and Organizational Process   467
Goal Displacement   467
Summary   469
Notes   472
References   472
Discussion Questions   474

Chapter 16   Measuring Performance: Consequences of the Process   476

Case: Outstanding   476
The Process of Measurement in Organizations   478
Defining Measurement   478
The Search for the Perfect Measure and Why   479
Case: Faust's First Law   480
The Fox and Henhouse Principle   482
Some Consequences of Different Approaches to Measurement   482
Measurement in The Agency   482
Box 22: Creating Crime by Measurement   483
Measurement in The University   487

Measurement in Business and Industry 488
Discretionary Control and Control by Standards 489
Organizational Goals and the Process of Measurement 491
Characteristics of Measures: A Summary 491
 Relation to Source 491
 Relation to Desired Outcome 494
 Formality of Procedures 494
 Number of Indicators 494
 Clarity 495
 Level of Aggregation 495
Measurement and Technology 495
Case: Agony 496
Summary 497
 What You Will Face, How You Might Act 497
Notes 499
References 499
Discussion Questions 501

Chapter 17 Systems for Feedback and Control: The Depersonalization of Management 503

Case: Breakthrough 503
A Point of View 507
Measurement and Feedback for Control 507
 Depersonalization of Control 509
 Output Control and Behavior Control 510
 Technology, Evaluation, and Control 511
Case: The Invisible Hand 513
What Went Wrong? 516
 Feedback and Control System 517
 Motivation System 519
 Mobility System 520
 Interaction System 520
 Systems Structure 520
Case: The One Best Way 521
Some Principles of Control Systems 525
 Examples from Organizational and Social Systems 525
Summary 528
Notes 530
References 530
Discussion Questions 532

Chapter 18 **Intergroup Relations: Conflict and Cooperation** 534

    Case: What's Best for The Company 534
    Conflict Defined 537
    Conflict as Process 538
        Conflict Aftermath 539
        Competition Versus Conflict 540
    Causes of Organizational Conflict 540
        Incompatible Goals 541
        Group Factors 541
        Social Structure 542
        Competition Revisited 544
        Conflict Escalation 544
        Box 23: Competition, Win-Lose, and Conflict 545
        Conflict Management 546
        Box 24: Knocking 'Em Off the Road 546
    Deescalation and Reciprocal Strategies for Conflict Resolution 549
        Box 25: An Eye for an Eye . . . 550
    The Superordinate Goal Idea 552
    Case: What's Best for The Company (II) 553
    Summary 554
    References 555
    Discussion Questions 557

PART V PROCESSES FOR ORGANIZATIONAL IMPROVEMENT 559

Chapter 19 **Understanding Organizational Change** 563

    Case: Friendly Persuasion 563
    The Dynamics of Change 567
        Change as a Way of Life 567
        Forces for Change 568
        Resistance to Change 569
    Strategies for Change 572
        Empirical-Rational Strategies 572
        Normative-Reeducative Strategies 573
        Power-Coercive Strategies 573
        Depth of Change 574
        Creating Expectations 574
    The Process of Change 575
    Change from the Bottom Up 577

Organizational Change and the Norwegian Experience 579
Sustaining Change 580
Summary 581
Notes 584
References 584
Discussion Questions 587

Chapter 20 The Research Foundations of Organizational Change 588

Case: Work Smarter, Not Harder 588
Research and Its Importance 592
Some Pitfalls in Attributing Causality 594
   Direction of Causality 594
   Multiple Causality 594
   Spurious Causation 594
Requirements of Proof 595
Major Study Designs 595
   The Before-and-After Experiment with No Separate Control Group 596
   The After-Only Experiment with One Control Group 597
   Before-and-After with One Control Group 597
Some Major Data Collection Techniques 599
   Attitude Surveys 600
   Interviews 601
   Group-Generated Data 601
   Checking for Reliability and Validity 603
   A Strategy for Data Collection 603
   Action Research: Theory to Practice 604
Summary 606
References 607
Discussion Questions 608

Chapter 21 Changing Interaction Patterns for Organizational Improvement 610

Case: I'm Okay, You're Okay 610
Why Interaction Patterns Should Be Changed 613
Methods of Changing Interaction Patterns 616
   Laboratory Training 616
   Attitude Survey Feedback 619
Team Building and Conflict Management 621
Some Research Evidence 624
Changing Hierarchical Interaction Patterns 627
   Participation and System 4 627

Box 26: Faculty Voice 630
The Weldon Experience 631
Summary 632
Notes 633
References 635
Discussion Questions 638

Chapter 22 Changing Motivation and Control Systems 640

Case: Better Lucky Than Right? 640
Changing a Changed Control System: PIP Is Modified 643
  PIP Is Introduced 644
  Data Analysis and Changes in PIP 645
  The Northland Experiment 646
  Ben's Response 649
Changes Compared: The Systems Effect of Three Programs 649
The Assembly Line and Organizational Controls 649
The Autonomous Work Group: Experiments in Alternative Modes of Production 651
  Job Enrichment and the Autonomous Work Group Compared 654
  Limitations of Autonomous Work Groups 655
  Box 27: We'd Rather Be Safe Than Switch 656
The American Experience 657
Management by Objectives as a Control System 659
MBO: The Bark and the Bite 661
The Scanlon Plan as a Motivation System 664
  The Suggestion System 664
  The Formula 665
  The Philosophy 666
  Box 28: Everyone Gets a Stake 667
As to the Future 668
Summary 670
Notes 672
References 673
Discussion Questions 677

Index 678

PART 1
Perspective

Chapter 1
Introduction: Perspectives on the Understanding of Organizational Behavior

Do Unto Others

"Forget it, Stan. It won't work. I'll guarantee you that. They're just not going to do it." Ted was speaking. "And after all, why should they? There's nothing in it for them."

"I might've known that's the way you'd look at it, Ted." Stanley was annoyed. "You're so used to asking what's in it for you that you just assume that's the way everybody thinks. But there's a lot of us who think first of what's best for The Company."

Stanley and Edward Wilson Shelby IV were locked in heated debate about the likelihood of success of Stanley's new idea, a "flash memo" system for engineers in The Company's research and development laboratories. Penny Scribner from the Communications Department was on hand to provide the expertise available from that function. The notion was that each engineer would file a brief paragraph describing his current project and then update this paragraph as significant "milestones" were reached. This information would be stored in a computerized information system.

The basis for Ted's contention that the system wouldn't work was that there were no particular benefits for either the engineering departments involved or the people who would have to do the work of preparing the memos. But let's listen to Ted and Stanley.

"So your first thought is for what's best for The Company, is it? And there's no thought for yourself, is that it?" Ted's tone dripped with sarcasm. "Why, that's good to know, Stan. I can use that money set aside for your next raise to keep Claude happy then."

"Now just wait a minute, Ted. You're deliberately distorting the whole thing. I didn't say I'd work for nothing, or that there's no benefit for me in this job. I just said that sometimes, *sometimes* we've got to put the good of The Company ahead of our own immediate selfish interest. That's all."

"But doing that makes you feel pretty good,

doesn't it? I mean, you wouldn't be doing it otherwise, would you?" Ted waited a moment for the logic to sink in. Then, "What I'm saying is that just by the fact that you do something, there must be something in it for you, right? Even people who give up their lives for the ideals they believe in do it because they feel good about it, right? Otherwise they wouldn't do it. Selfish motives again!" With this last Ted's tone was triumphant.

"No, no! You've got it all wrong. You're just turning it all around. Sure, those people who give up their lives for the things they believe in think they're doing the right thing. But they've given up their lives for the world, not just for themselves. So how can you say that's selfishness. Why, that's the highest level of . . . of. . . ."

"Altruism." Penny, the journalist, supplied the appropriate word.

"Yeah, altruism," Stanley echoed.

"Selfishness," countered Ted. "They're doing it because they're convinced they're right, and it makes them feel good to do it. Otherwise they wouldn't. And it's just the same in The Company. Why even when Mr. Marsh works for the good of The Company he's doing it because it's *his* company and he thinks of how everyone will remember what a good chief executive he was. So even Mr. Marsh basically must act on selfish motives."

By now Stanley was thoroughly confused. He knew absolutely that Ted was wrong. But he couldn't for the life of him find the hole in Ted's logic. But then, he was an engineer, not a debater.

Penny, seeing Stanley's obvious distress, came to the rescue. "Stan, you've fallen for the oldest debating trick in the world. You've accepted Ted's definition of the words you're using and you've also accepted his assumptions about why people do the things they do. If you start there, believe me, there's no way you can win your argument."

"Now wait a minute, Penny. . . ." Ted didn't want to see his fun spoiled. But even more, he believed his argument essentially to be sound.

"No, I get my turn, too," Penny cut in. "What Ted has done to you, Stan, is to use a definition of selfishness that is without meaning. He tells you that if we do something, then we must have had a reason for doing it. True, as far as it goes.

"Then he says that reason must relate either to something we want for ourselves or that we want for others. Therefore, because we *want* it to happen, our motives for trying to make it happen must be selfish, must be in our own self-interest.

"Now that's completely *circular* reasoning. Once you accept that definition, why then no matter what we do, *by definition* it must be for selfish reasons."

"Exactly," crowed Ted, pleased to see that Penny actually was on his side.

"Exactly wrong, Ted," Penny countered. "You see, Stan, if you accept Ted's definition you leave the word *selfish* without special meaning by making it logically equivalent to the word *motive*."

"Huh?" was Stanley's revealing if inelegant comment.

"Look at it this way, Stan," Penny continued. "According to Ted there are no other motives than those he calls selfish, correct?"

Stanley nodded in concert with Ted.

"Correct. And if that is so then does qualifying the word *motive* by the term *selfish* add meaning? No, of course it doesn't. For if all motives are selfish, then whatever meaning there is to the word *selfish* must be contained within what we mean by the word *motive*. Or, look at it another way; if all acts are selfish, then it is impossible to distinguish between a selfish act and some other kind of act. Therefore, the word *selfish* itself has no meaning."

Stanley shook his head slowly. That kind of talk was too heavy for him. And even Ted, still undaunted in his belief that he understood the essence of human motivation, was confused.

Rationality in Human Behavior:
A First Perspective

Motivation is a topic that interests us all. We continually seek to understand better the motives of other people in the hope that this understanding will make our own day-to-day affairs more manageable. In trying to understand why people do the things they do, each of us employs a somewhat different *perspective*. Ted's view of the world is that people do things only through selfish motivations, with *selfish* defined in his own peculiar way. Stanley has a different view of the world. In this chapter we will present our perspective on the study of organizational behavior and its dominant themes. We feel this is necessary to help you understand why we have arranged the text as we have, and why we have chosen to include or exclude various topics.

Our first concern is the same issue that Ted, Stanley, and Penny were discussing—human motivation. More precisely, it is our belief about rationality in human behavior.

Some people argue that human behavior is not essentially rational. They base their argument on the observation that people will turn down obvious benefits for themselves in order to uphold some ideal or to "go along with the group." Our view is quite the opposite. We contend that behavior is rational in the sense that individuals, where possible, seek to increase the utility to themselves of the outcomes of their actions. However, we see this not as an explanation of human behavior but rather as a model. As a model, such a viewpoint provides a useful framework within which to organize our knowledge of human behavior; as an explanation it is far too general to account for the particulars of observed behavior. Let us see what this means for understanding organizational behavior.

Reinforcement Theory

Reinforcement theory is a fundamental axiom of the school of psychology called *behaviorism*. A simple statement of reinforcement theory is that people are more likely to repeat behavior they find rewarding than behavior they find unrewarding. Similarly, people are more likely to avoid behavior that has a distasteful outcome—that is punished—than behavior that is not punished. That is, people try to do things that increase the *utility of their outcomes*. This is the first principle underlying rationality in human behavior—although we have greatly oversimplified it.

Further, the greater the frequency of reward for a given behavior, the more likely it is that such behavior will recur. In other words, the *perceived utility* of a given behavior depends on how frequently that behavior has been rewarded in the past. This implies that somehow we must be able to make the connection between a given behavior and the rewarding outcome, though this connection need not be conscious or explicit.

Reinforcement theory will be covered in more detail in later chapters. For now, we will present only a simplified outline of one cornerstone of our viewpoint.

Complexity in Human Behavior

How are we to use our model? And how does this model fit with our assumption of rationality?

First, people find a variety of outcomes rewarding. They bring a wide range of needs, goals, and expectations—not just material or financial needs—to the organization. The fact that, in a given situation, people may value social needs more than financial ones is not evidence that behavior is irrational. This limits the definition of *rationality* to mean only *economic rationality*. However, as we mentioned before, people value a wide variety of outcomes.

Next, the goals of people in an organization are not necessarily the same as those of the organization as stated by the management. Consequently, *rationality* does not mean responding only to the goals of the organization. Quite the opposite may be true. Often, personal needs and goals will conflict with those set forth by management.

Finally, people behave according to complex understandings and perceptions of the world about them that are often distorted or contrary to fact. What people define as real is real in its consequences. This last point needs elaboration.

What people find rewarding is defined, at least in part, by social perception. Internalized standards or norms of behavior, for example, may require someone to sacrifice immediate material reward to maintain the solidarity of the work group. Is this irrational? Not at all. Research tells us that people value membership in such groups, and so the utility of such behavior may outweigh that of the more tangible material return.

Social comparisons also affect perception. People expect their work efforts to be rewarded justly or equitably in relation to other people's efforts.

Finally, expectations affect perception. Each of us behaves according to an understanding of the world that we have pieced together from past experience. We have our own explanations of why things happen as they do, as well as expectations about the likely consequences of our own behavior and that of others. For most of us these explanations and expectations are reasonably accurate, though incomplete—but sometimes they are inaccurate. However, again, if someone believes a thing to be true and acts on the basis of that belief, then for that person the situation is real—the actual facts notwithstanding. In work organizations, therefore, people may misperceive the link between behavior and rewards and act on that misperception. This is a final complicating factor in our rationality model.

For these reasons reinforcement theory is useful primarily as a model rather than as an explanation of organizational behavior. The model says that people in organizations do things to increase the utility of their outcomes, whether this means getting greater positive returns or limiting losses. They do it under uncertainty and they do it because of expectations derived from an incomplete understanding of the organizational world. In spite of these limitations, the rule is the same.

Utility

If we act to increase the utility of our outcomes, then what are some of the things to which we generally attach utility?

Money is obviously one. And the inherent interest of the work. Then there is increased status or rank in the organization, that is, promotion. We also welcome the approval of our peers. Other valued outcomes are derived primarily from social situations: increased feelings of equity derived from reducing work effort while maintaining the same pay rate; revenge on management, one of the oldest human motivations; or good working conditions or job security. These are only a few of the things that human beings value, and they are not available in endless amounts in organizations. More to the point, we are often able to gain one only by sacrificing another. For example, we might give up an interesting work task to attain higher organizational status or money, or sacrifice additional wages to maintain peer approval.

The latter situation results in a subjective comparison of additional utilities. Is, for example, an increase in wages worth more to me at this point than an increase in peer approval? An aspiring executive might ask, "Does an increase in status offset a decrease in work interest?" Answers to these questions differ in different situations. A plant manager may feel, for example, that an increase in status adds less utility than an increase in work interest or leisure time. The professional aspiring to his or her first management position, however, is likely to feel just the opposite.

People, then, attach utility to a wide variety of material, physical, and social circumstances, and the comparative importance of these utilities varies from situation to situation. So what we mean by rationality is that people attempt to choose among alternatives in order to increase the utility of outcomes as they perceive them at a given time. Further, this choice process is neither endless nor infallible; people generally will not investigate all possible alternatives and often may misperceive the actual state of affairs.[1] None of this affects our model of rationality, however, for our principle describes what people are attempting to do, not their success in doing it.

Emotionality

Perhaps you are saying that our model describes a peculiarly *unemotional* human being.

That's true. It is true, too, that *emotional* and *rational* are terms most often used in contradistinction to one another. Actions taken in the heat of anger or bitter dispute can scarcely be said to be rational; that is, they are not likely to be based on some means-ends logic designed to increase the utility of outcomes. More often such actions simply "feel right" at the moment. This is one of the limitations of our model: it assumes that behavior is based, though perhaps not consciously, on means-ends logic.

We do not deny that emotion exists. It is one of the reasons why individual behavior is so difficult to predict. It is also the primary reason why we focus on the collective behavior of individuals in organizations. We shall get to this shortly. Right now let us summarize the first element of our perspective. Individual behavior in organizations is rational, with people acting to increase the utility of outcomes to themselves. They do this within a complex framework of needs, social perceptions, and constructed explanations of organizational reality.

Collective Versus Individual Behavior: A Second Perspective

Throughout this book we will use the phrase "understanding organizational behavior." For us, this means developing generalizatins that help us both to explain and to predict the likely outcomes of organizational situations. We believe that saying we "understand" must mean that some degree of *prediction* is possible. And the statements that help us predict must also help us explain what is taking place.

Just what do we wish to predict? We might wish to predict the behavior of individuals. Certainly managers would like to be able to predict the future behavior of individual employees. Yet experience tells us that predicting individual behavior is extremely difficult.[2] Therefore, since focusing on individual behavior is likely to be fruitless, we focus on *collective behavior,* the collective responses of individuals to organizational situations in which they find themselves. Notice that we understand that different individuals may attach considerably different utilities to similar outcomes, but that we also allow some degree of commonality among individuals. This, of course, forms the basis for successfully predicting collective behavior.

What is collective behavior? How does its analysis differ from the analysis of individual behavior?[3] First, a *collectivity* is a definable body of individuals involved in some common organizational circumstance. Examples of collectivities include the salespeople in The Company's Expandrium Products Division, the blue-collar workers in Ben Franklyn's expandrium mill, and the product design engineers in The Company's Portland plant.

A collectivity need not constitute a *group* as the term is commonly used to denote individuals who interact on a face-to-face basis. A group, or better, a *primary group* is a special case of a collectivity. To the extent that we observe collective behavior, then, we observe an aggregate of individuals responding in some characteristic fashion to a given circumstance. The analysis of collective behavior involves attempts to answer questions such as, "How will Ben Franklyn's blue-collar workers react collectively to the new wage incentive system? How will the product development engineers at Portland react to the new system of promotion?"

The answers to these questions are framed in terms of aggregate rather than individual responses. At the individual level of analysis the answer usually is, "Some will like it and some won't." Trying to predict which individuals will and which will not is difficult and not especially useful. Organizational policies are designed to deal with collectivities, not individuals, and we are interested in a policy's effect on collective behavior, not on individual behavior.

Figure 1.1 illustrates graphically the reaction of Ben Franklyn's blue-collar workers to a new wage incentive plan. It shows the change in level of motivated behavior in terms of productivity rates for the entire mill population.

The top figure shows the number of workers achieving a given productivity level before the introduction of the wage incentive plan. The average number of pieces produced by all workers is depicted as $\overline{X}_1$, the mean of the distribution shown.

The lower figure shows the productivity achieved by workers one month after the introduction of the plan. Several things should be noted. First, average productivity has gone up from 32 to 33.3 pieces per day. So in our terms, workers collectively have responded by boosting productivity. The next point is that the lower distribution is more spread out. This indicates that individual workers have reacted differently to the plan; some didn't change at all, but others increased performance markedly. That is, the wage incentive offered for increased productivity had different utilities for different individuals. Finally, notice the large group centered at 30 pieces per day in the lower figure. The productivity data for the individuals in that group show that most of them are actually producing less now than before the plan went into effect. Previously, most of them were producing at the earlier norm, 32 pieces per day. Why this should happen will be discussed in Chapter 13, along with group norms. For now it is sufficient to say that this is yet a third kind of individual reaction to the new plan, an attempt to restrict production in the face of what these particular individuals perceive to be a management attempt to raise productivity standards.

Different individuals, then, react in different ways to the same organizational circumstance. Some raise their productivity significantly, some continue at the same pace, and others lower their productivity. Predicting these reactions for individuals can be quite difficult, but collectively their behavior is quite predict-

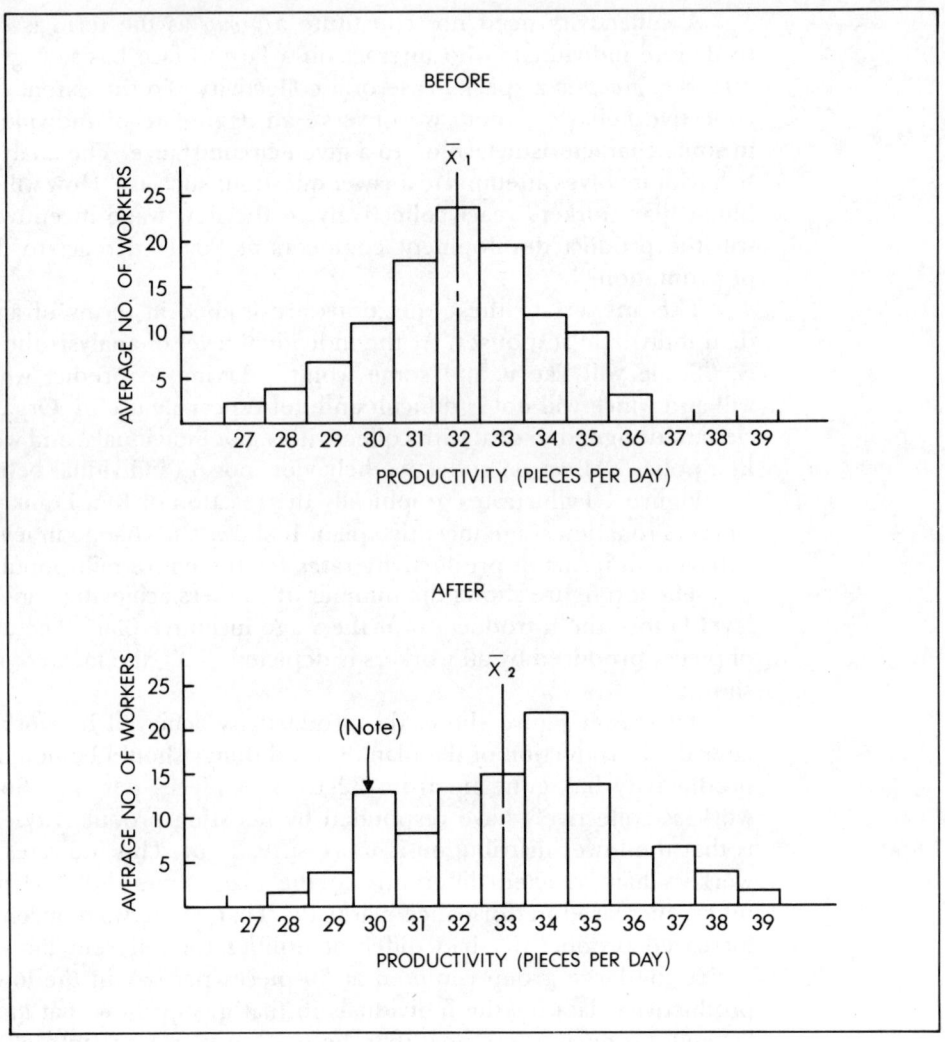

FIGURE 1.1 Productivity for Expandrium Mill Workers Before and After Introduction of Wage Incentive Plan (WIP)

able. In these circumstances, as has been observed repeatedly, productivity goes up.

This then illustrates the second major element in our perspective: a focus on the prediction and explanation of collective as opposed to individual behavior. We focus on the net result, the behavior of the entire body of individuals in response to common organizational situations.

The Effect of Social Structure: A Third Perspective

Thus far our model of organizational behavior shows individuals behaving rationally in seeking to increase the utilities of outcomes within the organizational context. Yet our model is still incomplete, for it essentially portrays the organizational person as responding to external situations strictly in terms of individual preference. A third element in our perspective must therefore be introduced—the powerful *impact of social structure* on human behavior.

What is *social structure* in terms of organizations? Basically it is a system of shared understandings and agreements as to what is and what is not appropriate behavior in a given social situation. It concerns our expectations about the behavior of others and what we intend by our own behavior in relation to the system of social positions and social roles in organizations. As an example, take the relationship between student and professor in the classroom. It is based on expectations that each has about the other's behavior. The expectations, in turn, are based on the *social roles* that each plays in connection with the *social positions* of student and professor. Each knows what the "correct" behavior for each should be despite the fact that the only knowledge they may have of each other as individuals is that one is student, the other professor. That is, the knowledge that shapes their behavior toward one another is based only on their shared understandings of what is expected in such organizational situations, not on particular knowledge they have of one another as human beings. Obviously, this is also true for manager and employee, union steward and foreman, "mail boy," and secretary.

These shared understandings may be explicit and formal, such as written rules and contractual obligations specified by the organization; or they may be implicit and informal—"the way we do things here in The Company." Examples of the latter include how to dress, who may and who may not arrive late for work, and exactly what constitutes a "fair day's work." For us, then, social structure is a *system of limitations or constraints on individual behavior* comprising two systems:

- a system of command and control: of authority relations, written work rules and contractual obligations; and
- a system of social roles and behavior norms: of understandings about "proper" behavior, and about "proper" attitudes, values, and motives.

Through the system of command and control management attempts explicitly to bring order and predictability into work activities, to harness the individual activity energized through the system of motivation. Yet, as with any formal system of rules and obligations it is incomplete and sometimes unworkable.

Partly because of this, and partly because it seems to be a universal consequence of human association, there arises a system of social roles and behavior norms that also brings order and predictability into the work activities of organizations. But this order is not necessarily in the service of management objectives. Often, the behavior dictated by the system of social roles and behavior norms will even be in opposition to these objectives.

Once again we should note the limitations of this model of behavior in organizations. First, by shared "understandings" about appropriate behavior we mean just that—*understandings*. We are not implying that everyone agrees actually to behave that way, or even that such behavior is desirable. There is simply a consensus as to how individuals are expected to behave. Understanding what is expected of us in no way ensures that we accept these expectations. And this, of course, paves the way for interpersonal and intergroup conflict.

Second, although there is considerable knowledge concerning the social structure of the organization, there also is considerable ignorance regarding it. Knowledge of social structure is *not* all pervasive, and is held differentially by members of an organization. This is because knowledge of social structure is generally gained through experience, through the process of *socialization* into the microsociety that is The Company. And this can be a second source of misunderstanding, tension, and conflict.

To summarize our third perspective, organizational behavior cannot be understood simply as a mechanistic system of rewards and punishments sought and avoided by individuals through work activities. The constraints imposed by social structures also have important consequences. These social structures are every bit as real as physical work activities and structures, and just as important to the purposes of the organization.

Focus on Problems and Process: The Final Perspective

In addition to studying organizational behavior, we have spent a considerable portion of our professional lives as researchers and managers in industrial organizations such as IBM, Western Electric, and Alcoa. We also have been consultants to industrial and nonprofit organizations. Each of us has served in the military and been a teacher and administrator in a university. This experience has had two effects: first, having been paid to detect and solve organizational problems has led us to develop a way of thinking about the affairs of organizations that centers on the problems they encounter. Second, because understanding these problems is impossible without understanding the processes that led to their development, we view the happenings in organizations not as discrete events, but rather as elements in a continuing process of change and adaptation.

This, then, is another perspective of our text. We feel you can learn more by looking at the problems that organizations encounter than by studying "business as usual." People cannot tell which elements are crucial in maintaining "business as usual" until something goes wrong. Then they say that things will not work until that problem is solved. Because we adopt this perspective, you may sometimes find yourself asking if anything ever goes right in organizations. The answer, of course, is yes, and most of the time. But we feel you are not going to learn much by assuming that all is for the best in this best of all possible worlds. These problems do exist—although perhaps they should not—and they are the outcomes of the *systems effects* of the complex interplay of organizational processes. Problems exist because organizations themselves are continually changing and adapting to changes in the social, economic, technological, and organizational environments. Problems also arise because organizations are sometimes slow to adapt to these changes.

We have tried to depict social processes within organizations in order to help you understand better the nature of organizational behavior. We have tried to avoid an evaluative stance in describing certain pervasive behaviors in organizations: workers restricting production, managers avoiding accountability, intergroup conflict, means-ends substitution in pursuing organizational goals, presenting oneself as advantageously as possible, to name just a few. Some people might regard these as problems in themselves, but we point out only that such behaviors do exist, and that it is impossible to understand organizational behavior fully without recognizing their existence. We are not advocating such behaviors, merely describing and analyzing why they occur and what their consequences are. Understanding the reasons why such behavior occurs will help you in managing your own career.

Problems in organizations have no universal solutions. Under appropriate conditions, the techniques of organization development can bring about real and beneficial change. But experience tells us that such change is neither universally applicable nor permanent. Because organizations are complex social systems, solutions to these systems problems are often only temporary. The environments of organizations are evolving continually, and it is difficult to predict where new problems will arise and old ones subside. This is perhaps best illustrated by the history of the study of organizational behavior. As you will see, largely in response to the social environment and to the research technology of the time, problems in this field have been defined in different ways at different times.

A Brief History of the Study of Organizational Behavior

A quick examination of any contemporary text in the field of organizational behavior will find major chapters devoted to organization structure, groups in organizations, leadership, motivation, technology and environment, and techniques of organization development. Suitable background material from psychology, sociology, or systems theory might also be included. We are tempted to take these topics for granted as the natural structure of the field. Yet it is important to understand how things got this way and what the concerns were that led to the concentration of effort on these topics. Learning about its history should help you understand the evolving nature of the field of organizational behavior and let you see how the topics we have chosen for this text reflect the concerns of the field. Our summary is admittedly sketchy, but we are trying only to illustrate the development of a set of concerns and ideas.

Work, Fatigue, and Effort: Individual Productivity As the Problem

We begin at the turn of the century with Frederick Winslow Taylor and the development of scientific management. At this time the problem was defined as how to obtain greater productivity from individual workers by rearranging task structure and providing monetary incentives for increased productivity. Taylor, the "father of scientific management," was much concerned with human motivation and the management philosophies detrimental to it. He wrote in 1915:

> Whatever the workingmen of this country are or whatever they are not, they are not fools. And all that is necessary is for a workingman to have but one object lesson, like that I have told you, and he [restricts his production] for the rest of his life. (14:32)

Through his scientific methods, Taylor demonstrated that individual productivity could be raised.

During the 1920s industrial psychologists in Great Britain did related studies concerning the effects of rest pauses and wage incentives on productivity. Boredom, they felt, was a key problem, and they gave this advice to industrialists:

> The amount of boredom experienced bears some relation to the conditions of work. It is less liable to arise (a) when the form of activity is changed at suitable times within the spell of work, (b) when the operatives are paid according to output produced instead of time worked, (c) when the work is conceived as a series of self-contained tasks rather than as an indefinite and apparently interminable activity. (17:43)

Perhaps the most famous researcher in this area was the psychologist Elton Mayo. Mayo spent a number of years observing individual workers in industrial settings and concluding that they exhibited clear signs of fatigue and reduced productivity even when they obviously were not physically exhausted. In 1924 he summarized his conclusions in terms of monotony and the quaint concept of "pessimistic revery":

> The investigation of revery seems to show that the essential problem is that as to the mental preoccupations induced in the workers by the condition of their work. Speaking generally it may be said that an individual's daily work or avocation may serve to minimize or to intensify any pre-existing tendency to pessimistic or paranoid meditation. (10:279)

Mayo's connection with the Harvard Business School involved him in the famous Hawthorne Studies conducted at the Western Electric Company in Chicago between 1927 and 1932. These studies were designed mainly to investigate the effects of rest pauses, incentive systems, the physical characteristics of the work setting on individual productivity, and the like. But unexpectedly the studies resulted in the discovery of the social nature of work and work organization. As the authors of *Management and the Worker,* the final report on Hawthorne, put it:

> An attempt has been made to point out that to state [productivity] problems in terms of "restriction," "faulty supervision," or "mismanagement" is to mistake symptoms for causes and to neglect the social factors involved (11:548).
>
> The point of view which gradually emerged from these studies is one from which an industrial organization is regarded as a social system (11:551).

The Hawthorne Studies marked a significant turning point in the study of organizational behavior [although it later turned out that the data hardly supported the authors' conclusions (1)]. From this point on it was generally acknowledged that understanding the productive behavior of people in organizations required more than just the study of individuals and individual "stimulus situations." This is not to imply that such an approach is useless, or that from this point such an approach was abandoned—it was not. Rather, people now understood the field and its problems at a higher level of complexity, with individual behavior being but part of the total picture.

With the Great Depression and World War II research in organizational behavior slowed.[4] During this time, one significant event affecting the field was the passage of the Wagner Act in 1935. This labor legislation established a firm legal basis for the activities of organized labor. It represented a major change in the social environment and also provided a new problem focus for people interested in the study of organizational behavior.

The Industrial Work Group: Social Relations As the Problem

In the late 1940s researchers returned to the study of organizational behavior in industry, but with a new focus on social organization, particularly on primary (face-to-face) groups and interpersonal relations. Concern for productivity remained, but the lessons of Hawthorne and an increase in union activity and consequent industrial strife brought about this new focus. Now we spoke of "industrial relations problems" and how the new science of "human relations" might be applied to solve them.

HUMAN RELATIONS IN INDUSTRY. One group of people including George Homans, William F. Whyte, and somewhat later, Chris Argyris and Leonard Sayles, studied human relations in industrial work settings in order to understand industrial strife and find possible remedies. A number of these people were associated with the Society for Applied Anthropology, an association that indicated both their viewpoint and methodological approach: observing and interviewing workers and foremen within "natural" industrial settings. The research task was one of observing work activities, interpersonal interactions, and sentiments, and relating these to one another in order to understand better how conflict comes about. Human relations researchers sought to understand better how people reacted to one another in given work settings, how people interpreted each other's verbal and symbolic communications, and how social and physical structure influenced these things. And although the aim was to explain industrial conflict in order to prevent or lessen its effects, there was still the implicit assumption that increased productivity would also result from improved human relations.

LEADERSHIP STUDIES. A second, related emphasis that developed at the same time was the study of the effects of first line leadership and its role in promoting good group relations. Most noteworthy was the effort at Ohio State University, which began partly from the concern during wartime for promoting effective military leadership. The Ohio State studies were models for the field. In particular, they were unique at the time in applying sophisticated psychometric methodology and developing quantitative measures of leader behavior.

As their understanding of leadership behavior grew, the Ohio State researchers applied their knowledge to the training of industrial managers. By training managers to become more "considerate" in their interpersonal relations with workers the researchers hoped that they could ease human relations problems and thus generally improve organizational effectiveness. Beyond this, their assumptions were similar to those of the theorists in human relations in industry—that is, that the relationship between workers and foremen could be studied profitably apart from the larger organizational context. This assumption was quite widely accepted when in 1953 Edwin Fleishman, an industrial psychologist, wrote:

> The problem in such training is much more complex than the simple addition of little positive and negative values to certain attitudes and ways of doing things. In order to effectively produce change in individual behavior some reorganization of the social environment also seems necessary. (3:206)

GROUP DYNAMICS. At about this same time researchers at the Institute for Social Research (ISR) at the University of Michigan began studying relations within the work group as the key to productivity and satisfaction. A number of interests converged at ISR, but two primary influences were Rensis Likert's Survey Research Center (SRC) and the Center for the Study of Group Dynamics, founded earlier by Kurt Lewin.

The people at SRC were leaders in bringing field survey techniques to the study of organizational behavior. Around 1950, two studies appeared that examined the relationship among productivity, "morale," and supervision. The studies reflected what would be the continuing concerns of the Michigan group over the next two decades (6, 7). The emphasis was very much in line with the human relations viewpoint. There was the belief that supervisory "style"—*democratic* supervisory style—could bring about both higher productivity and greater work satisfaction. Indeed, Likert's personal aim was to demonstrate scientifically that higher morale or job satisfaction resulting from improved supervision would be accompanied by higher productivity.

At the Group Dynamics Center the work was greatly influenced by the personality and teachings of Kurt Lewin, a refugee from Nazi Germany with a deep commitment to democracy and "an intense desire to apply the science of psychology to creating a better world" (13:86). Lewin founded his research group for group dynamics at MIT, after having conducted studies to demonstrate the superiority of democratic leadership at both the University of Iowa and MIT. Also as part of this early work in group dynamics, the researchers had investigated the effects on behavior change of group participation in decisions. These streams of work converged to form the cornerstone for the development of *participative management.* One such study, reported in 1948, demonstrated conclusively (at the time) that worker participation in decision making would lead to higher productivity. In the mid-1950s the research group moved to the University of Michigan.

An offshoot of Lewin's group dynamics enterprise was the founding of the National Training Laboratory's Institute for Applied Behavioral Science. During the mid-1950s NTL focused on the T-group, or training group. T-group practitioners were explicitly interested in developing interpersonal awareness through group dynamics. This concern has now evolved into the field of organization development (OD), although OD's relationship to its beginnings is primarily in its emphasis on planned change through remedying organizational interpersonal problems (12:618).

The Systems Approach: Our Contemporary Era

During the 1950s key ideas about organizational systems began emerging from a series of studies done at the Tavistock Institute in Great Britain. As set forth by Jacques, Emery, Trist, and others, the basic concept was that organizations are like cultures and can best be understood as "sociotechnical systems" (2, 5, 15). Through this concept they intended to emphasize the interdependence of the social structure of the work organization and its means of production or work technology. One of their early studies, for example, depicted dramatic changes in the social structure of a work group when mechanized methods of coal mining replaced the older "hand got" methods (15). These developing ideas about sociotechnical systems soon would be applied to entire complex organizations.

Just before 1960, three unrelated developments occurred that form a watershed in the study of organizational behavior. The first of these was the advent of the electronic computer. The other two were the publication in 1958 of two works that called attention to the fact that a larger systems perspective was necessary to understand organizational behavior: March and Simon's *Organizations* (9), and Joan Woodward's pamphlet "Management and Technology" (16). These works signalled the development of a new line of thought in the study of organizational behavior.

COMPUTERS AND THE STUDY OF ORGANIZATIONS. Studies that are commonplace today were virtually impossible before 1960. Today we regularly analyze large masses of data consisting of thousands of individual responses on hundreds of variables, and we compute multiple regressions, tens of thousands of simple correlations, factor analyses, and multivariate analyses of variance, computations possible only with the modern computer.

What has been the impact of this revolution? Primarily it seems to have changed the nature of the questions asked by people studying organizational behavior. Computational facility has made it possible to answer questions that previously could not be answered, and consequently were not asked. For example, complex models of individual motivation—expectancy models—require this kind of computational technology.

The computer has also changed our research methods—our ways of framing questions and of gathering data to answer those questions. Interviewing and observation have, to a great extent, been supplanted as primary research methodologies by questionnaires and by other means of gathering complex masses of quantitative data. Once again, the questions asked tend to be those which fit the method.

THE SYSTEMS APPROACH. These questions are now framed increasingly in terms of the complex interrelationships that characterize systems descriptions of organizations. The March and Simon and Woodward works were important here. They themselves did not necessarily bring about the change, but they did signal a developmental shift in concerns: it was becoming clear that a focus on the foreman and his group, on the relationship between satisfaction and productivity, was too restrictive, too simple an approach to be very useful. Forces in the organization as a whole had to be taken into account. The work technology employed by the organization and the environment of the organization were important. This awakening, together with the availability of the new computational technologies, has led us to our present concerns, concerns with organizations as systems of human behavior. These, in turn, have led us to increasingly more complex views of organizations and organizational behavior.

Summary

This brief history illustrates a major point: There are no final solutions to the problems of organizations. As environments and technologies evolve, organizations adapt and change, thus creating new problems and perhaps alleviating old ones. Even so, it seems incredible that in only fifty years we have come from Elton Mayo, who understood worker behavior in terms of "pessimistic revery," to our current understanding of organizational behavior as part of a complex system.

Unquestionably we understand more of the dynamics of organizational behavior than we did fifty years ago, but then, there is more to learn. In the 1920s organizations *were* simpler. Work technologies and environments were less complex. There were fewer external forces on organizations and these were more predictable. Perhaps the reason that we have evolved a more sophisticated view today is that organizational problems demand it. In any event, the history of our field indicates without question that the old problems persist, though perhaps in new, more complex forms. We still study the structure of work tasks, individual motivation, group relations, and leadership. At the same time, however, new issues have arisen through technological and environmental change. We have developed computerized information and control systems of enormous capacity; we must take account of affirmative action in our recruitment and promotion; and we have developed multiple management hierarchies, which are adaptive structures required by organizations whose work force is made up of thousands of professionals.

Our approach, then, is to provide a structure and logic with which you can analyze and understand human behavior in organizations. We focus on behavior within an organizational system that is continually adapting to changes in work technology and environment. And within this system, we seek to explain the collective behavior of individuals and the effect of organizational processes in directing motivated behavior in the service of organizational goals.

Notes

1. March and Simon (9) describe this process as *satisficing* as opposed to optimizing or maximizing.
2. An example of this difficulty can be found in the development of "expectancy theory"

in human motivation. Models trying to account for individual behavior in terms of differences in individual needs, perceptions, and task situations have become so complex that further progress at this time seems questionable (4, 8).
3. Our use of the term *collective behavior* is somewhat different from standard sociological usage. Sociologists distinguish between *institutional* and *collective* behavior: the former denoting "business as usual" under established norms and social agreements, the latter denoting some departure or change from normative behavior.
4. Behavioral science research in organizations didn't stop during World War II; however, most of it was channeled in the direction of the war effort.

References

1. CAREY, A. "The Hawthorne Studies: A Radical Criticism." *American Sociological Review* 32 (1967): 403–416.
2. EMERY, F., and E. TRIST. "Socio-technical Systems." In *Management Science, Models and Techniques*, Vol. 2, edited by C. W. Churchman and M. Verhulst. London: Pergamon, 1960.
3. FLEISHMAN, E. "Leadership Climate, Human Relations Training, and Supervisory Behavior." *Personnel Psychology* 6 (1953): 205–222.
4. HOUSE, R., H. SHAPIRO, and M. WAHBA. "Expectancy Theory as a Predictor of Work Behavior and Attitude: A Reevaluation of Empirical Evidence." *Decision Sciences* 5 (1974): 481–506.
5. JACQUES, E. *The Changing Culture of the Factory.* New York: Dryden, 1952.
6. KATZ, D., N. MACCOBY, and N. MORSE. *Productivity, Supervision and Morale in an Office Situation.* Ann Arbor, Mich.: University of Michigan Survey Research Center, 1950.
7. KATZ, D., N. MACCOBY, G. GURIN, and L. FLOOR. *Productivity, Supervision and Morale Among Railway Workers.* Ann Arbor, Mich.: University of Michigan Survey Research Center, 1951.
8. LAWLER, E., III. "Expectancy Theory and Job Behavior." *Organizational Behavior and Human Performance* 9 (1973): 482–503.
9. MARCH, J., and H. SIMON. *Organizations.* New York: Wiley, 1958.
10. MAYO, E. "Revery and Industrial Fatigue." *Personnel Journal* (December 1924): 273–281.
11. ROETHLISBERGER, F., and W. DICKSON. *Management and the Worker.* Cambridge, Mass.: Harvard University Press, 1939.
12. STRAUSS, G. "Organization Development." In *Handbook of Work, Organization and Society,* edited by Robert Dubin. Chicago: Rand McNally, 1976.
13. TANNENBAUM, A. *Social Psychology of the Work Organization.* Belmont, Calif.: Wadsworth, 1966.
14. TAYLOR, F. "The Principles of Scientific Management." *Advanced Management Journal* (September 1963): 30–39.
15. TRIST, E., and K. BAMFORTH. "Some Social and Psychological Consequences of the Longwall Method of Coal-Getting." *Human Relations* 4 (1951): 3–38.

16. WOODWARD, J. "Management and Technology." London: Her Majesty's Stationery Office, 1958.
17. WYATT, S., and J. FRASER. "The Effects of Monotony in Work." Industrial Health Research Board (Great Britain), Report No. 56 (1929).

Discussion Questions

1. State the four major perspectives adopted by the authors of this text. Explain what is intended by each.
2. How is the term *rationality* used in the description of human behavior in organizations? What is the relationship between this notion of rationality and the idea of increasing the utility of personal outcomes?
3. State in your own words what we mean by "collective behavior." What is the difference between a collectivity and a primary group? Give some examples of collectivities in your university or college.
4. What are the basic components of organizational social structure? What does "structuring" behavior mean in terms of this chapter?
5. The authors' emphasis on problems leads to the inclusion of many examples of things that go wrong in organizations. At times it may seem that we are focusing on "antiorganizational" behavior. Why do you think we have taken this approach?
6. From what you have read in this chapter, describe why you feel the authors say that there are no panaceas, no universal cures, for the problems encountered by complex organizations. Do you agree? Why? Why not?

Chapter 2
Organizations As Social Systems

Unfortunate or Incompetent?

"That's how I see it, Dr. Faust. It's just another example of top management sticking its fingers into things it should leave for local people to decide. The whole thing's crazy. Why, I could see that after just five minutes. Why can't they?"

The "they" in Stanley's last phrase referred to the corporate financial staff—in this case, people from the office of the vice president out of New York.

Dr. Faust had been listening to Stanley with some interest but hadn't said anything yet. Faust, as consultant to The Company on a new middle management study, was to "make sure that we are getting the kind of hard-hitting decision making we expect of our middle managers." Stanley, currently "on loan" to Dr. Faust, had been helping him gather statistical data. But now, in addition to the dry statistics, Stanley had brought back some interesting personal observations. In his last plant visit Stanley had been buttonholed by Kerry Drake (not one to let even the slightest opportunity go to waste) and given a graphic description of what Kerry thought was wrong.

"Too goddamn much second-guessing from Marsh's boys," had been Kerry's exact words. As the two of them had walked through Kerry's product development laboratory, Kerry had waved his hand about the half-empty room.

"Here, let me give you a case in point. See those empty desks. That's where half this project used to work. And you say Dr. Faust wants to know how to improve middle management effectiveness? I'll tell you! Just let us do what we know how to do without having to put up with the meddling of those corporate staff jackals." Kerry's emotional message had been clear, even if the logic hadn't been. Nevertheless, he must have noticed that Stanley was puzzled because he got quickly to the point.

"That damnfool Ted Shelby came out here this August to tell me that I was going way over budget by year's end and I'd have to find a way to cut back. Cut back! I said, why that's crazy. We're going great. And what am I going to cut back on? This is a product development project, not manufacturing. Ninety percent of my cost is in salaries and overhead. What do you want me to do? Burn the building? Fire my project people?" Kerry, satisfied that he had presented the alternatives absurdly enough to avoid action, had been unprepared for the answer—yes.

22

"So, to shorten my story," Kerry had continued, "that's where these empty desks come from. Shelby made me permanently transfer twenty people to other projects, some here, some at other locations. That's twenty out of seventy-five, mind you. And I'm sure you know that those transfers are permanent. That's a Company rule and a good one. We don't transfer people for three months and then bring them back. After all, we don't want our people to pay the price for the silly games we play. But that's not all, you see *next* year . . ."

Kerry had gone on to point out that next year the project would be moving into the prototype development phase and was scheduled to go from seventy-five to a hundred people. Simple arithmetic revealed that because of the transfers forced on Kerry by Ted Shelby, forty-five of these would be new people with all the confusion and delay inevitable under those circumstances.

"It's crazy! Nuts! I wish those staff smart alecks in New York had to manage something like this—just once! *Then* they'd sing a different tune."

This was the story Stanley had brought back to Dr. Faust. And now, after some thought, Faust was prepared to deliver *his* analysis. "So you agree with Kerry, do you? Well, I can see why. Kerry is very persuasive. And he deeply believes what he is saying. But you seem to have misplaced for the moment what you learned in our Management Systems seminar.

"All you see is the absurdity of Kerry's situation. He's been forced to act in a way that we might call . . . ah, counterproductive at the very least. But look at it from Ted's perspective. First, the facts." Faust ticked these off like a laundry list:

- "There are many such projects throughout The Company, all with some degree of cost overrun. But most are within the allowable limit of 10 percent.
- "Kerry is typical of middle managers in The Company; intelligent, persuasive people, not unwilling to engage in a certain amount of . . . ah, shall we say 'reconstruction' of the facts.
- "Ted's strength is not his technical ability; he's a financial man. And so he must rely on what he is told. More accurately, he must learn *not* to rely on what he is told.
- "All the young professional people on the vice president's financial staff—Ted included—have promising careers ahead of them, *if* they avoid the big blunder.
- "Decisiveness, crispness of manner is an important management attribute, and Ted has learned to cultivate that impression. So he'll make his decision *now*.
- "And perhaps most important of all, Ted's job is *financial* control, *not* product development.

"Well then, what do you suppose will be Ted's decision options given this situation?" Faust went on.

"First, to use one of Kerry's own phrases, one does not have time to separate the unfortunate from the incompetent. Another way of saying this is that the merits of the case carry very little weight. After all, Kerry's is only one of a number of such cases, and each justification is just as compelling as the others.

"Next, the person with the problem is Kerry, *not* Ted. And Ted keeps that firmly in mind when Kerry starts howling about 'taking it to Marsh himself.' Ted will reply politely, 'Well, that's your option. After all, you *are* 25 percent over budget. If Mr. Marsh wants to make that exception that's fine. But from where I stand I have no choice.'

"What follows directly is Ted's decision rule: the big loss comes only from letting the financial situation get out of hand—by being soft and indecisive. Product development is *not* his responsibility. He is a tightfisted financial manager; product development throughout The Company *will* come in on budget.

"So there you have it," said Dr. Faust, completing his summation. "What looks outrageous from Kerry's point of view is perfectly reasonable from Ted's. Conversely, what would be a reasonable solution from Kerry's point of view, and what indeed would save a great deal of waste and inefficiency for The Company, would be to make the exception in Kerry's case. Yet to make this exception would mean nothing but trouble for Ted. For if Kerry can win an exception, then why not this one, or that one? Ted instantly would find that there were dozens of cases with equal or greater merit and, surprisingly, each completely informed—better than Ted himself—on the details of Kerry's case.

"No, Ted just can't afford to let that happen. So he steels himself to the task of saying no and proceeds on the assumption that an ounce of prevention is worth a pound of cure and that the knowledge that financial sin has no redress in The Company will keep Kerry from overcommitting himself the next time. And so it may. Yet these things keep happening because there are other pressures on product development managers that keep them promising more than they can deliver. But that is another story."

Organizational Actions and Organizational Outcomes: A Systems Perspective

Jay Forrester, in his book *Urban Dynamics*, asserts that the interconnectedness of systems actions and their consequences is so complex that the human brain cannot accurately project the outcomes (7, 8). A computer is needed. We could make the same point about complex organizations, although we may not agree with Forrester concerning the use of the computer. Complex organizations have been described as *sociotechnical systems*, that is, systems where people and technology interact in producing outcomes. Technology refers not just to the machines of production, but also to systems in accounting, finance, marketing, and production control. Managers and professionals, like the people on the production floor, are also involved in a sociotechnical system.

This text is about the behavior of organizational and social systems comprising people and things. It is about the kind of problem Stanley observed in the vignette. From his place in this system, Stanley thought that top management's interference was responsible for a terribly unjust situation. Since it is within the power of management, and Ted in particular, to correct that situation, why, Stanley asked, did Ted persist in doing something so obviously wrongheaded?

Dr. Faust saw the situation differently. Perhaps experience helped him. He saw the problem as part of the complex economic, technical, and social system that is The Company. And he also saw that it was something quite likely to happen under the circumstances. The people who designed the corporate financial controls did not have that particular situation in mind—quite the opposite. Yet they could not hope to predict *all* the outcomes of the interaction of human motives and technical systems.

Let us take a brief look at two historically important instances of what we are talking about.

The Hawthorne Lighting Experiments

In the early part of this century, industrial psychologists hoped to improve worker productivity by discovering the relationship between effort and fatigue in the work task (13). In 1924, for instance, the Western Electric Company undertook an experiment to determine the relationship between lighting and worker efficiency (12). The results in each of the three experiments that evolved in the Hawthorne works of the company were completely unanticipated, however. Instead of a simple relationship between level of lighting and worker productivity, the bewildered experimenters observed a continuing increase in productivity regardless of lighting levels. In a second, more sophisticated experiment, a comparison group, measured and observed but not subject to lighting changes, was introduced; it too increased productivity along with the experimental group. In a third experiment all natural lighting was blocked out because the experimenters thought this might be the uncontrolled factor. Once again, however, productivity in both the test and control groups increased independently of illumination intensity until the lighting for the test group became so dim that the workers could hardly see what they were doing.

How can we explain what happened in those early illumination experiments at the Hawthorne works? There are at least two key points.

ASSUMING PASSIVITY OF WORKERS. The experimenters were assuming that the human materials with which they were working were little different from other experimental materials; they assumed they would "respond" to the stimulus rather than behave creatively or adapt in some other fashion. It apparently never occurred to the experimenters that the participants would create their own explanations for what was going on and act on the basis of these explanations. Yet this appears to be what happened.

IGNORING SOCIAL SYSTEMS STRUCTURE. The experimenters also failed to recognize that within the complex sociotechnical system of the organization, a great deal of information and many communications—both correct and incorrect—flowed directly from the changes taking place in the experimental situation. For example, management communicated interest in the workers by taking groups and moving them to special quarters, then adjusting the lighting. In the pervasive authoritarian atmosphere of the manufacturing industry in the 1920s this, in itself, was a powerful experimental change. The workers reciprocated by doing "a little more"—presumably to "reward" management so it would maintain its interest in improved working conditions.[1]

The Hawthorne lighting experiments, then, illustrate the complexity of systems outcomes, and the difficulty of predicting the consequences of systems actions without taking the total system into account.

Improving Industrial Relations Through Training

Our second illustration of the importance of considering the total system dates to the 1950s. At that time it was hoped that costly industrial conflict could be lessened by improving relations between management and production workers.

The direct object of attention was the foreman, the *interface* between organization management and the worker. Earlier research had shown that foremen were involved in two basic tasks: structuring worker activities and resolving human relations problems. It seemed reasonable, therefore, that training them to be more "considerate" in their human relations function would reduce conflict. On this basis, the International Harvester Company undertook a program of training to show foremen how to be more "considerate" in their direct relationships with workers (5, 6).

The procedures once again were simple enough. To ensure uniform training, foremen were brought to a central location and schooled in how to behave more considerately. Before the program began, the trainers, through questionnaires, had had workers describe their foremen so that appropriate after-training changes in the foremen's behavior could be detected. When the foremen returned to the job, the questionnaires were readministered to the workers and the results tabulated.

Surprisingly, the results showed that, if anything, the foremen were less considerate in their treatment of workers than before the training. The psychologists responsible for the experiment concluded that one possible explanation for this unanticipated result was the training procedure itself. That is, the very act of transporting the foremen to a central location and giving them "management" training had communicated directly to them the message that they were part of management. So they started to act more as they had seen "real" management acting—they were more directive and less considerate (5:214).

Once again, the industrial experiment foundered on the assumption of the passivity of the people involved and on ignorance of the effects of the sociotechnical system. The first assumption led to the belief that foremen could be trained by reading descriptions of considerate behavior and learning to recapitulate those descriptions to the trainers. In addition, there was no recognition of the message conveyed by participation in the training itself, of how the foremen would interpret that experience and how this might affect their behavior.

Second, from the systems viewpoint, during the experiment there was no recognition of the larger social system in which the foremen and workers functioned. The trainers saw the two groups interacting in isolation from the rest of the sociotechnical system of the organization. In the words of the participating psychologists:

> The purpose of [leadership] training is to produce a lasting change in behavior, but existing behavior patterns are part of, and molded by, the culture of the work situation. . . . In order to effectively produce change in individual behavior some reorganization of the social environment also seems necessary. (5:206)

Understanding Process

The Hawthorne lighting experiments and the International Harvester foremen training experiment illustrate the importance of looking at the ongoing process rather than at simple cause-and-effect events. We can distinguish between these two approaches by examining, for example, the function of recruitment. In looking at this function we might emphasize selection of the best personnel as "the problem." Or we might look at the entire process of recruitment, how organizations go about recruiting, and why they do it that way. Once again it is a question of emphasis. But with a process point of view, we also look at how recruitment relates to other aspects of the organization, such as intergroup conflict, motivation, and control. The distinction is that the former approach—the selection approach—focuses on attaining a desired outcome or solving a specific "problem," while the latter approach—the process approach—focuses on understanding what is taking place within a wider set of interrelated functions. And we must always keep in mind that an organization is a dynamic system of interrelated processes, rather than a static set of structures and related activities.

In the rest of this chapter we will outline some ideas about organizations as systems that will help us to explain organizational behavior. The ideas we will develop:

- emphasize the interrelatedness of structure, process, and behavior; and
- provide a framework to help you organize the knowledge presented in this text in terms of some basic building blocks of human organization (for example, the motivation system, the feedback and control system).

However, before moving ahead to this systems description of organizations let us, by way of comparison, look at what is called classical management theory.

Classical Management Theory

The writings of the French industrialist, Henri Fayol, best exemplify the approach of the classical management theorists. Writing at the beginning of this century, Fayol brought together his practical experience as a manager to create fourteen basic principles of management. His principles were formulated in terms of the characteristics of effective management, some of which are:

- a division of labor (people should be specialized to perform work more efficiently);
- unity of command (each employee should receive instructions from only one superior);
- unity of direction (operations of the organization having the same objective should be directed by the same manager); and
- subordination of individual interests to the common good (the interests of individuals should give way to the interests of the organization as a whole (4).

The classical theorists were striving for universal principles of organization. For example, they felt it important to arrive at the ideal span of control, the optimum number of subordinates to be supervised by a single superior. They seemed to agree that the maximum span of control should be no more than six. The classical management theorists believed that such principles could be achieved by any rational organization. Their assumptions were, first, that these principles could be applied to all organizations if some flexibility were allowed, and second, that all matters of consequence to management were internal to the organization and therefore within management's control.

In these two assumptions we find the differences between the classical view of organizations and the systems approach. First, we now generally believe that no single set of management principles applies to all organizations. Second, we now realize that external events influence behavior within organizations, and that these influences may largely be outside the direct control of management (11). However, before describing the systems view we should note that the observations of the classical management theorists were probably a fair representation of organizations at the turn of the century. If they are not adequate today, perhaps this is more the result of the rapid evolution of organizational environments than of the inadequacy of those theories at the time.

Some Systems Concepts Applied to Organizations

When we speak of organizations as systems the general impression is one of complexity and interrelatedness. But there are other basic systems concepts we need to understand. We must also remember that we *choose* what we wish to include in the system, with the remaining elements being termed the system's environment. For example, we might call a human being a system, and all social organization its environment. Or, moving up a level, we might regard a group of interacting individuals as a system and the organization as its environment. The choice is arbitrary and depends on what is most useful for the problem at hand. Since this text is about organizations, we choose to designate the complex organization as the system and whatever lies beyond its boundaries to be the environment.

There are a few basic concepts that support our analysis of organizational behavior (See Figure 2.1). Organizations as systems are:

- interrelated,
- open to the environment,
- purposeful,
- adaptive,
- constrained, and
- in need of feedback.[2]

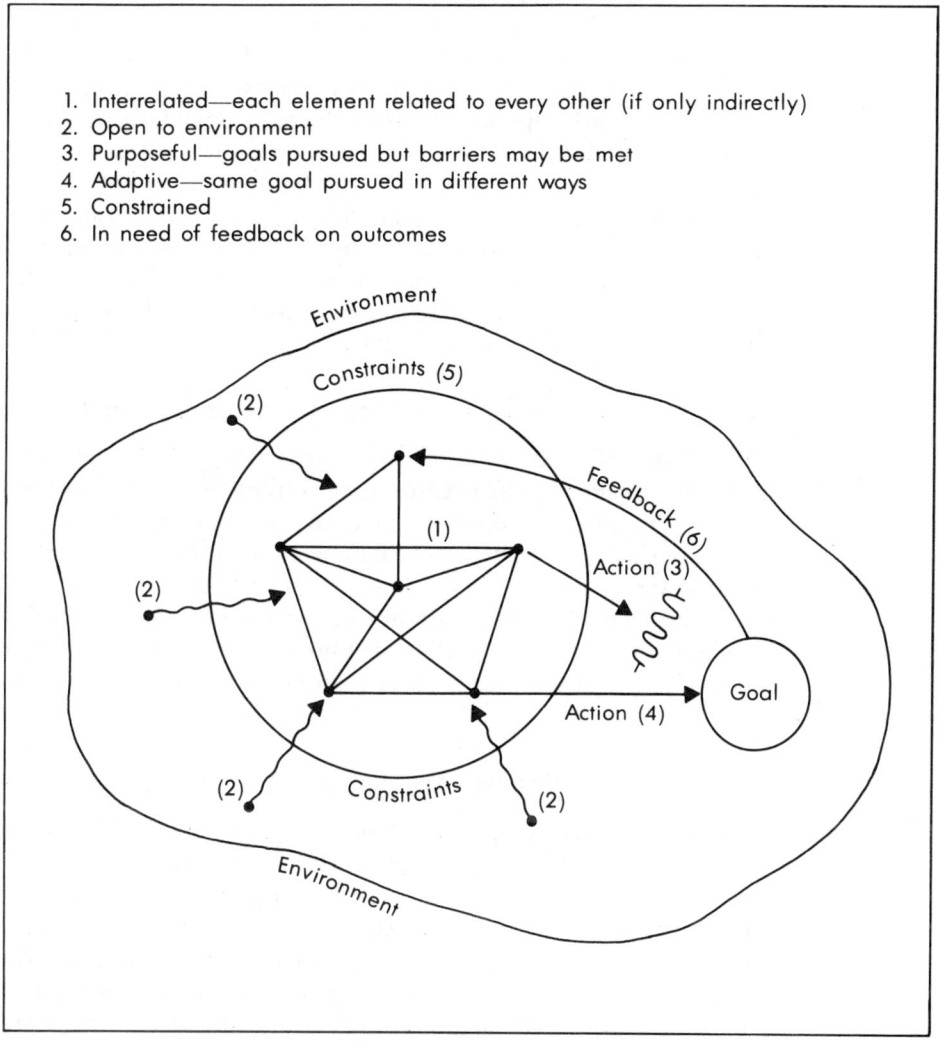

FIGURE 2.1 Major Characteristics of the Organizational System

Organizations Are Interrelated

Any action taken in some part of the organization has the potential to affect every other part of the organization. Its effect may be direct, as when changes in payment plans are made to spur the productivity of workers. They may also be indirect. For example, the attempts in the Hawthorne experiments to study the direct effect of the level of lighting actually produced an indirect effect on productivity through the workers' interpretation of what was taking place.

Because organizations are systems, outcomes resulting from actions taken within the organization must be interpreted as outcomes of an interrelated set of system elements. We often find ourselves saying, "If only the workers would do what they are supposed to, then this new manufacturing arrangement would work." Or "The problem is that those damn engineers don't realize that we are in business to make a profit." The tendency is to isolate a group or function from the rest of the system and blame it for any organizational problems. From a systems perspective, this cannot be so. All elements in a system work to allow the system to respond in purposeful, adaptive fashion to other forces in the system and environment. Hence, a problem is in the system as a whole—and it should be analyzed in that way.

Organizational Systems Are Open to the Environment

The shape of organizational structures and processes cannot be understood without considering the organization's interaction with its environment. Organizations cannot be understood as closed systems governed by a set of unchanging principles as assumed by classical management theory. For example, many studies of leadership behavior treat the leader and the work group as a closed system, assuming that the only important factors to be taken into account are the behavior of the leader and the reaction of subordinates. The leadership training experiment cited earlier in this chapter pointed to the inadequacy of a closed systems view.

Organizational Systems Are Purposeful

Organizations pursue goals (the desired outcomes of their activity). This seems simple enough. Yet the stated goals of an organization are many and complex. At executive levels the purposes of the organization are stated in general terms and may be realized only several years in the future. At the level of direct production activity, organizational purposes may be stated in terms of immediate, measurable outcomes to be achieved today. At times, difficulty arises in linking the longer-term, general goals of top management with the shorter-term, immediate activities of workers.

Organizational Systems Are Adaptive

Organizations as systems can adapt to changes in environment or internal structures in order to better pursue their specified purposes. In rapidly changing organizational, technological, and economic environments organizations continue to adapt their structures and activities in order to survive. However, organizations—because they are adaptive and purposeful systems—also resist change. For example, when procedures are introduced to increase productivity, lower levels of the organization may adapt to these procedures not by increasing productivity, but by capitalizing on the procedures introduced for measuring productivity. "Since it is often more efficient, in the short run, to devote effort to the accounts rather than to performance . . . a bottom-line ideology may overstimulate the cleverness of organizational participants in manipulating accounts" (10:568).

Organizational Systems Are Constrained

Constraint is a concept fundamental to understanding regulation or control. Some measure of *predictability* in a system can be achieved only if the possible actions of the system are in some ways constrained. Consider the familiar board game, checkers, a logical system. The players' moves are constrained to a few possibilities—forward only, and diagonally, for example. Because of this, outcomes are so highly predictable that, being given the choice of the first move, a master checkers player will never lose. Chess, with fewer constraints, provides even the master player with less certainty of control.

Organizational Systems Need Feedback

We cannot control a system without some constraint on its actions. Similarly, we cannot control a system without knowing the outcomes produced by those actions. Knowing the outcomes produced by action is called *feedback.* For example, the thermostat in a heating system senses the temperature in the room where it is located and tells the heat-supplying unit when it should turn on or off in order to maintain the desired temperature. The thermostat, then, provides feedback to the heat-supplying unit concerning the state of the system. If the feedback indicates the temperature is below the desired one, action is taken. This action (supplying heat) is ended when the desired temperature is restored. In this typical cycle, then, the current state of the system is measured, feedback of this information is supplied to the control mechanism, and any action necessary to produce the desired outcome is taken. The objective, in the case of the thermostat, is to maintain the room at a certain desired temperature.

All functions of an organizational system depend on feedback. When feedback is lacking or faulty, the organization cannot work satisfactorily toward its objectives. A large manufacturer of electronic components working in a government-regulated industry was allowed to produce solid-state components only for use within the company. When a vendor offered to sell the company identical components at considerably less cost, the group responsible for the manufacturing procedures for these components was shocked. The problem was lack of feedback. The group had been isolated from the marketplace and consequently had no sense of how well, or how poorly, they had been doing. They needed feedback to improve their performance. Within six months of receiving this feedback the group managed to cut costs by half.

The Organizational System

Fundamentally, organized behavior is the behavior of a collectivity of goal-seeking individuals whose actions are constrained in some ways, and channeled or motivated to achieve outcomes said to constitute the goals of the organization.

This definition assumes three basic features of the organizational system:

1. The organization comprises goal-seeking individuals; they seek to increase or maintain the utility of personal outcomes.
2. The organizational system has a structure that is the basis for organized activity; formal and informal social structures constrain the behavior of members of the organization in regular and predictable ways.
3. Systems for channeling motivated behavior constitute the control system of the organization and direct individual behavior toward the achievement of outcomes said to constitute the goals of the organization.

Within this framework the organizational system can be broken down into six component parts or subsystems (each of which we term a "system"). We will consider each of these component parts in turn, building the organizational system in complexity as we go.

The Formal Organization—Systems Structure (I)

Our first component is the formal organization. In the formal organization behavior occurs within a formal task structure to produce desired outputs (that is, transformed materials or people). Figure 2.2 depicts this system schematically. The arrows indicate that the formal task structures influence outputs, and that the outputs may also influence the formal task structures. Notice too the effects of technology and the environment. These are shown *outside* the systems structure because they are not part of the human organization. Rather they are additional constraints on the *form* of the organization as embodied in its formal task structure. The organizational system shown is open to its environment (dashed line).

Within the formal task structure we include both the social structure of the organization, which results from the way work tasks are broken down functionally, and the formal system of authority relationships. These ideas are treated in Chapters 3 and 4. Chapter 5 concerns the constraints on the formal structure that result from the requirements of technology and from interaction with the environment.

To illustrate these concepts, recall the Hawthorne lighting experiments. Changes in the task structure led to changes in both behavior and output. The changes in output led, in turn, to changes in the task structure—all within constraints of the technology and current social and economic environment. Each of these system elements played a role in the behavior of the system.

One note on interpretation. We do not intend that our schematic depictions

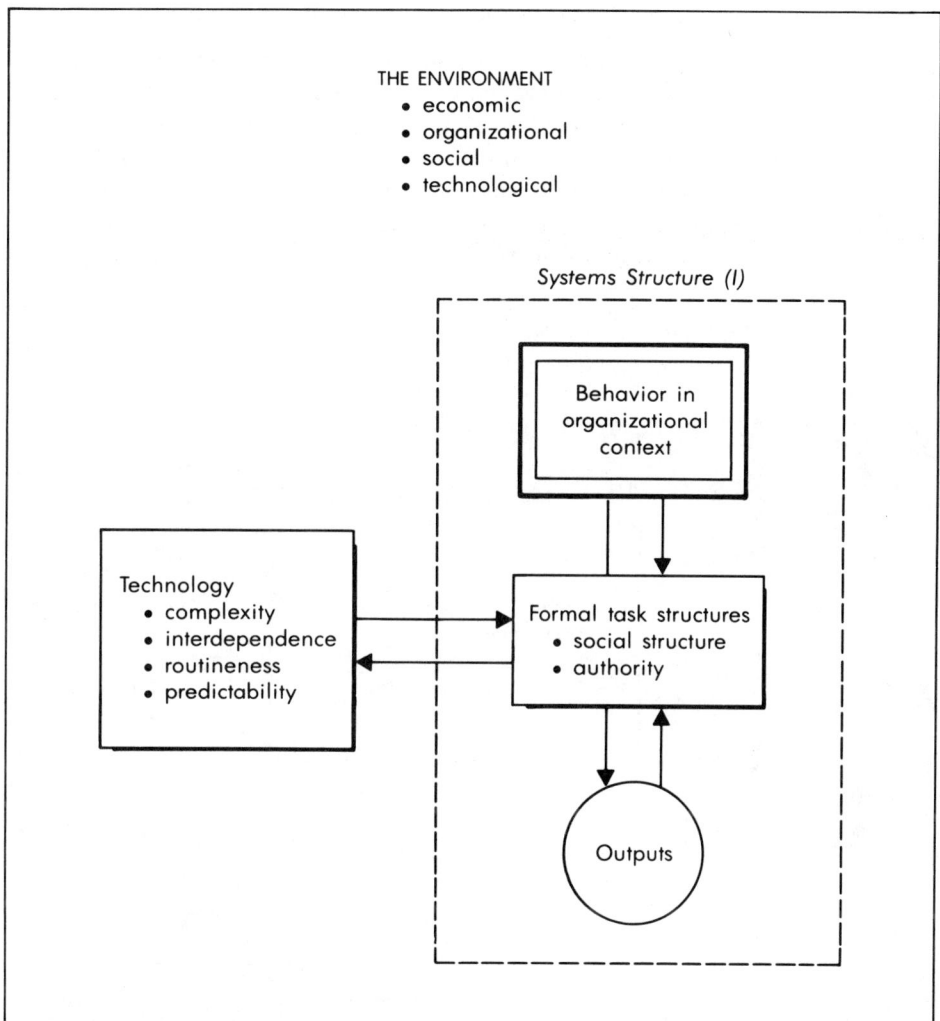

FIGURE 2.2 The Basis for Organizational Action: The Formal Organization—Systems Structure (I)

of the organizational system be taken literally and explicitly; they are only a teaching device. What we intend to convey is that behavior in an organizational context is related to the output of that organization through a formal task structure comprising interrelated (in a systems sense) constraints on behavior. Also, Figure 2.2 is incomplete—it is only part of the total organization and cannot function in isolation from the other parts; and it is *arbitrary*—we have chosen to carve up the total organizational system in this way for purposes of illustration.

Patterns of Social Behavior—Systems Structure (II)

The second set of constraints on individual behavior in our systems structure is the set of regular patterns of social behavior associated with positions in the formal organization. This second component is shown in Figure 2.3.

Each position in the organization involves a social role. *Social roles* are mutually understood expectations about ways in which people should behave. These roles limit organizational behavior. They also allow the behavior associated with each position to be regular and predictable. An understanding of these role

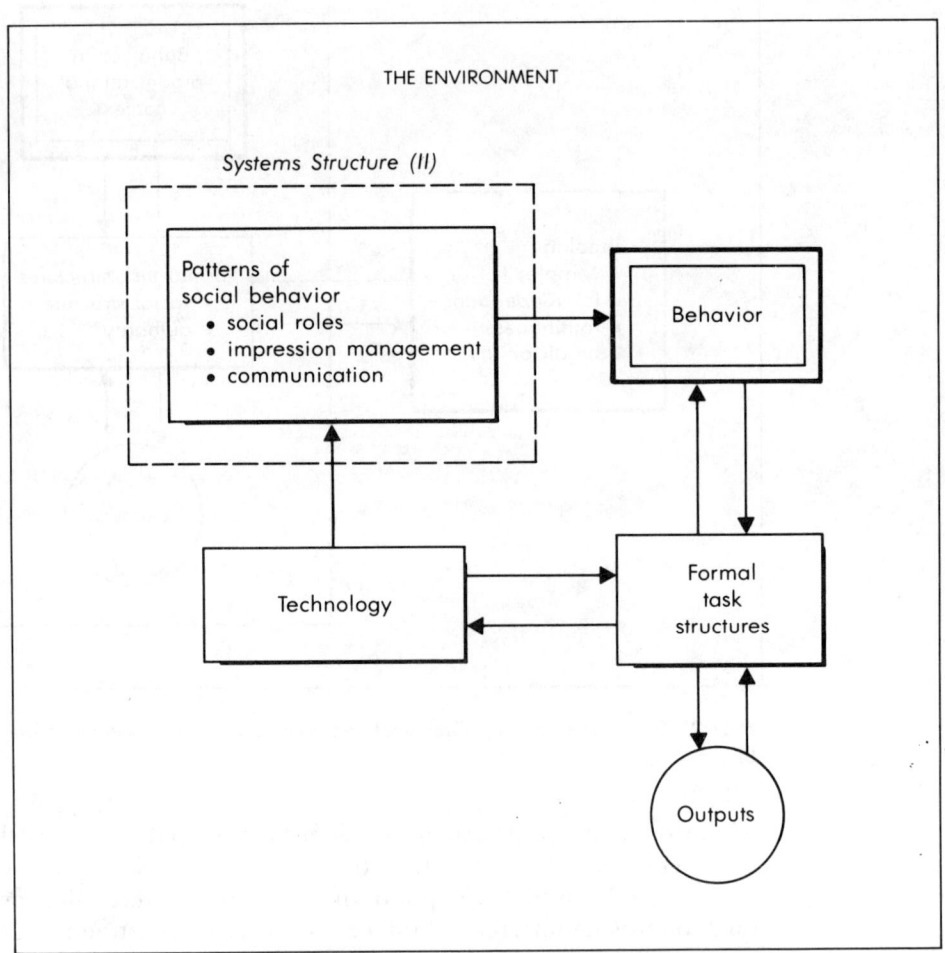

FIGURE 2.3 The Basis for Organizational Action: Patterns of Social Behavior—Systems Structure (II)

expectations is developed through the process of socialization, the organizational process discussed in Chapter 6.

A second set of behavior patterns is associated with what we call *impression management,* the topic of Chapter 7. By impression management we mean the ways in which individuals communicate important facts about themselves to others through appearances, nonverbal communication, and symbols. Such communication provides feedback about individuals to other members of the organization. The necessity of creating proper impressions also constrains individual behavior.

We will have a more general discussion of organizational communication in Chapter 8. Here we will provide a framework for understanding the relationship between patterns of social behavior and the ways in which word, action, dress, and symbol structure the interpretation of events in organizations.

This patterning of behavior in organizational positions is both purposeful and adaptive. For example, recall the industrial relations training experiment. Before the experiment foremen interacted with their subordinates in ways appropriate to the role of foreman as they had learned it through socialization. The apparent major effect of the training was to reinforce the foremen's personal identities as managers, in turn leading to changes in the way they managed their impressions for their subordinates. Apparently what was being communicated by action and symbol was quite different from what was being said (but not communicated) in the training sessions. The foremen's new posture emphasized somewhat less consideration—this was consonant with what they perceived to be the behavior of "real" managers (their own superiors).

The Motivation System

Goal attainment in organizations includes motivation, feedback, and control. The *motivation system* is our fourth system component and it is depicted in Figure 2.4.

The motivation system comprises those elements through which the organization provides incentives for desired behavior. As shown in the figure, this system influences behavior through individuals' personal goals. Two major types of incentives are available to control behavior through the motivation system: *financial and material rewards,* and *advancement in organizational status.*

Financial and material rewards relate to personal goals for economic well-being. In the systems sense, the availability of financial and material incentives shapes the personal goals of individuals, while incentive schemes for controlling behavior by providing financial and material rewards are shaped according to beliefs about the personal goals of organizational members. Once again we see the purposive and adaptive characteristics of organizational systems.

However, other personal needs are not met solely by financial and material incentives. The work task itself, for example, may be a powerful incentive for

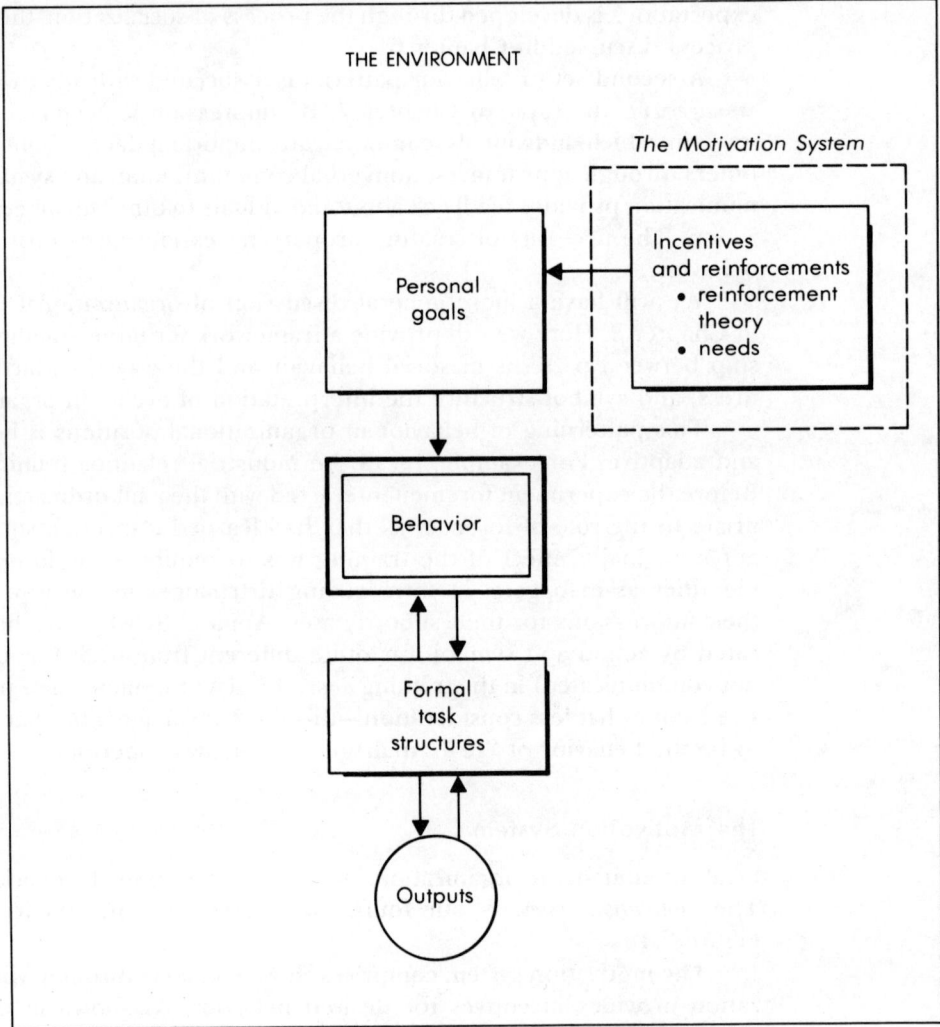

FIGURE 2.4 Achieving Personal Goals: Contingencies of Reinforcement—The Motivation System

goal-directed behavior. Chapters 9 and 10 will set forth what we know generally about theories of motivation and the personal goals of individuals.

The Mobility System

Our analysis of the mobility system follows directly from the logic of the previous Section. As shown in Figure 2.5, a similar relationship holds between personal

The Organizational System

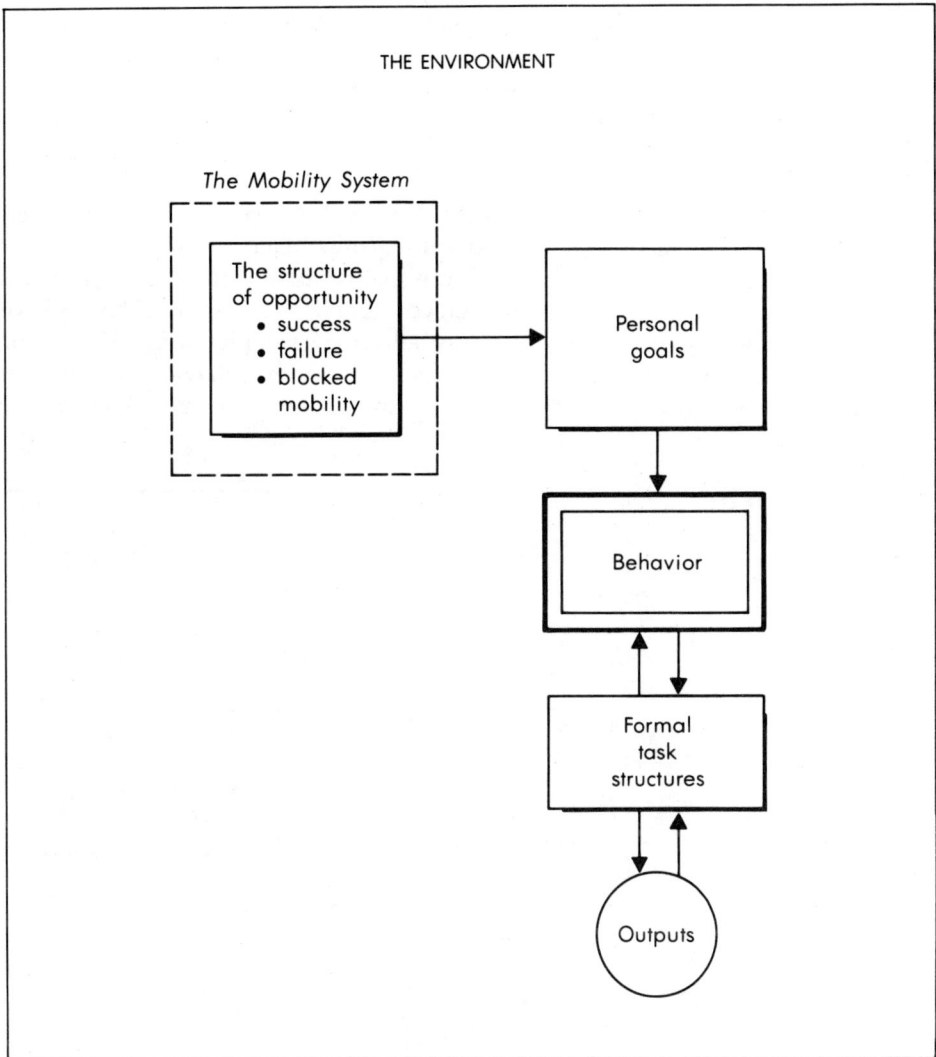

FIGURE 2.5 Achieving Personal Goals: Careers—The Mobility System

goals for status and power and the various organizational arrangements for providing upward mobility. The aim is to control behavior that is motivated by the incentives of increased status and power. Of course, other needs of the organization are filled as well, particularly the need to provide skilled management. But this practical concern can hardly account for all the details of the mobility process. In Chapter 11 we will describe the "structure of opportunity" that offers the incentives of prestige and esteem as people advance up the management ladder. In Chapter 12 we will analyze the motivational problems of people whose advancement is blocked.

The Interaction System

In the final section of Part II we will describe what we call the *interaction system*, those factors associated with group behavior, with interpersonal interaction. As in Sections I and II we will see the duality of achieving personal goals through activities designed to achieve organizational goals. Here we will be concerned with two aspects of group behavior as depicted in Figure 2.6. In Chapter 13 we will examine the dynamics of group behavior, in particular, how groups develop cohesiveness and norms of behavior, and then how they place direct

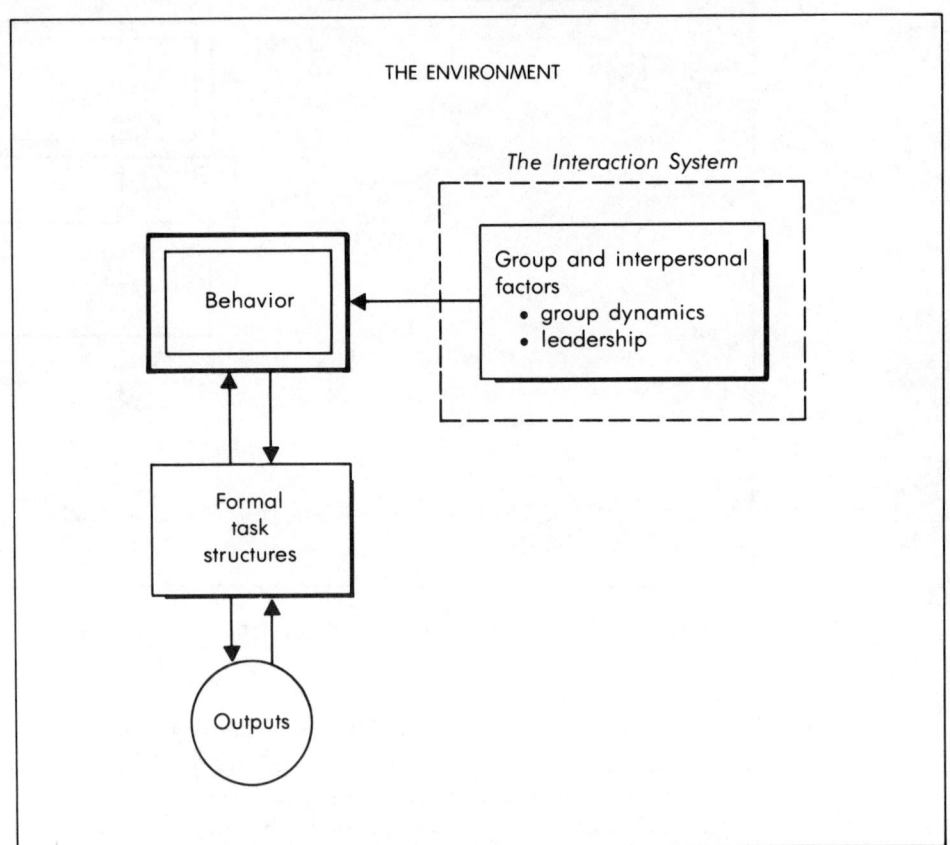

FIGURE 2.6 Achieving Personal Goals: Individuals in Groups—The Interaction System

social pressure on individuals to conform to these norms. In Chapter 14 we will inquire into the nature of leadership and how leaders enhance the ability of the group to modify individual behavior in the pursuit of group goals.

The Feedback and Control System

Our sixth, and final, systems component is the feedback and control system depicted in Figure 2.7. Controlling the outcomes of the organizational system

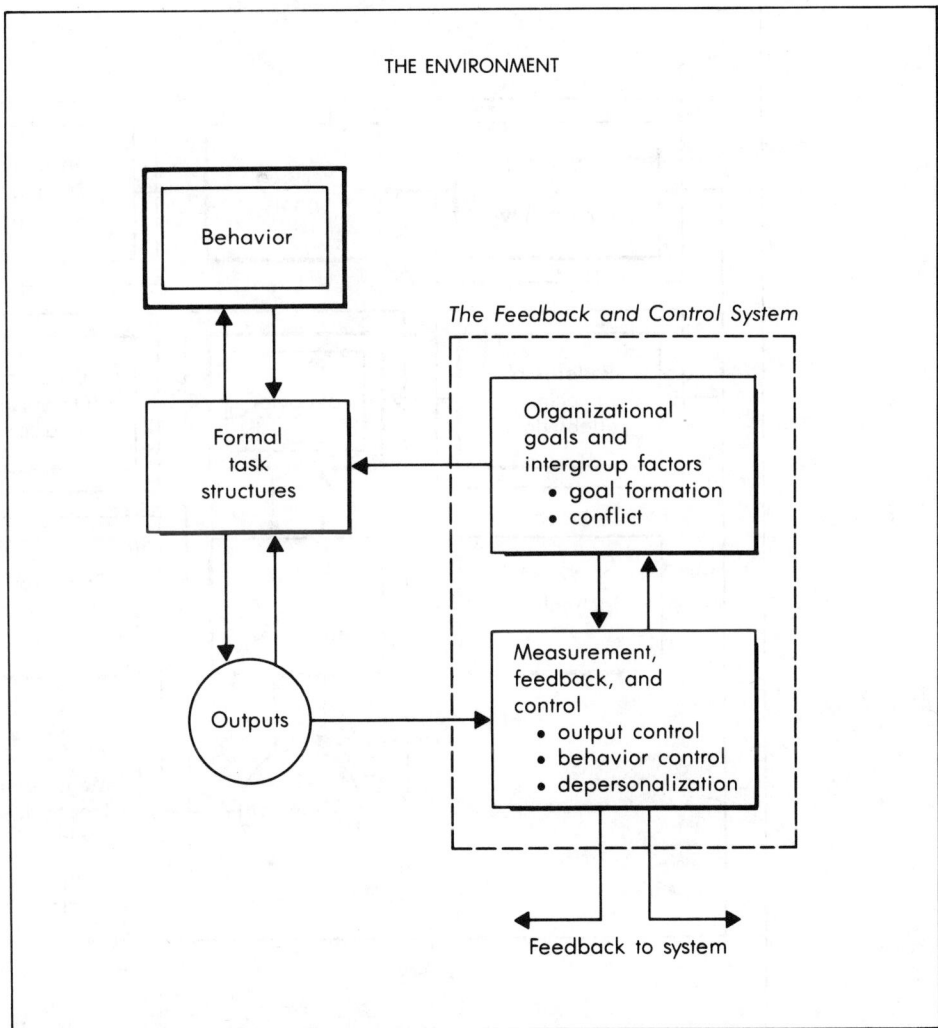

FIGURE 2.7 Achieving Management Goals—The Feedback and Control System

requires that outcomes be measured and that information be fed back to the system's control mechanisms—for example, to parts of the motivation and mobility systems. But as the systems diagram shows, goal formation is part of this process as well. Our analysis of the feedback and control function will consist of four chapters.

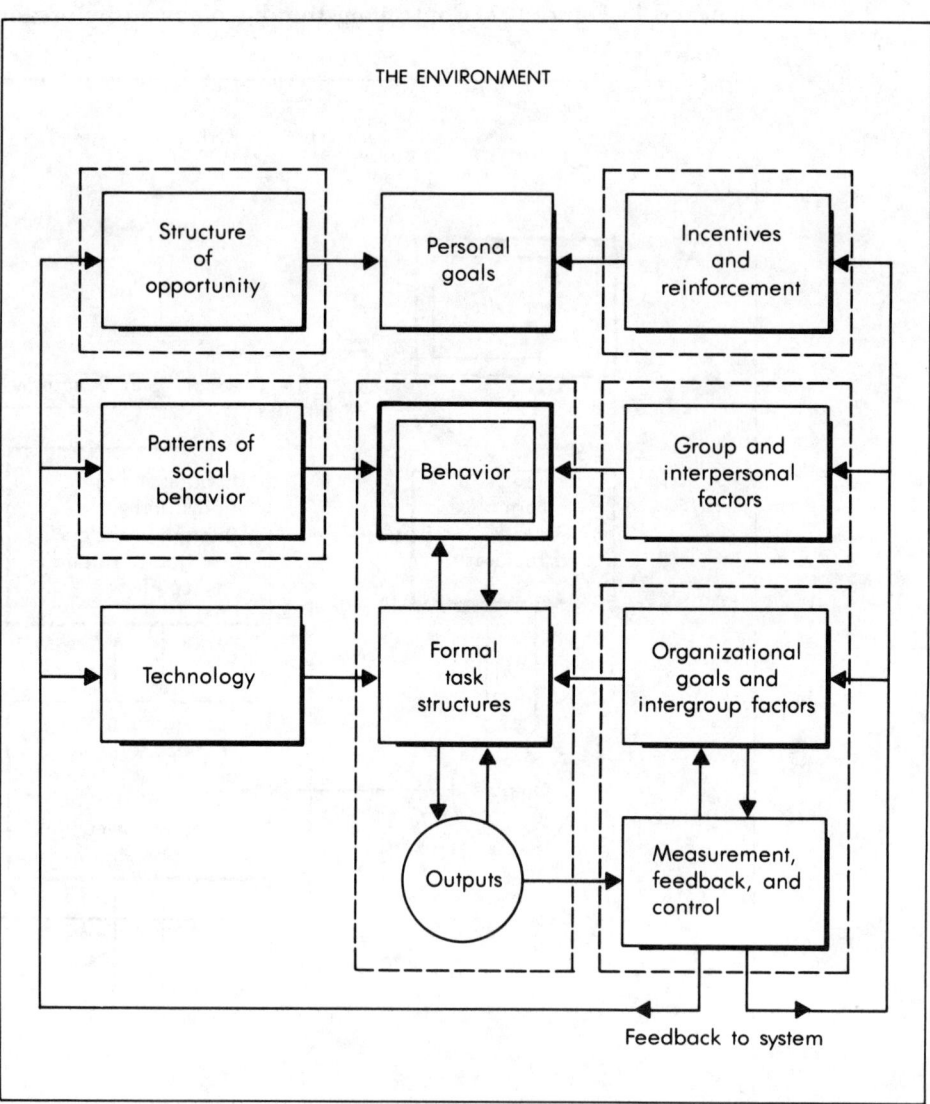

FIGURE 2.8   The Organization as a System

First, in Chapter 15, we will look at what organizational goals are, how they come into being, and how they affect resource allocation. Chapter 16 will be on the measurement of individual and organizational outcomes. Our concern is to develop an understanding of the nature of the process and the consequences of different ways of measuring outputs. We will find that there are important implications for the motivation system. In Chapter 17 we will look at how information is used in the feedback process to control behavior. We will see how the depersonalization of control through the construction of complex management information systems affects the entire organizational system. Chapter 18 will conclude this section with an analysis of the roots of intergroup conflict. All the factors we have named contribute, but certainly goal formation and the resulting reallocation of scarce resources are central to the problem. Chapter 18 completes our depiction of the organizational system but is also an appropriate introduction to our final part.

Processes for Organizational Improvement

Throughout this description of the six basic building blocks of the organizational system, our concerns have been to convey the interrelatedness of various organizational processes and to show how changes made in one element of the system are likely to have consequences (perhaps unanticipated) in others. For this reason, the processes of organizational improvement will be considered in the last part of this text. Our view of the process of organizational improvement is that for each change introduced one must take into consideration the entire organizational system (see Figure 2.8). For example, assume we try to change the motivation system by introducing financial incentives for higher worker productivity. The direct link to behavior is through individual goals for material well-being. However, there are also direct links back to the interaction system through the feedback and control system. Thus, schematically, we see what research has often shown: that workers' response to work incentive systems is modified by group pressure to restrict production.

These consequences of change aimed at organizational improvement will be illustrated in Chapters 19 through 21. Each major systems component will be examined and the probable consequences of change in each considered.

Summary

As you work through this text, there are a number of points you should remember. First, this text follows a building block approach. It starts with fundamental ideas about organizational structure and grows progressively more complex as principles concerning socialization, motivation, group process, leadership, and the like are added. With each new building block the organizational system becomes more complex and more realistic. We think this approach improves on the usual topical approach, in which each topic is presented completely before the next is introduced. Such an approach to the topic of authority, for example, would require that we present not only the key concepts of authority but take into account modifying principles of group process and leadership as well.

A more systematic approach is to proceed step by step through each building block, keeping in mind at each step that organizational behavior involves more than is being conveyed in the current discussion. At first our depiction of an organization will appear incomplete or impoverished, a mere shadow of a live organization. But remember that there is far more to it, as you will see in succeeding chapters.

Second, we believe that the principles of organizational behavior are equally applicable to all kinds of organizations. This means that there will be structures, systems of compliance, technologies, socialization processes, group processes, leadership, goals, motivation systems, feedback and control systems, and the like in all organizations. We describe these common principles and illustrate the wide variety of forms by which they are practiced in actual organizations. For example, the process of measuring performance in a manufacturing organization may be vastly different from the same process in, say, a social welfare agency; yet the basic principles are the same.

What is our point? Some of these common principles are illustrated more easily in one type of organization than in others. Socialization, for instance, may be illustrated particularly well through military organizations, because of their presumed need for uniform compliance. In such a case you may be tempted to say, "That is fine, but what does it have to do with me? I'm going to be a banker, not a military officer." The answer is that the principles of the socialization process are the same regardless of organization. If you understand the process as practiced in the military example, you will understand it as practiced in the banking industry and in your organization in particular. The forms may differ but the principles remain the same.

Thus, we have chosen examples from a variety of organizations, many of which you will never deal with firsthand. But you will be learning principles that will help you understand organizational behavior in a variety of contexts.

All in all, we hope you will find the analysis of organizational behavior as fascinating as do your authors.

Notes

1. This, together with the fact that the workers were primarily female, accounts for much of what took place in the Hawthorne experiments, according to Acker and Van Houten. For a discussion of this point, see Acker and Van Houten (1).

2. The concepts and some examples that follow are adapted from Ackoff (2). For other useful discussions of organizations as systems see Buckley (3) and Katz and Kahn (9).

References

1. ACKER, J., and D. R. VAN HOUTEN. "Differential Recruitment and Control: The Sex Structuring of Organizations." *Administrative Science Quarterly* 19 (June 1974): 152–163.
2. ACKOFF, R. L. "Towards a System of Systems Concepts." *Management Science* 17 (July 1971): 661–671.
3. BUCKLEY, W. *Modern Systems Research for the Behavioral Scientist.* Chicago: Aldine, 1968.
4. FAYOL, H. *Industrial and General Administration,* translated by J. A. Courbrough. Geneva: International Management Institute, 1930.
5. FLEISHMAN, E. A. "Leadership Climate, Human Relations Training, and Supervisory Behavior." *Personnel Psychology* 6 (1953): 205–222.
6. FLEISHMAN, E. A., E. F. HARRIS, and H. E. BURTT. *Leadership and Supervision.* Columbus: Bureau of Educational Research, Ohio State University, 1955.
7. FORRESTER, JAY W. "Counterintuitive Behavior of Social Systems." In *Search for Alternatives: Public Policy and the Study of the Future,* edited by Franklin Tugwell. Cambridge, Mass.: Winthrop, 1973.
8. ———. *Urban Dynamics.* Cambridge, Mass.: MIT Press, 1970.
9. KATZ, D., and R. L. KAHN. *The Social Psychology of Organizations,* 2nd ed. New York: Wiley, 1978.
10. MARCH, J. G. "Footnotes to Organizational Change." *Administrative Science Quarterly* 26 (1981): 563–577.
11. PFEFFER, J., and G. SALANCIK. *The External Control of Organizations: A Resource Dependence Perspective.* New York: Harper and Row, 1978.
12. ROETHLISBERGER, F. J., and W. J. DICKSON. *Management and the Worker.* Cambridge, Mass.: Harvard University Press, 1939.
13. RYAN, T. A. *Work and Effort.* New York: Ronald, 1947.

Discussion Questions

1. Our opening story is an actual case. Ted had the choice of going to top financial management to get an exception for Kerry. Where do the career risks lie for Ted? Under the criterion of personal utility, what are the likely consequences to Ted of his possible courses of action?
2. What do we mean by *Hawthorne effect?* What was it about the Hawthorne lighting experiments that produced the Hawthorne effect?
3. How would the systems model we developed in this chapter have helped the researchers in the leadership training experiment anticipate their lack of success?

4. Give a definition of *system*. What do we mean by *purposeful system*?
5. Give a definition of a purposeful, adaptive system. How does this definition relate to the importance of the notion of open systems?
6. Why is feedback important to a purposeful, adaptive system? Try to think of examples where feedback is important to your university or college department; to yourself.
7. As an exercise try to sketch out the main building blocks of the organization system from memory. Practice until you can place the major elements correctly.

PART II
The Basis for Organizational Action

Section One

The Formal Organization–Systems Structure (I)

Understanding organizational behavior requires more than understanding the sum of the parts of the organization; it requires comprehending the entire system as a system. To do this we must proceed step by step through the basic building blocks of the organizational system. In this section we take up the first of these building blocks, the *formal organization,* the basic framework within which organizational behavior takes place. The components of the formal organization are shown in Figure I.1.

Since the figure shows not only the structural elements of formal organization, but the factors of technology and environment as well, a better description of these components may be "the structure of the basic constraints on behavior and process within the organization." This structure includes:

1. the formal structure of positions, and the relationships among those positions that characterize the formal organization (the rights and duties attendant to those positions constituting the structure of formal authority), and
2. the structure imposed by the limitations of the work technology used in productive processes employed by the organization (the constraints imposed by the containing environment).

These are the basic attributes necessary to understanding the concepts of formal structure. We call them *system constraints* because they shape and limit organizational behavior.

Such a structure shapes behavior in several ways. First, since work activities

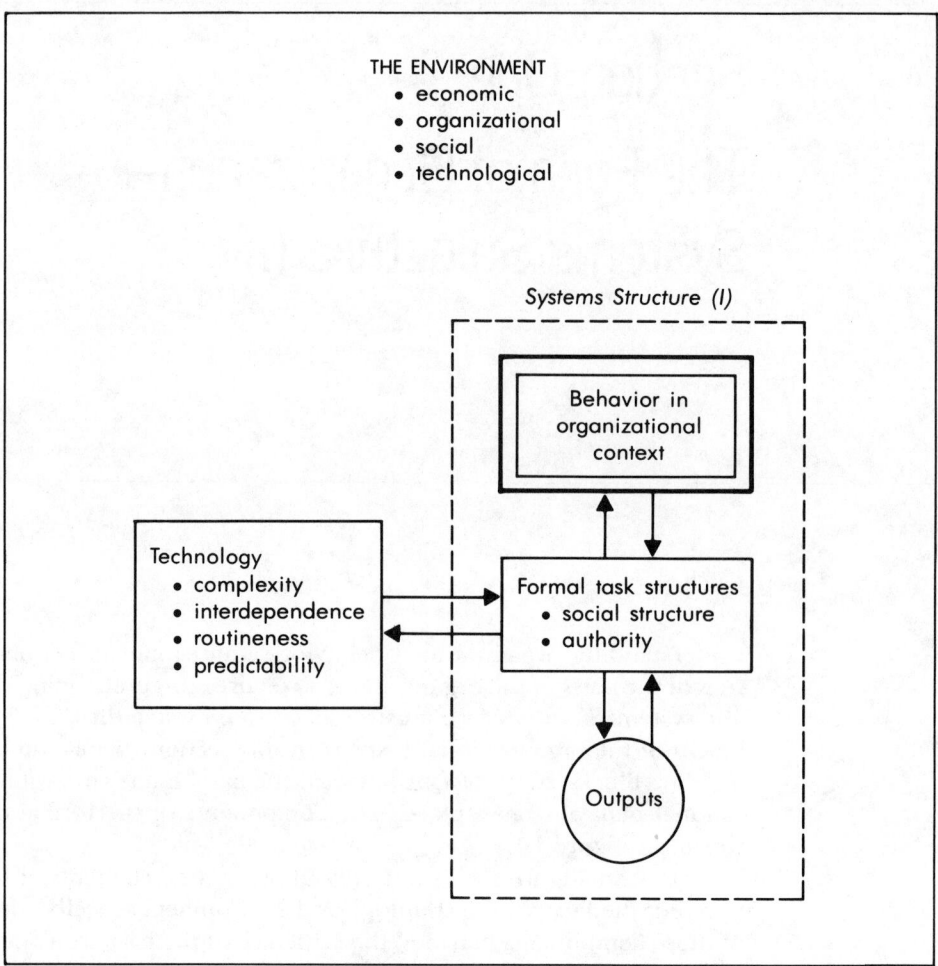

FIGURE I.1 The Basis for Organizational Action: The Formal Organization—Systems Structure (I)

in most complex organizations are differentiated, organizations need a structure for integrating these activities. For example, production work and sales need to be integrated. This need for integration leads to the beginning of the organization's formal structure since the duties and responsibilities of different production and sales positions must be specified. Then, presumably to ensure accountability in the performance of these functions, there is a matching authority structure—who has the right to tell whom what to do. These are the first elements of our systems structure or set of constraints on behavior.

A second set of constraints is derived from the limitation set by the work technology and the environment of the organization. Since technology and environment constrain the formal structure of the organization, they also shape behavior. For example, the formal structure of positions and authority relations in a chemical manufacturing plant will probably be different from that in an aircraft manufacturing plant. Furthermore, plants in rapidly evolving technological or economic environments will have formal structures that differ even more. Why this should be so is the topic of this section of our text. Thus, formal structures of positions and duties constrain organizational behavior, but are themselves limited or constrained by technology and environment.

Though the process of organizing behavior is one of shaping and constraining behavior, it is important *not* to think of a constraint as coercive or involuntary. Shaping and constraining is most likely to occur within a framework of positive inducements for modifying behavior.

In Section I, then, our task is to understand the first building block of the systems structure: the formal organization and the structural elements of technology and environment.

Chapter 3
The Social Structure of Organizations

Welcome Aboard

It wasn't Stanley's fault that his expectations of life in The Company were wildly unrealistic. When he had his first job interview, he and a few other young "technical people" were flown to Pawtucket in The Company's private plane. That's right, *flown* to a job interview in one of The Company's three executive jets. The recruiters knew (though the job seekers didn't) that the other way of getting to Pawtucket from New York was by rail, and that the Pawtucket railroad station was in such dismal shape that the recruiters were afraid it might convey the "wrong image."

But the recruits took no special notice of their treatment and blithely assumed that The Company thought them of sufficient worth to merit this special treatment. And in a way, they were right. It was just that this would be the last time any of them ever saw that executive jet again.

Stanley's final interview with Mr. Mason, the plant manager at that time, did nothing to change this self-image.

"How nice to have this chance to talk with you personally, Stanley." And "Yes, it seems to me that this is where you want to be, plant operations. That's the kind of experience we want our executives to have. We want people who know the range of The Company's operations, people who get outside their technical specialties and develop an understanding of how to run things."

Stanley conveyed to Mr. Mason with considerable ease that yes, that was how he felt. He wanted to be involved in a broad range of The Company's activities as soon as possible. After all, there was no time to lose—he was already twenty-one.

Poor Stanley. He knew so little of The Company and had such a distorted, egocentric view of his place in it. How could he know that this first, pleasant, personal chat with Mr. Mason would also be his last?

A week or so passed before The Company expressed its interest in "bringing him aboard," and Stanley reciprocated this interest by accepting. He was to report to Personnel at the beginning of the following week. On that day Stanley marched briskly through the special door to Personnel (you had to be escorted through the plant if you didn't have a Company badge) and proceeded to fill in forms for an hour or so. He knew no one, and no one seemed really to care. At regular intervals completed forms were carried away and new forms delivered. It all seemed so alien, so strange.

"Well, that's over, and the best of it is you won't have to do that again." The personnel manager was one of those hearty types who knew all the forms, knew all the rules, and, most of all, knew that everything was just as it should be.

"Mr. Franklyn said he would like to have some time with you this morning, so let's go up there and see if he's busy." On their way to Franklyn's office in the mill loft, the personnel man chattered continuously, pointing left and right, describing this and that and explaining why they were here and there. Utterly incomprehensible. Stanley did his best to reciprocate, but he knew so little. And he was also a little disappointed. He had been waiting to renew his conversation with Mr. Mason, but it was starting to look as though he would not have that opportunity today.

"Hello, son, nice to have you with us." With that greeting Ben Franklyn launched his first—and next to last—discussion with Stanley, revealing to him the importance and challenge of his new "responsibility." The challenge was here all right, on the mill floor. Ben knew that this was the heart of The Company. The rest he viewed as simply the supporting cast. Ben hoped Stanley understood this. He also wondered (being the quintessentially honest man) whether there was, in fact, a place in the mill scheme of things for a "college fella." Those were his words, "college fella."

Ben had a firm distrust of things he had not experienced personally, and higher education was one of them. It didn't seem to him—and perhaps he was right—that there was much about running a mill that could be learned from university classes. A person could learn mill work better and faster by actually working in the mill. When the talk ended, Stanley left Ben Franklyn's office to be taken by the mill clerk to lunch in the Company cafeteria. Stanley was disappointed not to have talked again with Mason, but he would have been even more disappointed had he known that this was the last time he would talk personally with Ben until he got his first pay raise.

Notables of the Pawtucket plant's society were pointed out to Stanley during lunch. Thoughts of success drifted through Stanley's mind as he headed back to the mill office. How long would it take, he wondered, to make it to the executive ranks. There wasn't much time.

In the office he was given Company manuals to read. They weren't very interesting, but the person in whose charge he had been placed (apparently someone in accounting) explained that it was important to get to know The Company and its operations well. The next day brought still more manuals. Where was the action? Boredom deepened. Finally, on the following day he was introduced to his new boss, the mill engineer. Apparently, having read the manuals, he was ready to go. The mill engineer didn't tell him he'd been too busy with something else to worry just then about a new employee.

Earlier, the mill engineer had been described to Stanley as "a genius with machines," a person totally involved in his work, a valuable asset to The Company. Stanley's acceptance of this description was reinforced now that he saw him since the engineer obviously did not pay much attention to appearance. His blue denim workshirt was stained with grease and oil, his safety boots ragged and equally oil-stained. His pants were nondescript gray twill (clean today, however). His face showed patches of beard that had been missed, and his hair had seen neither comb nor barber for weeks. But the thing that hit Stanley most forcefully was that this man was *old*. This very bright, successful, valuable engineer was probably over forty, possibly forty-five. Obviously a failure! Remembering Mason's words about Company operations being the road to executive success, Stanley was even more disappointed. What was there to learn from this man? *He* wasn't going anywhere.

"Have you seen the asset book? No. Well, that'll be up in Ray's [the manual pusher's] office. We've got to be sure that the asset book is up-to-date, and it's got to be correct. We find mistakes in it every now and then. We've let it go for a couple of years now, so you'll want to hop to it."

The engineer explained that Stanley's job was to verify The Company asset number on each piece of mill equipment and to update the book. He was warned pointedly not to yield to the temptation simply to assume that the number was correct. Even if it was difficult to find, obscured by grease and mill grime, he was to locate the tag with the number on it, clean it off and verify it, personally.

All the following week Stanley pursued this activity diligently. Soon it became apparent to him that this job would not be a matter of days, but of weeks, perhaps months. And it wasn't easy. The asset tags were in the damnedest places. In pursuing them Stanley was burned, soaked, shocked, cut, torn, and dirtied. But above all, he was profoundly bored and discouraged. The mill engineer had asked him, as a newcomer, to keep his eyes open for things the rest of them might not notice. He'd probably have some bright new ideas about the mill operations that they would all welcome. But, of course, when he did, no one ever paid any attention.

Stanley's only relief from the boredom came with his entry into the social life of the mill. He started spending a lot of time with Jimmy Szekely, who operated a finishing machine. The acquaintance had begun when Stanley had requested the whereabouts of the asset tag. When he found it, he asked Jimmy to tell him how the machine operated. And Jimmy did so. Stanley was impressed by what Jimmy knew about the machine—things Stanley would have assumed Jimmy wouldn't know. As their friendship grew Jimmy told Stanley about his family and about the electronics repair business he was getting started in the evenings. Stanley was genuinely impressed and Jimmy sensed that. It dawned on Stanley that Jimmy probably had more ambition than he did. And that seemed strange. For his part, Jimmy grew to trust Stanley, and so Stanley started to learn the lore of the mill. For instance, there *were* reasons why the expandrium shear never seemed to be able to operate above 30 percent efficiency. And those reasons—known to the men—were *not* to be shared with the industrial engineers.

Time passed, and still the only relief from the unrelenting boredom of the asset book were the stories and histories of the mill. This was how Stanley came to understand the social structure of the mill and the social order of The Company. And what were the things he learned?

About New York. Stanley learned that there was a place that contained all the intelligence and collective wisdom of The Company, and that was the New York headquarters, or simply New York. He learned that whatever policy or action took place, the ultimate justification was, "New York wants this," or when pressed, "I don't understand it either, but if New York wants it, it must be right."

About strife and social solidarity. Stanley learned that The Company was a society made up of two classes: management and workers. He learned that each viewed the other in an uncomplimentary way. He saw, or thought he saw, that there was a good deal of both misunderstanding and justification in these views. Mason and Shelby *did* think of the workers as machines, and not very efficient ones at that. The plant manager, one of the old guard, longed to return to the old days when workers didn't get a two-week vacation in the middle of July (thereby disrupting production terribly). On the other hand, if the workers put the energy and creativity into increasing production that they did into keeping it down, well, wouldn't things be better for everyone? The problem was simply too big for Stanley to grapple with.

About status hierarchies. Stanley learned that the status hierarchy throughout the plant was much more pervasive and complicated than he had ever dreamed. Sure, he knew that Mason and Franklyn were on top of things and that Mason was more important than Franklyn, Franklyn more important than Shelby, Shelby more important than Jimmy Szekely. But there were many other distinctions as well. It was more important to run the big rolling mill than to run the expandrium press. It was better to be an engineer than an accountant; and, strangely, it was more important to be a mechanical engineer than an electrical engineer. And finally, he found out that it was best of all to be from New York ("Those people really have something to say about what goes on here").

About the normative system. Stanley learned—though he wouldn't have put it that way—that there was a well-established set of unwritten should-dos and shouldn't-dos that was understood by everyone in plant society. He learned that everyone in The Company had to punch a time clock, including Mr. Marsh. Except that they didn't. That is, executives like Mr. Marsh and Mr. Mason had their time clock cards filled in for them by their secretaries. So did all the professional people in The Company—except that some didn't. So Stanley actually did punch the time clock for the first three months. Then he got his first raise, and Ben Franklyn told him it was now all right to go through the rear mill door. But that is another story. It is enough here to point out that because of plant security everyone had to leave through the two main entrance/exits—except that some didn't. And Ben Franklyn was the sole possessor of the unwritten knowledge and authority to say who did and who didn't have to.

This was how Stanley learned about the social structure of an organization. And that was the real worth of the asset book. Certainly it served the purpose of the mill engineer in acquainting Stanley with the mill equipment and with who knew what was where. But both the manuals and the asset book also served the incidental purpose of keeping Stanley out of the management's hair until they knew what to do with him. And in doing so it served the far more important purpose of socializing Stanley into The Company. What he learned of the social structure of organizations we are about to describe.[1]

Specialization and the Division of Labor

Two universal characteristics of complex human organizations are functional specialization and the consequent division of labor. For example, producing shoes involves many different tasks—there is functional specialization and division of labor. Producing a jet airliner is many times more complex—there is greater functional specialization of the organization, including the functions of design, test, and production, and, therefore, more division of labor. Within the broad functional areas there may be further specialization. Within the design function, for example, there is further functional specialization—in wings, engines, bodies, and the like. There are also the finance, marketing, and other functions supporting the basic production processes.

One result of this differentiation is the need for the structural integration of functions (wings need to fit bodies and engines to fit wings, and the whole thing has to fly). Each functional unit (wings, engines, bodies) has its boss. Above these bosses are bigger bosses (bosses of wings *and* bodies). Thus, the hierarchical pyramid is built up to achieve this integration of the subcomponents of the task (9, 15).

We have devised *organization charts* to portray organizational hierarchies and territories. Here are some examples.

The Organization Chart

Almost every organization has diagrams or charts depicting the relationships among positions in the organization. Depending on the size of the organization there may be one chart or many. Large organizations have many such charts, arranged in hierarchical fashion. For example, the first takes you from the board of directors through various functional vice presidents. The next from the vice presidents through local plant organizations, and so on. These charts convey both *position* and *rank;* that is, what that person is supposed to be occupied with—his or her territory—and the level. Position is conveyed through the job title—vice president for marketing, for example; rank, through location in the hierarchy (depicted by the chart, and to some extent through title as well).

The Company

Let us look at the charts of different kinds of organizations to see what they do, and do not, convey. The corporate management of The Company—the top level of organization—is shown in Figure 3.1. The chart shows how each position relates to others. It could be done in other ways, but this is how The Company does it. The chart shows who is responsible for what and at what level.

Everyone is responsible to Mr. Marsh. The board of directors presumably guides Marsh and approves key policy decisions. Yet this is not always the case. If the chairman of the board is elected because he controls the majority of stock (and Marsh, Sr., did until his recent death), then, in actuality, he may be the senior policymaking executive (and Marsh was). Also, the office of the president generally has a number of staff types in it—the "assistants to." These are usually the elect of The Company, bright young people putting in a tour of duty to familiarize themselves with the executive functions of The Company and, incidentally, becoming known personally to the president.

Notice that there is a distinction between *staff* and *line* relationships (although this distinction is not as clear in actual operations as it is on the formal organization chart; we will address this topic further in Chapter 4). Line relationships show the chain of authority. A position at one point on the line has the authority to direct the activities of those positions below it on the same line. In our chart line relationships can be seen by tracing a line downward from Mr. Marsh. For example, through the senior vice president for production and the group vice president for expandrium products, Marsh has a line relationship with the plant managers and those below them (see Figure 3.2). Staff relationships, however, are generally advisory. People in these positions do not have the authority to direct the activities of those in positions below them on the organization chart, hence the absence of lines of authority flowing downward from the position. For example, legal counsel is staff to the office of the president; it has an advisory relationship to the president, with no authority to direct the activities of the vice presidents.

After the president, the next step in the line of command is the vice presidents of the major functions within The Company. Notice that titles often convey more than the position indicates. For example, functions that have senior vice presidents, such as production and finance, are deemed more important to The Company than those which do not (personnel and industrial relations, for example). Within the personnel and industrial relations functions, industrial relations

The Organization Chart

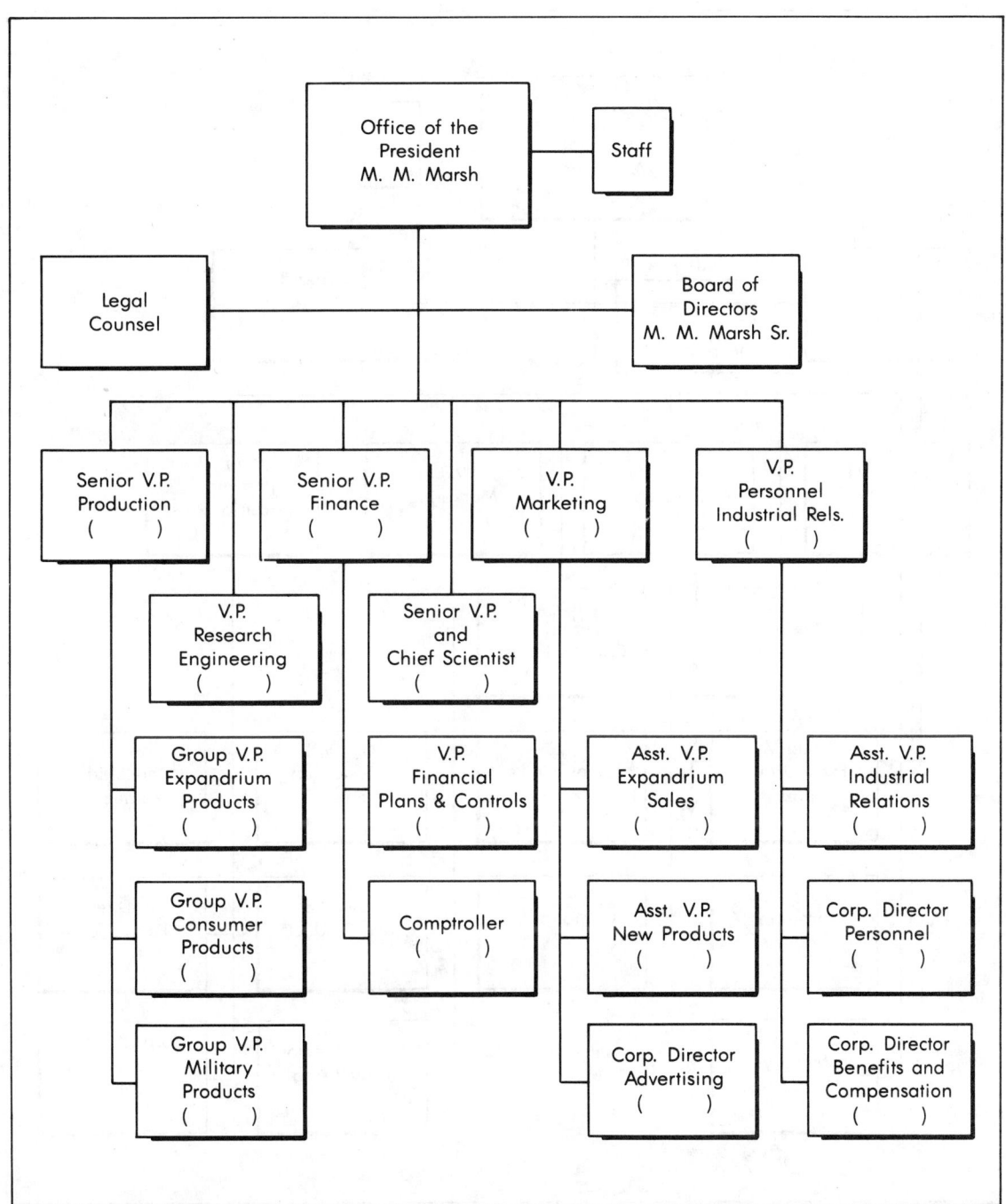

FIGURE 3.1   Corporate Staff Organization—The Company

56 Chapter 3 The Social Structure of Organizations

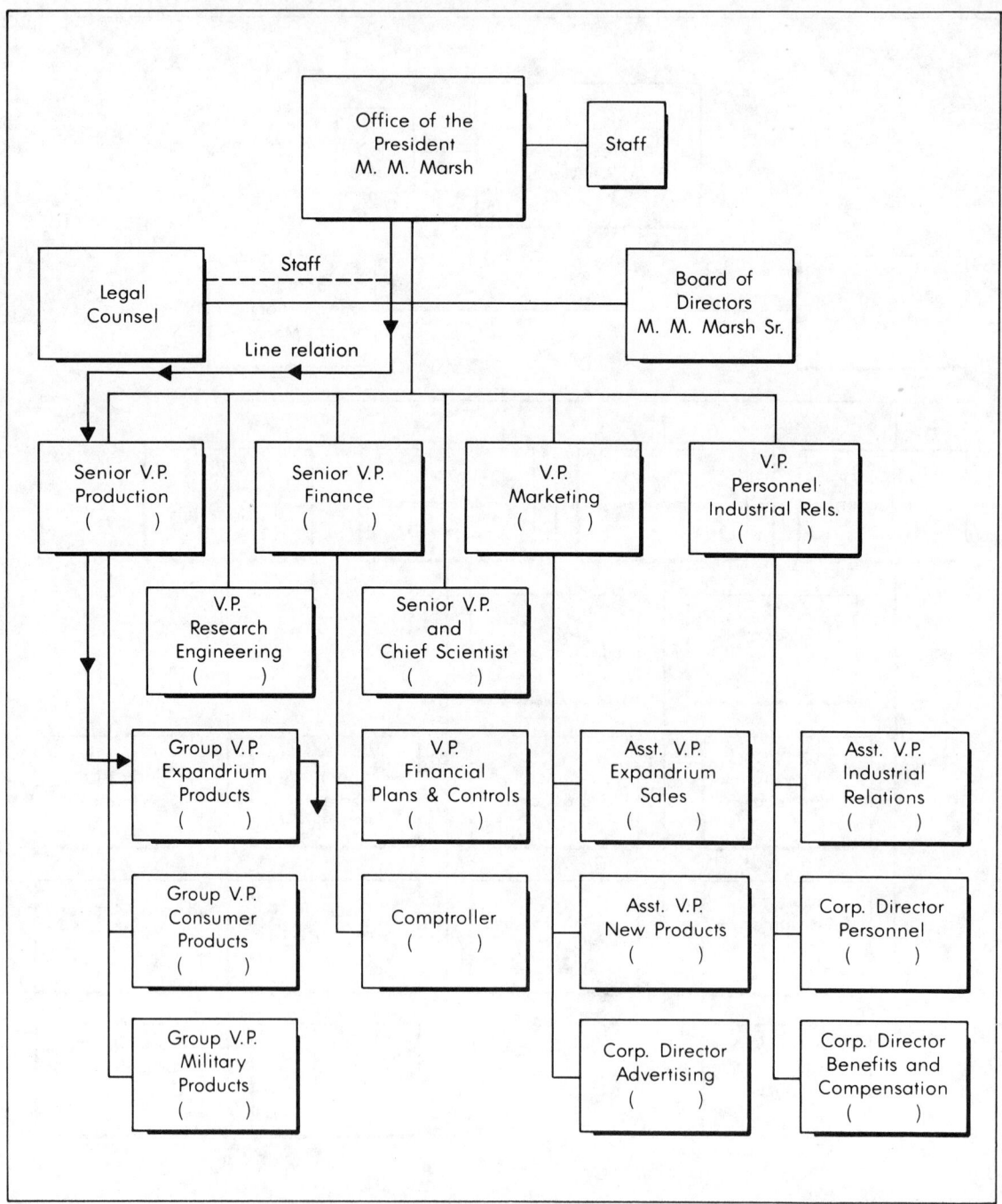

FIGURE 3.2 Corporate Staff Organization—The Company

is considered more important because it has an assistant vice president and personnel does not.

Having just established the importance of senior vice presidents we should now warn you that this is not always the case. Tucked away on the chart, and in addition to the vice president for research and engineering, there is a senior vice president and chief scientist. According to what we said, this should be a position and function of major importance in The Company, yet it is not. Why? Until now we have neglected a second important feature of the organization chart: *history*. Most organization charts today contain traces of their past. Some positions are there because "it has always been that way"; others, because at some point in the past a position was needed for a special purpose.

In this case, there was a time when certain basic patents became crucial to The Company's further development. Consequently, the holder of the patents, an outstanding inventor and technical mind, was "brought aboard" with great fanfare and made senior vice president for research and engineering.

For a while this worked well. But after several years of unprecedented growth and technical development (for which this senior vice president was largely responsible) the nature of the job changed. Because of that very growth and development, the job required a different kind of person, an executive rather than an inventor. The Company solved the problem by creating the position of senior vice president and chief scientist. They then moved the inventor into it and put a top-flight executive into the research and engineering vice presidency. This was a face-saving measure that added in no small way to The Company's current success.

This, then, is corporate organization, essentially a map of executive management. Let us now examine two very different kinds of organizations, the Roman Catholic Church and a large state department of public welfare.

The Church

The formal organization of the Roman Catholic Church is based on an interpretation of the relationship between Peter and the apostles, and on understandings of the initial form of the Church (history once again). For example, we might think of the position of the pope as corresponding directly to that of president of The Company, but this is not the case. For while the pope has the authority to instruct the bishops as a body, he does not have authority to command an individual bishop in the particular affairs of his diocese or archdiocese (geographical groupings of parishes). An interesting feature of the Roman Catholic Church is the "flatness" of the organization. The line of authority contains only three positions, the diocesan ordinary (the bishop or archbishop in charge), the head of the parish organization (the pastor), and the several curates or assistant pastors.

The Company has more levels of organization. Within The Company the number of different functions and the division of labor is great. Thus, there is a need for the coordinating hierarchy. This is not true of the Church, however. Within a basic framework of faith and moral teaching, dioceses pursue organizational activities largely independently of one another. There is no need for multiple levels of hierarchy to integrate functionally differentiated activities.

The Department of Public Welfare

Structurally, the Department of Public Welfare (DPW) resembles The Company more than the Church. In fact, though within the boundaries of one state, it has even more levels of hierarchy. The DPW has many functions: cash assistance and social services for the needy, child welfare, mental health, to name a few. A unique aspect of the DPW is that the central state organization lacks direct authority over the county organizations, for the DPW is essentially political. Thus, the central office maintains surveillance to ensure that legalities are observed, but county activities are up to the county commissioners and county board of assistance.

This political character extends to the central office as well. The secretary of welfare and the top deputies (corresponding to the first two levels of executive management) are political appointees, and thus are replaced when a new administration takes over. Rarely have they advanced through the ranks of the DPW, and they frequently understand little of its operations. As a result the lines of authority and responsibility are muddied, and policy is often tailored to short-range political aims. This situation is different from that in both The Company and the Church.

Thus, the organization chart tells us some things but not others. We need additional concepts to help us understand more of the social structure of organizations.

Position and Status

Position, as we have said, is found on the organization chart and can be stated in terms of the formal organization structure. *Status,* however, is a property of social organization and is not written down (1, 7). For example, there is a status hierarchy among presumably equal plant managers of The Company. Figure 3.3 shows the organization of the expandrium products group. Portsmouth is a newer and larger plant, and therefore its manager has a higher status than the managers in the other plants. Status, thus, is a property of position rather than of people. This can become confusing occasionally because people in positions of lower status may have greater influence than counterparts in positions of higher status. For example, Ben Franklyn in Pawtucket is more influential than Klein of Portland. Pawtucket is an older and smaller plant, and consequently the plant manager is lower in status than the plant manager at Portland. But over the years Franklyn has built up a special relationship with the group vice

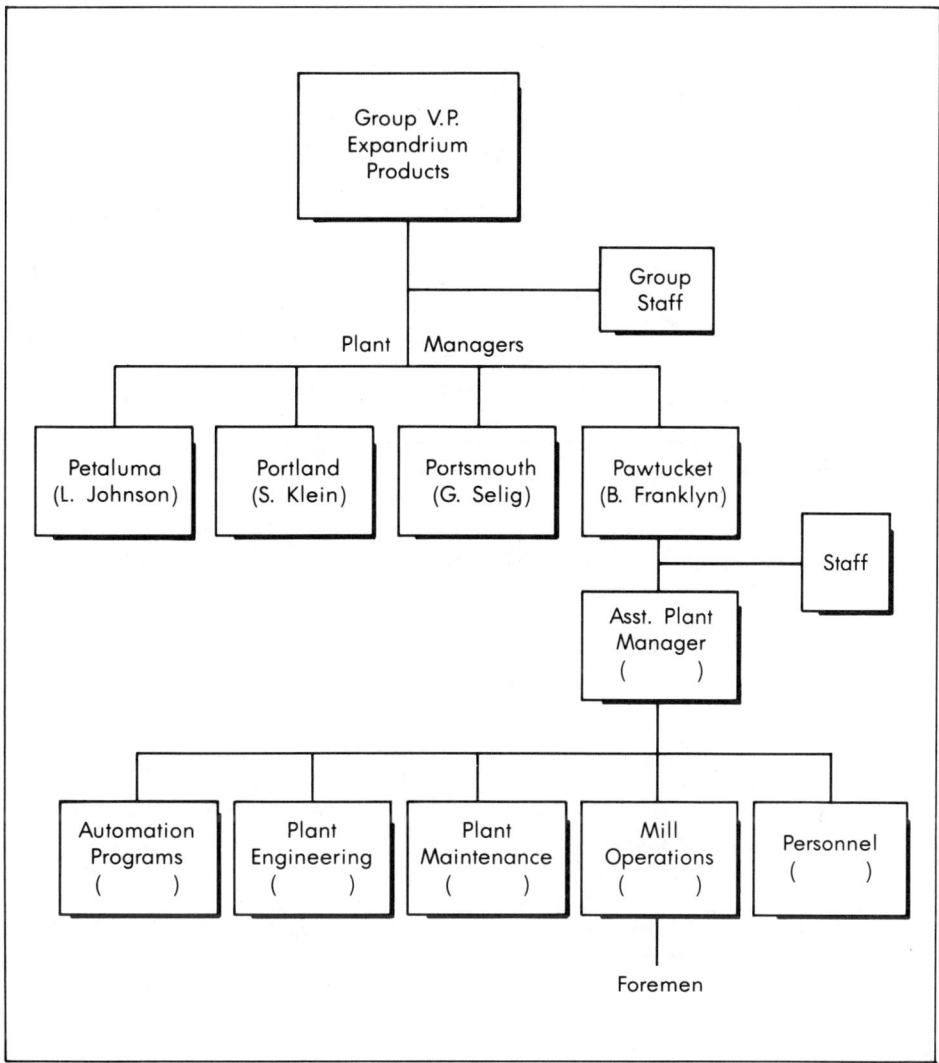

FIGURE 3.3 Organization of Expandrium Products Group

president. Because of this special relationship and the privileged communication that exists between the two, Franklyn is, in many ways, the most influential of the plant managers, though not the highest in status.

To summarize, status is a property of position in the organization, being related directly to the importance of that position. Plant manager of Portsmouth is a higher status position than plant manager of Pawtucket because Portsmouth is a bigger and more important plant. Vice president of marketing is higher status than vice president of personnel and industrial relations because people in The Company think that marketing is more important to the success of The Company than personnel and industrial relations. Finally, although influence generally coincides with status and importance, it is possible for lower-status individuals, because of special considerations, to have greater influence than higher-status individuals. (See Box 1 for more on status, power, and function).

Box 1

Power, Status, and Organizational Function

One way of accounting for differences in power or influence among managers is to suggest that this power comes from the importance of the subunit's function. A unit that deals with problems crucial to the existence of the entire organization will have the most power. In this research, Donald C. Hambrick uses the term "critical contingency" to describe the problems in the organization's environment that most affect its continued existence. Functions that are best able to cope with these crucial contingencies will be managed by higher-power, and hence, higher-status individuals.

Hambrick identifies two sources of critical contingencies: (1) the demands of the external environment, and (2) the organization's strategy for competing or prospering.

Hambrick identifies four types of environmental demand:

1. Output demands: requirements imposed by external product or market trends and events.
2. Throughput demands: new developments appearing in the environment in the processing or delivery of products or services.
3. Administrative demands: new developments in the determination of roles and relationships in organizations.
4. Regulatory demands: government regulations, taxes, sanctions, litigations, and the like.

Hambrick classifies his sample of organizations into two types. The first are those which can be considered "prospectors"—those whose strategy for coping is to develop new products or services. The second are "defenders"—organizations whose basic strategy is not innovation, but rather improving the efficiency and effectiveness with which they offer their present products or services.

A sample of 195 executives in twenty organizations provided data for the study. Three groups of organizations were chosen to provide generalizability: hospi-

continued

tals, colleges, and insurance companies. These organizations had been classified as either extreme prospectors or defenders. The power of each individual manager was measured by asking participating executives knowing the person in question to rate her, or his, influence on four types of decisions that were of major consequence to the organization. The executives were also asked to rate themselves as belonging primarily to one of nine functional areas such as accounting/finance, operations, marketing, product development.

Results of major interest here had to do with the relationship between the type of organization and the dominant critical contingency in its environment, the function of the executive, and that executive's perceived influence. The results provide a striking confirmation of the interrelationship between function, influence, and dominant environmental demands.

For example, the insurance company, whose basic environmental critical contingency is product/market innovation, showed significant positive correlation between executive influence and occupying a position in the marketing or product development functions. Because these correlations were controlled for the hierarchical level of the executive, we can rule out the possibility that people in these functions might simply be higher up in management and accordingly have greater power. By way of distinction, insurance executives in the accounting/finance and operations functions showed significantly lower influence.

If we now compare the results for hospitals, whose critical contingency is efficiency and cost control rather than marketing, we find exactly the reverse result. In hospitals influence was greater in the accounting/finance and operations functions. Executives in the marketing and product development functions were reported to have significantly less than average influence.

To summarize, the results confirm the direct relationship between the power or influence (and hence status) of management executives and the function they perform. The influence is greatest when that function is crucial to the survival and further growth of the organization.

(From D. C. Hambrick, "Environment, Strategy, and Power Within Top Management Teams," *Administrative Science Quarterly*, 26 (1981) 253–276).

Expected Behavior as Social Structure

With this discussion of the concept of status we have actually gone beyond the confines of the formal organization. Status is a property of position in the organization, but it is not part of the relationships among positions and the rights and duties attached to those positions as set forth in the written rules, regulations, and contracts of the organization. So the formal organization is but one aspect of the social structure of organizations. Organizational behavior also is constrained or structured by shared understandings among members as to what is proper behavior. These shared understandings are not set down as written rules and contracts of the organization, but exist as common expectations concerning behavior. Because of this, these elements of social structure are called the *informal organization* (3, 6).

Expectations concerning appropriate behavior on the part of others are said to constitute the *normative structure*. The rewards and penalties associated with adhering to or violating these expectations are termed *sanctions*. Sanctions used to support the normative structure may vary from social pressure to rewards such as promotion; they have definite consequences in the formal structure of the organization.

Two major components of the normative structure are *norms*, general expectations about how people in a given organization should behave, and *roles*, more restricted expectations about how people in specific positions should behave within particular organizational contexts.

Before proceeding, however, we must define behavior. Loosely, *behavior* refers to our actions. More specifically, in terms of normative structure, it refers to three kinds of actions: verbal behavior, activities, and displays.

Verbal behavior is what people say and how they say it. It is expressions of values, attitudes, beliefs, and motives; it is also tone and inflection. Words that mean one thing, for example, may convey the opposite meaning through tone and inflection.

Activities are what people do: how they move, how they act, when and where. Reporting late for work is an activity.

Display is dress and gesture.

All kinds of behavior, not just physical activities, are constrained by the social expectations that constitute the normative structure. Because role and norm are related concepts, with role expectations included under the wider normative structure, we first define the more specific term *role*.

Position and Role

The concept of *social role*, or simply *role*, is widely used in analyzing social organization. Roles relate to positions in the formal organization, not to people. We speak of the role of plant manager, the role of mill engineer, and the role of machine operator; not of Franklyn's role or Jimmy Szekely's role (except that it is all right, for example, to speak of Franklyn's role in such and such an event).

Let us say the divisional vice president (we will call him Martin) is putting in a ritual visit to Franklyn's mill floor. He does not much care how Szekely's expandrium scalper works, but he understands that, in his executive role, he is expected to ask Jimmy for an explanation and to listen patiently and nod, feigning interest while Szekely explains. He understands too that he should commend Szekely for his "important contribution."

Also predictable is that Jimmy addresses Martin as "Mr. Martin." Martin, however, after being introduced by Franklyn, talks with "Jimmy." Also, Martin calls Franklyn "Ben." But Ben, because Martin once worked for him as a young engineer, addresses Martin as "Marty" although younger plant managers probably would not (17).

Role, then, concerns a social relationship between occupants of positions, with shared expectations about the behavior that should characterize this relationship. These expectations are normative—they are expectations of what behavior should be (4:58).

Some role expectations are not illustrated directly in our example but can be easily imagined. For example, how is Mr. Martin dressed? How is Szekely dressed? Jimmy Szekely is wearing a ragged oil-stained coverall as are most of the millhands. This is not surprising—it is a very functional outfit for his job. Martin's gray pinstripe with tie and vest is no surprise either. Although not particularly functional, it is appropriate to his role and it is expected. We would probably be astonished if he came to work in a T-shirt and bluejeans. Thus, there are role expectations for *displays* as well as for verbal behavior and activities (4:63).

Finally, role behavior is specific to role pairs. That is, the role of father requires a complementary role of child; that of husband, the role of wife; and that of superior, the role of subordinate. Some roles have more than one complement. In our example, the role of plant manager has several. And different behaviors are prescribed for each of these complementary positions in his *role set* (the set of positions with whom the plant manager interacts) (4, 8, 10). The role of plant manager relates in one way to the role of machine operator but in another to that of company president. Martin, therefore, behaves differently toward Jimmy Szekely than toward Mr. Marsh.

Although this discussion may seem quite obvious, abstract considerations are very different from real life. What is expected is far from obvious to people in new positions, occupying new roles, who understand there *are* things expected of them but do not know what those things are. The social structure of role behavior must be learned by observation and experience—remember your awkward first date or first encounter with a head waiter. To summarize:

- Role is a concept used in analyzing social interaction between positions in an organization.
- Roles are understandings by members of an organization of how people in given positions are expected to relate socially with others.
- The expected behavior of a role occupant will differ when relating to different positions in the organization's hierarchy.
- The understanding of expected role behavior by the occupant of a given position may differ substantially from the understanding of others who interact with that position.

Norms and Rules

Behaviors covered by expectations applicable to all members of the organization, or to classes of members, but not to particular positions, are called *norms*. Most organizations have written rules specifying what is and what is not acceptable behavior within the organization. For example, people at The Company plant in Pawtucket must arrive at work at 8 A.M.; that is the rule. We use *rule* to refer to procedures or obligations explicitly stated and written in company manuals, military regulations, or the like.

Organizations differ widely in how extensive their rules are. Field manuals in the military, for example, are quite comprehensive. Rules governing the behavior of priests are also extensive. But formal rules governing behavior in The Company and other business organizations are relatively few. Some small businesses may even have no formal written rules.

Beyond these formal rules, and sometimes in conflict with them, are widely shared organization norms. These norms are unwritten, perhaps unstated, mutual understandings as to what is appropriate behavior under given sets of conditions. Some written rules may be incorporated into the normative structure and others not. But generally, the *normative structure* is far more extensive in its prescriptions and proscriptions than the formal, written rules. For example, in The Company's engineering and research laboratory, the rules require arrival at 8:30 A.M., one hour for lunch, and departure at 5:00 P.M. The normative order, however, says that those rules apply to everyone but the research scientists. They may come in when they wish and leave when they wish, or perhaps not come in at all on a given day. But the normative structure also says that for those scientists who choose not to follow the clock there is a price to pay: they must work more than the standard 37½ hours per week. If they choose to come in at 10:00 they must still be there at 6:00, or come in on Saturday or Sunday. Scientists who habitually violate the normative order will be told about it, *not* by the management, but by fellow scientists.

Perhaps it seems that we have used the terms role and norm to mean the same thing. That is partly true. Expectations about the behavior of people in a particular position are part of the normative structure generally. But role behavior is specific to a certain position and counterposition (for example, millhand and group vice president), and is related to a specific setting (such as the mill floor or a bowling party. Normative behavior is covered by general organizational norms and is not specific to a given position and counterposition (for example, the arrival time of scientists). Thus, for Jimmy Szekely the norms of the mill specify an appropriate level of production for a given day's work, a level different from that urged by Ted Shelby and his industrial engineers.

Since the normative structure is unwritten, the norms must reside in members of the social organization themselves. The social organization may be as small as the number of millhands in The Company's expandrium mill in Pawtucket (or even smaller), or as large as society itself. Jimmy Szekely's group ascribes to the quite specific norm, "Sixty percent of the production standard is too little, but 100 percent is too much," and to the societal norm, "Don't rat on your buddy."

Notice that norms are shared understandings about what *should* be, about correct ways for people to behave. They say little about how people actually behave, or how they wish to behave. So although it might be surprising to find commonly accepted behavior at variance with the normative order, it is possible. It depends on how central given behavior prescriptions are to organizational life. Some norms are seen as essential to the well-being of the organization. Hard work, commitment to execute a decision, observing codes of ethics and honor—these are key managerial norms. For Jimmy Szekely's group, control of production output is also key. But not all norms are deemed essential. Dress codes, for example, while central to outside salespeople, are less important for the manufacturing manager or accountant. Nevertheless, they are generally adhered to.[2]

Violation of norms seen as essential brings swift enforcement through the use of sanctions: verbal and perhaps physical abuse, the withholding of favors, the "silent treatment." Conformity to these norms, especially for managerial personnel, may be the path to rewards (such as promotion) within the formal structure of the organization. However, violation of norms seen as not essential to organizational well-being, such as dress codes, may be tacitly accepted, seen only as harmlessly deviant. To summarize:

- Norms are patterns of shared understandings concerning the behavior appropriate to a member of the organization.
- Norms include role behavior as well as work activities, beliefs, and sentiments.
- Norms may apply to members of the organization generally or may be specific to types of positions.
- Norms are distinct from the written rules of the organization though they may incorporate some of those rules.
- Norms are supported or enforced by sanctions invoked by members of the organization or subgroup of the organization. Example: the "silent treatment."

Summary

We began our discussion of social structure by describing the formal structure of the organization as set forth in the organization chart. We cannot discuss social structure fully, however, without looking at both the formal structure and the informal structure of the organization as constituted in status relationship patterns and role and norm systems.

This distinction between formal and informal organization is sometimes used as a basis for understanding organizational behavior (18). But we feel such a distinction is not terribly important. For one thing, an observer of organizational behavior would find it difficult to tell whether a given behavior was specified by the formal organization or stemmed from those shared understandings that constitute the informal organization. For another, it does not much matter. Constraints on behavior, whatever their source, are part of the structure of organizational systems. Our task is to examine the rules, expectations, and mutual understandings that constrain the behavior of individual organizational members and make that behavior "sensible" and predictable for other members.

Let us summarize some of these key elements of social structure. Specialization of work activities and the consequent division of labor characterizes most complex organizations. This division of labor is responsible for the complexity of the organization chart. Tasks are broken down or differentiated into subtasks and performed by different subunits of the organization. The organization chart shows how the work of those subunits is integrated. It describes relationships among positions as far as formal duties and rights are concerned. It indicates, for example, that Mr. Martin should be able to tell Ben Franklyn what to do, and to expect Ben to get it done. The organization chart also indicates who is more important than who else. But these distinctions are not as detailed as those actually existing in the social structure as it is understood by members of the organization. So the chart conveys the status of Mr. Mason compared to Mr. Marsh, but not the relative ranking of Martin compared to the senior vice president and chief scientist, or the status relationships among the various plant managers reporting to Mr. Martin. That knowledge is part of the status structure, which is not part of the formal organization. Yet the status structure helps us understand organizational behavior. Neither do the organization chart or the formal rules and procedures tell us about roles and norms. These too are part of social structure, and constrain behavior so as to make it "sensible" and predictable.

The point is that a great deal of behavior will not take place in certain organizational positions in specific organizational settings and with particular persons or groups. This is what we mean when we say that social structure constrains behavior. Mostly these constraints are important to the outcomes—whether related to increasing effectiveness or to cementing group solidarity—desired by members of the organization, from managers to millhands.

Sometimes these constraints are matters of style only—though some organizations have a strong commitment to style, whether it be in verbal behavior, in activities, or in displays. Whatever the case, rules and norms are part of a structure of shared expectations about behavior that are distinct from the formal organization, though no less a part of the systems structure.

With this background complete, we turn to an inquiry into the nature of authority, into patterns of command relationships. These authority relationships are also part of the systems structure. But, as with the formal organizational structure, formal authority relationships present but a partial depiction of structure.

Notes

1. For different kinds of "inside" accounts of life in the "mill" see Sprague (14) and Roy (12).
2. Schein (13) uses the terms *pivotal* and *peripheral* to refer to more important and less important organizational norms.

References

1. BARNARD, C. "Functions and Pathology of Status Systems in Formal Organizations." *Industry and Society,* edited by William F. Whyte. New York: McGraw-Hill, 1946.
2. BERGER, C., and L. CUMMINGS. "Organizational Structure, Attitudes, and Behaviors." In *Research in Organizational Behavior,* Vol. 1, edited by B. Staw, Greenwich, Conn.: JAI Press, 1979, pp. 169–208.
3. DALTON, M. *Men Who Manage.* New York: Wiley, 1959.
4. GROSS, N., W. S. MASON, and A. W. MCEACHERN. *Explorations in Role Analysis: Studies of the School Superintendency Role.* New York: Wiley, 1958.
5. HAMBRICK, D. "Environment, Strategy, and Power Within Top Management Teams." *Administrative Science Quarterly* 26 (1981): 253–276.
6. HOMANS, G. *The Human Group.* New York: Harcourt, Brace, 1950.
7. HUGHES, E. "Dilemmas and Contradictions of Status." *American Journal of Sociology* 50 (1945): 353–359.
8. KATZ, D., and R. L. KAHN. *The Social Psychology of Organizations,* 2nd ed. New York: Wiley, 1978.
9. LAWRENCE, P. *Organization and Environment: Managing Differentiation and Integration.* Homewood, Ill.: Irwin, 1969.
10. MERTON, R. *Social Theory and Social Structure,* revised ed. Glencoe, Ill.: Free Press, 1957.
11. MEYER, J., and B. ROWAN. "Institutionalized Organizations: Formal Structure as Myth and Ceremony." *American Journal of Sociology* 83 (September 1977): 340–363.
12. ROY, D. "Quota Restriction and Goldbricking in a Machine Shop." *American Journal of Sociology* 57 (1952): 427–442.
13. SCHEIN, E. *Organizational Psychology.* Englewood Cliffs, N.J.: Prentice-Hall, 1965.
14. SPRAGUE, L. "Needed Research in Organizational Behavior: A Production/Operations Management Perspective." *Academy of Management Review* 2 (July 1977): 504–507.
15. THOMPSON, J. *Organizations in Action.* New York: McGraw-Hill, 1967.

16. THOMPSON, V. *Modern Organization.* New York: Knopf, 1961.
17. WATSON, K. M. "An Analysis of Communication Patterns: A Method for Discriminating Leader and Subordinate Roles." *Academy of Management Journal* 25 (March 1982): 121–136.
18. WHYTE, W. *Men at Work.* Homewood, Ill.: Irwin-Dorsey, 1961.

Discussion Questions

1. Reread our opening case, "Welcome Aboard." What kinds of role behavior do you see attached to the position of new recruit?
2. At the end of this case we state that the "asset book" assignment served several purposes. How would you have felt if you had been in Stanley's position? What do you think was the most important organizational purpose of this assignment?
3. What do we mean by the terms *specialization* and *the division of labor*? What are the characteristics of complex, modern organizations that lead to functional specialization and a division of labor?
4. Take an organization with which you are familiar and try to construct an organization chart according to the principles of this chapter. What problems do you run into?
5. Discuss the distinction between *staff* and *line* relationships. How do these relate to the concept of "lateral" relationships?
6. Define the following: position, status, role, and norm.
7. As president of your student organization you are invited to a "tea" given by the president of your university. How will you address the president? Her or his husband or wife? Why? How do you think they expect you to address them? Are these things roles or norms? Where did you learn them?

Chapter 4
The Bases for Compliance: Authority, Power, and Persuasion

Peeping Tom

Stanley was becoming impatient. This was the morning he was scheduled to introduce Claude Gilliam to several department heads and show him around The Company headquarters. It was Claude's first week with The Company and there was quite a bit to show. The Company had moved to the suburbs several years ago and was now housed in a showcase building. It was very different from the old headquarters at 711 Gotham Avenue. Out here in the rolling, wooded countryside, in the middle of a 100-acre tract, the new building was all but invisible from the highway and accessible only by a quarter mile of winding road. On the top of the hill it stood, like a modern corporate fortress.

"Hey, where have you been?"

"I've been where you think I've been, on the road. Do you know how long it takes to get here? . . ." Claude didn't need to explain. Most of the employees at headquarters—except for the executives, of course—lived in the city before eventually relocating, and knew how long it took. The working hours of 8:00 to 4:30 (presumably to give employees time to appreciate country living in the summer) also made travel from the city difficult.

Claude continued, "I'm really sorry to make you wait, Stan, but listen, do you know what time I had to get up to get here at 8:00?" It was a rhetorical question. "Those aren't the hours us city folks keep. Look, I just can't get here before 8:30. I don't mind staying later, but I just can't get here by 8. Just can't! I'm going to have to shift my whole day back a little bit. It won't make any difference. It's still a day's work."

"Uh, listen, Claude, I think . . . well, maybe there's something you ought to know about that. Since I had to cancel our first meeting anyway we have some time. See, it was just about this time last year, oh, maybe a year and a half ago, that we ran into this problem. Mr. Marsh. . . ." And with that Stanley recounted the following story.

"Why me, I mean, *why me?*" Bonnie, Ted's secretary, was the picture of virtuous indignation. "*I* don't need that lecture, I'm probably the only one who ever gets here on time anyway. What a nerve! I've got an idea to just. . . ." Stanley, listening patiently, was hoping to find out sooner or later what had happened.

"Calm down, will you Bonnie? It can't be that bad. What'd he do now?" The "he," of course, was Ted.

"That's just what I mean. He didn't say anything to you about it," she said accusingly, "and I never see you here in the morning!"

Since Stanley was only getting more confused, and Bonnie really wasn't talking to him anyway, Stanley decided to find out directly from Ted what was going on.

"What's eating Bonnie?"

"Oh, is she upset?" was Ted's noncommittal reply.

"That's putting it mildly. Something about getting here at 8:00. I don't know."

"I see. That *is* too bad. She'll get over it though. Company policy you know. Here." With that he shuffled a memo across his tidy simulated woodgrain desk top. It read:

To: All Company managers
From: M. M. Marsh

It has been brought to the attention of this office that a number of our nonexempt personnel have been arriving late for work. I don't think that I need to remind you how this looks to our customers. We start business at 8:00 and they expect to find a businesslike office when they call.

I expect each of you personally to explain this to your nonexempt people.

Interesting memo, you say. But what does "nonexempt" mean? Well, it means not exempt from the provisions of the wages and hours law. That means you cannot put in overtime and not get paid for it. And that, in The Company, means that you punch a time clock. The nonexempts are mostly "lower participants," that is, secretaries, clerks, and the like—not managers and staff professionals. But back to Ted and Stanley.

"Where'd he get the 'um—inspiration for this?" Stanley floated the memo back across Ted's desk.

"I'm not sure, but it seems that some of Mr. Marsh's staff people noticed an increase in lateness and checked the time cards. I still find it hard to believe, but you know, almost a third of our people were in violation of Company policy."

"But that's taken care of now. It's just one of those things we have to shape up now and then. Looks bad to customers, you know."

Taken care of? Guess again, Ted. Barely two weeks had passed when another memo arrived.

To: All Company managers
From: M. M. Marsh

Once again it has been called to my attention that a surprising number of our staff-exempt people are not arriving on time. I do understand that many of you put in far more than an 8-hour day, staying after hours to finish important work. You must understand, however, that the issue involved here is one of fairness and equity with our nonexempt people. As always, I expect management to set the example for Company people. Please explain to your staff-exempt personnel that *everyone* is expected to be here at the start of business every morning.

How did this come about? Well, Stanley found it difficult to swallow—but Penny Scribner in communications knew the whole story.

"We got this, well, I guess you'd call it an open letter, addressed to Mr. Marsh and sent to the editor of The Company Clarion. It talked a lot about the unfairness of this thing to the working people here. And how there are lots of people, including managers who never show up on time, and maybe this is the time when everybody will finally realize why they need The Union in here after all." Penny was laughing now, "Well, you can bet that really scared the hell out of Marsh's staff boys.

"So you know what they did? Now I *know* you're not going to believe this, but I swear to God it's what happened. They send this spy up on the roof with a pair of binoculars. . . ." Penny had to stop for a minute to get her laughter under control, ". . . with a pair of binoculars, and he actually counts people coming in late for a week! Counts 'em! Then they divide that number by the total number of staff people we have here and figure it's almost a third of our staff that's coming in late. Can you imagine? 'Peeping Tom' up on the roof."

I suppose you think that was it, right? But no, Marsh's staff boys decided that a little "evaluation research" was needed. So up to the roof again went "peeping Tom," binoculars in hand. And, of course, nothing had changed.

A few more cycles like this followed, each with progressively stronger memos by Marsh and each followed by a quantitative evaluation showing identical results: no change. And what was the upshot?

"Why . . . that's the dumbest thing I ever heard of! Not me! I don't care what you do. *I'm* not punching any time clock. I'll quit first!" Stanley is now the one who is irate and Ted is trying to mollify him.

"Look, would it help if I said I agree with you? But *I'm* going to do it." This last was probably the worst thing Ted could have said, for it only confirmed Stanley's opinion of those who would knuckle under to such an outrage. "You just can't take things like this personally, Stanley. You've got to think of the good of The Company. After all, as Mr. Marsh said, it's up to management to set the example."

"And that's baloney, Ted. You know it, and I know it. Listen, you rated my work outstanding, right? [This is the top category in The Company's merit rating scheme.] So I must be doing my job, right? And I usually stay a lot later than the nonexempts. I'm a night person, not a morning person. So what does it matter?"

"Well, Bonnie . . ."

"Oh, no," Stanley wasn't going to listen to that line for a minute. "Don't tell me about Bonnie. I talked it over with her and *she* doesn't care. She knows I stay late, 'cause I leave stuff for her to type in the morning. She understands. Oh, no, don't use that one on me. That's just a coverup!"

As you might imagine this scene was typical of hundreds of Stanleys and Shelbys throughout Company headquarters that morning. Yes, it amounted to open insurrection. No siree, no time clocks, not for me!

So one Wednesday morning (at 8:00) every executive, middle manager, manager, staff professional, clerk and secretary (except for those answering phones), exempt and nonexempt, gathered in The Company cafeteria to hear what Mr. Marsh had called them together to say. What a scene! Sitting on the stage were Marsh himself and his vice presidents. Directly in front and facing the stage, arrayed in layers by rank, were the various assistant vice presidents, company directors of this and that, area managers, and first-line managers. Behind them were the rank and file. Marsh's executive vice president rose to introduce the featured speaker.

"The Company management committee [Marsh and his top VPs] decided that this issue was vital enough to warrant our calling this meeting so that we might all share Mr. Marsh's thinking on this. We believe there has been a communications problem on this lateness thing, so we're taking this opportunity to clear it up; so we all can, so to say, speak with one voice on this thing.

"Mr. Marsh."

"Good morning." Marsh was dignified and somber looking in his exquisitely tailored blue pinstripe. "I think most of you know what has made The Company the great organization it is today—values, the values of hard work, fairness and equity, and just reward for a job well done. And I think most of you also know that I have made it my own personal task to maintain these values, to fight the complacency that seems inevitably to flow from success.

"So I am here this morning to communicate to you directly my deep concern over what I see as a threat to one of these key values of our Company—that of fair and equitable treatment for all Company people, whatever their position. For all of you make a vital contribution. . . ."

And so it went. Marsh explained why the time clocks were necessary, and why he knew, when everyone saw it in this light—that is, when the issue had been properly communicated—that as always Company people would rise to the occasion, pull together, and do what was right. And why the time clocks? That was to show, through concrete action, The Company's firm belief in the worth of its people . . . *all* its people.

This is interesting, but what are we talking about here? Authority or power? Or persuasion? Actually, this factual episode raises several questions:

- Why was the issue of lateness so important to Marsh and his top management—important enough to have them devote considerable time and energy to it, to make a major issue out of it? Why didn't they just let it go with the original memo?
- Why did Marsh and his top management go to such great lengths to persuade all employees that Marsh's position was justified? Why did they try to persuade their exempt professionals that they ought to *want* to be on time? If top management was within its rights—and it was—why not just crack down on the offenders?
- Why did the professionals feel they didn't have to comply? After all, they knew the rules. Why, then, when it was so obvious that management felt it was important, did they choose to continue to break the rules?

An analysis of these issues involves understanding authority and power in organizations. It also involves understanding the limitations of formal structure as an explanation for human behavior in organizations. This chapter, then, is devoted to analyzing *compliance relationships* in organizations.

The basic motivation for the compliance relationship is the *power* of the superior over the subordinate. One of our tasks, therefore, will be to analyze the meaning of power, to look at different types of power, and to understand the limitations of its uses.

One specific form of compliance we will study is that relationship between superior and subordinate called *authority*. This authority relationship is the basic element in the formal structure of compliance; it occurs when the subordinate sees the superior's use of power as *justified* or legitimate.

We will conclude the chapter with a discussion of the problems that result when compliance is overdone, when getting members to exercise individual *discretion* may be more of a problem than gaining compliance.

Compliance and the Problem of Coordination

Organizations are broken down into divisions that represent the components of organizational tasks; that is, organizations are differentiated along functional lines. As we saw in Chapter 3 this functional differentiation is represented formally in the organization chart. On any given level of the organization chart we see a horizontal array of positions representing responsibility for different functions, and we see a vertical array of positions representing different responsibilities. This vertical array is called the *management hierarchy*.

The task of the people in this hierarchy is to *integrate*, to coordinate the functionally differentiated activities. Classical management theorists saw this problem of integration as essentially a technical one; they felt it could be resolved through a chain of command, that is, through links of authoritative instructions (11).

There are two key assumptions here. The first is that the formal organization adequately describes the activities required for the integration of functions. The second assumption is that gaining compliance should not be a problem in a well-run organization.

Are these assumptions correct? First, most of this text deals with structures and processes not described by the formal organization; the formal organization is only one part of the basis for action—the systems structure. The second assumption, that gaining compliance is not a problem, is the subject of this chapter.

Compliance involves a relationship between a superior and subordinate within a formal structure of command. In this relationship the subordinate behaves in accordance to a directive supported by the superior's influence (3). This definition will be broadened later, but for now, we are referring to these kinds of situations: the mill foreman asks Jimmy Szekely to run his machine to produce X pieces per hour, and he does it; Kerry Drake asks Ted Shelby to write a memo saying thus and so to Ben Franklyn, and Ted does so; Mr. Marsh sends his memos requiring managers to arrive on time, and they do.

We are not considering how well the resulting act is performed, or whether in similar circumstances in the future the subordinate will act on his or her own initiative. This is a larger question of motivation. Instead, we are considering here the motive that derives from the superior's influence. A superior exercises influence to gain compliance through the use of *authority, power,* and *persuasion.*

To illustrate these concepts let us see how The Company might handle the lateness problem. Ted calls Stanley into his office. "Mr. Marsh has sent a memo to all management, Stanley, asking that we make sure all our exempt nonmanagerial personnel are at their desks by 8:00 in the morning. I'm sure you understand. Mr. Marsh feels this is an area in which we've been a little lax lately. See you at 8:00 tomorrow." In this exchange Ted is operating on the assumption that Stanley will do what he says without any major objection, because Ted is justified in making such a request within the rules and formal structure of the organization. Ted is invoking his *authority.* If Stanley complies, then the compliance relationship is one of authority.

Here is a different approach. "Sit down, Stanley. I've noticed for some time that you make a practice of arriving here late in the morning. I've not said anything to you as yet because I've hoped this was a matter you would take care of yourself." Rolling the Marsh memo into a thin cylinder, Ted uses it as a pointer to underscore his instructions as he continues, "But now Mr. Marsh is onto this thing and there is going to be trouble. So I'm through asking. We start work here 8:00. Be here. And in case you don't think I mean business—

well, I've checked it out and we've got the authority to dock any one of you an hour's pay for any part of an hour lost through lateness. Think about it. And another thing. I know you're looking forward to a promotion this year, so I want you to know that one thing we look for in our managers is the willingness to set an example for other employees. I hope I don't have to draw a picture for you."

This episode illustrates another form of influence: *power*. In this form of influence the superior uses rewards and punishments directly to gain compliance.

Taking a third approach, Ted might say, "Look here, Stanley, I'm in no position to say that you have to do this, because I know you put in more than your share of hours here. But look at it this way, it's really not fair to the others."

Here Ted uses *persuasion* as the form of influence. Stanley's compliance would be based on the merits of Ted's argument, and a consequent decision that arriving on time is the right thing to do—but not because Ted ordered it, or because he feared that potential rewards might be withdrawn.

What we mean by persuasion should be clear enough from these examples, but we need to examine power and authority in more detail.

Power

Power is a relationship between superior and subordinate. You have power over another when you can induce the other to carry out your directions or wishes through control over rewards and punishments. Control over rewards and punishments is a key aspect of this definition. By ignoring this aspect we would ignore the fact that the term *power* involves coercion. In the compliance relationship, when power is exercised, the subordinate is less than free to do as he or she wishes.[1]

There are several bases for compliance. The oldest is fear—fear that if we do not do as we are told something undesirable will happen: physical harm, social ostracism, loss of possessions. In this case power is represented by the superior's ability to deprive the subordinate or inflict physical harm. Traditional military organizations and prisons use this basis for compliance.

Another basis for compliance is belief. The subordinate believes that what is being done is right. The church uses this basis for compliance; so do many civil rights organizations. Power is represented here by control over sentiment, and the allocation of symbols of prestige and esteem.

The basis for compliance most commonly used in business and industry is the dispensation of material rewards. In this case power is represented by control over material resources, that is, over material rewards and punishments.

Etzioni, in his discussion of compliance as a basis for the comparative study of organizations, characterizes these three types of power relationships as *coercive*, based on control of physical necessities; *normative,* based on the control of sentiments, of symbols of esteem and prestige; and *remunerative,* based on the control of material rewards and punishments (3).

These last two forms—power based on the control of sentiments and that based on the control of material rewards and punishments—are the ones of most interest to us here. Notice that although these forms of power are applied to organizational relationships they can also be applied to individual superior-subordinate relationships within a given organization. Furthermore, compliance may be based on a combination of control over material resources and control over resources of sentiment. In fact, this combination is likely when professional and managerial personnel are involved. The manipulation of sentiments and of symbols of prestige and esteem go hand in hand with the manipulation of material rewards and punishments.

We move next to a discussion of authority. Thus far we have said nothing about how the subordinate feels about the superior's use of power to gain compliance. Obviously, the subordinate may resent this use of power; prisoners in coercive organizations, for example, or blue-collar workers in organizations where compliance is based on control over material resources may be resentful. Yet in modern-day organizations the use of power is usually not resented; it is seen as *legitimate* or *justified.*

Authority as Justified Power

One justification of the superior's use of power is that the superior has "the right to decide." Most of us believe that the boss has the right to assign work tasks to subordinates. This vague usage of "right" is not troublesome as long as everyone behaves as though such a right exists. But if subordinates cease to act that way, if soldiers do not obey commands, or teams do not play as they are expected to, has the superior lost this right?

The term *right* is no more than a label describing a relationship between superior and subordinate. As Simon puts it,

> The relationship of authority can be defined . . . in purely objective and behavioristic terms. It involves behaviors on the part of both superior and subordinate. When, and only when, these behaviors occur does a relation of authority exist between the two persons involved. (21:125)

But authority means more than this; it means that the superior's use of power—his or her control over rewards and punishments—is seen as legitimate or justified. The crux of the authority relationship is that the request for compliance is not questioned by the subordinate; the subordinate "holds in abeyance his own critical faculties for choosing between alternatives and uses the formal criterion of the receipt of command or signal as the basis for his choice" (21:126).

This willing suspension of critical judgment characterizes the authority relationship and differentiates it from a simple use of power. Because the compliance relationship is seen as justified—because the superior's control over resources of sentiment and material rewards is seen as justified—the subordinate is willing to suspend critical judgment.

Why do organizational members accept authoritative commands instead of rejecting them? What legitimates or justifies authoritative requests? The great German sociologist Max Weber analyzed this question in his discussion of the three types of legitimate rule. Weber outlined three pure or ideal types of justification for compliance and labeled them *legal, traditional,* and *charismatic* (26, 27).[2]

Notice that the term *ideal* in "ideal type" is not used here in the sense of "a state of affairs to be sought after"; rather, it is used in the sense of "existing only in idea," hence not real or practical. Because of this confusion, Weber sometimes is understood incorrectly to be an advocate of bureaucracy, which he thought best represented the legal basis. But as we shall see later, the opposite is true (28). In the following pages we define these three types of justification for compliance, emphasizing especially what is and what is not meant by bureaucracy. We will also illustrate differences in organizations with different bases for justification of authority.

Bureaucracy: The Legal Justification

The pure type of the legal basis of justification is best embodied in bureaucracy since a key element of bureaucracy is *legality*. Compliance relationships are based on the law, on organizational regulations. Both superior and subordinate must obey the rules when giving orders or when receiving them. The right to give orders follows the organization chart, the line of command.

A second major feature of bureaucracy is *rationality*. One assumes that the holder of a superior office or superior position is there because of superior knowledge or competence. Hence, *rational* here means "for reasons of competence" or "for greater effectiveness" rather than simply "reasonable."

A third major element of bureaucracy is *impersonality*. This means that compliance is to a superior office, to a superior "box" in the organization chart, and not to a person. This feature is best exemplified by the military dictum that one salutes the uniform, not the man.

Perhaps you are saying, "Wait a minute. That's not at all what *I* mean by bureaucracy. I mean endless red tape and *in*efficiency. In fact, it seems to me that my notion of bureaucracy is just about the opposite of yours in every way."

You have a point. It is true that the common notion of bureaucratic behavior is quite different from what we just outlined. It is different for several reasons. First, ours is an abstract concept useful for analysis, an ideal type. Pure bureaucracies do not exist in the real world. The discussion of organizations as social systems shows this. Norms are not part of the codified rules of organizations, yet they are followed. People working together must establish personal relationships and assume social roles distinct from the formal requirements of the position. And, rationality assumes a knowledge of most of the important elements in organizations and the ability to measure and then relate them predictably to one another; this assumption, by and large, is not warranted. Real bureaucracies are not purely legal, are most certainly not purely rational, and are not purely impersonal.

But second, we believe that the term bureaucracy has become distorted because it is commonly used by the bureaucracy's *clients,* rather than by its *participants,* to explain their experience. Hence, when we are all treated the same (impersonally), although it is obvious to each of us that our case is different from the rest, we complain of "red tape." When bureaucrats meticulously follow the stated procedures (legally), even though they are obviously not directly relevant to our own case, we complain that the procedures are unnecessarily time consuming and inefficient. And filling out lengthy forms when half the information requested does not apply to our case strikes most of us as less than rational.

But remember that our discussion concerns why there is order in the structure of social affairs in organizations rather than chaos. That question involves the perceived legitimacy or justification of compliance by subordinates to orders of superiors. And one basis of that justification is the legal or bureaucratic basis.

The Traditional Justification

In contemporary organizations there are few examples of the traditional basis of justification. The church is one, traditional monarchies another. Justification for compliance rests in belief in the sanctity of the prescribed social order and the relationships established by hallowed tradition. So, for example, the relationship between the pope and the other bishops of the Roman Catholic Church is based on the model of the relationship between Peter and the other apostles. Also, other relationships among members of the church are patterned on the current understanding of those relationships in the early church (14).

Within the specifications of what has and has not been acceptable traditionally, a superior's actions are highly constrained. It is unthinkable, for example, for a member of the ruling hierarchy of the Roman Catholic Church to suggest a major reorganization of church structure for reasons of rationality; that is, because it might work better. However, in practices not prescribed by tradition, the superior in a traditional organization is free to exercise arbitrariness and favor, following purely personal considerations. And subordinates in such organizations are free to curry personal favor as they will. Appointments or promotions need be justified by nothing other than the will of the superior.

Besides the church and traditional monarchies, many voluntary and fraternal organizations also function on the basis of tradition.

The Charismatic Justification

A leader whose personal characteristics justify compliance to his or her authoritative commands is said to possess charisma. In the ideal type, the charismatic basis of justification is simply the personal qualities of the leader. Jesus Christ is often cited as an example of a charismatic leader. Martin Luther King and Fidel Castro are more recent examples.

Crucial to the charismatic leader is the subordinates' belief in his or her superordinary qualities and efficacy of command. This belief continues to justify compliance only as long as the leader secures success for the subordinates. An unsuccessful charismatic leader has no authority.

Power and Authority—One More Time

Before moving on we must discuss one other important framework for understanding power (see Box 2). This conceptualization of power is based on the study of group dynamics, and thus is an effort to provide a basis for the study of influence processes in groups. This is its only major difference from the other concepts we have developed. To anticipate a point we shall make later, leadership is a characteristic of groups and can be studied at the level of individuals and groups apart from considerations of formal structure. Management (or "managership") is a characteristic of formal structure and must be studied at the structural level, although group considerations are relevant.

The two ought not to be confused. Therefore, though the French and Raven framework relates to a broader range of influencing "others" than does ours, it obscures the structural distinction between power and authority which we consider to be extremely important. However, French and Raven's distinction between power and control is crucial, similar to ours between power and authority. Superior power may continue to exist while authority, the perceived legitimacy of exercising that power, does not. And authority is defined, as is control, in terms of the subordinate's *behavior*.

Legitimacy, however, is a social structural concept. It was just this idea that concerned Marsh in our opening vignette (though he would not have put it this way, of course). Marsh was concerned not with power, but with authority, a narrowing of what we shall call the "zone of indifference," that is, the range of authoritative requests to which the subordinate will automatically comply. Thus, if we fail to regard power and authority as different *types* of concepts, with different qualities, we cannot understand Marsh's concerns. Consequently, although we recognize the "power" of norms, roles, and groups to control

Box 2

The Bases of Social Power

To clarify the nature of influence processes in group dynamics, John R. P. French and Bertram Raven set out in 1959 to "identify the major types of power and to define them systematically." *Power* is defined in terms of the influence on a *Person* by some *Other,* where the *Other* may be a person, norm, role or group. Thus a norm is seen as exercising power over a *Person.* Power is, further, the maximum *potential* influence of an *Other* on a *Person.* Thus it continues to exist even when the *Other* may not choose to exercise it.

Power must be distinguished from *control.* Opposing forces within a *Person,* or from another, may be sufficient to resist an *Other's* power; thus the *Other* could not be said to be in control of the *Person.* Still, as *potential* influence, the *Other's* power exists nontheless. Finally, power is specific to aspects of a *Person's* behavior. Roles exert power only in situations to which they are relevant.

Five bases of power are identified:

1. reward power, the Person's perception that the Other can reward behavior;
2. coercive power, the Person's perception that the Other can punish behavior;
3. expert power, the perception that the Other has special knowledge;
4. referent power, the Person's identification with the Other; and
5. legitimate power, the Person's perception that the Other has a legitimate right to prescribe his or her behavior.

The last two need some further clarificaton. Referent power stems from a Person's feelings of oneness with the Other (for example, with a group) or from the desire for such identity. However, it may be difficult to ascertain that referent power is operating. Why does the Person conform to a group norm? If a Person fears expulsion from the group for not conforming, then it is *coercive* power; if the Person performs for praise, then reward power is operating. Only if a Person conforms for the sake of conformity, regardless of the possible actions of the Other, is referent power in operation.

Legitimate power is based on a Person's belief that the Other has the right to influence him, and that the Person has the duty to be influenced. This, French and Raven note, is very similar to legitimate authority, yet it need not occur in a role relationship. For example, its basis may be in a social norm. Thus, there are three bases for legitimate power: cultural values, social or organizational structures, and delegation from a legitimate Other in the structure.

Legitimate power in a formal organization is primarily a relationship between positions rather than persons. There it may also overlap with reward and coercive power if a Person considers the Other's attempts to influence through rewards or punishments to be legitimate.

(From J. R. P. French and B. Raven, "The Bases of Social Power." In *Group Dynamics,* 3rd ed. Edited by D. Cartwright and A. Zander. New York: Harper and Row, 1968.)

behavior, we believe that our more restrictive definition of position power is more helpful in clarifying the idea of managerial authority.

We now have a typology of justification for the use of power to accompany the typology of power developed previously. To understand how authority functions in organizations we must understand that the basis for justification is not the source of power itself. Theoretically, any basis of justification may apply to any form of power. Thus, for example, the legal-rational basis is most commonly associated with power over material resources and rewards. But charismatic justification may also be present where this form of power occurs. Charisma, however, is more likely to be the justification for control over resources of sentiment and symbols of prestige and esteem. Another pairing, one frequently observed in history, is an organization with authority deriving from charisma and typified by the use of fear or coercive power. Military, religious, and revolutionary organizations are examples. These relationships are summarized in Figure 4.1.

Notice the distinction between the justification of a particular action or decision and the justification of the superior's right to expect compliance. This goes to the heart of what we mean by authority. In an authority relationship there is no need to justify a particular action or decision because that justification is inherent in the authority relationship—it is what we mean by authority. That is, where authority exists, the subordinate may disagree with the wisdom of a request by a superior yet still see the request as legitimate within their relationship, and comply without question (21:132). Thus, do not misunderstand a superior's explanation (or justification) of a particular way of doing things because "we've always done it that way" as an example of the traditional basis of justification. Remember, we are talking about justification of the right of the superior to request compliance, not the rightness of the action.

This last distinction raises this issue, what happens when a superior issues an order and the subordinate does not comply?

The Zone of Indifference

There is a large range of requests a superior may make that, under ordinary circumstances, will result in subordinate compliance and the voluntary suspension of critical judgment. This range covers work duties assigned to the subordinate's position, as well as general rules of organizational procedure. It is called the *zone of indifference* (1). The subordinate is indifferent to commands or requests that fall within this zone; that is, he will comply with them while suspending his own critical judgment. For commands that fall outside this zone of indifference, the subordinate may feel free not to comply. For instance, the subordinate might not feel it necessary to attend departmental meetings on Sunday morning, and most likely would not be willing to accept an assignment with a high probability of physical harm. The zone of indifference, therefore, describes the limits

BASIS OF JUSTIFICATION	TYPE OF POWER		
	Remunerative	Normative	Coercive
	Examples		
Legal	Business corporation	Volunteer charity	Wartime military
Charismatic	Professional football team	Political organization	Certain utopian communities
Traditional	Craft guilds Apprenticeships	Church	Traditional monarchy

FIGURE 4.1 Organizations by Basis of Justification and Type of Power

of the authority relationship. A superior's use of power to gain compliance is no longer seen as legitimate for commands falling outside the zone. Thus, this concept of the zone of indifference is a key to understanding the effective use of authority in organizations. As Simon puts it, "in a very real sense, the leader, or the superior is merely a busdriver whose passengers will leave him unless he takes them in the direction they wish to go. They leave him only minor discretion as to the road to be followed" (21:134).

To gain compliance with an order that falls outside the subordinate's zone of indifference, a superior can take several courses. It is possible to invoke one's power. But this is a dangerous course. As we will see later in this chapter, not only is it ineffective, but it may further weaken the authority relationship. Another course is to use the third mode of influence we described—*persuasion*. In this course of action the superior acknowledges to the subordinate that the decision is up to him or her. Subordinate compliance then is based solely on the merit of the argument, whether that be an argument based on friendship, loyalty, logic, or ideology. But whatever strategy is used to gain compliance, the zone of indifference is important in determining it.

Several organizational factors help determine the extent of the zone of indifference. One factor is technology, the productive process involved in the work. Technology may be related to the type or extent of power used by the organization. For example, a superior's power over a subordinate is far greater in the military than in a volunteer charitable organization (21:134). If military subordinates understand the extent of the power of the military organization (to punish by death or reward with nationwide honor, for example) and if they accept this power as legitimate, then their zone of indifference will be great. The charitable organization depends on control over slight resources of sentiment and belief. Consequently, subordinates (who may not even regard themselves as such) will have a narrow zone of indifference, forcing superiors to rely more on persuasion as a means of influence.[3]

Technology differs by functional specialties. Generally, professionals and skilled crafts workers have narrower zones of indifference than workers of lesser skill, especially in their own fields (21).

If the superior's power, then, is associated with differences in technology or function, or if the subordinates expect to use individual discretion, then the zone of indifference will be affected.

The same is true of the economic and social environment. When jobs are scarce, the power of the superior to control rewards and punishments is great. The subordinate may have no alternative positions available, and the zone of indifference will therefore increase.[4] Also, in subcultures where the work ethic is strong, the zone of indifference is greater.

Authoritylike Relationships

The authority relationship can be summarized as follows:

- The compliance of the subordinate stems from the power of the superior.
- The superior's power is perceived as legitimate.
- The subordinate suspends critical judgment on receiving an authoritative request.

Sometimes the relationship between members of the organization has all these characteristics except that it is not between superior and subordinate, and thus a request is not backed by the power of a superior. That is, the relationship has all the behavioral attributes of the authority relationship except, properly speaking, it is not one of authority.[5] Such relationships occur in two general circumstances: the *authority of expertise* and the *collegial authority* situations.

THE AUTHORITY OF EXPERTISE. Directives may be accepted as though they came from a hierarchical superior because the organizational member issuing the directive is known to be correct—is an *expert* in the matter. Compliance of this kind is authoritylike because the expert's directive is accepted without question. The expertise in this situation may be technical, organizational (political), or both; it is based on knowledge and experience (2). If the authority of expertise accrues to a superior, however, then a true authority relationship actually exists.

The zone of indifference associated with the authority of expertise may be narrow, relating only to the expert's area of specialty. Consequently, when individuals accustomed to the authority of expertise speak out on unrelated issues, they may be surprised to find that their requests are not treated with accustomed compliance. On the other hand, directives on unrelated issues sometimes are followed because of the "halo effect" (the assumption of generalized competence). Nonetheless, it is this highly specialized zone of indifference that constitutes the important distinction between true authority relationships and authoritylike relationships.

COLLEGIAL AUTHORITY. The authoritylike relationship between a body of colleagues and one or more of its members has been called *collegial authority* (12, 26). Collegial authority is similar to the authority of expertise to the extent that colleagues are advisory only, having no power as we have defined it. This type of relationship is found most often in the academic world where requests from colleagues do not carry the weight of administrative decisions, and where the administration may independently control material resources and resources of sentiment.

Human Behavior and the Formal Organization

Since the formal model of the complex modern organization is that of the bureaucracy, we will discuss that system of authority in the rest of this chapter. Ideally, participants in the modern bureaucracy see the use of superior power as justified on the basis of legality, rationality, and impersonality. Also, from the formal perspective, superior power is based on control over material rewards and punishments.

The Real Versus the Ideal

Real bureaucracies differ from the ideal type described by Max Weber. Since you will probably work in a bureaucratic type of organization, we should talk about what this means for you. We begin with a description of classic bureaucratic intent attributed to Alfred Krupp, the German industrialist:

> What I shall attempt to bring about is that nothing shall be dependent upon the life or existence of any particular person; that nothing of any importance shall happen or be caused to happen without the foreknowledge and approval of the management; that the past and determinant future of the establishment can be learned in the files of the management without asking a question of any mortal. (24:15)

Though not a complete description of bureaucracy, certainly it catches the flavor. But how do real bureaucracies differ from this idealization?

LIMITED RATIONALITY. Formal bureaucratic structures are presumably constructed on rational bases; that is, they are created to achieve goals more effectively. But in real bureaucracies there are other considerations. Recall our earlier example of the vice president and the chief scientist in The Company. Purely rational organizations would have no such positions because they have no direct function in achieving effectiveness. But in this example of a real bureaucracy there is a compromise between rational (elements dictated purely by considerations of effectiveness) and political considerations. In this case, a position exists because of historical considerations involving compromise between contending factions within the organization. One does not maintain motivation in aspiring members of management by dumping a chief scientist when he is no longer useful.

LIMITED COMPETENCE. A key justification for compliance in bureaucratic organizations is the assumption that superiors are more competent than subordinates. And generally, superiors are older and have greater experience in the organization—hence, they have a greater knowledge of the operations of that organization. But in modern organizations we increasingly find conflict between hierarchical and specialist competency (24). The superior in the hierarchy generally has a greater knowledge of organizational operations, but probably inferior knowledge in special areas of expertise. This situation leads to problems in justifying compliance relationships based on competence. Subordinates may be told, "He wouldn't be where he is if he didn't know what he was doing," but they quickly perceive if this is not the case.

LIMITED LEGALITY. Most new organization members quickly realize that bureaucracies are rife with organizationally illegal acts. For example, everyone is supposed to punch a time clock—but not everyone does. And more importantly, granting favors within bureaucratic organizations usually (and necessarily) involves breaking rules or circumventing bureaucratic inflexibility. One reason superiors grant such favors is to help themselves establish a wider power base. A second reason is that rules are not, after all, entirely appropriate for all functions and all types of employees. Hence, rule breaking must be practiced by effective managers. For example, almost all budget estimates are arranged to make figures agree with the historical record or with the expectations of higher management. But in practice funds may be spent in very different ways. This rule-breaking practice generally occurs where subordinate management understands that no harm, and possibly a gain in organizational effectiveness, will result.

LIMITED IMPERSONALITY. The phrase "some are more equal than others" well describes the limited impersonality of real bureaucracies. Inevitably, some people stand out from the mass of employees simply because they happen to be sons or daughters of well-known executives. Thomas J. Watson, Jr., openly joked about the fact that at least one reason he was chief executive of IBM was that he was his father's son. Also, managers often have protégés whom they bring along for reasons other than competence; for example, superiors identify subordinates who can be trusted to protect the superior's position. Such subordinates will be judged by different standards than other employees.

There are also elements of charisma or tradition interwoven with bureaucratic justifications. Some superiors can engender a deep personal loyalty in their subordinates, and this allows them to act in nonbureaucratic fashion. Charisma, of course, may apply in the relationship to superordinates as well. Tradition may also apply. For example, IBM was Thomas Watson, Sr.'s, company. He made it what it is. Watson, Jr., quite properly, was the heir apparent and was so recognized by the IBM faithful.

Finally, despite the presence of other justifications, such as tradition, the bureaucratic justification is frequently acted out for the benefit of organization members. There may be no question that the son or daughter of the majority stockholder and chairman of the board will someday become president of the company. Yet in such instances (and there are quite a few) the heir apparent is moved carefully upward step by step through the organization, accompanied at each step by dutiful reports that his or her performance has equaled or excelled that of previous holders of that position. This little act is supposed to indicate to all that the rules of the game still apply; that, chairman's daughter or not, the heir apparent could have made it on her own. (For more on promotion criteria see Box 3.)

These are some of the ways in which real bureaucracies differ from the ideal type. Although the differences are largely due to discrepancies between

---

Box 3

Promotion Criteria in Public Bureaucracies

The Weberian model of bureaucracy describes a system of promotion to higher office that is based on either seniority or achievement, or both. In this research, Charles Halaby set out to identify the relative importance of seniority, examinations, and evaluation by superiors in making promotions. He also sought to identify the organizational conditions under which these criteria are used. He distinguishes between *fixed* criteria such as seniority and examination, and *discretionary* criteria such as supervisory evaluation. Three kinds of situation are hypothesized to predict the type of criterion that will be used.

continued

Control. Use of discretionary criteria such as supervisory evaluation places the control of career opportunity in the hands of the superior, thus supporting and strengthening the hierarchical system of discretionary authority.

Technical Uncertainty. The use of either discretionary or fixed criteria will depend on the superior's ability to assess the connection between work procedures and outcomes. When this means-ends relationship is evident, when skills and tasks are standardized, fixed criteria are feasible. When skills are highly technical, however, and tasks are variable and means-ends relationships poorly understood, discretionary criteria will be more appropriate.

Legal-institutional. When the legal-institutional framework of civil service regulations is placed on public organizations, we would expect to see examinations—fixed criteria—used at the expense of seniority and superior evaluation.

Data for this study come from nearly two hundred city, county, and state finance departments. Some of these departments are covered by civil service regulations and some are not. Furthermore, there were regional differences in the level of development of these regulations. The final model of promotion criteria use, derived from a sophisticated statistical analysis of many indicator variables, can be summarized thus.

- Departments composed of veterans rather than new hires tended to emphasize the fixed criteria of seniority and examinations at the expense of supervisory evaluation. Discretionary control was more likely to be applied to "newcomer" organizations. This pattern conforms to the control hypothesis—that the use of supervisory evaluation supports a system of hierarchical authority.
- When many members of a department held advanced degrees, that department tended to give more weight to examinations and less to seniority. However, the data otherwise gave little support to the technical uncertainty hypothesis.
- Finally, departments under civil service regulations tended to use examinations at the expense of all other criteria precisely because those departments were under these regulations.

The broad implications of this study are that the bureaucratization of promotion criteria is part of a broader process of rationalizing the careers of public officials. When civil service regulations are dominant, they govern not only promotion but also organizational processes affecting the use of discretionary control and hierarchical authority.

C. N. Halaby, "Bureaucratic Promotion Criteria," *Administrative Science Quarterly* 23 (1978): 66–84.

actual human behavior and a rational model of that behavior, they are also due to the fact that the model in some ways describes large, bureaucratic organizations only incompletely. In particular, the question of how functionally differentiated activities are integrated is not answered adequately by the bureaucratic model. In fact, much of the integrating activity that does take place does not conform to the formal, hierarchical model (10, 22).

Lateral and Diagonal Relationships

In Chapter 3 we saw that complex modern organizations are made up of multiple hierarchies, with lines of authority coming together near the top of the organizational pyramid. Large corporations, such as The Company, might have eight or more levels of management. Such organizations might have *product line* differentiation at the second or third level from the top. *Functional* differentiation (such as engineering, production, or sales) may take place at the next level. For this reason, actions involving *similar functions* but *different products* require coordination among subunits at the lowest level of different hierarchies, *lateral relationships*. Thus, the units requiring coordination may be five levels or so removed from the point of common authority. (See Figure 4.2.) Since disputes and minor disagreements among lower-level units are common, how are they to be resolved within the formal framework of authority?

Very few disagreements can be moved up the line for formal adjudication and then authoritative resolutions communicated down again. Remember that a superior position in one product line hierarchy, such as electric motors, has no formal authority over a subordinate position in, for example, the hierarchy of telecommunications products, a *diagonal relationship*. The formal structure of power and authority, therefore, turns out to be useful in explaining only a small fraction of the relationships involved in everyday business (6).[6]

Yet relationships that *look* like those of power and authority do occur. We believe the following are some of the reasons for this. Each may apply singly or in combination with the others.

THE GENERALIZED PRESUMPTION OF POWER. Although someone outside the direct line of authority cannot invoke superior power over a subordinate, subordinates still *presume* that somehow the superior has the power, or will have. They follow the bureaucratic wisdom: "Better be careful how you treat him. He might be your boss someday." And they act on the safer assumption that the remote superior does, in fact, have power. Consequently, an authoritylike relationship exists.

THE INVOCATION OF SPECIAL RELATIONSHIPS. Special relationships are invoked in several, related ways. The first of these is to call upon *special knowledge* of the will and procedures of the nearest common hierarchical superior, a superior

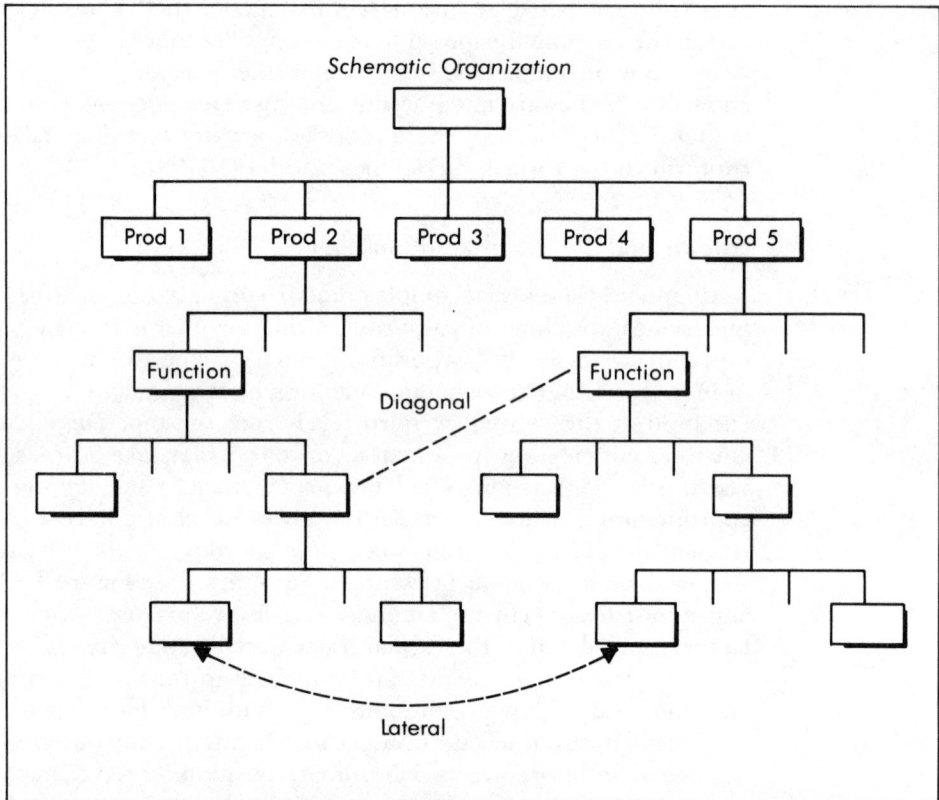

FIGURE 4.2 Lateral and Diagonal Relationships in Bureaucracy

who is usually inaccessible for the purpose at hand. For example, the accountant will state flatly that procedure in these matters is thus and so, and that the sales manager had better comply, that this is how the controller wants such matters handled. If the accountant manages his impression properly such claims are surprisingly rarely challenged. Special relationships may also be invoked by letting it be known that so and so "has the ear of" someone in the proper authority hierarchy. This conveys to the one who is supposed to comply that power may be invoked by remote control, as it were. And in the corporate poker game, it often seems safer to assume this is true than to call the other's bluff.

THE WEB OF FAVORS. Supporting the invocation of special relationships is the web of favors. By noting the needs of others in related hierarchies, and by providing these others with special means for meeting them (especially when bureaucratic regulations must be broken) the skilled practitioner can build up a set of organizational IOUs that can be called upon when needed. Of course, the very existence of these IOUs may make redemption unnecessary in practice. Others understand that these obligations can be called upon if necessary, and hence it is safer for them to comply—another authoritylike relationship.

THE POWER OF INTERDEPENDENCY. Related to the web of favors is the network of dependency of one function on another. Within a given product hierarchy, for example, people responsible for production may depend on those in development engineering to provide design features that make the product easier to manufacture. Conversely, development engineering may need the organizational support of production to get the go-ahead to develop a new product prototype. This form of interdependency means that neither manufacturing nor development engineering can afford to ignore completely the requests of the other. The same kind of thing is true as well at lower levels of the organization. Another example is the dependency between tool crib attendants and the skilled crafts workers using those tools. Once again, authoritylike relationships develop. And the basis for those relationships is the power of others to bring about organizational outcomes that indirectly affect material rewards and punishments.

THE AUTHORITY OF EXPERTISE. The authority of expertise is another basis for authoritylike relationships outside the formal chain of command. (See page 82.)

Bureaucracy, then, is a model of compliance relationships that, for real-world organizations, is both misleading and incomplete. Since real organizations can only approach the legal, rational, and impersonal ideal, the model is misleading if applied literally. And since it is doubtful that a real organization could survive being restricted to the use of designated channels of authority, the model is incomplete.

Existing bureaucratices differ from the ideal model in yet another respect—in the existence of what Victor Thompson calls *bureaupathology:* "Excessive aloofness, ritualistic attachment to routines and procedures, and resistance to change; and associated with these behavior patterns is a petty insistence upon rights of authority and status" (24:152).

Bureaupathology

Bureaupathology is not a characteristic of bureaucracy; rather it is a malady that at times affects such organizations. Bureaupathology is the unwillingness of superiors to exercise discretion—that is, to make choices under conditions of uncertainty as opposed simply to following "standard operating procedure." In bureaucracy, as an ideal type, those in superior positions must have the necessary skills, experience, and access to resources to carry out activities requiring the exercise of discretion. The expectation of compliance from subordinates is justified at least in part on this basis. When organizations must deal with uncertainty, the exercise of discretion by superiors becomes crucial (23). In examining bureaupathology, we are not interested in why some individuals develop "bureaucratic personalities," but in what makes entire organizations seem to (13).

James Thompson, assuming that "individuals exercise discretion whenever they believe it is to their advantage to do so and seek to evade discretion on other occasions," gives some situations in which bureaupathology may develop (23:118). It may occur when:

- uncertainty is large compared with the ability to predict the outcome of actions,
- the consequences of error are relatively severe for self and others, and
- performance is likely to be assessed in terms of adherence to rules and procedures.

To these we can add a fourth:

- performance is likely to be assessed on the basis of ambiguous, conflicting, or otherwise vague criteria (25:119).

Under these conditions we can expect to see a general unwillingness to exercise discretion, together with an unwillingness to communicate reasons ("excessive aloofness"), and an insistence on superordinate status and the right to decide—that is, bureaupathology. Perhaps it was observing these conditions that led Max Weber to give this opinion of bureaucracy as a form of social organization:

> It is still more horrible to think that the world could one day be filled with nothing but those little cogs, little men clinging to little jobs and striving towards bigger ones.... This passion for bureaucracy... is enough to drive one to despair. It is... as if we were deliberately to become men who need "order" and nothing but order, who become nervous and cowardly if for one minute this order wavers, and helpless if they are torn away from their total incorporation in it. (7:453)

Summary

This chapter is about organizations, not about individual relationships. Thus, our discussion is not about what may explain (or justify) a particular action of a superior. Organizations show a characteristic type of compliance relationship based on: a *type of power* (most commonly control over material rewards and punishments) and a *basis for justification* of the use of that power by superiors (most usually legal-rational).

Let us pursue this distinction between individual and organizational level concepts a bit further. What worried Mr. Marsh about the lateness he observed in our opening story was authority, an organizational concern. He was not happy about his exempt professionals arriving late, but not being a fool, he knows that, by and large, he gets more than a day's work from his professionals anyway.

What concerned Mr. Marsh in this case was the integrity of the authority relationship in The Company as a whole: understanding and accepting that compliance relationships are based in legal, rational, and impersonal rules, that, by definition, apply equally to all. Marsh felt a threat to this standing basis for justification of compliance to superiors' directives.

It is important to avoid having to cast such a superior-subordinate relationship in individual terms, as a particular relationship between you and your boss, where the justification for compliance appears to derive from the individual circumstances of your relationship. Such a situation implies a failure of the authority relationship. This is why we say that authority is an organizational rather than individual level concept.

The practical consequence of this for you in a business organization is that both you and your boss understand that you are expected to comply with requests for specific actions, and that your boss is justified in rewarding you for your compliance. You may not agree with the wisdom of the action, or be happy with the remuneration you receive for doing it, but that is not the point. The point is that a relationship of authority exists between you and your boss based on your relative positions in the organization. Of course, under the authority relationship there will be consequences of disagreement for you and your boss as *individuals*. Most likely these will concern your motivation to do the job well. This is a topic we shall address in Chapters 9 and 10.

Now consider another likely organizational context, a voluntary association between you and the local United Way. This is a very different situation organizationally. Power resides in your superiors' control over resources of sentiment, of symbols of esteem and prestige—things like congratulatory letters, certificates you can hang on the wall, acclaim in local newspapers. You and the other volunteers accept your superior's dispensation of these symbolic rewards as justified because you feel, as do those in The Company, that power is a property of the position. National charities, like business organizations, are bureaucracies. Local charities, however, might be somewhat different. Perhaps the charisma of the individuals heading the organizations provide justification in these cases.

What differences exist between this first and second situation? You would probably feel obligated to comply—to suspend your critical judgment—in a wider range of requests in the first than in the second. This is because most of us probably value a raise or promotion more than we value a paragraph or two in the local newspaper. In any event, you are likely to tell your United Way superior that you cannot canvass this Friday night despite her request. Your superior is even more likely not to make this request on the basis of her fragile authority. She would use persuasion to try to gain your compliance, making it clear that this was not an authoritative request. In comparison, your boss at The Company probably would make an authoritative request for a Friday evening meeting. Your zone of indifference in each case is a function of the organizational power of the superior.

This may seem confusing. Did we not say earlier that there were conditions where an authority relationship held even when the other had *no* organizational power?

Not exactly. There are authoritylike relationships not supported by superior power. In these relationships the person expected to comply suspends critical judgment nevertheless; that is, where there exists a zone of indifference characteristic of a true authority relation. Thus, one would not question compliance because one would "know," from past experience or reputation, that the other must be right. When Pat Jones, The Company psychologist, says to use a certain aptitude test, that test will be used. However, this authority of expertise, unlike authority based in power, is limited to the field of specialty, although people are always trying to extend their authority of expertise beyond their domain.

The model of organizational relationships described here—a model of the formal organization most likely justified on the legal-rational basis—is an idealized one, useful primarily for analysis and understanding. For example, most relationships in large, complex organizations are not hierarchical and authoritative; they are lateral and diagonal. Much of what you, as a professional, will be doing will not be supported directly by the "right" of authority. Therefore, when disagreement arises (and it will), referring the matter to a higher authority, you will quickly find, only complicates the issue further. Consequently, you will try to resolve your problems by bargaining, by using power others presume you to have, by invoking special relationships with powerful superiors, by cashing in on favors done earlier, and the like—that is, by being "political."

Also, sooner or later you will run into bureaupathology—someone's boss will be unwilling to act because of uncertainty, incompetence, or insecurity. This is troublesome, but there will not be much you can do about it. Most "bureaupaths," you will find, are well protected by their rigid adherence to the formal rules of the organization. The real problem comes when entire organizational units start behaving this way; this is a sure sign that something in the mission of the organization or its environment, not in the people, is terribly wrong.

Notes

1. This definition is based on that given by Etzioni (3), but we have modified it by adding "control over rewards and punishments." Since Etzioni's discussion is based explicitly on such control by superiors in organizations, our addition simply clarifies his use of the term *power*.
2. Yet another basis of justification or legitimacy—"value rationality"—has been proposed as one that characterizes modern professional organizations (17).
3. Fiedler's research on leadership effectiveness suggests that such a situation is not very favorable, calling for a task-oriented rather than relationship-oriented leader.

His conceptualization implies that power and direct authority are *not* useful under these conditions (4).
4. Sayles and Strauss illustrate such a labor market situation and relate it to differences in workers' preference for security (18). Our point follows directly.
5. Simon (21), while noting the difference in situations, states simply that, since all the attributes of the authority relation apply, the relation is one of authority. For consistency, since authority refers to a compliance relationship supported by superiors' legitimate use of power, we use the term *authoritylike*.
6. Galbraith (6) presents an extensive discussion of lateral and diagonal relations from the point of view of organization design. He argues that increased lateral relations are required to meet information needs in direct proportion to task uncertainty. Our own interest here is not design, however, but description.

References

1. BARNARD, CHESTER I. *The Functions of the Executive.* Cambridge: Harvard University Press, 1938.
2. BLAU, J. R. "Expertise and Power in Professional Organizations." *Sociology of Work and Occupations* 6 (February 1979): 103–123.
3. ETZIONI, AMITAI. *A Comparative Analysis of Complex Organizations.* Glencoe, Ill.: Free Press, 1961.
4. FIEDLER, FRED E. *A Theory of Leadership Effectiveness.* New York: McGraw-Hill, 1967.
5. FRENCH, JOHN R. P., and BERTRAM RAVEN. "The Bases of Social Power." In *Group Dynamics,* 3rd ed., edited by D. Cartwright and A. Zander. New York: Harper and Row, 1968.
6. GALBRAITH, J. *Organization Design.* Reading, Mass.: Addison-Wesley, 1977.
7. GOLDNER, FRED H. "Success *vs.* Failure: Prior Managerial Perspectives." *Industrial Relations* 9 (1970): 453–474.
8. HALABY, C. "Bureaucratic Promotion Criteria." *Administrative Science Quarterly* 23 (1978): 466–484.
9. HALL, RICHARD H., J. EUGENE HAAS, and NORMAN J. JOHNSON. "An Examination of the Blau-Scott and Etzioni Typologies." *Administrative Science Quarterly* 12 (1967): 118–139.
10. LANDSBERGER, HENRY A. "The Horizontal Dimension in Bureaucracy." *Administrative Science Quarterly* 6 (1961): 298–332.
11. LAWRENCE, PAUL R., and JAY W. LORSCH. *Organization and Environment: Managing Differentiation and Integration.* Homewood, Ill.: Irwin, 1969.
12. MARCSON, SIMON. *The Scientist in American Industry.* Princeton: Industrial Relations Research Section Report No. 99, 1960.
13. MERTON, ROBERT. "Bureaucratic Structure and Personality." *Social Forces* 18 (1940): 560–568.
14. *New York Times.* "Excerpts from Vatican Statement Affirming Prohibition on Women Priests" (January 28, 1977), A8.

15. PEABODY, ROBERT L. "Perceptions of Organizational Authority: A Comparative Analysis." *Administrative Science Quarterly* 6 (March 1962): 463–482.
16. ROY, DONALD. "Quota Restriction and Goldbricking in a Machine Shop." *American Journal of Sociology* 57 (1952): 427–442.
17. SATOW, ROBERTA L. "Value-rational Authority and Professional Organizations: Weber's Missing Type." *Administrative Science Quarterly* 20 (December 1975): 526–531.
18. SAYLES, LEONARD, and GEORGE STRAUSS. *Human Behavior in Organizations.* Englewood Cliffs, N.J.: Prentice-Hall, 1966.
19. SCOTT, W. RICHARD, SANFORD M. DORNBUSCH, BRUCE C. BUSCHING, and JAMES D. LAING. "Organizational Evaluation and Authority." *Administrative Science Quarterly* 12 (1967): 93–117.
20. SELZNIK, PHILIP. *Leadership in Administration.* Evanston, Ill.: Row, Peterson, 1957.
21. SIMON, HERBERT A. *Administrative Behavior.* 2nd ed. New York: Free Press, 1965.
22. STRAUSS, GEORGE. "Tactics of Lateral Relationship: The Purchasing Agent." *Administrative Science Quarterly* 7 (September 1962): 161–186.
23. THOMPSON, JAMES D. *Organizations in Action.* New York: McGraw-Hill, 1967.
24. THOMPSON, VICTOR A. *Modern Organization.* New York: Knopf, 1961.
25. WARNER, W. KEITH, and EUGENE A. HAVENS. "Goal Displacement and the Intangibility of Organizational Goals." *Administrative Science Quarterly* 12 (March 1968): 539–555.
26. WEBER, MAX. *The Theory of Social and Economic Organization.* Translated by A. M. Henderson and Talcott Parsons. Edited by Talcott Parsons. New York: Oxford University Press, 1947.
27. ———. "The Three Types of Legitimate Rule." In *A Sociological Reader on Complex Organizations,* 2nd ed., edited by Amitai Etzioni. New York: Holt, Rinehart and Winston, 1969.
28. WEISS, R. M. "Weber on Bureaucracy: Management Consultant or Political Theorist?" *The Academy of Management Review* 8 (April 1983): 242–248.
29. WHYTE, WILLIAM F. *Organizational Behavior: Theory and Application.* Homewood, Ill.: Irwin-Dorsey, 1969.
30. WHYTE, WILLIAM F., ED. *Money and Motivation: An Analysis of Incentives in Industry.* New York: Harper and Row, 1955.

Discussion Questions

1. In our opening case, exempt professionals regularly violated company rules by arriving late for work. Describe the situation in terms of the various concepts of authority developed in this chapter. How do you think the professionals involved would have accounted for their behavior?
2. Analyze the student-professor relationship using the concepts of power, authority, and persuasion outlined in this chapter. Use different situations to analyze each.
3. Distinguish between the concepts of power and authority, outlining a typology of power in organizations and a typology of justification or legitimacy. What do we mean by *ideal type?*

4. You have been fortunate enough to land a job as organization consultant to a prosperous petroleum-producing company wholly controlled by a tiny, Arab sheikdom in the Near East. What might you expect to find in terms of structures and processes of authority here?
5. What do we mean by *zone of indifference*? How does this concept help us to understand the exercise of authority? What individual and organizational factors might affect the extent of an individual's zone of indifference?
6. What do we mean by *lateral* and *diagonal relationships* in organizations? Are these authoritative relationships? Why? Why not? Why are such relationships essential to the functioning of a complex organization?
7. In this chapter we described a trade-off between the exercise of discretion and the demand for compliance. What do we mean by that trade-off?

Chapter 5
Technology and Environment: Constraints on Organizational Form

The Long and Short of It

"The beauty of this is that right here we have an actual example—a real-life success story—of what can be done, peoplewise, to improve our laboratory organizations." Ted's tone was triumphant as he continued, flipping to his next chart.

"The way Jim Fox [vice president, product development at Another Company] looks at it, why he's just got to delegate to his middle management with his laboratory structured this way. He can't possibly keep up with the details of what twenty-

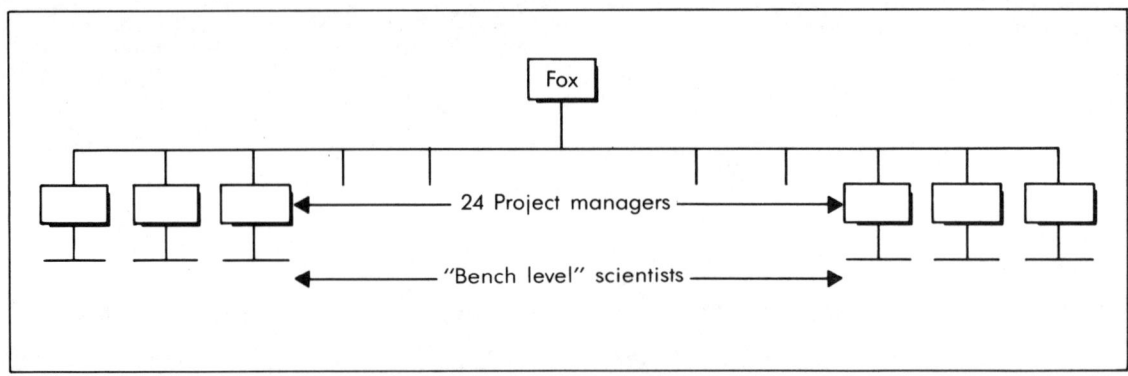

four—count them—twenty-four project managers are doing. That's why Fox says. . . ."

Ted was airing his latest discovery to a management team of personnel people. Sitting in were Dr. Faust as consultant, Pat Jones as Company psychologist, and Stanley, taking notes for feedback.

What was Ted's latest discovery? During his last AMA junket Ted had listened to a presentation by Jim Fox (Ph.D., chemical engineer) detailing how he had restructured his laboratory management. Fox, it turns out, is an ardent subscriber of Doug McGregor's Theory Y, that is, assume the best about your people and that's what you will get; assume the worst and you'll get the worst. "Assuming the best" means acting on the belief that your people will willingly take on responsibility and work as diligently as they can without external control. Still, Fox, as an engineer, was a detail man at heart, and he feared he wouldn't be able to keep his fingers out of the work of his subordinates. Consequently, he felt that implementing his beliefs might be a problem. The solution? He simply got rid of one layer of management, the second-level laboratory managers, and worked directly with the remaining twenty-four project managers. The result, Fox had reasoned, would be that despite his controlling predilections, he could not possibly keep tabs on all the activities of twenty-four busy managers.

But let's get back to Ted.

Benefits

- Better decision making
- Higher morale
- Lower turnover
- Increased productivity and creativity

TED'S CHART

"I'd say that's getting a lot for a little," Ted crowed, as his pointer ran down the list of benefits. "And it's so simple! I'm proposing that we form a task force, now, today, to study how we can move to get this system into our own laboratories as expeditiously as possible." Ted sat down.

Pat Jones was the first to make an observation. "Your list of benefits is impressive, all right. I take it there's some hard evidence of these changes you're talking about?"

"Why, er, of course."

"Creativity?" Pat pressed the point.

"Now, Pat, I know what you are getting at. You know as well as I that these kinds of things are subjective. But who would be in a better position to know than the laboratory manager?"

"Productivity?" Pat pressed on relentlessly.

"For God's sake, Pat, it's the man's own laboratory! Are you going to question his word?"

"No, not *really*." Pat's tone dripped with skepticism. "It's just that some facts are more like facts than other facts." Actually, Pat didn't really care one way or the other. But Ted's manner always managed to irritate her.

Following this exchange other personnel people made some laudatory comments about how this, once again, was proof of what personnel had to offer The Company. Finally, Faust, who had been silent until now, took a somewhat different tack.

"Let me see if I can recapitulate the line of reasoning as you have stated it, Ted.

- Product development laboratories in this company traditionally are difficult to manage. From time to time we experience morale problems and we have complaints about key decisions taking too long.
- Now you have come upon something that looks totally different from the way our laboratories are organized: far fewer levels and a much wider . . . ah, what do you call it, yes, *span of control*.
- Their laboratory head, Dr. Fox, feels that the changes he has introduced have produced attendant changes in morale and output, and presumably there is no reason to doubt this.
- Your conclusion, then, is that similar changes in The Company should produce similar desirable outcomes, is it not?"

Ted nodded, though from past experience he knew that Dr. Faust was not through.

"Now I have a question. What does our own

management have to say about your idea? Surely you have explored it with them."

"Er, actually, I haven't as yet. But I know what they'll say: 'Can't be done here. We're not like anyone else.' Hell, that's what they always say."

"They are wrong, of course." This last from Faust wasn't quite either a question or a comment.

"What do you think?" Ted was a bit annoyed. "It's not as though we were comparing engineers to sales or production. These people are all doing the same kind of work. How different can we be?"

"That *is* the question, is it not?" continued Faust. "Therefore, I would suggest, gentlemen—and Dr. Jones—that before we formalize a committee to study the implementation of Mr. Shelby's plan, we ought first to talk to our laboratory managers to get some sense of their understanding of this situation."

So after a brief discussion Martin, vice president, personnel, charged the group with getting a "hands-on feel" for what the differences might be, of whatever kind, between The Company's development organizations and that of Jim Fox. Dr. Faust, as a presumably unbiased outside source, would pull the facts together for the next meeting of the group, one month hence. Stanley, as Faust's former student at The University, would be "loaned" to Faust to assist.

Several weeks and several trips later, Dr. Faust and Stanley were collating the materials resulting from their explorations. Stanley's role for the most part had been to collect some descriptive statistics. Faust, in an appropriate higher status role, had been interviewing top-level managers.

This afternoon, with the package almost ready, Faust seemed pleased. When he was pleased he was also relaxed. Pipe lit, Dr. Faust was ready for conversation.

"Did anything in particular catch your eye when you visited Dr. Fox's laboratory, Stanley? Anything strike you straight off?"

Stanley thought for a moment, for even in casual conversation Faust's questions were not to be answered superficially. "Well, let's see . . . why, of course! It's so small. I mean, not really *small*, but compared to The Company's development laboratories at Portland or Portsmouth. . . ."

"Yes, the whole business is not the size of one large project at Portsmouth. Anything else?"

"Gee, I can't say. I guess everything seemed pretty much the same. At least to me. Not much to see in a product development laboratory except rooms and people and test equipment. But it really was a lot smaller than I expected."

"Then let us start there, shall we? What do you think accounts for the difference in size?"

"Ah, I suppose Another Company's just a lot smaller, that's all. No, wait." Stanley waved his hands as if to erase the first answer. "Another Company is smaller—but only maybe by a half or a third. Our laboratories, though, are bigger than theirs by at least ten or twenty times, easy."

"Quite right. So . . ."

"So I suppose it must be something else. But wait a minute, Dr. Faust, I have the feeling that I'm really getting farther away from the answer, not closer."

"Possibly. Possibly not. Why do you suppose our laboratories are, relatively speaking, so much larger?"

"Let's see, could it have something to do with our products? A lot of our business is in some pretty sophisticated systems and . . . yeah! I bet that's it. What do we call it? *High technology.* Sure. That stuff takes a lot of engineering."

"Compared to . . .?" Faust posed the obvious next question.

"Why compared to the synthetic fibers and plastics and stuff they do in Fox's laboratory."

"You *are* sure of that?" The tone of the question implied the answer.

"Well, no. But you know what I mean. It just seems like it would be less complicated. I'll bet I'm right, too."

"I see. But it will take more than your conviction to convince Ted. Here, how about these organization charts." Faust spread out charts from Portsmouth and Another Company side by side. The chart showing Jim Fox's laboratory was short and squat. And, sure enough, twenty-four different projects were shown reporting directly to Fox as laboratory head. By comparison, the shape of the Portsmouth organization was much taller and thinner, although in terms of numbers of projects, actually more extensive at the base. Yet it was steeper in appearance because it had three levels more than its counterpart.

"But that's just what Ted was talking about, Dr. Faust," said Stanley. "Look, Sawyer, the Portsmouth laboratory manager, has only five functional managers reporting to him, and so on down. So I can see where maybe you'd need another level because it's so much bigger, but. . . ." Stanley stopped, thoroughly confused for the moment.

"Now, I'm afraid, you have lost the thrust of the logic you were developing, Stanley. You had been talking about product development in The Company being more complicated. What evidence for that might there be here?"

Stanley silently struggled for a minute or two but no spark of insight was struck. Finally, Faust came to the rescue. "Why not concentrate on the simpler of the charts first? Consider this question: How would the head of that laboratory at Another Company go about coordinating or integrating the work of those twenty-four projects reporting to him? Would there be a problem?"

Stanley dutifully read the project titles, looked at the numbers of people in each of the projects, thought for a moment, started to speak, then stopped. Suddenly he knew he was right.

"Sure there'd be some problem, but, why, they really don't need any coordination . . . I mean, *integration,* Dr. Faust. Look, each of these is a complete project, self-contained, so to speak. The guys in 'Polyvinyl Applications' don't really have any need at all to work closely with these people here." He pointed to another project.

"Ah, quite right. And?"

"And, so Fox just doesn't have to worry about that. Yeah, I think that's what I mean about the job being less complicated."

"Than . . . ?"

"*Than?* Oh, than our guy's job, what's his name? . . . Sawyer at Portsmouth. Look, there's really only . . . wow! . . . only five big projects at Portsmouth. See, there's *Project Beacon,* the one using laser systems applied to manufacturing automation technology; then this one here on systems software. . . ." Stanley ran down the list of major projects, then continued, "And each one of these is broken into subparts at each step.

"But I wonder if they really had to do it that way?" Stanley's conviction suddenly melted under the realization that he knew nothing more of these activities than their labels on the chart.

"Yes, that is the question, is it not?" Faust was pensive. "Our managers tell me that it must be. 'Holding this mess together,' as they term the problem, seems to require the presence of far more levels of coordination than does the simpler situation at Another Company.

"I rather think that our people wish it were otherwise, you know. Even though they defend such an organization as necessary, they seem to like it even less than Ted. But the form of it seems to have just evolved under the pressures of the situation. As you say, Stanley, do they have to do it that way? Possibly, possibly not. But I for one would not wish to bet against it."

Work Technology, Organizational Structure, and Organizational Behavior

When we refer to structure in this chapter we will be talking about formal structure: about positions and the relationships among those positions, about the rights and duties attendant to those positions, and about the rules and formal procedures that shape the everyday work life of the organization.

Observations such as those made by Stanley and Dr. Faust raise a major issue in organizational design: is it possible to arrange the management structure of an organization any way we want, or are there constraints limiting our possibilities? That is, is there a *universal* theory of best design, applicable to all organizations, that would cause all *effective* organizations, regardless of their enterprise, to have a similar structural form?

Of course, we believe we already know the answer to that: no. However, if we accept this answer, we are left with this question: Why should this be so? Stanley and Dr. Faust have already provided some clues. The nature of the task being performed seems to constrain the structural form of the organization. The *complexity* of the task, the consequent division of labor, and the *interrelatedness* of the component *work activities* lead to certain types of organizational structure rather than others. In The Company, as a result, we saw more levels of hierarchy and smaller spans of control within that hierarchy; in short, it is a different structural shape than that supported by the technology in Another Company.

But there is also a considerable difference in the overall size of the organizations. The Company's product development operations are larger than those of Another Company's, so this factor, too, may enter in. This is what confused Stanley. Is the shape of the organization simply a result of size, or is there a relationship between technology and size?

Finally, as Faust noted, there seem to be some chronic "morale" problems in The Company's laboratories. These problems appear to have their roots in the "fragmentation" of the work task and the feelings of the scientists and engineers that they are little more than tiny cogs in a huge wheel.[1]

The task of this chapter is to illustrate and make plausible the assertion that organizations adapt in form and process to the technological requirements of the work that they do and to the demands of their environments. Since the research findings on the details of these relationships often disagree, we will primarily illustrate some of the basic ideas involved and offer examples of research findings.[2]

What Do We Mean by Technology?

At first, *technology* seems easy enough to understand. Most of us have a mental image of an auto assembly line, and we understand that this assembly line technology involves a conveyor moving at a fixed speed on which the bodies of automobiles are being assembled piece by piece. We also understand that at each of the many work stations arrayed along the length of the line a worker performs only one, or at most a few individual tasks (fastening tail lights in place, for example). And, most of us have some feeling about what this repetitious kind of work means for some aspects of organizational behavior—for the motivation system, for example.

Still, on further consideration, the meaning of technology might not be so plain. Few of us have much idea of what is involved in the technology of systems design that Stanley and Dr. Faust were investigating. Even the application of the term technology to such a process seems to be out of place. Nonetheless, the application of the concept seems useful, for the management structures accompanying systems design are quite different from those of the automobile assembly line.

A definition of technology that applies to the assembly line situation is this: *technology is the physical means used to produce designed outcomes.* Unfortunately, the applicability of this definition to the work of systems design raises questions. It is true that the work of the systems designer requires the use of a computer, and that clearly is technology by our definition. It also requires the production of physical documentation in the form of plans and layouts. Still, something seems to be missing. To identify what it might be, consider the work of an insurance salesperson. He or she must perform routines involving approaching possible clients and explaining the nature of the product in such a way as to convince the client to purchase the product. From this example it seems to us that there are also technologies that might be called behavior technologies, and that these are also part of the work of the systems designer. Therefore, we amend our definition of technology as follows: *Technology is the physical and behavioral means used to produce designed outcomes.*

As we discuss the meaning of technology for organization structure, we will be discussing the effect of technology at two levels: (1) as an overall system of work organization, and what this means for things such as specialization and the division of labor; and (2) as a task or tasks for the individual worker at the work station. So, for example, assembly line technology as an overall system of work organization has implications for the social structure of the factory, but it also has an effect on the nature of individual work tasks as they are presented to the worker. To the worker, it may mean monotony and boredom, for example (6).

Technology and Structure

Research studies show that different technologies require different supervisory structures, constrain social interaction in different ways, and have different effects on the motivation and feedback and control systems. For example, let us take a look at our assembly line and systems design technologies. Both require some level of skill, but the assembly line requires far less specialized skills. Next, the assembly line technology probably has no task-related requirements for social interaction. For the systems designer, however, it is just the opposite. Work tasks require continual communication with other systems designers. They also require formal meetings, although more than likely this requirement may be handled by managers responsible for coordinating the efforts of different task groups. And this, of course, is one of the reasons for differences in the formal structure of systems design efforts and other technologies. Other differences might be in work rules and regulations. For the assembly line these may not change much. For the systems designer proceeding on a new task, there may be no such work rules and regulations. In fact, the task may require keeping rather odd work hours in order to gain access to computers required to aid the design (20).

The point of all this is that the physical and behavioral means required to produce designed outcomes themselves require certain patterns of skills and physical and social activity that in turn give rise to patterns of structure, interaction, motivation, and control. In this chapter we hope to build a better understanding of the constraints on organizational behavior imposed by technology.

Technology as a Leading Factor

Some details of organizational structure, then, appear to be determined by the technology of the work process. These structural features in turn affect other aspects of the organizational system, and this sequence of relationships suggests that technology is the *leading* factor (or independent variable) whereas other aspects of the human organization are direct or indirect consequences of it. It seems that the technology is determined once the organization is in business; if that technology changes, so do factors dependent on it.

It may seem that we are forgetting everything but product development here. How does this apply to everything else in The Company? Are we suggesting that the whole company is set up according to the needs of product development?

Within The Company, the combined manufacturing, sales, accounting, and similar functions are larger by far, and more influential, than product development. There is no reason why the requirements of the work technology of product development engineers should affect these other functions. More precisely, there is no reason why these work requirements should affect other functional organizations in the same way (14, 19). A product system whose design requires many interrelated activities may be relatively simple to sell—and vice versa: it may take a complicated marketing system to sell a product of simple design. In fact, sales organizations in The Company are set up much differently from product development. They are much *flatter*, with far fewer levels of hierarchy than product development (29:198). Even more to the point, in a large multiproduct organization like The Company, the work technologies of similar functions differ widely from product division to product division. Not everyone works in high technology, so product development organizations themselves differ in structure.

Because of these differences we find it useful to think about organizations as being built around a "technical core" (36). The idea is that each of the suborganizations that constitute The Company—product development, production, sales—has its own core technology which, in turn, requires different structural forms for its support. Furthermore, as we shall see later in our discussion of the effect of environment, protection of this technological core from environmental shocks also gives rise to specialized structures and processes. (See Figure 5.1.)

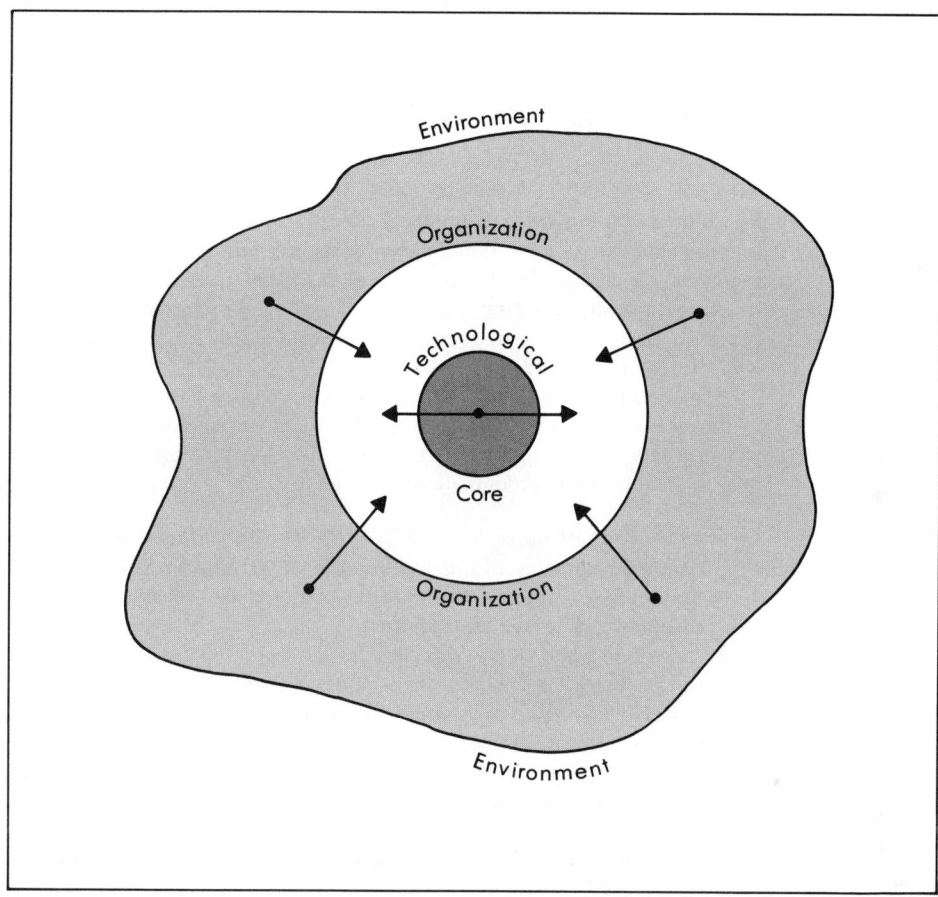

FIGURE 5.1 Technology and Environment as Causal Factors Shaping Process and Form: A Deterministic Viewpoint

Characterizing Core Technology

The relationship among work technology, the structure of the work organization, and human behavior is a theme that appears throughout the work of the early "human relations in industry" theorists (42). Yet it was not until the work of British sociologist Joan Woodward that a critical blow was dealt to traditional management theory. Until this time we generally assumed that the study of management was the search for a set of principles governing the "best" way to manage an organization. Woodward produced evidence showing that what was best for one kind of organization was not necessarily best for another (43). Historically, then, her studies provided the impetus for developing a contingency theory of management.[3] (See Box 4.)

Box 4

Technology, Structure, and Success

In a classic study of the relationship between technology and organizational structure, the research team initially came up with absolutely nothing. On examining the relationship between organizational structure and the success achieved in a hundred manufacturing organizations, Joan Woodward and a team of British researchers concluded that for a group who "spent so much time and effort on the teaching of management subjects, the lack of any interrelationship between business success and what is generally regarded as sound organizational structure was particularly disconcerting" (43:34).

However, as the team began to analyze possible relationships with a typology of technology they had developed, they found a number of striking relationships with aspects of organizational structure. The researchers found that they could reliably classify their organizations in three groups.

- *Unit and small-batch technology.* These were organizations whose business consisted primarily of producing units to customers' individual requirements, to the production of prototypes, and the like. Thus, each new job was essentially different from the last.
- *Large-batch and mass-production technology.* The business of these organizations involved making large numbers of similar units. A good example of this kind of technology would be the automobile mass-production line.
- *Continuous-process technology.* The business of these organizations was the manufacture of chemicals, gases, and similar types of products. An oil refinery or a brewery would be a familiar example.

The researchers concluded that these three types of technology corresponded to a continuum of technological development, with *unit* the simplest, and *continuous process* the most advanced. They also established that there was no relationship between technology and the size of the organizations in their sample.

Employing this typology of technological development, the research team now uncovered several striking relationships between technology and structure. Among them were these:

- The number of levels in the hierarchy increased directly with the level of technology.
- The ratio of supervisory staff to total personnel similarly increased.
- The ratio of indirect workers (those not actually engaged in the production task itself) to direct production workers was higher in the more developed technologies.

continued

Other relationships were found, but they were not so simple and direct.

- The span of control (the number of employees under a first-line supervisor) was greater in the midrange of technology than for either the simplest or most developed.
- Similarly, the formality of rules and procedures, the formalization of control procedures, was greater at the midrange.

Finally, when Woodward and her colleagues used technology as a mediating variable, they now found clear-cut relationships between structural form and success. Characterizing twenty organizations as above average in success and twenty as below average, they found that the unsuccessful firm had very different structural characteristics than were typical for their type of technology. For example, Figure 5.2 shows that for each type of technology, the average span of control of successful firms (white bars) clusters at the median, while unsuccessful ones (black bars) are dispersed about it.

(From J. Woodward, *Industrial Organization: Theory and Practice.* London: Oxford University Press, 1965.)

Woodward's studies showed that there was a relationship between the work technology employed by manufacturing organizations and the formal structure of those organizations. Even though her characterization of the core technologies was admittedly crude, the observed relationships between technology, structure, and business success were clear. Furthermore, they made sense. The direct relationship, for example, between number of levels of organization and technology, can be directly attributed to the increased need for coordination in the more developed technologies. Similarly, the greater proportion of indirect workers reflects the greater productivity of direct labor in the more developed technologies.

Explanations of the indirect relationships reflect first, the greater need for skilled workers in craft technologies and the need for technicians in the continuous-process technologies, with more supervision required for the more complex tasks of these workers. The formality of rules and procedures is explained by Woodward in the following way. First, in unit or prototype (one-of-a-kind) production, it does not pay in most cases to develop fixed rules for changing conditions. In continuous-process technologies, however, control procedures are built into the processes themselves and consequently fewer additional rules and procedures are necessary.

Woodward's findings were extremely influential, perhaps especially because

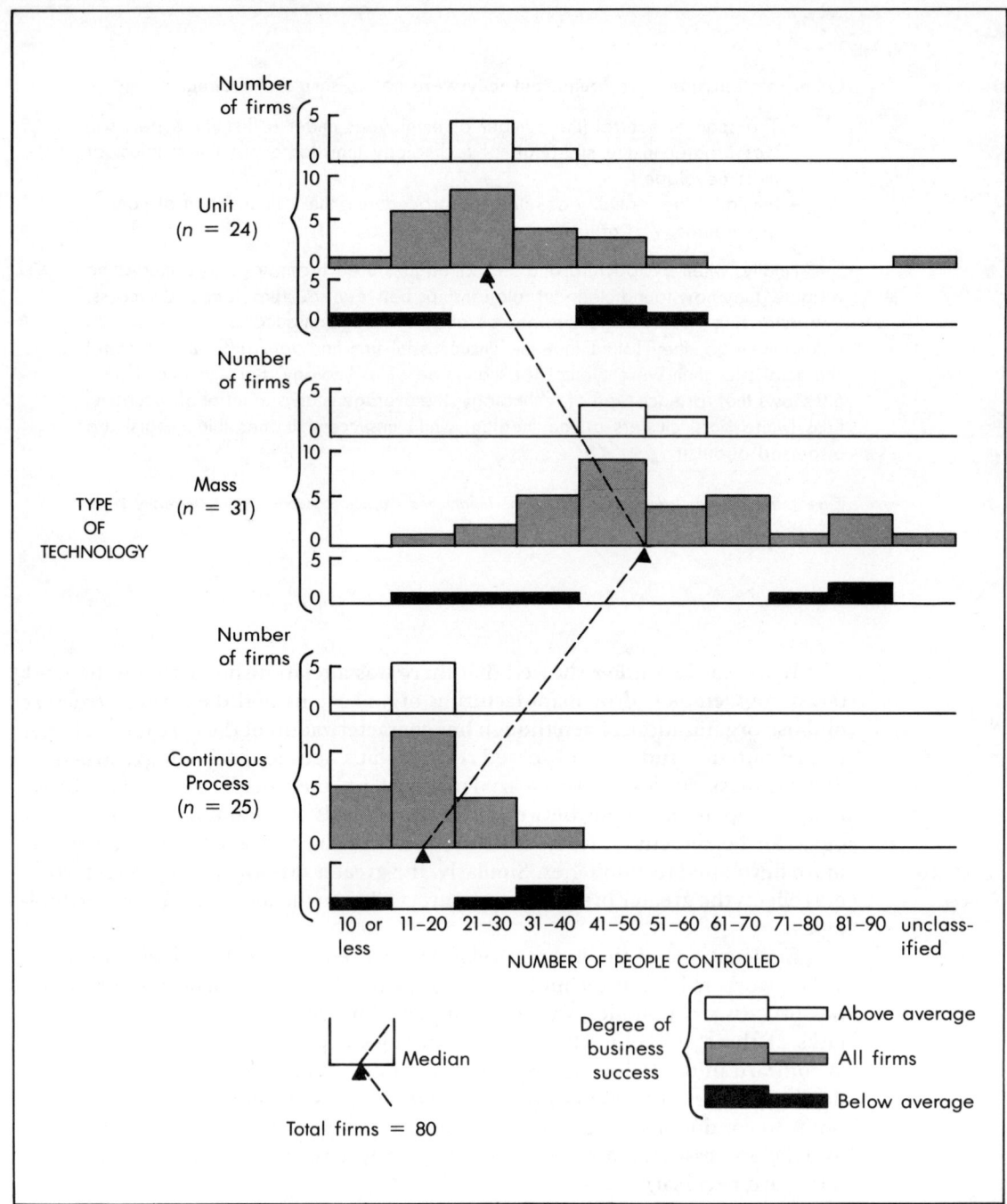

FIGURE 5.2 Average Span of Control of First-line Supervisor Analyzed by Business Success

of their directness and simplicity. However, attempts to duplicate the findings in other kinds of organizations have not been very successful, with the exception of a Japanese study (22). For one thing, all her organizations had a manufacturing core technology that could be easily characterized. Other research studies have had difficulty developing such a typology (13). For another, levels of analysis differ. It is one thing to characterize the technology of an entire organization, quite another to characterize a technology as it appears to an individual worker.

Still, this does not invalidate Woodward's basic principle. Whatever the particulars may be, manufacturing work technologies do affect manufacturing structures, engineering work technologies do affect engineering structures, and so on. For this reason we will now present a set of dimensions to help you in characterizing the technology of organizations. These dimensions include complexity, interdependence, routineness, and predictability of outcomes as summarized in Table 5.1.

Before we describe these dimensions, we need to make two important points. First, these are not independent characteristics. A given technology may show all these characteristics to a high degree or not. For example, a technology showing high interdependence among work tasks may or may not be very complex or very routine.[4] Second, to repeat a point that we made earlier, technology may occur on at least two levels: (1) it may be a core technology characterizing an entire organization or subunit, and (2) it may apply only to an individual at a work station. It is necessary to keep this distinction clear because the effect on structures and processes may differ at each level. For example, an automobile assembly line may have a highly developed core technology, yet the technology at the individual work station may be very simple.

Complexity

Complex technologies require more work operations to produce the designed outcome. Complexity is a result of the overall organization of work. Some products involve work tasks that are inherently simple. For example, the assembly

TABLE 5.1 Major Dimensions of Technology

Complexity	The number and kind of work operations required to produce the designed outcome
Interdependence	The extent to which successful performance of work tasks by one unit depends on the performance of others; the extent to which the quality of the final output depends on many organizational units
Routineness	The degree to which task requirements are fixed over time
Predictability of Outcome	The completeness of knowledge about means-ends relationships in the transformation process

of a flashlight is not complex at the organizational level or at the individual level. On the other hand, the automobile assembly line referred to earlier is at the middle range of complexity on the organizational level, but, through a planned division of labor, individual work tasks are exceedingly simple. The technology of computer systems design is inherently complex at both organizational and individual levels. Great technical skill is required to master the many and varied work operations.

The structural correlates of increasing complexity should be similar to those found by Woodward. The primary effect of complexity on organizational process would appear to take place within the motivation system. Simple, fractionated tasks seem to lead to a decreased motivation, whereas tasks enriched by increased complexity at the individual level lead to greater motivation (2, 10). Task complexity also affects the form of control processes (again as suggested by the Woodward findings).

Interdependence

A highly specialized division of labor with resulting specialization among organizational units creates an interdependence among tasks and among organizational units. These interdependent tasks will need to be coordinated. Consequently, there will be a need for specialized organizational units to coordinate them, and a need for more organizational levels (43, 18). This also agrees with the Woodward results. Formalization of control procedures also seems to be related to work unit interdependence as Dr. Faust and Stanley observed in the case of product development engineering (29).

An early study of coal mining methods in Great Britain demonstrated that problems may arise in the motivation system when the tasks performed by different work shifts are highly interdependent (38). Because satisfactory performance within each shift depended in large part on the work done by the previous shift, when that work was done poorly serious problems arose in the next shift's willingness to do its job well. A similar problem might arise in auto assembly line technology. The ease with which a worker at a more advanced work station can perform a task may in large part depend on how well previous tasks have been performed.

Routineness

Technologies involving routine work are associated with highly centralized organizational structures and use a more formalized control structure (16, 27). Where work operations are routine, and consequently repetitive, we might also expect to find a greater supervisory span of control since there would be fewer exceptional circumstances to require supervision and direct instruction. Again, the automobile assembly line technology is a good example of routine technology.

But, oddly enough, routineness may also characterize the work of a systems designer. For example, systems development engineers working in logic design find that their work tasks, though complex, rapidly become routine (29:20), and soon these engineers become concerned over lack of personal growth and development. Routineness, therefore, has implications not only for structure, but for the motivation and control systems as well. From the engineering example we see that routineness and complexity may both be attributes of the same work task.

Predictability

Predictability of designed outcomes is frequently included in typologies of work technology (21, 26, 36). Where designed outcomes are highly predictable, as in the automobile assembly line, we might expect organizations to develop highly centralized management structures since exceptions requiring lower-level decision making occur infrequently (21). A systems designer may be able to predict most outcomes at the individual task level. However, at the level of the entire organization the unpredictability of system performance is notorious. For this reason organization structures have specialized subunits to perform system analysis, debugging, and reliability analysis (20). Notice that predictability and routineness are not the same, although certainly they are related. For example, people in organizations often conform to existing procedures *because* the connection between work activities and desired outcomes is highly unpredictable or even unknown (25, 40). Routine or "ritual" performance serves as evidence that tasks are being performed "well," that is, according to prescribed methods.

These four dimensions do not represent all the possible aspects of technology, yet they do illustrate technological effects than can be seen within an organization. As a future participant you should be aware that organization structure and process are shaped generally by the constraints of technology. To summarize,

- Technology affects organizational structure but in ways that are neither simple nor universal. For example, product development engineering in an electronic systems organization will probably lead to different structures than that same function in a chemical plastics organization.
- Technology affects organizational processes. We have tried to illustrate here through examples that differences in work technology may affect the interaction, motivation, and control systems. Thus, the complexity of tasks, interdependence, and routineness, all potentially affect different aspects of the motivation system.

We close our discussion of technology with a comment concerning *technological determinism*, the notion that once a form of technology is given, then the form of the organization and certain particulars of its internal processes are fixed. Technology is viewed as the *given,* and the effects on human behavior, the *consequences.* This concept, however, is an overly simplistic way to interpret the research findings we have reviewed. The form of technology does place constraints on the organizational system, but there is a range of structures that "fit" a given technology (12). Furthermore, there is no inherent reason why technology should not be as subject to change as other variables (7). The practitioners of "job enrichment" are leaders in showing how work tasks can be restructured to produce important effects on the interaction, motivation, and control systems of organizations.

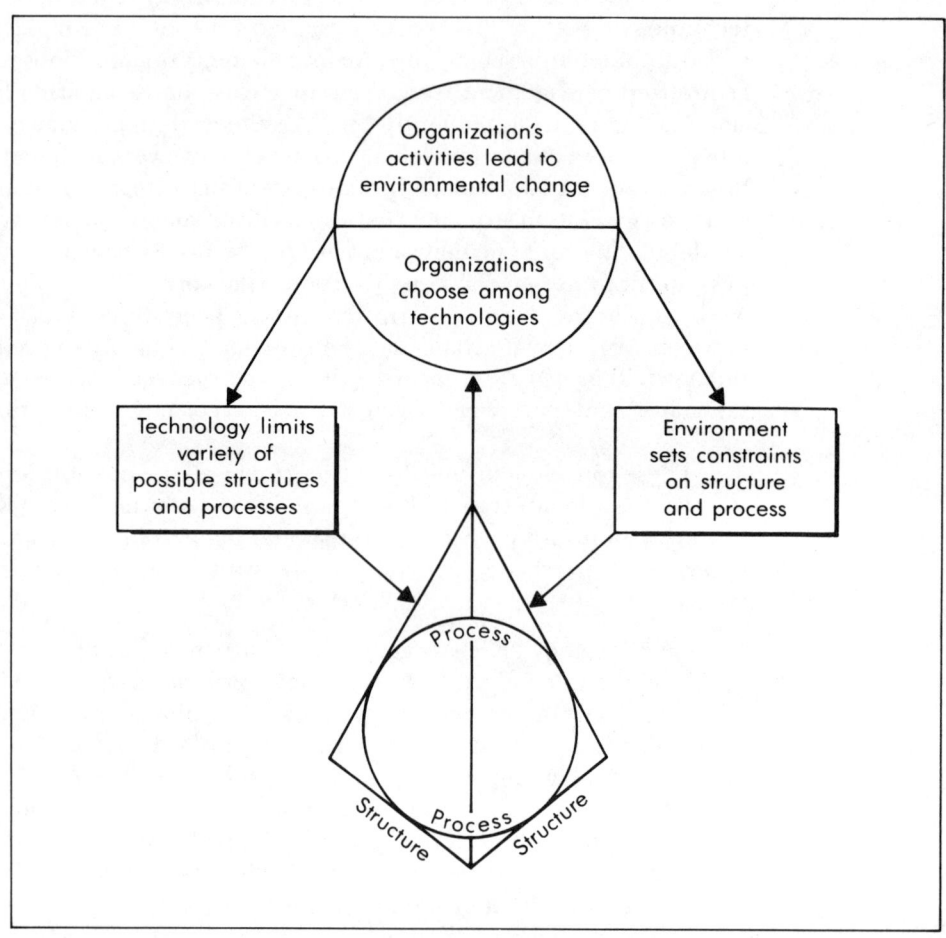

FIGURE 5.3 Technology and Environment as Causal Factors Shaping Process and Form: A Systems Viewpoint

Technology, then, within a systems framework, is mainly a set of constraints on the structure and processes of the organizational system. Another set of factors also shapes and limits structure and process, the organization's environment. From a systems perspective, we see these factors influencing one another rather than acting unidirectionally (see Figure 5.3).

Organizational Environment, Organizational Structure, and Organizational Behavior

We define environment in this way: the social, economic, technological, and organizational forces that directly or indirectly affect the structure and process of a given organization but lie outside the boundary of that organization.[5]

Recall from Chapter 2 that the choice of what to include in the system and what in the environment is arbitrary. Therefore, in this definition of environment, from an open-systems viewpoint, it is impossible to define exactly what constitutes the "boundary" of an organization. Still, "competition from the Japanese" is in the environment of the General Motors Corporation, as are equal employment opportunity laws, the Organization of Petroleum Exporting Countries, and advances in microchip technology.

Our major point should be evident. Organizations, as open, purposeful, adaptive systems, will change their structures and processes to meet the demands and opportunities presented by their environments.

It is this feature of organizations that has led some writers to adopt an explicitly evolutionary framework to analyze the effect of environmental forces. Organizations are seen as struggling for survival in environments characterized by limited resources (1). Organizations with appropriate characteristics (for example, Woodward's successful manufacturing firms) survive through processes akin to biological natural selection. Over the short term, there is adaptation to a particular ecological niche, perhaps a set of business opportunities or intergovernmental service relationships. Over the longer term, forms of organization that cannot adapt further simply disappear.

The result is an ever-changing population of organizational forms adapted more or less well to the current environmental conditions. Taking this view to an extreme position, some writers have argued that the task of management is not so much attending to the internal affairs of the organization as it is to be a "processor of external demands" (28). Whether or not this is management's primary task, environmental surveillance is certainly one way in which environment shapes organizational behavior.

The rest of this chapter thus will be devoted to characterizing the environment and the ways in which organizations adapt in structure and process. We will particularly look at how organizations attempt to cope with the uncertainties generated by rapidly changing environments. Finally, we will describe some interesting ideas on how management constructs an understanding of their organization's environment.

Characterizing Environments

The most important feature of organizational environment to affect structural adaptation is the predictability of events in that environment. This problem generally is framed in terms of uncertainty (8, 36). Under high uncertainty, organizational decision makers have difficulty in developing enough information to decide whether their actions will produce the desired result. The question, then, is what characteristics of the environment lead to predictability, or conversely, to uncertainty. The most generally cited characteristics are:

- stability—the static or dynamic character of the environment,
- concentration—the simplicity or complexity of the environment (the number of factors that must be attended to), and
- turbulence—the interdependence among environmental elements together with the rate of change in those interdependencies. (1).

Environments presenting the most uncertainty to decision makers would be highly dynamic, complex, and turbulent. In such environments it may be impossible *in principle* to predict the outcomes of courses of action. You might frequently hear the comment, "Well, it's a whole new ball game now." In simpler environments, demand for products is steady and predictable, competition is stable, and technological development is slow, but in turbulent environments just the opposite is true: demand is unpredictable, competition unstable, and technological development explosive. If you add a strong dose of governmentally generated economic instability, then, as of this writing, the environment surrounding organizations such as those in the microcomputer industry might well be characterized as turbulent.

Adapting to Environmental Uncertainty

As we noted earlier, the population of organizational forms changes by individual adaptation in the short term and through natural selection over the longer term. A snapshot view of the population at any given time will not reveal which process is occurring in an organization, but we might assume both are taking place. Existing organizations modify themselves to fit their opportunities, and new organizations arise to replace poorly adapted older ones. Two major ways in which structural adaptations take place are:

1. the innovation of specialized organizational subunits—buffering—and
2. decreasing the short-term dependency of key organizational units on the units most subject to environmental shock—loose coupling (15, 41, 36).

Buffering by specialized organizational subunits is easiest to illustrate through our example of the automobile assembly line. The function of buffering is to insulate the technological core from environmental uncertainty, thus to allow the core to run at maximum efficiency. In the simplest example, specialized subunits are set up to stockpile raw materials so that the assembly line does not depend on a day-to-day external supply. Similarly, finished automobiles are warehoused to smooth out fluctuations in demand. In electronic systems production, a company such as IBM may want to develop its own microchip design and production subunits to help absorb environmental uncertainty that might otherwise affect the smooth operation of its production core technology. Still another example might be the development of specialized long-range planning units.

Making crucial organizational subunits less dependent on the units that are most likely to be directly affected by environmental uncertainty can be effected through loose coupling. Organizational subunits are set up such that the failure of one does not immediately affect the functioning of another. For example, IBM, understanding that its long-term competitive success is based on a combined technical and marketing strategy, created an independent Advanced Systems Development Division with loose coupling in mind. This division was to develop products and marketing strategies to take effect within five to ten years, thus relieving the division of pressures for time sequencing product developments to fit near-term market needs. Thus, in theory at least, even if current products were doing poorly in the marketplace, the resulting pressures on the existing product development divisions would not be transferred to the Advanced Systems Development Division with its five- to ten-year time horizon.

Although they are related strategies there is a distinction between loose coupling and buffering. In buffering, new organizational subunits are created and the technical core is very dependent on the functioning of these newly created units. In loose coupling just the opposite is true.

Recently, researchers interested in public organizations have been developing a theory of organizational adaptation to environment that is in some ways quite different from the adaptations we have been discussing here (24). The basic idea is that public organizations depend for their support on public funds, and that these are obtained best by organizations that most clearly represent "what everyone knows" about effective organizations. Thus, because the technical efficiency of these organizations is extremely difficult to determine otherwise, growth and survival are aided by adopting structural innovations that mirror "what we all know" about the structural form of successful organizations (for more detail, see Box 5).

Adaptation in Organizational Process

There is also some evidence to indicate that organizations adapt to uncertainty in their environments with changes in the interaction, motivation, and feedback

Box 5 Organizational Adaptation to Institutional Environments

In this research Brian Rowan sought to learn the extent to which the environment accounts for the innovation and stabilization of new organizational subunits. To do so, he drew upon the distinction between *technical* and *institutional* environments. Briefly, in technical environments organizations add subunits as needed to stabilize and promote the efficiency of the technical core. In institutional environments, as Rowan theorizes, the organizational innovations that come about tend to reflect society's norms, values, and beliefs about what constitutes effective technical relationships.

Innovation in institutional environments proceeds in three stages. First, "new service units are defined and rationalized by lobbying publics, professions, legislatures, and regulatory agencies. As institution building proceeds, emergent services gain legitimacy and are perceived as useful additions . . ." (30:259). A period of diffusion follows as other organizations adopt the innovation. Finally, as the innovation becomes widespread, diffusion slows and a period of stabilization begins.

To investigate these ideas Rowan examined the historical development of three service "domains": the health, psychological, and curriculum services units in thirty California school districts. He counted a district as adopting a structure when it "listed an administrative officer with a job title relevant to the type of work done in a domain" (30:264). In health, for example, this would mean a Director of School Health, a school physician, or a nurse.

Rowan's thesis was that growing organizations will add new structures that have the support of "key actors" in their institutional environment. School systems were a good test population since it is difficult for them to justify most of their innovations because of the high level of uncertainty inherent in their technology. Educational organizations have difficulty *proving* their effectiveness. Instead, they try to gain acceptance for their structures and functions on the basis of current institutionalized beliefs about what works best. Consequently, the acceptance of *new* structures and functions is likely to be based on currently institutionalized beliefs held by key environmental actors.

The key actors in this study were defined to be the state and federal legislatures, the state education agency, the state-level professional agencies, and the teacher training agencies. These groups authorized new programs, defined types of professional personnel needed, prescribed the training and credentials required, and developed administrative channels to regulate the operation of innovative programs. An important hypothesis of Rowan's research is that innovations will become widespread and stable only when a state of "balance" exists among these key actors

continued

in the environment. Balance exists when a network of actors "develops ideological consensus and coordinated working relationships . . ." (30:262). The organizational innovations that survive are likely to respect the beliefs of the key environmental actors who both reflect and certify as correct "what everyone knows."

Examining the life histories of the important events in each domain, Rowan found out the following.

Health subunits were most widespread, but currently in a state of environmental imbalance. Following the advent of compulsory immunization in the 1950s, which did away with the need for frequent health inspections, key actors had been unable to agree upon a new rationale for the existence of health subunits. As a result diffusion ceased and some health units were being dropped.

Curriculum services revealed a history fraught with disagreement, particularly over the adoption of a progressive, child-centered approach. In this state of environmental imbalance, most schools did not adopt the innovation, and those that did frequently dropped it after a few years.

In contrast, psychological services subunits, while initially lagging behind the others, showed a history of continued diffusion and stability. Again, examination of the historical record showed that an ideological consensus had been long in coming, but that now the network of key actors had achieved a state of balance.

Two major conclusions come out of Rowan's research.

- Organizations do not grow simply by adding additional new units as decided by the needs of individual districts. Rather, the choices are determined at least in part by views current in the institutionalized environment.
- The persistence of structural innovations is not inevitable, but depends on the maintenance of balance among influential actors in the environment. Where both consensus as to the value of these units and harmonious working relationships exist, so does a state of balance, which in turn guarantees continuing support for a given structural innovation.

From B. Rowan, "Organizational Structure and the Institutional Environment: The Case of Public Schools." *Administrative Science Quarterly,* 27 (1982): 259–279.

and control systems. Two early but influential studies indicated that organizations reacted to environmental uncertainty with structural changes, but also made changes in role definitions, communication patterns, and management behavior (4, 21).

In a study of British electronics firms, researchers identified two approaches to management that they called *mechanistic* and *organic.* The mechanistic systems they found to be relatively inflexible in procedures, whereas the organic systems were more adaptive. For example, mechanistic systems were characterized by specific role prescriptions for each member, vertical communication patterns (between superior and subordinate), an emphasis on the leader's right to decide and superior knowledge, and an emphasis on obedience. Organic systems were quite the opposite, with general role definitions and an emphasis on task accomplishment, diffuse structures of control and authority, both vertical and horizontal communications, knowledge assumed to belong to others besides the formal leader, and so on. The chief point of the study was not that either the mechanistic or organic system was superior, but that each seemed to be adapted to a different environment. The mechanistic system seemed most appropriate for static environments, those with a low degree of environmental uncertainty. And organic systems seemed to be better adapted to what we have called turbulent environments, those with high levels of uncertainty.

In a study done in this country researchers found similar results. Their work paralleled the Woodward study in that they were interested in the relationships among environment, structure, and the success of the organization. One interesting finding of that study was that patterns of decision-making influence in the control system differed for successful firms operating in different environments. Specifically, in highly uncertain environments, lower-level managers were more involved in influential decisions than their higher-level counterparts. In stable, predictable environments just the opposite was true (21:143). These results, of course, follow the pattern we have been observing here, that mechanistic management systems seem to be effective in stable environments, whereas organic systems seem most appropriate in turbulent, uncertain environments.

Perception and the Social Construction of Environments

In the preceding discussion, we have made the implicit assumption that the managements of organizations can, and are motivated to, make accurate and exhaustive searches of their environments. However, there is good reason to doubt that this is the case, especially in a turbulent environment. For one thing, perceptions of the environment tend to be distorted by beliefs about it. People perceive facts selectively, in accord with what they already "know." They also choose facts that provide plausible explanations for management difficulties they may be experiencing. This process of socially constructing the organization's environment has been called *enacting* the environment (41). For example, in Pennsylvania the Public Utility Commission cannot, by law, terminate winter service to utility consumers who have failed to pay bills for a number of months. Utility company executives perceive the problem as being created by "deadbeats," who use more than their share of utility services and then simply refuse to pay. To them, termination of service is a way of bringing these people back into line. However, consumer surveys sponsored by the Public Utility Commission reveal a vastly more complicated picture. In fact, a major cause of the problem is bad management practice, putting off attempts to collect past due bills until the consumer would need to send several months' wages to pay off the bill.

A more familiar example is the plight of the American auto industry. Serious analyses point to the fact that the problem is due as much to the auto makers' enactment of an environment that did not exist and their unwillingness to attend to environmental signals as it is to the organizational skills of the Japanese. Obviously, however, it is in the personal interests of auto executives to enact an environment of Japanese invasion rather than one of American blundering (31).

Summary

In our opening story, The Company has been having problems in its product development laboratories. Ted's proposal is to restructure them more along the lines of Another Company's laboratories. We could simplify this situation in two ways: (1) we could attribute the problems in morale to the complex structural form in the Company laboratories; or (2) we might suppose that both the morale problems and structural forms are attributable to yet a third variable, or set of variables, the effects of technology and environment. This latter is the conclusion favored by our discussion. We might even infer that to change the structure of The Company's product development laboratory radically would be disastrous because the technology and environment could not accommodate such a structure.

The Company operates in a turbulent technological and organizational environment. Rapid change characterizes both. New technologies are continually developing and new organizations with new approaches to the business are appearing all the time. All are trying to get a piece of the action. As a consequence of this environment, product development in The Company must be programmed to meet these challenges. Each product line must be kept ahead of its competition. Time cannot be wasted.

Typically, then, a large project may be planned for a hundred man-years. This may mean five years with twenty people, or two years with fifty. The difference is that the two-year approach involves a greater division of labor and, consequently, greater specialization. The technology of systems development requires that each element of the project be closely integrated with all others, so a great deal of coordinating apparatus is needed to integrate these highly differentiated activities. The structural form of the organization mirrors these requirements of technology and environment, and the observed human consequences flow from this structure. This is the viewpoint of environmental and technological determinism. It is the principle behind the contingency theory of organizations: Proper and effective structures and processes are contingent on conditions given by the technology and environment.

As with all such comprehensive principles this one can be misleading if taken deterministically. Structure and process are indeed constrained by the technological imperative—The Company's systems development laboratories cannot, for example, use the flat structure of Another Company—but within these constraints a range of structural forms *is* possible, each associated with somewhat different sets of systems outcomes. There is a range of possibilities in the interaction system, such as cross-departmental teams; there are different patterns of motivation systems available, such as lateral reassignment to relieve the boredom resulting from task fragmentation. Possibilities are endless. Thus, in place of the principle of technological and environmental determinism we pose a less stringent principle of organizational constraints (3). Some things are not possible if these constraints are to be satisfied—that is what we mean by constraint. But more than one structural form or process is possible. Many forms may satisfy a system of constraints. Understanding organizational behavior means understanding how and why these constraints affect behavior. We may successfully quantify, measure, and control the work behavior of a salesperson, but doing the same for a researcher is an entirely different matter. Within the technology and likely environment of sales, such an approach is consonant with the constraints; for the researcher it is not.

Our discussion has concerned only the most general of principles. Yet, as we have seen, they can be powerful principles. They suggest that you, as a participant in your organization, should learn to understand the constraints of environment and technology before attempting to understand the significance of other factors in the organizational behavior you have observed. Not all things are possible.

Notes

1. The work technology of systems development engineers is described extensively by Ritti (29).
2. Summary reviews of the literature on the effects of technology from different perspectives may be found in Davis and Taylor (7), Gillespie and Mileti (14), Steers (33), and Gerwin (13). Summary discussions of the literature on organizational environments from different viewpoints may be found in Starbuck (32), Perrow (27), Steers (33), and Aldrich (1).
3. Evidence for such a contingency theory had been presented earlier by Burns and Stalker (4), but this work did not receive the general attention that was later given the 1965 Woodward volume.
4. One major problem running through the literature on work technology is the effect of organizational size (6, 18). The need in larger-sized organizations for a large volume of production may lead to high subunit interdependence because a highly specialized

division of labor is necessary to cope with the volume. Similarly, process complexity and product complexity with low volume may lead to very different structural forms than with high volume. However, our concern is not with organization design per se, and our intent here is only to illustrate that the effects of technology constrain form and process.

5. Some writers have used the concept of "task environment" as a less inclusive definition. The task environment includes only those factors related to the goal-achieving activities of the organization.

References

1. ALDRICH, H. *Organizations and Environments.* Englewood Cliffs, N.J.: Prentice-Hall, 1979.
2. BLAUNER, R. *Alienation and Freedom.* Chicago: University of Chicago Press, 1964.
3. BUCK, V. "The Organization as a System of Constraints." In *Approaches to Organization Design,* edited by J. D. Thompson. Pittsburgh: University of Pittsburgh Press, 1966.
4. BURNS, T., and G. M. STALKER. *The Management of Innovation.* London: Tavistock, 1961.
5. CHANDLER, A. *Strategy and Structure.* Cambridge: M.I.T. Press, 1962.
6. COMSTOCK, D., and W. R. SCOTT. "Technology and the Structure of Subunits: Distinguishing Individual and Workgroup Effects." *Administrative Science Quarterly* 22 (1977): 177–202.
7. DAVIS, L., and J. C. TAYLOR. "Technology, Organization and Job Structure." In *Handbook of Work, Organization and Society,* edited by Robert Dubin. Chicago: Rand McNally, 1976.
8. DUNCAN, R. "Characteristics of Organizational Environments and Perceived Environmental Uncertainty." *Administrative Science Quarterly* 17 (1972): 313–327.
9. EMERY, F., and E. L. TRIST. "The Causal Texture of Organizational Environments." *Human Relations* 8 (1965): 21–32.
10. FORD, R. *Motivation Through the Work Itself.* New York: American Management Assn., 1969.
11. FRY, L. W. "Technology-Structure Research: Three Critical Issues." *Academy of Management Journal* 25 (September 1982): 532–552.
12. GALBRAITH, J. *Organization Design.* Reading, Mass.: Addison-Wesley, 1977.
13. GERWIN, D. "Relationships between Structure and Technology." In *Handbook of Organizational Design,* Vol. 2. Edited by P. Nystrom and W. Starbuck. New York: Oxford University Press, 1981. Chap. 1.
14. GILLESPIE, D., and D. S. MILETI. "Technology and the Study of Organizations: An Overview and Appraisal." *Academy of Management Review* 2 (1977): 7–16.
15. GLASSMAN, R. "Persistance and Loose Coupling." *Behavioral Science* 18 (1973): 83–98.
16. HAGE, J., and M. AIKEN. "Routine Technology, Social Structure and Organization Goals." *Administrative Science Quarterly* 14 (1969): 366–376.

17. HASENFELD, Y. "People Processing Organizations: An Exchange Approach." *American Sociological Review* 37 (1972): 256–263.
18. HICKSON, D., D. S. PUGH, and D. C. PHESEY. "Operations Technology and Organization Structure: An Empirical Reappraisal." *Administrative Science Quarterly* 14 (1969): 378–397.
19. JELINEK, M. "Technology, Organizations, and Contingency." *Academy of Management Review* 2 (1977): 17–26.
20. KIDDER, T. *The Soul of a New Machine.* Boston: Little, Brown, 1981.
21. LAWRENCE, P., and J. W. LORSCH. *Organization and Environment: Managing Differentiation and Integration.* Homewood, Ill.: Irwin, 1969.
22. MARSH, R., and H. MANNARI. "Technology and Size as Derminants of the Organizational Structure of Japanese Factories." *Administrative Science Quarterly* 26 (1981): 33–57.
23. MEYER, A. D. "Adapting to Environmental Jolts." *Administrative Science Quarterly* 27 (December 1982) 515–537.
24. MEYER, J. W., and B. ROWAN. "Institutionalized Organizations: Formal Structure as Myth and Ceremony." *American Journal of Sociology* 83 (September 1977): 340–363.
25. OUCHI, W. "The Relationship Between Organizational Structure and Organizational Control." *Administrative Science Quarterly* 22 (1977): 95–113.
26. PERROW, C. "A Framework for the Comparative Analysis of Organizations." *American Sociological Review* 32 (1967): 194–208.
27. ———— *Organizational Analysis: A Sociological View.* Belmont, Calif.: Wadsworth, 1970.
28. PFEFFER, J., and G. SALANCIK. *The External Control of Organizations: A Resource Dependence Perspective.* New York: Harper and Row, 1978.
29. RITTI, R. *The Engineer in the Industrial Corporation.* New York: Columbia University Press, 1971.
30. ROWAN, B. "Organizational Structure and the Institutional Environment: The Case of Public Schools." *Administrative Science Quarterly* 27 (1982): 259–279.
31. SMIRCICH, L. "Implications of the Interpretive Perspective for Management Theory." In *Communicating and Organizing,* edited by L. Putnam and M. Pacanowky. Beverley Hills, Calif.: Sage, 1983.
32. STARBUCK, W. "Organizations and Their Environments." In *Handbook of Industrial and Organizational Psychology,* edited by M. Dunnette. Chicago: Rand McNally, 1976.
33. STEERS, R. *Organizational Effectiveness: A Behavioral View.* Santa Monica, Calif.: Goodyear, 1977.
34. TERREBERRY, S. "The Evolution of Organizational Environments." *Administrative Science Quarterly* 12 (1968): 590–613.
35. THOMPSON, J. "Organizational Management of Conflict." *Administrative Science Quarterly* 4 (1960): 389–409.
36. ————. *Organizations in Action.* New York: McGraw-Hill, 1967.
37. THOMPSON, J., and W. MCEWEN. "Organizational Goals and Environment." *American Sociological Review* 23 (1958): 23–31.

38. TRIST, E., and K. W. BAMFORTH. "Some Social and Psychological Consequences of the Longwall Method of Coal Getting." *Human Relations* 4 (1951): 3–38.
39. WAMSLEY, G., and M. N. ZALD. "The Political Economy of Public Organizations." *Public Administration Review* 33 (1973): 62–73.
40. WARNER, W., and E. A. HAVENS. "Goal Displacement and the Intangibility of Organizational Goals." *Administrative Science Quarterly* 12 (1968): 539–555.
41. WEICK, K. *The Social Psychology of Organizing.* Reading, Mass.: Addison-Wesley, 1969.
42. WHYTE, W. *Human Relations in the Restaurant Industry.* New York: McGraw-Hill, 1948.
43. WOODWARD, J. *Industrial Organization.* London: Oxford University Press, 1965.

Discussion Questions

1. Referring to our opening case, explain what we mean by "flattening" the management structure of an organization. What advantages were projected by Ted Shelby for his project to flatten Company management structures?
2. Using the dimensions of technology outlined in this chapter, describe the production technologies of your university or college. What effect can you see of these technologies on university structure?
3. Compare The Company's product development organization structure to the structure of a large university. (Consider students as employees for this exercise.) How would you expect these structures to differ? Why?
4. What do we mean by *technological determinism*? What are the two sides of this issue? Why is this an important issue for people interested in the design of organization structures?
5. Using the various dimensions of environment and work technology, how would you describe a combat infantry division? A state department of public welfare? Do you feel that the term *technology* is applicable to such organizations?
6. A high degree of interdependence among work tasks seems to lead to a high degree of complexity in work tasks, yet we state that these are separate dimensions of technology. In your own words tell what is meant by independent dimensions, and why tasks may be highly interdependent, or highly complex, but not necessarily both.
7. Give the definitions for *technology* and *environment* used in this chapter. Try to apply these to several kinds of organizations.
8. What do we mean by *turbulent environment*? Give some examples of environmental turbulence.

Section Two

Patterns of Social Behavior—Systems Structure (II)

In our description of the formal structure of organizations we showed first, how positions are patterned to provide differentiation of subunit functions; and second, how the relationships between these subunit functions are structured into patterns of compliance and authority among positions. We tried to show both in theory and in practice how these formal arrangements impose structure on organizational behavior.

Now we will move to a second aspect of structure, depicted in Figure II.1: the *patterning of social behavior* by positions. Just as the authority structure specifies the rights and duties of positions, so too does the *structure of social expectations* make a wide range of behavior in these positions predictable and interpretable. We learn of this structure of social expectations through the organization processes of socialization. More precisely, socialization is the process through which we learn *roles*, patterns of behavior appropriate to specific positions in specific organizational contexts; and *norms*, more general patterns of behavior appropriate to a given organizational context. Together these constitute part of the normative structure. Socialization also conveys attitudes, values, and beliefs about what is proper in *this* organization.

In this section we will first discuss how people learn the expectations that constitute organizational roles in particular, and the normative structure in general. This process of socialization starts even before recruitment into the organization and continues throughout a person's career or careers. Individuals select organizations, and organizations select individuals with the proper values, attitudes, and motives—and, of course, abilities. Within organizations people work

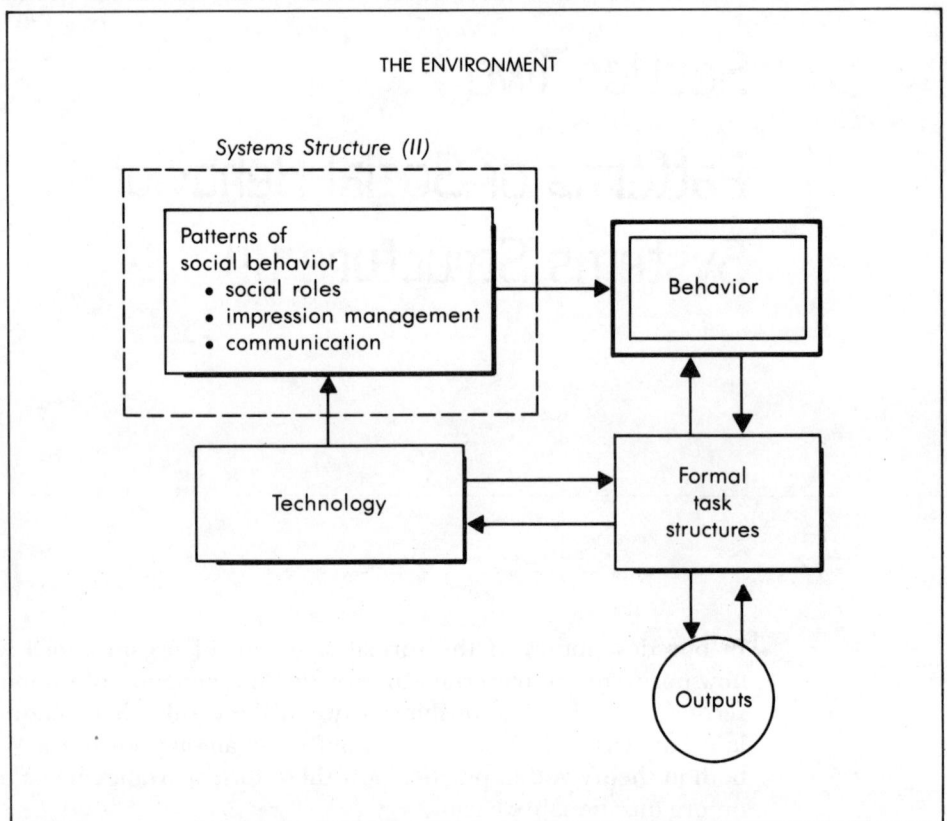

FIGURE II.1 The Basis for Organizational Action: Patterns of Social Behavior—Systems Structure (II)

toward positions that provide attractive roles: lawyer, manager, salesperson. Individuals modify, restrict, or amplify their behavior to fit roles associated with these positions. In turn, organizations with positions to be filled may have to modify structures in order to provide attractive roles as necessary inducements in recruiting new members. The process, therefore, is reciprocal: individuals adapt to organizational needs through socialization, and organizations adapt to the needs of individuals through recruitment and structural change. Nevertheless, organizational socialization mainly concerns how individuals modify themselves and their attitudes to fit the needs and desires of the social system that is the organization.

We will also discuss *impression management,* a less emphasized aspect of the patterning of behavior in positions. Impression management is somewhat the opposite of role assumption. Individuals' role performances are constrained by organizational expectations, that is, individuals modify their behavior to conform to these expectations. However, through performances that are managed in order to convey a favorable impression—for the *presentation of self*—individuals modify organizational expectations. These presentations generally are "true" (though they need not be); they convey aspects of self that the individual considers important but cannot directly verbalize ("I'm really very capable, you know"), or that are not otherwise directly apparent or evident. Impression management, then, describes the ways in which people convey symbolically important attributes of their organizational selves to others in the organization.

As with role expectations, people learn to interpret these symbolic performances of impression management as part of the socialization process. The organizational social facts necessary for proper role performance and for proper impression management, then, are parts of the systems structure of the organization; they are an important part of the uncodified rules within which the organization's activities are carried on.

These organizational social facts are also part of the structure of organizational communication. And that is the final topic we shall take up in this section, to provide a more general framework for understanding how information is conveyed by word, action, dress, and symbol. We shall explore how the exact words and symbols we use structure the interpretation of events in organizations and ensure that those events are understood correctly. You will see, for example, when the corporate communications people announce that Ted Shelby has been "assigned to a new responsibility," that most definitely does not mean "promoted." In fact, it just might mean, "he fouled up in his present position and is being moved laterally out of the way."

Chapter 6
Socialization: The Assumption of Roles

You're in the Army Now

The absurd is humorous, say the philosophers. If that were so, then the humor of his present situation was lost on Stanley. Yesterday had been his last day with The Company; today, his first day in the Army. Actually, he would only be in the Army for the next six months, fulfilling his part of an earlier bargain with the military. And actually it hadn't been his last day with The Company; it was a leave of absence. Nonetheless, here he was, a new private E-1, the lowest order of enlisted man. The absurdity of his situation was rooted in the fact that yesterday evening, as he had taken his personal effects out of his desk at his office in The Company, a hired cleaning man had been dutifully buffing the office floor. Today—or rather tonight—Stanley was dutifully sweeping the floor of the Orderly Room. Absurd. And the thought of it absorbed him as he labored through his first assigned night duty.

His position in The Company and his position in the Army were quite different. As a young professional man in The Company he had some status; that is, he could locate himself somewhere in the lower middle ranks of The Company "totem pole."

Here, as an unwilling conscript, his status was the lowest of the low. Still, there was some humor in it. Everything was so turned about, so upside down, that surprises were the order of the day. And surprise is an element of humor.

* * * * *

"All right, you mens. Fall in down by A building—on the double." The persistent compound plural, favored by Army noncoms from the rural South, was a puzzle to Stanley, though the meaning was clear enough. "Take yourself a broom and get to sweeping."

Stanley gaped in disbelief as the noncom demonstrated the morning's duty: to sweep the parade yard free of the loose gravel that littered the surface. In itself that task was not so extraordinary—except that the parade yard wasn't paved; it was simply compacted gravel full of new, emerging pebbles waiting to take the place of old.

But they were going to do it all right. They might as well get to it. So Stanley and his fellow conscripts fell to the task, working to complete the unrewarding labor in order to return to the shade of the barracks. Or so they thought. For just as they finished, their pebbles all in neat piles on the far side of the yard, the noncom returned.

"Figure you're done, do you? I don't think I like the looks of the yard. You didn't do a good job. Pebbles all around. Go back over it and get 'em all."

At noon they broke for chow, the task still not complete. That afternoon they were carted off for some shots. They never worked the parade yard again. Stanley felt there was something to be learned from that experience but he wasn't quite sure what.

* * * * *

Thanksgiving Day for the new conscript was dismal (any holiday for that matter). New surroundings, no real friends, no pass to town—only the dingy, dilapidated buildings of the recruit reception center. But things could have been worse. Stanley learned that Army cooks *could* make a good meal, and the noonday dinner had been enjoyable. Now most of them were upstairs in the barracks lying around, talking or reading. Well, it could be worse.

"All right, you mens, on you feets. I'm gonna need some of you for a while." Then the noncom continued, "I hear a few of you are college boys. Is that right? Let's see your hands." Six or seven hands shot up immediately, as if vying with one another for recognition. They assumed something good was in the offing for those so qualified, something more appropriate to their former civilian status.

"All right, let's go. You volunteers get down to the mess hall. KP tonight."

And that was how Stanley learned the meaning of the time-honored dictum: never, *never* volunteer.

Only it wasn't so easy, somehow, to tell when you were volunteering.

* * * * *

Some say the Army has its own way of doing things. That may be an understatement. The standard joke was that the only way you could *not* be assigned a given job was if you had some previous skill or training in it. You could forget about being a cook, for example, if that's what you had done in civilian life. And that was because you might be tempted to do something your own way. What the Army wanted was uniformity—in dress, action, and speech.

Sometimes this caused trouble. There were people who didn't understand why this uniformity was so necessary. For example, a most troublesome point was the insistence of the training cadre that the weapon that was their constant companion during basic training was a *rifle,* not a *gun.* Stanley noticed that this was particularly vexatious to some of the Southern boys for whom hunting, and guns, were a way of life. But the noncoms were unrelenting. There were even little exercises in self-debasement contrived to punish violators. The offender was made to recite and act out: "This is my rifle, this is my gun. One is for fighting, the other for fun." One day a youth in Stanley's barracks finally could take no more of it, and, when ritually asked, "Your what, soldier?" shouted back at his tormentors in ripe Southern dialect, "Guun! Guun! It may be a rahfle to you, but it's a Goddam guun to me."

Ah well, that's how you get "volunteers" to paint the mess hall.[1]

Socialization: An Overview of the Process

Possibly the military has changed since Stanley's day, but the experience is a powerful one because the *norms, roles,* and *symbols* are generally beyond the experience of previous everyday life, and are contrived and amplified. Stanley's first experiences in The Company were not as stark. There were new aspects in The Company, to be sure, but the new roles were more an extension of, a building on, earlier experiences. In the Army Stanley was transplanted into a foreign organizational world. There were new roles to be learned that were appropriate to the position of private. And the new norms, statuses, symbols, and symbolic acts were all the more exaggerated because the military organization intrudes on more aspects of life than the ordinary work organization. This is why the military experience is so instructive—it etches in bold relief elements common to all organizations.

The military actually wants just a few things. It wants *uniformity*—things must be done the Army way. It wants complete *compliance* to authoritative commands. And it wants *commitment*, the knowledge that new members will continue to participate. These few things add up to *predictability* of action, and that is what the military organization is geared to produce (11, 50). Still, in itself this is not unique. All organizations want the same thing from members, though not to the same degree. Socialization mechanisms are not so intrusive either.

Why is this so? First, most organizations in both the public and private sector offer substantial material rewards for participation, and, hence, compliance is more easily achieved through voluntary means. Furthermore, potential physical risk is usually far less than in the military, and hence, the total predictability of action necessary to ensure the safety of group members is not as great. But these are differences in degree, not in kind.

In this chapter we will examine how organizations add new individuals and turn them into members with a commitment to the organization and its values, and with a sense of shared identity with others in the organization. We will focus on the process by which we assume new roles in new organizational contexts and come to share a wide range of attitudes, values, commitments, and motives with fellow members, giving, in turn, some predictability to our organizational actions (24).[2]

Career Stages in the Socialization Process

Organizational socialization takes place throughout your career, but the effects of its processes are more intense during some periods than others (25). Intense socialization occurs particularly at the beginning of a career, and during transitions into new organizations or functions. Edgar Schein of MIT's Sloan School of Management outlines these career stages as shown in Table 6.1 (38).

Let us review the entire process first. In Stage 1 is the process known as *anticipatory socialization* (29:265). Through this process we come to adopt the key values and beliefs characteristic of the anticipated career. Its function is to ease transition into later roles.

Anticipatory socialization takes place in several ways. First, we learn proper attitudes, values, and motives. These are conveyed through occupational myths, the beliefs shared by members of our society; they tell us what to expect of physicians, police officers, athletes, scientists, or business people. We also learn by directly observing the activities of people in these occupations.

And we learn through *presocializing institutions* such as universities or acade-

TABLE 6.1 Basic Stages, Positions, and Processes Involved in a Career

Basic Stages and Transitions	Statuses or Positions	Psychological and Organizational Processes: Transactions Between Individual and Organization
1. Pre-entry	Aspirant, applicant, rushee	Preparation, education, anticipatory socialization
Entry (transition)	Entrant, postulant, recruit	Recruitment, rushing, testing, screening, selection, acceptance ("hiring"); passage through external inclusion boundary; rites of entry; induction and orientation
2. Basic training, novitiate	Trainee, novice, pledge	Training, indoctrination, socialization, testing . . . by the organization, tentative acceptance into group
Initiation, first vows (transition)	Initiate, graduate	Passage through first inner inclusion boundary, acceptance as member and conferring of organizational status, rite of passage and acceptance
3. First regular assignment	New member	First testing by [member] of . . . own capacity to function; granting of real responsibility (playing for keeps); passage through functional boundary with assignment to specific job or department
Substages		
3a. Learning the job 3b. Maximum performance 3c. Becoming obsolete 3d. Learning new skills, et cetera		Indoctrination and testing . . . by immediate workgroup leading to acceptance or rejection; if accepted, further education and socialization (learning the ropes); preparation for higher status through coaching, seeking visibility, finding sponsors
Promotion or leveling off (transition)		Preparation, testing, passage through hierarchical boundary, rite of passage; may involve passage through functional boundary as well (rotation)
4. Second assignment	Legitimate member (fully accepted)	Processes under no. 3 repeat

TABLE 6.1 (*Continued*)

Basic Stages and Transitions	Statuses or Positions	Psychological and Organizational Processes: Transactions Between Individual and Organization
5. Tenure	Permanent member	Passage through another inner inclusion boundary
Termination and exit (transition)	Old-timer, senior citizen	Preparation for exit, cooling the mark out, rites of exit (testimonial dinners, and so on)
6. Post-exit	Alumnus, emeritus, retired	Granting of peripheral status, consultant or senior advisor

Reproduced by special permission from the *Journal of Applied Behavioral Science*, "The Individual, the Organization, and the Career: A Conceptual Scheme," by Edgar H. Schein, Vol. 7, No. 4, 1971, Table 1, pp. 415–416, NTL Institute for Applied Behavioral Science.

mies, and through training programs, which are presocializing activities for future roles (although these programs often occur after initial recruitment but before acceptance into full membership). For example, for years the Bell Laboratories has sent its newly recruited technical people through a master's degree program. The labeling may be ambiguous, but the function is clear enough: The presocializing experience takes place in a formal setting and is aimed at inculcating proper values, attitudes, and motives, often in the context of skills training.

Recruitment is another key stage in the socialization process. We will examine two aspects of recruitment. The first is the viewpoint of an organization trying to select individuals who already possess desirable skills and appropriate values. This is the organization's attempt to select individuals who will adapt easily to its "culture." The second is the effect of individuals on organizations, that is, the processes by which organizations adapt to the attributes of recruits.

Stage 2 of the Schein schema concerns the initial stages of the socialization process *within* the organization. It starts with *resocialization*, the substitution of new values for old (11, 48, 50). This function occurs in formal training programs provided for new recruits. Resocialization is commonly necessary because the values, attitudes, beliefs, and motives developed during anticipatory socialization and in presocializing institutions may be somewhat at odds with organizational realities.

This gap between the ideal and the real leads to a condition that has been called *reality shock* (19). Each previous stage of socialization has its own function and its own special view of the career; the reality of workaday life may be different still. The first "real job" in a career also brings first encounters with organizational reality. Military officers learn they cannot "go by the book"; business students find that technical rationality is not necessarily the touchstone of organizational success (37).

Finally, a *rite of passage* brings the person into full membership status (44). The rite of passage is an event or series of events signifying that a formal change in status has taken place. For example, fraternities and sororities have hazing practices that signify the transition from pledge to brother or sister.

Stages 3 and 4 involve building a *commitment*. During these stages proper values, attitudes, and motives are internalized; that is, we come to accept the organization's outlook as our own. This process is helped by the accrual of power and material rewards through which we become bound ever more strongly to the organization.

Stages 5 and 6 are the final career stages. We will examine these topics in Chapters 11 and 12, where we will consider the dynamics of managerial advancement, the management of definitions of success and failure, and procedures for "cooling out the mark," that is, for making demotivating role transitions more acceptable.

We will use this basic outline to organize our presentation of the processes involved in the assumption of new organizational roles.

Characteristics Affecting Recruitment and Socialization

Stanley did not have much choice about whether or not he wanted to become a member of the United States Army. The recruiting process was swift and impersonal. On the other hand, Father Douggan has spent most of his life deciding to become and remain a priest. This is a continuous lifetime decision for both him and the church. Jimmy Szekely became a member of The Company by answering a want ad and standing in line for forty-five minutes, whereas Dr. Faust's experience with The University was different still.

Why do people have different experiences in joining organizations? There are obvious factors such as the supply and demand for recruits, the geographical location of available jobs, and the percentage of available recruits who, if hired, could perform the work ably. But there are other important considerations in recruitment and socialization, particularly for organizations that want their members to hold a strong value orientation.

THE VALUE ORIENTATION. In our previous discussion we outlined three major bases of organizational power: coercive, normative, and remunerative. We noted also that most organizations are not pure types but combine something of each, usually remunerative and normative. Normative organizations differ from the remunerative in having a strong commitment to a core of values, beliefs, or ideologies—a *value orientation*.[3] This core of values may even be the reason for being of the organization; an example is the Catholic Church.

The organizations of primary interest to us, however, are likely to reflect both types of concerns. Although material returns to the organization and its members may be the chief concern there will still be some concern in maintaining a central core of values, beliefs, or ideologies.

Let us look at two common value orientations found in organizations: ideology and elitism. By *ideology* we mean that the organization has, *central to its function,* a belief in a set of value principles. Social work agencies, universities, and medical groups are organizations where the proper value orientation is most important. Recruiting for these involves as much determining whether the recruit has a "proper view" of the profession as it does whether she or he has the proper accomplishments. Subsequent socialization emphasizes the superiority of "our" approach over "theirs."

Elitism is another value orientation. Organizations with aspirations of being "best" strive to recruit individuals who conform to a "model" image. Examples might be elite military organizations, the so-called great universities, "white shoe" law firms (those who recruit from the law schools of Ivy League universities), some industrial basic research laboratories in companies such as AT&T, General Electric, and IBM. Such organizations have special, elaborate recruiting procedures, perhaps developed into several stages, with accompanying ideological requirements (45). Such procedures are formal and carefully planned, and there will be well-developed safeguards against recruiting errors. Elite business organizations recruit primarily from top schools, which have already screened students. Much money and time are devoted to recruiting, for these organizations feel success depends on the effectiveness of this effort. Once recruited, the new member is continually presented with models for emulation. The military has ritual occasions and medals; the academic world, society meetings and publications; and business organizations, conventions and "100 percent clubs" for successful salespeople.

WORK TECHNOLOGY. A second organizational characteristic affecting recruitment and socialization is work technology. In certain work technologies the key factor in the organization's success may be its ability to recruit appropriately, and then maintain necessary values, attitudes, and motives. Collegiate athletic organizations and research organizations are good examples. However, recruiting may not be problematic at all in machine-paced manufacturing work. The knowledge that the organization occasionally recruits new workers may be enough of a recruiting program. Socialization, then, is largely informal, taking place primarily within the immediate workgroup.

THE ENVIRONMENT. There is a clear relationship between recruiting and socialization strategies and the social and economic environment of an organization. For example, equal opportunity recruiting programs require new types of recruits from new populations; and new recruiting procedures and new recruiters are needed to attract women, blacks, and Chicanos. Further, since these new types of employees may not have "appropriate" values, attitudes, and motives—may, in fact, have the opposite (13)—organizations often find supplementary training programs necessary. These are for skills training, but equally for "remedial socialization." Furthermore, success models are necessary. Providing the necessary motivation to "fit in" requires that these groups be able to hold realistic aspirations to upper management positions. And "token" minority representation will not suffice.

Recruiting and socialization procedures are also tailored to other environmental factors, such as the clientele served. Elite law firms, investment bankers, and similar client-oriented organizations want workers who match their clientele. This usually means born to wealth, Ivy League educated, a conservative viewpoint, and a good game of tennis (42). Drug rehabilitation agencies, on the other hand, find it suitable to hire ex-addicts, and welfare agencies are under considerable pressure to have their professional and working staff drawn from the same population they serve: inner-city minorities and "people in the community" (9, 17). Figure 6.1 illustrates recruitment patterns.

Welcome Aboard!—Patterns of Recruitment

We will now turn to a more detailed examination of the basic processes involved in recruiting—Stage 1 processes in the Schein outline. First we will consider how prospective recruits prepare themselves for membership in the organization through anticipatory socialization and presocializing institutions. Next, we will look at what recruiting means for the organization; the long-range effects of certain recruiting strategies; and organizations' need to alter themselves structurally to adapt to recruiting needs.

When Does Recruiting Begin?

Preparing for organizational roles may start long before actual organizational membership. Anticipatory socialization takes place as the future recruit prepares for organizational roles by adopting appropriate attitudes, values, and motives.

ANTICIPATORY SOCIALIZATION. Recruiting individuals into occupations where the work demands a high degree of personal commitment to the ideal of the profession or the organization involves the *occupational myth*. Generally, information is available about all occupations in our society. For example, you may have some idea about the work on an automotive assembly line, or the work of scientists, social workers, architects, and physicians. We all feel we know something of the work done by these people, and possibly of the organizational context in which it is done. For the latter occupations this knowledge is often idealized and positively valued, though the media sometimes present us with negative images as well.

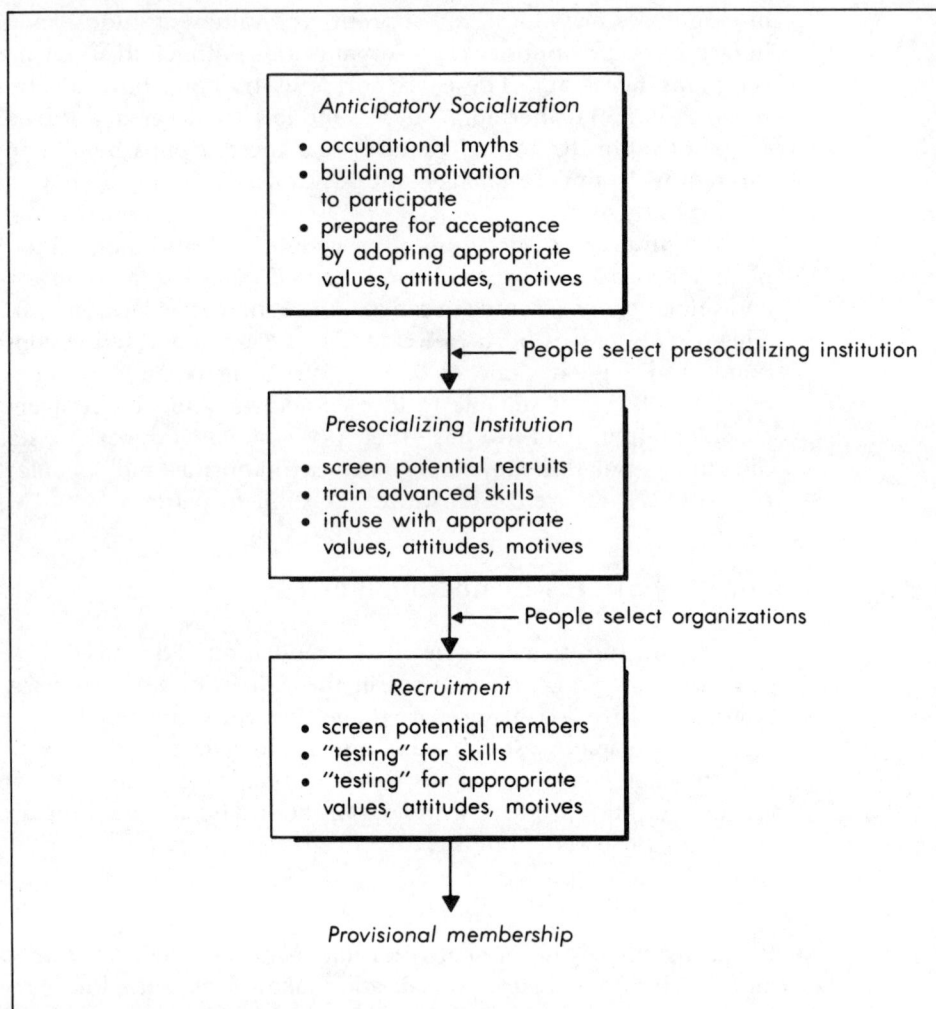

FIGURE 6.1 Patterns of Recruitment

The role, then, of the occupational myth—these positively valued images—is to help induce recruits to enter a training or apprenticeship period where immediate rewards must be deferred to the future. The more rigorous the training the more pervasive will be the positively valued occupational myths concerning the role to be performed when training is complete.[4]

PRESOCIALIZING INSTITUTIONS. A presocializing institution is an organization that conveys values and norms appropriate to anticipated organizational roles. Participants in its training programs move to a different position and status in their organization when the training period is completed. The presocializing institution is not necessarily part of the parent organization in which the entry position will be held. And this can be confusing for the purposes of definition.

Universities and military academies are good examples of presocializing institutions. An industrial training program for new recruits would not be, *unless* the training program was distinct from the initial work assignment, and where movement to a "final" assignment was anticipated on completion of training. Notice that the difference is one of degree rather than kind.

Presocializing institutions fulfill several functions, including:

- preselecting and screening out inappropriate recruits,
- providing training in advanced occupational skills, and
- infusing proper attitudes, values, and motives.

Presocializing institutions are generally found where future roles will be especially demanding, or where a great idealistic commitment is required—sometimes both, as in preparing for the Roman Catholic priesthood (18). Here the lack of material rewards and the requirement of a deep commitment to an idealistic belief system make a presocializing mechanism absolutely essential. The same thing is true of medicine; the role of physician is extremely demanding, so presocializing involves not only the university, but medical school and internship.

The function of these periods is commonly understood to be primarily one of implanting the skills required for a difficult profession. We feel, however, that the functions of *screening* and of *implanting appropriate norms and values* are of even greater importance (47). For example, the elite of the business trainees are those working for a Master of Business Administration (MBA) degree. During this period of training skills appropriate for entry roles are learned. But, far more importantly, this period acts as a selection and screening device for later executive management positions. Something about this training, therefore, is even more important than the skills: the values, attitudes, and motives; the belief that all problems can be solved using rational techniques; that efficiency—optimization—is possible; and mostly, that management means decision making based on facts and not on emotion. The whole ethos of the MBA is one of learning to approach problems, human or technical, with confidence in the efficacy of rational solutions.

If the organization and its requirements have an effect on individual recruits, so too does the process of recruiting affect the organization and its procedures.

Recruiting Traps: Systems Consequences of Selection

Selection procedures, especially selection technologies such as aptitude tests, are often geared to recruiting individuals who will be able to perform entry roles successfully. Problems arise when these procedures inadvertently screen out attributes necessary for performance of later roles. Typically, testing procedures are developed to predict entry position requirements or perhaps performance in even less related roles. Law Board (admission) exams are developed to predict grades in law school, for example. But there may be some problem in this if, as some guess, law school grades are not indicative of later career performance. This type of problem may be particularly severe where later creativity is desired.

In a different context, one large corporation was continually dissatisfied with the performance of engineers in executive positions. Somehow these engineer-executives did not seem to match up to corporate executives from other specialties. The problem, of course, was that this corporation emphasized exceptional technical ability in recruiting engineers for entry positions. And, unfortunately, characteristics that lead to success in technical problem solving seem to promote the opposite in managerial problem solving (27).

Another recruiting problem is that informal recruiting and screening procedures may derive from simple preference or bias. For example, traditionally, public welfare organizations have been value-oriented. How you felt about the poor—how you related to the poor—was the key. The emphasis was on feeling, on possessing the right outlook. Consequently, there was a continuing, built-in selection bias *against* hardheadedness and *for* feelings. And, of course, people trained in social work carried these values with them when they moved later to executive roles. The managerial values of efficiency and objectivity—the hardheaded values—were not, therefore, strong suits among executives of public welfare agencies. They had almost been screened out deliberately.

As a result of this situation, when public welfare became big business in the late 1960s and early 1970s, few people in the system were prepared to deal with the large-scale managerial problems that arose. As one solution to these problems, people from business schools with appropriately hard-headed managerial values, attitudes, and motives were brought in. It should not be difficult to imagine the consequent conflict that took place (1, 45).

Organizational consequences of recruiting strategies can also be seen in the results of a study of the banking industry. Although it surely is dated, the study illustrates a situation that could occur in any enterprise (2, 28).[5]

The study concerns personnel problems in banks. Citing low morale and a lack of qualified candidates for executive positions, it concludes that four conditions contribute particularly to this situation. The first stems from the fact that senior bank officers usually enjoy a position of prestige and distinction in their communities. They are regarded as authority figures comparable to physicians and clergy; they have superior status as the result of their economic power over the borrower. Because of this, bank officers tend to develop an exalted concept of their importance, and this fosters the growth of *authoritarian tendencies*. The elegance of the officers' quarters themselves and the awe they create in the average citizen further contribute to bankers' idealized conception of themselves.

The second contributing factor is the *routine nature* of bank operations, with their major emphasis on checks and balances, and the almost total structuring of each activity. Except at the very top levels of management no decision making or risk taking of consequence is required. Every contingency that might occur at the lower levels has been provided for. This makes regimentation and autocratic management almost inevitable; there is little room for much freedom of action.

Third, over the years a stereotype of the "right type" of bank employee has developed. This person is neat, clean, well-groomed, comes from a good family, speaks quietly, uses good grammar, and is properly deferential to authority figures. He or she is the *submissive type* who has always done as told. This type fits in well in the hushed, unhurried, cathedral milieu of many older banks.

Finally, men and women who can conform to this stereotype have been sought and hired by banks for many years. Most of them have stayed (those who were less submissive and conformist left, either voluntarily or by request). Through seniority many of these "right types" have become officers. In turn, they have been charged with hiring new employees. They have thus tended to *perpetuate their type,* to hire in their own images.

The author of the study concludes that it is "this 'right type' of employee who is now being recognized as lacking in the capacity to become the bank's chief executive officer. While he is well adapted to the role of deferential subordinate in an autocratic, regimented and structured bank environment, he is less well suited to the rough and tumble of today's competition; as business pressures become more acute, the inadequacies of this type of employee become more apparent" (28:90). The study, then, is an excellent example of the kinds of pathology, the recruiting traps, that can accompany recruiting based on role expectations at entry-level positions.

Environment and Organizational Adaptation

There are many stories concerning the conformity that organizations demand of recruits. And some of these are certainly true. Less often do we hear of or examine the opposite case, that is, organizations adapting to their recruits, or to recruiting necessities. Such organizational adaptation occurs through redefinition of role requirements and restructuring of organizational positions. Military organizations, for example, have spent considerable time in recent years polishing their images and redefining roles in order to accommodate recruiting needs. When the draft was abolished and it became evident that traditional recruiting methods were not producing the kind of recruit desired, military organizations had little choice but to modify old authoritarian ways, becoming less rigid and more tolerant of individuality. As a result, we now have the New Army, the New Navy and, just possibly, the New Marines (20, 43, 50). In business and other organizations equal opportunity requirements have brought changes (14).

Organizations, then, cannot afford to think of recruiting as something done through newspaper advertisements and let it go at that. Change, perhaps fundamental change, may be necessary. For example, the large law firms of Wall Street, catering to a socially elite clientele, have for years attempted to recruit a very special type of lawyer for future promotion to partnership positions. However, because manpower needs greatly exceed the numbers of socially elite recruits available to any one firm, it has become necessary in recent years to recruit others who do not meet qualifications of lineage and social background. Since these "others" are not considered for full partnership, however, organizational accommodations must be made to ensure that new recruits understand their position in the firm (42). Here is a description of the recruiting process as adapted from Erwin Smigel (42).

The Giants of Wall Street

Large law offices and especially the giants of Wall Street want people with ability who also have pleasing personalities, are from the "right" schools, have the "right" social backgrounds and clean-cut appearance, and are endowed with tremendous stamina. A former dean of a law school states:

> To get a job they [students] should be long enough on family connections, long enough on ability or long enough on personality, or a combination of these. Something called acceptability is made up of the sum of its parts. (42:57)

These Wall Street firms see themselves as an elite and view their work as highly important, and they want to perpetuate this image. There is keen competition for the preferred lawyer—who is personable, comes from one of the select eastern law schools, graduated with honors from an Ivy League college, and was at the top of the law school class.

There is increasing competition among firms for these elitists. Because of this competition the following organizational adaptations can be observed.

- Formalization of the role of hiring partner. The hiring partner, one of the most attractive and personable of the partners, saves the valuable time of other partners by relieving them of the duties of visiting various law schools, weeding out the poorer prospects, and inviting better ones to visit the firm in New York.
- Establishment of training programs. With size, there is the inevitable division of labor and consequent specialization. Since most recruits fear early specialization and a consequent loss of their own marketability, firms provide formalized training programs as a recruiting device to allay such fears.

- Provision of simulated advancement. One thing that concerns recruits about large firms is that they don't get ahead fast enough—"It takes forever to make partner." Therefore, some firms have created additional titles such as junior partner to create the illusion that associates are moving up faster than they actually are.
- Management of mobility. Firms have adopted an "up-or-out rule." Lawyers who are not going to be made partners must leave the firm so as to ensure a flow of new talent. Thus, to provide continued job security, some offices function as employment centers, providing their corporate clients with good legal and executive talent. The consequent reputation for "taking care of their men" is an obvious aid in recruitment.
- Provision of models of success for minorities. Traditionally, large Wall Street law firms, especially the "white shoe" firms, composed largely of lawyers from Ivy League schools with social register backgrounds, have discriminated against Jewish lawyers. With increased competition for the brightest graduates, however, it has become necessary to appoint Jewish lawyers as partners in recognition of the fact that it is good recruitment policy to provide models of success.

(By the way, much the same situation is true in the "big eight" accounting firms. But our example isn't quite complete.)

Sixteen years after the study was published the following story appeared in the *New York Times,* headlined "Lawyer Says Firm Denied Partnership on Ethnic Grounds."

> The lawyer . . . says in his complaint that [the law firm] . . . pursues a "continuing pattern and practice of discrimination in favor of white, Protestant males, generally of northern European ancestry."
>
> The suit is said to be the first attempt to challenge the professional personnel policy of a large Wall Street law firm. . . . One of the partners . . . yesterday described [the] action as "a totally baseless law suit."
>
> [The lawyer], who was graduated second in his class at Notre Dame Law School . . . said the law firm discriminated by selecting most of its employees from "just four selected law schools"—Harvard, Yale, Columbia, and Virginia. . . . He said he was hired on an "up-or-out" policy under which he would be promoted to a partnership if he proved satisfactory and, if not, would be asked to leave.
>
> When he protested [on being told that he was not going to be recommended for promotion to partnership] he said he was told among other things "to go see a psychiatrist."
>
> As of [the date of the law suit, he said, the firm] did not have, and had never had, a partner of Italian ancestry or an Italian-surnamed partner.(33)

Apparently, although things do change, it takes time. The message is clear, however. The organization seeks to recruit those who subscribe to the "right" values, accept the conventional occupational myths associated with the roles they are recruited for, and come from the presocializing institutions that encourage such values and myths. The organization attempts to arrange reward and mobility structures consonant with these recruitment objectives, *but*, is subject to constraints beyond its control. Adaptation takes place, albeit slowly, in response to the available manpower, technological requirements, and societal demands.

Socialization: The Way We Do It Here

> There's only two things you gotta know around here. First, forget everything you've learned at the Academy because the street's where you learn to be a cop; and second, being first around here don't mean shit. Take it easy, that's our motto. (48:225)

This advice, from a veteran police officer to a novice, is an astute analysis of how to survive on the force. Giving this sort of advice constitutes a major part of the socialization process in organizations (see Figure 6.2).

Socialization into the First Position

The initial stage of recruitment and its attendant processes is followed by a period of intensive socialization into organizational roles. This period, constituting Schein's Stage 2, involves resocialization, reality shock, and the rite of passage.

RESOCIALIZATION: NEW VALUES FOR OLD. In our depiction of Stanley's early military experience we touched on an aspect of socialization that involves the *un*learning of values, attitudes, and motives appropriate to former positions. The military stresses the irrelevance of earlier statuses in order to establish a firm basis for new ones. Uniforms mask clues to individual differences, but organizational differences *are* emphasized. Status-leveling busywork is assigned to entire groups of recruits, and tasks clearly inappropriate to former statuses are the rule—college boys first to KP, for example (21, 30).

The function of all this is to clear the way for appropriate new norms. Dornbusch, in describing the functions of the Coast Guard Academy, calls this the "suppression of preexisting statuses."

> Uniforms are issued on the first day and discussions of wealth and family background are taboo. Although the pay of the cadet is very low, he is not permitted to receive money from home. The role of the cadet must supersede other roles the individual has been accustomed to play. There are few clues left which will reveal social status in the outside world. (11:317)

The Catholic seminary is another, even more pervasive, mechanism for promoting the loss of previous identities. Social isolation is fostered and, as in the military, the uniform, the clerical habit, masks individuality. To exert

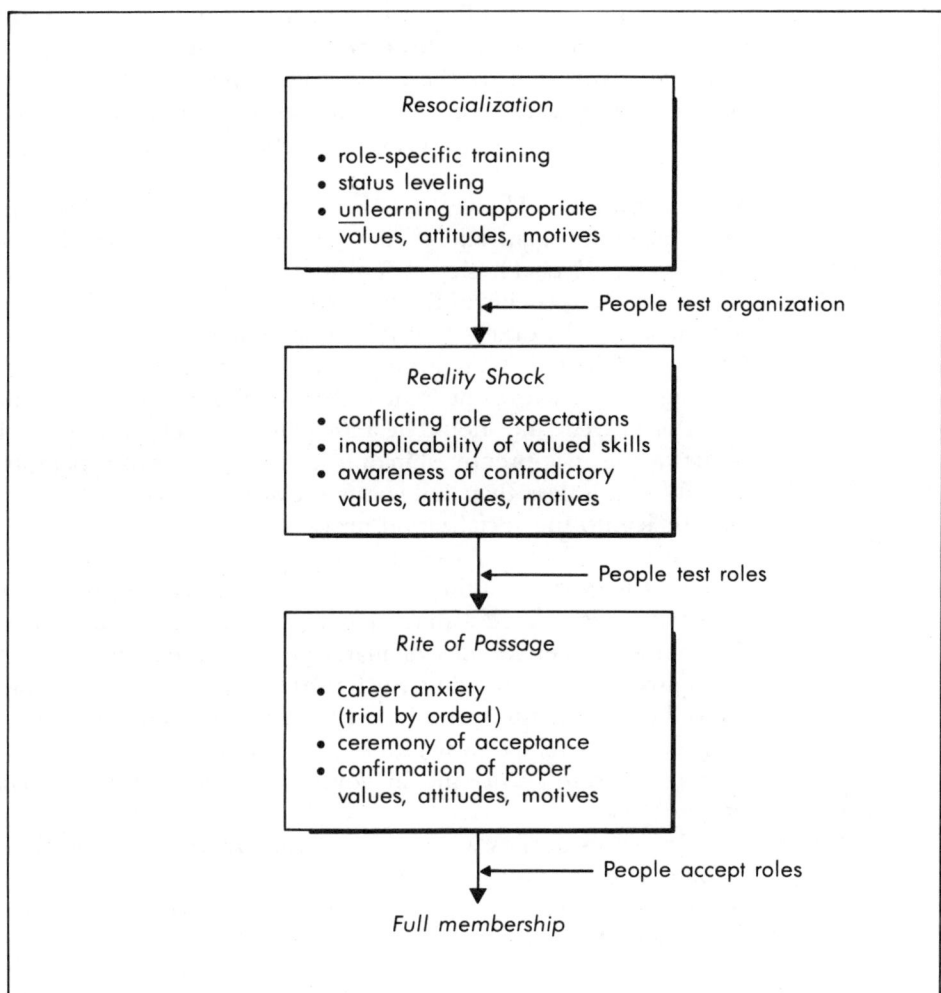

FIGURE 6.2 Patterns of Socialization

individual will or express forcefully your individual viewpoint is termed the "sin of pride" and is relentlessly criticized. All this prepares the seminarian to be a priest like all other priests, not an individual (16, 35).

These examples are dramatic illustrations of a process that occurs less dramatically in less value-oriented organizations. Business graduates, for example, on becoming management apprentices, should adopt a "balanced" view of labor so that an appropriate managerial stance is possible (though this does not mean adopting an outright antilabor view). It is a question of perspective, since university socialization has perhaps produced values that are "unrealistic" in the new context. This process of value change has been documented by Schein. Students enrolled in a management program showed considerable change in the direction of values expressed by the faculty. However, within a year of returning to a business organization, most of this resocialization disappeared and a change in the direction of former values was observed (36, 37).

REALITY SHOCK. The realization by recruits, and especially those in value-oriented or elite organizations, that their occupation falls short of expectations is called *reality shock*. Physicians find their skills are not nearly as effective as they had been led to believe. Engineers find their work highly specialized and constrained; social workers find the poor unable and unwilling to be helped; and MBAs find that there is little room for innovation and independent decision making in entry-level positions. Reality shock may last through the first few years of a career and should be anticipated by every professional. Only in professions having an apprenticeship or internship, where the final stage of socialization is only a little less than full-status membership, is the transition from ideal to real built into the socialization process (6, 23).

RITES OF PASSAGE. Anthropologists note that almost all societies have rites or ceremonies associated with the passage from one membership status to another. Examples are ceremonies of marriage and ceremonies attending the passage from juvenile status to adult. Such rites take place in contemporary organizations as well (44). The function of the rite of passage and its attendant ordeal (which is generally psychological rather than physical) is to mark a change in status with a concrete event, and in doing so *provide a deeper commitment* to the new status.

Examples of rites of passage in organizations are the "hazing" of fraternity initiates and the basic training of elite military organizations such as the Rangers. A particularly dramatic example is the way in which a new member is initiated into the Mafia.

> Being initiated, or "made," carries great honor and prestige in organized crime. . . . For the initiation, . . . the prospective member is brought into a room where the members and bosses are waiting. A gun and a knife are placed on a table in front of him and he is told: "This represents that you live by the gun and the knife and you die by the gun and the knife."
>
> He then is told to make a cup of his hands in which a paper is placed and set afire. As the paper burns he is told to repeat several times, "This is the way I will burn if I betray the secret of this Cosa Nostra."
>
> The initiate is assigned a kind of godfather from the various members present, usually the man who sponsored his membership and who is to look after him and be responsible for him. . . . [An informer] said that, "until the new guy establishes his trust, he goes through his sponsor in all his dealings with the family's bosses." (32)

This kind of process sets the stage for subsequent behavior, for there is evidence that the first job in an organization serves as a rite of passage that can have a significant effect on career progress. Thus, AT&T management trainees who were assigned jobs with demanding performance expectations performed significantly better four and five years later than trainees whose initial jobs had lower performance expectations. Apparently this initial socialization experience created positive attitudes that carried over to subsequent assignments (7). (See Box 6 for a model of this socialization process.)

> **Box 6**
>
> ## Socialization as Surprise and Sense Making
>
> Although researchers have paid considerable attention to the structural aspects of socialization, their models do not explain the change that accompanies socialization into new settings. However, Meryl Louis proposes a process model to account for newcomers' sense making in organizational situations to which they have moved. She proposes three key features of the entry experience: change, contrast, and surprise.
>
> *Change.* The experience of change results from those features of the new situation that are objectively different. These are things that are publicly knowable, such as location, job title, or organizational affiliation. With the start of a new job, the individual will experience a change in role and perhaps professional identity; for example, from student to financial analyst, from professional to supervisor. In principle, the existence of change is knowable before the actual transition.
>
> *Contrast.* Contrast is a personal rather than objective feature. It necessarily involves both past experience and present, and a comparison of differences between the two. Even so, two people undergoing exactly the same change may perceive different contrasts. This is because different aspects of the situation may be perceived differently by different individuals. The process of giving up old roles also may produce contrast. Former role behaviors will persist in new settings as new roles are being learned. But, as socialization proceeds, the developing awareness of demands to shift role behavior evokes continuing contrast.
>
> *Surprise.* Differences between what is anticipated and actual experience in new settings produces surprise. These differences come about in a number of ways.
>
> Conscious expectations about the situation or about one's own abilities to perform in the new situation may not be met. There also are unconscious expectations for situations with which one has no previous experience. For example, it may not occur to an individual that working in an office without windows would be

continued

unpleasant. Next, it may be difficult to forecast one's own reactions to a situation that has been anticipated, but not previously experienced. The person may not realize how he or she will react to a steady diet of sixty-hour work weeks. Finally, assumptions about organizational cultures brought from the old setting may not be appropriate in the new setting.

Sense making. People employ *cognitive scripts* in producing behavior in everyday situations. Such scripts can be thought of as "trustworthy recipes for thinking-as-usual" . . . (25:239). Therefore, people do not think much about what they are doing; they just follow the recipe. Cognitive scripts also provide implicit explanations for events. Consequently, when scripts fail, when expected outcomes do not occur, conscious thought is required to explain why, and to construct new explanations and revise the script. This is why the sense-making process is a recurring one. One is continually updating anticipations and revising assumptions.

Newcomers in particular differ from insiders in two important ways that make surprise, and hence sense making, more frequent. First, newcomers have not yet developed local interpretation schemes, the context-specific dictionaries of meaning used by members of the setting. Second, newcomers cannot avail themselves of insiders' interpretations since they have usually not yet been accepted as full members within a network of insiders. As a result, the newcomer tries to interpret events with schemes developed in former settings. More often than not, the responses based on these previous schemes are inappropriate, and thus constitute yet another source of surprise and subsequent sense making in the process of socialization.

(M. R. Lewis, "Surprise and Sense Making: What Newcomers Experience in Entering Unfamiliar Organizational Settings." *Administrative Science Quarterly,* 25 (1980) 226–251).

Key Characteristics of Socialization Settings

Thus far we have been analyzing socialization as a sequence of events. Now let us look at it from a cross-sectional perspective, that is, at how socialization processes occurring at the same career stage differ among organizations. Following are five key characteristics of socialization settings in which organizations may differ (48, 49).

FORMALITY—THE DEGREE TO WHICH THE SETTING IS SEGREGATED FROM THE ONGOING WORK CONTEXT. In very formal settings, the role of the recruit is differentiated clearly from later roles, and the focus of socialization is on the recruit's internalization of the proper organizational perspective. Consequently, little of this experience will be transferable to the workaday reality of the organization, and the recruit will be able to generalize little of the ability or skills learned in the socialization setting. Highly formal settings therefore concentrate more on attitude than act. Management training and development programs are examples.

INDIVIDUAL OR COLLECTIVE PROCESSING. Collective socialization settings provide recruits with shared understandings of the occupation. Homogeneous results are promoted in collective settings through peer pressure on the individual to conform to organizational norms. However, group standards and managerial objectives may differ, for the group is more likely to ignore or redefine the demands of the organization than are individuals.

THE SERIAL CHARACTER OF SOCIALIZATION SETTINGS. Serial socialization means that experienced members groom recruits who are about to assume similar roles in the organization. This contrasts with socialization by members occupying other kinds of positions and hence different roles. Serial socialization is perhaps the best guarantee that the organization will not change over a long period of time. Innovation is unlikely and stability is maintained—even, perhaps, in the face of a rapidly changing environment.

LENGTH OF THE FORMAL SOCIALIZATION PERIOD. The longer the socialization period, the greater the amount of culture, tradition, and everyday assumptions that can be absorbed by the recruit. Longer periods also provide a greater opportunity to assess the recruit's motivation, trustworthiness, ability, and loyalty. Although the longer process may be more demanding and perhaps frustrating, the endurance of such ordeals promotes a strong fellowship among recruit cohorts and engenders a greater commitment to the organization later.

THE PRESENCE OR VISIBILITY OF A "COACH." A one-on-one relationship between the recruit and a socializing agent of the organization leads to an intense value-oriented socialization program where an affective bond is built between the recruit and the socializing agent. In this situation the recruit is more concerned with satisfying the expectations of the coach than the expectations of the organization. The organization's assumption, of course, is that the two sets of expectations are congruent.

Drawing on our earlier analyses, we expect that for each of these characteristics the stronger form of the process will be associated with a greater need for organizational members to fulfill their roles in uniform, predictable fashion. Therefore, to the extent that organizations are value-oriented—either ideological or elite—and to the extent that they are subject to stress from the external environment, one should expect the stronger form of the socialization process to be employed by the organization.

Building Commitment

With passage into full membership status, the initial processes of making the organization man or woman are complete. But socialization continues; it continues as new positions bring new insights into the organization from a different, and usually more privileged, perspective; it continues as new functions are assumed. As these things occur, an increasing commitment to the organization is built (52). By *commitment* we mean (1) identification—adopting as your own the goals and values of the organization; (2) involvement—immersing yourself psychologically in the activities of your work role; and (3) loyalty—feeling affection for and attachment to the organization (8:533). In the rest of this chapter we will introduce some aspects of the commitment concept, examine mechanisms for building commitment, and illustrate some consequences of its loss. This is only an introduction, however; throughout the text—especially in our consideration of the motivation system—the processes of building commitment to the organization remain key considerations. Figure 6.3 illustrates graphically patterns of commitment.

Not too long ago Stanley, Penny, and Claude learned something of the ways in which The Company used to build commitment.

Let's Have a Song

Stanley and Penny Scribner were laughing wildly as Claude Gilliam turned down the hall leading to the Company communications department. In fact, Claude didn't quite believe what he saw. Yes, Stanley was singing something—that was obvious. Claude thought he had heard the tune before but he couldn't make out the words.

Penny, for her part, was orchestrating Stanley's performance with her hands. Possibly they'd both gone mad.

"What in hell are you doing?" was Claude's blunt reaction.

"Hey, just in time. Come on, join in. Here." At Stanley's invitation, Penny thrust a slim booklet in front of Claude. Then Penny continued, "Here, this one. The one that says 'To Mason M. Marsh, President, The Company.'" Then, pointing to a by-line under the title, "See, you're supposed to sing it to 'Pack Up Your Troubles'; you know, the one that goes. . . ." With that, Penny hummed a few bars and Stanley started in again:

Pack up your troubles—Mr. Marsh is here!
And smile, smile, smile.
He is the genius in our Company,
He's the man worthwhile.
He's inspiring all the time,
And very versatile—oh!
He is our strong and able president!
His smile's worthwhile.
Great organizer and a friend so true,
Say all we boys
Ever he thinks of things to say and do,
To increase our joys . . .

As the song continued, a small group gathered about them and Penny had to explain what was going on. One day, while rummaging through old files she had come upon a thin booklet—maybe forty or fifty pages—entitled *Songs of The Company*, probably from the time when Marsh Industries, Inc., had just been renamed The Company. The

Building Commitment 147

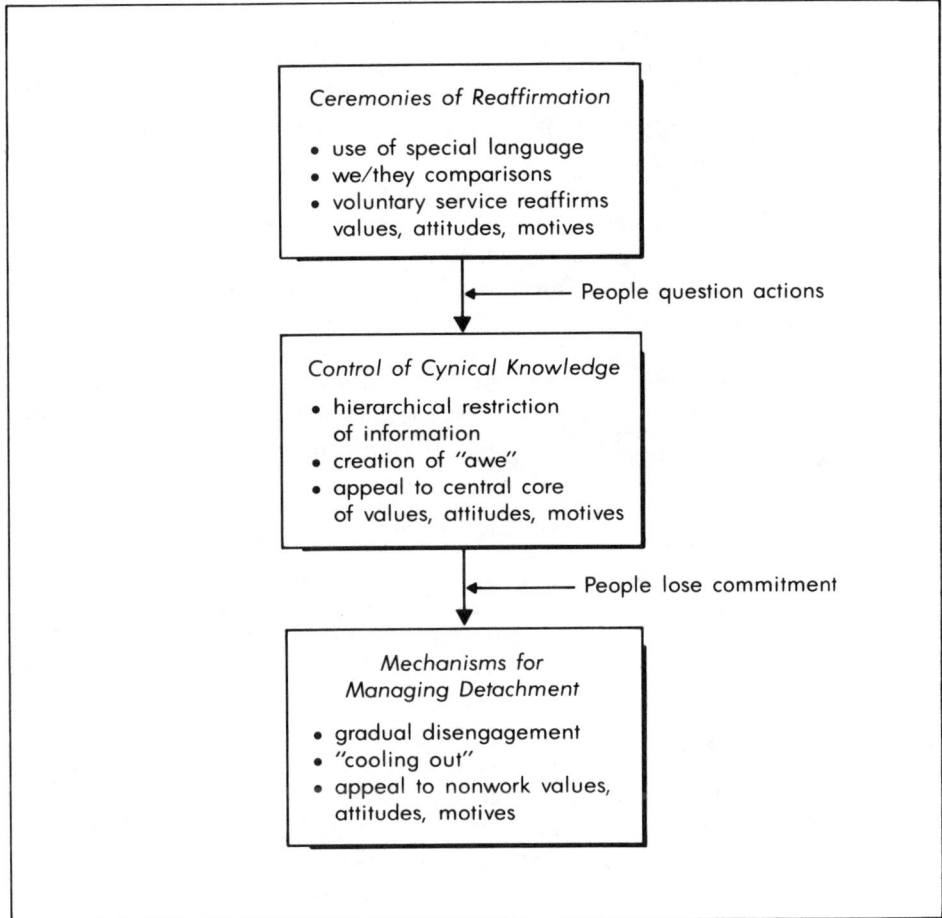

FIGURE 6.3 Patterns of Commitment

Marsh of the song was probably M. M. Marsh, Sr., the old man. It was rumored that everybody in The Company in those days used to start the day, and every Company gathering, with a song or two. Unbelievable!

"Hey, look at this one." Now Claude was in the act. "Hey, *hey!* Look at this! Here's one to Ben Franklyn. Can you beat that?"

Company songs strike most of us as strange because the organizations we know usually rely on material rewards rather than value orientation to build commitment. Nevertheless, singing as a device for building commitment is an interesting *particular* example of a general phenomenon. Our real interest, however, is the mechanisms organizations use for reaffirming commitment to the organization, its roles, and its purposes. Although The Company no longer uses songs, many business organizations do have a strong value orientation, especially in the higher ranks. The value is a belief in the company itself—in its rightness, its altruism, its service ideal, its place in our system of free enterprise (usually equated with democracy and patriotism). And since many people in managerial positions find the material rewards insufficient in themselves, there is a real need to believe in the rightness of the enterprise.

We see, therefore, an array of symbols and rituals of reaffirmation: personal financial investment in the organization, special language and special dress, competitive organizations being characterized as morally inferior, regular group meetings, and the expectation of additional voluntary labor in group context, to name but a few. These and other mechanisms—including institutional songs at special occasions—are generally present in varying degrees in all organizations and serve the continuing purpose of reaffirming commitment (22).[6]

Controlling Threats to Commitment

Members highly committed to the organization perform their duties in extraordinary fashion if so required. Consequently, a highly committed membership is useful to management. New recruits, in the early stages of their careers, are less committed to a particular organization than are the managers or executives who receive greater rewards and who consequently have a greater stake in the organization's success.

For this reason, most organizations screen information that goes to newer, less committed members, especially information that might shake their tenuous early commitment. For example, new recruits must believe in the superior competence and ability of higher management, so information that may not support this belief is screened out. Such a belief is necessary to counter the inevitable queries from lower members as to why something was done as it was, or why a particular decision was made. The ritual answer is: "Don't worry. They know what they're doing. They wouldn't be where they are if they didn't." Belief in the superior's competence helps in getting compliance to authoritative requests. The detailed reasons for decisions are seldom known to lower members, and so the superior wisdom of management is invoked. Further, barriers are constructed and symbols used to screen lower members from easy fraternizing with higher levels of the organization. The plush office on the seventeenth floor, the executive dining rooms, the key to special washrooms are not only privileges of office, but serve as symbols maintaining distance between those who make decisions and those who must execute them. As Victor Thompson puts it,

> Incumbents of high office are held in awe because they are in touch with the mysteries and magic of such office. . . . Since one knows less and less about the activities of superordinates, the farther away in the hierarchy they are, the greater is the

> awe in which he holds them. . . . The hierarchy is a highly restricted system of communication, with much information coming in to each position; but the amount sent out to subordinates . . . for strategic and other reasons is always limited. There results an increasing vagueness as to the activities at each level as one mounts the hierarchy, and this vagueness supports the prestige ranking which we call the status system (46:70).

This situation is useful in dismissing any suspicion of incompetence or of self-serving motives on the part of executives. Maintaining "awe" is at least one reason for the endless briefings by subordinates of their own managers to convey detailed information about projects under way. Higher-level people are then the ones who attend the meetings where confidential matters are discussed. Recruits or lower organizational members seldom are invited to attend these meetings and seldom witness the decision process directly. Questions raised about the wisdom of such decisions therefore tend to be naive—hence, easily discounted. And since no one wishes to appear naive, we accept the premise that top management judgment is correct; in doing so, we increase even more our commitment to the system of hierarchy and its values.

What happens, however, when we discover that decisions were not made for "the good of us all," but rather for organizationally self-serving motives? What happens when cynicism replaces faith, when the presumed basis for organizational procedures or actions is revealed as having been misrepresented, and the actual purpose is far different and self-serving to the management? What happens when the assumption of rightness is dissipated? (10, 16).

Consequences of the Loss of Commitment

Consider the Watergate incident. Despite an almost overwhelming will by Americans to believe in the rightness of the president—that is, believe in the office—the evidence of cynical pursuit of organizationally self-serving motives finally became indisputable. This affected many agencies of government and resulted in a questioning of administration functions in a wide range of matters.

The military underwent a similar crisis during the unpopular war in Vietnam. Military and government leaders so focused on providing the illusion of winning the war that political deception and its attendant cynical revelations became widespread. For example, just before the Tet offensive in 1968, top military officers and their civilian representatives deliberately distorted intelligence estimates of enemy troops in order to gain political goals. General Abrams is quoted as saying,

> We have been projecting an image of success over the recent months. [If the true number of Vietcong troops became public] all available caveats and explanations will not prevent the press from drawing an erroneous and gloomy conclusion. All those who have an incorrect view of the war will be reinforced and the task will be made more difficult. (10)

The troops in the field were unaware of these deceptions, as apparently were many high-ranking military officers. Consequently, the military was caught off guard by the fury and success of the Vietcong offensive. Such situations hardly instill rank-and-file confidence in leadership.

Finally, in our own research in The Company, your authors observed the effects of the introduction of a new work measurement program for production workers. The catchy slogan of the new program was, "Work smarter, not harder." But catch phrases did not mask the reality. Workers interpreted this as a breach in the traditional trust between themselves and management, and an abandonment of the traditional emphasis on pride and quality of workmanship. Morale plummeted while production barely rose. Workers, long accustomed to doing within reason whatever jobs were asked of them, became less willing to cooperate and eventually The Company wisely curtailed the entire program.

Among the general consequences of a loss of commitment are these:

- In value-oriented organizations, increasingly perfunctory performance of duties and an increasing demand for material incentives for special effort
- Increasing difficulty in getting compliance to authoritative requests; increased questioning of the right of superiors to request unusual duties
- An increased turnover of personnel and problems in recruiting new personnel, especially in organizations where a high level of commitment is required to maintain organizational membership
- A decrease in the availability and effectiveness of socializing agents; increasing difficulty in finding highly committed personnel who are effective in socializing new members into the values of the organization and its norms.

The loss of commitment, then, is far more serious than what is implied by a "loss of morale." It pervades the organization and can reduce effectiveness in almost every sphere of activity (7, 8).

Summary

The Socialization Process

Socialization is the process through which members of organizations derive a sense of identity with others in the organization, and the organization achieves some predictability of action from participants. Socialization occurs as a result of both formal, planned activities and informal, on-the-job experience. It is the process of fitting individuals to roles—roles attendant to organizational positions. For our summary, then, what should you know about this process in order to understand what is taking place in your organization and, more directly, what is happening to you?

ANTICIPATORY SOCIALIZATION. Preparation for your future roles began before recruitment when you began building an identification with an occupation or profession. Selectively you learned proper values, attitudes, and motives: efficiency and dispassionate respect for the facts—a value for business; empathy with the poor and a desire to help others—a value for the helping professions; a belief that facts speak for themselves, and a commitment to value-free inquiry—in itself a value for science. You also observed proper behavior, both firsthand and in the media. You began to understand something of the ways in which people in these positions fulfill their roles; you learned something, for example, of the courtroom, boardroom, and bedside manner. You may not have understood, however, that these are distorted images that serve, though not intentionally, the function of recruiting future lawyers, doctors, police, priests, engineers, businesspeople, and the like.

THE FUNCTION OF THE PRESOCIALIZING INSTITUTION. The university and the training academy are generally seen as institutions whose function it is to convey skills necessary to future occupations. But we feel that the functions of selection and indoctrination are even more important. People in widely differing professions and occupations complain that only a small fraction of what they learned during training is used later in actual professional practice. What is the necessity, then, of such training? One function is weeding out those who are unable to support the values, attitudes, and motives that support the work ethic, for example. So look at your institutional experiences from this perspective. Be aware of the value components, and understand both the process of preparing for roles you will fill later, and the multiple functions of skill training.

RECRUITING. One of the genuine curiosities of the recruiting experience is that nearly everyone believes that recruiting is done on the basis of ability, yet almost no one acts that way when being recruited. That is, in your recruiting interviews you will almost certainly try to stress aspects of yourself other than those directly reflecting ability. Your personality, values, interests, and other nontechnical aspects about you convey the worth of the "whole person." You will probably do this because, to all intents and purposes, the technical capabilities of most recruits are more than sufficient to do the job; so, both you and the recruiter will be looking ahead to future roles. There will be an implicit agreement between you that what is being tested is outlook, an approach to problems or to work, an understanding of what organization is all about. This is why organizations prefer to recruit MBAs—not so much for what they can do now, but for how they approach a problem, for what they believe about business problems. Remember, then, that outlook can be just as important as skill—once you have the skills, that is. If the recruiters know what they are doing, they are looking past the entry position, testing to see if you are future executive material.

REALITY SHOCK. As the motto says: "Be prepared"—not for what will be asked of you, however, but rather for what will *not* be asked of you. You will *not* be asked to make major decisions or take major responsibility (although your assignment descriptions may sound like it). You will *not* be expected to use most of the skills you learned at great physical and mental expense. And you will probably *not* seem to be going anywhere in the organization particularly rapidly (37). Most of you, regardless of organization, are in the management incubator. Your progress is being watched, but an organization can take just so many executives at one time. Just be prepared!

THE DEVELOPMENT OF COMMITMENT. Organizations strive to build commitment through the process of socialization. In your organizational roles, therefore, you will be rewarded and approved for behavior appropriate to your role, and punished or criticized for behavior that is inappropriate. In value-oriented or elite organizations acceptance as a member, by itself, is rewarding. This builds commitment. So do the material and psychological rewards of increased salary, influence, and status in the organization. Increased commitment, in turn, means that you will have more to lose if something goes awry for you organizationally. Consequently, increased commitment leads you to increased effort to perform well and meet role expectations. This is the cycle of developing commitment—for most people in organizations it is desirable and expected.

Notes

1. Such "debasement" procedures aimed at destroying members' individual identities are common features of "total institutions" like the military, mental hospitals, and prisons (15, 41, 50).
2. Kroeber and Kluckhohn describe socialization as the process of producing "overt, patterned ways of behaving, feeling and acting, [deriving from] unstated premises and categories," (24:157). Van Maanen terms it the sharing of common "values, attitudes and motives" (47:86).
3. Thompson (45), for example, makes a similar distinction between ideological and "Giant Corporation" types of organizations.
4. These myths and the consequences for professionals discovering subsequent organizational reality are documented for a number of professional occupations (4, 5, 23, 34, 35, 48).
5. The following description of a bank is adapted directly from McMurry (28). Argyris (2) reached very similar conclusions in a study done at about the same time.
6. While this list is drawn from Kanter's (22) description of commitment mechanisms in utopian communities, it applies nonetheless to other kinds of organizations.

References

1. ABELS, P. "The Managers are Coming! The Managers are Coming!" *Public Welfare* 31 (1973): 13–15.
2. ARGYRIS, CHRIS. *Organization of a Bank.* New Haven, Conn.: Labor and Management Center, Yale University, 1954.
3. ARONSON, E., and J. MILLS. "Effect of Severity of Initiation on Liking for a Group." *Journal of Abnormal and Social Psychology* 59 (1959): 177–181.
4. BASSIS, M. S., and W. R. ROSENGREN. "Socialization for Occupational Disengagement: Vocational Education in the Merchant Marine." *Sociology of Work and Occupations* 2 (1975): 133–149.
5. BECKER, H. S., and B. GEER. "The Fate of Idealism in Medical School." *American Sociological Review* 23 (1958): 50–56.
6. BECKER, H. S., B. GEER, E. C. HUGHES, and A. STRAUSS. *Boys in White: Student Culture in Medical School.* Chicago: University of Chicago Press, 1961.
7. BERLEW, D. E., and D. T. HALL. "The Socialization of Managers: Effects of Expectations on Performance." *Administrative Science Quarterly* 11 (1966): 207–223.
8. BUCHANAN B., II "Building Organizational Commitment: The Socialization of Managers in Work Organizations." *Administrative Science Quarterly* 19 (1974): 533–546.
9. BULLINGTON, B., J. G. MUNNS, and G. GEIS. "Purchase of Conformity: Ex-Narcotic Addicts Among the Bourgeoisie." *Social Problems* 16 (1969): 456–463.
10. *Centre Daily Times.* "Enemy Forces Underestimated, Analyst Says." State College, Pennsylvania, September 18, 1975, p. 1. Reprinted with the permission of the Associated Press.
11. DORNBUSCH, S. "The Military Academy as an Assimilating Institution." *Social Forces* 33 (1955): 316–321.
12. FELDMAN, D. C. "The Multiple Socialization of Organization Members." *The Academy of Management Review,* 6 (April 1981): 309–318.
13. FERMAN, L. A. *The Negro and Equal Employment Opportunities: A Review of Management Experiences in Twenty Companies.* New York: Praeger, 1968.
14. FERNANDEZ, J. P. *Black Managers in White Corporations.* New York: Wiley, 1975.
15. GOFFMAN, E. *Asylums.* Garden City, N.Y.: Doubleday, 1961.
16. GOLDNER, F. H., R. R. RITTI, and T. P. FERENCE. "The Production of Cynical Knowledge in Organizations." *American Sociological Review* 42 (1977): 539–551.
17. HELFGOT, J. "Professional Reform Organizations and the Symbolic Representation of the Poor." *American Sociological Review* 39 (1974): 475–491.
18. HUGHES, E. C. *Men and Their Work.* Glencoe, Ill.: Free Press, 1958.
19. ———. "The Study of Occupations." In *Sociology Today,* edited by R. K. Merton, L. Broom, and L. Cotrell. New York: Basic Books, 1958.
20. JANOWITZ, M., ed. *The New Military: Changing Patterns of Organization.* New York: Russell Sage Foundation, 1964.
21. JOSEPH, N., and N. ALEX. "The Uniform: A Sociological Perspective." *American Journal of Sociology* 77 (1972): 719–730.

22. KANTER, R. M. "Commitment and Social Organization: A Study of Commitment Mechanisms in Utopian Communities." *American Sociological Review* 33 (1968): 499–516.
23. KRAMER, M. *Reality Shock: Why Nurses Leave Nursing.* St. Louis: C. V. Mosby, 1974.
24. KROEBER, A. L., and C. KLUCKHOHN. *Culture.* New York: Vintage, 1963.
25. LIGHT, D., JR. "The Sociological Calendar: An Analytic Tool for Field Work Applied to Medical and Psychiatric Training." *American Journal of Sociology* 5 (1975): 1145–1164.
26. LOUIS, M. R. "Surprise and Sense Making: What Newcomers Experience in Entering Unfamiliar Organizational Settings." *Administrative Science Quarterly* 25(1980): 226–251.
27. McCLELLAND, D. *Power, the Inner Experience.* New York: Halstead (1975). See Chap. 6, "Power Motivation and Organizational Leadership."
28. McMURRY, R. N. "Recruitment, Dependency and Morale in the Banking Industry." *Administrative Science Quarterly* 3 (1958): 87–117.
29. MERTON, R. K. *Social Theory and Social Structure,* rev. ed. Glencoe, Ill.: Free Press, 1957. See chap. 8, "Contributions to the Theory of Reference Group Behavior."
30. MOORE, W. E. "Occupational Socialization." In *Handbook of Socialization Theory and Research,* edited by D. A. Goslin. Chicago: Rand McNally, 1969.
31. *New York Times.* "False Troop Data in Vietnam Cited." September 19, 1975, p. 7.
32. ———. "Five Mafia Families Open Rosters to New Members." March 21, 1976, p. 1. © 1976 by The New York Times Company. Reprinted by permission.
33. ———. "Lawyer Says Firm Denied Him Partnership on Ethnic Grounds." February 12, 1976, p. 25. © 1976 by The New York Times Company. Reprinted by permission.
34. RITTI, R. R. *The Engineer in the Industrial Corporation.* New York: Columbia University Press, 1971.
35. RITTI, R. R., T. P. FERENCE, and F. H. GOLDNER. "Professions and Their Plausibility: Priests, Work, and Belief Systems." *Sociology of Work and Occupations* 1 (1974): 24–51.
36. SCHEIN, E. H. "Attitude Change During Management Education." *Administrative Science Quarterly* 11 (1967): 601–628.
37. ———. "The First Job Dilemma." *Psychology Today* 1 (1968): 26–37.
38. ———. "The Individual, The Organization, and The Career: A Conceptual Scheme." *Journal of Applied Behavioral Science* 7 (1971): 401–426.
39. ———. "Management Development As a Process of Influence." *Industrial Management Review* 2 (1961): 59–77.
40. SCOTT, W. G. "Executive Development As an Instrument of Higher Control." *Academy of Management Journal* (September 1963): 191–203.
41. SHILOH, A. "Sanctuary or Prison—Responses to Life in a Mental Hospital." In *Total Institutions,* edited by S. E. Wallace. Chicago: Aldine, 1971.
42. SMIGEL, E. O. "The Impact of Recruitment on the Organization of the Large Law Firm." *American Sociological Review* 25 (1960): 56–66.

43. STARLING, J. D. "Organization and the Decision to Participate." *Public Administration Review* 52 (1968): 72–89.
44. STRAUSS, A. *Mirrors and Masks.* Glencoe, Ill.: Free Press, 1959.
45. THOMPSON, J. "Organizational Management of Conflict." *Administrative Science Quarterly* 4 (1960): 389–409.
46. THOMPSON, V. *Modern Organization.* New York: Knopf, 1961. Excerpt from page 70 reprinted by permission.
47. VAN MAANEN, J. "Breaking In: Socialization to Work." In *Handbook of Work, Organization, and Society,* edited by Robert Dubin. Chicago: Rand McNally, 1975. Chap. 3.
48. ———. "Police Socialization: A Longitudinal Examination of Job Attitudes in an Urban Police Department." *Administrative Science Quarterly* 20 (1975): 207–228.
49. VAN MAANEN, J., and SCHEIN. "Toward a Theory of Organizational Socialization." In *Research in Organizational Behavior,* Vol. 1, edited by B. Staw. Greenwich, Conn.: JAI Press, 1979. Pp. 209–264.
50. WAMSLEY, G. L. "Contrasting Institutions of Air Force Socialization: Happenstance or Bellwether?" *American Journal of Sociology* 78 (1972): 399–417.
51. WHEELER, S. "The Structure of Formally Organized Socialization Settings." In *Socialization After Childhood,* edited by O. G. Brim and S. Wheeler. New York: Wiley, 1966.
52. WIENER, Y. "Commitment in Organizations: A Normative View." *The Academy of Management Review* 7 (1982): 418–428.

Discussion Questions

1. Our opening case in Chapter 3 found Stanley spending several months checking the asset tags on machinery in Ben Franklyn's mill. Do you see any similarities between that situation and the opening case in this chapter? Any dissimilarities?
2. Think of some organization that you belong to or have belonged to. Try to reconstruct your recruitment and socialization experiences in terms of the key stages outlined in this chapter.
3. Most likely you are currently in some kind of preprofessional program. What key values, attitudes, and motives did you bring to this program? Which of these does your program seem most to emphasize? Are these different from your earlier ones?
4. Give some examples of recruiting traps. How does understanding the organization as a system help us to see the consequences of recruiting new members solely on the basis of how well they meet entry requirements?
5. We used the term *suppression of preexisting statuses* to identify a key stage in the socialization process. Explain what this term means. In what kinds of organizations generally would this stage be most important?
6. All of us have participated in group singing of organizational songs. Think of at least three such common examples. Do you think these occasions reaffirm commitment to the organization and its purposes? Why? Why not?
7. State four general consequences of the loss of commitment. Do these seem to be important consequences to you? Why? Why not?

Chapter 7
Impression Management in Organizational Life

Clothes Make the Man

"I mean, why should they care? What's it to them?" Stanley was in a state of considerable agitation as he described for Dr. Faust his meeting in New York with The Company's sales trainees. They were gathered for the commencement of that year's sales training class, and Stanley was present as Ted Shelby's "observer" from Personnel.

The Company is quite conservative about the dress of its sales "representatives." Consequently, Stanley—who had lately been experimenting with "styling" (complete with floppy, wide-brimmed hat and necklace)—stood out from the crowd. But let's rejoin Stanley as he recounts the incident to Dr. Faust.

"Things go O.K. until we break up into work groups. Everybody introduces himself and someone says to me, 'Where do you work, Stan?' So I say, 'The Company, just like you.' The guy says, 'Come on, you're kidding me. *You* work for The Company?' So he starts laughing, I mean uncontrollably. Then he says, 'Hey, this guy works for The Company, he really does, can you believe it?'

"Well, this breaks them all up. They all sit there, sort of pointing their fingers at me and saying, '*He* works for *The Company!*' I won't drag it out any longer, but what I want to know is what the hell do *they* care? How come they get so excited about something like that?"

Faust waited to make sure Stanley was indeed through. Then repeating the obvious he said, "Well, they *do* care. But don't misunderstand, they weren't mocking you. They were simply amazed. Why should they be amazed?" Faust continued, giving words to the thought that had formed in Stanley's mind. "They were amazed because they had never seen anything quite like you before." Faust puffed his pipe in silence for a moment to give proper emphasis to his next words, then he went on. "They were amazed in the same sense as a primitive who has just seen the violation of an ancient taboo without visitation of the promised retribution by the gods. It is amazing and a little frightening, and suggests also that the one committing the violation may just be a bit special. Beyond this I can't really *explain* anything more to you except by way of example."

Stanley prepared himself for one of Faust's Socratic exercises. "Now consider this situation and tell me what you think is going on," said Faust.

"Think carefully about it, and tell me why you retain or discard the possible explanations." Faust went on to describe a meeting involving a dozen or so lower and middle management people at The Plant. They were working out a long-range manufacturing automation strategy that had great consequence for the entire Company. All were suitably attired (coats and ties) save one. This one had on an old, faintly grease-stained flannel shirt, with sleeves rolled up to the elbows, exhibiting a muscular pair of forearms.

"Well?" Dr. Faust signaled that the exercise was to begin.

Stanley thought. "I guess you want me to account for the guy in the flannel shirt."

"Precisely," Faust puffed slowly.

"It wasn't just that he didn't have time to change, because then you wouldn't have asked me to explain it."

Faust nodded in acknowledgment.

"And I guess since they're all management people he'd have to know better."

Another nod.

"Does he dress this way all the time?"

"Almost invariably, except when he travels to New York."

"Then he's trying to prove something?"

"That is essentially the question I have posed for you, not the answer," Faust intoned.

"O.K., O.K. Then he's advertising that he's something special. But what? Yeah. It's that he's not *just another* middle management guy. He's something else, and more."

Dr. Faust gave no visible encouragement, but Stanley felt he was getting somewhere. "Yeah, the grease . . . the arms. Here's a guy that not only knows management, but knows The Company right where it lives, the manufacturing floor. Gets along with the men, too, I'll bet." Stanley could hardly contain himself as new inferences raced through his head.

"Go on."

"He's so good that he doesn't have to give a damn about wearing a stuffy old shirt and tie, except when he goes to New York . . . and that's good, too, because that way he gets to show that he can suit up when he wants to." Stanley actually felt himself developing a deep admiration for this phantom of his imagination. "Now I'll bet. . . ."

"Enough, enough." Faust held up his hands. "You now feel that you know this fellow, don't you? And I've told you almost nothing about him. You yourself have supplied the details through logic and deduction. And so, of course, do all the others who meet him. This is the point I wished you to see." Faust continued, "You must understand that none of us knows another very well, and especially in organizations such as The Company. We continually call on our store of knowledge about the world, and our sense of what is and is not reasonable to interpret what is going on about us. We seem to have a need for consistency that compels us to come up with reasons for what appears at first to be unreasonable. So each creates for himself or herself a phantom endowed with qualities and capabilities to fit the image received.

"That's part of the answer to why your friends got so excited about your appearance. Each believes that The Company is a superior company and fittingly hires superior people—and, by George, they ought to *look* that way."

"I understand," said Stanley. "But let's get back to your example. If what you say is true, then why doesn't *everybody* manufacture an image for himself?"

"They do," said Faust enigmatically.

"Now, wait a minute, you said. . . ."

"No, *you* wait a minute." Dr. Faust punctuated his command with a thrust of his pipestem at Stanley. "And *think* before you talk. I said that everyone presents an image to others that to some extent is calculated and shaped. In large measure these presentations of self are consistent and raise few questions. Managers look like managers, workers like workers, and so on. I presented an extreme case, for—ah—heuristic purposes."

"No, what I meant was, since there seems to be some advantage in it, why doesn't everybody pretend to be something he isn't?"

"When did I say anything about pretense?"

"Sure you . . ." Stanley caught himself. "I mean, isn't this guy pretending to be something he isn't?"

"Did I say that?" The tone of Dr. Faust's query

answered the question. "What I pointed out, quite simply, was only that *you,* not I, nor he, had supplied the details as to his status in The Company, his ability, his social relations with the mill hands and the like. In fact, I doubt if any *pretense* is involved, as I understand the word. Obviously, this man is acting out something he *wants* to be. And I doubt that this could be done convincingly through sheer calculation. Even the complete charlatan at one level of his consciousness must believe that, indeed, he *is* a doctor or psychologist or whatnot." Faust was no longer speaking directly to Stanley. "After all, in an existential sense, which of us knows what he *really* is? What is more real: what we pretend we are, what we think we are, what we are afraid we are, what others think we are . . .?"

Faust suddenly remembered Stanley and returned to the situation at hand. "No, I don't think this is consciously calculated behavior—quite the opposite. I am quite sure that this fellow would not be able to articulate what he was doing. His pattern, his display, has more or less evolved because it "feels right," and because he likes the things that happen to him in this mode. He likes the questions people ask, the inferences they draw. What they make of him is what he wants to be. And who are we to deny that that is what he really is?"[1]

What Is Impression Management?

Dr. Faust's Socratic exercise with Stanley may have raised more questions for you than it answered. First, you may say, we all know that appearance is important. Clothes *do* make the man, as the saying goes. So why is "impression management" so important? Also, the anecdote seems to suggest that the appearance of things really is more important than fact; that is, that you can be whatever you want just by looking or acting like it. But that is clearly not true.

Let us first define *impression management* exactly.[2] We are talking about *communication* and *perception,* neither of which can be understood apart from the other in an organizational context. Communication, at bottom, is a *transfer of information* from one person to another or perhaps from an organization to a person.[3] This received impression may be conveyed verbally or symbolically, but, as a communications authority has pointed out, "There is no meaning in a message except what the people put into it" (33). Another way of saying this is that *perception* is a key element in both verbal and nonverbal communication. Messages are filtered through *perceptual screens:* We add information, and ignore and distort information in arriving at conclusions (4). And we organize this information in ways which are systematically biased. The *management* of impressions, then, concerns our conscious or subconscious use of these perceptual principles to convey information about ourselves to others.

The Importance of Impression Management

Why is impression management so important? One answer is illustrated in our opening story. People used bits and pieces of information to construct complete images of others. Company salespeople at the convention found it difficult to believe that Stanley worked for The Company. And Stanley, presented with the same kind of fragmentary information about Dr. Faust's management friend, constructed his own phantom, complete with acceptable (to Stanley) explanations as to why in *this* instance *this* style of dress was *not* inappropriate. He also made inferences about other kinds of behavior and abilities that were likely to be present.

Impression management, therefore, is important primarily because we know very little firsthand of others with whom we must work in organizations, yet we must make judgments about people every day. We are unaware of the abilities, motivations, and intentions of these people for several reasons:

1. Most of us do not stay very long in one position, organizationally or geographically—one or two years is the rule, especially early in the career.
2. In most professional positions business interactions with others take place mainly outside our immediate departmental territory. This is especially true of nonspecialist positions, where the person is expected to move into management.
3. We do not have access to performance records (such as course grades), which provide objective evidence of the motivation or ability of others.
4. Most tasks require only limited and specialized abilities; they do not require our full capability. That is, it is often as difficult to fail as it is to shine on the basis of talent alone.

Consequently, we make judgments based on impressions that past experience tells us (or we *think* tells us) are associated with certain traits: crispness of manner with decisiveness, warmth of tone with friendliness, somber dress with responsibility, promptness with dependability, and so on.

Even supervisors have little concrete information on which to judge the performance of their subordinates; consequently, they too go on impressions (19). As Victor Thompson has pointed out,

> Since much of the information conveyed to the audience is by visible rather than by verbal symbols, appearances and mannerisms of the performers cannot be overlooked. . . . Physical appearance, dress, mannerisms, office behavior—all are important. Impressions fostered at work are probably as important as accomplishment. (35:148)

Consequently,

> The control of information . . . and the management of impressions, become important techniques in the struggle for authority, status, and power. (35:139)

Thus, the crux of impression management is not that appearance is important, but rather that we must understand the *circumstances* and *situations* that define favorable impressions.

As to impression management being synonymous with misrepresentation, it *is* possible to misrepresent key facts about yourself, creating a "false impression." But our interest is in attempts to communicate to others, verbally or symbolically, consciously or subconsciously, information that helps define for others significant aspects of ourselves. As Erving Goffman has put it,

> The individual typically infuses his activity with signs which dramatically highlight and portray confirmatory facts that might otherwise remain unapparent or obscure. (11:30)

By "confirmatory facts" Goffman means facts that help confirm the truth or reality of the social self the person is presenting. For as Dr. Faust tried to explain to Stanley, part of what we are is what we are trying to become. Impression management, then, far from being a misrepresentation of what we are, consists of our own attempts to communicate to others, both in concrete and symbolic ways, facts about ourselves that we consider important and meaningful in our relationships with those others.

Impression Management: An Overview

Courtesy in everyday life requires that we accept as truth the impression presented by another person. The Oriental concept of "face," for example, allows each member of the group "an honest, decent face," simply by virtue of that membership (16). Another example is the "word of a gentleman." That "word" is not to be doubted. Mutual acceptance of each other's impressions or presentations of self is one thing that keeps organizations (and society at large) going.

Remember that norms and roles involve the expectations others in your organization have about your behavior. For example, Stanley expects to have little personal interaction with Mr. Marsh. But if he does, he will know pretty much what to do. He also knows that the situational context—a Company meeting as opposed to a Company picnic, for example—certainly will influence how both will act.

Beyond this core of normative expectations there remains a latitude of speech, dress, and behavior that is the basis of impression management. Dr. Faust's friend in our opening story even transgressed some norms related to his position in his presentation of self, yet this was effective symbolic communication. Nevertheless, when he traveled to the New York headquarters, he modified this image considerably. To Mr. Marsh the symbolic presentation would have had a different meaning (27). Impression management, then, provides a behavioral counterpoint to the normative structure's prescriptions.

In this chapter we will first outline some key principles of person perception—principles concerning how information is transmitted and perceived, and how those perceptions are organized. Next, we will examine dramaturgy, the art of stagecraft. We will consider the use of voice and gesture, body language, the importance of appearance, and the use of stage props—symbolic communications.

Then we will look at the rules of impression management appropriate to certain key roles in organizations: superior, subordinate, lower participant, and specialist. Each has features that differentiate it from the others. We will also consider the use of stage props, concrete symbols of power and privilege. Finally, we will look at examples of how entire organizations manage their impressions to create desired images.

Perceiving and Organizing Impressions of People

Impression management is important because in many organizational situations impressions are our major source of information. It is awkward to say to another, "I hear what you are saying, but how can I know that is really what you believe?" Indeed, questions like this communicate something about ourselves. Further, it is not a proper question from subordinate to superior in any event—the normative structure specifies that. Yet a decision has to be made: "Yes, I'll take that assignment, Mr. Mason," or "No, I'm afraid that . . ."

In these situations we try to glean as much as we can from partial cues and limited information, then organize it and interpret it as best we can. In doing so, the following happen:

- We fill in, ignore, or distort information to make it *consistent* with the overall impression we are organizing of the person (4).
- We attribute to the person motives and causes that are consistent with our derived impressions (9).

These impressions, however, may be erroneous, filtered and distorted by our expectations. For example, in an important meeting a subordinate may perceive an executive to be abrupt and aggressive, when the executive is actually unsure of himself and very nervous. Research shows that a wide range of personal characteristics attributed to people may be based on our perception (perhaps faulty) of a single important attribute (38:96).

Several basic mechanisms *bias* or *distort* our perceptions of people. Let us examine a few of these.[4]

CULTURAL CONDITIONING. Different cultures may interpret the same behavior quite differently (15). If two interacting individuals do not understand this, the communication between them can be distorted. For example, the physical distance thought comfortable for interpersonal interaction differs considerably among cultures. The face-to-face distance comfortable for the Latin is quite uncomfortable for the North American. The North American may see the Latin as pushy and aggressive, when the Latin is simply trying to adjust the face-to-face distance to a closer, more comfortable gap (20). This principle is also true of *organizational subcultures*. Salespeople are expected to be crisp and hardhitting, engineers to be thoughtful and methodical. Such impressions of individuals, however, can be quite erroneous.

STEREOTYPING. Stereotyping means attributing characteristics to individuals based on a belief we hold about a group with which we identify that individual. The usual basis for stereotyping is ethnic identification, although such group labels as union member, banker, or social worker serve like functions (39). We know what "they" are like, how "they" think.

An example of the effects of stereotyping involves the experiences of black managers in industry (8). Appearance is the primary factor affecting the hiring of black managers. (In this case, "informal" appearance is given as the reason for not hiring.) White managers look for individuals who resemble themselves. One white manager is quoted as saying, "Someone who dresses rather bizarrely indicates a lack of maturity, and it would be an obstacle to his or her promotion to management" (8:70). Styles of dress, speech, and personal mannerisms are all cited as evidence of the doubt of blacks' ability to perform managerial roles. Of course, black American subculture currently differs in some particulars from the predominantly white business subculture. White managers, perceiving these differences, and interpreting them within this business subculture, draw unwarranted conclusions about the competence of black candidates for managerial positions.

CATEGORIZATION. The role expectations associated with positions in organizations are similar to stereotypes: we ignore individual characteristics and attribute instead certain expected characteristics of the category. Identical performances by Stanley and Mr. Marsh would be interpreted quite differently by observers. Your position in the organization influences the impression you make. In this view Goffman speaks of the "general impression of the sacred compatibility between the man and his job" (11:46). Thus "executives often project an air of competency and general grasp of the situation, blinding themselves and others to fact that they hold their jobs partly because they look like executives, not because they can work like executives" (11:47).

HALO EFFECT. General impressions influence the perception of specific traits. For example, a professor who is favorably impressed by a student's classroom participation may find this impression unduly influencing his or her grading of that student's term papers or final exams. For this reason some professors grade term papers "blind," that is, without knowing the student's name. The same is true of various merit rating schemes used in organizations; employees who are well liked tend to be judged as more capable than others, though they may actually be equal in ability (39).

PROJECTION. We often attribute our own motives and attitudes to others in interpreting their actions. If we are intimidated by a domineering supervisor, we tend to project our reactions to this person onto others. If our own key motive is getting ahead in the organization, we tend to interpret others' actions as stemming from like motivations.

First impressions. Research shows that the first impression we receive of a person greatly biases our perceptions of subsequent information. We tend to fill in, ignore, and distort new information to be consistent with our first impression. Thus, first impressions resist change. As a master of stagecraft put it:

> You cannot erase a spoiled first impression any more than you can recover lost maidenhood. (34:79)

Attribution of motives. Research also shows that observers of a person's behavior tend to attribute different reasons for that behavior than does the person being observed. You tend to explain your *own* actions in terms of the situation in which you find yourself at a given time. Someone observing you, however, when asked to account for your actions, will probably give an explanation in terms of your personal attributes, rather than in terms of the situation (9). For example, assume you have been asked to perform a long and boring task. You are doing your best to complete it before it drives you crazy. If you become distracted easily and need frequent breaks to reenergize yourself, you blame the job. Your boss, however, is likely to perceive the problem as being not the situation, but *you*: you lack responsibility; perhaps you are immature. This is one reason why Ted Shelby tackles every assignment in his best eager/responsible manner.

Figure 7.1 illustrates these factors that affect our perceptions of people.

Principles of Dramaturgy

In his classic essay on the presentation of self in everyday life, Erving Goffman used dramaturgy, the art of stagecraft, as the organizing framework within which to analyze impression management. We shall do the same. But before getting into the dramaturgical principles that underlie impression management, we will briefly explore the roots of dramaturgy in human organizations (17).

Ritual occasions have performed key functions in the human organization since the early agricultural communities. For example, everyone participated in the dance and music of harvest rites and like ceremonies that were deemed necessary to ensure the survival of the group. As the social organization of these communities became more complex, so did the rites. Specialists (priests) became necessary to explain and instruct others in the meaning and power of the rituals.

Costumes helped symbolize the power of participants in the ritual over nature. Masks were especially important: The bigger the mask, the greater the

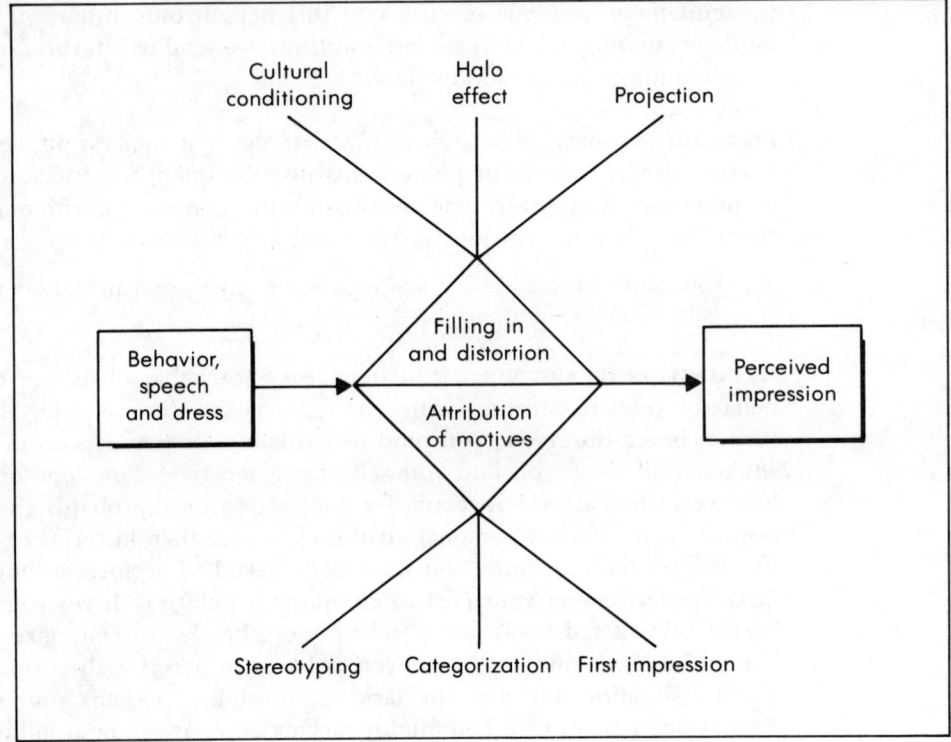

FIGURE 7.1 Factors in Person Perception Important to Impression Management

power. In fact, the wearer of the mask was more than a representation of the "god," he *was* the god; he *had* the power (6).

Dramaturgy, then, did not begin as entertainment. It began because the human organization, in order to maintain itself, needed some part of a ritual performance to come true. If a successful harvest were portrayed, their harvest would be successful; if the group were portrayed winning a war or making a profit, these events would come true. Similar rituals exist today throughout the world, though in "modern" societies most of us have lost our wholehearted belief in the efficacy of such rituals.

The dramaturgical impulse seems to remain, nevertheless, even in modern organizations. There are elements of ritual in the departmental meeting. And speeches by company executives often carry more than the hint of atavistic ritual. That is, the need remains to convey by symbol and by word the values, attitudes, and motives that "dramatically highlight and portray confirmatory facts that might otherwise remain unapparent or obscure" (11:30). (For an example, see Box 7.)

Box 7: Managing the Impression of Competence in an Environment of Uncertainty

In all professions, but especially in medicine, students who are being socialized into the profession are subject to "ritual ordeals of uncertainty." Student physicians are faced with a body of knowledge so huge that it cannot be learned completely. Faced with frequent and difficult examinations, they are made painfully aware that they will often face situations in which they are unsure of their knowledge and themselves. Students adapt to this situation in medical school by developing "cloaking behavior," that is, using "interaction skills to suggest a degree of confidence and knowledge that the emerging, but also established, practitioner may or may not possess."

A study was made of an innovative medical program intended to develop community oriented physicians who understand how to work as a team. The study involved participant observation and interviewing over the entire three-year period of training of a class of eighty student physicians. Students worked in small groups of five students and one tutor. There were no written tests or grades. Evaluations were based on discussions among students and tutors of each other's strengths and weaknesses.

Since the threat of tests and grades was absent, the researchers hypothesized that the degree of cloaking behavior would be reduced. Yet these students displayed such behavior even earlier than students in traditional programs. Reviewing the situation, the researchers came up with this: unlike students in traditional medical programs, students in this team-oriented approach have three major sources of uncertainty.

1. They have direct contact with patients from the very first day. They simply have no experience in this and thus no guidelines for enacting a "professional physician-like role."
2. Because there are no exam grades, these students cannot compare their progress with others'. Furthermore, without examinations to point the way to the core knowledge of medicine, they have no assurance that they are building a base competence.
3. Because evaluation occurs in a group interaction, students must be attuned to nuances. Since reputations are created and defined in these settings, with students being the object of display and discussion, this self-exposure produces anxiety but also early interactional skills.

The result is that students in this tutorial-based program learned to negotiate interactional evaluation much *earlier* than their peers in traditional programs. They

continued

learned to "cover" themselves by deflecting others from probing their ignorance, by developing cloaking behavior that is often accompanied by initiative-taking behavior intended to impress others with their competence. In short, they begin to master an interaction ritual that will aid greatly in later professional performances under uncertainty. So it is that students learn not only professional skills, but impression management skills as well. With these they demonstrate competence and thereby legitimate claims of trustworthiness in serious or fateful matters. The symbolic communication of professional competence is, in fact, a hidden curriculum.

From J. Haas and W. Shaffir, "Ritual Evaluation of Competence: The Hidden Curriculum of Professionalization in an Innovative Medical School Program." *Work and Occupations* 9 (1982): 131–154.

Elements of Dramaturgical Performances

The impression manager has basically three "materials" to work with:

1. voice and manner of speaking,
2. body language—facial expression and gestures, and
3. appearance—costumes and stage setting.

Each of these contributes in the communication of an overall impression.

Psychological research has found that information can be carried by *voice* alone, although this information may be incorrect. But correct or not, listeners receive relatively uniform impressions and make assumptions about the speaker's personality on the basis of voice (18:64). Combining this principle with cultural conditioning and stereotyping helps explain how different speech patterns or accents convey impressions. Ted Shelby understands this well and tailors his speech to the occasion.

Facial expressions, particularly the eyes, can convey a great deal of information that, at times, may contradict what we are saying. This is because facial expressions are difficult to control (2:52). Nonfacial gestures are also meaningful. Students of *body language* suggest that a great deal of symbolic communication takes place through gesture. For example, the military salute is supposed to be a symbolic act of deference to officers from enlisted personnel. This conventional and symbolic gesture seems to be a simple act, but apparently this is not so. Enlisted personnel vary the components of the salute in subtle ways through differences in stance, facial expression, and duration and timing of the movements, as well as the choice of context. The result is that officers may receive a "proper salute" that is symbolic of insult or ridicule rather than deference (2:79).

Costuming and *stage setting* are obvious tools of impression management. Although requirements for appropriate attire have relaxed since the days of the gray flannel suit and IBM's essential white shirt, there are still limitations. A *New York Times* article on office attire reported that "not quite anything goes" (25).

For instance, the Chase Manhattan Bank felt this way:

> "Leisure suits?" the interviewer asked.
> "Yes."
> "Pants suits?"
> "Yes."
> "See-through blouses?"
> "See-through blouses?" the bank man repeated, puzzled.
> "Yes, the braless look," said the interviewer.
> "The braless look," he said a bit aghast, "at the Chase Manhattan Bank?" (25:F10)

Costuming and stage setting must work together to form a right impression. Jimmy Carter, in the peanut fields in Plains, Georgia, wearing jeans and an open-necked shirt, presented a coherent impression of a man with the "common touch." In 1924 Calvin Coolidge had tried the same thing and created a "spoiled" impression. Photographs of Coolidge walking through the fields showed him in starched, creased overalls and well-shined, black business shoes. The resulting incongruous impression left him an "object of national ridicule" (26).

Another example of the use of organizational stage settings comes from the description in Chapter 6 of the recruiting problems of the conservative bank. The stage setting was described as fostering the authoritarian tendencies of bankers. The "very elegance of many banking houses and of the officers' quarters in them and the awe they create in the average citizen may contribute further to the banker's idealized conception of himself." This, combined with the fact that the properly deferential and submissive type favored by recruiters, "is a type which fits in well in the hushed, unhurried, cathedral-like milieu of many of the older banks," provides a stage setting that helps both to create and to enhance dramaturgical impressions (21:89).

Symbols and Symbolic Acts

Symbols play an important part in communication and perception. One school of thought even advances the proposition that social reality exists only in our culturally conditioned interpretation of symbols and symbolic acts (3). Less abstractly, experience tells us that a great deal of impression management in organizations is carried out symbolically—through word, gesture, and artifact whose meaning is learned as part of the socialization process. These symbols may be concrete or abstract, embodied in interaction between roles, or performed alone. The student wearing a multifunction calculator on one hip is managing an impression, as is the professor who affects blue denim jackets and jeans in the classroom. It is *because* these items are displayed as they are, in this specific context, that they take on symbolic meaning. Other examples of this principle are the shoe buffing machines installed in all the washrooms at Company headquarters, and careful reference always to "Mr. Marsh" when speaking to superiors about the president of The Company.

ORGANIZATIONS MANAGE SYMBOLIC IMPRESSIONS. The principles of impression management also apply to entire organizations. To be more precise, individuals responsible for the impression made by the organization manage impressions of the organization. For example, management consultation organizations put a great deal of effort into conveying the impression that they are well managed themselves. Also, rational planning techniques such as PERT (Program Evaluation and Review Techniques) are probably more useful as symbols of management effectiveness than as tools for achieving effective management (13:182).

In another example, both of us worked for IBM when their new corporate headquarters was being constructed. The new building was elegant in a typical subdued manner, with the main structure built around two strikingly landscaped Japanese gardens. In stark contrast to this were vinyl tile floors in the hallways and elsewhere (except in the management offices). This tile seemed out of place; carpeting would have been more in harmony with the overall decor. One day quite by accident, in conversation with an industrial engineer, we found out why this was so. We had assumed expense was involved, but it was not. Vinyl tile actually is more expensive than carpet over the life of the covering, once the labor costs of waxing and buffing are added on. However, most management people of our generation perceived carpeting as *symbolic* of luxury, hence cost. IBM top management, always sensitive to customers' suspicions that its products were more expensive than necessary, reasoned that any suggestion of unnecessary opulence might support this erroneous reasoning; hence carpets were taboo. Impression management was at work.

SYMBOLIC ACTS. Symbolic acts are an integral part of the social structure of organizations; they mediate and structure communication among members. One of the most widespread uses of symbolism is to ensure appropriate behavior in deference relationships (10). In the well-ordered society of The Company, cues to proper deference behavior are generally provided through costuming and stage setting. But occasionally, if the territory is unfamiliar, or it is not clear what the deference relationship should be, symbolic behavior may be necessary. Take, for example, the day that Dr. Faust visited The Agency.

Dr. Faust Visits the Agency

Dr. Faust was doing his best to get the attention of the executive deputy secretary for operations of The Agency, but the damn phones kept ringing. There were three of them on the spacious desk.

The ringing stopped Faust in mid-sentence.

"Ah, excuse me, Dr. Faust. Yes, Bill. Yes, of course. Say, how did that deal on HR-131 come out? Oh, yes? Yes. Well, listen. . . ."

Stanley and Dr. Faust knew they had been lucky to get this appointment. The executive deputy secretary wasn't easy to see. But so far, in the first half hour, they had managed only five minutes of uninterrupted discussion. No sooner did they seem to be making progress—to be getting their point across—when the phone would ring, the secretary would say "Excuse me," and proceed to talk for several minutes, apparently oblivious to his visitors. Then, returning his attention to Faust and Stanley he would apologize profusely and say, "Now then, where were we?" seemingly having forgotten all that had gone before.

And so it went for the entire appointed hour.

Afterward, though Stanley was disappointed that they didn't get much accomplished, Faust was livid. And he was not saying much. To break the ice, Stanley volunteered that it was a shame they had so little time to "make their pitch" to the secretary. But then, obviously he was quite busy, an important man in the department. But, strangely, all Faust had to say was, "Yes, isn't he? Isn't he, though? Yes, it certainly would seem that way."

Four Key Roles: Superior, Subordinate, Lower Participant, and Specialist

Thus far we have set forth and illustrated principles regarding the perception of people, and examined the dramaturgical tools available to the impression manager. We have tried also to illustrate how symbolic meaning becomes attached to objects or acts through association with a given organizational context, or stage setting. From these principles we will now derive a corollary principle for impression management: Different organizational roles call for different techniques to create favorable impressions; and conversely, identical techniques applied in different roles can create very different impressions. For example, Mr. Marsh runs his meetings in an overbearing, autocratic, tension-producing manner. Yet, the impression is favorable: crisp, hard-hitting, a sense of urgency, as befits a top executive. If Stanley were to use the same approach, however, in running a peer group meeting, the result might not be so favorable. For this reason we must consider the major roles available to organizational members and to examine the appropriate dramaturgy for each role.[5]

Remember that references to superior and subordinate describe *complementary roles*, a *relationship* between positions, not the positions themselves. And although the farther up the hierarchical ladder you go the more your relationships will be that of superior to subordinate, until you reach Mr. Marsh's level you will still be subordinate to someone. That is, our discussion concerns impression management appropriate to roles in relation to one another. This explains why we need to treat the role of *lower participant* distinctly. Although all lower organizational participants are subordinates, not all subordinates are lower participants. The genuine lower participant—the secretary, the millhand, the mail carrier—is without hope or aspiration of attaining a position carrying the role of superior. The organizational role of lower participants will be treated thoroughly in Chapter 12. We differentiate the *specialist* from the *subordinate* for much the same reason. The specialist may accrue status and power, but will not perform in the role of superior. Remember too that we are describing pure types, concepts that illustrate principles well but are found seldom in real roles in real organizations (see Figure 7.2).

Dramaturgy of the Superior

The proper superior impression is to appear sincere, competent, and poised—and busy. Busy, however, seems self-evident (29).

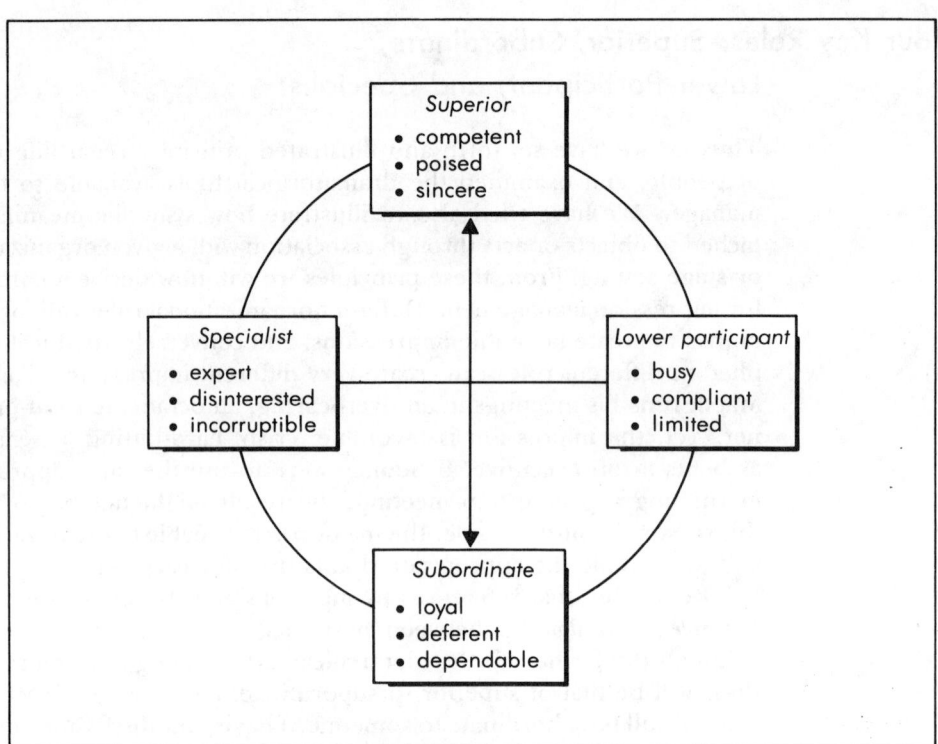

FIGURE 7.2   Four Key Roles in the Dramaturgy of Organizations

SINCERITY. Ideally this element needs no impression management by executives. They should really care. The superior who does not care cannot expect subordinates to care. The superior is the paragon and the transmitter of the normative structure of management; the sincerity of the superior's commitment provides at least one answer to subordinates as to why things should be done as they are.

COMPETENCE AND POISE. Victor Thompson feels the basic problem of modern bureaucratic organization is "maintaining the legitimacy of hierarchical roles in the face of advancing specialization" (35:142). Thus, the impression of superior competence must be cultivated and maintained. This aura of superior competence, however, except under special circumstances, need not be one of greater *specialist* competence. As we noted in Chapter 6, restriction of the flow of information downward through the hierarchy surrounds the executive position with mystery, creating in itself the impression that important and difficult duties are being carried forward, and thus supporting the assumption of specialist competence.

The superior must also cultivate an air of general competence and poise. He should be on a first-name basis not only with other important people in his own company but with those on the outside as well.

Dramaturgy of the Subordinate

Subordinate describes an organizational *role,* not a position. Kerry Drake, for example, is Ted Shelby's superior, and that relationship calls for him to act the role of the superior; yet Kerry is subordinate to Mr. Mason, and the proper impression for that relationship requires a different dramaturgy. The dramaturgy of the subordinate conveys the impressions of loyalty and deference: loyalty to the organization, and both loyalty and deference to the superior.

LOYALTY. Loyalty to the company is perhaps the basic requirement of membership in an organization. But loyalty to superiors is also necessary. The superior must know, for instance, that the subordinate will not reveal confidential information at inopportune times. Subordinate loyalty ensures that the superior will be able to carry off his or her own dramaturgical performances convincingly. In return, the subordinate understands the superior's sincerity in intending to help build the career of the subordinate. This is the complementarity of role expectations we discussed earlier.

DEFERENCE. Deference, like loyalty, conveys the impression of *dependability.* Acts of deference may be important symbolic communications, especially in large bureaucracies where the exceptional competence of a subordinate may raise questions of loyalty. Perhaps you think we are underestimating the importance of competence; suggesting that competence does not count; just loyalty and deference.

We agree that competence is important, of course, but in a discussion about the impression management involved in the complementary relationship between two organizational roles—superior and subordinate—it is somewhat irrelevant.

The appropriate subordinate impression, then, is one of deference, one of emphasizing that the competent performance of the subordinate is due in no little measure to the coaching and instruction of the superior. If this is true (and it often is) so much the better.

Dramaturgy of the Lower Participant

Lower organizational participants are different from subordinates in that they cannot hope to aspire to superior roles in the organization. Secretaries, enlisted personnel in the military, machine operatives in industry (millhands), janitors, hospital attendants, are all examples of lower participants.

From the lower participant's point of view material rewards from the organization—inducements to participate—are fixed. But his or her productive activities—contributions to the organization—are not. Others in the organization may want to increase their contributions in order to obtain a higher level of rewards from the organization, but this is not possible for the lower participant. Therefore, in order to achieve a more favorable balance of inducements to contributions, he or she reduces the level of contributions and seeks other rewards from the job situation, for example, from social interaction.

Impression management helps the lower participant accomplish this successfully. The dramaturgy of the lower participant is that of appearing to be always busy, ever compliant, yet innocent of management's work rules and limited in competence beyond the specific task he or she is to perform.

BUSY. The Calvinist epigram that "idle hands do the devil's work" finds current expression in modern organizations. The lower participant must appear to be busy even when there is nothing to do, since superiors may supply distasteful busy work to an idle lower participant. Thus, the lower participant feels it is better to appear busy than risk being assigned work that may be worse.

COMPLIANCE AND INNOCENCE. Superiors generally understand that organizations have no reason to expect loyalty from lower participants, but they do expect compliance. How do lower participants manage the impression of compliance, when obviously in a situation where they are not complying with the work rules of the management? One strategy is to feign innocence of the transgression. Compliance is essential; but inadvertent noncompliance can be explained by innocence. "After all," the superior may say, "what more can one expect?"

LIMITED COMPETENCE. Like innocence, limited competence fits well the dramaturgy of the lower participant. Projecting the appearance of limited competence helps lower participants reduce their contributions. The impression of limited competence, for example, may mask "illegal" activities. The machine operative may want to demonstrate convincingly to the industrial engineer that he cannot operate the machine at the desired speed without continually burning out tools. Then, when not observed, he may use his special knowledge to run the machine at twice the speed for his own purposes (32, 37). The impression of limited competence also serves to fend off the assignment of additional or unusual tasks for which there is no significant increase in material rewards: "No, Mr. Shelby, I just can't seem to get the hang of how to run that new tape memory typewriter." Naturally, it may be necessary to produce several batches of badly botched work to substantiate this impression.

Dramaturgy of the Specialist

The role of specialist is as ancient as human organization itself. Early hunting bands were at the mercy of luck and nature. Consequently, they felt the need for more direct control over the natural events upon which their lives depended. What evolved was the *shaman,* a unique "spiritual helper" whose personal visions could ensure a successful hunt or battle, and who also could perform healing arts. The shaman's prestige came from his special knowledge and *not* from his position in the group. He remained a unique individual, for though he was in the group he was not a part of its structure, as was the "priest" who filled a conventional and prescribed position (7). Furthermore, because of his specialist status, the shaman could be called on for help by the tribal chief yet not be seen as a competitor for the chief's status.

Shamanistic costumes also bespoke the office. Indians of the Northwest coast area used "symbols of office," including shaggy, tangled hair, bone necklaces, and a special bone tube with which to blow away sickness and catch souls. Songs were accompanied by carved rattles. The costuming and performances were mainly individualistic, reflecting the "mystery" of individual power.

Specialists still perform today in much the same way for much the same reasons and rewards—though not by dancing and singing, of course. The pure specialist is someone whose contribution to the organization is solely that of giving expert advice derived from special expertise. Good examples might be the Ph.D. economist, employed by the organization to perform econometric forecasts; or the Ph.D. behavioral scientist, employed to give advice on the mysteries of modern behavioral technologies. But the true specialist is rare—like the shaman, there are few such roles required in modern organizations. True specialists derive power from the impression that they care little about the mundane matters of organizational policy; in fact, they care little about this organization per se and its material rewards. Their interest is in the truth revealed by their specialty, regardless of consequences. The impression to be conveyed is that they can be believed because their motives are pure. The specialists' strength is this aura of incorruptibility; their weakness, dubious loyalty.

The principle is this: the specialist, like the shaman, gains exemption from the usual rules of the superior-subordinate game by declaring him- or herself out of the management/hierarchical race and disinterested in the game of status and position power. The key elements of specialist dramaturgy, then, are organizational asceticism and the mystery of specialty. Ideally, the specialist is not supposed to do anything. He or she is supposed to give advice but not care whether or not that advice is followed. This is the essence of the specialist role. Someone on whom the organization depends for the day-to-day performance of necessary activities must be placed within the authority structure of the organization, and hence, bound to superior-subordinate dramaturgy. Specialists can be exempt from this only because the organization does not require their routine performance. Nevertheless, with proper impression management and a properly esoteric profession, specialists may accede to great power in organizations.

Outside consultants, some of whom regularly serve one organization, share many of the characteristics of the specialist (13). They share the exemptions of the specialist, and the usual rules of superior-subordinate interaction do not apply to them.

To summarize, the impression conveyed must be appropriate to the role. The impression that is right for the superior is wrong for the subordinate. The cynicism of the specialist is entirely inappropriate for the superior; expressing superior competence is wrong for the role of subordinate; and indulging in the specialist dramaturgy that allows you to ignore expressions of loyalty and deference is inappropriate for a nonspecialist. Others may begin to see you as truly a specialist, and out of the management game.[6]

Summary

Impression management is important because we possess so little detailed information about others in organizations. Certainly this is true of social interaction in everyday life. Consequently, we become accustomed to accepting self-presentation as factual. This, in turn, leads each of us to develop a personal dramaturgy that conveys to others the essence of what we are or believe we are. A great deal of effort is devoted to impression management—to creating an "image" that is appropriate to the situation and the personal needs of the individuals involved.

Is everyday life in The Company, then, all sham and pretense and no substance? No. When Mr. Marsh gives his semiyearly address to The Company's sales club, it is invariably crisp and hard-hitting. Marsh himself exudes that image in gesture, tone, and dress. He works at it. But then, that is how he believes himself to be. To paraphrase the old saying: "It is not enough to be decisive, you must *appear* decisive as well."

This is the problem of the theater, the dividing line between belief and truth. The actor, in one part of himself, *is* the role, but he must reserve another part of himself to observe. A loss in balance either way faults his impression. This confusion between belief and truth is conveyed very well by Kurt Vonnegut, Jr., in *Mother Night*. In this short novel, Howard Campbell, an American agent operating in Germany under the guise of a propaganda broadcaster, is extremely effective in both functions. He gets information to the Allied forces encoded in diatribes of racist propaganda that he himself writes. After the war he is adjudged a "war criminal." Unjust? Campbell defends himself to the agent who recruited him, one of the three people in the world who knew his true identity.

> "Three people in all the world knew me for what I was—" I said. "And all the rest—" I shrugged.
> "They knew you for what you were, too," he said abruptly.
> "That wasn't me," I said, startled by his sharpness.
> "Whoever it was—" said [the agent], "he was one of the most vicious sons of bitches who ever lived."
> "You think I was a Nazi?" I said.
> "Certainly you were," he said. "How else could a responsible historian classify you? Let me ask you a question—"
> "Ask away," I said.
> "If Germany had won, had conquered the world—" he stopped, cocked his head. "You must be way ahead of me. You must know what the question is."

Campbell then gives what he himself describes as a "corrosively cynical answer" to the implied question.

> "There is every chance," I said, "that I would have become a sort of Nazi Edgar Guest, writing a daily column of optimistic doggerel for daily papers around the world. And, as senility set in—the sunset of life as they say—I might even come to believe what my couplets said: that everything was probably all for the best." (36:143)

As Vonnegut sums it all up, "this is the only story of mine whose moral I know. I don't think it's a marvelous moral; I simply happen to know what it is: we are what we pretend to be so we must be careful about what we pretend to be" (36:v).

Notes

1. This story is adapted from an earlier account of Stanley and his cohorts in The Company by Ritti and Funkhouser (30). For an analysis of how "clothes make the person" see Leonard Bickman (1).

2. This term is taken from Erving Goffman, the well-known sociologist of "everyday life" (10, 11, 12).
3. It seems impossible to come up with a simple, agreed-upon definition of *communication*. See Porter and Roberts (28).
4. This list appears in a number of basic social psychology texts under the general topic of person perception (9, 18, 38). Zalkind and Costello (39) have applied some of these directly to organizations.
5. This section draws on a similar discussion by Victor Thompson (35) in his chapter on dramaturgy.
6. Evidence for this kind of categorization in a technical organization is noted in Rosen, Billings, and Turney (31:182).

References

1. BICKMAN, L. "Social Roles and Uniforms: Clothes Make the Person." *Psychology Today* 11 (1974): 48–53.
2. BIRDWHISTELL, R. *Kinesics and Context: Essays on Body Motion Communication.* Philadelphia, Pa.: University of Pennsylvania Press, 1970. See part II, "Isolating Behavior."
3. BLUMER, H. *Symbolic Interactionism: Perspective and Method.* Englewood Cliffs, N.J.: Prentice-Hall, 1969.
4. BUCKHOUT, R. "Eyewitness Testimony." *Scientific American* 231 (1974): 23–31.
5. CALDWELL, D. F., AND C. A. O'REILLY, III. "Responses to Failure: The Effects of Choice and Responsibility on Impression Management." *Academy of Management Journal* 25 (March 1982): 121–136.
6. CAMPBELL, J. *The Masks of God: Primitive Mythology.* New York: Viking, 1959.
7. DRUCKER, P. *Indians of the Northwest Coast.* Garden City, N.Y.: The Natural History Press, 1963. See Chap. 5, "Religion."
8. FERNANDEZ, J. P. *Black Managers in White Corporations.* New York: Wiley, 1975.
9. GAMSON, W., and A. MODIGLIANI. *Conceptions of Social Life.* Boston: Little, Brown, 1974. See Chap. 2.
10. GOFFMAN, E. *Interaction Ritual: Essays on Face to Face Behavior.* Garden City, N.Y.: Doubleday, 1967.
11. ———. *The Presentation of Self in Everyday Life.* New York: Doubleday, 1959.
12. ——— *Stigma: Notes on the Management of Spoiled Identity.* Englewood Cliffs, N.J.: Prentice-Hall, 1973.
13. GUTTMAN, D., and B. WILLNER. *The Shadow Government.* New York: Pantheon, 1976.
14. HAAS, J., and W. SHAFFIR. "Ritual Evaluation of Competence: The Hidden Curriculum of an Innovative Medical School Program." *Work and Occupations* 9 (May 1982): 131–154.
15. HALL, E. T. *The Hidden Dimension.* Garden City, N.Y.: Doubleday, 1966.
16. HO, D. "On the Concept of Face." *American Journal of Sociology* 4 (1976): 867–884.
17. HUNNINGHER, B. *The Origin of the Theatre.* New York: Hill and Wang, 1961.

18. Krech, D., R. Crutchfield, and E. Ballachy. *Individual in Society.* New York: McGraw-Hill, 1962. See Chap. 2, "Cognition."
19. Levinson, H. "Appraisal of *What* Performance?" *Harvard Business Review* 54 (1976): 30 ff.
20. McGough, E. *Understanding Body Talk.* New York: Scholastic Book Services, 1974. See Chap. 9.
21. McMurry, R. N. "Recruitment, Dependency and Morale in the Banking Industry." *Administrative Science Quarterly* 3 (1958): 87–117.
22. Marquand, J. *Sincerely, Willis Wayde.* Boston: Little, Brown, 1955.
23. Mechanic, D. "Sources of Power of Lower Participants in Complex Organizations." *Administrative Science Quarterly* 7 (1962): 349–364.
24. *Newsline.* "The Phony Dr. Fox." *Psychology Today* 5 (1973): 19.
25. *New York Times,* "Office Dress: Not Quite Anything Goes." December 28, 1975, p. F10. © 1975 by The New York Times Company. Reprinted by permission.
26. *New York Times,* "Report on Men's Wear." "All the Candidates' Clothes." September 19, 1976, p. 64.
27. Pfeffer, J. "Management as Symbolic Action: The Creation and Maintenance of Organizational Paradigms." In *Research in Organizational Behavior,* Vol. 3. Edited by L. Cummings and B. Staw. Greenwich, Conn.: JAI Press, 1981.
28. Porter, L., and K. Roberts. "Communication in Organizations." In *Handbook of Industrial and Organizational Psychology,* edited by M. D. Dunnette. Chicago: Rand McNally, 1976, Chap. 35.
29. Rice, B. "Adventures in the Image Trade." *Psychology Today* 16 (September 1982): 6–11.
30. Ritti, R., and R. Funkhouser. *The Ropes to Skip and the Ropes to Know: Studies in Organizational Behavior.* Columbus, Ohio: GRID, 1977.
31. Rosen, N., R. Billings, and J. Turney. "The Emergence and Allocation of Leadership Resources over Time in a Technical Organization." *Academy of Management Journal* 2 (1976): 165–183.
32. Roy, D. "Quota Restriction and Goldbricking in a Machine Shop." *American Journal of Sociology* 57 (1952): 427–442.
33. Schramm, W. "The Nature of Communication Between Humans." In *The Process and Effects of Mass Communication,* edited by W. Schramm and D. F. Roberts. Urbana: The University of Illinois Press, 1971.
34. Stanislavski, C. *Creating a Role.* New York: Theatre Arts Books, 1961.
35. Thompson, V. *Modern Organization.* New York: Knopf, 1961. Excerpts from pages 139 and 148 reprinted by permission.
36. Vonnegut, K., Jr. *Mother Night.* New York: Delacorte, 1966. Copyright © 1962, 1966 by Kurt Vonnegut, Jr. Reprinted by permission of Delacorte Press/Seymour Lawrence.
37. Whyte, W. *Money and Motivation.* New York: Harper, 1955.
38. Wrightsman, L. *Social Psychology.* Monterey, Calif.: Brooks/Cole, 1977.
39. Zalkind, S., and T. Costello. "Perception: Some Recent Research and Implications for Administration." *Administrative Science Quarterly* 7 (1962): 218–235.

Discussion Questions

1. In our opening case Dr. Faust uses the example of a middle management person in a manufacturing plant who violates the norms of dress. How would you verbalize the message he conveys with this presentation of self? If he is promoted to the corporate staff in New York, will he continue to manage his impression this way? Why?
2. Give four reasons why we have very little information about the abilities, motivations, and intentions of people with whom we work. Compare and contrast the applicability of these reasons (a) for a professional commission salesperson, and (b) for a copywriter in an ad agency. Is this difference due to work technology?
3. Explain why perceptions of people may be quite erroneous and distorted. Explain six mechanisms by which this perceptual distortion occurs.
4. Assuming that you are looking ahead to a career in management, think about your upcoming job interviews. What impression will you try to convey to the recruiter? How will you do this symbolically? Verbally?
5. Impression management is not limited to business organizations. Think about impression management in the classroom. Spend part of your next class noting instances of presentation of self by various actors.
6. In our discussion of symbolic acts we relate the story of Dr. Faust's visit to The Agency. In your own words, what was the executive deputy secretary trying to convey to Dr. Faust? Why do you think he chose to do it this way?
7. As an exercise, observe in detail as many faculty offices as you can. Using this information only and the principles of this chapter, what do you think you can infer about the relative status of different faculty members in your major concentration? Be as specific as you can. What are the major kinds of differences that you see?

Chapter 8
Communications in Organizations

His Master's Voice

". . . and so I know there's no need to tell you people here about the continuing concern that our chairman has about the price of success, how an organization such as our Company can grow fat and complacent." One of Marsh's top staff aides was speaking, "So I'm here today, on the personal request of Mr. Marsh, to emphasize once again to you just how important your role in this project is. The need, the spirit, and the benefits of our Procedures Improvement Program (PIP) must be communicated fully and convincingly to everyone in The Company. Not just to our blue-collar people—to *everyone!*"

Well, now, this is interesting, isn't it? What in the world could this PIP program be that makes it so important to Marsh? And here assembled to put together a communications package was a group of very important people: Marshall B. Mason, vice president for manufacturing; Bill Banfield, of Banfield Associates Consultants; Ted Shelby IV to work as liaison; Dr. Faust; and an assortment of corporate staff types for "informational purposes." Also attending were Claude and Penny. Penny had drawn the assignment from communications to prepare the actual written text of the various communication packages. Claude, as an industrial engineer, was to work with Penny to provide the "technical input." Oh yes, and there's Stanley, almost hidden in the corner. Once again he's "on loan" to Dr. Faust, Faust's gopher (go-fer) as it's said.

Now it was Bill Banfield's turn to orient the group to the basic technical thrusts of the PIP project. Just the net of it, so that the communications people would have a working understanding of the basics.

Banfield moved to the head of the table, pulling down a projection screen. "Would you turn on the projector, Stanley?" Banfield had the latest technology of "the presentation."

"Our Procedures Improvement Program has two basic objectives." Scrrp, up went the first slide. Now, with a light pencil to indicate what and where he was reading, "First, through the introduction of standard methods we have a planning tool to estimate accurately, to *forecast* the manufacturing costs of new products with which we have *no previous experience*. We will also be able to *control* costs more closely. Second," again pointing, "by training workers in the use of better individual methods we achieve higher production *without* increased effort.

"So that's our two-fold approach: greater control over costs, planning-wise; and greater efficiency methods-wise, with *no additional costs for either management or employees.*

"And how do we do this?" Scrrp, up went the next slide. "We do it through the use of what we call [pointing again] *synthetic standards.* Now previous to. . . ."

To save some time here let's examine only the essence of what Banfield told the assembled group. Work standards trace their genesis to Frederick Winslow Taylor and the "scientific management" movement. Scientific management, or Taylorism as it came to be known, is a way for systematically determining the proper pace and the "one best way" in which a work task should be performed. The output that can be achieved using this best method working at the prescribed pace constitutes the performance standard for that job. Additional effort might result in performance greater than 100 percent of standard, whereas lack of diligence or improper work methods might result in lower than standard performance, say 60 to 70 percent of standard.

Standard times (the times necessary to complete the unit tasks) can be set in two basic ways. First, the job might be timed with a stopwatch by an industrial engineer. The worker, using the approved method, would be timed to see how long it took to do the job. The pace with which he or she did the work would be estimated by the engineer. The time it took to do the job would then be adjusted for the pace of the worker as *estimated* by the engineer and a *standard time* to do the job would be derived. Obviously, a major source of error in such a procedure might be the accuracy with which the engineer is able to estimate the workers' pace.

Partly because of this problem, engineers subsequently devised *synthetic standards.* To develop a synthetic standard the engineer consults a book of *standard times* that are to be allowed for certain "unit movements" of arms, hands, legs, bodies, or whatnot that are required to do a given job. When the "one best way" to do the job is devised (by the engineer) the job is then broken down into its component unit moves. These, by the way, are called therbligs, or Gilbreth spelled backward to confer immortality on the innovator. Then the appropriate times are applied. The sum total required for the work task is the synthetically constructed standard time for the job. Direct and very scientific.

Since the worker is expected to produce 100 percent of standard on whatever job, certain allowances must be made for unforeseen contingencies. Thus, there are time allowances available for substandard material, machine breakdown, and the like. Time allowances also are added for "rest pauses."

Now back to Bill Banfield. "So there you have the basic thrust of our proposal, gentlemen. As you can see, this is an *educational* program, to train our people in improved work *procedures.* Why, it's as much a program for our blue-collar workers as it is for management. Right here they have the opportunity to make more money by increasing their output, and with the same, or possibly even *less* effort. For management it means a long-range planning tool that we've never had before."

"Thank you, Bill, good show," concluded Mason. "I've asked Ted Shelby to work with Bill to develop some themes for our group that will convey the true meaning of PIP to our people. What have you got for us, Ted?"

With that introduction Ted unrolled his flip charts and mounted them on an easel at the front of the room. Ted preferred the technologically inferior charts to slides because it made *him* the center of the presentation. And now, in the sincere/urgent tone that seemed best to fit the situation, he flipped to his first chart. It said simply, but in huge caps, COMPETITION.

"That's the bottom line today, gentlemen. Meet and beat the competition. The theme we want to stress here is that savings cost-wise in manufacturing will ensure The Company's continuing leadership position in our field." Then, nodding to a raised hand, "Van?"

"That's all well and good, Ted, but why should our people really care about The Company's being number one? Understand, I'm just playing the devil's advocate on this. To me it means one hell of a lot."

"Good point, Van. That's what we're all here

for, to brainstorm this thing." Ted looked about the room, "Anybody?"

"I'll tell you why," Mason cut in. "It's as simple as ABC. The more profitable we are, the more we grow. The more we grow the more opportunities for promotion there are for all of us."

The group nodded and murmured approval of this piece of vice presidential wisdom. And Ted quickly picked up the cue, "Ver-ry good! Got that Penny?"

Yes, she nodded, she had.

"Now then, our next theme—EFFICIENCY." Ted tapped the easel vigorously with his pointer. "The key to efficiency in manufacturing is to improve our productivity without additional capital expenditure. And that's where our Banfield Associates study comes in. Bill, here, has shown us how we can up productivity by 20 to 25 percent just by applying better procedures at the workplace. That's why we call this a procedures improvement program. The net of it is that we can certainly produce more with just the same . . . why, possibly even with *less* effort!" Ted was positively glowing with just the thought of it.

"Claude?"

"Yeah, I know that's true, Ted. But I also know that there's lots of folks down on the floor who won't believe it. It's going to take more than just saying so to convince them that they're not just going to be working harder."

That was the moment it flashed through Penny's mind, the slogan for the whole communications pitch. "Hey, how about this, Ted—'Work smarter, not harder'?"

The room was silent for a moment, then Ted burst out, "Dynamite idea, Penny!"

Everyone agreed, nodding in congratulation toward Penny. And so it went, Ted setting out several more major themes, such as education, and a Company family effort. With each, questions were raised and the themes consequently modified and embellished. And even though several meetings were necessary, to "iterate this thing again," in Ted's words, within just a few weeks the group had hammered out a framework for one of the most important total communications efforts ever to be undertaken by The Company.

The theme of the campaign was taken from its slogan: Work smarter, not harder. In his kickoff announcement, Company chairman Marsh put it in the following way.

TO: All Company Managers
FROM: Office of the Chairman

M. M. Marsh, president and chairman, and Marshall B. Mason, vice president, manufacturing, announced jointly today the initiation of a new manufacturing program aimed at significantly reducing the manufacturing costs of all Company products. This program is to be called The Company's Procedures Improvement Program.

In making his announcement Mr. Marsh had these comments. "As you are all well aware, the business environment of The Company has changed dramatically over the past decade. We have entered a highly competitive era. For this reason, it is more important than ever that we tighten our cost control efforts to get the maximum return on every dollar of capital investment. Our new Procedures Improvement Program has been designed to help all Company personnel reach still higher levels of productivity through careful analysis and refinement of the procedures by which work is performed."

Company vice president Mason commented, "This is first and foremost an educational program. I see procedures improvement as a joint effort by the entire Company family to help us all approach our jobs more intelligently and, as a result, achieve still higher productivity levels with the same effort. This is why I have adopted as our motto—Work smarter, not harder."

This vignette depicts an intent on the part of the top management to establish an attitude among its millhands through a communications program. The intent took the form of a package of messages that was sent through a variety of channels and media. The rank and file were supposed to get the message and accept the program without too much fuss. But did they? To some extent, they did, but not nearly as well as hoped. And a lot more was communicated than intended. The reasons will be the major theme of this chapter.

Communications in Organizations: Some General Comments

Communications are pervasive. They are the life blood of an organization. Almost all major transactions occur through communications and without them the organization would come to a grinding stop. Because of communications' pervasiveness and necessity, and because we communicate from birth to death, you would think that communicating would be one of the simplest things in the world. Yet, it is not!

Communication is part of a social fabric that has norms and a context that allows people to interpret messages and sometimes to distort them. Consequently, messages are sometimes taken according to the intent of the communicator. Also getting in the way of intended interpretations are elements of the communication process such as the message source, the message itself, and the characteristics of the receiver of the message. Any one of these can be a source of error. And many communications are not just to inform but also to change things, such as a person's behavior or attitudes; they make you do something you might not do freely. Finally, a lot of words have several meanings—not just dictionary meanings but symbolic ones. It is often the symbolic meanings that cause the difficulties.

In our treatment of communications we will deal with the problems we have mentioned. In doing so we will try to account for why some communications succeed and others fail.

Elements of the Process of Communication

All communications are made up of: the *source*, the *message*, the *receiver* and the *social context*. These are depicted in Figure 8.1 along with a *feedback loop* back to the source. That feedback loop is essential in order for the source to understand the effect of the message and to change it if necessary.

The Source

Each of the elements has important characteristics. The source has degrees of credibility and a variety of possible motives (31, 45). These characteristics are,

Elements of the Process of Communication

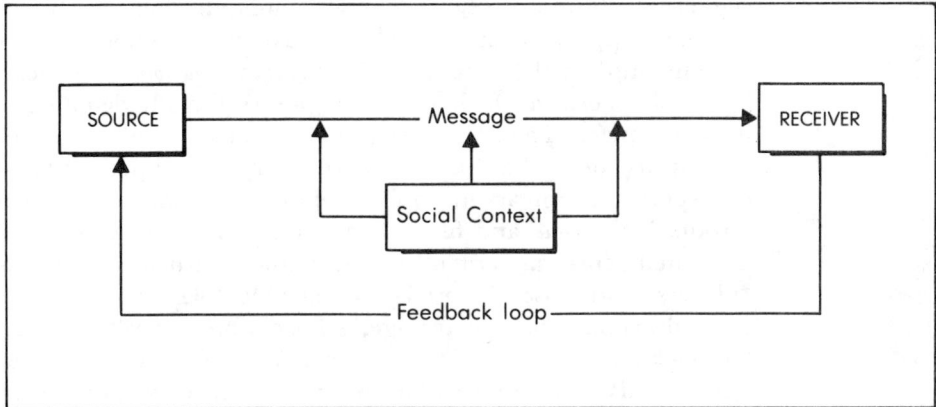

FIGURE 8.1 The Basic Elements of the Communications Process

of course, related; each has some bearing on the success of the communication. As an example, if the intent is to influence the actions of the receiver then it helps enormously if the source is seen as entirely credible, of high status, and with a good purpose—in short, trustworthy. Communicators spend a lot of time worrying about such things.

The Message

The content of the message is important. Job-related information normally takes the form of instructions, directives, performance evaluations, or procedure (37). In other words, what to do, how to do it, when to do it, and how well it has been done. Such task-oriented communiqués are important for two reasons. First, subordinates have to know how to do things according to specific procedures and standards. In other words, organizational expectations concerning behavior and outcomes need to be communicated (50). Second, clear role requirements reduce role ambiguity, which is a correlate of job dissatisfaction and job-related stress (50, 51, 58).

Several things seem important with respect to the clarification of role requirements. First, the message must be specific enough to foreclose important misinterpretation. Second, the message must carry redundancy, the same content said in different ways (59). Third, the message must be repeated, preferably through different channels and from different sources (59). This is because there are many error sources within the social structure and the individual, even when the message is simple (17, 37).

The sensitivity to possible misinterpretations is particularly important when the message carries symbolic as well as literal meaning (16). The idea that a significant portion of organizational communications is symbolic is gaining increasing support. As an example, the use of metaphors to convey impressions is commonplace (59). *Webster's New Collegiate Dictionary* defines metaphor as "a figure of speech in which a word or phrase literally denoting one kind of idea is used in place of another to suggest a likeness." And so business organizations wishing to convey hard-headed agressiveness, competition, and winning often use sports or military metaphors. Lower participants are considered to be "troops" or "rank and file." Top management engages in "strategy, tactics, and intelligence gathering," organizational participants are considered to be "players" and those who are knowledgeable "play the game." People who make good decisions "hit for average," those who make "dynamite" decisions are "heavy hitters." Project directors or task force leaders are "quarterbacks" who "call signals," and those who are moved out of a position because of a bad decision are put in "the penalty box."

Such metaphors are colorful and descriptive in ways that other language is not, but the impressions conveyed are not always precisely those desired. For example, women, not always experienced in military ways or knowledgeable in locker room language may feel excluded from groups engaging in such metaphorical discussion, whether or not that is the intent.

Still, metaphors convey meanings important for developing organizations' self-concepts and support beliefs concerning what the organization is all about. Through the use of such symbols important beliefs are communicated and reinforced that in turn provide coherence and stability to organizational actions. The "think" sign at IBM, for example, does not warrant a thinking response every time it is read, but rather, signifies the company's commitment to judicious action.

The choice of symbols is determined by what they are intended to convey (16, 54). Some symbols are intended to direct attitudes toward certain ends. "The Star Spangled Banner" and "America the Beautiful" are constructed grammatically to trigger sentiments of patriotism. The Coke commercial showing an exhausted and beat-up "mean" Joe Green receiving a Coke from a little boy and then tossing the boy a piece of his football uniform in return symbolizes a common bond between black and white, big and small, sophisticated and innocent. The message is that everyone shares the quality of humanity, and that one element of this quality is a fondness for Coca Cola.

Organizations do similar things with respect to organizational happenings. Messages concerning important transactions—promotions for example—are constructed to convey to members the image of organizational rationality and purposiveness (46).

SYMBOLS, MYTHS AND ORGANIZATIONAL REALITY. Recall that authority in most large organizations rests on the functional grounds of bureaucracy and that bureaucracy has tenets that are sound in the abstract but imperfect in the execution. Legality, impersonality, and rationality support authority and justify compliance; yet they are frequently violated in most bureaucracies for practical reasons. Consequently, effort must be directed to make it appear that the principles ordinarily are operating. To do this communications are designed to construct a social reality that supports the principles and thereby justifies requests for compliance (16). And as the "knowledge" circulates, is repeated, and acts as a perceptual screen, the social reality becomes ever more certain. Yet there is nothing we can point to and say "that is real."

The process has been well known among communicators for a long time. It is well known too, that constructed images, if repeated frequently enough, can become part of the organizational store of truths (45, 46). Once that is done, the social reality is secure. And so symbols, myths, and rituals are important parts of the communications process.

For example, many events for which there is no apparent reason occur in organizations. The explanations for such events should not be left to people who may question the ability of those responsible for the events. Rather, the interpretation should support the wisdom of the decision makers and thus support the organization's rationality. The same reasoning pertains to promotions and accounts for the litany of accomplishments attached to those who are promoted (59, 76).

Goals, objectives, performance, effectiveness, and efficiency are common organizational words and are indicators of organizational purposes. Further, these words attached to groups or to individuals create impressions that not only help others evaluate those groups or individuals but also create expectations of their future behavior. Hence, commonly "known" characteristics of people also set the stage for future actions (7). For example, a simple statement that Ted Shelby was recently promoted to corporate director of planning will not do. The impression needs to be created that Shelby is a highly competent person in an organization that values competency. That impression justifies his promotion, reaffirms the organizational values, and supports organizational rationality. Put another way, information is both given and withheld in order to create mythical explanations of events that then provide the framework for the subsequent consensual interpretations of such events. That framework is constructed to increase the probability that people will see the organization as effective and higher management as heroic (16, 46, 59).

To summarize, much of the organizational information flow downward is symbolic. Its intent is to create or to change attitudes that serve organizational purposes. Because organization reality is partly a function of what is said and partly of what is part of the record, organizational management is careful to pad its communications with a grammar of bureaucratic justification. Furthermore, when notable accomplishments are communicated or change is justified the vocabulary of effectiveness is used. This supports two important factors: the organizational norm of effectiveness and the bureaucratic concept of rationality. The first is purposive or goal-oriented and the second justifies the authority structure and hence, authoritative requests.

How effective are such communications? The answer to that depends a lot on the other elements of the model in Figure 8.1.

The Receiver

Perception is the essence of reception. We perceive a message and that perception depends on the message structure, its content and vocabulary, the source, the social context, and the personal history that we bring to the situation. If the message comes from a trusted source, is couched in easily understood terms, and is consistent with our experiences and our thinking, we will probably see it for what it is (30, 31, 53, 61). But if any of those factors is questionable, we may have a problem of perceptual error.

We talked of perceptual errors in the previous chapter. There are other ways a person tends to distort communications—leveling, sharpening, and condensation (61). *Leveling* involves subjective omission of information. In many communiqués, particularly those which are fairly complex, people find it difficult to remember everything. They typically omit factors that do not correspond with what they see as appropriate elements of the message. The omitted material ordinarily is not seen as important by the receiver, but there are other reasons that it may be unconsciously left out. The perceptual errors that we described before play an important role in what people tend to omit.

Sharpening is selective retention. That is, receivers select elements of the message that correspond with their overall view of the subject matter. Together, leveling and sharpening will tend to distort the message in favor of the receiver's predisposition toward the object of the communication.

Condensation has to do with reducing uncertainty and is the logical assimilation of the leveling and sharpening processes (61). If the message is complex and much of it is ambiguous, the psychological tendency is to compress the message by eliminating the uncertain elements and retaining that part of the message that makes sense.

Recently, the Ford Motor Company, reorganizing one of its plants because of the increasing weakness of the domestic car market, presented its workers with two alternatives: (1) give back management's prerogatives of moving people from job to job according to need and according to the best utilization of manpower, or (2) lose the opportunity to have more work allocated to the plant. At the time, the plant was operating with a reduced workforce, and the short-run projections were that more reductions were likely. If the union (UAW) would agree to the givebacks, then not only would the laid-off workers be recalled but there was a strong possibility, according to Ford management, that additional work would be created that would require more employment in the plant.

The message in simple and clear terms contained the following elements:

(1) The company had to choose which of two plants would receive the work; (2) the plant that did not receive the work allocation would have its workforce reduced further; (3) the economic forecasts made it highly improbable that both plants could ever have what had been known as full employment before the recession; (4) the union givebacks would not be financial, but would have to do with management prerogatives; and (5) in any event, the company could not guarantee full employment of either of the plants regardless of how the workers voted, although there was a good possibility that the increased work would require substantially more workers.

Even though about half of the membership was laid off at the time, and the economic prospects of that geographical area were not bright, the workers voted against their best interests and the union leadership's recommendations; they voted *not* to allow the givebacks. How did that happen?

According to interviews of the workers, those who voted against the givebacks simply did not trust, and hence, believe management. The history was adversarial with very tough bargaining. The workers, through their conditioning and their experience, had developed stereotypes of management. The norms of distrust provided a context within which they either overlooked or chose not to focus on the promised jobs and job security (leveling). They did not believe that management was changing; they rather thought that it was capitalizing on the uncertain economic times to take advantage of the union. The workers focused instead on the givebacks, the loss of control over job territory and the seniority provisions of the previous contract (sharpening). They zeroed in on words like "*try* to allocate the work at," "will make a *great effort* to," and "*nothing can be guaranteed.*" The message finally came out that "management is asking us to give up our seniority protection with no guarantees of anything better" (condensation). Needless to say, management was shocked by the outcome. Yet, given the history of the industrial relations between Ford and the UAW, and the current social context, the perceptual distortions should not have been surprising.

The Social Context

Normally, people respond to messages in a social environment and take many interpretative cues from that environment. For example, one study suggested that people perceived their manager's leadership characteristics through their perceptions of the total job context (10). Another study suggested that people develop attitudes about their job according to how others feel, not necessarily according to the job's characteristics. Furthermore, management constructs messages to fit their own view of social reality and how they would like that reality to appear to the receiver of the message (24, 26, 40). Consequently, there are social constraints placed on both the interpretation and the construction of the message.

The management of cynical knowledge is a constraining factor of the communications flow of any organization. Recall that many things transpire in organizations that should not be known by the lower participants if they must comply with authoritative directives. Decisions made higher up must be seen as rational and related to organizational effectiveness. Consequently a lot of communications are justifications that follow hard-to-understand action (16).

The norms constrain communication also. In the chapter's opening vignette, the norm that all organizational participants are members of an organizational family and as such have rights of influencing their work environment constrains the communication's content and form. It would simply not do to say that the reason for the new manufacturing system is that the workers were not performing up to a reasonable industrial standard. Such a message would have violated the norm, been misinterpreted, and caused significant industrial relations problems. Instead the messages needed to be constructed in such a way as to recognize the workers' past accomplishments, to emphasize the company's concern with their well-being, and to play on their sentiments to "do right by the company." As you shall see, to construct such a message is very difficult and takes much time and concern.

Thus, the social context affects communication in at least three ways: it provides social cues, which limit interpretation; it offers judgments about what should or should not be communicated, which limit the flow and content; and it contains norms, which provide a framework for the meanings attached to the message by both the communicator and the recipient (59).

UPWARD INFORMATION DISTORTION. The hierarchy devised partly as a means of facilitating communications often does the opposite. Information moving upward in the organization is often purged of real problems. People tend to report successes and hide failures. The reasons are obvious, but the obviousness of the phenomenon does not diminish its importance. The threat inherent in the hierarchy of authority causes subordinates to shield their superiors from bad news, and to distort discrediting information. Consequently, means need to be devised to reduce the distortion and encourage accurate feedback.

Feedback

Feedback seems to be an essential form of communication (50, 51, 58). People want to know whether they have communicated well, but even more, they *need* to know. Ample data show the importance of feedback for work effectiveness (56). If communication is task directed, feedback tells the communicator that the task will be performed according to instruction and standard. If the feedback indicates that things are not going according to the intent of the communications, corrections can be made.

Feedback is a clarification process in its own right (50). Without timely feedback, the communicator has no real idea of how his or her messages are being received. In the Ford illustration, management thought it was getting accurate feedback through the union leadership but was not listening to the workers.

In our opening vignette, the problem was to convey the impression that The Company had to meet increasingly stiff competition without violating any of its values, and without in any way implying criticism of past efforts. What were those values? First was that the company regarded all of its employees as part of a family. Another was the idea of elitism, based on the self-concept of effectively meeting competitive challenges through tough-minded application of intelligence and cooperative efforts. Thus, words such as "education," "joint effort," "family," "we," and "still higher levels of productivity" are sprinkled through the memo. Notice, too, the name of the program, "Procedures Improvement Program," and the new motto, "Work Smarter, Not Harder." All such words are loaded with the symbols that support The Company's belief system and nothing in the memo challenges its basic values. Indeed, the memo went through several dry runs such as the one depicted in the vignette and then numerous drafts until the right feeling emerged.

Finally notice who sent the memo and to whom it is addressed—the chairman of The Company and his management respectively. The chairman is assisted by Mason, the vice president of manufacturing. This structure does two things: it produces strong credibility and it does so through the management structure, adding strength to the message (75). It seems as though Ted and Penny had covered all the bases, but had they? We will see later that problems did emerge.

What is *our* message so far? It is simply this: communiqués will likely be interpreted, and often misinterpreted, by people subject to the frailties of human perception and according to their own motives and biases. The biases are a function of what people bring with them: history, tradition, social learning and the like, and the social context that provides guidelines for interpretations (14, 15, 29, 31, 46, 59). Organizational communicators, understanding those problems, try to counter them by constructing messages carefully and having them delivered by highly credible sources (17, 18, 48). The degree of success is due to several factors, but especially the extent to which the message is intended to change attitudes and through them, behavior.

Attitudes and Communication

Communications often are designed to create, support, or change attitudes—to influence the way employees view their working environment and thence the organization itself. The assumption here is that in some ways attitudes affect actions. As an example, if you believe that your organization is ethical, moral, and useful to society, authoritative requests may seem more justified and commitment to organizational goals more rational than if you believed otherwise. Consequently, you would be more likely to honor the requests and seek those goals. Such reasoning seems apt but is it correct?

Attitudes and Behavior

The answer to the question we have just posed is yes and no. Certainly, if we ask you, "Do you believe that the Republican candidate is more in tune with your thinking than the Democratic candidate?" we know that if you say "most assuredly yes" and if you take the trouble to vote, you are likely to vote for the Republican. On the other hand, if you believe that your boss is a fool, will you behave accordingly? If you have any sense at all, it is not likely. Therefore, we can see that attitudes are antecedents of actions only when there are no other important constraints on behavior.

Several review articles indicate that the correlation between attitudes and

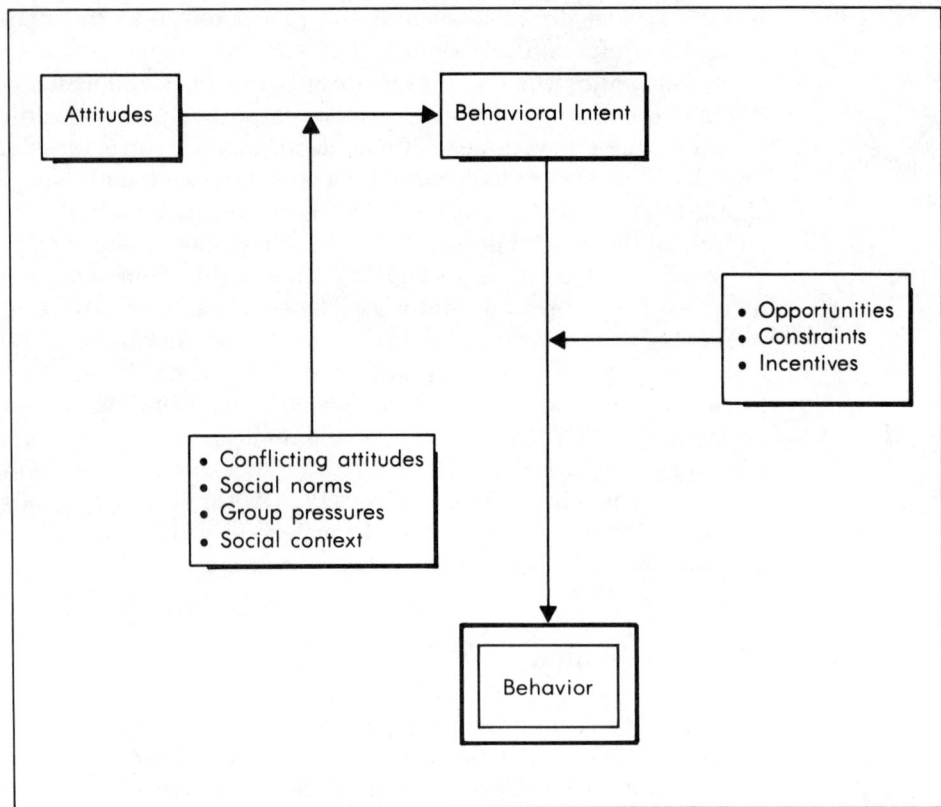

FIGURE 8.2 Modifiers of Attitudes as an Antecedent of Action

actions rarely is above 0.30 and usually is much lower (15, 20, 31). Consequently, simply identifying, measuring, and then changing attitudes may not be productive work. We know for example, that we can get experimental subjects to administer extreme shock to others with a bad heart, to plow through garbage and sort it into piles, and other equally nasty things even though their attitude toward those behaviors is negative (8). If the subjects had been asked whether those were good things to do most would have said no.

Furthermore, we have found that subjects often change their beliefs and attitudes after engaging in acts that they do not view as appropriate (7, 9, 11, 61). In other words, people seem to justify their actions after the fact, by changing their beliefs to correspond to those actions (15, 19). The actual behavior seems determined more by prevailing norms, roles, situational pressures, rewards, and reference groups than by beliefs or attitudes (1, 8, 15, 30, 31). What then is the role of attitudes as an antecedent of behavior?

Beliefs and attitudes seem to set the stage for action because they act as psychological screens on information about social events that occur within the organization. Attitudes provide a means of interpreting events. They filter, distort, and embellish perceptions and in this way set the stage for action, but then the actions themselves are normally triggered by other more pressing factors that encourage or restrain them (1, 8, 15, 21, 61). Hence, organizational members may view acts as immoral, unethical, or just plain wrong, but engage in them nevertheless because others do or because they are afraid not to. We conclude that attitudes are often important antecedents of actions even though there may not be a direct and immediate correspondence between the two. Figure 8.2 summarizes this discussion.

Attitude Change

There are several things under consideration when a communications program is designed to change attitudes. These are shown in Figure 8.3. The first is simply getting people to pay attention to the message. Indeed, much organizational communication, which is only peripherally related to employees' interests, is often ignored. Evidence tells us that people will attend to the information that is relevant to their interests but not to the information that is peripheral (17, 18, 26, 48).

The second major factor that contributes to attitude change is something we discussed earlier—confidence in the source, as depicted in box 1 of Figure 8.3 (17, 27, 33, 53). That is typically related to such factors as past experience with the source's credibility, the source's expertise in the subject matter (33), and the source's status—including rank or position in the organization (17, 24). It also seems to help if the source is likeable (33). In some instances, likeability is more powerful in changing an attitude than is technical competence.

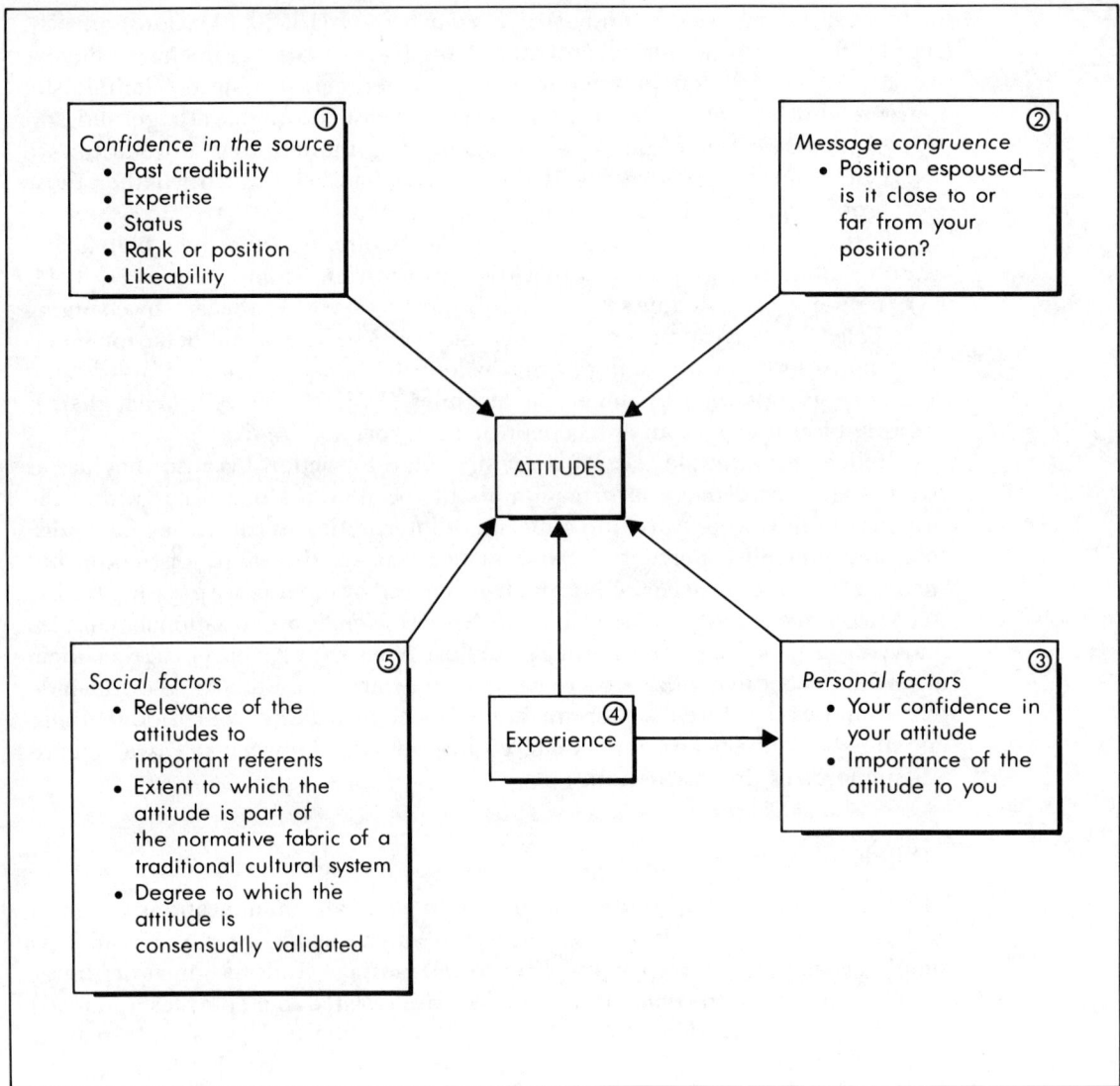

FIGURE 8.3 Factors Affecting Attitude Change

A third major factor is the message's congruence with the receivers' views (42, 53), as depicted in box 2 of Figure 8.3. Highly discrepant information may not be effective in changing attitudes because of what has been called the *contrast effect* (53, 61). That means that the messages considerably at odds with one's own position will be viewed as extreme, and therefore, not credible.

Research has shown that when the message is substantially discrepant from the receiver's attitudes the source is ridiculed and hence loses all credibility (31, 53, 61). On the other hand, positions close to one's own will benefit by the so-called *assimilative effect* (53). That is, when you see many similarities to your own position in a communiqué, you will see it as credible, even if there is some discrepancy.

A fourth factor—depicted in box 3—is the confidence you have in your own views (27). Associated with this idea is your strength of feeling about your views. Some attitudes are simply unimportant in your overall scheme of things; when you are given credible sources and sound arguments, you are likely to change such attitudes. On the other hand, some attitudes may be central to your concept of life and these have proven very resistent to change (6, 53).

Several other ideas seem relevant to confidence. For one thing, how does one gain confidence in one's own attitudes? Experience seems to be a major factor here (8). It is hard to change perceptions of what you have experienced as reality, particularly if that experience is repeated. Another factor is *consensual validation* (8, 21, 24, 53, 61). If many others share your attitudes, this gives validity to that attitude and you are likely to reject discrepant communications. Furthermore, if those others are important and credible referents—your friends, family, and respected teachers for example—you will probably reject discrepant information regardless of its merits (53). The others who help to consensually validate your attitudes or beliefs are part of the social context which we discussed earlier and which is depicted in box 5 of Figure 8.3. An example of some research on attitude change is presented in Box 8 on page 194.

Finally, many attitudes are normative, part of the fabric of our social network. Those attitudes are strong and resist change. An example is the attitudes toward women as career professionals. Although women perform similarly to men they often are not treated similarly with respect to salary and promotions (36, 55). That is because, until just recently, women were allocated certain roles in our society—mother, wife, teacher, and so forth. The allocation was justified by social attitudes, together with the view of women as naturally more supportive, more nurturing, less aggressive, and less decisive. Such attitudes are so fundamentally a part of our thinking that despite overwhelming contradictory evidence, many still feel that women are not suited for important managerial positions. For example, one study disclosed that early job assignment to challenging work was predicated on the expectations of later success in the organization. Despite evidence that they could handle the job challenge as well as men, women were systematically excluded from those challenging jobs because they were not expected to succeed later on (55). These attitudes will not change easily.

To summarize, attitudes are relevant to behavior and they can be changed, although not easily. The major factors that limit attitude change are depicted in Figure 8.3. They are contained in the source, the social fabric, the message, and the receiver. The effect of the receiver's experience is demonstrated in

Box 8

Confidence in Your Belief

The researcher interested in developing a theory of belief change was concerned with the relative strengths of three variables thought to produce change. They were: (1) the discrepancy between one's own position and the position of the communication's source, (2) the confidence of the target population in their own belief, and (3) the confidence of the target population in the source of the message.

The subjects were 270 women college students. Each subject was tested at a microcomputer and told that the study concerned aviation safety and job performance of an air traffic controller. Further, she was told the specific research questions were whether a controller could make better judgments working alone or in cooperation with a co-worker, and how each team member would use the information supplied by her partner. Each subject was asked to perform and then was given false feedback indicating high, moderate, or low performance. This was designed to manipulate the subject's confidence in her own beliefs.

Each subject was then told that her partner had high, medium, or low performance. This was designed to manipulate the subject's confidence in the source of the message. Subjects were then shown the judgment of their partner. This judgment might be close to, fairly far from, or very far from the subject's judgment and represented the discrepant manipulation. Hence, there were measures of high, moderate, or low on the three independent variables: (1) confidence in one's own belief, (2) confidence in the partner's judgment (the source of the message), and (3) the discrepancy between one's own estimate and the judgment made by one's partner. The subjects were then asked to repeat their judgments. The extent to which their judgments changed was the measure of their change in belief.

All three variables produced significant belief change and each tended to amplify the other. Subjects who had low self-confidence, high confidence in the source, and a large discrepancy between the positions changed their beliefs the most. However, whenever a subject's confidence exceeded her confidence in the source, she changed very little, regardless of the discrepancy between positions. The experimenter concluded that if someone has greater confidence in herself than in the source she will not change regardless of discrepancy, but if her confidence in the source is greater, then change will be directly related to the size of the discrepancy. According to these results, the relative degrees of confidence in one's self and in a message source, is a major, indeed *overriding* variable when belief change is at issue.

"Toward Theories of Persuasion and Belief Change," James Jaccard, *Journal of Personality and Social Psychology* 40 (1981): 260–269.

. . . Not Harder?

Yes, Ted was uneasy. Stanley was getting to know Ted pretty well, and it was evident that Ted felt things were not going well at all. You see, Ted was out of his element here at the plant, dealing with a bunch of production department supervisors. He was much more at home with his fellow corporate staff people who dealt with words, not with realities. And in particular, there was this person who kept muttering, "Bull," every time Ted made one of his very best points.

"How can these people not want PIP?" Ted was thinking. Why, Mr. Marsh himself has given it his top priority. It's been thought through carefully by our very top corporate people. And everyone here has received that dynamite communications package that sets out the whole agenda of the program in great detail. So why isn't it absolutely clear to everyone just what a first-rate program this is? How in the world can there be a problem?

But a problem there was.

Now the one who had been muttering to himself finally spoke up. "What you're telling us, then, Mr. Shelby, is that *we're* supposed to go down on the floor now, and explain to our guys that they ain't been doin' the job all these years. And that we're . . . no, your industrial engineers are gonna finally show 'em how to do it right. And me, and these other foremen here, are gonna explain that when they finally *do* learn how to do their jobs right, that they're gonna be able to make a lot more pieces, only now it's gonna be even easier?"

As his questioner paused for effect, Ted almost thought he heard someone say, "Bull." Then the questioner continued, "So I'm gonna 'explain' to this guy who's been working his machine for thirty years now that he don't know how to do it right, that my asking him to up his production ten pieces an hour ain't really asking him to (how'd you say it) work harder—just to work smarter!" Again the pause.

"Bull!"

Now Ted definitely was on the defensive, "What you seem to be saying then, Mr. ah—"

"Mr. Szekely."

"What you apparently are saying then, Mr. Szekely, is that we've got a communications problem here, aren't you?" Ted began hopefully.

Szekely paused for a moment trying to find words to express what he felt . . . no, what he *knew* to be true. "I guess that depends on what you mean by a communications problem, Mr. Shelby. If it means that my men aren't going to agree with what you've been saying, then, you're right, there's a communications problem. And if it means that I don't buy what you're selling, then you're right again. We've got a communications problem. But if you mean that we don't understand what you're saying, believe me, there's no communications problem at all! Fact is, I think we understand what you are saying better than you do."

Ted was about to say something in defense of his "facts package" but Szekely had more to say. Now, however, his tone was different. And though apparently he still was addressing Ted, he was looking directly at Martin, the plant manager. "No, I don't like it, Mr. Shelby. But don't misunderstand me. I'm thirty some years with The Company now, and it's been a damn good thirty years. If this is what The Company wants, then Jimmy Szekely is going to do it the very best he can. Still, I have to say, I wonder. I wonder if you really know what you are saying to these guys, the message you are giving them when you say they've got to work *smarter*."

Communications Programs and Their Problems

Szekely understood well what corporate types like Ted do not. People know their own experiences better than anyone else. Trying to tell them that one thing is true when they know another thing is, is futile and dangerous. And telling them that strangers—even experts—can help them do their work "smarter" is condescending and insulting. They will not believe you, they will not like you, and they will feel demeaned because of your obvious disregard for their competence. Such feelings are hardly useful. What should have been done?

Building a Communications Program

There are many commonplace statements that we can make here: "build the source's credibility," "make sure the messages are clear," and so forth. However, these are obvious and not helpful.

Let us go back to our basic communications model. The primary source for communications in any organization should be the line management, and the primary objectives of a communications program should include, at the very least: (1) allowing employees to form impressions about the organization that may positively affect their attitudes, motivations, and productivity; (2) allowing them to influence the organization by communicating problems and concerns upward (2, 28), and (3) focusing on work- and career-related issues with the idea of solving problems or disclosing information of organizational relevance (48, 50, 51). Performance evaluations are an example. To meet those conditions the unit supervisor must be a key link in the process and the free flow of relevant information must be an organizational value and norm (45). How can this be done? It is not easy; and simple exhortations to communicate clearly, honestly, and directly will not help much. We must look to the organizational structure and process to find some solutions.

SOME STRUCTURAL ADAPTATIONS TO COMMUNICATIONS PROBLEMS. Formal structures may be devised to protect against misperceptions and distorted feedback while allowing free-flowing job-relevant information.

The first mechanism is the feedback and control system.* Such systems incorporate data about work standards and how well the standards are being met (4, 12, 38, 56). When there is no direct measure of performance, formalized procedures may be substituted; conformity to such procedures is then recorded and fed back to a central office. These measures serve as a basis for regulation

---

* We deal with the feedback and control system in greater detail in Part IV, pp. 439 ff.

and are used to get feedback on operations. The process is depicted in Figure 8.4. However, the depicted process is not so straightforward as it might seem. When the process is used to measure performance and allocate rewards and punishments, people respond defensively and learn how to beat the system (12, 56). Consequently, participants need to be involved in developing both the standards and the measures, and they also should be the first recipients of the feedback. Self-regulation is the key here. In this way, because the participants have a stake in the information process under nonthreatening conditions, they are more likely to give valid information (28, 50).

A second avenue is to create special staff units whose mission is to seek out information and then provide it to the line for further dispensation. Usually, the departments report well up in the organizational hierarchy and are independent of the normal line hierarchy. This helps to ensure that the information will not be corrupted by special interests (54). Long-range planning departments scan the environment, identify social, economic, and technical trends, and analyze the data that help set the direction of the organization. Communications depart-

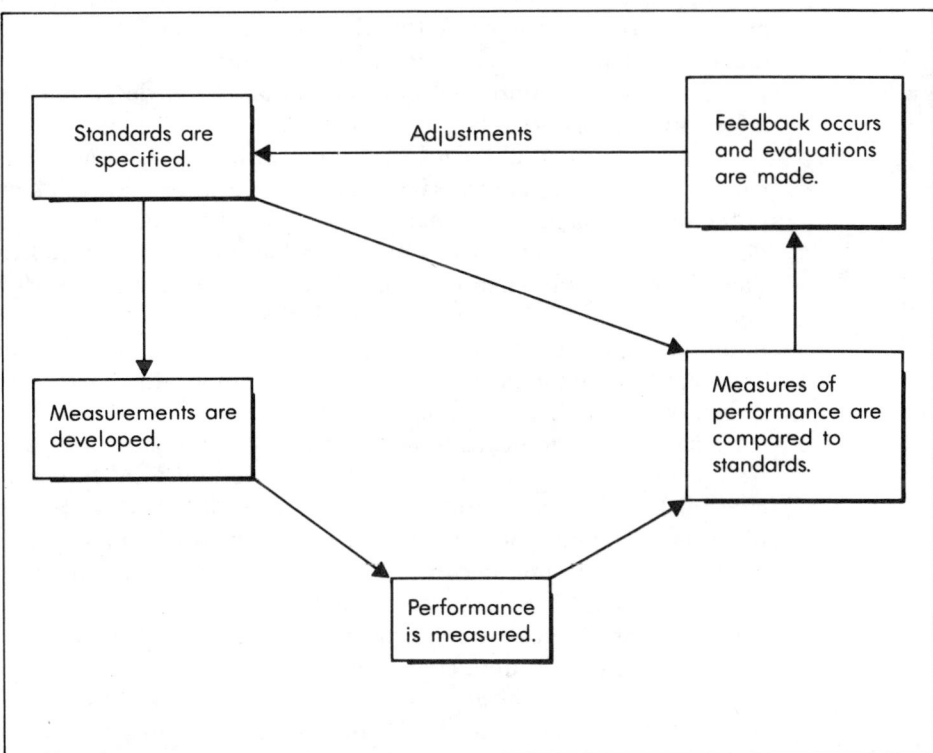

FIGURE 8.4 Feedback Process for Control

ments seek information that might be of interest to organizational participants and then devise means of getting it across. Such departments often manage the information process by deciding who should get what information and in what form and then develop a means of executing the decisions. However, ultimately, it is line management that bears the responsibility of communicating (12, 23, 56).

We worked in such a department when we were employed by The Company. The department was called *Basic Personnel Research* and one of its responsibilities was to gather information about employee work attitudes and motivation. We reported to a director in the corporate headquarters personnel function who was responsible for initiating all personnel programs. Our data came primarily from within the company; we devised means of getting information periodically from each employee in the organization. Some of these means were attitude surveys, extensive interviewing, and examining the company records. Our outside sources included the professional literature and experts in job attitudes and worker motivation. We gathered and analyzed these data frequently, summarized them and then fed them back to the line management for action. A major feature of the process was that once we fed the data back to top management our major role was to ensure that the data were then fed back to each organizational unit *through* line management. Through this process the organization was able to gather unbiased information and then devise means of using the information appropriately.

Another structural means of dealing with the communications problem includes establishing several channels that are independent of each other and of the normal chain of command (45). When the information from one channel does not square with that from another, additional checks are indicated. Although the use of multiple channels contributes to information overload, it seems a good management practice to have such channels. Examples are regular communications meetings with employees, suggestion systems, and an open door policy. The regular communications department should also have some people who search out additional information channels.

Finally, a major means of opening up the information flow is to institutionalize certain management practices that are designed solely for information exchange. In this case, communicating is considered to be part of the normal management work, and the adequacy with which information is communicated up and down the line becomes a facet of the normal management evaluation procedure (38, 39, 48). As an example, building on the previously discussed basic personnel research departments' efforts, one aspect of the total program was the feedback of intended actions by management personnel to their superiors. Data from attitude surveys were collected from all employees analyzed and then fed back to each manager in the company. Because the intent of the survey was to disclose problems and then deal with those problems effectively, each management person responsible for any given department was to devise corrective plans of action. These plans, along with objectives and time tables, were then sent to their superiors, and so on up the hierarchy.

Note that each of the means just discussed is designed to avoid channel congestion and to legitimize information exchange as part of the organizational normative structure. To make such activities effective and regular requires continual reiteration and support from the total management system. It is difficult management work.

Summary

We have chosen to deal with communications in a nontraditional way by discussing its uses and the problems associated with communicating. Our focus was on interpretations that develop in organizations—why they develop as they do, and how they often differ from the intent of the communicators.

We began our analysis by presenting a very traditional model of the communicating process. The elements of the process include: the source, the message, the receiver, the social context, and the feedback loop. Each element is a source of problems for understanding and interpreting communiqués.

We noted that many communiqués are designed to support the bureaucratic tenet of rationality and the organizationally desirable norm of effectiveness. Messages of this sort are couched in the grammar of purposiveness and success, particularly when they are used to justify decisions or personnel actions. As a consequence symbols designating rationality and effectiveness are often invoked to convey impressions. "Performance Improvement Program" and "Work Smarter, not Harder" are examples.

We dealt with the problems of misinterpretation and disbelief. We suggested that they come mainly from the individual—his or her background, attitudes, and experiences—and the social context—how others feel, what they believe, and what is historically normative. Further, we suggested that the focus of many communication programs was to change attitudes with the hope of changing behavior. But because attitudes and behaviors are not always tightly coupled, the intent of those programs may not be realized. Finally, we suggested that attitudes are difficult to change for reasons similar to those presenting problems for the acceptance of messages, namely, lack of source credibility, the social context, and personal experience.

We ended by describing structural facilitators of the communicating process. Apart from the usual bromides exhorting clarity, sensitivity, and listening, we suggested that there are structural means of easing the process. An important one is to build a norm of effective communicating by making it part of the usual management task and the evaluation system.

References

1. AJZEN, I., and M. FISHBEIN. "The Prediction of Behavior from Attitudinal and Normative Variables." *Journal of Experimental Social Psychology* 6 (1970): 466–487.
2. ALDERFER, CLAYTON P. "Improving Organizational Communication through Long-Term Intergroup Intervention." *Journal of Applied Behavioral Science* 13, 2 (April–June 1977): 193–210.
3. ALKER, H. A. "Is Personality Situationally Specific or Intrapsychically Consistent?" *Journal of Personality* 40 (1972): 1–16.
4. ANSARI, S. L. "Behavioral Factors in Variance Control: Report on a Laboratory Experiment." *Journal of Accounting Research* 14 (1976): 189–211.
5. BEEHER, TERRY A., and D. C. GILMORE. "Applicant Attractiveness as a Perceived Job-Relevant Variable in Selection of Management Trainees." *Academy of Management Journal* 25, 3 (1982): 607–617.
6. BEM, D. J. "Self-Perception Theory." In *Advances in Experimental Social Psychology*, Vol. 6. Edited by L. Berkowitz. New York: Academic Press, 1972.
7. BEM, D. J., and A. ALLEN. "On Predicting Some of the People Some of the Time: The Search for Cross-Situational Consistencies in Behavior." *Psychological Review* 81 (1974): 506–520.
8. BRANNON, ROBERT. "Attitudes and the Prediction of Behavior." In *Social Psychology: An Introduction*. Edited by Bernard Seidenberg and Alvin Snadowsky. New York: The Free Press, 1976, pp. 145–198.
9. BRANNON, R., G. CYPHERS, S. HESSE, S. HESSELBART, R. KEANE, H. SCHEIMAN, T. VICARRO, and D. WRIGHT. "Attitude and Action: A Field Experiment Joined to a General Population Survey." *American Sociological Review* 38 (1973): 625–636.
10. BREHM, J. W. *A Theory of Psychological Reactance*. New York: Academic Press, 1966.
11. ———. *Responses to Loss of Freedom: A Theory of Psychological Reactance*. Morristown, N.J.: General Learning Press, 1972.
12. CAMMANN, C., and D. A. NADLER. "Fit Control System to Your Management Style." *Harvard Business Review* 54, 1 (1976): 65–72.
13. CAMPBELL, A., P. E. CONVERSE, W. E. MILLER, and D. E. STOKES. *The American Voter: An Abridgement*. New York: Wiley, 1964.
14. CHAIKEN, S. "Heuristic vs. Systematic Information Processing and the Use of Source vs. Message Cues in Persuasion." *Journal of Personality and Social Psychology* 39, 5 (November 1980): 752–766.
15. CIALDINI, ROBERT B., RICHARD E. PETTY, and JOHN T. CACIOPPO. "Attitude and Attitude Change." *Annual Review of Psychology* 32 (1981): 357–404.
16. DANDRIDGE, THOMAS C., IAN MITROFF, and WILLIAM F. JOYCE. "Organizational Symbolism: A Topic to Expand Organizational Analysis," *Academy of Management Review* 5, 1 (1980): 77–82.
17. D'APRIX, ROGER. "The Oldest and Best Way to Communicate with Employees." *Harvard Business Review* 60 (September–October, 1982): 30–32.
18. FAHS, MICHAEL L. "Communication Strategies for Anticipating and Managing Con-

flict. Developing a System of Positive Interaction." *Personnel Administrator* 27 (October 1982): 28–34.

19. FESTINGER, L. *A Theory of Cognitive Dissonance.* Stanford, Calif.: Stanford University Press, 1957.

20. FISHBEIN, M. "The Relationships Between Beliefs, Attitudes, and Behavior." In *Cognitive Consistency.* Edited by S. Feldman. New York: Academic Press, 1966.

21. FISHBEIN, M., and I. AJZEN. *Belief, Attitude, Intention, and Behavior.* Reading, Mass.: Addison-Wesley, 1975.

22. GREENBAUM, H. H. "The Audit of Organizational Communication." *Academy of Management Journal* 17 (1974): 739–754.

23. GRIFFIN, RICKY W. "Supervisory Behavior as a Source of Perceived Task Scope." *Journal of Occupational Psychology* 54 (1981): 175–182.

24. HARKINS, STEPHEN G., and RICHARD E. PETTY. "Effects of Source Magnification of Cognitive Effort on Attitudes: An Information-Processing View." *Journal of Personality and Social Psychology* 40, 3 (March 1981): 401–413.

25. HOM, PETER W., and CHARLES L. HULIN. "A Competitive Test of the Prediction of Reenlistment by Several Models." *Journal of Applied Psychology* 66, 1 (1981): 23–29.

26. IRELAND, R. DUANE, PHILIP VAN AWKEN, and PHILLIP LEWIS. "Investigation of the Relationship Between Organization Climate and Communication and Communication Climate." *Journal of Business Communication* 16 (Fall 1978): 3–10.

27. JACCARD, JAMES. "Toward Theories of Persuasion and Belief Change." *Journal of Personality and Social Psychology* 40, 2 (1981): 260–269.

28. JACKSON, SUSAN E. "Participation in Decision-Making as a Strategy for Reducing Job Related Strain." *Journal of Applied Psychology* 68 (1983): 3–19.

29. KIESLER, C. A. *The Psychology of Commitment: Experiments Linking Behavior to Belief.* New York: Academic Press, 1971.

30. KIESLER, C. A., B. E. COLLINS, and N. MILLER. *Attitude Change: A Critical Analysis of Theoretical Approaches.* New York: Wiley, 1969.

31. KIESLER, C. A., and P. A. MIRSON. "Attitudes and Opinions." In *Annual Review of Psychology,* Vol. 26. Edited by M. R. Rosenzweig and L. W. Porter. Palo Alto, Calif.: Annual Reviews, Inc., 1975. Pp. 415–456.

32. LALEIMIA, JAMES, and THOMAS BAGLAN. "Choice of Strategies for Attitude Change: An Exploratory Analysis." *Psychological Reports* 48 (June 1981): 793–794.

33. MCGINNIES, ELLIOT, and CHARLES D. WARD. "Better Liked than Right: Trustworthiness and Expertise as Factors in Credibility." *Personality and Social Psychology Bulletin* 6 (September 1980): 467–472.

34. MILLER, DANNY, and PETER H. FRIESEN. "Structural Change and Performance: Quantum versus Piecemeal-Incremental Approaches." *Academy of Management Journal* 25 (1982): 867–892.

35. MITCHELL, TERENCE R., and LAURA S. KALB. "Effects of Outcome Knowledge and Outcome Valence on Supervisors' Evaluations." *Journal of Applied Psychology* 66 (October 1981): 604–612.

36. MOBLEY, WILLIAM H. "Supervisor and Employee Race and Sex Effects on Perfor-

mance Appraisals: A Field Study of Adverse Impact and Generalizability." *Academy of Management Journal* 25 (1982): 598–606.

37. MUCHINSKY, PAUL M. "Organizational Communication: Relationships to Organizational Climate and Job Satisfaction." *Academy of Management Journal* 20 (December 1977): 592–607.

38. NADLER, DAVID A., C. CAMMANN, and P. N. MIRVIS. "Developing Feedback Systems for Work Units: A Field Experiment in Structural Change." *Journal of Applied Behavioral Science* 16 (1980): 41–62.

39. O'REILLY, CHARLES A. III. "Variations in Decision Makers' Use of Information Sources: The Impact of Quality and Accessibility of Information." *Academy of Management Journal* 25 (1982): 756–771.

40. O'REILLY, C. A., and D. F. CALDWELL. "Informational Influence as a Determinant of Perceived Task Characteristics and Job Satisfaction." *Journal of Applied Psychology* 64 (1979): 157–165.

41. ORGAN, DENNIS W., and CHARLES N. GREENE. "The Effects of Formalization on Professional Involvement: A Compensatory Process Approach." *Administrative Science Quarterly* 26 (June 1981): 237–252.

42. OSGOOD, C. E., and P. H. TANNENBAUM. "The Principle of Congruity in the Prediction of Attitude Change." *Psychological Review* 62 (1955): 42–55.

43. PETTY, RICHARD E., JOHN T. CACIOPPO, and RACHEL GOLDMAN. "Personal Involvement as a Determinant of Argument-Based Persuasion." *Journal of Personality and Social Psychology* 41 (November 1981): 847–855.

44. PLAX, TIMOTHY G., and LAWRENCE B. ROSENFELD. "Individual differences in the Credibility and Attitude Change Relationships." *Journal of Social Psychology* 111 (June 1980): 79–89.

45. PORTER, LYMAN W., and KARLENE H. ROBERTS. "Communication in Organizations." In *Handbook of Industrial and Organizational Psychology*. Edited by Marvin D. Dunnette. Chicago, Ill: Rand McNally, 1976.

46. RITTI, R. RICHARD. "The Social Bases of Organizational Knowledge." Working paper, The Pennsylvania State University, 1982.

47. ROBERTS, K. H., C. A. O'REILLY, III, G. E. BRETTON, and L. W. PORTER. "Organizational Communication: A Communication Failure?" *Human Relations* 27 (1974): 501–524.

48. ST. JOHN, WALTER. "In-House Communication Guidelines." *Personnel Journal* 60 (November 1981): 872–878.

49. SALANCIK, G., and PFEFFER, J. "A Social Information Processing Approach to Job Attitudes and Task Design." *Administrative Science Quarterly* 23 (1978): 224–253.

50. SCHULER, RANDALL S. "A Role Perception Transactional Process Model for Organizational Communication-Outcome Relationships." *Organizational Behavior and Human Performances* 23, 2 (April 1979): 268–291.

51. ———. "Communicating with Employees for Productivity and Quality of Work Life Improvements." Working paper, 1980.

52. SCHWARTZ, NORBERT, DIETER FREY, and MARTIN KUMPF. "Interactive Effects of Writ-

ing and Reading a Persuasive Essay on Attitude Change and Selective Exposure." *Journal of Experimental Social Psychology* 16, 1 (January 1980): 1–17.
53. SHERIF, M., and C. HOVLAND. *Social Judgement.* New Haven, Conn: Yale University Press, 1961.
54. SIMONSON, MICHAEL R. "Media and Attitudes: A Bibliography: II. *Educational Communication and Technology* 28, 1 (Spring 1980): 47–61.
55. STEWART, LEA P., and WILLIAM B. GUDYKUNST. "Differential Factors Influencing the Hierarchical Level and Number of Promotions of Males and Females within an Organization." *Academy of Management Journal* 25 (1982): 586–597.
56. TODD, J. "Management Control Systems: A Key Link Between Strategy, Structure, and Employee Performance." *Organizations Dynamics* 5 (1977): 65–78.
57. TUSHMAN, MICHAEL L., and THOMAS J. SCANLON. "Boundary Spanning Individuals: Their Role in Information Transfer and Their Antecedents." *Academy of Management Journal* 24 (June 1981): 289–305.
58. VAN SELL, N., A. R. BRIEF, and R. S. SCHULER. "Role Conflict and Role Ambiguity: Integration of the Literature and Directions for Future Research." *Human Relations* 34 (1981): 43–72.
59. WEICK, KARL E. *The Social Psychology of Organizing,* 2nd ed. Reading, Mass: Addison-Wesley, 1979.
60. WEISS, HOWARD M., and CHRISTINE E. NOWICKI. "Social Influences on Task Satisfaction: Model Competence and Observer Field Dependence." *Organizational Behavior and Human Performance* 27 (June 1981): 345–366.
61. WRIGHTSMAN, LAWRENCE S. *Social Psychology,* 2nd ed. Monterey, Calif.: Brooks/Cole, 1977.

Discussion Questions

1. What are the elements of the communications process? How is each a source of error?
2. In what ways are symbols used in organizations? Why are they used in the ways that they are? What function do metaphors perform?
3. Explain how the Ford Company illustration incorporated the concepts of leveling, sharpening, and condensation. What could Ford have done to "get its message across"?
4. Are attitudes antecedents of behavior? In what ways? How are they not? Explain.
5. What are the main factors that encourage or impede attitude change?
6. How would you have built a "communication package" to help sell PIP? What errors did Ted make? Why do you feel that way?
7. "Much of downward communications is intended to support the bureaucratic facet called 'rationality'." Explain that statement.

PART III
The Process of Goal Attainment

Section One
Meeting Personal Goals: The Motivation System

Chapter 9
Motivation in Organizations: The Process of Directed Behavior

Who Could Have Known?

"You can bet that if *I* had my hands on a million dollars, *I* wouldn't be wondering what to do with it." The voice was that of Pat Jones, responding to a news story coming over the car radio. It was one of those "human interest" stories about a twenty-six-year-old millionaire who had given his fortune to an animal hospital and gone off somewhere to seek "inner truth." The remark was directed at Kerry Drake, listening while Pat did the driving. Their destination, several hours hence, was a Company retreat devoted to "Modern Middle Management—Problems and Prospects."

"So you think that you'd know how to handle it, do you? Maybe so. But it's not all that easy. You know, I was a millionaire once—on paper at least." Kerry's matter-of-fact statement came as a complete surprise to Pat.

"You?"

"Sure, back during the last housing boom. Remember? Everything looked great. The Feds were putting a lot of dollars into low rent housing and we had this idea to really cut costs and build volume. We'd build housing units in the factory and simply assemble them on site."

With that, Pat cut in, "But that's an old idea, isn't it? Prefabricated housing."

"Oh, no! Yes, I know what you mean. But this was *prebuilt*. All that was left to do in the field was to assemble the major housing modules. No, this was the ultimate in prebuilt housing. And I still think it was a good idea. But there *were* problems."

"And you say you made a million from this business?"

"No, I said I became a millionaire on *paper*. And that's a big difference. We've got nothing better to do—let me tell you the story.

"Most people don't know that I left The Company some years ago and went into business with a friend of mine who was a builder with this great idea. He was the technical man, and I was going to handle the management. I also put every last dime I had into it.

"We got things going pretty well. We found solid financing, leased a plant, and built some prototypes. Everything seemed to be going fine. All the while, our stock was going up. Now the first real job we had went up pretty well. But, for some reason, we lost money. Later, I found out that the modules weren't going together in the field as well as expected and that a lot of extra work was required. But my partner, the builder, didn't tell me that. He really believed that his method couldn't miss. So all he told me was not to worry; we were having the usual problems shaking the thing down. I think he really believed it, too.

"Well, now, our next big job lost money, too. I guess you know me well enough to understand I wasn't going to put up with that. So I decided it was time for management to provide some extra motivation. So, I called these birds together and laid it on the line. I still remember the scene. I said, 'Listen carefully, because I'm not going to tell any of you again. The next man, the *next* man, who reports a loss from the field doesn't have to bother coming back for his paycheck, because it's his last. We'll mail it to him. I don't want to know anything. Produce or else!'"

"And you know, that seemed to work pretty well. Things started looking a lot better from that point. At least for a while."

At that point, Pat, who had been listening quietly, couldn't contain herself. "But you know what people do under circumstances like that, don't you? Why, it's basic psychology."

"Sure, I know. They just stop telling you. And that's what my people did." And then with a wry smile, "There I was, out there whipping on the sales staff and losing 15 percent on every job." Kerry was shaking his head.

"Then why . . . ?"

Kerry didn't answer Pat's half-formed question. For really, there was no answer. How *could* he have known? Everything seemed to be going fine until the hidden (displaced, if you will) expenses started showing up. And by that time, it was too late. That, together with some unfortunate changes in the money market, brought Kerry's dream to a quick end—and rendered some $2 million on paper worthless.

Pat Jones would analyze the situation by saying that Kerry had tried to bring about productive behavior by severe punishment. But punishment for what? For *reporting* losses. And so it was the reporting behavior that was affected. The threat of severe punishment effectively suppressed negative reports and rendered the feedback system invalid. Kerry had *hoped* for increased effectiveness and *got* feedback that made the reporters look good or at least not bad. Nothing changed except the nature of the information that people chose to disclose.

Why do people behave as they do in organizations? Those of you with organizational experience know that behavior is not wholly predictable. And it is almost impossible to construct a motivation system that will enable managers to get the behavior they want all the time from the majority of the people they supervise. Let us briefly summarize the reasons for this.

First, motivation is extremely complex. Thus, people respond to a variety of stimuli and cues according to a variety of motives. And, of course, it is the way they see things that really counts. Consequently, behavior depends as much on individual factors, hidden from objective observers, as it does on structural and social factors that are part of the environment (6, 14, 80, 96).

Second, the decision to act is often based on some calculation of marginal utility to the actor, and not everyone's calculation is the same (22). Where one person sees conformity to group norms as being more valuable than the increased wages from increased production, another may not.

Third, some behavior is unquestionably emotional, and we have few means of predicting specific emotions and, hence, the response (10).

Much could be said about individual differences in organizations, particularly as these pertain to performance (61, 62, 65, 90). However, it is not our intent to dwell extensively on this subject. Our focus is on organizational factors designed to create regularities in behavior—that is, in collective behavior. Thus we will focus also on general factors. We will look at motivational features that individuals share, rather than at those which create differences. We hope in this way to get you to understand better the development of motivation systems that are generally useful for organizational purposes.

Several misconceptions about motivation are held by both practicing managers and students of organizations. Among the most prominent of these is that people should be motivated to reach organizationally defined work goals. If they are not, then they are not motivated. Our view is different. People, assessing their work situation in personal terms, rarely try to reach work goals unless those goals have personal value. It is the incentive attached to the work goals that people go after. That is, people seek work goals because of their personal goals: money, advancement, recognition, a sense of accomplishment, avoiding punishments, and so forth. Work goals are often other people's goals; it is management's job to attach meaningful incentives to them. Without such incentives, people may not be motivated to reach work goals, even though they may be motivated to do something else.

We assume then that actions in organizations are motivated. Further, we assume that people usually respond to organizational cues consistent with their own goals and with the incentive properties of these goals.

Many antecedents of behavior can be described in organizational terms. For example, people generally respond to what they perceive as a legitimate request from an authoritative figure. Further, they respond to what they perceive as valued incentives within the organizations. Specifically, people tend to sort out organizational rewards such as pay, advancement, or recognition, and they assess how their behavior can gain these payoffs.

We assume, too, that a variety of desired organizational outcomes result from people's actions. For example, management may wish to attract and keep people in the organization only while they perform satisfactorily. Or it may wish to have people internalize the organizational goals and perform beyond the prescribed standards. Management may wish to have people conform to organizational procedures and role prescriptions, or it may wish to have them behave creatively and innovatively, going beyond such procedures and prescriptions (32). Each of these desires suggests different strategies for designing motivation systems and, as we will see, behavior is usually a consequence of such systems, though it may not be a consequence of the intent behind the system.

Finally, we assume that people generally respond as we have stated, given the variety of needs, goals, and expectations they bring to the organization. If, on the average, they do not behave according to the intent of the organizational motivation system, then managers must look to that system and determine its malfunctions.

Definitions of Key Terms

Reinforcement and Punishment

Let us distinguish between rewards and punishments. Rewards are simply things that have positive personal value. Punishments are things that are painful, physically or psychologically. People seek rewards and try to avoid punishment. Getting a reward for a given behavior is receiving *positive reinforcement* for that behavior and avoiding punishment by behaving in the "right" way is receiving *negative reinforcement* for that behavior. However each reinforcement is a kind of reward—getting something good or losing something bad. And so reinforcing is the administration of rewards on behavior.

It is also important to distinguish between the consequences of punishment and negative reinforcement. Since negative reinforcement is the removal of something negative, it should be contingent on the performance of appropriate behavior. For example, report writing is inherently distasteful to most of us, and few organizations routinely reward reports. Reports are written, therefore, to escape the consequences of not writing them (84, 97). One can feel good about that.

Punishment is the occurrence of something negative as a consequence of behavior, as a method of inducing goal-directed behavior. There are two kinds of punishment: something distasteful that is given as a consequence of undesired behavior, or something tasteful that is taken away. Thus, it is quite different from negative reinforcement. With punishment, an inappropriate response is punished, but the correct response is not indicated. Consequently, we do not know if a correct response will follow. The only thing we do know is that punishment will have a direct bearing on the probability of the punished response's occurring again (10).

There is another problem with punishment, however. We assume that most activities are motivated and not random. But punished responses are motivated before the punishment occurs. Therefore, unlike the desire to engage in appropriate behavior as a consequence of negative reinforcement, no motive is associated with the correct response under punishment—only motives to avoid the punishment (81). Hence, it is likely that, in the absence of the punishing agent, the punished response will recur (97). Or, more significantly, one of a set of mixed behaviors is likely to occur (16). For example, a worker who wants to punch a foreman is motivated at least by hostility toward that foreman. Knowing that such an act would result in dismissal (punishment), however, the worker refrains. But there are other aggressive behaviors. So the subordinate may make life miserable for the superior without engaging in a direct and punishable act of aggression. Such things happen all the time (2).

The main distinction between punishment and negative reinforcement, then, is that negative reinforcement is the removal of something negative when the appropriate behavior occurs, whereas punishment is the application of something

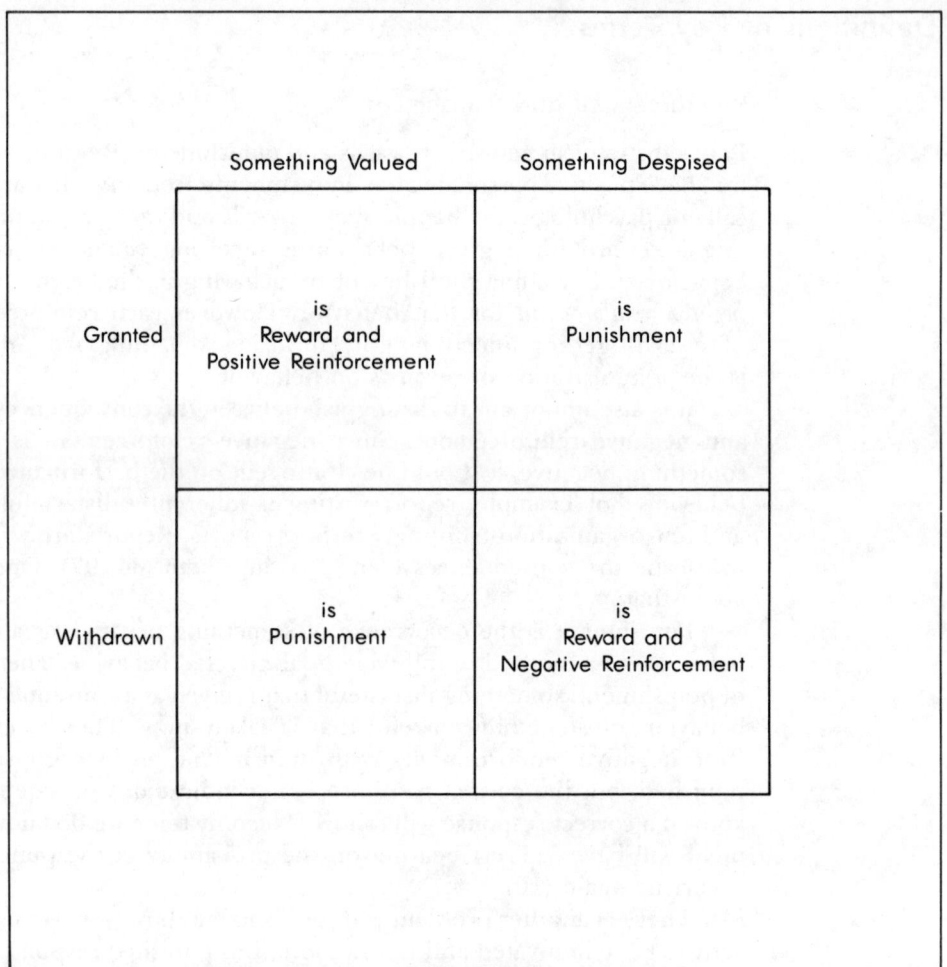

FIGURE 9.1 Rewards, Punishments, and Reinforcements

negative for undesired behavior. If punishment is used to promote positive behavior, therefore, it is likely to be ineffective (19). You saw this happen in the vignette at the beginning of this chapter when Kerry punished his field men. Figure 9.1 illustrates our points with respect to rewards, reinforcements, and punishments.

Accordingly, reinforced behavior is more likely to recur than nonreinforced behavior; this principle is called the law of effect (88). Punished behavior is less likely to occur under similar circumstances than either reinforced or nonreinforced behavior (10). Furthermore, the more often a response pattern is reinforced in a given situation, the more likely it is that the pattern will be connected to that situation; this principle is called the law of exercise (88). In other words, responses will continue in a given situation, depending on the frequency and nature of the reinforcement for those responses. If a response is reinforced one time, it is more likely to recur than if it is not reinforced; and if it occurs many times and reinforcement follows, then it is more likely to recur than if the sequence occurs infrequently.

Incentives

Perhaps all this seems a bit mechanical. People still behave according to how they think and feel, don't they? Yes, they do, which brings us to our next definition. *Incentives* are things of value that people strive for. We might call them "reinforcements of the future." Incentives are tied to rewards directly. That is, when people experience or witness rewards occurring consistently as a consequence of certain behaviors, they come to expect that such behaviors will result in these rewards in the future. Hence, they strive for the rewards. The rewards then become incentives, and are said to motivate behavior because behavior is considered instrumental in gaining the rewards. The meaning of these rewards, however, varies depending on each individual's need or want state. People's desires to satisfy needs or wants can be considered their motives. Thus, motives are modifiers of incentives (10).

It is important to know that it is the incentive attached to the work goal that people seek. Goal reaching itself, or even the instrumental behavior, may be rewarding (1), but if the rewards of reaching the goals do not offset the costs, it is unlikely that either will recur. We make this distinction because it is often thought that organizationally defined goals *should* be sought, and it may be puzzling when they are not. However, the puzzle can be cleared up if we understand that other people's goals may not be an incentive for us (47, 48, 49).

Generalization

When people are reinforced for behavior under one set of circumstances, that behavior is likely to recur not only under those conditions, but under similar conditions as well. This is called *generalization*. For example, if someone learns to work hard because hard work is reinforced, then this learning should be generalized to similar circumstances. That is, through the process of generalization, after a series of linkages occur between working hard and gaining rewards (and developing incentives), then the general pattern of working hard should be established and repeated in most circumstances where work is important.

Let us take a moment to summarize what we have just said. Reinforcement is the giving of a reward for a certain behavior. The reward is either something given that the person finds pleasurable or something taken away that the person has found distasteful. The former is often called positive reinforcement; the latter, negative reinforcement. In either case the reinforcement is given for desired behavior and tends to increase the probability that the behavior will be repeated. The anticipation of gaining the reward in the future makes that reward an incentive. When rewards are attached to behaviors there is an incentive to engage in those behaviors, but the strength of the incentive depends on what meaning the reward has for the individual. A basic model representing these ideas is depicted in Figure 9.2.

We now have most of the basic components of a motivation system. But other concepts are also useful when we address the issue of actually constructing the system.

Extinction

If we follow the reasoning associated with the law of effect and the law of exercise, we can conclude that behavior that is not reinforced tends to disappear. For example, assume that you are trying to be creative in class by interjecting new ideas. If your instructor ignores these creative attempts and reinforces only a recapitulation of the book or the lectures, you are unlikely to continue to be creative for that class. You might continue, of course, if the act of creation is intrinsically satisfying. In that case, you will be giving yourself rewards for being creative (6).

The same holds true in organizations. Many activities in organizations are not reinforced in a formal sense. Unless these activities are reinforced by other means, such as your own feeling of satisfaction, then it is likely that they will have no utility for you as an individual. Frequently among blue-collar workers work of superior quality is not counted in an evaluation scheme. Still, the workers may continue trying to turn out high-quality work because of their sense of craftsmanship and the intrinsic satisfaction associated with such craftsmanship. A company is more likely to reward high productivity and punish low productivity. Therefore, the workers will probably produce as much work as necessary to gain rewards and, at the same time, meet the minimal quality standards to avoid punishment. In other words, the response tendency for turning out superior quality is likely to become extinct because it is not reinforced.

Quantity and Quality of Rewards

QUANTITY. Performance often depends on the size of reward associated with it. The larger the reward, the greater the performance. However, there are problems with this notion. First, there is a problem of *satiation*. It is unlikely, for example, that most people will respond with ever greater performance once they have received what they think is enough of the reward (10). Further, the

Definitions of Key Terms

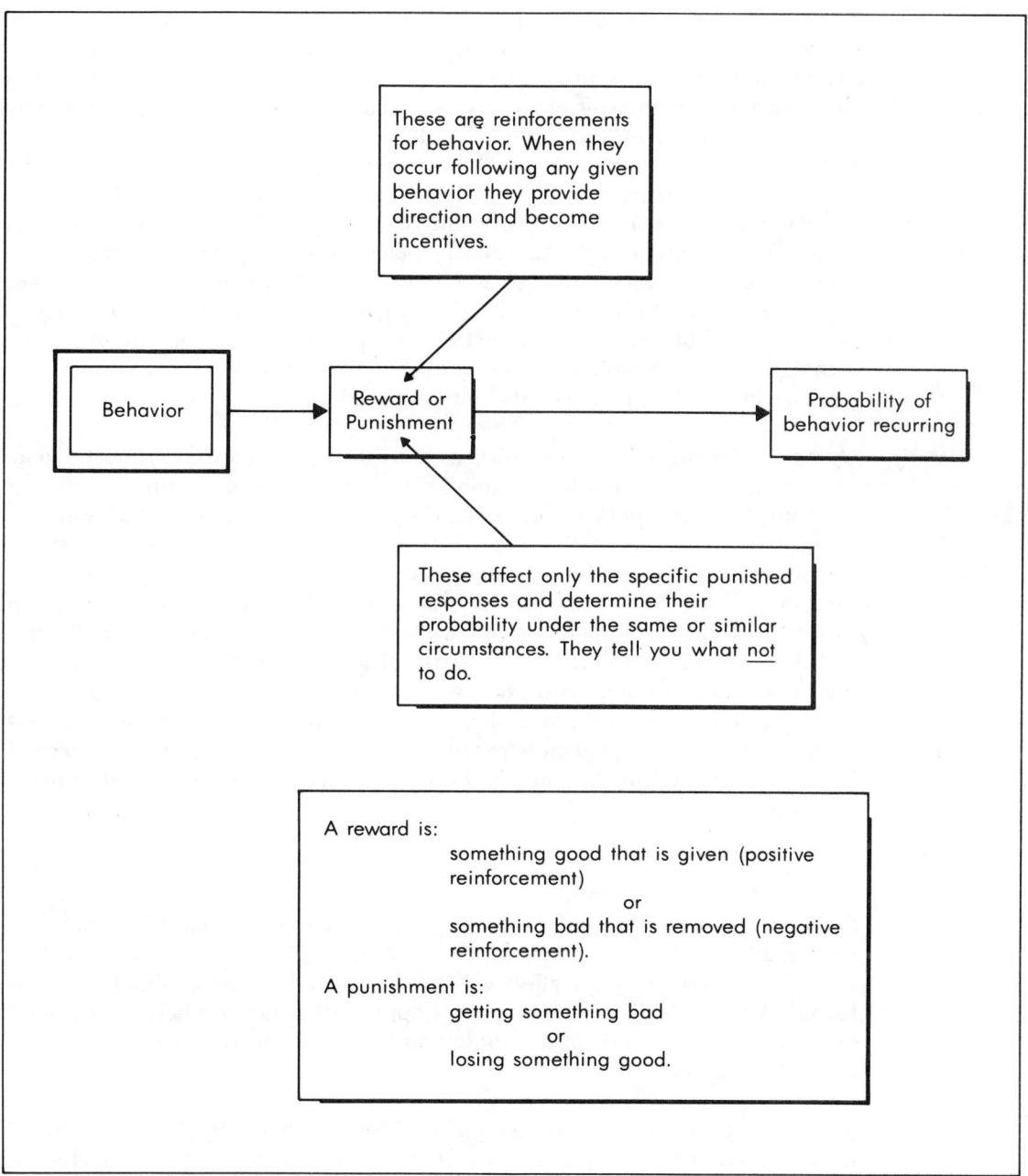

FIGURE 9.2 Our Model of Reinforcement

marginal satisfaction that people gain from such things as praise and recognition, or even money, may decrease as the cost for increased performance becomes greater. In other words, people tend to assess whether the rewards gained from the behavior more than offset the costs associated with it. It becomes increasingly difficult to increase performance when the rewards lose value because of satiation. Therefore, people make a subjective cost-benefit analysis and the results are directly associated with the individual's question, "Is it worth it?"

Another factor associated with this issue concerns the individual's *capacity* to increase performance. As this capacity reaches the upper limits set by previous reinforcements, it takes ever greater rewards to induce performance at ever higher levels (5). Eventually, a point is reached where higher performance is not possible. The results are predictable: people level off at the rate of performance most comfortable to them, considering the net returns. Few incentive schemes in organizations take this into account.

QUALITY. Quality of rewards concerns individual preferences. Obviously, some rewards are more valued by some individuals than by others. And things that are valued by one person may not be by another. If an individual values a particular reward, then it is considered to be a quality reinforcer (33). For example, suppose there are two people, one with a high need for achievement, and the other with a high need for material things. For the first person, we can expect that achieving something significant on the job will be a quality reinforcer, and if good work is followed by a sense of achievement, then we can expect the responses associated with good work to continue. For the second person, the opportunity to achieve something substantial on the job may be unimportant compared to the amount of money associated with high performance. The second individual works for money, and, in this case, money may be considered a quality reinforcer.

Frequency of Reinforcement

Frequency of reinforcement has to do with the number of times behaviors are reinforced. Are they reinforced some of the time, all of the time, or never? As we shall see, frequency can affect whether all desired behaviors should be reinforced. All other things being equal, it appears that desired behaviors should be rewarded consistently, if not continuously—but that observation, too, is limited by satiation (5).

The concepts of satiation, size and quality of rewards, and frequency of reinforcement are relative concepts in organizations. For example, it is unlikely that workers will ever get enough money, in an absolute sense. However, because the available money is limited, and because many rewards are attached to behaviors that are not organizationally valued, it is likely that people will compare the utilities of various behavioral options. Knowing that so many dollars are attached to an increase in performance, but that fatigue, loss of leisure, or group rejection is also attached, employees may decide not to pursue the money. A point of satiation may have been reached because the available quantity or quality of rewards attached to organizationally valued outcomes is not sufficient to motivate that behavior.

Schedules of Reinforcement

The way in which reinforcements are administered is called the *schedule of reinforcement*. There are two basic kinds of schedules: continuous reinforcement and partial reinforcement. *Continuous reinforcement* is the administration of the reward after each appropriate behavioral act. The effect of such reinforcement is a quick bond of association between a behavior and reward but also quick extinction when that behavior is no longer reinforced (75).

Partial reinforcement occurs when a desired behavior is not always reinforced. There are two basic types of partial reinforcement: fixed and variable. Reinforcement may be *fixed* by being given only after a certain time has lapsed—a fixed interval—or after a certain number of desired responses are made—a fixed ratio. In both cases the person knows the reinforcement is coming and expects it. Fixed schedules, therefore, are like continuous reinforcement in an individual's mind (97); that is, people consider a given amount of time or of behavior as a *unit* of behavior.

There are some differences between fixed interval and fixed ratio schedules in terms of predicted responses. Interval schedules depend on time as well as response. Therefore, responses will diminish directly after reinforcement, and pick up again as the time approaches for the next reinforcement (5). Using midterm and final examinations is somewhat like using a fixed interval schedule. The reinforcements may be positive and negative, but studying is likely to intensify as examination time approaches and is likely to diminish just after the exam.

Ratio schedules depend entirely on response, so an individual knows how much response is required for reinforcement. For example, you know that if you complete *x* lab assignments, you will receive an evaluation. In this case, we can predict that, by and large, *x* assignments will be completed (5).

In either interval or ratio schedules, because blocks of time or responses are thought of as units, extinction is likely if reinforcement does not occur after the units of responses.

It is important to remember that continuous and fixed schedules produce expectations of reinforcement, and if these expectations are not met, a person may have perceptions of punishment. Consequently, if you are led to believe, through past reinforcement history, that you will receive a reward for certain behavior, and if you do not receive the reward, then in your mind, you have received punishment. In such a case, not only extinction but negative emotional responses such as resentment and hostility may occur. These unfulfilled expectations of rewards go beyond the behavior-reinforcement linkage and affect other behaviors of organizational relevance.

Variable schedules are quite different. With these, reinforcements do not occur after specific time intervals or specific numbers of responses. Individuals know only that reinforcements will be coming eventually. However, although the association between response and reinforcement may take some time to establish, once established, they are very resistant to extinction.

These different schedules of reinforcement have different behavioral consequences. For example, fixed interval schedules using pay as the reinforcer empirically have never been associated with increases in performance, whereas fixed ratio schedules have (38, 39, 42, 95).

Regardless of schedule, people must understand that reinforcement is contingent on certain kinds of behaviors. A fixed interval schedule of reinforcement may be contingent solely on showing up at work and performing at a minimal level. A variable interval schedule should be contingent on good performance, but it is uncertain as to when these reinforcements can occur. Fixed ratio schedules are contingent on a certain amount of adequate performance, and the level and magnitude of the reinforcement should be contingent on the level and magnitude of the total pattern of behavior. Variable ratio schedules are contingent on responses, but the number changes and is therefore uncertain. In Table 9.1 we summarize the major concepts.

So far we have emphasized the more mechanistic aspects of the response-reinforcement linkage. Some feel that since behavior is largely a function of its consequence it is enough to know what behavior is wanted, and what is seen by those behaving as rewarding; then one can reinforce the desired behavior with desirable rewards (33, 52). Accordingly, the desired behavior is thought to occur with increasing frequency until it becomes a matter of course. Once that happens, reinforcements need to be provided regularly enough to ensure

TABLE 9.1 Basic Motivation Concepts Summarized

Concept	Definition/Consequence
Law of effect	Reinforced behaviors have a higher probability of recurring than those not reinforced.
Law of exercise	The more often reinforced behaviors occur in a particular situation, the stronger the linkage between the situation, the response, and the reinforcement.
Generalization	Reinforced responses occurring in one situation are likely to occur in similar situations.
Positive reinforcement	The occurrence of something rewarding is contingent upon a desired response.

Definitions of Key Terms

TABLE 9.1 (*continued*)

Concept	Definition/Consequence
Negative reinforcement	The removal of something punishing is contingent upon a desired response.
Punishment	Disapproved responses are followed by something disliked or painful.
Extinction	There is a tendency for nonreinforced responses to disappear.
Continuous reinforcement	Reinforcement occurs after every desired response. The response-reinforcement linkage is quickly established under continuous reinforcement; extinction likewise occurs quickly.
Partial reinforcement	Reinforcement occurs after a time or a frequency of responses; slower response-reinforcement linkages and extinction occur.
1. Fixed interval schedules	Reinforcement occurs after a specific time has lapsed. Slower learning occurs and there is moderate resistance to extinction. Response rates decrease after reinforcement and pick up again as reinforcement time approaches.
2. Fixed ratio	Reinforcement occurs after a specified number of responses occur. Slower learning, higher continuous levels of response, and moderate resistance to extinction are likely.
3. Variable interval schedule	Reinforcements occur after an uncertain amount of time has lapsed. Slower learning and high resistance to extinction occur.
4. Variable ratio schedule	Reinforcements occur after an uncertain amount of responses. Slower learning occurs and there is great resistance to extinction.
	(Both variable schedules may be dangerous to use in organizations because expectations of reinforcement may not be met, and frustration or hostility may result.)
Amount of reward	Associated with stronger response tendencies until satiation occurs or the point is reached when a subjective assessment suggests that the reinforcement is not worth the costs of response.
Quality of reward	This is directly associated with the value an individual places on the reinforcement. It is variable from one person to the next.
Expectation	This is an individual's assessment as to the consequences of his or her actions.
Incentive	This is a combination of the amount and quality of the expected reward.

the continuation of the behavior (84). Thought processes are generally excluded from this line of reasoning. The behavior is conditioned automatically.

One of the most reported study areas thought to support this line of reasoning deals with absenteeism. One study had workers who came to work drawing a card for a poker hand. At the end of the week, the workers in each work group with the best hand got the $20 pot. Another study had hospital employees participating in cash drawings if they were not absent during a three-week period. In these cases, as well as in others, absenteeism went down under the experimental condition (70, 85). Another example is contained in Box 9.

Still another study examined occupational safety behavior as a function of behavior-contingent rewards. Workers were told what standards of behavior were desired and why, and then how well they were conforming to those standards (feedback). Baseline measures of behavior were obtained before the study, and behavior during the course of the study was compared to that baseline. The results showed a significant increase in safety behavior so long as feedback (reinforcement) was present. Once feedback was taken away the behavior returned to the baseline (35).

Each of the studies indicates the importance of reinforcement. Each is thought to demonstrate the efficacy of organizational behavior modification. None in fact does so, because it is impossible to extract the cognitive aspects

---

Box 9

Incentives and Behavior

This study concerned the work behavior of department store sales personnel. The store noted that a lot of people frequently were absent from their work stations. Several university professors were consulted to help solve the problem. The professors selected sixteen departments at random and assigned eight to an experimental group and eight to the control group. Five kinds of behavior were recorded: idle time, time away from work stations, and three others which were combined in an index called "aggregate retail performance." Subjects in both groups were measured on their performance and were given the same specific performance standards—standards higher than previously experienced. The experimental group was also given paid time off and became eligible for a vacation lottery if they met performance standards. The experimental group showed substantial improvement in aggregate retail behavior, absence from work stations, and idle time. The control group showed no improvement.

(Luthans F., R. Paul, and A. Baker. "An Experimental Analysis of the Effect of Contingent Reinforcement on Salespersons' Performance Behavior." *Journal of Applied Psychology* 66 (1981), pp. 314–322).

from the reported studies (45). As an example, how can one separate out the *expectations* of reward in the persons engaged in less idle time or less time away from the work station from the effects reported in the department store study? Not only would it be difficult, it would also be unwarranted because clearly people make conscious connections between behavior and outcomes and then behave accordingly.

It is this process of making conscious linkages that is most important for our subsequent discussion. In the next section we will concentrate on the process underlying directed behavior in organizations.

Motivation Systems for Directed Behavior: Enter Cognition

Why do people choose one behavior over another? Generally they do so because they expect the chosen behavior to help them more in reaching their own goals (3, 24, 36, 42, 91). Hence we have another term. *Instrumentality* is an act or pattern of behavior that leads to or is followed by a reinforcement.

Many studies suggest that people shoot for measurable task goals or standards irrespective of objective incentives (48, 49, 67). That is, if they accept task goals, they intend to reach them and will direct efforts toward them. Reaching them is apparently reinforcing. However, since the process is entirely cognitive, the problem is to get people to accept appropriate task goals at the outset. Our model, then, must include a cognitive aspect; this is illustrated in Figure 9.3. However, the conditions themselves are partly a product of individual orientations. That is, the same sequence of events has very different meanings for different people, and thus different behaviors may be anticipated.

In 1916 Frederick Winslow Taylor, who is considered "father of scientific management," provided some interesting observations on workers and their motivation. Although Taylor was primarily concerned with relatively unskilled workers, his statements can be generalized to virtually everyone who works. In an article entitled "The Principles of Scientific Management," Taylor tried to account for both high production and the development of what he called "soldiering." Soldiering is activity similar to what we call productivity restriction; in other words, people purposely hold down production. Taylor wrote:

> If, for example, you are manufacturing a pen, let us assume for simplicity that a pen can be made by a single man. Let us say that the workman is turning out 10 pens a day and that he is receiving $2.50 a day for his wages. He has a progressive foreman who is up-to-date and that foreman goes to the workman and suggests "Here, John, you are getting $2.50 a day and you are turning out 10 pens. I would suggest that I pay you $.25 for making that pen." The man takes the job and through the help of the foreman, through his own ingenuity, through his increased

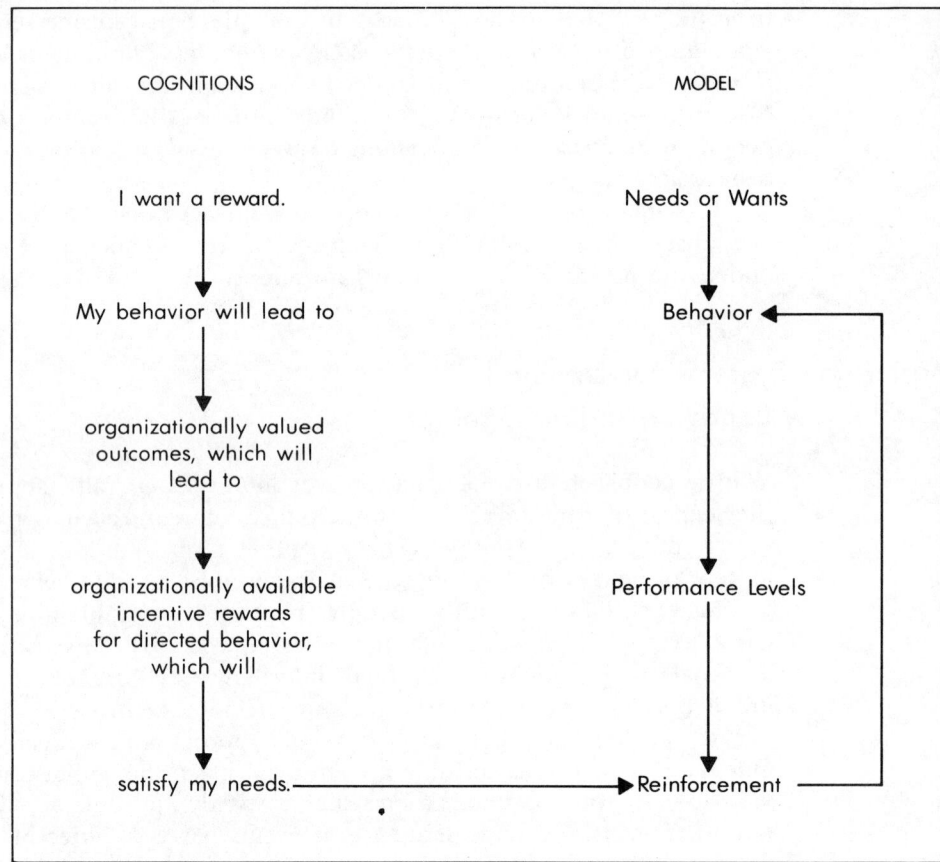

FIGURE 9.3 Cognitive Aspects of Our Model of Directed Behavior

work, through his interest in his own business, through the help of his friends, at the end of the year, he finds himself turning out 20 pens instead of 10. He is happy, he is making $5.00 instead of $2.50 a day. His foreman is happy because with the same room, with the same men he had before, he has doubled the output of his department and the manufacturer himself is sometimes happy, but not often. Then someone on the board of directors asks to see the payroll and he finds that we are paying $5.00 a day when the standard rate of wages is $2.50. What is the result? The foreman goes back to his workman in sadness and depression and tells his workman, "I'm sorry, John, but I have got to cut the price down for that pen; I cannot let you earn $5.00 a day; the Board of Directors has got on to it and it is ruining the labor market; you ought to be willing to have the price reduced. You cannot earn more than $3.00 or $2.75 a day and I will have to cut your wages so that you will only get $3.00 a day." John of necessity accepts the cut, but he sees to it that he never makes enough pens to get another cut (86: 31, 32).

The results are predictable. In the first instance, John, who is working for money, produces more pens and thereby gets more money. Then his wages are cut. He still wants to make more money, but he no longer sees making as many pens as he can as a means toward that end. Therefore, a new set of goals emerges: to make his maximum daily wage, to avoid fatigue, and to do nothing that would maximize the company's profits with no benefits to himself. Before the wage cut, he received reinforcement for increased production in the form of doubled wages. Once his wages were cut, he received punishment for high production and rewards for "soldiering." What, then, were John's incentives? (See Figure 9.4.)

To summarize, we know, first, that directed behavior is partly a function of the reinforcement history of an individual. Second, we know that people often expect similar rewards in similar circumstances (generalization) and that their behavior may be instrumental in gaining such rewards. Hence, behavior depends partly on reinforcement history and on expectations, which are related. Third, we can infer that because people tend to seek rewards, these rewards become incentives. That is, although both behavioral conditioning and unconscious motives may be important behavioral determinants, our concern here is with conscious goal seeking. That is because organizations develop their motivation systems in order to gain conscious responses to consciously determined incentives. And that is precisely where cognitions come in.

Expectancies as Part of the Cognitive Process

There is ample evidence that piece rates are associated with higher levels of performance than other means of compensation such as hourly or day rates or salaries (42, 58). Several recent studies or reviews indicate that monetary incentives substantially increase performance. One of these compared four groups of foundry workers under two monetary incentive conditions (76). Both conditions substantially increased and sustained performance levels over three months. The study also shows consistency of performance over that time. This consistency could be used to indicate incentive effectiveness.

A review nicely summarizes the literature on the effect of *individual* wage incentives on productivity by noting that 100 percent of the reported studies show increases in performance, with a median improvement of about 30 percent, and a range of 3 percent to 49 percent (50). A more recent review, which includes group as well as individual incentive plans, reports that all but one of the studies show increases in performance after the plans go into effect, and the range of increases is between 4 and 62 percent (31). Clearly, then, monetary incentives have a substantial effect on performance. However, virtually everyone who studies the effect of incentives is puzzled by two things: (1) performance fluctuates around a mean and within a specific range (not too high and not too low) both between and within days; and (2) performance is rarely as

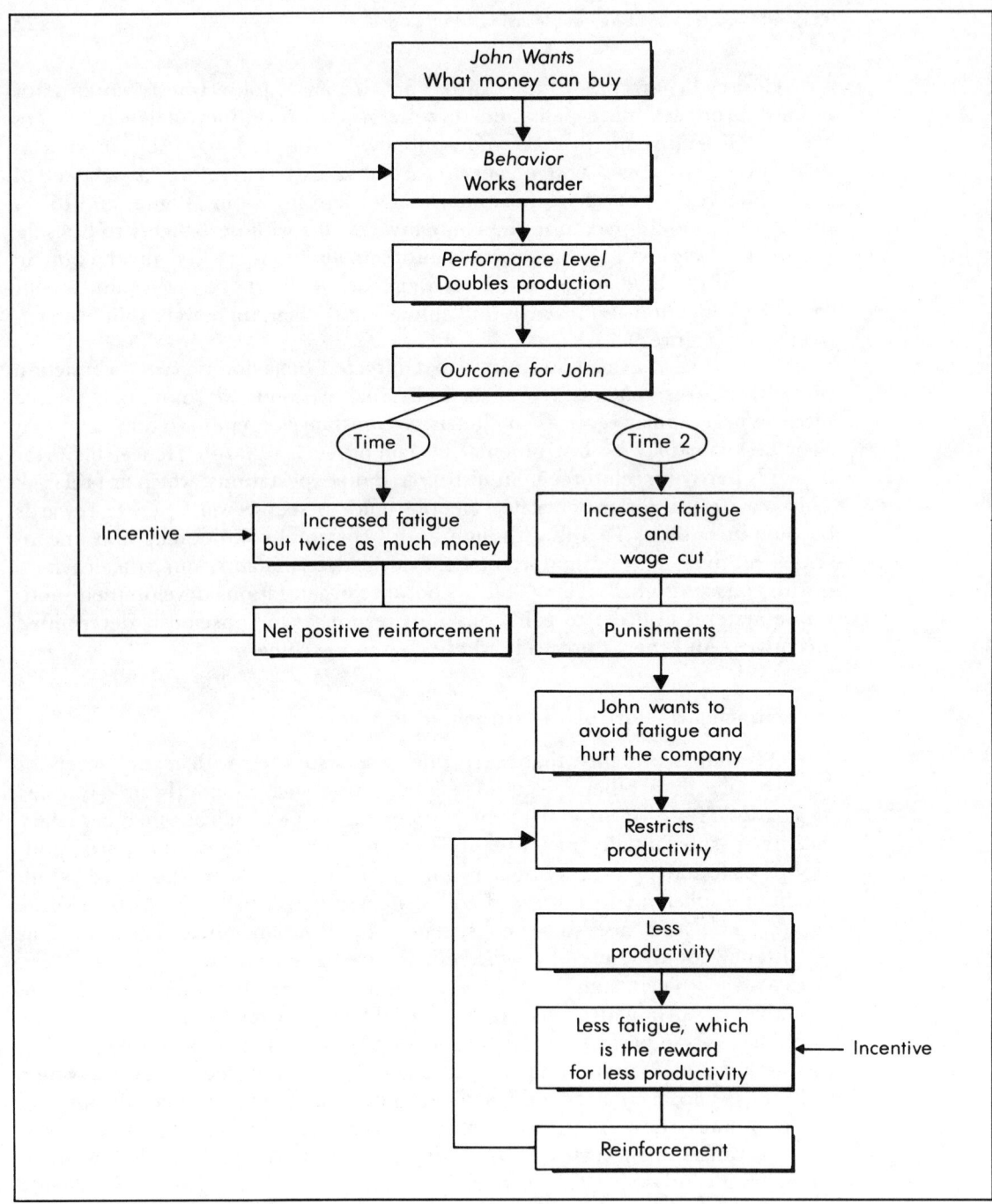

FIGURE 9.4 John's Motivation

high as the possible upper limit (94). Indeed, the data consistently show that where incentive systems are installed, after an initial adjustment period, productivity improves rapidly to a point but not beyond, even though there is a clear capacity to do more (58, 94). Why?

The general answer to that question is clear enough. There are factors that modify the value of money as a reinforcement. Perceptions concerning the probability that the reinforcement will occur as a consequence of effort is one of the factors. The meaning that people place on the reinforcement and the events leading to it is another. To illustrate, let us examine the use of money as a reward and a reinforcer (25).

Money as a Generalized Reinforcer

Money has value because it is instrumental in satisfying a variety of needs (23). It is the common denominator in industrialized society, and it is for money that most of us work (20, 58). These statements may seem commonsensical to you, but common sense is often overlooked when complexity enters the picture.

It is probably this complexity that causes many behavioral scientists to play down the significance of money as a motivator. A host of research dating to the Hawthorne studies has emphasized factors other than money as important to the work motive. It is undeniable, and our discussion so far would support this, that people come to an organization with needs for things other than those associated with money per se (94). Money, in a sense, is a given, part of the bargain that people strike when they decide that money is a background factor (42). When money is viewed as a given that is shared by all according to their contribution, then other things seem more important. But when people are threatened with reduced incomes, are enticed by opportunities to make substantially more income, or see income as inequitably administered, money becomes a powerful incentive (58).

Historically, money has come to summarize the contract between worker and employer. Once people worked for grain, shelter, clothing, and so forth, but they now work for money in order to buy such things. Thus, money is related to a host of needs in a most elementary way. Lawler states, for example:

> The evidence rather clearly suggests that pay can be instrumental for the satisfaction of a variety of needs and that it is likely to be seen as more instrumental with respect to some needs than to others. The evidence is perhaps clearest with respect to the ability of pay to satisfy esteem and recognition as well as basic physiological needs. . . . The evidence also suggests that pay can be an anxiety reducer in the sense that it leads to feelings of security: Higher-paid people feel more secure. (18:33, 34)

Let us extend this point a bit. When people enter employment, they may examine their needs and assess the extent to which their monetary compensation can satisfy these needs. Does money buy appropriate levels of food, shelter, or other physical comfort? If the answer is yes and if employment is ensured, then money may become part of the background, so long as these needs remain satisfied. But money is associated with other needs as well. Money buys status—serves as a yardstick so to speak—and in this way is related to esteem. It helps us to gain power and it is directly associated with achievement. In fact, as McClelland (55) points out, money is one of the concrete bits of evidence that achievement has taken place. An outstanding contributions award, or a significant salary increase, demonstrates that the organization acknowledges such achievement. If there is enough, money even helps justify behavior that, for moral or ethical reasons, we might not otherwise engage in.

Money, then, has a substantial symbolic potential that is directly associated with how we view ourselves and others. This point is brought home when salary increases are distributed according to merit, even though only marginal differences in terms of purchasing power separate the top and bottom increases. The feelings generated by such differences typically cannot be explained by the size of the differences, only by their existence (57).

Why, then, should there be any confusion as to the role of money as an incentive in organizations? Our assessment is that the use of money as an incentive must meet four conditions, and, because these conditions are rarely met, money has not been used effectively as an incentive (94).

1. Money has to have sufficient incentive value. It has to stand up in a comparison with other incentives that might work against its use, such as the incentive for social acceptance.
2. There has to be an opportunity to do what is required to gain the sufficient incentive. That is, *can* the individual for whom money is offered as an incentive actually do what is required to gain that incentive?
3. There has to be a clear tie-up between the path and the sufficient incentive. In other words, if I can do what is required to get that sufficient incentive, *will* such incentive follow?
4. There has to be clear justification for the manner in which money is distributed. That is, people must know and accept the grounds on which money is related to job classifications and to performance.

If these four conditions do not exist, then money is not likely to be an effective incentive and, in fact, incentives attached to other kinds of needs may be more dominant. When money is the incentive, when productivity is the path toward gaining the incentive, and when clear differences in performance are the determining factor for differential allocations, virtually all the data examining monetary incentive systems indicate higher, not lower, productivity compared to a day or hourly rate (6). If it does not work that way, the conditions are probably not being met.

One author thoroughly discusses the use of money as an incentive (6). He feels that when money is not effective, it is because the avenue for gaining more money is being blocked by other important needs. For example, an employee who sees that increased production will result in layoffs is not likely to increase production. Neither is he or she likely to increase production if such an increase would result in disapprobation by other members of the group.

The numerous paradoxes are explained in this way. The goals of workers and the goals of management are usually different and frequently irreconcilable. A goal of management is to increase production and decrease costs, whereas goals of employees are often to protect job security and make substantial increases in monetary outcomes. However, if these were the sole goals of each group, there might not be a problem. All management would have to do would be to assure workers of their job security and provide substantial incentives for increasing productivity so that countervailing incentives would be overridden. But the fact that this rarely happens suggests that those responsible for determining wage policies do so with a complex set of goals that is different from the stated goal of profit maximization—for example, maintaining a wage structure that is not out of line with the prevailing wage rates of surrounding communities. At the heart of incentive systems' ineffectiveness is the way the management responsible for such things constructs incentive systems to service goals besides the stated goal. Rarely is enough funneled into an incentive system to compensate for such factors as increased fatigue, lost overtime, or social pressures to restrict production. Let us go a step further.

William F. Whyte, an old hand at studying the use of money as an incentive, identifies variables that confound the use of incentives in organizational life. The first he calls *conflicting stimuli*—that is, workers are faced with several sets of incentives contingent on different kinds of behaviors. As an illustration, take a monetary incentive system juxtaposed with a suggestion system. Under the incentive system, people are rewarded according to how much they produce. If job improvements that help toward that end are made, the improvements will be hidden from the industrial engineers (IEs). In this way, people can produce more without having the rates adjusted upward. That is, it is to the employees' advantage to make method changes, hide them, beat the rates, and make more money. And that is what they do (94).

Under the suggestion system, however, people are rewarded according to those very job changes that helped them beat the rates. The incentive is a one-shot payoff for submitting an awardable suggestion. Measure this against the continued payoffs that employees gain by their increased performance using the new method—the one the company is not notified about. Furthermore, only the person submitting a suggestion gains a reward. Others in the workgroup do not share it; instead they face a tightening of the rates. Is it any wonder that few suggestion systems are successful for a blue-collar work force that is under a piece-rate system? As Whyte states, if workers conceal inventions successfully, all involved make out (94). What, then, are the *real* incentives under such conditions?

Another factor that Whyte identifies as having an important bearing on financial incentive systems is a so-called *time lag and trust*. Whyte notes that most financial incentive systems have a time lag between the behavior and the reinforcement. During that time, people may operate on faith that good performance will be followed by a reward that is better than rewards gained by performing at a lower level. Faith, in this case, constitutes the incentive. However, if, either through past experience or through the observation that performance is not followed by reward, or that performance will result in negative incentives, then statements by those who are empowered to offer rewards may be viewed as unreliable.

For example, management may *promise* not to adjust rates even if workers substantially and consistently beat standard. There are two important considerations when such a thing happens. First of all, the IEs are reinforced to maintain tight rates. When workers consistently beat these rates, attention is inevitably drawn to them, and the IEs are compelled to change the rates. That is part of their job. Furthermore, as workers learn the ropes and make a series of small method changes, these may add up enough to warrant reengineering the job, so that the rates are cut. So, promises to the contrary, workers must reckon with IEs, who are doing their jobs and who get substantial and objective justification to adjust the rates and thus break the promise. Under these circumstances, problems of trust emerge and the prevailing motive is to beat the rates by not too much, only enough to make out.

Let us recast the above points in a somewhat different way. Although an organization may provide reinforcements for desired behavior, those reinforcements may not be incentives because they are not valued enough, reinforcement attached to competing behaviors may be more attractive, the behavior itself may be uncommonly distasteful, or the routes to the reinforcement may not be entirely clear. Any of these may interfere with the effectiveness of a motivation system. How then ought we view the construction of such a system?

The Expectancy Framework

Several authors have suggested a systematic framework for viewing motivation in organizations that has been called instrumentality theory, expectancy theory, and path-goal theory (24, 25, 66, 73, 74). The basic terms of this theory include expectancy, which is the expectation that something will occur given a sequence of events; instrumentality, which is the perception that a behavior brings valued outcomes; and valence, which is the extent to which people prefer a certain outcome. The valence depends on the value of the outcome. The model is depicted in Figure 9.5.

The effort devoted to a task and the behavior associated with that effort

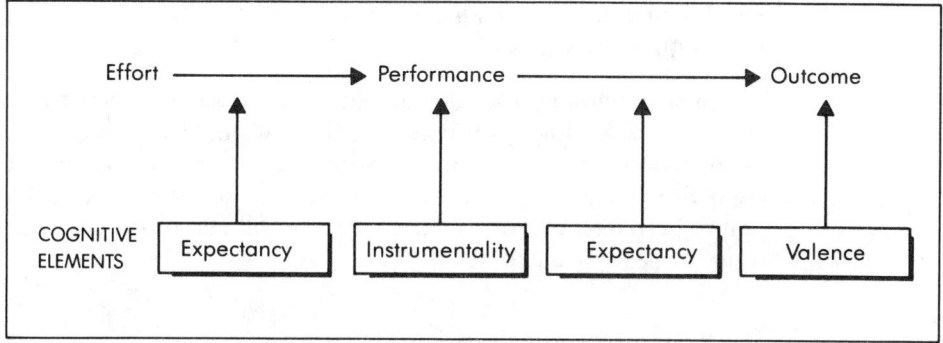

FIGURE 9.5 An Expectancy Model of Motivation

lead to levels of performance. The levels of performance are instrumental in gaining outcomes. The expectancies are the subjective probabilities that effort will lead to performance and that performance will lead to outcomes, each of which carries valence. Hence, the amount of effort will depend on how strongly the person feels (1) that the effort will lead to variation in performance, (2) that performance will lead to rewards, and (3) that variations in performance will be differentially rewarding. If the outcomes are strongly and positively valent, and if the expectancies and instrumentalities are high then strong effort should be forthcoming (66, 91). Put somewhat differently, until people consciously link effort to performance and performance to reward or punishment, the motivational system should not work to the best advantage of the organization (11, 12).

Managing Cognitions

Four elements in the process of managing cognitions require attention: (1) the effort-performance expectancy, (2) the instrumentality of performance, (3) the performance-reward expectancy, and (4) the value of the reward.

The Effort-Performance Expectancy

Several factors are important here. People must be competent enough to perform at desired levels. Also, they should know what they have to do, how to do it, and what level of performance will act as their standard. Finally, they should have available the resources to do the job (42, 73, 91).

The Instrumentality of Performance for Desired Outcomes

The instrumentality question is what behaviors are seen by the organization members as leading to things that they want. Many things that people do in organizations are potentially rewarding. It is up to management to define precisely the linkage between desired behaviors and the rewards that the organization is prepared to give so that workers will see those behaviors as the surest route to desired outcomes (91).

The Performance-Reward Expectancy

Specific rewards should be attached to specified performance levels, and people should experience appropriate reinforcements either directly or vicariously. Without clear calibration, perceptions of inequality will creep in and the value of the reward will be diminished accordingly (11).

Value of the Reward

One of the main reasons that monetary incentive systems work only to a point is that the rewards for increasing performance are not large enough. People do not feel that the benefits of more money, for example, offset the costs of increased effort (11). Our quote from F. W. Taylor (pp. 221–22) illustrated that point nicely.

Each of the elements above is largely controllable by management and provides a link to leadership, a subject we will deal with in Chapter 14. As an illustration let us examine Figure 9.6.

In Figure 9.6 the factors that we call dependencies are largely the responsibilities of management although they are rarely totally controllable. Management does not always have the right people for the job, the flexibility to reward primarily according to performance, or the resources to facilitate performance or to reward it adequately. If the compensation system is geared primarily to performance, the perception of equity is more likely than if it is not, but for a variety of reasons, perceptions of inequity seem to abound where evaluations of performance are an issue. Still, it is management's responsibility to clarify, set standards, gain resources, facilitate performance-oriented behavior, and then reinforce it appropriately.

The research directed to the expectancy theories shows a lot of support although by no means unanimity (9, 12, 54, 66). To date, the expectation that performance will be followed by some reward seems to be the most important factor (12, 37).

One study compared two plants. One had a piece rate system that specified the relationship between performance and wage rates. The other had no such

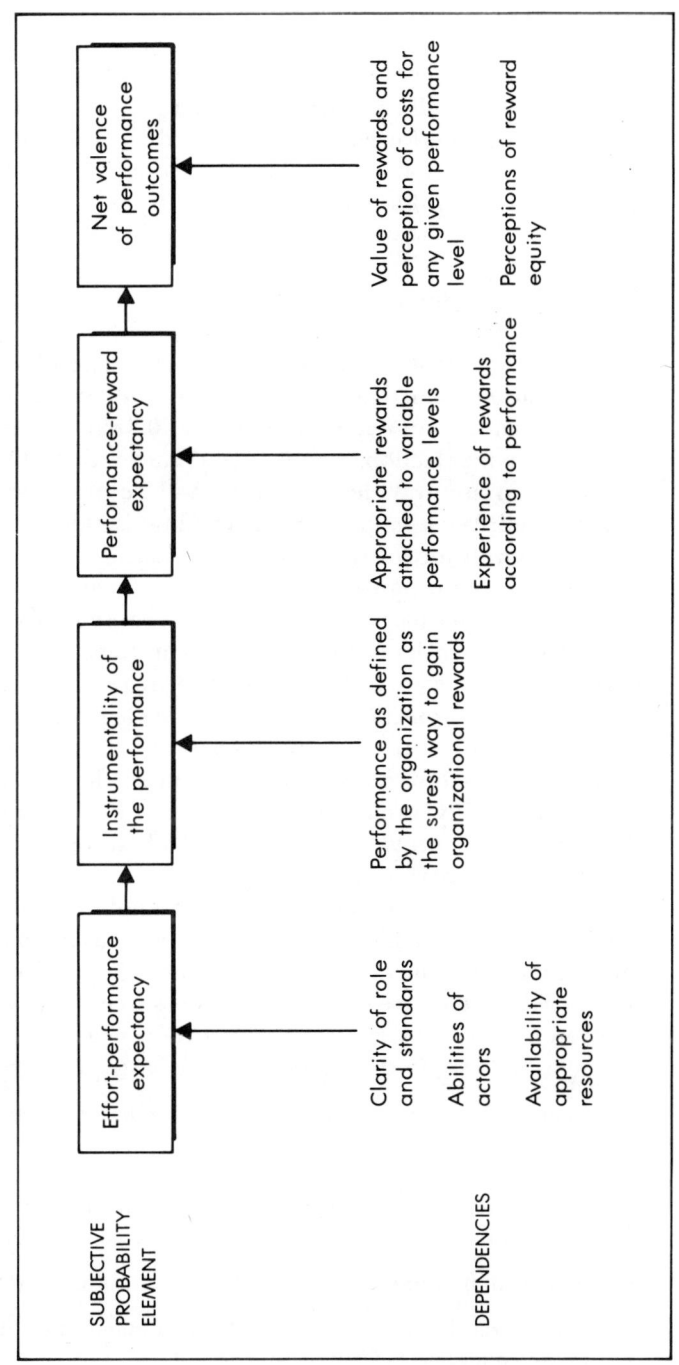

FIGURE 9.6 Managing Expectancies: Making a Motivational System Work

system. As a consequence the first plant produced strong and consistent relationships between peoples' expectation that performance would be followed by reward and their level of performance. No such relationship existed in the second plant (61). This tells us that only when a clear and explicit relationship really exists between performance and rewards will people perceive it and behave accordingly. A system-wide example is provided by Mitchell Fein when he discusses the Lincoln Electric Company (20).

The Lincoln Electric Experience

Fein recognizes that "in practically all plants and offices, if the workers do anything to raise productivity, some of them will be penalized. The instrumentality of performance is not readily apparent" (20:489). Fein goes on to say, "If employees increase production, reduce delays and waiting time, reduce crew sizes, or cooperate in any way, less overtime will be available or some employees will be displaced. What employee will voluntarily raise his production output, only to be penalized for his diligence?" (20:489).

Now, recognizing these problems and having worked as an industrial engineer for the better part of three decades, Fein suggests that certain preconditions are necessary in order for incentive systems to be effective. First of all, employees must have job security. That is, if they increase productivity, they should not work themselves out of a job. Second, management must recognize that there is a built-in conflict between their goals and the workers' goals. Third, management must structure its incentive system so that the goals coincide in at least one facet, namely, around productivity itself. He suggests that the *only* way to do so is first to provide job security and, second, to give employees the full fruits of higher performance.

Fein uses Lincoln Electric as an example of a company that meets these conditions. Lincoln Electric is a Cleveland-based company that manufactures arc welding equipment and supplies, and AC integral horsepower motors. It is a world leader in each area, and its success has been due to its ability to innovate and to manufacture quality products at low prices. Lincoln has a management philosophy that rests on three basic premises. First, that:

> There will be a greater growth of man under continued profit incentive (43:7).

Second, that:

> Competition is the foundation of man's development. . . . [The] danger is [that a] man's life [may be] made dull by lack of competition (43:33).

Third, that management and labor have common interests:

> Our standard of living could be doubled immediately if labor and management would cooperate (43:35).

> There is all the difference in the world between the grudging, distrustful, half-forced compliance and the eager, . . . vigorous cooperation of men working together for a common purpose (43:35).

Lincoln Electric chooses to operationalize these concepts through a rigorous merit and incentive system. And the reality? Fein describes it:

> Most unusual is Lincoln's employees' identification with their work. At one station I saw a worker operate five different machine tools to produce a rotor shaft from a blank; he operated a tape-controlled engineer lathe, a tracer lathe, two small milling machines, a hydraulic press, and he performed all his own inspections; he made a finished part to close tolerances ready for assembly. I saw another worker make finished gasoline tanks; he took two tank halves, soldered on the fittings, submerged arc-welded the two halves into the completed assembly, repaired it if necessary, sprayed it in a paint booth, and delivered the first tank to the main assembly line (20:510).

Fein goes on to state:

> The employees participate in work to a far greater extent than visualized by psychologists in their writings. The key to this participation is that the employees want to do it; there is no holding back (20:511).

Why should this be so? Fein suggests four reasons: (1) The employees' job security is fully protected and their raised productivity does not penalize them; (2) employees at Lincoln see that their increased productivity and identification with management's goals are reflected in *both* increased take-home pay and job security; (3) the increased productivity is passed along to Lincoln's customers, which increases their competitiveness and further protects job security; (4) Lincoln continually plows back earnings to develop their product and, hence, their position in the market.

How does Lincoln do this? Its compensation package includes a bonus that is almost *four times* the stockholder dividend. This bonus is based on earnings and is distributed to everyone at Lincoln. It is distributed according to each employee's annual paycheck and according to merit. The year-end average bonus has ranged from 78 percent to over 130 percent of wages during the past thirty-three years. Furthermore, the pay is *based directly on performance ratings.* There is no guaranteed minimum—all production work is on an incentive schedule. And all employees are *guaranteed* 52 paychecks a year at a minimum of thirty hours paid work per week.

The entire system points in one direction and that is to increase productivity and reduce costs. And a noteworthy feature of the Lincoln Electric system is that management, in pursuing its goals, is apparently seen by employees as pursuing theirs as well. That is because, as management increases the product market share and as costs are reduced, the employees share equally through the distribution of earnings.

Let us examine this in light of what we said previously. First, the rewards for employees are substantial, clear, and unequivocally associated with performance. Second, performance is manifestly the only path to gaining rewards. Third, according to Fein, there are few competing incentives. Fourth, there are reinforcements for appropriate behavior. These reinforcements occur several times during the year, and the job reinforcement is a big chunk of money at the end of the year distributed according to job level and performance level. From Fein's description, then, apparently all of the necessary conditions for an effective motivation system are met at Lincoln Electric. Indeed, as reported by Lincoln's employees, high productivity norms are established in work groups because individual performance affects other group members. And low performance is viewed negatively by others in the social system (7). Further, promotion is from within, and only those with high performance ratings are considered.

Goal Setting and Performance

We must address one last issue in this chapter; in a sense it ties a lot of things together. We refer to personal goals and their relationship to organizational work goals. So far we have learned that performance needs to be reinforced, through rewards, that the incentive value of the rewards is largely a function of the expectation that performance will be followed by a reward together with the subjective net value (valence) of the reward. We will now see how work goals are associated with or merge into personal goals.

Work Goals as Personal Goals

The ends that an individual intends to reach may be considered her or his goals. People do seek rewards, which may be considered their goals, and behave in ways to get these rewards, but that does not explain behavior directed toward performance standards defined by others (83), and for which there are no obvious rewards (47, 48, 49). The explanation is that although reinforcement history may explain such behavior more straightforwardly, the standards themselves have reinforcing properties. A sense of accomplishment, or of meeting a challenge, or the goal-directed behavior itself may be rewarding (3, 4, 55). Goals, therefore, are ends that people intend to reach because of their reinforcing properties. Once these properties are determined, they become incentives. Goals established by the organization are not personal goals unless they become personally valued. Personal goals are things like "making more money," "getting promoted," "avoiding fatigue," "having good personal relations," "staying out of trouble," and so forth. To reach these goals one may or may not choose to meet standards of performance that are the organization's goals (13). In other words, meeting organizational performance standards may or may not be viewed as instrumental to personal goals (47).

However, goals are neither constant nor static variables, and activities do not cease when the goals are reached (78, 89). The individual may even intend to reach the goal again if the goal state is reinforcing (38). For example, an individual intends to get a promotion. That is her goal. She then pursues the "right" course of action and the promotion follows. This is her reinforcement. Assume, however, that the promotion has some positive and some negative consequences, say salary increases and status on the positive side, and increased pressure and other people's problems on the negative side. The relative strength of the positive and negative reinforcements will determine the subsequent incentive properties of further promotions. The initial course of action, to get the promotion, has been successful and reinforced, but the intent to pursue a similar course of action for further promotion depends on what the promotion itself has come to mean to the individual. If promotion continues to have a positive meaning, it may be set as a goal again. If the meaning becomes negative, the goal may be to get out. And so the process goes. In each instance the initial reinforcement (promotion) is the same, but the anticipated behaviors are different depending on the ongoing rewards or costs associated with the goal.

If we say the goal attainment is reinforced, then, we are adding to the fact that goal reaching is itself reinforcing and the goal state has both good and bad aspects (14, 17). It is important to distinguish between the reinforcing properties of goal reaching and those of what follows, if we are to understand the motivational nature of goals. To summarize, work goals become personal goals as a consequence of at least three things: the expected rewards contingent on goal reaching, the expected rewards from the process of goal reaching, and the expected rewards inherent in the goal itself (40). Let us develop these ideas more thoroughly.

Goal Setting

MOTIVES. Several things contribute to goal setting. First are personal motives. Motives are enduring characteristics of an individual denoted by persistent goal-orientation and primarily comprising the needs or wants the individual brings to a situation (1, 10, 16, 71). People consciously pursue activities that are goal-directed (47).

INCENTIVES. As we have said, personal goal setting is determined partly by the perceived incentive properties of the goal, that is, how well the results of reaching a goal satisfy one's needs.

PATH AVAILABILITY. Goal setting is often determined by the availability of the paths toward the goal. In other words, one may desire a goal, but if no means are available for reaching it, one is not likely to accept that goal (24).

REWARDS AND COSTS OF THE PATH. The available paths will involve activities that themselves carry rewards and punishments. Goal setting is determined by the costs of the paths, compared to the value of the outcome (32). Although data suggest that difficult goals are more valued, at least to a point (50, 54), people assess other things associated with goal reaching before they intend to get the goal. That is, what does it take to reach the goal? For example, suppose making a lot of money is your goal, but the only paths available entail either an extraordinary amount of work, which will interfere with other important goals, or being unethical, which may interfere with your goal of being an ethical person. Your decision to act will be based on the relative worth of making a lot of money and the costs associated with the path toward the goal (15, 60).

COMPETING GOALS. How attractive are competing goals and goal-directed activities? For example, recall that workers are often placed in a quality-quantity goal dilemma. How this dilemma is solved depends on the workers' comparison of benefits to be derived from reaching each target. In other words, they set as performance goals some combination of quantity and quality according to their assessment of the relative worth of each.

AUTHORITATIVE REQUESTS. Goal setting may be determined by those in positions of authority (18, 56). The effectiveness of authoritative requests touches goal setting directly. A considerable body of evidence, for example, suggests that people will accept the goals of authoritarian figures and then intend to pursue those goals (46, 48, 50). Whether people comply with authoritative goals because they accept those goals and see the authoritative requests as legitimate or because they wish to please the person in authority, the result is the same (28, 47, 48, 50).

INDIVIDUAL DIFFERENCES. Goals are often individualistic, and therefore the incentives associated with performance may vary from person to person. For example, you might need to be left alone after a hard day at work, in which case you would be motivated to seek solitude. Others in the same circumstance might need to socialize or blow off a bit of steam, in which case they would be motivated to do something quite different. Neither motive is necessarily associated with future job performance, but each is a different consequence of what happened previously, and the shape of the action is determined by a combination of personal attributes and experience. This statement has two important aspects. First, people may respond differently to the same circumstances, depending on their motives, and second, these motives, though goal-directed, produce entirely different behavior (41, 53). Hence, if increased worker performance is our aim, we must find the motive that encompasses the broadest range of individual motives and then attach it to the incentive system of the organization. Or we can seek to create an environment that triggers the motives that many of us share, in order to direct behavior appropriately (44, 55, 56). This is precisely why money and advancement are used universally as inducements to behave. Each represents a wide range of potential motive patterns associated with such needs as achievement, recognition, status, and power (11, 67). And so goals are set according to present needs, past actions, present circumstances, and anticipated outcomes (63, 64, 87).

Variations in Work Performance

Every study so far shows that people perform better when they have specific goals than when they do not. Furthermore, a recent review article disclosed that the average increase in performance due to goal setting alone is 16 percent and the range is between 2 and 57.5 percent. And to a point it seems the higher the goal set, the better the performance (50).

There seem to be three primary reasons for the relationships between goal difficulty and performance. Each is related to the reason that goal setting is more effective than no goal setting in gaining high performance. First, goal difficulty is probably related to effort. If an *accepted* goal is hard to reach, it is logical that more effort will be directed to that goal (47). Furthermore, as we have said, difficult goals are probably more valued (54). Therefore, people will be more motivated to reach those goals. This explanation fits well with expectancy theory.

A second explanation is that goals provide a direction for behavior, and more difficult goals provide a more continuous source of directed behavior (21, 28). In other words, knowing what the performance goals are and that they will be hard to reach lessens the probability that a person will expend unfocused effort on activities that are not performance related (51). This too corresponds with our discussion of expectancy theory.

A final and related reason that explicit and difficult goals produce increased performance has to do with feedback. Difficult goals are likely to take longer than easier goals and consequently offer more opportunities for feedback (8, 26, 27, 64). This is particularly likely under complex conditions, where feedback can be given during the monitoring process and then again when the goals are to be achieved (87, 90). Since feedback is related to reinforcement, the greater the frequency of reinforcement, the higher the motivational levels ought to be. An interesting study on goal difficulty appears in Box 10.

The major lesson to be learned from this research is that harder goals seem to lead to higher performance even though it is less likely that the harder goals will be reached. Apparently, the value placed on accomplishment by the subjects offsets the lower likelihood that hard goals will be reached (as compared to easy goals). However, had the expectancy for goal attainment been a lot lower, a different result would be likely.

Two other studies conducted at General Electric showed the effects of setting

> **Box 10**
>
> ## Valued Goals Seem Best
>
> The study was designed to test postulates from expectancy theory and from goal-setting theory. According to expectancy theory easier goals are more attainable than more difficult goals; more difficult goals are more attractive, hence they carry more valence. Goal-setting theory merely states that more difficult goals will lead to higher performance. The question posed was: Will the more difficult goals with their considerable valence result in greater performance even though they are seen as unattainable. That they seem unattainable is called a low effort-performance expectancy.
>
> The task required quick checking to detect discrepancies between two lists of paired sets of three-digit numbers. The easy goal condition was to do one better than the average score on five practice trials. The hard goal condition was to do one more than the best score on the practice trials. Six of the subjects, 98.4 percent, were able to attain the easy goal, whereas 66.7 percent attained the more difficult goal.
>
> Measures were obtained for the effort-performance expectancy. As predicted, the harder goals received lower expectancy scores. Measures also were obtained for the valence of outcomes (achievement, self-confidence, ability to concentrate, clerical ability, and persistence) and then the extent to which goal attainment would lead to those outcomes (instrumentality). As expected, goal attainment in the hard goal group was seen as substantially more instrumental to desired outcomes.
>
> The results were:
>
> 1. Hard goals resulted in higher performance.
> 2. Although the expectancy of goal attainment was substantially greater in the lower goal condition this had little effect on performance.
> 3. The valence of goal reaching was substantially greater for the hard goal condition and seems to be the determining factor directing behavior.
>
> The authors conclude that the motivational force generated by the valence of the hard goals is substantially greater than the negative factor of low expectations. They go on to say that 66.7 percent of the subjects were able to reach the hard goal and therefore, at best, it was moderately difficult.
>
> Matsui, T., A. Okada, and R. Mitzuguchi. "Expectancy Theory Prediction of the Goal Theory Postulate, 'The Higher the Goals, the Higher the Performance'." *The Journal of Applied Psychology* 66 (1981): 54–58.

performance standards in an organization. In both cases when targets were set, they were met—presumably because people come to value the outcomes of such actions for whatever reason.

Although the basic relationship between goal difficulty and performance levels appears well supported in the empirical literature, there is ample evidence that the relationship is true only to a point (30, 38, 87). When the goal is too difficult and hence seen as unattainable many people may cease to pursue it (53, 54). This fact too fits well with expectancy theory. At this time we do not know the limits of the goal difficulty–performance relationship, nor do we know how people's individual differences might affect the relationship. We only know that goals are better than no goals as productive of directed behavior, and that difficult goals seem more efficacious than easier ones.

Summary

We began this chapter by treating in some detail the reinforcement model of motivation. We did so because in our judgment, much of any motivation system is predicated on the consequences of behavior. People can be told what to do, how to do it, and what the likely outcomes will be, but in the end it is what really happens that counts. Therefore we emphasized behavior-contingent reinforcement—the provision of rewards or the taking away of punishments when desired behavior occurs. Many of the antecedents of a motive to act are what an individual brings to a particular situation and are typically beyond an organization's control. However, the motive to act in a particular circumstance also depends on organizational factors: incentives and reinforcements for action and outcomes of action, path and goal availability, standards of performance for any given work role, authoritative requests, and competing incentive and reinforcement properties of different actions and outcomes. Goals are accepted on the basis of these variables and, once accepted, imply an intent to act. Actions are then followed by certain outcomes that also have reinforcement properties. The consequences of the outcomes then become antecedents for further actions.

There are several important aspects to all of this. The first is that goal acceptance depends on one's motives to act. The motive to act depends in turn on personal factors, organizational history, and perceptions and expectations of what the organization has to offer.

Second, because the motive to act is determined by so many perceptual variables and subjective assessments of relative payoffs, any organization has only partial control over people's behavior. And this is true despite the adequacy of both the control system and organizational inducements such as pay.

Third, goal acceptance is only partly controlled by an organization. An organization may have an elaborate scheme for developing and setting goals, but it is not the goals themselves that people shoot for. Rather it is the subjectively determined payoffs—a combination of incentives attached to the organizational goals and to the paths toward the goals—that they go after. These payoffs are the real goals, and if they are valuable enough to individuals, they will be accepted and pursued (72).

Finally, the complexity associated with the intent to act compounds the problems of predicting action. All of these things contribute to the somewhat disappointing results of most empirical studies that have used similar models for predicting performance levels. They have not explained many of the variances of behavior. However, the studies do predict the direction of behavior; that is, if people see their effort as leading to organizationally defined performance levels or if they see levels of performance as associated with levels of incentives, then performance tends to be somewhat higher.

For example, money is an inducement for action. It is important to most of us who work and, indeed, getting more money is commonly thought of as an important goal. Is it more important than friendship, group cohesion, autonomy, avoiding fatigue, family, personal integrity, or consistency? We do not know. We do know, however, that monetary incentive systems work only to a point, and then no more. That is, people will do only so much for monetary inducements, or at least for those which are available in organizations. Getting more money is only one of a series of goals that individuals have and its relative importance can be gauged only by their behavior as they go about their organizational business. If the monetary inducements are large enough, then making more money will probably be an important goal because it does cut across several need areas, such as status and recognition. However, this idea rarely has been tested empirically.

Finally, the organization does have partial control of our perceptions, expectations, and reinforcements. It can create role clarity, path-goal clarity, certainty of reinforcements for reaching organizationally defined goals, and so forth. We call these organizational triggers. The problem has always been the inability to identify, with reasonable certainty, all the variables that people respond to and the linkages that people make between that behavior and what they see as the organizational payoffs. And so we have a Kerry Drake, wanting behavior that will contribute to his profits, but getting instead suppression of negative information.

The next chapter may help you develop your own perceptions of the types of linkages people make, determined primarily by the needs they bring to a given organizational setting and by the inducements for need satisfaction that exist in organizations.

References

1. ALLPORT, G. *Personality: A Psychological Interpretation.* New York: Holt, Rinehart and Winston, 1937.

2. ARVEY, R. D., and J. M. INVANCEVICH. "Punishment in Organizations: a Review, Propositions and Research Suggestions." *Academy of Management Review* 5 (1980): 123–132.
3. ATKINSON, J. W. *An Introduction to Motivation.* New York: Van Nostrand Reinhold, 1964.
4. ATKINSON, J. W., and N. T. FEATHER. *A Theory of Achievement Motivation.* New York: Wiley, 1966.
5. BANDURA, A. *Principles of Behavior Modification.* New York: Holt, Rinehart and Winston, 1969.
6. BANDURA, A. *Social Learning Theory,* Englewood Cliffs, N.J.: Prentice Hall, 1977.
7. BAUMEISTER, ROY F. "A Self-Presentational View of Social Phenomena." *Psychological Bulletin* 91 (January 1982): 3–26.
8. BECKER, L. J. "Joint Effect of Feedback and Goal Setting on Performance: Field Study of Residential Energy Conservation." *Journal of Applied Psychology* 63 (1978): 428–433.
9. BERGER, C. J., L. L. CUMMINGS, and H. G. HENEMEN. "Expectancy Theory and Operant Conditioning Predictions of Performance Under Variable Ratio and Continuous Schedules of Reinforcement." *Organizational Behavior and Human Performance* 14 (1975): 227–243.
10. BIRCH, D., and J. VEROFF. *Motivation: The Study of Action.* Monterey, Calif.: Brooks/Cole, 1965.
11. CAMPBELL, D. T., M. D. DUNNETTE, E. E. LAWLER, III, and K. E. WEICK, JR. *Managerial Behavior: Performance and Effectiveness.* New York: McGraw-Hill, 1970.
12. CAMPBELL, J. P., and R. D. PRITCHARD. "Motivation Theory in Industrial and Organizational Psychology." In *Handbook of Industrial and Organizational Psychology,* edited by M. D. Dunnette. Chicago: Rand McNally, 1976. Pp. 63–151.
13. CAMPION, MICHAEL A., and ROBERT G. LORD. "A Controls Systems Conceptualization of the Goal Setting and Changing Process." *Organizational Behavior and Human Performance* 30 (October 1982): 265–287.
14. DAVIS, T. R. V., and F. LUTHANS. "A Social Learning Approach to Organizational Behavior." *Academy of Management Review* 5 (1980): 281–290.
15. DAWIS, R., LLOYD LOFQUIST, and DAVID WEISS. *A Theory of Work Adjustment.* Minnesota Studies in Vocational Rehabilitation 23, Bulletin 47, 1968.
16. DOLLARD, J., and N. E. MILLER. *Personality and Psychotherapy.* New York: McGraw-Hill, 1950.
17. DOSSETT, D. L., G. P. LATHAM, and T. R. MITCHELL. "Effects of Assigned vs. Participatively Set Goals, Knowledge of Results, and Individual Differences on Employee Behavior When Goal Difficulty is Held Constant." *Journal of Applied Psychology* 64 (1979): 291–298.
18. DULANEY, D. E., JR. "Awareness, Rules and Propositions: A Confrontation with S-R Behavior Theory." In *Verbal Behavior and General Behavior Theory,* edited by D. Horton and T. Dixon. Englewood Cliffs, N.J.: Prentice-Hall, 1968. Pp. 340–488.
19. EMURIAN, HENRY H., CLEEVE S. EMURIAN, and JOSEPH J. BRADY. "Appetitive and Aversive Reinforcement Schedule Effects on Behavior: A Systematic Replication." *Basic and Applied Social Psychology* 3 (March 1982): 39–52.

20. FEIN, M. "Motivation for Work." In *Handbook of Work, Organization and Society,* edited by R. Dubin. Chicago: Rand McNally, 1976. Pp. 465–530.
21. GARLAND, HOWARD. "Goal Levels and Task Performance: A Compelling Replication of Some Compelling Results." *Journal of Applied Psychology* 67 (April 1982): 245–248.
22. GELLER, E. SCOTT, LISA PATTERSON and ELIZABETH TALBOT. "Deterrence and Income Tax Cheating: Testing Interaction Hypothesis in Utilitarian Theories." *Journal of Applied Behavior Analysis* 15 (Fall 1982): 403–413.
23. GELLERMAN, S. W. *Motivation and Productivity,* New York: American Management Association, 1963.
24. GEORGOPOULOS, B. S., G. M. MAHONEY, and N. W. JONES. "A Path-Goal Approach to Productivity." *Journal of Applied Psychology* 41 (1957): 345–353.
25. GRAEN, G. B. "Instrumentality Theory of Work Motivation: Some Experimental Results and Suggested Modifications." *Journal of Applied Psychology* Monograph 53 (1969): 1–25.
26. HOM, PETER W., ANGELO S. DE NISE, ANGELO J. KINICKI, and BRENDAN D. BANNISTER. "Effectiveness of Performance Feedback from Behaviorally Anchored Rating Scales." *Journal of Applied Psychology* 65 (October 1982): 568–576.
27. ILGEN, A. R., C. D. FISHER, and M. S. TAYLOR. "Consequences of Individual Feedback on Behavior in Organizations." *Journal of Applied Psychology* 64 (1979): 349–371.
28. IVANCEVICH, J. M. "Different Goal Setting Treatments and Their Effects on Performance and Job Satisfaction." *Academy of Management Journal* 20 (1977): 406–418.
29. IVANCEVICH, J. M. "Effects of Goal Setting on Performance and Job Satisfaction." *Journal of Applied Psychology* 61 (1976): 605–612.
30. JOHNSON, DAVID W., GEOFFREY MARUYAMA, ROGER JOHNSON, DEBORAH NELSON, and LINDA SKON. "Effects of Cooperative, Competitive, and Individualistic Goal Structures on Achievement: A Meta-Analysis." *Psychological Bulletin* 89 (January 1981): 47–62.
31. JUDD, R., and J. LAWRENCE. "Effects of Wage Incentives on Productivity." Paper presented at the MBAA meetings, Chicago, 1982.
32. KATZ, D., and R. L. KAHN. *The Social Psychology of Organizations,* 2nd ed. New York: Wiley, 1977.
33. KAZDEN, A. E. *Behavior Modification in Applied Settings.* Homewood, Ill.: Dorsey Press, 1975.
34. KIM, J. S., and W. C. HAMNER. "Effect of Performance Feedback and Goal Setting on Productivity and Satisfaction in an Organizational Setting." *Journal of Applied Psychology* 61 (1976): 48–57.
35. KOMAKI, J., K. D. BORWICK, and L. R. SCOTT. "A Behavioral Approach to Occupational Safety: Pinpointing and Reinforcing Safe Performance in a Food Manufacturing Plant." *Journal of Applied Psychology* 63 (1978): 434–445.
36. KOMAKI, JUDITH L., ROBERT L. COLLINS, and PAT PENN. "The Role of Performance Antecedents and Consequences in Work Motivation." *Journal of Applied Psychology* 67 (June 1982): 334–340.

37. KOPELMAN, R. E., and P. H. THOMPSON. "Boundary Conditions for Expectancy Theory Predictions of Work Motivation and Job Performance." *Academy of Management Journal* 19 (1976): 237–258.
38. LATHAM, GARY P., LARRY L. CUMMINGS, and TERRENCE R. MITCHELL. "Behavioral Strategies to Improve Productivity." *Organizational Dynamics* (Winter 1981): 5–23.
39. LATHAM, G. P., and D. L. DOSSETT. "Designing Incentive Plans for Unionized Employees: A Comparison of Continuous and Variable Ratio Reinforcement Schedules." *Personnel Psychology* 31 (1978): 47–61.
40. LATHAM, G. P., and G. A. TUKL. "Effects of Assigned and Participative Goal Setting on Performance and Job Satisfaction." *Journal of Applied Psychology* 60 (1975): 299–302.
41. LAURIE, JOHN. "The HRD Ladder: Changing Attitudes and Motivations." *Personnel Journal* 61 (November 1982): 820–822.
42. LAWLER, E. E. *Pay and Organizational Effectiveness: A Psychological View.* New York: McGraw-Hill, 1971.
43. LINCOLN, J. F. *Incentive Management.* Cleveland, Ohio: Lincoln Electric, 1951.
44. LITWIN, G. H., and R. A. STRINGER, JR. *Motivation and Organizational Climate.* Cambridge, Mass., Harvard University Press, 1968.
45. LOCKE, E. A. "The Myths of Behavior Mod in Organizations." *Academy of Management Review* 2 (1977): 543–553.
46. ———. "The Nature and Causes of Job Satisfaction." In *Handbook of Industrial and Organizational Psychology,* edited by M. D. Dunnette. Chicago: Rand McNally, 1976.
47. ———. "The Ubiquity of the Technique of Goal Setting in Theories of and Approaches to Employee Motivation." *Academy of Management Review* 3 (1978): 594–601.
48. ———. "Toward a Theory of Task Motivation and Incentives." *Organizational Behavior and Human Performance* 3 (1968): 157–189.
49. LOCKE, E. A., J. F. BRYAN, and L. M. KENDALL. "Goals and Intentions as Mediators of the Effects of Monetary Incentives on Behavior." *Journal of Applied Psychology* 52 (1968): 104–121.
50. LOCKE, E. A., D. B. FEREN, V. M. MCCALEB, K. N. SHAW, and A. T. DENNY. "The Relative Effectiveness of Four Methods of Motivating Employee Performance." In *Changes in Working Life,* edited by K. D. Duncan, M. M. Greenberg, and D. Wallis. New York: Wiley, 1980.
51. LONG, J. SCOTT, and MCGINNIS, ROBERT. "Organizational Context and Scientific Productivity." *American Sociological Review* 46 (August 1981): 422–442.
52. LUTHANS, FRED, ROBERT PAUL, and DOUGLAS BAKER. "An Experimental Analysis of the Impact of Contingent Reinforcement on Salespersons' Performance Behavior." *Journal of Applied Psychology* 66 (June 1981): 314–323.
53. MATSUI, TAMAO, AKINORI OKADA, and TAKASHI KAKUYAMA. "Influence of Achievement Need on Goal Setting, Performance, and Feedback Effectiveness." *Journal of Applied Psychology* 67 (October 1982): 645–648.
54. MATSUI, TAMAO, AKINORI OKADA, and REYI MIZUGUCHI. "Expectancy Theory Predic-

tion of the Goal Theory Postulate, 'The Harder the Goals, The Higher the Performance.'" *Journal of Applied Psychology* 66 (February 1981): 54–58.

55. McClelland, D. C. *The Achieving Society.* New York, Van Nostrand Reinhold, 1961.
56. McClelland, D. C. *Power, the Inner Experience.* New York: Irvington Publishers, 1975.
57. Meyer, H. H., and W. B. Walker. "Need for Achievement and Risk Preferences as they Relate to Attitudes Towards Reward Systems and Performance Appraisal in an Industrial Setting." *Journal of Applied Psychology* 45 (1961): 251–256.
58. Milbourn, G., Jr. "The Relationship of Money to Motivation." *Compensation Review* 12 (1980): 33–44.
59. Milgram, S. "Some Conditions of Obedience and Disobedience to Authority." *Human Relations* 18 (1965): 57–76.
60. Miller, Lynn E., and Richard M. Weiss. "The Work-leisure Relationship: Evidence for the Compensatory Hypothesis." *Human Relations* 35 (September 1982): 763–771.
61. Miner, John B. *Theories of Organizational Behavior.* Hinsdale, Ill.: The Dryden Press, 1980.
62. Miner, John B. "The Role of Managerial and Professional Motivation in the Career Success of Management Professors." *Academy of Management Journal* 23 (1980): 487–508.
63. Miner, John B., and Donald P. Crane. "Motivation to Manage and the Manifestation of a Managerial Orientation in Career Planning." *Academy of Management Journal* 24 (September 1981): 626–633.
64. Miner, John B. and Norman R. Smith. "Decline and Stabilization of Managerial Motivation Over a Twenty-year Period." *Journal of Applied Psychology* 67 (June 1982): 297–305.
65. Mitchel, James O. "The Effect of Intentions, Tenure, Personal, and Organizational Variables on Managerial Turnover." *Academy of Management Journal* 24 (December 1981): 742–751.
66. Mitchell, T. R. "Expectancy Models of Job Satisfaction, Occupational Preference and Effort: A Theoretical, Methodological and Empirical Appraisal." *Psychological Bulletin* 81 (1974): 1053–1077.
67. Mower, John C., R. Dennis Middlemist, and David Luther. "Joint Effects of Assigned Goal Level and Incentive Structure on Task Performance: A Laboratory Study." *Journal of Applied Psychology* 65 (October 1981): 598–603.
68. O'Reilly, C. A., and K. H. Roberts. "Supervisor Influences and Subordinate Mobility Aspirations as Moderators of Consideration and Initiating Structure." *Journal of Applied Psychology* 63 (1978): 96–102.
69. O'Reilly, C. A., and B. A. Weitz. "Managing Marginal Employees: The Use of Warnings and Dismissals." *Administrative Science Quarterly* 25 (1980): 467–484.
70. Orpen, C. "Effects of Bonuses for Attendance on Absenteeism of Industrial Workers." *Journal of Organizational Behavior Management* 1 (1978): 118–124.
71. Peak, H. "Attitude and Motivation." In *Nebraska Symposium on Motivation,* edited by M. R. Jones. Lincoln: University of Nebraska Press, 1955. Pp. 149–188.
72. Perry, Lee T., and Jay B. Barney. "Performance Lies Are Hazardous to Organizational Health." *Organizational Dynamics* (Winter 1981): 68–80.

73. PORTER, L. W., and E. E. LAWLER, III. *Managerial Attitudes and Performance.* Homewood, Ill.: Irwin, 1968.
74. PORTER, L. W., and RICHARD M. STEERS. *Motivation and Work Behavior.* New York: McGraw-Hill, 1983.
75. PRITCHARD, R. D., ET. AL. "The Effects of Varying Schedules of Reinforcement on Human Task Performance." *Organizational Behavior and Human Performance* 16 (1976): 205–230.
76. ROTHE, H. F. "Out Put Rates Among Industrial Employees." *Journal of Applied Psychology* 63 (1978): 70–76.
77. SALOMONE, PAUL R., and ROBERT B. SLANEY. "The Influence of Chance and Contingency Factors on the Vocational Choice Process of Nonprofessional Workers." *Journal of Vocational Behavior* 19 (August 1981): 25–35.
78. SAMPSON, E. E. "Cognitive Psychology as Ideology." *American Psychologist* 36 (1981): 730–743.
79. SCHREISHEIM, C. A., and A. S. DINISI. "Task Dimensions as Moderators of the Instrumental Effects of Instrumental Leadership, a Two-Sample Replicated Test of the Path-Goal Leadership Theory." *Journal of Applied Psychology* 66 (1981): 589–597.
80. SCHREISHEIM, J. F. "The Social Context of Leader-Subordinate Relations: An Investigation of the Effects of Group Cohesiveness." *Journal of Applied Psychology* 65 (1980): 183–194.
81. SIMS, H. P., JR. "Further Thoughts on Punishment in Organizations." *Academy of Management Review* 5 (1980): 133–138.
82. SORCHER, M. *The Effects of Employee Involvement on Work Performance.* New York: Personnel Research Planning and Practices, General Electric Co., 1969.
83. SPECTOR, PAUL E. "Behavior in Organizations as a Function of Employees' Locus of Control." *Psychological Bulletin* 91 (May 1982): 482–497.
84. SPENCE, K. W. *Behavior Theory and Learning.* Englewood Cliffs, N.J.: Prentice-Hall, 1960.
85. STEPHANS, T. A., and W. A. BURROUGHS. "An Application of Operant Conditioning to Absenteeism in a Hospital Setting." *Journal of Applied Psychology* 63 (1978): 518–521.
86. TAYLOR, F. W. "The Principles of Scientific Management." *Advanced Management Journal* (September 1963): 30–39. The text on pages 221–22 is quoted by permission of the publisher from the *Advanced Management Journal,* September 1963. © 1963 by the Society for the Advancement of Management, pp. 31, 32. All rights reserved.
87. TERBORG, J. R. "The Motivational Components of Goal Setting." *Journal of Applied Psychology* 61 (1976): 613–621.
88. THORNDIKE, E. L. *The Psychology of Learning.* New York: Teacher's College, 1913.
89. TOLMAN, E. C. *Purposive Behavior in Animals and Men.* New York: Century, 1932.
90. TOWNSEND, JOHN M. "Job Involvement of Intrinsically and Extrinsically Motivated Indian Managers: To Each According to his Need." *Human Relations* 35 (September 1982): 785–804.
91. VROOM, V. H. *Work and Motivation.* New York: Wiley, 1964.
92. WHEELER, KENNETH G., and THOMAS A. MAHONEY. "The Expectancy Model in the

Analysis of Occupational Preference and Occupational Choice." *Journal of Vocational Behavior* 19 (August 1981): 113–122.
93. WHITE, S. E., and T. R. MITCHELL. "Job Enrichment Vs. Social Cues: Comparison and Competitive Test." *Journal of Applied Psychology* 64 (1979): 1–9.
94. WHYTE, W. F., JR. *Money and Motivation.* New York: Harper, 1955.
95. ———. "Skinnerian Theory in Organizations." *Psychology Today* (April 1972): 67–68, 96, 98.
96. WOOD, ROBERT E., and TERENCE R. MITCHELL. "Manager Behavior in a Social Context: The Impact of Impression Management in Attributions and Disciplinary Actions." *Organizational Behavior and Human Performance* 28 (December 1981): 356–378.
97. WOODWORTH, R. S. *Experimental Psychology.* New York: Holt, Reinhart and Winston, 1938.

Discussion Questions

1. Discuss Kerry's and John's behavior (John is the worker Taylor described) in terms of positive and negative reinforcement.
2. Discuss positive and negative reinforcement and punishment in terms of gaining desired behavior.
3. Discuss generalization, extinction, and satiation as they apply to the probability of gaining desired behavior.
4. Why is the process of directed behavior a dynamic rather than static condition? Illustrate using the concepts of needs, goals, incentives, and reinforcement.
5. Construct a motivation system for students in which learning rather than getting good grades is the desired outcome. Explain.
6. Why must we add the concept of expectations to those of needs, goals, incentives, and reinforcements for a more complete understanding of motivation in organizations?
7. Research has disclosed that the higher the goal and the more specific it is, the higher the performance. Using the concepts of reinforcement, expectations, and feedback, explain why. When may that relationship *not* be true?

Chapter 10
Motivation: Need Theories, Incentives, and Reinforcements

Virtue Is Its Own Reward

This was the afternoon of The Company picnic. Specifically, it was the afternoon of The Company corporate headquarters picnic, and Company people from very different callings had come together to celebrate The Company way of life. As is usual in these things, people couldn't avoid "talking shop," though not in the usual way. In this informal setting they were willing to talk about things they usually wouldn't.

So it was on this lazy, hot July afternoon that Stanley, Penny, Ted, and Dr. Faust were sitting together around the table, sipping beer under a big shade tree. Somehow the conversation had come around to how each had gotten where he or she was. There were stories of past ambitions and future aspirations. Now Penny was recounting her first job.

"I suppose I thought that government service would give me the fairest shake. The starting salaries were good and they said it didn't matter whether you were a man or a woman. But after I'd been there awhile I just couldn't take it any longer. It just seemed to me that nobody gave a damn that they weren't going anywhere—that no matter what you did you only moved up after a certain amount of time had passed. And nobody seemed to care about what they were doing. Not that there was anything to do.

"Fact is, they all seemed to *hate* their work. But maybe that's too strong a word. Anyway, a lot of them, especially the men, were there because there was something about applying their time in military service toward seniority on the job, and that way they got more pay than they could someplace else."

"How could you know they hated their work?" Ted queried.

"How do I know? I just know, that's all. You could see it in everything. Listen, I'll tell you how I know. The high point of the day for them was quitting time. I think it was really the most creative thing most of them did all day. Here, let me give you the picture." Penny took a broken twig and started sketching on the bare earth.

"This place was what they called a 'secure facility.' It was spread out over acres and acres like this. It was all fenced in and there was only one exit. Then the buildings were scattered all over the place for security, I guess. Everyone drove their own automobile and parked near the building where they worked.

"Now you can see what happens. Come five o'clock, everyone's trying to get out this one gate and the line really backs up. Why sometimes it's backed up all the way to here." Penny pointed to the middle of her sketch.

"If you got stuck towards the end of that line, it might take you as much as half an hour to get out. The real problem was that you had to show your security pass at the gate so you could be cleared to leave. You couldn't just zip through."

Now Penny's tone changed as she simulated the drama of the scene about to unfold. "Get this picture: Here it is, oh, maybe 4:57. You look around outside. Not a soul to be seen. But here and there—behind trees, in driveways, even behind shrubbery on the lawn—what do you see? Cars, lots of 'em. The motors are all running and the doors are open. Over the entire laboratory grounds, nothing but cars pointed in one direction, warmed up and ready to go. Now it's 4:59. Still no sign of life outside. But look through the exit doors. There they are, backed up ten deep, waiting to break with the gun.

"There it is! The siren screams—5 o'clock." Penny waved her hands to signify the tumult. "Here they come, tumbling from doorways and exits. And, what's this? Some have even been hiding behind those trees. So they've got a head start. They leap into those open car doors, tromp on the gas, and the daily Grand Prix is under way. So ends another day."

The group applauded Penny's dramatization.

"Now ask me how I know they hated their jobs. I couldn't work at a place like that. They were just putting in their time."

Now Stanley joined in. "I know *just* what you mean, Penny. If you're not going to give it your best, why—why bother?"

Then no one spoke for a while. They all seemed to be thinking how lucky they had been to be able to work for The Company. Finally, it was Ted, somewhat mellowed from the beer and late afternoon heat, who offered his own observations.

"I have to admit that sometimes I have difficulty in understanding you kids. (In reality, he wasn't *that* much older than Stanley and Penny.) What does liking your job have to do with it? You're given a job to do and you do it. What more is there to say? Look, the way I see it, if I take care of *my* end of things, why, The Company will take care of theirs. I'll get my promotions and pay raises, and sooner or later I *will* have the kind of job I want.

"Hell, you can't expect every job to be interesting. And that's not what you're being paid for. You're being paid to do what The Company needs done. It's as simple as that.

"Why are we all working, anyway? For the money, that's why. Otherwise you wouldn't be working, would you? Listen, I've never had a job that I didn't find interesting, even if it was just to find a way to get it done as quickly as possible so I could get through with it. But that's what Mr. Marsh pays us for. Don't forget it. We need him a lot more than he needs us. Any of us."

With this last statement Dr. Faust rose to the bait. Indeed, he too was feeling a bit mellow, a bit less reserved.

"That is what you believe, isn't it, Ted? And if that's how you feel, fine. But don't ask the rest of us to agree. I, for one, do not.

"I suppose you all know that I worked for Another Company for a time some years ago. I suppose I had a very good position there. So good, in fact, that my salary was just about cut in half when I joined The University. I've never regretted that move. I admit, as Ted suggests, that occasionally I think about what I might have been making had I stayed. But it was worth it."

"Worth it? How? How can you possibly say that?" Ted was perplexed. This made no sense to him whatsoever.

"Yes, others have asked me the same thing. The best answer I can give you is to tell you how it came about. I had been working with a staff group attached to the corporate director of manufacturing. We were doing research in applying some newly developed optimizing techniques to manufacturing operations. For a while I felt that we all had the best of both worlds. We were applying our knowledge in a real-life laboratory, so to speak.

"But there was always a tension between management and our group. As Ted says, we were only there to do what Another Company wanted done. We had to justify our group's existence continually.

"Then, after several years of this, the work started to become routine. We saw the same old problems again and again. I started to feel that nothing more lay ahead of me but more of the same. Then one day I was asked if I wished to take a new position, that of assistant to the vice president for manufacturing. To be honest about it I was quite flattered. But I didn't want it. And if I didn't take that position, that would mark a turning point in my career. From then on, if I stayed with Another Company I would be looked upon as someone who didn't have what it took to make it into management. Sooner or later I would be seen as a failure."

Faust paused, distracted by Ted's look of sheer disbelief. "You didn't want it! I can't believe it. Don't you know why they offered you that kind of job? They were going to groom you for top management. That's how much they must have thought of you. And you threw it away?"

"I don't expect you to agree, just to understand. I didn't, and I still don't, want a career in management. To me, you see, that would be the end of freedom. From that point on I would be doing only what I was told, working on problems that somebody else wanted solved."

"Is it really that different at The University?" Penny ventured. Faust thought for a moment. Then chuckled, "No, I'd be lying if I claimed it was. But it is to some extent. Take those never-ending reports we produced at Another Company. I don't think anyone ever read them, you know. We cranked them out because we had to justify ourselves; we had to produce some concrete evidence of the worth of our research activities. But we had no interest in them, really."

"How very different from your articles in the Journal, eh, Faust?" Ted chimed in. Ted had Dr. Faust dead to rights there.

"Well, ah—possibly I don't see your point, Ted," replied Faust.

"Oh, sure you do. Those things in the Journal are as dull as dishwater and you know it. Who reads 'em? A handful of people maybe. How are they so different from what you did for Another Company?"

"I see. Possibly you are right. But there *is* one big difference. Those articles in the Journal represent my own interests—what I choose to work on, not what I've been *told* to work on. Possibly you will not see that much difference in the actual content, but there is a world of difference in the motivation." There was no mirth in Faust's tone.

Not so for Ted. He was genuinely enjoying himself. "I've really got to hand it to you, Doc. If that makes sense to you, then you're really your own man." Ted's tone was half mirth and half amazement. "I can't think of many people who would have the moral fortitude to take a 50 percent cut in pay—at least—and give up a top executive post just so they could write reports that nobody will read, *but* what they wanted to write instead of what the company wanted them to. Yep. That's a *real* achievement."

It is possible that Ted had a little too much beer, but Faust didn't mind. After all, he'd never had a great deal of success in explaining what he'd done. And, after all, there was the real possibility that it *didn't* make any sense.

In Chapter 9 we noted that people seek to gain rewards. When attached to work goals, they are incentives—things people want. Therefore, it is the incentives that people seek and that serve as reinforcers. Thus, incentives are goals that people shoot for and, if obtained, they are likely to reinforce the goal-directed behavior. As a consequence, motivation systems are, in part, incentive systems. But what makes an incentive?

In this chapter, we will examine an issue that has puzzled psychologists for some time, namely, why do things that seem rewarding—or that seem like punishment—for some do not for others? What we address is the complexity contained in the relatively simple framework of Chapter 9. It is this complexity that presents difficulties for designing motivational systems.

We will begin with a historical perspective of the various need theories; then go through the development and refinement of such theories as they pertain to organizations. After this, we will try to place the current knowledge within the framework that we provided in Chapter 9. We will conclude with the idea that it is possible to design incentive systems that touch the majority of people, at least to the extent that many—but not all—desired behaviors can be predicted. However, we leave you to develop your own conclusions as to why only a handful of organizations seem to have developed the kinds of incentive programs that encourage substantial directed behaviors toward what the organization defines as its primary operative goals. But first, let us go back to The Company.

It is easy to say that the motives of Penny and Faust are better, somehow, than Ted's—but they are not. Each is responding to a system in which his or her own individual needs can best be met. Penny was upset with her experience in government work. But she was not upset because of the money or the security provided by the government, for each was substantial. What bothered her was the lack of opportunity for advancement, and the facts that the work itself was uninteresting and the work climate contrary to her own value system.

Why couldn't Ted understand? Clearly he viewed the role of work in his own life differently from the way Penny viewed it in hers. He saw work as mostly instrumental for making more money and for moving ahead in the organization. We suspect that Ted also had certain needs to be controlled by others and told what to do. What, then, motivated Ted? Money seemed to be the key. But status was also important to him. The job itself had little to do with his motivation.

To Faust, clearly, the job was the end. He wanted a job that would offer him more autonomy and new challenges—not more power. This kind of thinking was beyond Ted's comprehension.

So it is with each of us. Although we are motivated differently by different basic needs we may have other needs as well. For example, Penny joined the government because the starting salaries were high and she had an opportunity, as a woman, to move ahead. At that time, then, Penny was motivated by things other than those which led her to leave the government. Faust's story suggests that he, too, had a number of needs—even power needs. But the need for autonomy and the need not to be seen as a failure in the organization were more important to him than any other at that particular time.

Thus, different people are motivated to act by different needs; and these differences are not so much a function of the total presence or absence of specific needs, but rather of the extent to which a given need is important to the person at that time. What, then, are the needs that motivate action?

Need Theories

The Need Hierarchy

In 1943 Abraham Maslow, a clinical psychologist, developed a theory in which he classified the major needs shared by the majority of people he observed in his clinical practice. These needs were identified as (1) physiological, including hunger, thirst, elimination, and so on; (2) safety needs, including freedom from physical and psychological harm; (3) belongingness, including friendship, love, affiliation, and affection; (4) esteem, such as self-respect, respect of others, and a general feeling of being worthwhile; and (5) self-actualization, which concerns reaching one's potential as a total human being.

Underlying Maslow's theory are two assumptions that were shaped by the work of his predecessors (72). These are:

1. Satisfied needs are not motivating, whereas unsatisfied needs are.
2. All people, to a greater or lesser extent, have the identified needs.

Maslow's contribution is his contention that the needs are arranged in a hierarchy of importance or prepotency. That is, the lowest needs are the most important until they are satisfied. Then the next need level becomes prepotent. Higher-level needs are not motivating until lower-level needs are satisfied. For example, if an individual is hungry or fears for his personal safety, then that is what dominates his thoughts and motivates his actions. He cannot concern himself with affiliation, self-esteem, and so forth, until he is no longer hungry or in danger.

Although these notions generally make sense and have generated considerable interest among organizational theorists like Douglas McGregor (63), there are some problems with the theory. First, one may possibly satisfy one's physiological and safety needs most of the time, but higher order needs seem relatively insatiable. That is, can one get enough love, self-esteem, or self-actualization? We think not, and the empirical evidence substantiates this thought (53).

Second, the hierarchy assumes that each need level operates discretely and that the simultaneous operation of levels is unlikely. Maslow recognizes this problem (57), but others have taken him too literally. In fact, a person can strive for love, self-esteem, and self-actualization all at the same time (57). Then the question becomes, how much love or esteem does one require before the need is satisfied and the next level becomes dominant? We would guess that the requisite amount of need satisfaction varies among individuals and depends greatly on the relative strength of each person's needs.

Third, Maslow's initial formulation predicted behavior quite different from reinforcement theories. For example, reinforcement theory predicts that need satisfaction is reinforcing and, therefore, leads to repeated behavior. The need hierarchy predicts that need satisfaction leads to other concerns *unless* the need is again aroused. This difference can be reconciled if we assume that continued satiation is unlikely and that the higher-level needs become more important the more they are reinforced (19). For example, are you likely to stop doing the things that will bring you more self-esteem? Or, if you do something that increases your self-esteem, isn't it likely to have been pleasurable enough that you would strive for that feeling again? Most people will answer that they take any opportunity to perform actions associated with self-esteem. It is not surprising, therefore, that the evidence supports this logic (41, 53, 89). In other words, higher-order needs, being relatively insatiable, present opportunities for continued and highly valued reinforcement and, consequently, offer considerable potential for building organizational incentives.

Maslow extended his theory to some extent by classifying needs into deficiency and growth needs (57). The deficiency needs include physiological needs, safety, belongingness, love, respect, and self-esteem; when there are deficiencies people are motivated to remove them. The growth needs, on the other hand, sensitize people to things that cannot possibly be totally satisfied, and therefore are always operating.

Lawler and Suttle suggest the following conclusion:

> On the lowest level of the hierarchy are the basic biological needs . . . all other needs are on the second level. The lower level needs are clearly distinguished from the high level ones in that they are biologically based; the base can be specified with some confidence. It is not clear what the biological bases for the higher level needs are. Further, all the lower level needs show a linear inverse relationship between satisfaction and importance; higher satisfaction leads to lower importance. No such clear cut relationship exists for the needs that are classified as higher level. (53:284)

Indeed, as Wahba and Bridwell (88) point out, evidence exists that the relationship between importance and satisfaction for higher-level needs is positive and linear, which supports Maslow's final statement (41). In other words, the more the growth needs are reinforced, the more important they become.

Finally, whether or not Maslow's need hierarchy is a valid theory is debatable. Even if we assume that the so-called deficiency needs are reasonably satisfied by the organization, which of the higher-level needs will then become prepotent and when (3)? We suspect that this depends a great deal on the individual's personality and past learning. It is, therefore, impractical to specify anything definitive with regard to the Maslow need hierarchy other than the points we have already made. Individual differences are so obvious and empirical support so sketchy that a more final statement would be misleading.

Alderfer reformulated the Maslow hierarchy into existence needs, relatedness needs, and growth needs (2). Existence needs are desires for material things associated with food and shelter, though money falls into this category too. Relatedness needs have to do with other people; the need for affiliation, sharing one's thoughts, interaction, and esteem from others are examples. Growth needs are the development of whatever abilities and capacities the individual feels at any given time. Growth needs could include self-esteem and self-actualization, but the concept is less confining than Maslow's self-actualization, since any form of personal development can be included in the category. However, additional evidence helps us redefine our thinking to some extent.

The Herzberg Motivation-Hygiene Theory (M-H Theory)

According to the M-H theory there are two classes of work factors: extrinsic and intrinsic.

EXTRINSIC FACTORS. Extrinsic factors are things the organization itself provides. They are substantive and nonpsychological and include money; supervision; interpersonal relations; company policies such as rules, regulations, and fringe benefits; working conditions or physical surroundings; and job security. They are part of the given work environment and are not necessarily job-related; hence, they are "extrinsic." According to Herzberg and his colleagues, extrinsic factors are usually not associated with motivation. That is, they may have incentive value, but since none are part of the job itself, they tend to be short term. They are also related to pain-avoidance needs (negative reinforcement) that either pull or push a person toward an action. The individual can be pulled to act by an incentive such as more money for production—the pain being deprivation of extra money—or pushed to act by the incentive of avoiding being fired. A major review of the M-H theory and its empirical research states:

> In either case (push-pull) the forces move the individual by acting upon him from the "outside." The pain avoidance needs themselves have the basic characteristic of being cyclical in nature. The feeling of deprivation is recurring and progressively requires an increase in incentives for its satisfaction. The performance implications are as follows: the effect of hygiene factors is short term; the level of performance will never be above the minimum effort necessary to eliminate a state of psychological or physical pain or discomfort. In order to get performance (movement) one must create a pain situation or play upon an already existing pain. Otherwise, there is no reason to expect movement. (32:842)

However, as Katz and Kahn (50) point out, extrinsic factors are related to the motivation to join and stay in an organization, as well as to the subsequent minimal performance levels that are required for continued employment.

INTRINSIC FACTORS. According to Herzberg, intrinsic factors are part of the job itself and of the person's psychological relationship to the job. These factors are *achievement* or completing an important task successfully, *recognition* for doing a good job, *responsibility* for the outcomes of one's own or others' behavior, *advancement* to a better job, and the *interest* or *challenge* inherent in the job. Each is embedded in the job, can be a consequence of job performance, and, hence, has incentive value and potential reinforcing properties. Consequently, these factors are thought to be long lasting and directly associated with an individual's maximum potential. Herzberg's theory is summarized in Figure 10.1.

The M-H theory has come under a great deal of criticism. Often, these criticisms concern methodology and are not relevant to our discussion here. However, several independent studies conducted for other purposes tend to corroborate Herzberg's formulations [see Broedling (14) for a review]. Furthermore, the evidence by no means refutes Herzberg (32), except as M-H theory relates to job satisfaction, a topic we will cover later in this chapter. Indeed, evidence suggests that there are general classifications of intrinsic versus extrinsic outcomes, much as Herzberg suggested (14, 17, 18, 19). Furthermore, the theory not only fits with reinforcement theory, it also fits with the Maslow need hierarchy and with Alderfer's extension. Extrinsic factors are associated with the lower-order needs, and intrinsic factors with the higher-order or growth needs (see Figure 10.2). And if our previous discussion is correct, the intrinsic factors, being associated with the relatively insatiable higher needs, would more continuously provide the reinforcement and consequently the incentives for which people strive.

Notice that intrinsic factors are often outcomes or reinforcements that people can provide for themselves, whereas extrinsic factors are almost wholly granted by others. And each is important since each has different implications for designing motivation systems. For example, motivation systems that rely to a large extent on extrinsic factors must create incentives related to job behav-

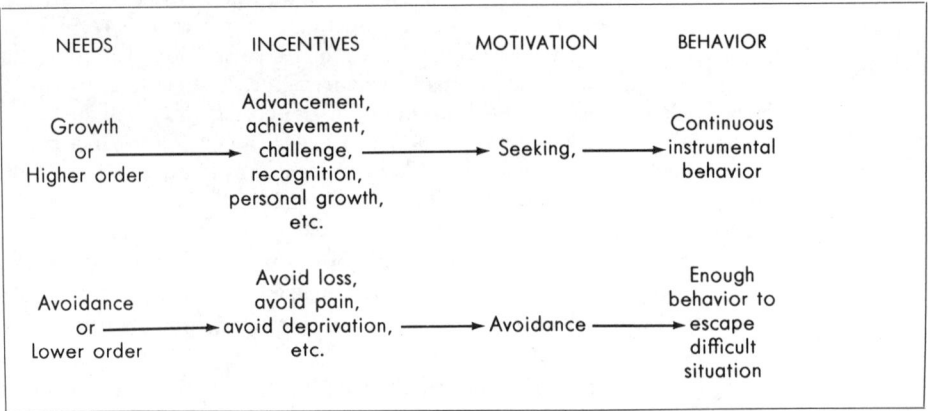

FIGURE 10.1 Dynamics of the M–H Theory

Need Theories

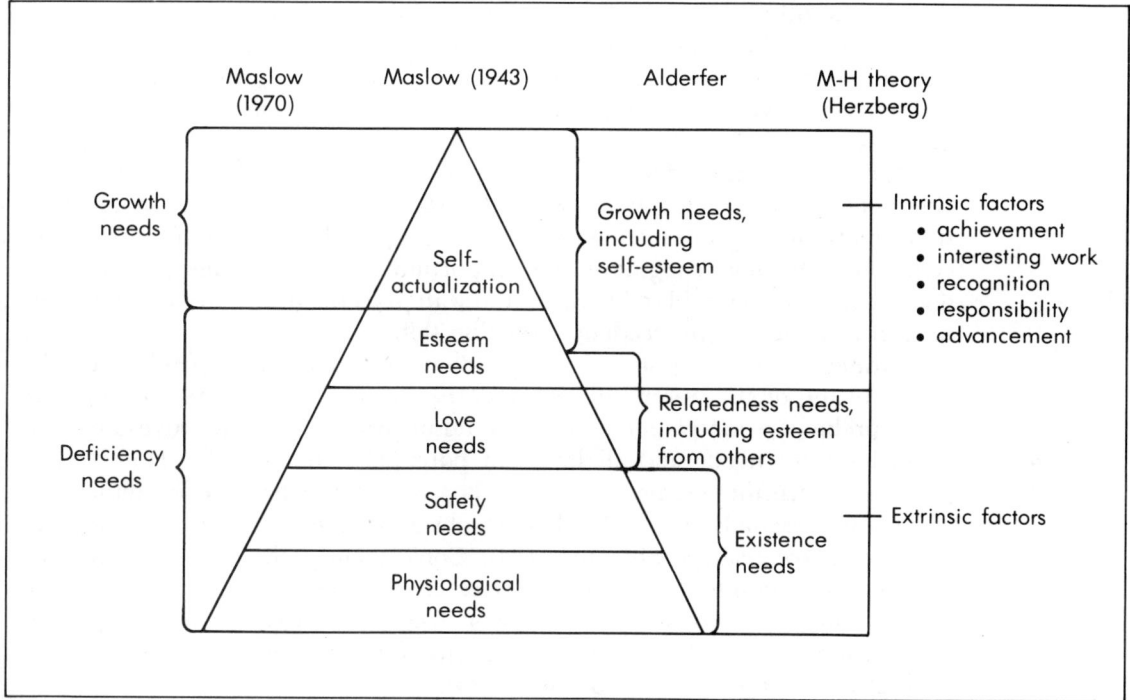

FIGURE 10.2 Needs Hierarchy, Existence-Relatedness-Growth, and M-H Theories Compared

ior. Money is often used this way. However, motivation systems that take intrinsic factors into account will likely focus on job design. Or, as we have argued, various combinations may be appropriate because of the variety of possible definitions of incentive value. Further, evidence suggests that where extrinsic rewards are used as a primary mode of reinforcement, then intrinsic or self-mediated rewards tend to lose some of their incentive properties (19). And reinforcements associated with higher-levels needs or intrinsic factors seem to make these needs stronger, not weaker, whereas the opposite is true for lower-level needs or extrinsic factors (see Alderfer (2), Deci (19), Lawler and Suttle (53), and Maslow (57)).

It is useful to classify these needs as we have done, because each class suggests different strategies for building motivation systems. If, for example, an organization wants to increase performance, it may have several strategies to pursue, either separately or together. To provide incentives related to extrinsic factors, it can directly attach money to performance, or use the opportunity to associate in a satisfactory manner with other people or groups as an incentive.

On the other hand, motivation systems that include better working conditions, increased benefits, or more palatable company policies may satisfy needs but cannot be directly tied to performance. Hence, they provide no incentive for behavior other than the general intent to become a part of and stay in the organization (50, 52).

Intrinsic incentives focus on the job itself—that is, on job designs that provide opportunities for completing an important task successfully, assuming responsibility, having interesting and challenging work, and, on successful task completion gaining recognition and opportunity for advancement. These job dimensions are then said to be associated with psychological states or cognitions that, in turn, are the antecedents of action (39).

Strategies may be pursued independently or together, depending on the nature of the organization and the tasks that people are expected to perform. A comprehensive motivation system should incorporate the incentives attached to all levels of needs and all levels of potential outcome (49). However, in practical terms, this seems impossible. For example, it has proven difficult to restructure assembly line technologies substantially so that the intrinsic reinforcements are realistic outcomes (24). Consequently, the organization must pay more attention to money and other externally mediated rewards to provide sufficient incentives for directed behavior. Under such circumstances organizations generally try to have clear-cut incentives, work rules, and procedures so people will work at a satisfactory level (24).

Special Cases of Higher Order Needs

NEED FOR AFFILIATION. Special cases of higher-order needs have been identified as particularly important for organizational motivation systems. Indeed, each was considered at one time a major motivational source for organizational behavior (59, 81). These needs are needs for *affiliation, achievement,* and *power.* Affiliation is undeniably powerful for many people. Its organizational pertinency, however, is confined primarily to two things: (1) the relationship that people have to their group; and second, (2) their relationship to the leader of that group. Rewards to be gained from establishing and maintaining good interpersonal relations have been shown over and again to be related to a number of job behaviors. Group cohesion is an example.

However, the need for affiliation has never consistently been shown as a motive for organizational effectiveness, except in organizations specifically established to satisfy the need. Consequently, though it may be a powerful need, it moderates behavior only when directed by other needs. For example, group cohesion is associated with high productivity *only when* the group norms support high productivity. If the incentives attached to other needs conflict with the incentives for satisfying the affiliative need, then we must examine the way the incentives are being applied, for the intended behavior may not be what actually occurs. If the need for affiliation builds on other organizational incentives—for example on *group* monetary incentive systems—then potential conflict created by different incentives may be minimized.

NEED FOR ACHIEVEMENT. The need for achievement has been defined as a need to excel in relation to a competitive or internalized standard (6, 7, 86). People motivated by the need for achievement tend to concern themselves with goal attainment; they also spend a great deal of time thinking about plans for achieving these goals and for overcoming obstacles or blocks toward that end (60). They tend to take personal responsibility for solving problems, set task goals that are moderately but not exceptionally difficult, take calculated risks, desire feedback about performance, and strive for personal accomplishment. Accomplishment is the incentive and its value is enhanced by the moderate goal difficulty and amount of risk. That is, people with high need achievement avoid easy goals with no risks, for these provide no incentive value even though they may be reachable (8), and also avoid very difficult or risky goals for these are virtually unreachable and consequently offer no realistic incentives (6, 7, 10, 71).

NEED FOR POWER. A third major need that has been identified as organizationally pertinent is the need for power. The need for power is defined as the need to have an effect on one's environment including the desire to take strong action—acting aggressively; giving help, assistance, or advice; controlling others by influencing, persuading, or trying to impress them; taking actions that produce emotions in others; and, finally, by being concerned for one's reputation, but only insofar as this reputation has an obvious effect on others (59).

People with high needs for power tend to accumulate whatever symbols give them prestige in a group to which they belong. Moreover, they tend to engage in competitive activities, particularly person-to-person competition, and try to dominate the situation (12).

McClelland identifies four stages of power orientation. The first he calls "it strengthens me"; this is the tendency to draw strength from others or from things. During this stage one wants to be around people who give one strength and who inspire one. According to McClelland, people in this stage enter occupations in which they can serve powerful others (59).

The second stage he calls "I strengthen myself." An individual at this stage of development tries to control his or her environment through willful self-assertion and by accumulating possessions closely associated with status. The goal of such power motivation is to feel comparatively powerful by collecting prestige possessions or by disciplining oneself in order to feel strong. That is, "I am better than you because I have these nice things and you do not," or "I am more disciplined, hence stronger than you."

Stage 3 McClelland calls, "I have impact on others"; this is a natural extension of Stage 2. Individuals at this stage are aggressive or, as they become socialized, behave in more subtle ways such as by persuasion, bargaining, maneuvering to control the behavior of others, or by giving gifts or help to others and thereby gaining symbolic acceptance of their own superiority.

Stage 4 is the most advanced stage of the power need. It has been identified by McClelland as "it moves me to do my duty." This is the most socialized stage of the power need. Persons at this stage see themselves as *instruments* of higher authority, which then moves them to try to influence or serve others. At this stage personal goals are subordinated to a higher authority, in whose name the individual then seeks to influence others.

As we shall see, one of the main features of leadership is the ability to influence others to gain organizational or group goals. Thus, influencing people or exercising power means using organizational support systems, such as authority or the administration of rewards and punishments, to get things done (59, 61, 62).

In most organizations where clear-cut authority relationships exist, the organization itself presents the mechanisms required for directing actions. Hence, it may be illegitimate to go beyond what is required by the authority structure in expressing power needs. Remember, too, that organizations cannot function without some kind of authority relationship. It is both necessary and desirable for people to work through the authority relationships to influence others and achieve organizational or group goals (66, 67, 69), but one does not have to express *power needs* in terms of personal dominance. Stage 3, then, is expressed in acts of personal dominance, which have only marginal organizational legitimacy, whereas Stage 4 is expressed in more *socialized* and typically more organizationally legitimate ways.

The stages of power and likely organizational consequences of behavior representing each stage are shown in Figure 10.3. Notice that Stage 1 can produce functional behavior if it is confined primarily to the followers of the organization. Stage 4 power behavior is more consonant with organizational structures and goals; Stages 2 and 3 may create levels of interpersonal and hierarchical conflict.

Role Motivation Theory

A related theoretical domain that has received research support is Miner's role motivation theory (66, 67, 69, 70). The manager's job can be broken down into several facets. It is logical to assume that those who are most motivated to perform the managerial role facets will be more successful than those who are not. The facets include actions toward supervisors, peers, and subordinates and to routine administrative functions. Briefly, the theory states that successful managers will have:

1. positive attitudes toward authority,
2. a desire to compete,

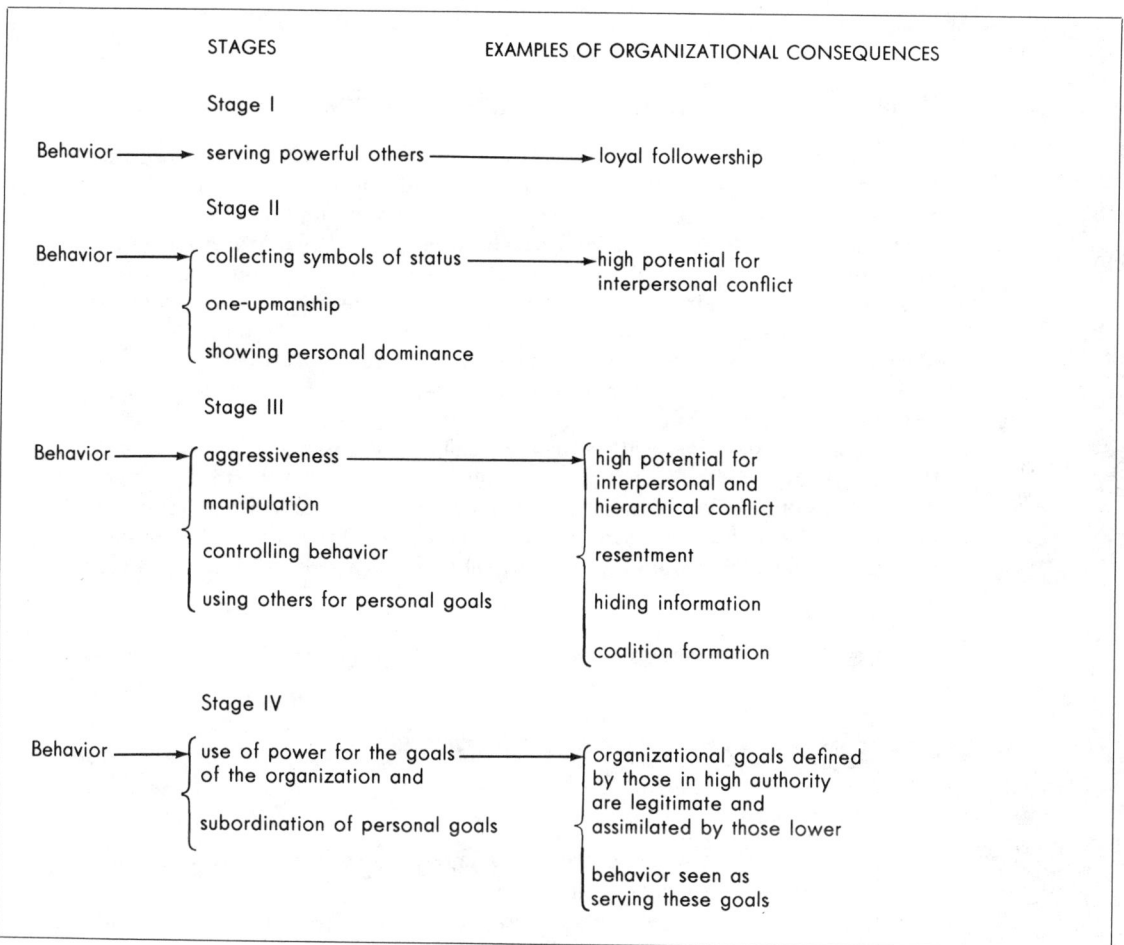

FIGURE 10.3   Stages of Power and Organizational Consequences

    3. a desire to be assertive,
    4. a desire to exercise power,
    5. a desire to stand out, and
    6. a desire to perform routine administrative functions.

Although all of the role facets receive research support, the strongest support pertains to hierarchical relationships (69). These facets are:

    1. positive attitudes toward authority because managers need to obtain resources from superiors and rely on their support,

> **BOX 11**
>
> ## Role Motivation and Executive Success
>
> This study focused on the role motivation theory. The subjects were drawn from sixty-eight large companies in the southeastern United States. Seventy-five top executives were compared to lower-level managers of the same age and from the same companies. Another comparison was made between professional executives—those who rose through the ranks of an organization—and entrepreneurial executives—those who either founded the organization or who were related to the founder.
>
> The measure of comparison was the Miner Sentence Completion Scale (MSCS) which asks the respondent to fill in incomplete sentences, each of which is related to a role motivation facet. This projective instrument is designed to elicit responses that reflect the respondents' motives.
>
> The results show that the most successful executives were more favorable toward authority and more competitive, had stronger desires to stand out from the crowd and to exercise power, and felt more responsible for fullfilling administrative duties. The professional managers were more favorable toward authority than the entrepreneurs but scored the same on all other facets—a result predicted by the theory.
>
> Fred Berman. "Managerial Role Motivation Theory Among Top Executives." *Dissertation Abstracts,* 1980.

2. a desire to compete because managers must "win" resources and support for their goals and their efforts, and
3. a desire to exercise power because power represents the control over and use of desired resources to gain compliance from subordinates.

An example of the research on role motivation theory is in Box 11.

Need Arousal in Organizations: A Perspective

Although most theorists consider the needs we just described as predetermined, programmatic research suggests that most of us have these needs in varying intensities (6, 7, 59). Since they can be aroused through training and through organizational incentives, they must be considered in the total motivation system devised by any organization (11, 58, 59, 61, 68). According to our framework, these needs are antecedents of motives to act, awaiting only the organizational factors to arouse them. At the same time, the organization can provide incentives that inhibit antecedent needs. In our vignette, Penny's experience with the government is an example of that. Thus, whether or not the motives are aroused—or to what extent they are aroused—depends on how the individual sees his or her environment (6). Experimental support for this statement is provided by Litwin and Stringer (55). The experiment was designed to arouse needs for affiliation, achievement, and power. Matched subjects were split into three groups of fifteen each. Each group constituted an organization.

The first organization, designed to arouse the power motive, emphasized authority relationships and the relative status of the membership. The second organization, designed to arouse the affiliative motive, was loosely structured and friendly, and cooperative behavior was stressed. Group decision making was encouraged at every level, and the atmosphere was one of relaxed encouragement and assistance. The third organization, designed to arouse the achievement motive, emphasized high productivity, individual goal setting, and taking personal responsibility for results. Rewards were dispensed for innovation, creativity, and excellent performance, and though competition was stressed, it was relative to an external standard, that is, against another group.

Results showed that each organization aroused the intended need significantly more than did the other organizations. The experimenters conclude that distinct organizational climates can be created, and that once created, they can have a dramatic effect on motivation (55). Furthermore, as two distinct lines of research show, the need for achievement and the role facets of role motivation theory can be induced or increased through training. It would seem fair to say, then, that such factors can be shaped by the environment. Figure 10.4 depicts some of these environmental factors and their likely consequences.

The motive to act, then, is determined by both the individual's need strengths and the organizational incentives that arouse or inhibit these needs. And since people have a variety of needs, we conclude that the organization, through its incentives, reinforcements, expectations, and training, can construct a motivation system that arouses or inhibits specific needs (see Figure 10.4). How well it can do this towards its own purposes will determine the extent of appropriate directed behavior.

We will turn now to a theory of motivation that is as applicable to attitude change as it is to the decision to act. Since attitudes are often a predisposition to act, the theory has relevance for organizational behavior (3, 21).

Cognitive Balance Theory

According to the cognitive balance theory, people need psychological or cognitive balance, and, if that balance does not exist, then they are motivated toward gaining it. The main elements of cognitive balance or imbalance are: (1) attitudes about oneself, about others, and about things or objects; and (2) behavior of

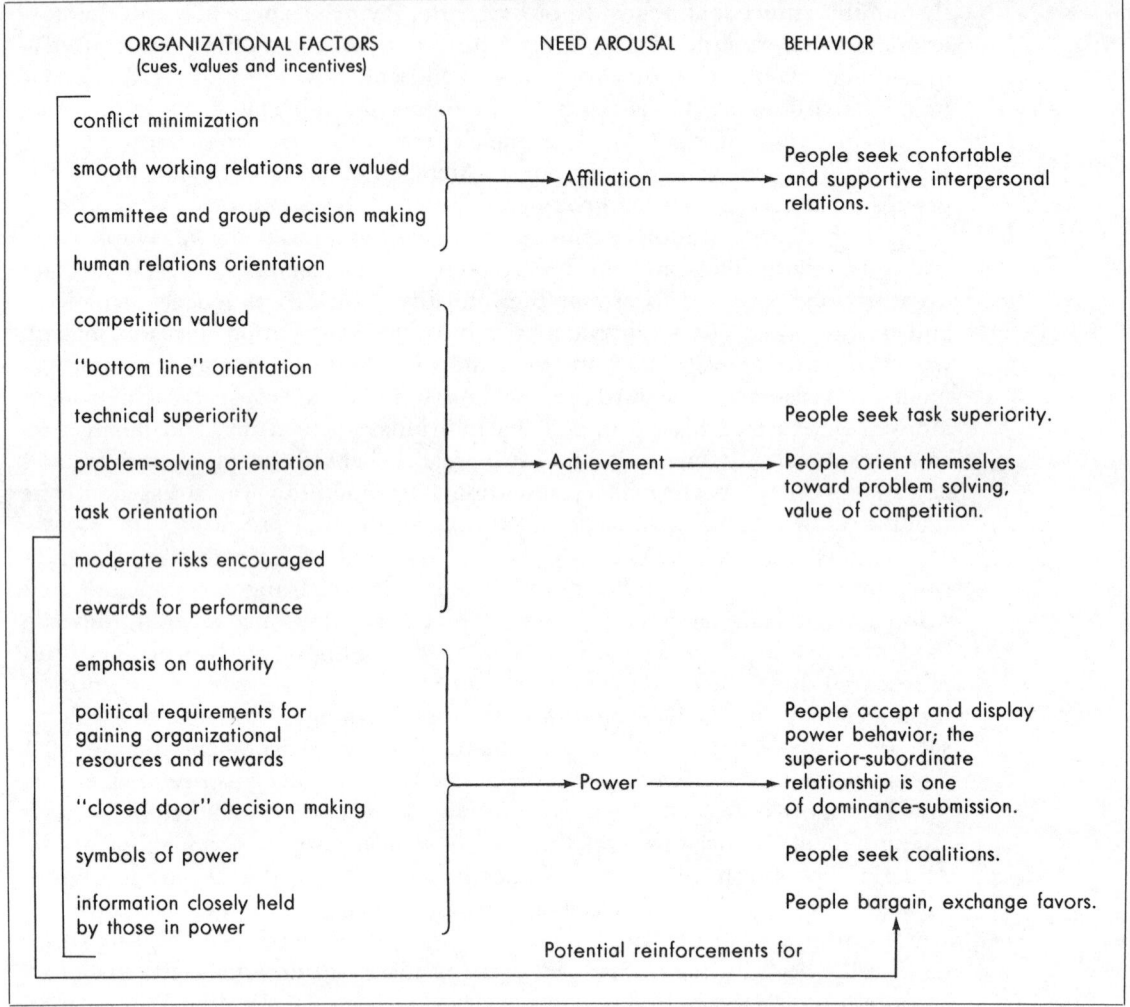

FIGURE 10.4 Organizational Factors and Need Arousal

self and others (15, 41, 73, 76). These elements must relate in some logical way if cognitive balance is to occur.

If you view yourself, for example, as highly competent, have a high regard for your supervisor, but you receive a negative performance evaluation, it is likely that you will be in a state of cognitive imbalance. You can restore balance by changing your views of yourself or your views of your supervisor since you have no control over an already received negative evaluation. Or, you can resolve to do what is required to receive a positive evaluation next time. That is, you can accept the evaluation as justified this time, but plan to work to correct the reasons for it, so next time you will get a positive evaluation. You can also attribute the cause of your negative evaluation to environmental factors beyond either your control or the control of your supervisor. Any of these means of restoring balance are possible—in fact, this list is by no means exhaustive—and the one chosen depends on the circumstance.

Suppose, that this was your second negative evaluation, received after you had taken corrective action that everyone *but* your supervisor thought effective. What might you do to restore the balance then? Most likely you would change your view of your supervisor, for you have validated your self-concept and thereby rejected your supervisor's evaluation as invalid. Hence, his judgment no longer deserves respect.

There are several balance theories,[1] but the most intensively researched is called the theory of cognitive dissonance (26). Cognitive dissonance theory deals with psychological states that arise as a consequence of simultaneously holding incongruous beliefs or attitudes. To extend the definition, dissonance exists between at least two pieces of information when the expectations of outcomes of action are not the same as the actual outcomes of such action; or when you believe something is true or right—something you value—and you get discrepant information from a reliable or valued source; or when you do something less than desirable with no objective justification. In each case you will be in a state of dissonance (54).

Dissonance can be reduced by taking alternative actions or by discovering in the situation values and rewards that are associated with other motives. This is theoretically significant, for reinforcement theory predicts alternative actions, whereas dissonance theory predicts either course. Indeed, dissonance theory explains why people persist in nonreinforced courses of action even when there is no probability that the originally expected reinforcements will occur. That is, since people are motivated to reduce dissonance, they can do so by seeking other justifications for their behavior than those which originally produced it. Hence, continued behavior, for which objective reinforcements do not occur as expected, is a consequence of psychological justifications that occurred after the fact (54).

Dissonance theory has three basic hypotheses: (1) the existence of dissonance creates psychological tension and, hence, motivates the person to reduce the dissonance; (2) when dissonance exists, the person will try to avoid situations that would increase the dissonance; and (3) the greater the dissonance, the greater is the motivation to reduce it. The magnitude of the dissonance depends on the importance of the elements that are in dissonance (51). For example, if the elements are central to your self-esteem, the dissonance will be strong, but if they touch you only peripherally, dissonance will likely be weak.

Suppose you took a job, agreed to a certain salary, and were led to believe that the working conditions were good, management treated its employees decently, and the work was challenging and offered opportunities for advancement. After reporting to work, you found that the pay and the management were as you expected, but that the work was not challenging, and that only limited opportunities existed for advancement. This is particularly irritating because you had rejected other jobs that at the time did not seem to fulfill these important dimensions. So you are stuck in a job for which the expectations did not materialize, knowing that if you had accepted another job, things might have gone better for you. You are now in a state of cognitive dissonance.

To reduce this dissonance you are likely to select the least costly means over which you have a good measure of control (25, 26). There are two general categories of possibilities: attitudinal and behavioral. To reduce dissonance attitudinally you could: redefine your job as important and challenging; begin to place more value on the things you know will happen as a consequence of your employment—good money, for instance; devalue the importance of job challenge; or reaffirm to yourself that the other jobs you were offered were not as challenging as this one and seek evidence to support that reaffirmation. Reducing dissonance through changing attitudes is particularly likely when you perceive that you have no choice for an alternative action. That is, you have taken the original action and there is little that you can do about it. So you will make the best of it.

Suppose you do have a choice of action. Now it is likely that you might use a behavioral means of reducing dissonance. For example, you might attempt to restructure your job by finding additional responsibilities or by redefining the responsibilities you already have, expecting that by doing so you will increase your visibility and hence your opportunities for mobility; or you might quit; or—though a less likely course—you might reduce your inputs to coincide with the outcomes you receive from the job. That is, you could work less diligently. This is unlikely because at the beginning stages of your career, you might not want to risk that.

These courses of action are not trivial. Each has significant consequences for organizational behavior. For example, if you decide to leave the organization, the recruiting and training costs to that organization might be substantial. If you decide to stay and reduce your inputs, this too would be costly. However, since cognitive dissonance is psychological, the basis of reducing dissonance will probably be psychological as well. Hence, what changes is often how you assess the situation and learn to live with it, not the situation itself. In psychological reassessment, the importance of dissonance theory lies in the number of people who have chosen to reduce dissonance not by deed but by thought, and the extent to which the situation remains stable. Numerous people may take action when the justifications for a bad situation no longer exist. That is, when, collectively, they can no longer justify a terrible state of affairs.

These, then, are the basic elements of the balance theory and a special case of that theory. The theories are psychological and are applicable primarily to psychological constructs such as attitudes—not necessarily to action. Although attitudes may be the precursors of action, you may question the place that such theories have in a chapter on motivation. Let us, then, illustrate the applicability of cognitive balance-imbalance for understanding action.

The Lordstown Plant Case and the Notion of Equity

The following analysis is based on equity theory, another variant of balance theory. According to equity theory, what people get from their efforts or inputs should be commensurate with those efforts or inputs relative to someone else (1), to some other job, or to a previously determined and satisfactory standard (48). It is typified by the phrase, "A fair day's work for a fair day's pay." That is, if you are getting x for doing y, so should I, and if I am doing x for y outcome, then so should you if you are getting y outcome.[2] For example, if two people with similar abilities and similar output work side by side, but one person, for unknown reasons, makes more money, then both people will feel a sense of inequity (cognitive dissonance). Each will probably seek a different way of restoring equity (reducing dissonance). The more highly paid worker might try to increase productivity (1) or perhaps find other characteristics—say, seniority—to justify the higher pay. The lesser paid worker might reduce input or seek justifications similar to those the higher paid worker did, such as, "He has higher seniority and things really are equitable." In either case, the potential for action because of a sense of inequity is substantial even though there are psychological means available for restoring equity (1).

Another example is when an employee or group of employees feel they are not getting a fair share of their productive efforts (24, 48). Such was the case of Lordstown. The General Motors Lordstown, Ohio, plant was opened in 1966 to manufacture Chevrolet Impalas. Two management groups were involved: Fisher Body and Chevrolet. Initially, the line was geared to produce sixty cars per hour. Things ran smoothly for four years. The union-management relationship was reasonably good and the period was marked by low grievance rates, no unauthorized work stoppages, and acceptable quality.

In 1970 the Vega was introduced and, along with it, an hourly rate change to 100 cars. The retooling also generated unprecedented automation—for example, 95 percent of the welding was done by industrial robots called Unimates. The automation and the fact that the car was smaller meant that, despite the line speedup, the amount of work for each employee remained much the same as before the Vega was introduced.

In 1971 the management changed from Chevy-Fisher Body to General Motors Assembly Division (GMAD). Shortly after it took control, GMAD studied the work standards and determined that the same work could be done by substantially fewer employees. Between 400 and 800 hourly employees were laid off.[3] The employees soon realized they were turning out more work with fewer people and for the same money than before the advent of GMAD and the Vega.

Several things happened then. Grievances skyrocketed from 300 per year to over 5000; despite a "zero defects" program, the plant's repair lab was frequently overflowing; industrial sabotage such as slashed upholstery was commonplace. The story goes on to include disciplinary layoffs and ultimately a strike, but for our purposes the main point is that management in this case was seen by the employees as violating a previously agreed-on, though unofficial, contract. These kinds of contracts have been called, variously: psychological contracts (81), social contracts (64) and effort bargains (29). Under these unstated contracts, the employee expects to give something—compliance to authority, for example—in return for organizational rewards. Management expects a certain amount of production in return for a certain amount of reward. When either party gives or receives less than is called for by the implicit contract, feelings of inequity may follow.

At Lordstown, the employees thought GMAD management had violated the implicit bargain by speeding up the line and reducing the work force. The employees were motivated, as a consequence, to engage in counterproductive behavior to set things right. In their own minds, such behavior was completely justified because of the inequities they saw. As Gary Bryner, then president of UAW Local 1112, said in an address to a class at a local university in the spring of 1975:

> All that talk about a young work force wanting more interesting work was overblown. The basic reason we walked off was that management changed the standards on us and sped up the line. If they hadn't done that, none of the rest would have happened." [An allusion to sabotage, slowdown, grievance actions, and the ultimate strike.] The speedup caused it all. It was all give and no take for us. [Paraphrase of an answer to the question: "Wouldn't job enrichment help the labor relations at Lordstown?"]

Since then, several things have happened. First, the Vega has been phased out and a larger auto replaced it. Second, the employees lived through a difficult economic time from 1973 through 1977—a recession and a drop in demand for the Vega put more than 1000 employees on indefinite layoff. Under such conditions, justification for less militancy and more compliance to authoritative requests is likely, for according to dissonance theory, people tend to choose their justifications according to availability and the course of least resistance. Third, line speed was cut to eighty-five cars per hour, with the expectation of a further drop to seventy-five. Fourth, a new plant manager, more sympathetic to employees' needs, took over. Currently, labor relations appear good (16).

Figure 10.5 illustrates a post facto analysis of the Lordstown case. Plug in a number and you will see for yourself that the amount the employees got

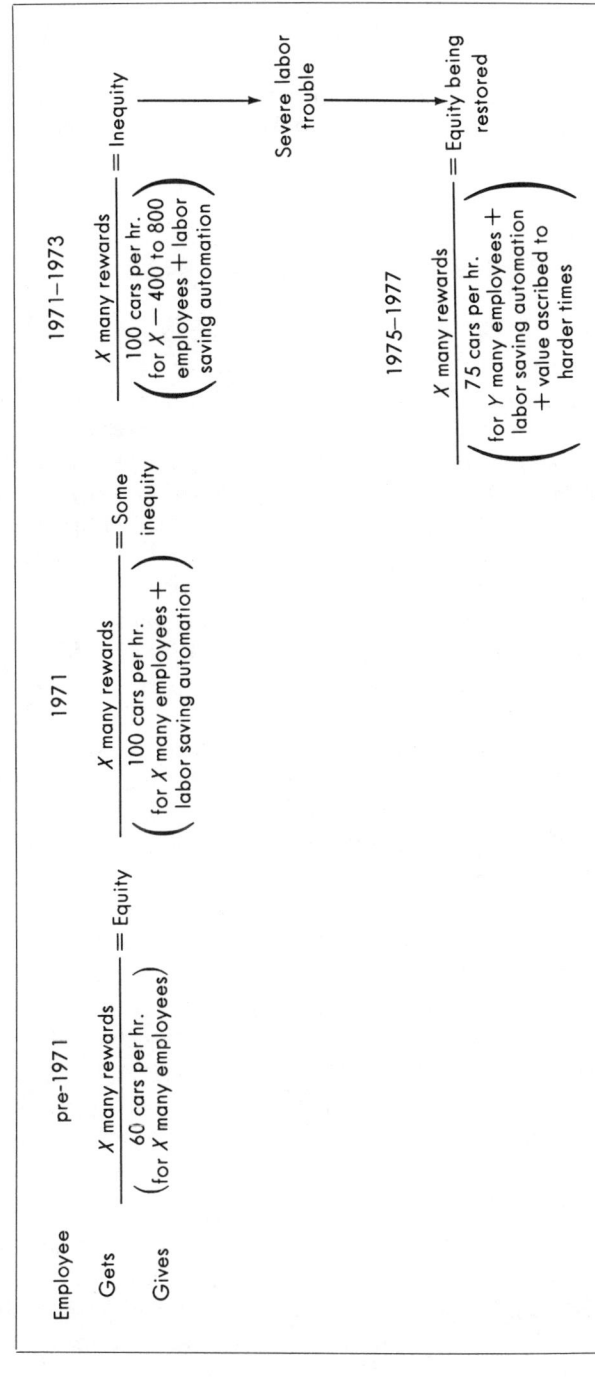

FIGURE 10.5 Equity Theory and Lordstown

relative to what they gave diminished over time. In other words, "A fair day's work" was adjusted upward, but "a fair day's pay" was not. Feelings of inequity resulted and doubtless were a major contributor to subsequent events.[4] Attitudes created by cognitive imbalance can therefore determine behavior of considerable consequence to the organization.

Job Satisfaction and Motivation

Job satisfaction is defined as a positive feeling that one gets after evaluating one's job situation (5, 83). There are degrees of satisfaction and there is dissatisfaction, defined in terms of negative feelings. The concept of job satisfaction is comprised of several components. The chief ones appear to be: (1) the work itself, which includes its interest, difficulty, opportunities for control over pace and method, and variety; (2) salary; (3) interpersonal relations with peers; (4) responsibility; (5) opportunities for advancement; (6) opportunities for achievement; and (6) supervision. If all or most of these factors are amply present job satisfaction should be high (17, 68).

Herzberg's M-H theory has generated the most systematic research about job satisfaction. The motivators are thought to be satisfiers as well. So, a person with ample amounts of achievement, advancement, recognition, responsibility, and challenging, complex work, should be satisfied; but a person without them should not be dissatisfied. On the other hand, so the theory goes, if the hygienes such as pay, supervision, peers, working conditions, administrative policies, and benefits were *not* sufficiently present, people would be dissatisfied; and if they were sufficiently present, then more of them would *not* lead to greater satisfaction (42, 43).

Although there is some merit to the argument, independent research has disclosed that the motivators–satisfiers tend to be more important determinants of both satisfaction and dissatisfaction than the hygienics, and that for low-skilled occupations where the motivators are not probable, the hygienics appear to have satisfying characteristics (35, 68, 83, 87). Perhaps the important outcome of the M-H research has been to focus on the nature of the work rather than on the work's context.

Job Satisfaction and Performance

Our concern here is on motivation to work hard and well. Although there is reason to study job satisfaction in its own right—it is a co-variant of absenteeism, turnover, and some physical and mental health problems—it is job satisfaction's relationship to job performance that we will analyze in this chapter. There are basically two assumptions here. The first is that satisfaction for some reason "causes" job performance (79). The second is that job satisfaction acts as a moderator between some other factor (or factors) and job performance (79).

AS A CAUSE OF JOB PERFORMANCE. Let us put one issue to rest. Job satisfaction as we have defined it does *not* by itself lead to job performance. Research on this issue has been plentiful and by and large the relationships between performance and satisfaction have been small (45, 68). Furthermore, when there is co-variation between the two factors, often it is due to other variables leading to each—such as equitable pay for performance. Or sometimes performance, because of its inherent value to the person, leads to satisfaction (48, 68, 85). In either case the instrumentality of performance for satisfaction and the expectation that satisfaction will again occur as an outcome of performance is the likely causal chain (50). And so it appears that when there is a correlation between job satisfaction and job performance, the direction is not from satisfaction to performance but often the other way around (77, 87). To pursue this point a bit further look at Box 12.

AS A REWARD FOR PERFORMANCE. If job performance in any way causes job satisfaction, it is as an incentive associated with outcomes of performance (75, 77). Indeed the incentive properties of job satisfaction are implicitly inherent in M-H theory and expectancy theory (85). In the first case the quality is implied because people seek the motivators and are satisfied when they get them. In the second case, it is implied because the value attached to outcomes is defined in terms of satisfaction. And so if people are or expect to be satisfied as a consequence of performance (intrinsic) or as a consequence of the outcomes associated with performance (extrinsic or intrinsic), then there will be an incentive to perform (45, 46, 47).

AS A MODERATING VARIABLE. One final point with respect to where job satisfaction fits into motivational systems. It seems that satisfied people are easier to deal with and hence more compliant. Furthermore, job satisfaction seems to be one element in an even more complex concept called commitment, which is known to have a bearing on motivation (4, 23, 92, 93). Consequently, it is not unreasonable to speculate that job satisfaction modifies the relationship between organizational requests for behavior and the occurrence of that behavior. Indeed, that is one of the reasons that so many in management want high levels of employee satisfaction even without evidence that satisfaction leads directly to high levels of performance. Thus, although most of the evidence suggests that: (1) there are far more powerful predictors to performance than job

> **Box 12**
>
> ## Do Well, Feel Good
>
> This research was designed to test the hypotheses that performance would be well related to satisfaction when (1) organizational pressure for performance and (2) time pressures were low. The reasoning behind these predictions was that if employees could attribute their performance to themselves and not to pressures that required them to perform then they would derive satisfaction from that performance.
>
> The subjects were 104 department store managers. They were rated by their supervisors on a variety of work-related dimensions such as technical know-how, competence, organizing, delegating, amount of work performed, and accomplishing sales targets. These dimensions were added together to become a single factor called "job performance." Job satisfaction was measured by a commonly used scale called the Job Diagnostic Survey. Organizational pressures were measured by self-ratings and ratings of supervisors, and time pressures were measured by self-ratings developed and validated elsewhere.
>
> Using two different statistical analyses the following findings emerged:
>
> 1. Overall there was a 0.35 correlation between performance and satisfaction.
> 2. When organizational pressure to perform was low, as determined by self-ratings, the correlation between satisfaction and performance was 0.51; under medium and high pressures the correlations were −0.10 and +0.11 respectively.
> 3. When pressure determined by supervisory ratings was low, the correlation between satisfaction and performance was 0.61; under medium and high pressures the correlations were 0.18 and −0.09, respectively.
> 4. The same pattern emerged for time pressures as a moderating variable.
>
> These findings support the idea that high performance leads to high satisfaction if people can attribute that performance to their own efforts and volition but not if people feel they are forced to perform.
>
> Rabi S. Bhagat. "Conditions Under Which Strong Job Performance–Job Satisfaction Relationships May be Observed. A Closer Look at Two Situational Contingencies." *Academy of Management Journal* 25 (1982): 772–789.

satisfaction; (2) if there is a satisfaction-performance relationship, performance is likely to come first; and (3) job satisfaction may be related to other psychological states, such as commitment, that in turn affect job behavior; still, job satisfaction does have an indirect relationship to behavior (see Figure 10.6).

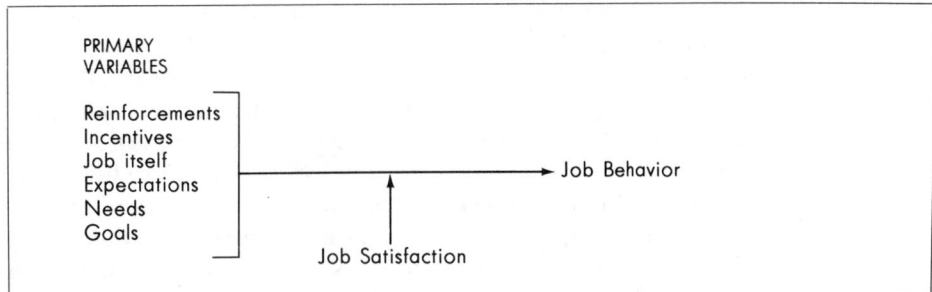

FIGURE 10.6   Job Satisfaction as a Modifier of the Causal Job Behavior Relationship

Job Enrichment as a Part of a Motivation System

Much has been written about the motivational characteristics of the job itself. And it makes good sense to ascribe such characteristics to jobs since most of us have experienced both boring jobs that we complete only because we have to and exciting jobs that we cannot wait to tackle. Positive reinforcement in the latter case is inherent in the job itself. The exciting job has been called *enriched* (42).

Job enrichment has its theoretical foundation in the M-H theory of motivation, which states that motivation is provided by the job itself. The job factors include opportunities for (1) responsibility and personal achievement, (2) interesting work, (3) growth and learning, (4) recognition, and (5) advancement. Job enrichment seeks to provide some or all of these factors. For example, suppose you were on a typewriter assembly line. The line would start with a stamped frame, and as the frame moved down the line, keys, keyboard, carriage, cover, and so forth would be added to it, with each assembly operation being provided by one individual. The operations are fairly simple and routine, and the responsibility is confined to each operation. That is not an enriched job. Now suppose instead that you had before you all of the parts and from these parts had to assemble the entire typewriter. Furthermore, you could decide how to do it and, within limits, how fast to proceed; and you would be responsible for the entire assembly process and the outcome. In this case, the job is much more complex and the responsibility for an entire machine is contained in that one job. That is an enriched job.

There have been several reports on the effect of job enrichment. Herzberg reports an experimental job change that incorporated the major features of job enrichment (42). The job to be changed was that of stockholder correspondents of a major utility. The major responsibility of the correspondents was to answer any questions or complaints or provide any information requested to the stockholder. Before the experiment, productivity and morale were considered low, and turnover was high. The changes were as follows: (1) the correspondents were given the responsibility of dealing with complex and specialized questions (the supervisors had done this before); (2) the correspondents were held personally accountable for the letters they wrote (the supervisor had signed off on all letters before); (3) the correspondents were given the responsibility for proofreading their letters, and supervisory verification of such letters dropped from 100 percent to a randomly selected 10 percent; (4) the correspondents were told only that high performance was expected (before, the supervisors continuously stressed the number of letters that required answers); (5) the letters were no longer routed through the supervisors before going to the mailroom; (6) the letters were personalized (before, they were mostly sent out pro forma).

According to Herzberg, increases in responsibility, personal achievement, recognition, growth, and learning—all motivators per the two-factor theory—were more probable with these jobs after the experimental change occurred. The results, as reported by Herzberg, indicated an initial drop in the performance index, followed by a substantial and rapid increase, and culminating in sustained superior performance. Furthermore, the job attitudes improved markedly over the life of the experiment. Similar results are reported by other proponents of job enrichment (87).

Why should enriched jobs provide more motivation than unenriched jobs? That is, although it may be obvious that people would rather have an enriched job than its opposite, it is not so obvious that such jobs provide the incentives necessary to motivate superior performance. A model developed through a series of studies can help us out on that score (36–39).

The model states that work motivation is a function of at least three sets of variables: job core characteristics, psychological states of the employees, and the employees' growth need strengths. The job core characteristics are:

1. skill variety—the degree to which different skills and talents are required for the job,
2. task identity—the degree to which the job performed is a whole, identifiable piece of work with visible outcomes,
3. task significance—the job's importance to the organization or to other people,
4. autonomy—the individual's freedom to decide independently on how much to do and how to do it, and
5. feedback—the degree to which there is concrete and accurate information as to the consequences of a person's job efforts.

Each of these characteristics is said to lead to certain psychological states:

1. experienced meaningfulness, which is a consequence of skill variety, task identity, and task significance;

2. experienced responsibility for task outcomes, which is a consequence of autonomy; and
3. knowledge of work outcomes, which is a consequence of feedback.

The model is shown in Figure 10.7. Note that the core job dimensions cause the psychological states. Once these states are aroused, the work outcomes follow. The rationale for these relationships is well described by Hackman and Oldham:

> This positive effect is reinforcing to the individual and serves as an incentive for him to continue to try to perform well in the future. When he does not perform well, he does not experience an internally reinforcing state of affairs, and he may elect to try harder in the future so as to regain the internal rewards that good performance brings. The net result is a self-perpetuating cycle of positive work motivation powered by self-generated rewards, that is predicted to continue until

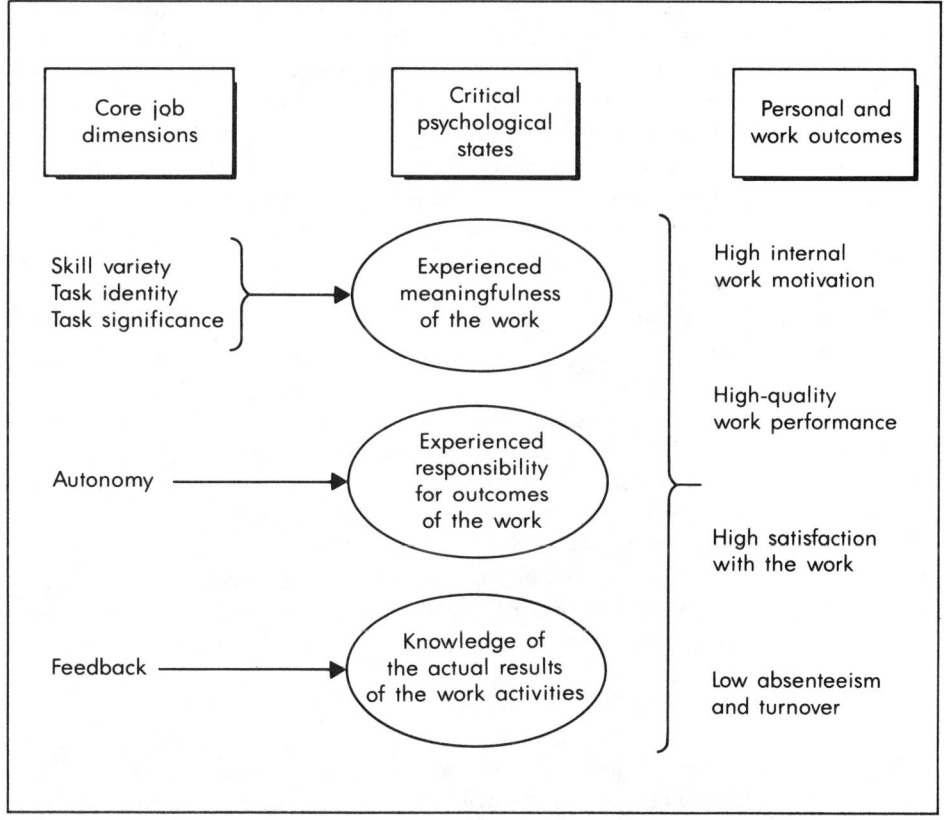

FIGURE 10.7 Motivation Dynamics of Job Enrichment (Adapted from Hackman and Oldham 38: 256)

one or more of the three psychological states is no longer present, or until the individual no longer values the internal rewards that derive from good performance.

It should be noted that self-generated motivation should be highest when all three of the psychological states are present. If the performer feels fully responsible for work outcomes on a meaningful task, but never finds out how well he is performing, it is doubtful that he will experience the internal rewards that prompt self-generated motivation. Similarly, if he has full knowledge of the results of the work, but experiences the task as trivial (or feels no personal responsibility for the results of the work), internal motivation will not be high. (38: 256)

This quotation helps us understand the possible dynamics of motivation associated with job enrichment. Furthermore, by breaking the job into component factors, each of which may be associated with specific psychological states, we may be able to diagnose deficiencies in any given job and then "enrich" it on the deficient dimension.

But is the model correct? The evidence at this time is promising, but by no means conclusive. For example, one study indicates that core job dimensions do, in fact, relate to the employees' psychological states (38). As hypothesized, skill variety, task identity, and task significance correlate with experienced meaningfulness, and knowledge of results correlates highly with feedback. All relate to experienced responsibility equally well, though in no case are the correlations very high. Contrary to the hypothesis, however, the job characteristics seem to relate better, on the average, to the more objective measures of performance such as absenteeism and rated work effectiveness. In other words, the objective characteristics of the job seem to affect performance as hypothesized but not necessarily because of the employees' psychological states.

Another comprehensive review questions the adequacy of job design theory and of task characteristics measurement. One of the main points of that review and of subsequent research is that people assess the job partly on the basis of its objective characteristics and partly according to social cues and definitions (78). One study varied information coming from fellow workers (positive or negative) and the nature of the task (enriched or unenriched) and found that the information was a much better predictor of perceptions of the job than the job characteristics (91). Another study using somewhat different methods found that enrichment did predict to job perceptions, but so did social cues (13). Furthermore the social cues were better predictors of satisfaction and performance. Therefore, it seems that job enrichment, at least in these laboratory situations, is hardly robust. Is that also true of field research?

Virtually all reported job enrichment studies suggest some success. The success is said to be a function of the motivating characteristics of the changes in the job itself. Let us examine that supposition. Tausky and Parke reviewed fifteen reported job-enrichment studies that are used as the evidence to support such efforts (87). They found that in every case, although the intent of the enrichment may have been to increase autonomy, job complexity, and challenge—thereby capitalizing on people's need for such things—two other crucial aspects of the total change effort invariably emerged. First, in every case, individual accountability was built into the change. For example, in the AT&T studies, before job enrichment was installed, it was unclear who had committed clerical errors in the work process. After the enrichment, errors were directly traceable to specific employees. Results of work effort were highly visible and, as a consequence, the workers' accountability for performance and, perhaps most important, management's ability to hold individual workers accountable for their performance, increased.

Second, in most of the reported enrichment studies, financial incentives were either explicitly changed as part of the enrichment program or were being explored as a means of shoring up an unsuccessful enrichment attempt.

Furthermore, if we tie accountability or incentives with other elements of enrichment, such as giving a person a complete and natural unit of work, and assigning individuals to specific or specialized tasks as Herzberg suggests, not only have we increased potential accountability, but we have made the work more complete and clearly identifiable. It is no wonder, then, that the reported job enrichment studies are as closely akin to traditional industrial engineering as they are to enrichment theory (24, 65). In addition, such changes increase the potential positive and negative objective reinforcements associated with job outcomes.

To illustrate these points, let us examine an excellent study of an enrichment experiment (56). The study included three experimental groups composed of federal government clerical workers and matching control groups. Each unit ranged in size from ten to forty employees. Before the experiment, the jobs were routine and the division of labor, definitive. Each employee worked pretty much on the same job day after day, and assignments were determined by the supervisor.

After enrichment it was noted that the three experimental groups had the following characteristics:

Unit A: There were four 6-person teams working independently. Three teams worked on sorting and one worked on miscellaneous mailroom jobs on a rotating basis. The employees could decide for themselves how to divide up the various operations and were not assigned to specific tasks. Each team kept track of and posted its own daily productivity.

Unit B: The employees were allowed to decide for themselves what needed to be done. When the work was completed, they—not their supervisors—decided where to send it. The clerks themselves allotted time to the tasks according to what needed to be done rather than to what was assigned to them. They kept their own time records. Members were assigned the job of captain on a rotating basis. They were responsible for screening incoming work, compiling unit time records, dispatching outgoing work, and so on. Unit B had meetings with other units to go over common problems.

Unit C: This unit was taken off production standards; employees could switch back and forth between the tasks, and were trained to do more advanced tasks. They kept track of their own production and individual and unit production was posted each day. The accuracy of the self-kept production figures was checked by supervisors and other units.

Autonomy, feedback, and variety were increased for all groups, and responsibility, as determined by accountability for performance, was increased for groups A and B.

This study indicated that absenteeism, turnover, complaints, disciplinary action, and productivity all improved when the experimental groups were combined and then compared to the combined control groups. The attitudes, however, showed an unexpected result. The responses from both the experimental and control groups were negative. The control groups were dissatisfied with the same things they were dissatisfied with before the study, but the experimental groups stated that the enrichment experiment did not go far enough and, most importantly, that they had not received any *extrinsic* rewards such as increased pay or promotion for the new skills that they had learned.

The experimenters concluded that the changes in productivity were due to *more efficient manpower* usage; the employees could work where they were needed rather than where they were assigned; some unnecessary work procedures were eliminated; there was more precise feedback concerning performance; and in two of the groups, performance accountability was increased. They further stated that "it is evident that the above changes, especially the first three, involve elements of sound industrial engineering . . . *as much or more* than those of the cognitive growth school of Herzberg." Further, they attribute the changes in absences and turnover to the initial change in attitudes, which seemed positive, but then changed toward the negative as the experiment progressed. Finally, they concluded that the lack of attitude change was attributed to two factors: (1) the lack of sufficient enrichment; and (2) the *lack of any practical payoff* for the workers. And, according to their interpretation, the second factor was more significant than the first (56).

By implication, the same or better results could have been gained solely by reengineering the methods for efficiency, goal setting, holding people accountable to the goals, and providing financial rewards for reaching and exceeding the goals. Of course, we do not know what might have happened had enrichment been extended to its logical conclusion. It is our guess, however, that the predominant factors still would have been efficient methods, accountability, work standards (goals), and concrete organizational incentives. That is, rather than the outcome variables being primarily a function of psychological states, they seem a function of the perceived aggregation of positive and negative incentives.

There are other problems with job enrichment. For example, technological factors may make job enrichment difficult. If the means of production include assembly-line operations in which there is an enormous amount of capital invested and which has a relatively good history of efficient operations, it may not be advisable to make job changes.

Furthermore, certain types of employees are not as receptive to job enrichment as others. Indeed, it seems that only a minority of workers even want job enrichment (24, 44). For example, several studies have found that white-collar people are more affected by job enrichment than blue-collar people; rural people more than urban people; those who accept the so-called work ethic more than those who do not; and those with higher needs for growth more than those with low growth needs (27, 28, 38, 44, 82, 83). Finally, there is some evidence that the intrinsic satisfaction derived from stimulating jobs is distracting, and thereby detracts from objectively measured performance. That is, people may become so involved with the interesting aspects of a job (it is reinforcing) that they neglect such things as cost efficiency (45).

Indeed one of the leading researchers in the enrichment area has recently concluded that realistically job enrichment may not have much of a future because of organizational constraints such as technology and control systems (33, 34). Each of these places great credence in simplicity of process and numerical measures, as we shall see later.

To conclude, we do not reject the hypothesis that individuals' so-called growth needs are better served through enriched jobs, for it has been shown that many people do require autonomy and task complexity as fundamental features of their work. This requirement has been amply demonstrated for a minority of people, and certainly many studies support such a hypothesis. Furthermore, a recent review suggested that job enrichment, together with employee participation in developing the new job designs, has been associated with increases in performance measures (80, 82). However, in order to understand the motivation to perform at high levels, it is also important to understand the outcomes the employees get as a result of high performance. These outcomes empirically and historically have been the objective reinforcements and the consequent incentive values of traditional organizational emoluments, such as increased pay, enhanced opportunities for promotion, and avoidance of punishment. The psychological reinforcements from sustained experience on enriched jobs, despite their association with work satisfaction, have yet to be empirically associated in reasonable consistency with high performance in well-controlled studies.

Summary

The complexities of motivation are caused—at least in part—by the variety of needs that people bring to an organizational setting. Organizations, being complex themselves, also contain many cues to which people can respond. These two factors—variety of needs and multitude of organizational cues—make predicting directed behavior problematic. One thing is sure, however: taken collectively, people seem to respond according to their perceptions of what is best for them, of where the net profits are. Consequently, motivation systems for directed behavior must take into account general need states and the general incentives that address such need states. Organizations seem to structure motivation systems according to their views of need generalities. Figure 10.8 summarizes these conclusions. Let us go through the model point by point.

First, we previously concluded that the need areas are important antecedents of the motive to act. If people are responsive to their own needs, then the available rewards in an organization should be attached to the desired behaviors and at the same time related to needs. If they are not, the desired behaviors are unlikely. If they are, the desired behaviors become more likely.

Second, the rewards ought to satisfy needs adequately. Further, the rewards ought to be commensurate with effort and seen as equitably distributed. If they are, the desired behavior is likely to occur; and if they are not, such likelihood decreases. Third, other behaviors than those desired may have reward value and compete with desired behaviors. If they do not, the likelihood of the behavior occurring increases. If they do, however, a new value enters the picture: if the competing rewards and behaviors are of greater value to the individual than the desired behaviors, such desired behaviors are less likely. If, however, they have less value, then the probability of the desired behaviors occurring will not be affected negatively.

Fourth, are the desired paths for gaining rewards seen as available? If they are not, the desired behaviors are unlikely. If they are, then the probability of such behaviors increases. Fifth, are alternative paths available for gaining the rewards? That is, are there other ways of gaining the same desired outcomes than through the appropriate designated behavior? If there are, an individual must decide which behaviors he or she will engage in to get the desired outcomes; therefore, the desired behavior becomes problematic. This is particularly true if the alternative path is inherently more rewarding than the one desired by the organization. If there are no such alternative paths for getting the rewards, then the likelihood that desired behaviors will occur increases.

Finally, we have reinforcement, the actual gaining of the rewards. The history of reinforcement is the basis for expecting that future rewards are likely to follow similar behavior, and hence, undergird the *incentive* system.

Motivation in organizations, then, is a function of needs, their relative strengths, and the extent to which they are seen as being satisfied by available organizational rewards. The task of organizations is to determine which rewards apply to which classes of employees, to attach these to the desired behaviors, ensuring that their quality and quantity are greater than those attached to other less desirable behaviors, and to reinforce the desired behaviors. Reinforcement is the precursor of incentives. However, because of the complexities we have discussed, motivation systems typically fall far short of their intent.

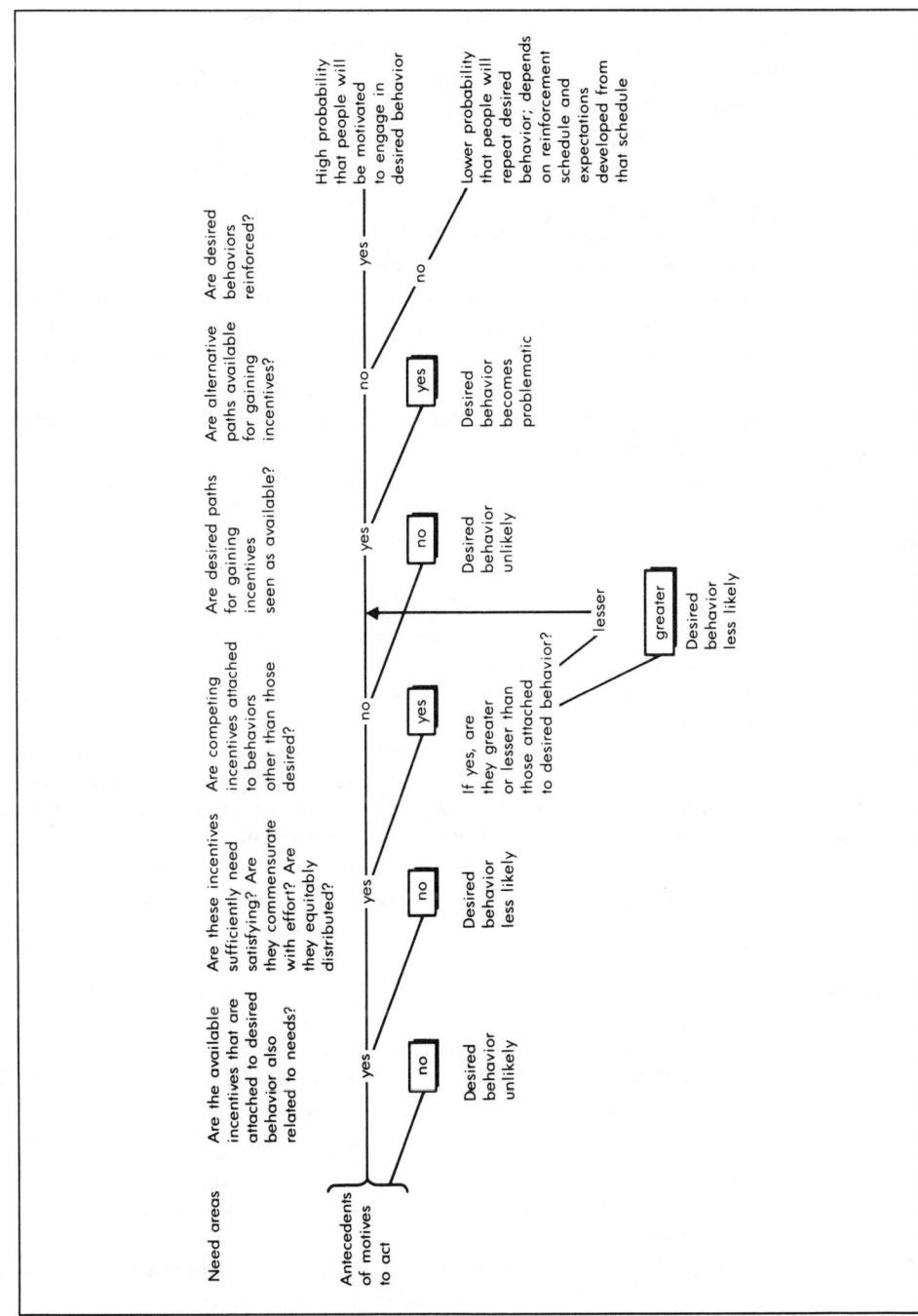

FIGURE 10.8 Conditions Pertaining to the Motives to Act

Yet many motivation systems do what is intended. People usually act according to the incentives they observe. Many motivation systems fail because they tend to confuse people: the incentives may be unclear; there may be competing incentives that suggest different behaviors; the desired behaviors may not be specified or available; and the reinforcements may be uncertain. Further, action goals may be incentives for a few people, for though these goals may be an end state to their creators, they may be only a means to an end for others. Meaningful incentives must therefore be attached to the desired goals and the relevant behavior; each must be achievable and clearly spelled out. These limitations are especially important since people come to an organization with a variety of needs, and the organization provides a variety of inducements, cues, and sanctions to which people respond. Thus, the structure of the motivation system should be sufficiently consonant with the motive patterns the organization wants from its people to ensure that most of the employees will behave as desired most of the time (32).

Notes

1. For a discussion of these theories, see Keisler, Collins, and Miller (51).
2. For a complete and elegant treatment of equity theory, see Adams (1), Goodman and Friedman (29), and Jacques (48).
3. Management estimated that about 400 employees were laid off, whereas the union estimated about 800.
4. Post facto analyses are always subject to the criticism that the data are made to fit a theory and that, for this reason, other explanations made to fit other theories are possible. For example, theories of aggression (10), from which a frustration-aggression hypothesis (19) is derived, handles the Lordstown situation about as well as equity theory. However, it is our contention that the source of frustration is very likely contained in the workers' sense of inequity.

References

1. ADAMS, J. S. "Inequity in Social Exchange," *Advances in Experimental Social Psychology*, Vol. 2. Edited by L. Berkowitz. New York: Academic Press, 1965. Pp. 267–300.
2. ALDERFER, C. P. *Human Needs in Organizational Settings*. New York: Free Press, 1972.
3. ALLPORT, F. H. *Social Psychology*. New York: Houghton Mifflin, 1924.
4. ANGLE, HAROLD L., and JAMES L. PERRY. "An Empirical Assessment of Organizational Commitment and Organizational Effectiveness." *Administrative Science Quarterly* 26 (March 1981): 1–14.
5. ARGYRIS, C. *Integrating the Individual and the Organization*. New York: Wiley, 1964.
6. ATKINSON, J. W. *An Introduction to Motivation*. New York: Van Nostrand Reinhold, 1964.

7. ———. "Toward Experimental Analysis of Human Motivation in Terms of Motives, Expectancies and Incentives." In *Motives in Fantasy, Action and Society,* edited by J. W. Atkinson. Princeton, N.J.: Van Nostrand, 1958. Pp. 288–305.
8. ATKINSON, J. W., and D. CARTWRIGHT. "Some Neglected Variables in Contemporary Conceptions of Decisions and Performance." *Psychological Reports* 14 (1964): 575–590.
9. BERKOWITZ, L. "The Judgemental Process in Personality Functioning," *Psychological Review* 67 (1960): 130–142.
10. BIRCH, D., and J. VEROFF. *Motivation: A Study of Action.* Belmont, Calif.: Brooks/Cole, 1966.
11. BOYATZIS, R. E. "A Two-Factor Theory of Affiliation Motive." Doctoral dissertation, Harvard University, 1973.
12. ———. *The Competent Manager: A Model for Effective Performance.* New York: Wiley, 1982.
13. BRASS, DANIEL, J. "Structural Relationships, Job Characteristics, and Worker Satisfaction and Performance." *Administrative Science Quarterly* 26 (September 1981): 331–348.
14. BROEDLING, L. A. "Relationship of Internal-External Control to Work Motivation and Performance in an Expectancy Model." *Journal of Applied Psychology* 60 (1975): 65–70.
15. CARTWRIGHT, D., and F. HARARY. "Structural Balance: A Generalization of Heider's Theory." *Psychological Review* 63 (1956): 277–293.
16. CHILD, J. "Lordstown Revisited: What Has Happened to Those Blue Collar Blues?" Unpublished working paper, Kent State University, Kent, Ohio, 1977.
17. DAWIS, R. V., L. H. LOFGUIST, and D. J. WEISS. "A Theory of Work Adjustment (Revision)." *Minnesota Studies in Vocational Rehabilitation 23.* Minneapolis: University of Minnesota, 1968.
18. DECHARMS, R. "Affiliation Motivation and Productivity in Small Groups." *Journal of Abnormal Psychology* 55 (1957): 222–226.
19. DECI, E. L. *Intrinsic Motivation.* New York: Plenum Publishing, 1975.
20. DOLLARD, J., L. W. DOOB, N. E. MILLER, D. H. MOWRER, and R. R. SEARS. *Frustration and Aggression.* New Haven, Conn: Yale University Press, 1939.
21. DOOB, L. W. "The Behavior of Attitudes," *Psychological Review* 54 (1947): 135–136.
22. EBELING, JOHN S., and MICHAEL KING. "Hierarchical Position in the Work Organization and Job Satisfaction: A failure to replicate." *Human Relations* 34 (July 1981): 567–572.
23. FARRELL, DANIEL, and CARYL E. RUSBULT. "Exchange Variables as Predictors of Job Satisfaction, Job Commitment, and Turnover: The Impact of Rewards, Costs, Alternatives and Investments." *Organizational Behavior and Human Performance* 28 (August 1981): 78–95.
24. FEIN, M. "Motivation for Work." In *Handbook of Work, Organization and Society,* edited by R. Dubin. Chicago: Rand McNally, 1976.
25. FESTINGER, L. "A Theory of Social Comparison Processes." *Human Relations* 7 (1954): 117–140.

26. FESTINGER, L. *Conflict, Decision and Dissonance.* Stanford, Calif.: Stanford University Press, 1964.
27. GILES, WILLIAM F. "Volunteering for Job Enrichment: Reaction to Job Characteristics or Change?" *Journal of Vocational Behavior* 11 (1977): 232–238.
28. GILES, W. F., and W. F. HOLLEY, JR. "Job Enrichment vs. Traditional Issues at the Bargaining Table." *Academy of Management Journal* 21 (December 1978): 725–730.
29. GOODMAN, P. S., and A. FRIEDMAN. "An Examination of Adams' Theory of Inequity." *Administrative Science Quarterly* 16 (1971): 271–288.
30. GREENBERG, CARL I., YAN-DE WANG, and DENNIS L. DOSSETT. "Effects of Work Group Size and Task Size on Observers' Job Characteristics Ratings." *Basic and Applied Social Psychology* 3 (March 1982): 53–66.
31. GRIFFIN, R. "Relationships Among Individual Task Design and Leader Behavior Variables." *Academy of Management Journal* 23 (1980): 665–683.
32. GRIGALIUNAS, B., and Y. WIENER. "Has the Research Challenge to Motivation-Hygiene Theory Been Conclusive? An Analysis of Critical Studies." *Human Relations* 27 (1976): 839–71.
33. HACKMAN, J. RICHARD. "Is Job Enrichment Just a Fad?" *Harvard Business Review* 53 (1975a): 129–138.
34. HACKMAN, J. RICHARD. "On the Coming Demise of Job Enrichment." In *Man and Work in Society,* edited by E. L. Cass and F. G. Zimmer. New York: Van Nostrand Reinhold, 1975b. Pp. 97–115.
35. HACKMAN, J. RICHARD. "Work Design." In *Improving Life at Work: Behavioral Science Approaches to Organizational Change,* edited by J. Richard Hackman and J. Lloyd Suttle. Santa Monica, Calif.: Goodyear, 1977. Pp. 96–162.
36. HACKMAN, J. R., and E. E. LAWLER, III. "Employee Reactions to Job Characteristics." *Journal of Applied Psychology,* Monograph 55 (1971): 259–286.
37. HACKMAN, J. R., and G. R. OLDHAM. "Development of the Job Diagnostic Survey." *Journal of Applied Psychology* 60 (1975): 159–170.
38. HACKMAN, J. R., and G. R. OLDHAM. "Motivation Through the Design of Work: Test of a Theory." *Organizational Behavior and Human Performance* 16 (1976): 250–276. The quotation on pages 273–74 is reprinted with permission of the publisher.
39. HACKMAN, J. R., G. OLDHAM, R. JANSON, and K. PURDY. "A New Strategy for Job Enrichment." In *The Organization Game,* edited by R. Miles and W. A. Randolph. Santa Monica, Calif.: Goodyear, 1979. Pp. 130–145.
40. HALL, D. T., and K. E. NOUGAIM. "An Examination of Maslow's Need Heirarchy in an Organizational Setting." *Organizational Behavior and Human Performance* 3 (1968): 12–35.
41. HEIDER, F. *The Psychology of Interpersonal Relations.* New York: Wiley, 1958.
42. HERZBERG, F. *Work and the Nature of Man.* Cleveland: World Publishing, 1966.
43. HERZBERG, F., B. MAUSNER, and B. SNYDERMAN. *The Motivation to Work.* New York: Wiley, 1959.
44. HULIN, C. L. "Individual Differences and Job Enrichment—The Case Against General Treatments." In *Organizational Issues in Industrial Society,* edited by J. M. Shepard. Englewood Cliffs, N.J.: Prentice-Hall, 1972. Pp. 387–408.

45. IVANCEVICH, JOHN M. "High and Low Task Stimulation Jobs: A Causal Analysis of the Performance-Satisfaction Relationship." *Academy of Management Journal* 22 (1979): 206–222.

46. IVANCEVICH, J. M., and J. T. MCMAHON. "A Study of Task-Goal Attributes, Higher Order Need Strength, and Performance." *Academy of Management Journal* 20 (1977): 552–563.

47. JACKSON, SUSAN E., and SHELDON, ZEDECK. "Explaining Performance Variability: Contributions of Goal Setting, Task Characteristics, and Evaluative Contexts." *Journal of Applied Psychology* 67 (December 1982): 759–768.

48. JACQUES, E. *Equitable Payment.* New York: Wiley, 1961.

49. JAMAL, MUHAMMAD, and SALEHA M. JAMAL. "Work and Nonwork Experiences of Employees on Fixed and Rotating Shifts: An Empirical Assessment." *Journal of Vocational Behavior* 20 (June 1982): 282–293.

50. KATZ, D., and R. L. KAHN. *The Social Psychology of Organizations,* 2nd ed. New York: Wiley, 1978.

51. KEISLER, C. A., B. E. COLLINS, and N. MILLER. *Attitude Change,* New York: Wiley, 1969.

52. KNOKE, DAVID. "Commitment and Detachment in Voluntary Associations." *American Sociological Review* 46 (April 1981): 141–158.

53. LAWLER, E. E., III, and J. L. SUTTLE. "A Causal Correlation Test of the Need Hierarchy Concept." *Organizational Behavior and Human Performance* 7 (1972): 265–287.

54. LAWRENCE, D. H., and L. FESTINGER. *Deterrents and Reinforcement.* Stanford, Calif.: Stanford University Press, 1962.

55. LITWIN, G. H., and R. A. STRINGER. *Motivation and Organizational Climate.* Boston: Harvard University, Graduate School of Business Administration, 1968.

56. LOCKE, E. A., D. SIROTA, and A. D. WOLFSON. "An Experimental Case Study of the Successes and Failures of Job Enrichment in a Government Agency." *Journal of Applied Psychology* 61 (1976): 701–712.

57. MASLOW, A. H. *Motivation and Personality,* 2nd ed. New York: Harper, 1970.

58. MCCLELLAND, D. C. "Is Personality Consistent? In *Further Explorations in Personality,* edited by A. I. Rubin, J. Aronoff, A. M. Barclay, and R. A. Zucker. New York: Wiley, 1981.

59. MCCLELLAND, D. C. *Power: The Inner Experience.* New York: Irvington Publishers, 1975.

60. ———. *The Achieving Society.* Princeton, N.J.: Van Nostrand, 1961.

61. MCCLELLAND, D. C., and RICHARD E. BOYATZIS. "Leadership Motive Pattern and Long-Term Success in Management." *Journal of Applied Psychology* 67 (December 1982): 737–743.

62. MCCLELLAND, D. C., and D. BURMHAN. "Power is the Great Motivator." *Harvard Business Review* 25 (March–April 1976): 159–166.

63. MCGREGOR, D. *The Human Side of Enterprise.* New York: McGraw-Hill, 1960.

64. MERTON, R. K. *Social Theory and Social Structure.* New York: Free Press, 1957.

65. MEYER, H. H. "Achievement Motivation and Industrial Climate." In *Organizational*

Climate: Exploration of a Concept, edited by R. T. Tagiuri and G. H. Litwin. Cambridge, Mass.: Harvard University Press, 1968.

66. MINER, JOHN B. *Motivation to Manage: A Ten-Year Update on the "Studies of Management Education" Research.* Atlanta, Ga.: Organizational Measurement Systems Press, 1977.

67. MINER, J. B. "The Early Identification of Managerial Talent." *Personnel Guide Journal* 46 (1968): 586–591.

68. ———. *Theories of Organizational Behavior.* Hinsdale, Ill.: The Dryden Press, 1980.

69. ———. "Twenty Years of Research on Role-Motivation Theory of Managerial Effectiveness." *Personnel Psychology* 31 (1978): 739–760.

70. MINER, J. B., and NORMAN R. SMITH. "Decline and Stabilization of Managerial Motivation Over a Twenty-Year Period." *Journal of Applied Psychology* 67 (June 1982): 297–305.

71. MOSSHOLDER, K. W. "Effects of Externally Mediated Goal Setting on Intrinsic Motivation: A Laboratory Experiment." *Journal of Applied Psychology* 65 (1980): 202–210.

72. MURRAY, H. A. *Explorations in Personality.* New York: Oxford University Press, 1938.

73. NEWCOMBE, T. M. *The Acquaintance Process.* New York: Holt, Rinehart and Winston, 1961.

74. OLDHAM, G. R. "The Motivational Strategies Used by Supervisors: Relationships to Effectiveness Indicators." *Organizational Behavior and Human Performance* 15 (1976): 66–86.

75. ORPEN, C. "The Effects of Job Enrichment on Employee Satisfaction, Motivation, Involvement, and Performance: A Field Experiment." *Human Relations* 32 (1979): 189–217.

76. OSGOOD, C. E., and P. H. TANNENBAUM. "The Principle of Congruity in the Prediction of Attitude Change." *Psychological Review* 62 (1955): 42–55.

77. RAKESTRAW, T. L., JR., and H. M. WEISS. "The Interaction of Social Influences and Task Experience on Goal, Performance, and Performance Satisfaction." *Organizational Behavior and Human Performance* 27 (1981): 326–344.

78. ROBERTS, K. H., and W. GLICK. "The Job Characteristics Approach to Task Design: A Critical Review." *Journal of Applied Psychology* 66 (1981): 193–217.

79. ROUSSEAU, DENIS M. "Technological Differences in Job Characteristics, Employee Satisfaction, and Motivation: A Synthesis of Job Design Research and Sociotechnical Systems Theory." *Organizational Behavior and Human Performance* 19 (1977): 18–42.

80. SALANCIK, GERALD R., and JEFFREY PFEFFER. "A Social Information Processing Approach to Job Attitudes and Task Design." *Administrative Science* 23 (1978): 224–253.

81. SCHEIN, E. H. *Organizational Psychology.* Englewood Cliffs, N.J.: Prentice-Hall, 1965.

82. SEEBORG, I. S. "The Influence of Employee Participation in Job Redesign." *Journal of Applied Behavioral Science* 14 (1978): 87–98.

83. SHEPARD, J. M. "Functional Specialization, Alienation, and Job Satisfaction." In *Organizational Issues in Industrial Society,* edited by J. M. Shepard. Englewood Cliffs, N.J.: Prentice-Hall, 1972.

84. STAW, B. M., and G. R. OLDHAM. "Reconsidering Our Dependent Variables: A Critique and Empirical Study." *Academy of Management Journal* 21 (December 1978): 539.
85. STEERS, RICHARD M., and LYMANS W. PORTER. *Motivation and Work Behavior.* New York: McGraw-Hill, 1983.
86. STEERS, RICHARD M., and DANIEL G. SPENCER. "The Role of Achievement Motivation in Job Design." *Journal of Applied Psychology* 62 (1977): 472–479.
87. TAUSKY, C., and E. L. PARKE. "Job Enrichment, Need Theory and Reinforcement Theory." In *Handbook of Work, Organization and Society,* edited by R. Dubin. Chicago: Rand McNally, 1976. Pp. 531–561.
88. TZINER, AHARON, and YOAV VARDI. "Effects of Command Style and Group Cohesiveness on the Performance Effectiveness of Self-Selected Tank Crews." *Journal of Applied Psychology* 67 (December 1982): 769–775.
89. WAHBA, M. A., and L. G. BIRDWALL. "Maslow Reconsidered: A Review of Research on the Need Hierarchy Theory." *Organizational Behavior and Human Performance* 15 (1976): 212–240.
90. WHITE, J. KENNETH. "Individual Differences and the Job Quality-Worker Response Relationship: Review, Integration, and Comments." *Academy of Management Review* 3 (1978): 267–280.
91. WHITE, S. E., and T. R. MITCHELL. "Job Enrichment Vs. Social Cues: A Comparison and Competitive Test." *Journal of Applied Psychology* 64 (1979): 1–9.
92. WIENER, YAOSH. "Commitment in Organizations: A Normative View." *Academy of Management Review* 7 (1982): 418–428.
93. WIENER, Y., and Y. VARDI. "Relationships Between Job, Organization, and Career Commitments and Work Outcomes—An Integrative Approach." *Organizational Behavior and Human Performance* 26 (1980): 81–96.

Discussion Questions

1. Discuss the responses of the characters in our opening story to Penny's description of her government agency experience. How might each character have behaved in that situation? Why?
2. Discuss the strengths and the shortcomings of the need hierarchy theories for understanding organizational behavior.
3. How are the motivation–hygiene and need hierarchy theories related? How do they differ?
4. How would you integrate need theory and reinforcement theory?
5. Discuss needs for affiliation, achievement, and power. How might each have organizational consequences? Relate your discussion to the concept of socialization.
6. Discuss the theories of cognitive balance as they may pertain to motivation and to organizational behavior.
7. According to need theory how might job satisfaction relate to motivation? Why? How might job satisfaction relate to motivation according to reinforcement theory? Why?

8. Describe job enrichment as perhaps one important element of a motivational system. Be sure to relate job enrichment to our discussions of the process of motivation. Also, relate it to effective organizations in general.
9. Under what conditions might job enrichment succeed? Under what conditions might it fail? Why?

Section Two
Careers: The Mobility System

In the previous section we examined motivation—the processes and some substantive theories about what motivates people. Simply put, motivation stems both from intrinsic and extrinsic factors, from the noncontrived outcomes of a job well done, and from the properly applied reinforcers of pay and promotion.

From this perspective, the unfolding sequence of job-related activities which is said to constitute a career also offers a series of opportunities for providing interesting work, increases in pay, and promotion that are crucial to maintaining motivation over a lifespan of work. Therefore, in this part we will view a career as providing a structure of opportunity.

In keeping with the approach we have adopted for this text, our analysis of careers is *not* going to be one of career management, of how to do it. Rather, we are interested in building an understanding of the forces that shape careers, of how people in organizations understand careers, and of how they develop perceptions of success and failure. We are also interested in the structural adaptations that organizations make to maintain the motivation of people whose careers have come to rest, as it were. Thus, the chapters that constitute Section Two focus on these features of the mobility system as shown in Figure II.1:

- a description of the *structure of opportunity*, those organizational mechanisms which structure advancement upward through the ranks of management, and provide symbols of success or failure; and

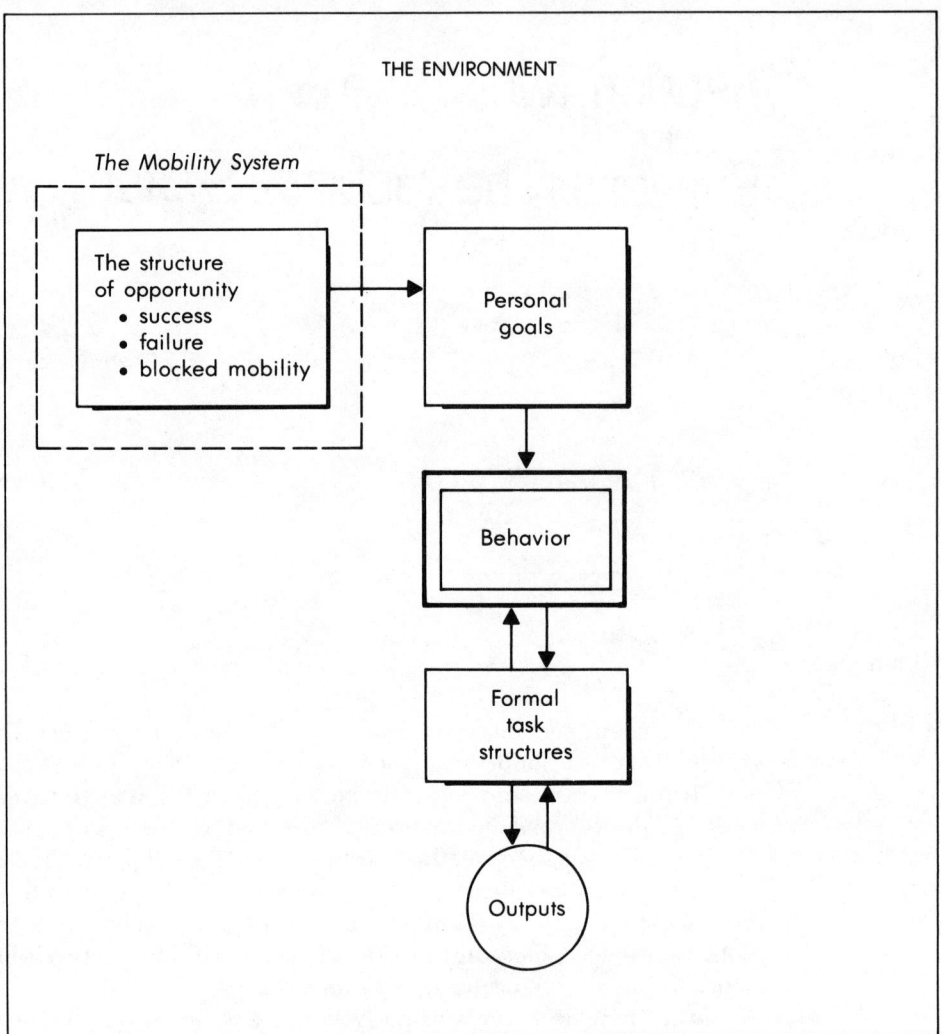

FIGURE II.1 Achieving Personal Goals: Careers—The Mobility System

- an analysis of situations in which people find the paths of advancement in position and status blocked, and of how individuals and organizations adapt to these situations.

Our aim is to provide an understanding of the ways in which organizations attempt to arrange for the continuing motivation of people through those unfolding sequences of job-related activities called careers.

Chapter 11
The Structure of Opportunity

Nothing Succeeds Like Success

Ben wasn't saying much. He didn't think he had to. Just let Shelby talk a bit longer, he thought. That ought to take care of it. Naturally, Ted obliged.

". . . since almost all of our management development actually has been directed at those of us *already* in management. What we've failed to see—and I'd be the first one to admit that I've missed the boat here, too—what we've *failed* to see is that we are absolutely wasting six or seven years of management potential in every one of our future managers. Think of it, nearly *one-quarter* of a working career!"

What was Ted up to now? More of the usual. He was selling a new management development program to help The Company survive in "the most competitive climate we've experienced since Mr. Marsh, Sr., etc." Today's agenda called for a sales pitch to Ben Franklyn and various others from plant operations. Pat Jones and some staff people were also assembled for the meeting.

Ted is explaining the program.

"Let me make this perfectly clear, HYPO (high risk, high potential) is a tough, hard-hitting program designed to produce tough, hard-hitting managers. That's why we've pegged the survival rate at less than 50 percent—*less* than 50 percent." Ted paused for effect. "That means that every recruit accepted for HYPO is more likely to fail than succeed. We're throwing 'em in to see who swims.

"But the boys who keep their heads above water, why, look what they have accomplished career-wise for themselves, and experience-wise for The Company. Within only two years of their entry date these men will be experienced first-line managers. And, you know, I wouldn't be a bit surprised if some of those people might not even be ready for their *next* promotion. Look what we've gained." Ted flipped to the next chart and took pointer in hand.

Ted now recited the virtues of HYPO point by point, explaining how, by moving new recruits directly into first-line managerial positions, The Company could increase its decision-making effectiveness. The rapid development of young, energetic management was the key. The high failure rate, a natural outcome of inexperience and of the uncertainty of the selection process, was also a plus. This was because the ones who couldn't "cut it"

289

knew that they had nothing to be ashamed of. After all, this was tough, tight-fisted competition, and that's what The Company is all about.

HYPO

- Early indentification of high-potential managers
- No time to pick up bad work habits
- Trial by fire; tough but fair
- Managerial ability put to early use
- Ensures competitive environment; promotes crisp decision making

---

TED'S CHART

Ted was especially pleased with himself as he concluded, asking for "your input on this." There followed a few scattered comments from staff people—favorable, of course—to get the discussion rolling.

Ben was still holding off. He'd decided that the program didn't mean much for Pawtucket anyway. Because they were an older plant they weren't growing at all and there just weren't any new management openings. No, he'd let the others do the talking for a change. Then Pat spoke up.

Pat always made Ted uneasy, and this time was no exception. "I must have missed part of your explanation somewhere along the line, Ted. Would you go over the part again that says just how you make this a high risk program?"

"Why, er—certainly, Pat. That is, I'm not sure that I covered that point, detail by detail. But then it's obvious, isn't it?"

Pat's look made her reply unnecessary.

Ted started to fidget, "Why *sure* it is. Look, here we've got a group of young men (another look from Pat) just four to six months with The Company and now we throw them without experience directly into what is probably the most demanding job in The Company—first-line supervision. How do I know it's high risk? Just look at the time it *usually* takes to prepare for that position—six to seven years at the minimum. And that's the *shortest* period of preparation before promotion. So our HYPOs have got a big order to fill. They're learning two jobs at once. That's what it amounts to."

"I see," said Pat, "and maybe I don't. Ted, what makes you think it takes seven years to learn how to be a manager. What are these people learning in that seven years?"

"Now you wait a minute, Pat. That's the kind of game you always play." Ted really was irritated now. "How do we know *this* for sure, how do we know *that* for sure?" Ted's imitation was not particularly convincing. "You always want to run a ten-year controlled experiment before you are willing to say we '*know*' anything."

Pat was about to reply but Ted continued on, "No, let me finish. What I *know* is that if it takes seven years before we feel a man is ready for management, then there's *got to be* a good reason for it. Otherwise—why, otherwise, we'd be moving 'em up sooner, wouldn't we." This last was not a question, simply a declaration of fact.

Again Pat started to reply, but this time Ben cut in. Finally, he'd heard enough. "I'm kind of enjoying this argument between you experts. Why, I'm even willing to allow that I don't know—that's right—I really *don't know* how long it takes to figure out how to be a good manager. From what I see, most of the time it doesn't *ever* seem to happen." Ben chuckled.

"Never mind. There's something else you really ought to be thinking about. Yeah. Something else." This was Ben's turn to pause for effect. "Who's going to be doing the work that all the managers are going to be managing? Maybe I can't tell you how long it takes to get to become a good manager, but I can tell you why it doesn't happen in less than seven years. That's because we need someone to do the *work*, that's why. You can't have all chiefs and no Indians, that's why."

Silence followed Ben's analysis. No one wanted to challenge Ben—and they particularly didn't want to antagonize him. Yet everyone knew that Ben was awfully old-fashioned about these things. So what he said was mostly ignored.

In the end some top corporate staff people bought the program and in about a half a year HYPO was underway. This is how Claude Gilliam became one of The Company's first HYPOs. Which meant, incidentally, that he was also one of the last. How so? Let's move ahead about two years and have Claude explain. He's just been moved to a headquarters staff position and he's explaining his feelings to Pat Jones.

"No sense in staying, Pat. Just no sense. Look, I've *shown* that I can do a job that now I've got to wait six, seven, hell, maybe ten years for. So I can't hang around here and just *wait.* No, I'm putting together my resume and I'm gonna start knocking on some doors."

"Oh, now. I can understand, I think, how you must feel, Claude. And I'm not trying to tell you what to do—but you knew HYPO was—what'd Shelby call it?—a 'high risk opportunity,'" Pat mouthed the words with distaste. "So I wouldn't blame it on The Company."

"But that's just it, Pat. Don't you see? I didn't fail! Listen, I could take that. Nothing's ever come easy to me, you know. But I *didn't fail.* Every performance rating I got from my boss was above average. I was doing the job. That's how I know I've got to move on. I'm not going to rot doing corporate staff make-work for ten years just to get another chance."

"Maybe I don't understand then," replied Pat. "If you *did* do the job, then what happened? Do you think . . . I mean, ah, do you suppose that, ah, because . . ."

"You can say it, I don't mind," Claude interrupted. "You mean do I think 'cause I'm black they knocked me out. Yeah, I thought about that. But that's not it. The Company's pretty fair, I'd have to say. And anyway, it turns out that there's lots of others in the same fix as me. And they feel just about the way I do. Fact is, I'd have to say that I don't know anyone in HYPO who failed. Oh, maybe one or two did. But I don't know 'em."

"I think I'm beginning to see," Pat brightened. "So what we had was a group of bright young people like yourself all doing jobs that ordinarily they would not have had for at least six or seven more years; and probably doing them better than anyone before, I'll bet."

"Of course. Ted was right, in a way. You people were highly motivated and you brought some fresh ideas to the job, too. Certainly you did. You hadn't had them beaten out of you yet. So while you made plenty of mistakes, that's only natural, but you . . ."

"We gave it everything we had. Hell, this was our big chance." Claude cut in. After all, it was his story. "Yeah, our big chance. But you know, I think the problem was they really didn't know what to do with us when we *did* make it. Some of those jobs were kind of *created,* I think. Anyway, they didn't seem to be all that necessary. And then there were the guys who had been waiting their turn, the guys who had been hanging around for those however many years just so they could become managers. Yeah, I think that was the *real* problem."

And so in the end it was Ben who foresaw most clearly what the outcome would be. Ted, with his "modern behavioral technologies," had lost sight of what Ben knew: not *how* long it took to learn to become a manager, but *why* it took that long.

Perhaps Claude's experience in the HYPO program is a bit unusual.[1] Yet it illustrates a major dilemma of organizations: how to maintain the motivation of all when the structure of opportunity provides room for only a few. This is the problem that led the *Wall Street Journal* to proclaim in 1975,

BATTLE OF THE BULGE

Firms Fight an Effect of 1950's Baby Boom: Young-Executive Glut
They Try Lateral Transfers, Extra Titles and Urging of Lowered Expectations
From Woodstock to Reality (41:1)

The problem with the HYPO program was not that it would not produce more capable managers; most likely it would. What HYPO failed to realize was that a strategy for maintaining the motivation of the larger group of professionals may be more important than a strategy for the rapid advancement of the most talented. That is, there is a trade-off—one comes at the expense of the other. As The Company found out, potential managers are lined up awaiting their own opportunity. And in large measure the motivation of the people in this line stems from the expectation of future promotion.

Our task in this chapter, then, is to examine how organizations manage the structure of opportunity in order to maintain motivation, and how they attempt to manage definitions of success and failure in order to cope with the demotivating consequences of limited opportunities for advancement.

Theory tells us that the *expectation* of promotion to higher-level positions is motivating. We know also from the preceding chapters that this is not as simple a situation as it might seem. For one thing, people's expectations differ. For another, the rate of advancement is important. The experience of success is a relative thing, keyed to changes in status, with the rate of change judged against both individual expectations and comparisons to other people. We discuss this at length in this chapter, but the principle is, the link between the rate of upward mobility and motivation is forged by the experience of success. Success feelings build greater commitment, greater willingness to comply, and greater motivation.

Unfortunately, we do not know as much about the consequences of failure. One reason for this is that failure has not been a popular topic for study. Another is that individuals and organizations go out of their way to provide alternative explanations and reasons for events that otherwise would be experienced as failure. What happens when a person no longer has the expectation of future success, when that expectation ceases to be a motivating force? To answer this question we need to understand how expectation dies. We need to understand the individual and social processes involved in the development of organizational definitions of success and failure. With this understanding we will see why organizations try to manage the structure of opportunity, where they succeed, and where they fail.

To summarize, we will examine the link between the structure of opportunity and motivation within the following framework:

- The expectation of promotion into higher-level managerial jobs is a major factor in the motivation to work. With advancement come greater status

and authority, increased monetary rewards, greater recognition, and similar desirable benefits.
- The ability to grant or withhold promotion is a major component in the power, and hence the authority, of superiors. Consequently, the expectation of promotion is a key incentive for compliance.
- The typical pyramidal shape of hierarchy increasingly constrains the structure of opportunity as managers move upward. Therefore, since success and failure are defined relative to others in the social structure, the failure of some is inevitable.
- A major problem with which organizations must cope is that of providing sufficient upward mobility to maintain motivation while avoiding the negative consequences of the failure implied by lack of movement.

The Structure of Opportunity

In our opening chapters we took a close look at the social structure of organizations, at systems of roles, and of power and authority. We saw superior authority as rooted in the justified power to dispense rewards and punishments. We viewed authority basically as a mechanism for integrating the different functions of a large and complex organization.

Now, we would like to turn this organization on its head, so to speak, to examine social structure as a structure of opportunity—the system of authority as a system of motivation. Each of those coordinating or integrating positions arrayed along the hierarchy of the formal structure brings with it increased status, increased prestige, increased material benefits, and power. Let us see how Stanley learned about the structure of opportunity.

In his first years with The Company Stanley probably spent as much time learning about the structure of opportunity as he did learning to do his job. The question continually on his mind was, where do I go from here? The more he learned, the more he came to realize that from his place in The Company's scheme of things opportunities were truly limitless. He was young, with a good technical education, and he was personable. If he was also innocent in the ways of The Company, well, time would take care of that. Let us summarize what Stanley saw in those first days.

First, he saw promotion *within categories*. You are promoted from engineer to staff engineer, from accountant to senior accountant, and the like. These are the nominal signs of progress, of success. That is, your work does not change very much from category to category, but the new title does signify that you are moving ahead satisfactorily.

Then he noted *lateral* movement. This is perhaps the most common form of movement. For young people on the way up, the lateral is generally akin to a promotion within categories. It definitely is a step ahead. However, for older people in The Company, people no longer on the way up, a lateral may signify the end of a career, that they have been found unsuitable for the job and are being moved out of the way.

He also saw that promotion from *professional to manager* is the big step. This is the step certifying that you are capable of performing managerial work. This is the step that opens up opportunity in other management positions. It may take place within a given function, but in large organizations it is equally likely to be a *diagonal* step to a higher position in a different function.

The *diagonal* promotion is most common, however, after your first step into the managerial ranks. It is commonly designed to broaden your experience in a different function or geographical area of The Company. It is extremely unlikely that anyone who has not gone through a number of these diagonal promotions will ever reach the executive levels of The Company.

Finally, Stanley learned that careers are typically made up of lateral, diagonal, and direct upward moves. For example, as a young manager you are typically moved from a plant or sales office for a stint in a corporate staff position. The move itself may be lateral, but it is designed to broaden your experience. Even more important, it is designed to give you increased exposure to corporate executives and middle management. If you perform well, the next step will very likely be a diagonal promotion into middle management at one of The Company's locations. An interesting model of this process has been developed by Rosenbaum (33). (See Box 13.)

With this in mind we will examine the structural and organizational considerations involved in managing opportunity, and look at how these affect the organization's motivation system.

BOX 13

Careers as Tournaments

Since a career may be defined as an unfolding sequence of jobs, James Rosenbaum asked, "Is there some way of generalizing about the process by which careers unfold?" In answer he describes three possible types of career process:

1. In the contest model, individuals have complete freedom to compete and past career history has no effect on present chances for movement upward; that is, the model is totally ahistorical.
2. The sponsorship model has individuals being selected very early for their ultimate careers and allows no freedom for departure from this choice. The sponsorship

continued

model also is ahistorical in that later positions are predicted only from the position just before them, and not from earlier career history.
3. In the tournament model the career is a sequence of competitions, each of which affects future positions. Winners gain the opportunity to compete for higher levels, but there is no guarantee of achieving them as there is in the sponsorship model. Losers are permitted to compete only for lower-level positions or perhaps not to compete at all. Thus, the model is historical in that early outcomes have irreversible consequences for the losers.

Rosenbaum set out to determine the validity of the tournament model by gathering data over a thirteen-year period on a cohort of 671 employees of a Fortune 500 company. Personnel records were the source for information on career mobility.

From these data it was evident that the contest model did not apply. The simplicity and orderliness of the career paths evident in the data did not at all support the random, open-opportunity situation of the contest model. Careers followed only a limited number of paths.

Investigating the tournament model presented some difficulties since there are no explicit competition events and decisions about losers are not publicly announced. Thus, the model assumes that competitions occur every three to four years and that an individual has lost if not promoted during that period. Aside from this, however, Rosenbaum's data provide strong support for the tournament model. Perhaps the most important finding is the crucial role of early promotion. Only employees promoted in the earliest time period of the study attained middle-management levels in this study.

In discussing his results Rosenbaum notes these implications of the tournament model:

- Survivors of the tournament are likely to be labeled winners, a fact that may enhance the leader's future effectiveness.
- There is some likelihood that a self-fulfilling prophecy is in operation, in which early winners are viewed as having high potential and thus will be socialized differentially into strong developmental opportunities. Losers will be given little chance to prove themselves again and will receive "custodial" socialization—to "homogenize" them to fit undemanding roles.

To conclude, from the tournament model we come to understand the pressure experienced by upwardly mobile managers. If any loss will have a permanent negative effect on an entire career, then certainly the price of victory is eternal vigilance.

From J. E. Rosenbaum, "Tournament Mobility: Career Patterns in a Corporation." *Administrative Science Quarterly* 24 (1979): 220–241.

Definitions of Success and Failure

Advancement upward through the organization and into the ranks of management is the accepted norm for professional employees. A professional employee is embarked on a career, and the steps and timetable for such upward mobility are fairly well defined (27, 34). A competent person is more likely to have high mobility expectations. Something is amiss if this is not the case. One manager, on learning that a subordinate turned down an opportunity for advancement, observed, "My estimate of his abilities and his work has gone down a lot. I have to question his motivation and ambition" (11: 611).

Such ambition is celebrated in the business media, and this helps to mold the pattern of expectations of young professionals. *Fortune* devoted an entire article to analyzing the histories and future careers of exemplary members of the MBA crop of 1977. The theme of the article was the search for the "fast track" upward through the corporate ranks. The extraordinary young women and men described will not be satisfied, the magazine said, with the ordinary rate of progress. No, advancement commensurate with their superior skills requires the fast track (26).

The point of all this is not that extraordinary young people seek extraordinary success, but that the yardstick of that success, the measure of their worth, is in terms of their *relative rate of advancement.* These people define success. Do the others, then, define failure? That depends on comparisons with their own past aspirations and with their *reference groups,* that is, groups of people like themselves in organizations—for example, the class of 1956, production managers in The Company, blue-collar workers in Pawtucket. Fundamentally, both comparison to expectations and social comparison are social processes based on comparison to socially defined norms that define "fast" or "good." Judgments of success are tested and molded within the normative system and keyed to each person's background characteristics and the organizational situation.

Before moving ahead, we should note two points that put our analysis in perspective. First, there are *individual differences* in people's aspirations. Movement to the top of the management hierarchy is all-important to some, but certainly not to everyone. Second, there is growing evidence that emphasis on position and extrinsic rewards is decreasing in aspirants to professional and managerial positions. For example, a study by AT&T compared the aspirations of people hired for entry-level management positions in the 1950s and 1970s. What the data show is that the level of aspiration in the 1970s group is only about half that expressed by their 1950s forerunners (24). There is good reason to believe that this adjustment in aspiration is a realistic adaptation to the demographics of the baby boom generation.

Still, we wonder how much behavior will change. The plain fact is that most of you now reading these pages would not be doing so if you did not have your eye on advancement within the ranks of some organization.

Terminology of Success and Failure

Success and failure are relative. You might balance for a while at "neither success nor failure," but sooner or later judgment will be rendered within the normative system. If you are not a success, then in some ways you have failed; this is the essence of it (11, 37). Let us identify some organizational categories that will help us understand how success and failure are defined.

SUCCESS. All organizations have their "stars," "hypos," "comers," "rockets"—people on the fast track. The management knows who these people are. So do others. These are the elect, the elite, people earmarked for top executive positions. They are the people with outstanding credentials, with personalities, and motivation to match.

For the larger group of management aspirants with more ordinary talents these people are the yardstick against which success may be measured. And these stars are to some extent "mystified" within the normative system; that is, they are endowed with qualities and judgment they may not even possess, for they represent the ideal of the normative system of management.[2] Thus, *Fortune's* top representatives of the MBA crop all have remarkable qualities that few, if any, ordinary mortals can ever hope to possess.

One utilitarian function of this mystification is to provide an explanation for lesser degrees of success. Surely you, as an ordinary person, cannot hope to match their performance. The question then becomes, how rapidly are you moving compared to this standard? The answer depends on your current career stage, for upward progress slows as the organizational pyramid starts to narrow at upper levels. Nonetheless, it is relative upward movement that defines relative degrees of success.

FAILURE. Clear-cut failure is more difficult to identify than success. Since motivational problems may attend failure, organizations and their members attempt to disguise failure where possible. Outright termination is an obvious instance of failure, yet it is fairly rare among management aspirants. Termination generally is reserved for gross negligence or moral turpitude, since, as a *policy*, termination can have major dysfunctional consequences within the motivation system.[3] *Demotion* is the more common procedure, and demotion also constitutes evident failure—the reduction of a superior to a subordinate position within the same function. Demotion signifies that an individual has been tried and found wanting. In many organizations, though not all, demotion signifies the end of a career.

A variant procedure is the *transmotion,* as Kerry calls it: being transferred and demoted. The transmotion is really a disguised demotion. The superior is transferred to a different function, possibly at what appears to be the same level but at a lower status in a less problematic function. Thus, failure, like success, is evidenced by movement relative to that of others, in this case downward through the organization.

BLOCKED MOBILITY. Perhaps the largest group of careers in organizations comprises those people who, for various reasons, find the paths of upward mobility nonexistent or blocked. These people may be defined as either success or failure depending on their circumstances and on their final level in the organization. The motivational consequences also vary. If the final step of your career is a high-level executive position, then, under most circumstances you will be reckoned a success. Your motivation at this point will probably stem from the necessity of providing a proper role model for aspiring young managers. If your final position is considerably lower, your success may be questionable.

Blocked mobility can present motivational problems for the organization. For one thing, the organization has few incentives for performance or compliance to offer these people. For another, it is likely that they will become disaffected and demotivated if they come to see themselves as failures. Finally, nonmobile managers block upward pathways for younger managerial aspirants, creating still further motivational problems. Because this situation of blocked mobility is both complicated and important in its motivational and behavioral consequences, we shall treat it fully in Chapter 12.

Perception of Success

In our opening story Claude is unhappy with what has occurred. In one sense he has achieved more than many young people in The Company; yet, he is so dissatisfied that he is threatening to "look elsewhere." He won't, of course. But the paradoxical fact is that Claude is *less* satisfied now than if he had never met the challenge offered by HYPO. Why should this be?

Once again, the basic laws of perception, of perceptual adaptation to accustomed conditions, explain a great deal about how success and failure are defined. When we combine these *adaptation level* principles with those of socialization, whereby people come to share understandings of social events, we can develop some powerful principles for understanding the consequences of the structure of opportunity.

ADAPTATION LEVEL. The basic principle of adaptation level theory is the following: "The subjective experience of stimulus input is a function *not of the absolute level* of that input but of the *discrepancy* between the input and past levels" (8:287; emphasis added). An excellent example of this principle can be seen in any baseball game. Just before coming to the plate the batter adds a metal ring to the fat end of the bat. The net effect is to increase markedly the swing weight of the bat. Swinging this bat shifts the batter's adaptation level toward "heavier." When the batter removes the ring and comes to the plate, the normal bat feels considerably lighter and easier to swing than it usually does. Whether this exercise improves performance is questionable, but it certainly does change the perception of task difficulty.

Thus, the first principle for the formation of adaptation level to "stimulus input" is this: averaging of past experience provides the background against which current outcomes will be judged.[4]

A second way in which adaptation levels are formed is by averaging current outcomes over several factors. Let us take another example from sports. A friend of ours, a fine athlete, refuses to take tennis seriously as a game. The reason is that, although he is not a poor tennis player, he is far worse at tennis than at golf, basketball, or just about any other game. So every time he plays tennis his experience is that of failure—despite the fact that he wins often enough. He compares his outcomes to an adaptation level based on sports in which he is far superior.

Finally, adaptation level is also formed through social comparison—comparing your own outcomes to those of another person, or to some average of outcomes in a reference group. For example, as an above-average student you are quite happy with your B in quantitative methods, until you discover that your buddies got As. Had those people gotten mostly Cs, your judgment of your own accomplishment, of course, would have been far more favorable.

These observations demonstrate the derivative principle of *relative deprivation* (28, 35). This principle has been used to explain the dissatisfaction of better-educated soldiers in the Army. Better-educated soldiers actually have greater opportunities for advancement than their less-educated counterparts. Still, their social comparisons are based on an adaptation level established by people of similar education and background, that is, the commissioned officers, and those fared better still. Thus, better-educated soldiers are "deprived" relative to their social reference group, even though objectively they are better off than their less-educated counterparts.

This same principle explains the lower satisfaction of soldiers with promotion policies in organizations providing greater promotion opportunities. In organizations with a high rate of promotion, being promoted is the norm, and everyone expects it. Therefore, the adaptation level in those organizations is "being promoted." Soldiers in organizations with low rates of promotion have an adaptation level of "no promotion." Comparing the two situations, those in the low promotion organizations who exceed the adaptation level by being promoted experience positive outcomes; the rest, being at the adaptation level, experience neutral outcomes. Conversely, those in the high promotion organizations are found to experience lower average levels of satisfaction than those in the low rate of promotion organizations (35).

Using these principles, let us try to account for Claude's feelings about his experience in HYPO. First, and most obviously, Claude's adaptation level had been raised by his very rapid movement into management. Because of this, his level of expectation about the future, his *level of aspiration*, had increased and was higher than his adaptation level, as generally occurs in achievement tasks (8:290). When he returned to about the same situation in which he would have ordinarily found himself without HYPO, he experienced failure.

His adaptation level was also raised by his proven ability to perform various managerial tasks. This is our second principle: averaging across different factors. Having shown that he could perform these tasks, and then being reduced to a status not commensurate with that performance, he was again considerably below his adaptation level.

Finally, Claude will make social comparisons. The question is, which reference group, which social grouping, will be used for the comparison. Possible comparison groups for Claude might be other black males in the labor market, people of his own age and education in The Company, other black professionals, and the like. Each of these will produce a different subjective experience of success in comparative terms. Yet Claude's adaptation level has probably shifted upward because he now has a *new* reference group: first-level managers in The Company.

Thus, had Claude never participated in HYPO, had he never experienced this extraordinary situation, he would have been more satisfied in The Company than he is. Now his adaptation level, as well as his level of aspiration, have soared far above what The Company can offer under the principle of equity.

THE PRINCIPLE OF EQUITY. In Chapter 10 we introduced the principle of equity as a basis for judging the appropriateness of rewards: *people unequal in abilities, past accomplishments, or effort should be rewarded unequally, preferably in proportion to their merits* (1). This principle seems to be the rule within the normative system of most American organizations, even for blue-collar workers, whose pay scales are keyed to types of work. For example, Klein found that workers' preferences for different pay systems accorded with the principle of equity. Basically, then, *unequal* success seems to be perceived as fair if such perceptions are congruent with relevant social comparisons.

The most fundamental basis for comparison under the principle of equity is return on investment in human capital. That is, human capital theorists have demonstrated that rewards accrue to individuals in direct proportion to their investment in the development of *general skills* (greater education) and *specific skills* (on-the-job experience) (5). Judgments concerning effort expended also enter in. The principle of equity, then, says that people with greater investment in human capital, and those people perceived as putting out the greatest effort, should move ahead the most rapidly. And people who have moved the most rapidly should possess superior credentials and should manifest the greatest effort if that movement is to be perceived as equitable.

Figure 11.1 illustrates both the adaptation level and the equity comparison processes involved in maintaining motivation.

ORGANIZATIONAL CONSEQUENCES. These formulations have direct consequences for the structure of opportunity. First, organizations tend to structure opportunity in consonance with equity theory. People with the greatest investment in human capital are most likely to receive the greatest returns. Whether this is

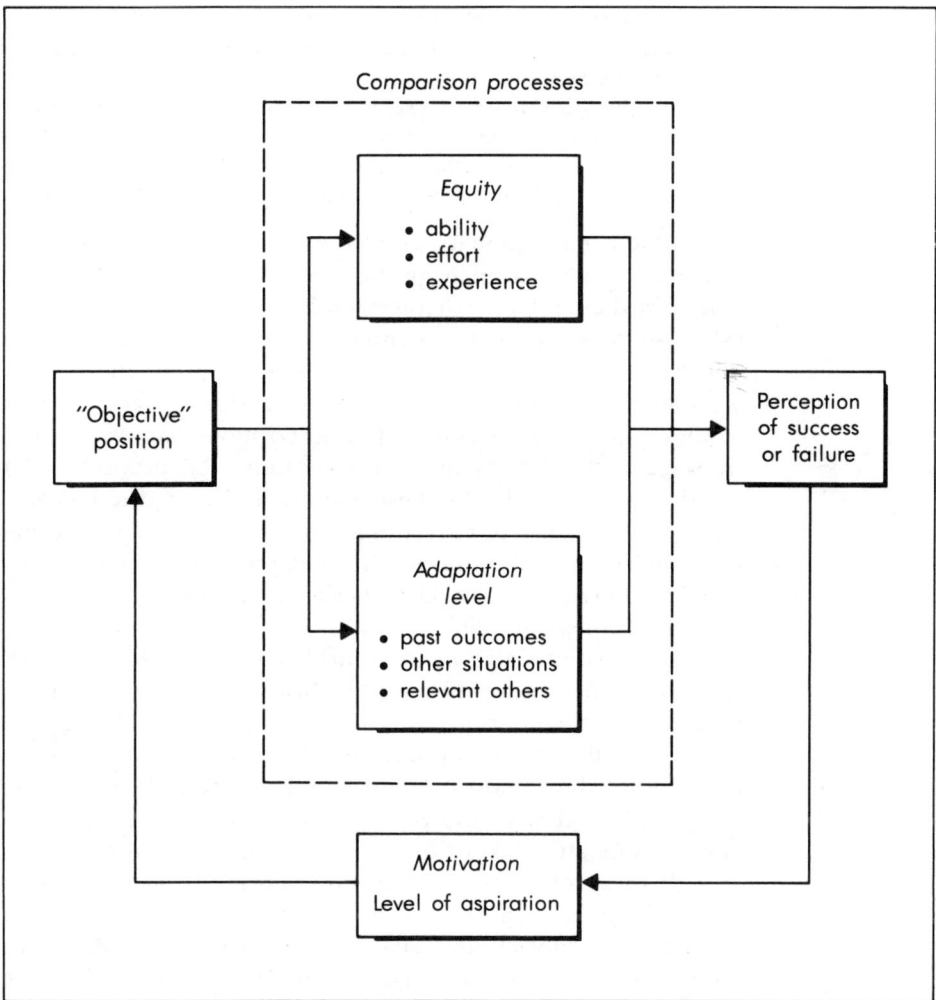

FIGURE 11.1 Maintaining Motivation: Schematic Diagram of Comparison Processes

because organizations receive greater return from this increased human capital, or whether it is simply a process of credentialing—that is, educational institutions performing the selection process for organizations—or some combination of these is irrelevant. People act on equity theory in the most direct way: by obtaining stronger credentials and increasing their own expectations (6). One consequence of these inflated expectations is plain in this letter written by an MBA in response to the "fast-track" article in *Fortune*.

> Graduate business schools teach management skills which are used mainly by middle to upper level administrators. However, most MBAs are not recruited into these decision-making positions. . . .
>
> The MBA therefore experiences increasing frustration and pressure in his first two years due to the dilemma between what is and what he feels should be. . . . [Business schools] cannot continue to create executive-potential graduates without infusing some reality into the program *vis-a-vis* the fast-track. (12:68)

Other organizational actions stem from fear of the consequences of inequity. Organizations try to manage the structure of opportunity by striving to create equity in their salary structures both in fact and in impression. Industry-wide salary surveys are made so companies can peg their average salary levels for different types of employees at some desired point above or below the industry standard. Within the organization a great deal of care is taken to ensure equity among different types of jobs. Job descriptions are written and studied carefully by wage and salary analysts to determine the proper level of compensation for the duties involved. These hierarchically adjusted salary levels may then be adjusted further to reflect differences in status among organizational hierarchies; that is, organizations may have different salary levels for presumably equal positions to reflect status differences among functions such as engineering, manufacturing, or plant maintenance.

Organizations also contrive artificial hierarchies to provide opportunities for promotion that would not otherwise exist. For example, large research and development laboratories may employ thousands of engineers, relatively few of whom will have the opportunity to advance into management. Yet, as our own studies show, most of these people aspire to be part of management some day. One solution to the problem is to provide an "alternative management ladder" so status distinctions necessary to maintain equity can be made, even though these distinctions carry no managerial powers. We shall say more of this in the next chapter.

Other organizational adaptations arise within the normative structure, though they are not "managed" in the formal sense. One such adaptation to the need for equity is found in the social control over perceptions of similarity and merit. As noted in Chapter 6, direct access to information about superordinate management is controlled by restricting subordinates' opportunities to interact directly with superiors in work settings. This makes it easy to create an impression of greater generalized competence. If subordinates do not know why a particular action is being taken, they have to assume that the people at the top know something they do not. Thus, superiors are there not only because they have been with the organization longer, but because they have superior skills and talents (4, 18, 37).

Conversely, we ascribe to lower participants characteristics that fit their position in the organization, further testifying to the equity of the assignment.

If secretaries are mostly female, we say it is because females are better suited to the work, more interested in the home than in the company, and happier to socialize than make decisions (25). Since the incentives for task-oriented activity are generally lacking in such lower-participant positions, this kind of ascription neatly becomes self-fulfilling.

To summarize, advancement into the ranks of management, into positions of greater status and power, is synonymous with success. But the subjective experience of success is comparative and relative, rooted in past experience and in comparison with others. Therefore, to understand how organizations provide motivating success experiences, we must first understand the principles of adaptation level and equity, and how they apply in an organizational context.

Rapid movement upward for some people brings about an upward shift of adaptation level for all. Since this can be dysfunctional for an organization, steps should be taken to counter to some extent the effects of this rapid movement. Such steps include (1) moving very few so rapidly, and (2) mystifying those few—that is, according them vastly superior abilities and achievements.

This second step invokes both social comparison and equity. People bringing greater human capital to the situation *ought to* move ahead faster, and comparisons with such outstanding people justify differential success. Yet equity applies as well to effort and service. So the larger group of "ordinary" professionals expect, in time, their own reward for faithful service. This expectation maintains their motivation, and is violated only at risk to the organization's entire motivation system.

Organizations, therefore, must carefully manage the structure of opportunity. Promoting everyone would be no more successful a strategy than promoting no one. The principles of adaptation and equity must be served. The consequences of success and failure must be attended to.

Success: Consequences and Structures

From a motivational standpoint organizations would like to be able to provide success experiences for all. That would be ideal; it would also be impossible. Success is a subjective and comparative judgment, and organizations are constrained by considerations of equity and by the diminished opportunity reflected in the shape of the hierarchical pyramid. Within this structure of opportunity there are also individual differences in ability, personality, energy, and appearance. However, presuming that organizations would like to provide success experiences for their members, what do we know of the motivational consequences of success?

Success breeds success. This is what we conclude from studies of the motivational consequences of successful careers (21). Briefly, the reasoning is this:

- Achieving desired career outcomes provides the subjective experience of success. Success leads to increased self-esteem, with the likely outcome of increased job involvement.
- In consequence, the level of aspiration for further achievement shifts upward, leading to greater task motivation.
- Where the structure of opportunity allows this greater motivation to be translated into performance, the "success cycle" is then closed through increased performance and the achievement of new career outcomes (21:125).

Evidence that success and organizational commitment are related within the adaption level/equity framework is provided by studies of the relationship between organizational commitment and a manager's education and sex (19). Managers who bring a lower investment in human capital to the job—either through lower education or through the burden of lower ascribed status (women, for example)—should experience greater feelings of success and, hence, show greater commitment to the organization than others in the same position but with a higher investment in human capital. And this is what the studies show. The subjective experience of success is greater because the adaptation levels are lower.

The "success breeds success" model allows a further conclusion: the anticipation of success should widen the zone of indifference to authoritative requests. Since authority is based in the superior power to dispense rewards and punishments, the subordinate anticipating rewards clearly has more to lose through noncompliance than the subordinate who does not anticipate rewards.

Thus, from several points of view we can see that success, commitment, compliance, and task motivation are all outcomes of the success cycle. This state of affairs is highly desirable for the organization. Let us identify some of the organizational, situational, and individual factors that foster success.

Organizational Factors

Most obviously, the organization's rate of growth fosters success. Where growth is rapid, new career opportunities open up. Functions grow vertically by the addition of new levels of hierarchy, and horizontally by the subdivision of existing components. Entire new hierarchies may be formed as new products are introduced or new markets entered. Geographical dispersion takes place as new manufacturing or product development facilities are created. Such was the case with the IBM Corporation, for example, during its rapid growth years in the 1950s and 1960s. At least one writer has even advanced the thesis that corporate *expansion* has replaced *profit* as a major goal of corporate managers—in part because of the new opportunities growth creates (14).

Another precondition for success is that people have the opportunity to employ and sharpen their skills through challenging work. As present tasks are mastered, professionals look to new jobs and the opportunity to develop new skills. Thus, advancement or lateral movement to new functions is necessary, although not always possible. One of the major complaints of professionals, especially those in large R and D organizations, is that assignments to routine and fragmented tasks frustrate career development (23, 29, 32). And this frustration seems to stem from the structure of the work itself, a product of the task technology and division of labor (31).

Situational Factors

A second set of conditions leading to success stems from different situations within the organization—for example, the fast track. Organizations try to provide a fast track—a managed situation for growth and advancement—for people identified as future "stars," or perhaps for people with needed specialties currently in short supply. For example, during the explosive growth of systems and programming specialties, when this profession was becoming established, organizations provided a fast track for the professionals involved. Thus, we can find situations for certain people or in certain subunits of organizations in which the potential for rapid mobility is far greater than in others, regardless of the overall organizational growth rate.

Interesting opportunities may present themselves in any organization. A clever example of career planning was that of a friend of ours, an engineer, who is now a vice president of a major corporation. At the time he was recruited engineers in that particular organization were unionized, a condition viewed with distaste by most professionals. The company also had a reputation for lack of innovation and stodginess. Our friend recounts how, on graduation, his professors urged him against accepting a job offer from that company, since he had too much potential to consign himself to a career with such a second-rate outfit. But that was the job offer he accepted. Fifteen years ago he explained his choice this way, "I figured that the bright guys all over the country probably were getting the same advice. But the company was too big to die. So at some point, when they needed to replace their retiring managers, they were going to look around and not be able to find anybody. So right there I figured, this is the place for me. There wouldn't be that much competition." He was right.

Another situational condition favorable to success is the strategic position. Organizations employing different technologies and existing in different environments find certain functions and career lines more problematic to their success than others. Marketing, finance, or perhaps manufacturing will be thought to be most crucial to the success of the organization. People who match their career lines to these beliefs are less likely to enter a career cul-de-sac somewhere along the line. Conversely, functions such as personnel generally are *not* seen as problematic. So even though it may be difficult to resist that fast promotion from, say, marketing into personnel, the long-term consequences may be detrimental in a marketing-oriented organization.

Finally, be aware that situationally favored specialties may change with time. For example, with the advent of advanced electronic and systems technologies in the 1950s, the fast track in the IBM Company shifted toward people with "systems" experience. People with career lines in older specialties were generally perceived as not having the proper background to cope with what commonly were understood to be the problems of the future (30).

Personal Factors

Ability and personality are obviously important personal factors in success. Yet the complexity of the career situation, involving as it does judgments by different superiors in different environments, may be equally important (10). For example, we should not neglect the importance of having an organizational sponsor. It is common in organizations for the career of a junior person to become enmeshed with that of a senior manager (27). The tacit agreement seems to be: "You take care of my interests lower down in the organization and I'll take care of your career." The bargain involves loyalty, commitment, and compliance in return for advancement. It may seem rather ordinary, but it works and is probably the most common mechanism for upward mobility.[5]

People in large organizations do not get to know many others very well, except by reputation. Furthermore, since mobility opportunities occur most often through diagonal moves, potential subordinates may be completely unknown. For these reasons managers like to bring with them subordinates who are known and trusted for both their competence and loyalty.

Finally, an understanding of the complexity of the organization seems to be indispensable to success. One interesting study showed that managers' perceptions of their organizations, recorded in an earlier period, predicted their success five years later (17). The managers who achieved the greatest success over this period were those who saw the complexity of the organization and accepted it. The least successful, those managers who were demoted during that period, were naive about the nature of the organization. They neither understood the complexity of the situations with which they were dealing nor perceived the nature of their position in the organization. Thus, the ability to manage the work of subordinates, although necessary to success, is insufficient. In complex organizations the ability to build relationships with peers and with superiors in other functions seems crucial.

To conclude, we can identify certain organizational, situational, and personal factors that promote success. But success is relative, so for some, sooner or later, the subjective experience will fall short of success. And for a few this experience will be unambiguous: they will have to adjust to failure. (For a similar conclusion see Box 14).

Box 14   **Motivation Chickens or Advancement Eggs?**

For the past quarter century the Bell System has conducted an ongoing research project with a group of managers first identified in the late 1950s. As reported by Douglas Bray and Ann Howard, both of the Bell System, two aspects of this research are particularly striking, both for the findings and for the uniqueness of the data.

Surveys conducted over a period of time on the same group of individuals—often called panel studies—provide developmental insights that cannot be obtained from studies conducted at a single time—cross-sectional studies. For example, if we measured "leadership drive" in a cross-sectional sample of managers and found that the higher-level managers had higher leadership drive, we still would be unable to answer the proverbial chicken-and-egg question: did drive lead to promotion, or promotion to drive?

A clearer, but more complex picture, drawn from the Bell management progress study (MPS), is given in Figure 11.2. The data are drawn from personal interviews of the MPS participants coded by a clinical psychologist for the relative importance of nine "life themes." The occupational involvement theme is shown here, charted over a nineteen-year period, and broken down by the final level of management that had been attained by that *final year*. So, for example, the occupational involvement at the start of the study—year zero—is shown as it corresponds to the managerial level attained nineteen years later.

The picture is interesting indeed. At the outset all the entering first-level MPS managers had nearly an identical level of involvement. Yet almost immediately some began to "turn on and move up," whereas others equally quickly began the process of disengagement. Notice that some of the group were never again promoted, remaining at level 1, whereas others had moved as high as level 6 and are likely to continue to move.

How are we to interpret these data? It does seem likely that involvement and motivation lead to advancement at the very early stages. But over time the process becomes more complex. It does seem reasonable to infer that early promotion feeds involvement, which in turn makes further promotion more likely. Yet also evident from the data is a process beginning with the tenth year where managers at levels 1–3 apparently have gotten the message that further advancement is not likely. Notice the downturn in involvement past this point. At this point the process appears to be just the opposite of that in the earliest stage: lack of advancement produces lack of involvement.

This study does not tell us why some turned on early and why others did not. But there is striking evidence of major structural differences in early work assignments, in suitable role models, in challenging assignments, and in the availability of unstructured tasks.

From D. W. Bray and A. Howard. "The AT&T Longitudinal Studies of Managers." In *Longitudinal Studies of Adult Psychological Development,* edited by K. W. Schaie. New York: Guilford Press, 1983.

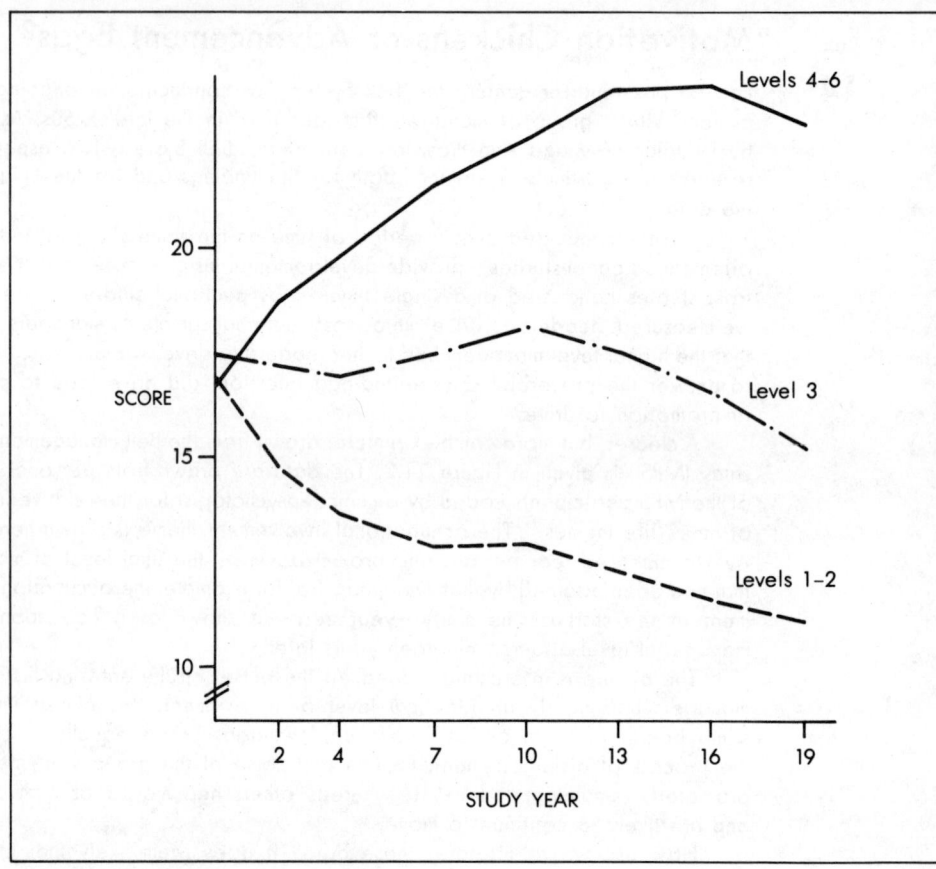

FIGURE 11.2 Importance of Occupational Life Theme by Study Year Shown for Management Level as of Nineteenth Year of Study
Adapted from Bray and Howard, 1983 (7), with permission of Guilford Press.

Misfits and Malcontents[6]

Stanley gazed out the window only half listening as Sherman March paced the length of his office, engaged in a monologue of pessimism. The view to the north overlooking the lake was considerably more interesting than March's incessant complaining.

"What it boils down to is a blatant overemphasis on status and power to the utter neglect of technical issues," March went on. "We've been held up four months on this project because top management can't decide how to merge two project groups into one. Now any damn fool can see that one group of managers will no longer be in charge. So one group won't be managers any longer. That's why I say status and power is the issue. Right now it's like waiting for the gods on high to decide and then throw something down to us."

Stanley had been requested by Ted to visit the Portland product development laboratory as a "personal representative" of corporate personnel. March, a second-level engineering manager, had asked for an interview with someone from corporate personnel in order to explain a problem he felt was "eating away at The Company." So the corporate staff had obliged, suspecting that they were dealing with a "problem person" and hoping to pour some oil on troubled waters.

The trouble, it seemed, was that March had sensed that *he* was destined to be one of the group who would soon no longer be managers. Therefore, at an appropriate pause in the monologue Stanley decided to ask the natural question: Why, under these circumstances, would such a change be such a problem? Would there be a big cut in salary?

"Oh no, quite likely not," replied March, "but that's not the point! It's a loss of face—they take your manager's book away. And I don't mean that to be funny. You don't get any information anymore. You're not able to go to those management classes. You don't get the hot scoop and you're not allowed to go to these new organization meetings." March went on to list a lot of things in which management people participate, but staff engineers do not. He went on, "Another thing, they'll move me out of this office. Even though they don't have to. They'll move me over there somewhere (pointing to the interior of the building). And it'll be smaller and it won't have any rug. They don't *have* to do that, you know. There's plenty of space for everyone. That's what I mean by a status issue.

"If you treated a manager as only an administrator, why then there would be much less interest in being a manager. So then if they changed you from manager to staff engineer there wouldn't be that much of a problem. Then you're not joining a class of malcontents and misfits. You can see that there's a lot of good people there. You see that they also have a lot of money and sports cars."

"Er, malcontents? I'm not sure I get your meaning, Sherm." Stanley was puzzled.

"Well, that's exactly what I mean. The feeling around here is that the poor residue of staff engineers [senior technical professionals] either didn't have what it takes to make manager or they simply were not interested. But look, every staff engineer I ever had working for me wanted to become a manager. Look at the performance appraisals. There it is—manager, manager, manager—they *all* want to be managers."

"But I guess I still really don't see why," Stanley said.

"I guess I'm not sure either. I think The Company wants our engineers to do this: they want them to take responsibility. But people have a natural desire for *power*. And how could things be otherwise given the way we treat them? Most of the knowledge of what The Company is doing is just not available to the staff engineer, but it *is* to the manager. And the staff engineers, why, we've spit on them in every way. We use a bunch of unnecessary titles for managers and this makes our staff people seem even less.

"And when our new products people from marketing come in—my God, they're the ultimate. They won't even talk to you unless you have a title. *That's* why it's important. That's why I say it's status and power. Listen, you don't go into a carpeted office and say to the guy sitting there, 'Look you jerk, it's not that way; it's this way.' "

Suddenly March stopped, staring out the window for a minute or so at nothing in particular. Then, in a different tone he said, "You know, Stan, it's the end of the line once you slip. It's in your personnel file that you were a manager once and now you're nothing. Doesn't even matter how it happened. They'll forget why soon enough, and something like that always looks suspicious in your file. So, well, you're through."

March looked so completely deflated now that Stanley felt sorry for him. The interview was over soon after that, and Stanley promised to carry the word to corporate—and not as a personal matter but as a general issue for The Company to examine.

But what was the issue? Stanley was still puzzled. Nothing much had happened to March, had it? He hadn't lost any money and that was the important thing, wasn't it? Yet March had seemed so hopeless there at the end, as though life itself were about to end. What struck Stanley as particularly strange was that most engineering managers didn't particularly seem to enjoy managing. They complained about "administrivia," and were always recalling the good old days when they were "bench" engineers. One manager, while complaining about his burden of paper work had ruefully observed, "It's like a dog and his fleas. Thinking about his fleas keeps him from thinking about being a dog." No, it didn't make any sense.

March's experience, though in some ways like Claude's, is different in important particulars. Claude was moved from his first-level managerial position at one of The Company locations back to a staff position at corporate headquarters. He was moved geographically and organizationally. Claude is unhappy about this, but no one in The Company feels that Claude has been demoted. The interpretation of horizontal moves is always difficult. Not for Sherman March, however. His feelings about his future were right. He is in the same organization, in the same building, and even in the same project (one combined from its two predecessors). But there is little ambiguity in what happened to him. As he put it, he was "un-managed"—demoted.

We can expect Claude to adapt to his situation and move ahead once more with his usual motivation, wiser and perhaps more wary. But what of March? Can we expect the same about him? We do not really know. What March will do seems to depend on whether or not he can find another *valued role* and *status* to replace the one that he lost. Our "success breeds success" principle does not seem to operate in reverse; that is, failure does not necessarily breed further failure—though it may (21:127). March may become bitter about his demotion and spend his time trying to justify his own position by continually pointing up the errors of management. That course would likely lead to further failure. However, he may become comfortable in a different role, one emphasizing new positive aspects of his current position. But then this depends partly on the individual personality involved, doesn't it?

In fact, it does—to some extent. But equally important is the management of the situation by The Company.

Failure: Consequences and Adaptations

Although organizations would like to provide success experiences for everyone, under the principles of adaptation level and equity this is not possible. In fact, some failure is actually essential. Failure helps to define success by establishing its opposite; the presence of failure justifies the efforts of the successful. If there are no visible consequences of incompetent or indifferent performance, then questions of equity will be raised and people will question the necessity of their own efforts. There may be serious consequences for the maintenance of both authority relationships and high levels of motivation. It seems likely that both managers and professionals occasionally like to see "dead wood" pruned back (16). What is defined within the social system of the organization as "not good enough" sets the level of aspiration.

On the other hand, though organizations want compliance to authority, they also want subordinates to exercise discretion. Where there is excessive fear of failure there is excessive bureaucratic rigidity as well—bureaupathology. If the consequences of failure are too severe, subordinates will not act on their own judgment but will choose unnecessarily conservative alternatives. The question, then, is not how to *prevent* failure, but how to *manage* its motivational consequences.

Motivational Consequences of Failure

Keep in mind that in this section we are talking about clear-cut failure, about demotion. Demotion serves two distinct organizational functions: *selection* and *punishment*. Selection weeds out incompetent individuals. Its primary purpose is to improve the quality of management, though as noted, there are also motivational consequences. The punishment function, the meting out of harsh treatment, is intended primarily to serve people who might otherwise be tempted to behave similarly. Punishment is given for willful noncompliance or for serious errors of omission or sloth. A demotion serves notice to others that management will not tolerate this kind of behavior.

In other instances management may wish to disguise the demotion, or ease its effect as much as possible—for example, where a well-liked manager has served faithfully and well for many years but now is no longer up to the job. If these people are treated harshly, that lesson will not be lost on organizational observers. So once again, the extent of failure, or whether it even is failure, is left to be defined within the social system of the organization.

The motivational consequences of punishment (demotion) are not simply the opposite of the consequences of positive reinforcement (promotion). For this reason demotion, or the *threat* of demotion, produces different motivations from those caused by the expectation of success. Consequently, if failure is unavoidable in organizations, then how the experience is managed becomes quite important, as does whether it is defined within the social system as punishment or, more neutrally, as "replacement by superior talent."

Finally, little research evidence is available to support our analysis of the effect of failure on managerial motivations. Thus, our purpose in this section is not to spell out the sure consequences, but rather to establish a way of thinking about the consequences of different modes of failure within the social system of the organization. Given a more or less fixed rate of advancement, what might we expect to be the consequences of different rates of failure? The answer to this question again depends on a number of organizational, situational, and individual factors.

ORGANIZATIONAL FACTORS. Our discussion centers on two major organizational aspects: the *rate* of failure and the *severity* of the consequences. Although the rate of failure is linked to the rate of success, the two need not be identical. For example, there will be organizations where little movement of any kind, up *or* down, takes place. In other organizations there may be a great deal of both. Therefore, we are talking about factors that characterize the policy or condition of the entire organization. *Rate,* then, refers to how often or how *likely* it is that someone will be demoted. By *severity* of consequences we mean primarily how likely it is that upward movement can be resumed, although other factors, such as the size of the salary cut, are involved.

We examine severity first. To the extent that there is an organizational norm for how demotion will be handled, you can be sure that it will be known within the social system. When the consequences are typically severe—termination, for example, or permanent removal from further consideration for management—the motivational consequences may also be severe. Recall Kerry's experience in "Who Could Have Known?" (Chapter 9). The threat of severe punishment resulted in complete disruption of upward communication. People suffering severe consequences, having lost hope for advancement, will also have lost the incentive provided by hope for future advancement.

To understand better the effect of severity of consequences we need to know the rate of failure. Where a high rate of failure is the organizational norm, we can expect some lowering of the adaptation level for success. Furthermore, since failure is not uncommon, some of the stigma will be removed from it (16). Our analysis also suggests that the rate of failure will have the following effects depending on the severity of the consequences:

1. Where the rate of failure is low but the consequences severe, we are likely to find the organizational situation described as bureaupathology, the unwillingness to exercise discretion (16, 36, 37). In such organizations the old saying, "If you don't do anything you can't do anything wrong," holds true.
2. Where rates of failure are low but the consequences *not* severe, we might find general indifference and apathy. This is the kind of organization Penny was describing in the vignette in Chapter 10.
3. Where both rate and severity are high, it is difficult to guess the consequences. Since this situation seems to characterize certain elite organizations, we speculate that the rewards for success, both remunerative and normative, must be great enough to maintain participants' willingness to remain.
4. The situation in which the rate of failure is relatively high, but the consequences generally are not severe has been suggested as producing highest overall levels of motivation (16:717). Demotion is frequent enough to be not excessively stigmatizing, and hope remains for renewed upward

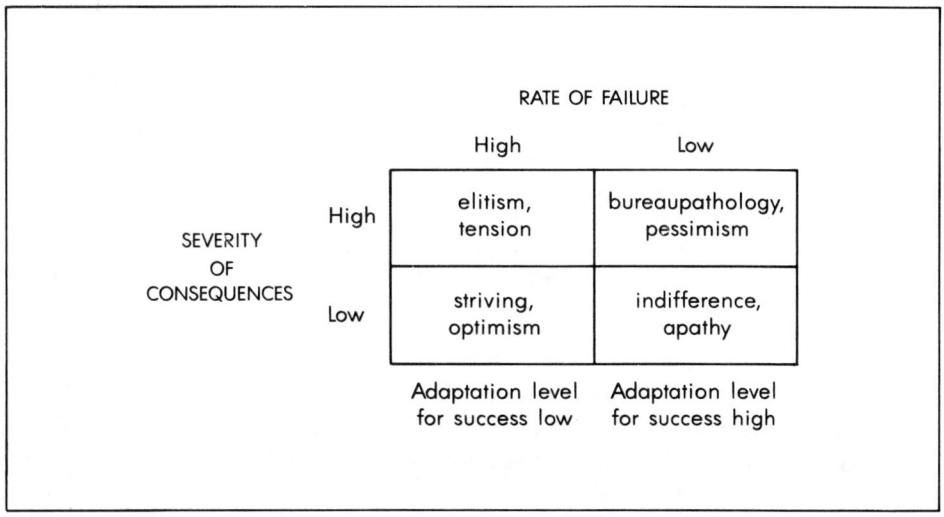

FIGURE 11.3 Possible consequences for Motivation System of Rate of Failure and Severity of Consequences

mobility. Furthermore, by lowering the adaptation level for success, that experience is made more meaningful.[7]

Figure 11.3 summarizes these possible consequences.

Again, what we are suggesting is a way of thinking about the organizational consequences of failure that goes beyond looking at demotion as simply a way of removing incompetent managers. We are not suggesting hard and fast rules for organizational policy.

SITUATIONAL FACTORS. A key factor in lessening the negative consequences of a demotion is the ambiguity of the situation. If the situation in which the demotion occurs is clear-cut, the consequences may be far different from the situation in which the intent and reasons for the move are neither clearly stated nor easily interpreted. The following Company announcement is an example of this latter situation. What do you think is going on?

NEW CORPORATE STAFF, EXECUTIVE APPOINTMENTS ANNOUNCED

Company chairman, M. M. Marsh, today announced the creation of a new Corporate staff: technical personnel development.

The new group will promote the technical vitality of The Company's professional, engineering, technological, and scientific communities throughout the world and will work to enhance the exchange of technical information among The Company's laboratories and its business units . . . .

Company Vice President C. Marsh Bell has been appointed vice president, technical personnel development, to head the new staff.

Succeeding Mr. Bell as vice president, engineering, systems and technology, is Company Vice President Marshall B. Mason. . . .

Commenting on the new corporate staff, Mr. Marsh said, "Company leadership in our fast-moving industry is heavily dependent upon our ability to help our technical people maintain professional vitality and ensure open communications among our engineers, scientists, and businesspeople. I think this is an important milestone along that road."

Here are some clues for interpreting the announcement: Read carefully for words like *promoted, appointed, creation.* Ask yourself what you know about the relative status of functions such as manufacturing, engineering, personnel, and so on. Look at the jobs involved and ask yourself how important they are to maintaining a sound profits picture. As a final question, what has happened to C. Marsh Bell? Bell, you should know, has served long and faithfully in The Company.

PERSONAL FACTORS. Where there is no stigma attached to demotion, the motivational consequences may be slight. One example of this is the professional athlete who has grown too old to compete (16). The professional athlete may lose his or her preeminent position before retiring without loss of honor. The athlete may be used in spot appearances or otherwise held in reserve in case of injury to a regular player. Similar situations occur in other kinds of organizations. For example, a manager who has had a severe illness or a heart attack can generally be demoted to lesser responsibilities with no stigma. And someone who has served faithfully and well for many years may at some point become unable to cope with the changing nature of the business (C. Marsh Bell?). For such individuals, like the overage athlete, no stigma is attached to demotion. The situation will be managed carefully by the organization.

Situations where no stigma is attached are relatively rare compared to the numbers of people actually demoted. Therefore, to maintain motivation, organizations look for ways to help individuals adapt to failure.

Individual And Organizational Adaptations to Failure

Erving Goffman, in his analysis of the consequences of failure, suggested that we use an analogy to the "cooling-out" of the "mark" in a confidence game (11). The aim of the con game is to set up the mark so that he or she willingly turns over a sizable sum of money to one of the players, in the hope of receiving a much larger sum in return. The mark's understanding is that the money will be used to finance an illicit scheme which, however, is a sure thing. Unfortunately the scheme is being perpetrated on the mark. Since the success of the con game often depends on the mark's being unwilling to go to the police to report the loss, one of the players stays with the mark after the "sting"—the point at which the loss is realized—to "cool out" the mark, to provide sufficient reason to accept the loss stoically.

How is this done? Often the loss of the money is less important than the humiliation, the loss of self-image. As Goffman put it:

> A mark's participation in a play, and his investment in it, clearly commit him in his own eyes to the proposition that he is a smart man. . . . When the blow-off comes, the mark finds that he has no defense for not being a shrewd man, [therefore] it is no wonder that the mark needs to be cooled out and that it is good business policy for one of the operators to stay with the mark in order to talk him into a point of view from which it is possible to accept a loss. (15:452)

Thus, the objective of the "cooler" is to restore enough of the mark's self-image to allow him or her to accept what has happened without open protest—to provide reasons and a new definition of the social situation that allow the mark once again to sustain a positive self-concept.

Applied to the process of demotion in organizations, the cool-out has a similar function. If the organization provides no ego-rebuilding mechanisms, the demoted manager may deny the validity of what is taking place. Aside from the consequences for task motivation and compliance, then, we might expect the development of antimanagement attitudes and of an "individualistic orientation"—that is, of managers who have been demoted from higher levels developing possessive attitudes toward their new departments, coming to regard them as their own private territories (27:109). Whether the demotion was right or wrong, the demoted manager will seek ways to rebuild his self-image. Hence, the desirability of the managed cool-out.

Goffman suggests the following as typical cool-out procedures (15:457):[8]

- Offering the demoted manager *a different status,* a new role providing an opportunity for something to become. Some typical ways of doing this would be (1) offering a position of similar rank but in a different hierarchy with a less important function (example: transferring a manufacturing executive to become corporate director of safety programs); (2) offering a position of unique merit and prestige but no power (example: The Company has a "distinguished scientist" program reserved for individual contributors with records of outstanding achievement. These positions carry a high salary and many Company perquisites. There are perhaps a dozen of these honorific positions in The Company, but more than one is occupied by a technical executive who has outlived his usefulness); (3) being kicked upstairs, usually to a corporate staff position, possibly to a "newly created" function—sound familiar? (examples: The Company

retires an obsolete plant manager within the community by establishing the corporate position "resident vice president"; a vice president of engineering and technology becomes the new vice president and chief Company scientist).
- Allowing the demoted manager to keep the *same role* but to carry it out in a "safer," possibly geographically more attractive context. Examples: a district sales manager may be moved from a competitive territory to a "safe" one, perhaps in a climate where year-round golf is possible; a plant manager is moved to a less important location, perhaps one making a routinized product out of the mainstream of Company business.
- Allowing the demoted manager to *blow-up*, let off steam, give vent to attitudes, values, and motives that, in other circumstances, would be unacceptable. Others understand that this is a ritual cool-out, and, consequently, will be freed from norms that otherwise would require them to censure such behavior. The weakness of the blow-up as a method of cooling the mark out is that it fails to provide an alternative valued role.
- Offering *bribery*, that is, allowing the demoted manager to pretend it is he or she who has taken the initiative in the change of position. This form of cool-out requires the cooperation of the audience to maintain the plausibility of the drama. When the demoted manager announces to all, "I decided that ten years of this kind of administrative responsibility was more than enough for anyone, so I've asked the president to let me return to . . . ," the faithful of the organization are required ritually to admire the person's judgment, courage, and dedication to the professional aspects of his work.

The cool-out may also be applied to entire categories of employees, and in particular those who have lost out early in the "mobility tournament." From the viewpoint of this chapter, this lack of opportunity for advancement presents a potentially serious motivational problem in organizations whose entire work force is primarily made up of college-educated professionals, few of whom actually can be placed in management positions. High-technology organizations, service organizations such as hospitals, and technical sales organizations are examples. The cooling out process in these organizations is managed with a career counseling program where the attempt is made to persuade professional employees to accept alternative definitions of success. The rewards of careers other than those in management, and the "fit" of these to the employees' abilities are presented in a stepwise counseling process.[9]

1. *Provide opportunities for alternative success.* Substitute opportunities can be made to appear not very different from what has been denied. People accepting the alternative status are invited to interpret the new status as more in keeping with their particular abilities.
2. *Gradual disengagement.* Likely candidates are urged to see the alternative

status as more fitting. Self-assessment is encouraged and evidence of performance is produced to suggest that the alternative status is more appropriate.
3. *Objective denial.* This reorientation is aided by confrontation with the facts. Appraisals and other "objective" data provide the professional with accumulating evidence that he or she, rather than the organization, is responsible. Such procedures help to detach the organization and its managers from the emotional aspects of the cooling out work.
4. *Agents of consolation.* Career counselors are available to explain patiently to unaccepting professionals the necessity of changing their intentions. "They believe in the value of alternative careers . . . and are practiced in consoling" (9: 575).
5. *Avoidance of standards.* The organizational cooling out process avoids reference to standards that allow only one set of criteria for success. They employ rather a soft-sell treatment, assuming that many kinds of ability are valuable, with each in its place. Proper *placement* is paramount and standards are relative.

Finally, to be effective, the cooling out role of the organization must not be perceived clearly or understood by these professionals. Otherwise, the value of the procedures would be impaired.

Summary

What is the function of management? Although there are other answers, we have presented a view of management as a *structure of opportunity*. We consider this to be a major, if not *the* major motivational force for professional employees.

With this in mind we ask, how does the structure of opportunity and the process of movement through the ranks of the organization affect the motivation system? Our answer invokes two major theoretical ideas: *adaptation level* and *equity*. Adaptation level, we explained, is the pooling of past experience and social comparisons that establishes the reference point for judging new experience. Adaptation level also helps set the level of aspiration for future outcomes that will be judged satisfactory. The higher the adaptation level, the higher the level of aspiration. The idea of *equity*, on the other hand, concerns how people judge outcomes to themselves as being fair or unfair. Equity is judged by comparing your own experience to that of others in the organization.

The motivational consequences of upward movement through the organization derive from comparisons to adaptation level and from feelings of equitable treatment. To illustrate, let us reconstruct some of the early stages of Stanley's career in The Company and examine the motivational consequences of his perceptions of the structure of opportunity.

From the very first Stanley was looking "to get ahead." He was not sure quite why this was, but he knew it was expected of him by himself and by his friends and family. The idea of "being a success" was a key part of his own developing understanding of who he was. His level of aspiration was quite high, perhaps unrealistically so since he knew almost nothing of what real organizations were like.

When the time arrived for him to take his first job, he was actively recruited by a number of large corporations. His choice of The Company was based largely on the structure of opportunity he saw; the technology and the environment of The Company seemed to offer a potentially interesting and dynamic experience. Recall from our earlier chapters that Stanley picked a position in plant operations because he was told that The Company's management came from there. Of course, he did not understand it fully at the time, but he was choosing a line function as opposed to a staff function in engineering.

Next came a period of intense socialization. Stanley probably learned more about the structure of opportunity in those first six months than in any subsequent time. Specifically he learned (1) that the people just above him had been in their jobs much longer than he had thought they would be, and (2) that the work he was asked to do seemed ridiculously simple. He feared that he was forgetting more than he was learning, and there was no foreseeable change in the situation. In fact, he was learning a great deal about some very important things in organizations, although he did not see it that way.

At this point he became highly dissatisfied. His anticipated progress was far below his level of aspiration. One result of this was that he spent considerable time looking about him and talking to other people in different functions. He got to know them and they got to know him. The impression he conveyed was that of a restless young man eager to move ahead.

Partly because of this and partly by chance Stanley was soon given the opportunity for his first *lateral move.* He was transferred to Kerry's group in New York (we introduce the details of this episode in Chapter 13). Stanley now went through a second period of intensive socialization. Kerry stressed to all that (1) this group was select and therefore they had greater responsibility than others in The Company might, and (2) since they had this greater responsibility they ought to work harder. Kerry held forth the expectation of promotion into "a responsible management position." Let us look at the motivational consequences of this move for Stanley.

First, this was Stanley's key break from the pack. People in his peer group who had entered The Company with him at Pawtucket were still all there. Stanley had been the first to move, and to New York at that. Second, there was greatly increased responsibility in this new job. Kerry had made that clear to them, and the group around Kerry reinforced this feeling. Finally, there was that explicit promise of promotion as well as the implicit suggestion that great things lay in store for those who could "cut it."

One motivating result of this situation was that Stanley was well ahead of his adaptation level for progress. He had exceeded his adaptation level on each of the three mechanisms: by comparison with his past experience, by averaging across different job factors, and by social comparisons with his reference group. An immediate consequence was a rapid rise in his aspiration level. Stanley was probably never more highly motivated than during his stay with Kerry.

A second motivating factor was based on our notion of equity. Stanley felt his progress was *more than equitable.* Given the skills, training, and background he brought to the job, plus his work experience to date, he felt that he was actually doing better than he should be. So again the disparity was motivating: increased effort would restore the balance of equity.

What happened to Stanley in his career with The Company from this point on is more complicated. But that is another story.

Notes

1. Work by Hall (21, 22) indicates that Claude's predicament is not as unusual as it might appear at first.
2. Barnard (3, 4) describes the status system of management and concludes that, "Men are eager to be 'bossed' by superior ability. . . . So strong is this need of assigning superior status that . . . men will impute abilities they cannot recognize or judge [leading] often to profuse rationalization about status and *even to mythological and mystical explanations of it . . .* " (4:59); (italics added).
3. Recall Kerry Drake's experience in "Who Could Have Known?" in Chapter 9.
4. This principle and the discussion of those that follow are adapted from Brickman and Campbell (8).
5. The lack of such sponsors for women and minorities is one factor in their difficulty in achieving executive positions (25).
6. This vignette is taken directly from an actual interview. Martin and Strauss also note that merging departments is a common mechanism for downgrading managers (27:108).
7. Grusky's data suggest that rapid managerial succession may reduce organizational effectiveness (20). But individual motivation and organizational effectiveness are different matters, as we will see in Chapter 17. Furthermore, Grusky's athletic teams are small organizations with the turnover occurring at the top.
8. Brickman and Campbell discuss the cool-out and suggest that such procedures fit well within the adaptation-level framework (8:294).
9. This description is adapted from Clark (9).

References

1. ADAMS, J. S. "Inequity in Social Exchange." In *Advances in Experimental Social Psychology,* Vol. 2, edited by L. Berkowitz. New York: Academic Press, 1965.

2. ANDERSON, J. C., G. MILKOVICH, and A. TSUI. "A Model of Intra-Organizational Mobility." *The Academy of Management Review* 6 (October 1981): 529–538.
3. BARNARD, C. *The Functions of the Executive.* Cambridge, Mass.: Harvard University Press, 1938.
4. ———. "Functions and Pathology of Status Systems in Formal Organizations." In *Industry and Society,* edited by W. F. Whyte. New York: McGraw-Hill, 1946.
5. BECKER, G. *Human Capital.* New York: Columbia University Press, 1964.
6. BERG, I. "Rich Man's Qualifications for Poor Man's Jobs." *Trans-Action* 6 (March 1969): 45–50.
7. BRAY, D., and A. HOWARD. "The AT & T Longitudinal Studies of Managers." In *Longitudinal Studies of Adult Psychological Development,* edited by K. W. Schaie. N.Y.: Guilford Press, 1983.
8. BRICKMAN, P., and D. CAMPBELL. "Hedonic Relativism and Planning the Good Society." In *Adaptation-Level Theory,* edited by M. H. Appley. New York: Academic Press, 1971. Pp. 287–302.
9. CLARK, B. R. "The 'Cooling-out' Function in Higher Education." *American Journal of Sociology* 65 (1960): 569–576.
10. DILL, W., T. HILTON, and W. REITMAN. *The New Managers.* Englewood Cliffs, N.J.: Prentice-Hall, 1962.
11. FERENCE, T., J. STONER, AND E. WARREN. "Managing the Career Plateau." *Academy of Management Review* 2 (1977): 602–612.
12. *Fortune,* Letters to. " 'Fast Track' M.B.A.'s." *Fortune* 96 (1977): 68.
13. FRIEDMAN, T. "The Baby Boom Comes of Age." *New York Times,* Section 12, January 10, 1982, p. 18.
14. GALBRAITH, J. *The New Industrial State.* Boston: Houghton, Mifflin, 1967.
15. GOFFMAN, E. "On Cooling the Mark Out: Some Aspects of Adaptation to Failure." *Psychiatry* 15 (1952): 451–463.
16. GOLDNER, F. "Demotion in Industrial Management." *American Sociological Review* 30 (1965): 714–724.
17. ———. "Success vs. Failure: Prior Managerial Perspectives." *Industrial Relations* 9 (1970): 453–474.
18. GOLDNER, F., R. RITTI, and T. FERENCE. "The Production of Cynical Knowledge in Organizations." *American Sociological Review* 42 (1977): 539–551.
19. GRUSKY, O. "Career Mobility and Organizational Commitment." *Administrative Science Quarterly* 10 (1966): 488–503.
20. ———. "Managerial Succession and Organizational Effectiveness." *American Journal of Sociology* 69 (1963): 21–30.
21. HALL, D. *Careers in Organizations.* Pacific Palisades, Calif.: Goodyear, 1976.
22. ———. "Potential for Career Growth." *Personnel Administration* 34 (1971): 18–30.
23. HALL, D., and E. LAWLOR, III. "Unused Potential in Research and Development Organizations." *Research Management* 12 (1969): 339–354.
24. HOWARD, A., and J. A. WILSON. "Leadership in a Declining Work Ethic." *California Management Review* 24 (Summer 1982): 33–46.

25. KANTER, R. *Men and Women of the Corporation.* New York: Basic Books, 1977.
26. LAMB, R. "A New Crop of M.B.A.'s Goes Looking for that 'Fast Track.'" *Fortune* 95 (1977): 160–170.
27. MARTIN, N., and A. STRAUSS. "Patterns of Mobility within Industrial Organizations." *Journal of Business* 29 (1956): 101–110.
28. MERTON, R., and A. KITT. "Contributions to the Theory of Reference Group Behavior." In *Continuities in Social Research: Studies in the Scope and Method of "The American Soldier,"* edited by R. K. Merton and P. F. Lazarfeld. Glencoe, Ill.: Free Press, 1950.
29. RITTI, R. *The Engineer in the Industrial Corporation.* New York: Columbia University Press, 1971.
30. ———. "Engineers and Managers: A Study of Engineering Organization." Ph.D. dissertation, Cornell University, 1960.
31. ———. "The Underemployment of Engineers." *Industrial Relations* 9 (1970): 437–452.
32. RITTI, R., T. FERENCE, and F. GOLDNER. "Professions and Their Plausibility: Priests, Work and Belief Systems." *Sociology of Work and Occupations* 1 (1974): 24–51.
33. ROSENBAUM, J. E. "Tournament Mobility: Career Patterns in a Corporation." *Administrative Science Quarterly* 24 (June 1979): 220–241.
34. SCHEIN, E. "The Individual, the Organization, and the Career: A Conceptual Scheme." *Journal of Applied Behavioral Science* 7 (1971): 401–426.
35. STOUFFER, S., E. SUCHMAN, L. DEVINNEY, S. STAR, and R. WILLIAMS. *The American Soldier: Adjustment During Army Life,* Vol. 1. Princeton, N.J.: Princeton University Press, 1949.
36. THOMPSON, J. *Organizations in Action.* New York: McGraw-Hill, 1967.
37. THOMPSON, V. *Modern Organization.* New York: Knopf, 1961.
38. VARDI, Y. "Organizational Career Mobility: An Integrative Model." *The Academy of Management Review* 5 (July 1980): 341–356.
39. VEIGA, J. "Mobility Influences During Managerial Career Stages." *Academy of Management Journal* 26 (March 1983): 64–85.
40. ———. "Plateaued Versus Nonplateaued Managers: Career Patterns, Attitudes, and Path Potential." *Academy of Management Journal* 24 (September 1981): 566–578.
41. *Wall Street Journal.* "Firms Fight an Effect of 1950's Baby Boom: Young Executive Glut." *Wall Street Journal,* August 18, 1975, p. 1.

Discussion Questions

1. Our opening case describes a program of rapid advancement for high potential managerial candidates. Describe the motivational consequences for Claude when, after the program, he was moved to a corporate staff position. Consider the effects of such a program in which young managers are identified and promoted early within (a) organizations having a rapid growth rate, (b) those stable in size, and (c) those which are retrenching. What will be the motivational consequences in each case on the entire group of professionals in each organization? Why?

2. In Chapter 7 we set forth a framework for understanding the factors in person perception. Using this framework, what do you think might be the effects of a program of early identification of high potential on the future success of candidates?
3. Recall our discussion of the hierarchical structure of The Company and the Catholic Church. Think also of the structure of a large state department of public welfare. Does the concept of "structure of opportunity" apply equally well to each of these organizations? Why? How would each differ in this regard? How about the structure of opportunity in your university or college? In each kind of organization how does the structure of opportunity relate to the idea of maintaining motivation?
4. What are your own aspirations for success? Do you intend to pursue a career in management? How far do you think you will advance? Try to picture your position at ages thirty, forty, and fifty. What will it take at each point for you to feel you are successful? Compare these aspirations with those of some of your friends.
5. State the three bases for comparison in setting adaptation levels for success. In your answer to the previous question, which of these did you use to establish your success goals? What else are you taking into consideration?
6. Do you feel there are any potential "stars" or "rockets" among your classmates? What seem to be the essential differences between these people and others? How much impression management is involved? When you consider your own future career, how do you think your own success will compare with theirs?
7. Do you know anyone in an organization who might be called a failure? Why? Why not? Do you know how this person reacted to the situation of failure? In terms of our discussion, why do you think open knowledge of failure is relatively rare?
8. Consider the positions of (a) head coach of a professional football team and (b) director of personnel for a public utility. Each is terminated from his or her position. For which of the two will the personal effect be greatest? Why? What organizational mechanisms for the management of failure might be used in each case?
9. Using the story in our case "Misfits and Malcontents," set down some of the cool-out procedures that might have been used on Sherman March. Were any of these used? Can you speculate why or why not? What likely symbolic evidences of failure will accompany March's demotion?

Chapter 12
Maintaining Motivation: The Consequences of Blocked Opportunity

Mac's Shop

"So here's where you will want to come when you're trying to get a story out on plant automation or some such, right, Penny?" Actually, Ted was speaking to Lesley, not Penny, for he was escorting Lesley on a tour through the halls and byways of The Company's corporate headquarters.

Lesley? Oh, yes, she was the new systems analyst in the office of the Corporate Director for manufacturing. Fresh from Portsmouth, she was new to the corporate picture, and so Ted, in his role as Assistant to the Vice President of Human Resources, was showing her around. Right now they were visiting Corporate Communications.

"I'll bet this is all pretty confusing right now, isn't it, Lesley?" said Penny. "I remember my own first couple of days. But don't worry. The main thing is that you just get the big picture right now. You'll never keep all of us straight, but we'll remember you." Penny was trying to be helpful.

"I certainly hope so," was the hopeful reply, "but, as you say, I'm getting a pretty good idea of the big picture. Really, I had absolutely no idea of just how many interesting things are going on in human resources."

"Yes, it's true, isn't it?" Ted's tone carried conviction. "The fact is, even I'm amazed by how we've moved ahead in this field. Why, it wasn't all that long ago that all we did here was some of the traditional personnel activities. And, of course, there was Mac's Shop then, too."

"Mac's shop?" queried Lesley.

"Yes, Jack MacPherson. I guess we haven't been down to that end of the hall, have we? It just slipped my mind." Then, as an afterthought, "Oh, well, I guess Mac's kind of easy to forget. I don't know that you'll be interacting much with those folks, Lesley, but anyway, let's go have a look at Psychological Services."

As they moved off down the hall, Ted described the psychological services "folks," with gestures appropriate to his language. "Mac's one of our old timers in Human Resources, you know. I think he goes back all the way to Mr. Marsh, Sr.'s time," Ted explained. "He used to handle pretty much all the psychological testing, placement, and counseling programs in The Company but, well, I don't know, it seems as if the times have passed him by."

"I don't think I understand, Mr. Shelby. I mean, passed him by how?" queried Les.

"You'd have to know something about the human resources field to really understand, I suppose. But you see, behavioral technology has undergone a simply explosive development of new knowledge in the past ten years," Ted illustrated with a wave of his hands. "We've had new ideas about human resources management, organization development, job enrichment, assessment centers. These are all exciting, new, science-based techniques."

Ted was waxing lyrical at the very thought of it all and almost forgot the topic at hand. But Lesley's curious look brought him back to earth. "Oh, yes, Mac," Ted continued. "But you see, Mac didn't really grow with us." Then, dropping his voice, and adopting his best sincere/concerned tone, "The fact is, he actually has fought some of these ideas."

Here they were. You should understand that Mac had been with The Company since he was a brand new college graduate, about thirty years ago. Along the way, as part of The Company's employee development plan, Mac had earned his Ph.D. in industrial psychology from a top midwestern university. But you wouldn't know that he was one of The Company's own just to look at him. Mac was one of those people who would never look comfortable in The Company's corporate uniform, the white shirt, regimental striped tie, and three-piece suit, even though he wore it religiously. Somehow the collar ends always seemed to turn up just a tad in carrying out the seemingly appointed task of choking the florid face just above. And the vest seemed ready to give up in its contest with the slightly sagging paunch. Likewise the trousers. Otherwise, Jack MacPherson was amiable, though serious, and certainly, *most certainly*, not crisp and hard hitting.

"Mac is the original manager of psychological services, Lesley," Ted was saying. "He started up shop here, how long ago?"

"Twenty-two years," Mac replied. "Yes sir, I've seen them come and go all right. I'll bet I'm the only manager in The Company today who's the personal acquaintance of every darn one of the last, um, let's see, five generations of plant managers. Just incidently, starting with your dad, Ted, right on down to young Mason who moved up in Pawtucket just last week."

The conversation went on in this vein for a while, with Mac reminiscing about past heroics and heros of the company. Then Ted rose, signaling the end to the interview.

"Nice to meet you, Mr. MacPherson," Lesley concluded.

"Oh, come on, Lesley, just call me Mac. Everyone does, you know."

Ted was thoughtful as he moved on back up the hallway. "It's really a shame, you know. I wonder what the missing ingredient was. Here's a bright young guy starting out great. Here's The Company growing like a mushroom. And what? Nothing." Ted really was talking out of turn now, but careers were extremely important to him and this bothered him. It bothered him so much that he really didn't think about the etiquette of the situation.

"You know, nobody pays much attention to Mac anymore. He's more like, well, just more like a tradition than anything. He still has some ideas now and again but, you know, you've got to think twice about them. After all, here's a guy whose been in the same slot, never moved up in twenty or so years, so you've just got to know that something's missing. Somebody has looked at him in the past and said 'This guy just doesn't have it.' So you tend to discount his judgment. And yet. . . ."

What *had* happened to Jack MacPherson? At another time, in another situation, Stanley had asked that exact question of Dr. Faust. What Faust had told him was this.

"There indeed is a lesson for you here, Stanley. Most people in The Company seem to have forgotten that Dr. MacPherson has been responsible for some truly outstanding achievements in personnel administration. You may know that he is the inventor of the SPACE (systems programmer aptitude check exam) test, and at the time when no other such instrument existed. And from the most rudimentary beginning he developed the entire selection, placement, and career guidance system of The Company.

Again, ahead of its time and before any other corporation had such a comprehensive and well-validated set of procedures.

"Then where lies the problem?" The question by Faust was purely rhetorical, of course. "First, in his position there was no evident avenue for promotion within his field. And since he did not want to move outside of it, there quite simply was no position to which he could advance.

"Second, Dr. MacPherson is not, ah . . . how would you say it . . . ?"

"An empire builder, I think you mean, don't you, Dr. Faust?" supplied Stanley.

"Yes! Precisely. He believed that the correct way to proceed was to limit the size of his corporate staff and build instead at the plant level. A most productive strategy for The Company, but not so productive a strategy for a career. And so, over the years, he gained the image of someone who once had been considered, but was passed over, for promotion."

Faust continued, "Now, as you may or may not know, Dr. MacPherson has always opposed those faddish ideas in personnel that are so dear to the hearts of our corporate program hucksters. Yes, and very often, in the long run, he was quite correct. Yet it is in the nature of these things that few remember when the program fades from view that it was Dr. MacPherson who had been right, and they wrong. No, what is remembered is only that he is a chronic naysayer, a corporate Cassandra who is afraid of risk. He is looked upon as being, ah . . . backward-looking.

"So it is that over the years a consensus has evolved in our corporate management culture that this is not the man to be consulted on important matters. And in the end that belief becomes truth."

Faust has spelled it out pretty well for Stanley. First, partly by circumstance and partly by choice, there were no avenues upward for Mac beyond that first-level spot he occupies, so there he stays. Now we witness the kind of reasoning that attends the situation of blocked opportunity. When a manager or professional has not moved ahead within the usual timetable, people start asking why. The situation calls for explanation. Ultimately, these explanations come to have the taint of failure. It would be dissonance-producing for younger managers and professionals to admit that the organization has only limited opportunity for competent people. Consequently, we "explain" the situation by the *attribution* of personal characteristics; by attributing lack of ambition, lack of ability, or motivation to them. Now we start perceiving our "failures" in the light of these newly constructed explanations. We start expecting them to behave in ways consistent with our explanation. And that is what we see. So we begin to treat them differently, in ways consistent with our new perception of their behavior. Finally, to close the ring, the persons in the blocked position themselves will start to behave more in accordance with the way they are being treated under these developing expectations.[1]

Why should this be so? Some of the reasons were given in Chapter 7 on impression management. The processes of perceptual filling in and distortion are at work. We also know that people naturally construct explanations for events that take place in organizations. People want to have reasons for what has happened. Dissonance theory, as we pointed out earlier, tells us that these explanations are likely to be internally self-consistent. When we observe failure our explanations for what has happened likely will be consistent with the assumption that the organization, by and large, is correct, informed, and justified in what it has done. To believe the opposite would be to raise troublesome questions, such as, if this is such an arbitrary organization then why am I here? This question in turn raises additional dissonance-producing observations. It is far simpler to assume the rightness of the organization and the correctness of the situation, and to attribute the failure to individual shortcomings (34:122).

This kind of analysis helps us to understand better the position of people whose upward aspirations are blocked because of lower ascribed statuses: women and minorities, and people with little formal education from lower socioeconomic backgrounds. By *ascribed* status we mean social position allocated on ascriptive characteristics such as sex, race, religion, or nationality. For a variety of reasons such people are assigned within the organization to lower-participant roles and are expected to behave in ways consistent with the attitudes, values, and motives attributed to such people. This is Penny's problem. How can she convey to her superiors that she is not only a *woman,* but a *person* as well; that the usual female roles, and hence *positions,* assigned by the organization are not the positions to which she aspires. This also is Claude's problem and one of the reasons why he was so sensitive to the outcome of HYPO: people might explain his "failure" through the attribution of characteristics consistent with his ascribed status.

Types of Blocked Opportunity

Status ascription is one of the ways in which people may be blocked from access to the structure of opportunity. Here we shall describe three main types of career situation in which further advancement is blocked: plateaued careers, completed careers, and deadend careers.

1. *Plateaued careers* are those of managers who have risen to a point in the organization where further advancement is unlikely. Why? They may be caught in the squeeze at the top of the pyramid. There simply are no jobs left to be filled. Or they may have taken a career line seen as inappropriate for further advancement, for example, Personnel. Yet another reason might be that the manager has missed a career step providing experience felt to be indispensable in the performance of the next position. Finally, it may be that superiors see him or her as lacking desire or some key ability.
2. *Completed careers* are similar to plateaued careers with one exception: further advancement has been terminated by the choice of the manager. People in such completed career positions usually are satisfied with their present status, performing the duties so well that executive management

is unwilling or unable to remove them by way of lateral transfers. Managers with completed careers are most commonly found in terminal positions such as plant manager. We know a few of these people personally. The reasons they give for staying put are strong geographical preference for their present location and an abiding dislike of corporate executive life.

3. *Deadend careers* are career lines that have few steps to begin with. These are the career lines of lower participants: secretaries and foremen in industry, people in various clerical and nonprofessional specialties, noncommissioned officers in the military.

There is yet another group of deadend careers that, because of its importance, we would like to treat separately.

4. *Ascribed careers* are those allocated to women and minorities. The key distinction between ascribed careers and other deadend careers is that ascribed careers are based on *statuses ascribed* to women and minorities in the larger society. The positions, and hence roles, provided by organizations for women and minorities are similar to those occupied in the larger society and are consonant with the attitudes, values, and motives attributed to the occupants of those roles.

Let us now examine each of these situations of blocked opportunity to see how they are defined within the social system of the organization, what the organizational and motivational consequences might be, and how both individuals and organizations adapt to these consequences.

Plateaued Careers

The Peter Principle illustrates well the popularity of explanations of failure based on individual shortcomings (25). Briefly, the Peter Principle explains that the plateaued manager has been promoted to his or her "level of incompetence." Each promotion brings the manager closer to the point where he or she will be unable to perform. Perhaps the Peter Principle was proposed with tongue in cheek; still, it has become a popular part of management folklore. And it does provide an organizationally self-justifying explanation for plateaued careers. After all, if a manager gets no farther, it must simply be because he does not have what it takes.

Yet in one sense the Peter principle *is* correct. As the organizational pyramid narrows, the few positions that remain will probably go to the more able, more aggressive, the more personable and politically astute managers. Demographic projections indicate that this problem will mushroom with the coming of age of the baby boom generation. An indication of the magnitude of the problem is shown in Figure 12.1. American organizations for the first time will face a

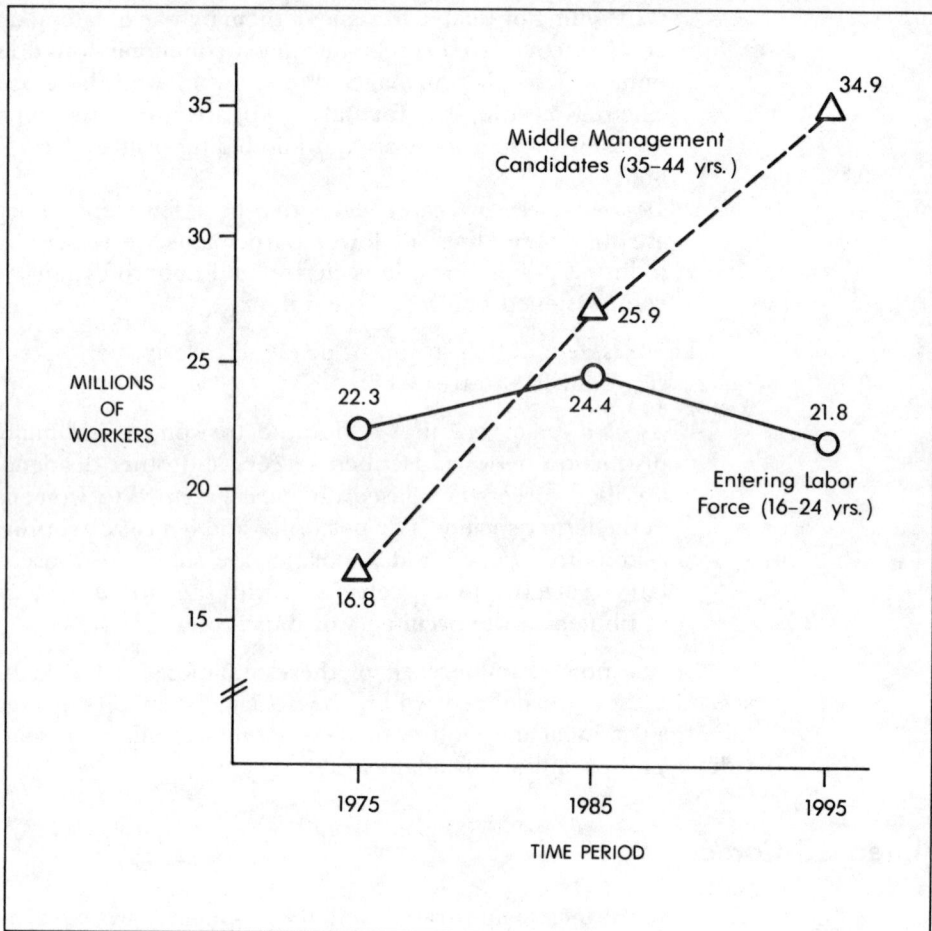

FIGURE 12.1 Size of Civilian Labor Force in Two Age Groups Projected for 1985 and 1995 (Millions of Workers)

Source: Graph constructed from information provided by the Bureau of Labor Statistics' *Moderate Growth Projection*, as cited in T. Friedman, "The Baby Boom Comes of Age." *New York Times*, January 10, 1982, Section 12, p. 18.

situation in which the numbers of potential middle-management candidates far exceed the numbers of young people entering the workforce (10). Together with the fact that many more of these people are college educated, this means greater competition for fewer slots. Whether or not the adjustment in leadership expectations noted in the previous chapter will ease these difficulties remains to be seen. Still, the basic problem is a structural one: the squeeze at the top of the pyramid. The alleged incompetence and lack of motivation of the plateaued manager, where it does exist, is more likely the motivational *result* rather than the *cause* of the situation. Plateaued managers exist in a world of social definitions that suggest they are failures (8: 611). Career plateaus also place limits on incentives of increased salary and status. Under the theory of equity, salary and symbols of status must be allocated according to position. It is little wonder, then, that plateaued managers come to seek different kinds of satisfaction from their jobs and ultimately may become organizational deadwood (8: 607).

Motivational Consequences

One major consequence of such organizationally defined failure is the *disengagement* of the plateaued manager. Rosabeth Kanter explains in vivid detail how these people are felt to be in the "write it off" stage of their careers.

> They were known as "mummies" or "zombies" or "mystery men in the office." They walked around doing only what they were told, taking no initiative, and responding only to crises, if then. Sometimes they stopped participating in office social functions. (18:146)

Certainly this is a gloomy depiction of the plateaued manager. And so we must ask, how common is this kind of situation? One estimate is that plateaued managers constitute the majority of the managerial work force, but that the deadwood—the people corresponding most closely to Kanter's description—probably are only a small group (8: 607). In addition to the nonmobile *managers* there also are groups of plateaued *professionals,* for example, technical professionals in large professional organizations.

So now we must ask, how do people in plateaued careers adapt to their situations? What prevents them from becoming "zombies"? The most obvious answer is that it depends on the *level* of the *plateau* and the individual's *level of aspiration* based on the human capital he or she brings to the job. Where the plateau corresponds to level of aspiration, where the situation seems equitable, motivation may be more a function of the intrinsic interest of the work than of anything else (8: 609). Where the career plateau occurs in upper management, the probability of disaffection seems even less likely. Providing a proper role model for lower-level managers and attending to their socialization become satisfying activities in themselves. Consequently, the problem resides primarily with lower-level managerial and professional people, especially where the plateau results from blocked opportunity. We feel it important to reemphasize here that this situation has important motivational consequences *regardless* of the adequacy of selection and promotion procedures. Even if promotion procedures are *entirely* accurate and equitable, there still remains a large group of potentially disaffected and demotivated managerial and professional personnel whose efforts we must assume are important to the success of the organization.

Individual and Organizational Adaptations

The essence of adaptation to a situation that otherwise might be interpreted as failure lies in adopting alternative goals, or alternative statuses and organizational identities (11, 12). Organizations assist individuals in this by reminding them of other aspects of their position which, though less important, are ones that upwardly mobile people are more likely to trade for continued opportunity: geographical location, job stress, hours of work, and the like (4: 294). Stressing "professional" aspects of the job is another common mechanism. But emphasizing *professionalism* as an alternative to *advancement* may have unanticipated motivational consequences. Take, for example, the professional salesman.

When a supplier develops enough business with a key customer a resident salesman located within the customer organization may be assigned to handle that account. Such accounts need not be pursued as aggressively as new accounts, and so the sales representative often is an older, more experienced person. The job may require diplomacy rather than energy. And very likely that salesman also will be one who no longer is under consideration for managerial responsibility. Thus,

> Permanent salesmen evidently become more attached to the customer relationship than to the relationship with those above them in the organization. Salesmen become more dependent on their customers than on their bosses when they forsake promotion into management. They frequently take the customer's point of view. . . . They feel they are involved in a professional-client relationship. As one put it: ". . . I feel as though we are more or less professional in filling the need we may create for an individual. We speak with people who are on the management level most of the time and aren't trying to con people but doing them a service. There are times we actually don't recommend our equipment—that is professionalism." (13: 501)

Surrounded by the customer organization, the professional salesman becomes too familiar with customer problems, too imbued with the customer's point of view to aggressively promote new sales and new products. The sales representative comes to take on an objective, professional attitude, perhaps advising the consumer there is no need to replace an old item with a new one, or suggesting perhaps that a competitor's product is preferable. Therefore emphasizing the rewards of professionalism helps to provide a valued alternative to the status foregone through blocked opportunity.

This strategy of emphasizing professional achievement as a substitute for managerial status may require structural adaptations to make the strategy plausible in situations where organizations "need not only to motivate achievement but also to mollify those denied it in order to sustain motivation in the face of disappointment and to deflect resentment" (5: 569). In the face of a structure permitting only limited opportunity, organizations need some mechanism that still permits everyone to succeed. This kind of problem occurs commonly in organizations that have mainly professionals in their work force: large accounting firms, legal firms, research and development laboratories, and the like. Some of these, such as the legal firms noted in Chapter 6, use "outplacement" as a solution; lawyers and accountants go on to individual careers in corporate organizations.

The research and development laboratory presents a different problem. Here there are many highly trained professionals who certainly will not have access to the customary managerial careers. Nevertheless, these professionals do aspire to managerial careers (27, 29). One solution is to create a parallel management hierarchy based on *professional achievement* rather than on managerial responsibility. This hierarchy is meant to provide an alternative definition of success for professionals to whom the usual avenues of advancement are inaccessible (13).

A typical dual ladder of management is structured as shown in Figure 12.2. Beginning from the entry-level position of assistant engineer, the professional is promoted through the nonmanagement levels to the rank of engineer.[2] The understanding is that this level 3 position will be the terminal professional position for those who have not shown themselves capable of further advancement. All remaining positions are described as management, either staff management or administrative management. Thus, although the two sides of the ladder use different titles, they are described in Company personnel literature as having equal rank and pay. Advancement through these positions within each side is said to reflect professional achievement, the difference being that this professional achievement reflects purely technical leadership in the one and a mix of administrative and technical leadership in the other. Finally, again as shown in Figure 12.2, there is yet another set of position titles that reflect levels in the administrative hierarchy of the organization. These titles are held only by people on the administrative side of the ladder but do not necessarily coincide with the rank accorded to professional achievement, as indicated by the dotted lines. Therefore, a department manager might be at level 4, 5, or 6 in professional rank. Finally, there are further positions in general management, such as laboratory manager, that extend beyond the ladder structure.

Company publications describing their own dual path of opportunity are scrupulous in describing this structure. Much emphasis is given to the need for, and value of, the "individual contributor." When, as sometimes happens, a level 4 staff engineer is moved across to a level 4 project engineer position, this move is never described as a promotion (although everyone thinks of it as such) but as a new assignment. And, although it is possible in principle, care is taken to avoid having a function manager of lower professional rank, such as project engineer, supervising a department manager of higher professional rank, such as group engineer. All in all, operating the system can be quite complex, and the communications people who announce promotions and reassignments must be careful that appropriate language is being used.

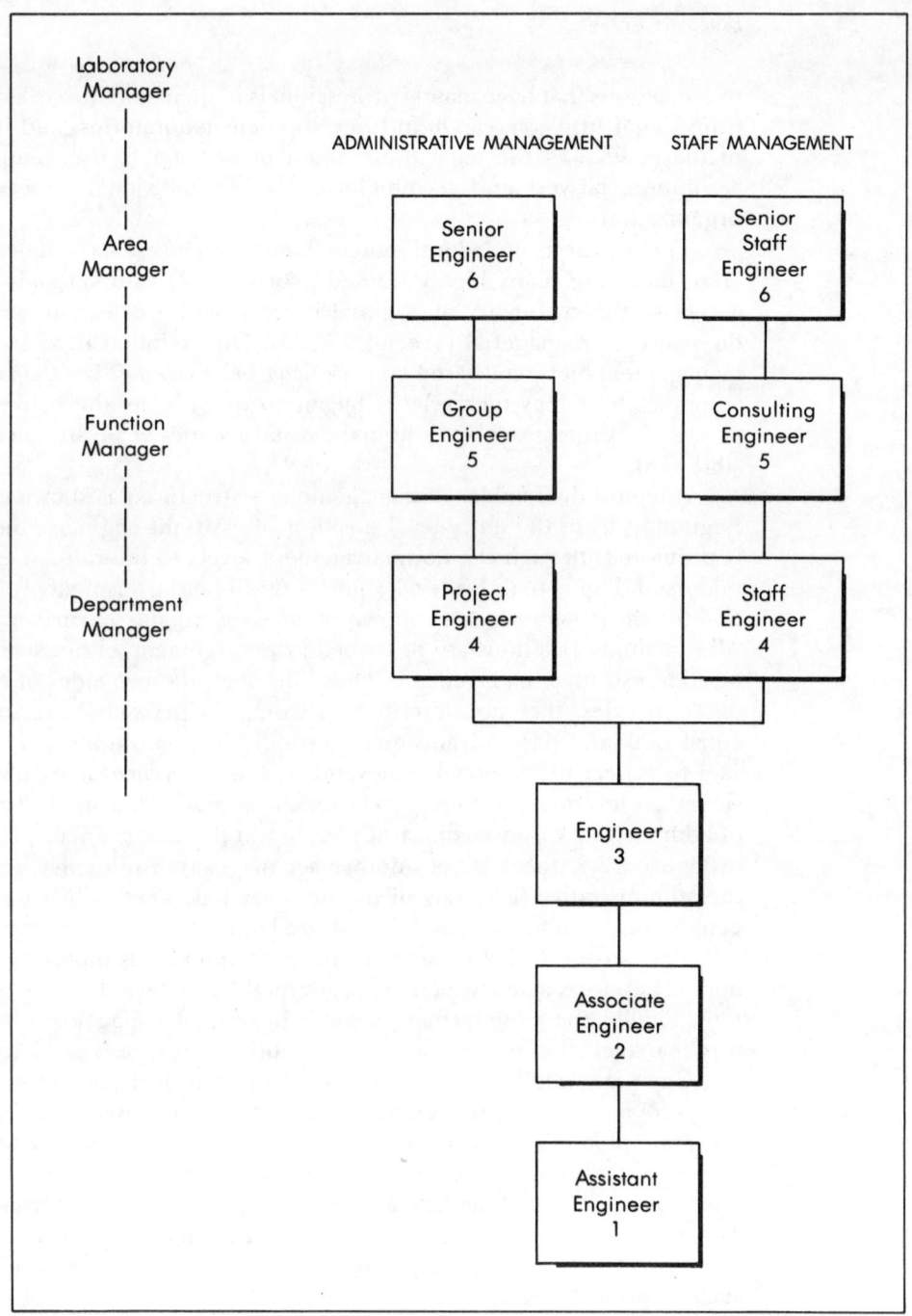

FIGURE 12.2 The Dual Ladder of Opportunity in The Company

Looking to the future we would guess that this kind of arrangement will become increasingly common, for it provides an alternative structure of opportunity in organizations whose entire work force is made up of college-educated professionals. Pairing the demographic trends depicted at the beginning of this chapter with the increasing level of education in our work force, it seems certain that some such arrangement will be necessary in most organizations. For example, we already have seen proposals for using some such systems with police and with nursing professionals. In light of this, we might ask, how well does it work? For one answer see Box 15.

Box 15

The Dual Management Hierarchy: How Well Does It Work?

As part of a comprehensive study of engineers in high technology organizations, Ritti addressed some questions concerning the motivational consequences of the dual management structure used in the engineering laboratories of one organization. Personnel officers described the intent of this dual structure as one of providing an incentive for engineers to remain in technical work instead of moving into managerial positions. They cited the great need for "individual contributors" and described staff engineers as being involved in technical decisions whereas their counterparts in administration were involved in personnel and budget decisions. Overall, the logic is one of providing an opportunity for advancement for those who are best fitted for, and whose interests lie in, purely technical work.

In this case study several interesting initial facts became evident. First, there is little or no difference in the work goals chosen by staff engineers and by managerial engineers. By and large, these are consistent with a future career in management. Second, of all engineers entering the organization, only 15 percent have not been promoted into a staff or managerial position within their first ten years.

With these facts in mind, 787 supervisors, 328 staff counterparts, and 933 nonmanagement engineers were asked to compare the staff technical positions to their supervisory management counterparts on thirteen attributes of the dual hierarchy. For each they could indicate that the staff technical position had more of the attribute, the managerial position more, or that both positions were about the same. Comparing the rating given by current staff engineers to those from current managerial engineers shows considerable consensus. For example, 80 percent of the staff engineers felt that managers had "greater potential for getting action on your ideas." More surprisingly, on attributes such as "recognition of your contri-

continued

butions" and "chance to make important technical decisions," the staff technical engineers felt that the manager had more of each attribute by a two-to-one margin, roughly 55 to 20 percent. Only on such things as "interesting work" and "utilization of skills" did the picture reverse. In summary, on every attribute involving some element of organizational influence the staff positions were judged lacking in comparison to the supervisory management positions.

To complete the picture, we can see how the views of engineers change over time as the early losers in the mobility tournament adjust their career goals. Figure 12.3 shows that those promoted neither to staff nor to supervisory management after seven years expect lower goal achievement but show higher preference for the staff technical position and an increased expectation that the staff position will utilize greater individual skill.

In conclusion, this study indicates clearly that the availability of the staff technical side of a dual management hierarchy provides a valued alternative to engineers who come to realize that they are not going to move up in supervisory management. Although the attribute of managerial influence is lacking, engineers come to focus on the alternative attributes of more interesting work and greater utilization of technical skills.

R. Richard Ritti. *The Engineer in the Industrial Corporation*. New York: Columbia University Press, 1971.

To conclude, the fundamental problem of plateaued careers is the taint of failure. For those higher up in the organization this is less of a problem than for lower-level managers and professionals. Motivational consequences may be severe if alternative valued roles and statuses are not adopted. Consequently, although individuals may provide these for themselves, most often organizations and the social system within the organization provide adaptive mechanisms whereby suitable explanations and career alternatives are made available.

Completed Careers

Recall that the completed career is similar to the plateaued career except that it occurs through personal choice. And this one exception can mean a world of difference for motivation. Plateaued managers or professionals see themselves turned down by the organization before their career goals have been reached. Managers with completed careers have decided that their current position in the organization best achieves their career goals.

Completed Careers

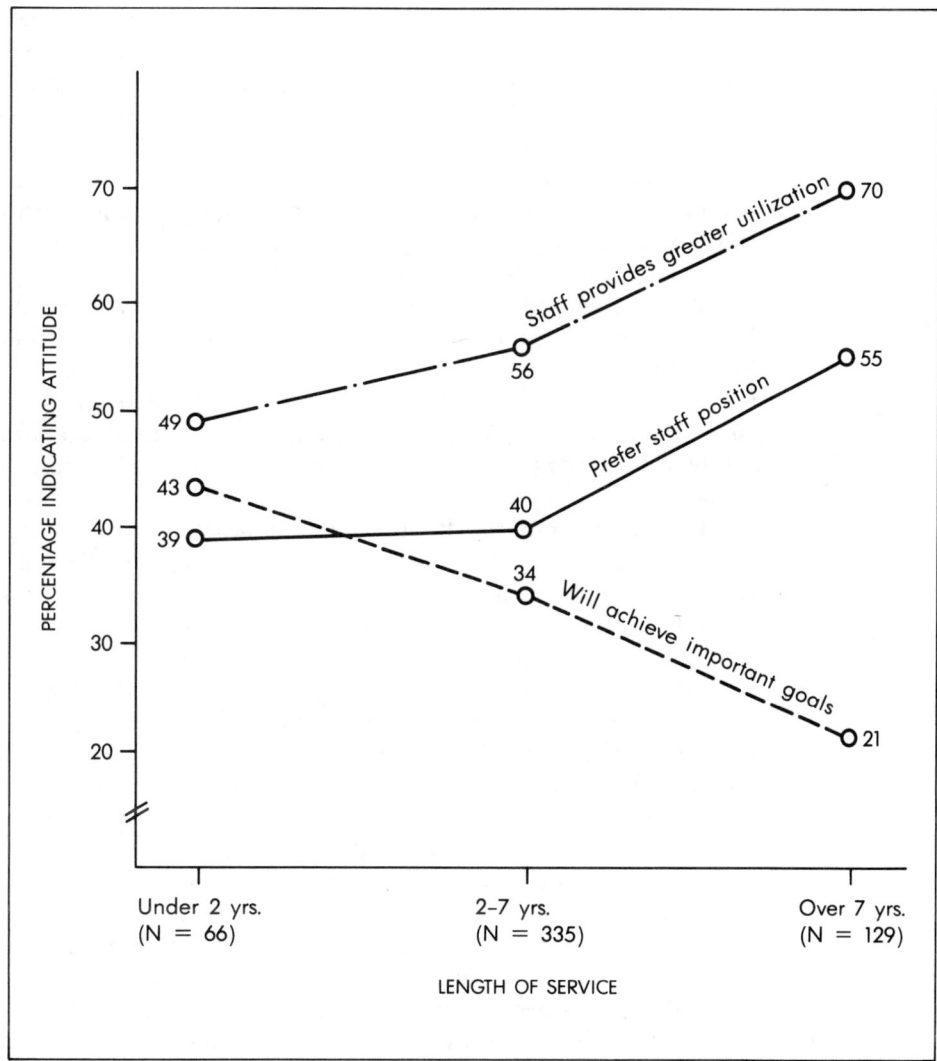

FIGURE 12.3 Attitudes about Staff Position and Achievement of Important Career Goals as a Function of Length of Service (B.S. degree only, Engineers 1, 2, and 3 only)

They are not people who simply have given up the idea of further advancement. That attitude is more characteristic of plateaued managers who find the game not worth the struggle. Instead, we are talking about people who consider themselves successful, whom the organization would promote if they would have it, who have not lost their taste for corporate battle.

Typically these managers are in a powerful position, what we have called a terminal position. For example, we have talked to branch office sales managers who would not hear of being moved up the ladder. Running their branch office is just like running their own business, they say. They talk of power, independence, geographical preference, and especially of freedom from the "sterility" of life on the corporate staff. They talk of being out in the real world. These people are experienced, politically astute high performers with extensive networks of loyal supporters. And these are the characteristics that prevent them from being removed by lateral transfer.

But why should The Company want to remove such an effective manager? The answer is that these managers present more than their share of problems for the organization, problems mainly of gaining compliance. Why is this? Simply for the reason that the organization has very few positive inducements for compliance left to offer; but responsible executives otherwise are afraid to risk what surely will be recognized as an arbitrary removal of a noncompliant but effective manager.

Let us elaborate on the motivational situation of the completed career by looking at two of our acquaintances. We know both these people well. The first is our plant manager, Ben Franklyn. Time and time again he has been offered various executive positions on the New York corporate staff, but he will not move. As plant manager, he is an important person in his pleasant, small community. He is extremely popular with local management and workers, inspiring fierce loyalty in his subordinates. Manufacturing people in The Company generally agree that his plant is among their most productive. He was the only plant manager not to go along with the new Company-wide work measurement program, despite unrelenting pressure from his vice president who threatened, wheedled, and cajoled.

Another exemplar of the completed career is R and D manager Kerry Drake. He has a history of major technical achievements and, like Ben, the unswerving loyalty of his scientists. The Company's problem with him is that he can not tolerate the new corporate strategy of "planned innovation"; that is, working on products dreamed up by the corporate staff long-range planners. He believes in following his own instincts. Though now and then his laboratory produces a major technical breakthrough, still this is not quite what the planners want. Kerry is thus a nettlesome burr under the corporate saddle.

What *does* The Company do with such people? We suppose it can just learn to live with them, continually trying to bring them around. Or the corporate executives in charge can develop a strategy of negative reinforcement. First, the corporate people could create a noxious stimulus, later to be withdrawn as an incentive for compliance. (Recall the meaning of negative reinforcement.) So our two friends will find that they have special requirements to meet, or that the corporate people require special commitments in return for allowing noncompliance. The New York people could let Ben Franklyn escape the work measurement program, but only after he promised to deliver higher production his way than would have been achieved the corporate way. For his part, Kerry has been burdened continually by corporate visitors and watchdogs, by bureaucratic requirements, administrivia, and paperwork. The negative reinforcement comes about when future compliance is rewarded by the removal of these special requirements.

A final organizational adaptation to these troublesome people in completed careers is the cool-out. The key to the success of this strategy is to convince the loyal following of the manager that in fact he or she has not been treated badly. "Kicking upstairs" to a created position is sometimes arranged so that the manager is allowed to stay in his or her community. Actually, in Kerry's case, he was offered the position of "distinguished scientist" and found it too attractive to turn down.

To summarize, people in completed careers are both powerful and irksome to the organization. The usual incentives for compliance are unavailable and there is powerful support for them within the norms of the organization. Furthermore, the presence of these nonmobile managers upsets the structure of opportunity, blocking the avenue of advancement for subordinate managers.

Deadend Careers: The Motivations of "Lower Participants"

What is a deadend career? First, it must in fact be a *career* rather than simply a job; that is, there must be some continuity from position to position, a beginning and end, with some *differentiation of roles* along the way. However, the career ladder is short, terminating in a position still of relatively low formal status. We have used the examples of noncommissioned officers in the military, stenographers and secretaries, and people in various nonprofessional white-collar specialties. Ben Franklyn's millhands also are lower participants, but to the extent that they just fill jobs rather than being embarked on careers they do not fit our definition of being in deadend careers. Another key characteristic of deadend careers is that the formal rewards, both material and normative, are not great. Nor are the performance obligations great. The formal duties of lower participants are specific and clearly defined.

So lower participant is a *position* in the organization, and that position is one of a series that constitutes the deadend career. What kinds of people are we likely to find in those positions? We will find people who we assume fit the roles offered by those positions; people who under the theory of equity bring little human capital to the job, or people whose social characteristics lead us to assume that they will be satisfied with such roles. Typically these are people with little education, from lower socioeconomic backgrounds; they are likely to be women and minorities, people of lower *ascribed* statuses in our society. Since we will treat the special issues of ascribed careers next, now we will note only the tendency to attribute to lower participants characteristics that are consonant with their subordinated roles. We attribute abilities as well as attitudes, values, and motives that help us explain why these people are lower participants. For example, we might say that secretaries are more interested in home and family than a career; they lack the training, interest in, and motivation for professional work. Similarly, we may say that noncommissioned officers lack the background and education necessary for commissioned status, although occasionally a "battlefield commission" is awarded through sheer necessity.

The role imagery of lower participants differs also from that of subordinates. As we said earlier, the role of subordinate is held by someone preparing to become a superior. The lower participant, however, manages an impression as one who has no aspirations for higher position, who simply wishes to perform a job as satisfactorily as possible. The lower participant presents an image to those in higher authority of one who is compliant, and neither interested in nor knowledgable about the political aspects of organization. For these reasons people in positions of formal power in the organization feel secure in sharing with lower participants their access to information, people, and organizational resources normally withheld from subordinates. Executive secretaries and master sergeants are examples, as are dispatchers (people who decide which units of goods and services are provided to whom and in what sequence) and purchasing agents (21, 33). Think of "Radar" Riley of M*A*S*H fame.

What are the motivational consequences of deadend careers? Rewards for compliance are few, especially since these positions are not well paid to begin with. Also, since lower participants' duties are constrained and routine, rewards from the intrinsic interest of the work are few. The upshot of this is that the lower participant is more difficult to control than the subordinate and can afford to have a cavalier attitude toward the formal rules (7:16). Therefore, since lower participants may have informal access to the power of their superiors, and since the available inducements to compliance are few, lower participants actually may be in a position to wield considerable power in the organization. As one writer puts it, "Organizations, in a sense, are continuously at the mercy of their lower participants." (21:350).

Sources of Power of Lower Participants

Let us examine for a moment the organizational situation of an exemplary lower participant. First of all, he or she works for a boss who is moving through the organization both upward and laterally. This means that our lower participant, who does not need such experience-gathering movement, will have considerably longer tenure in his or her organizational niche and consequently will know more of the details of the organization, its operations and its participants—lower *and* upper.

The boss will be thinking of bigger things than routine details of everyday operations. He or she will be busy learning the "professional" aspects of the new position and nurturing a career. In addition, because administrative responsibilities grow with advancing position, more than ever it will be necessary to delegate the administrivia. This situation sets the stage for the lower participant who is inclined to use the available power.[3]

EXPERT KNOWLEDGE. Because of having long tenure in a position the lower participant will build up a substantial store of knowledge about the details of technical operations as well as organizational politics. The astute lower participant will know where the skeletons are buried—who owes whom for what. Take the computer specialist who has certain critical aspects of the system only in her head. She can render judgments on which jobs are possible and which not, which will take a great deal of effort and which are easy. And no one else knows enough to argue. Therefore, people in the good graces of the computer specialist will have jobs performed for them that are impossible for others. Consider also the secretary who arranges the order in which documents are processed, recovered, or typed. The work of some people will never emerge from the bottom of the pile. The secretary also will have access to a wide network of friends in the organization who know how to achieve within the informal network that which is formally impossible. Finally, we have the accounting specialist who continually invokes obscure company rules to alter policy decisions. No one else has the time and patience to separate accustomed practice from ironclad company rules.

LACK OF INTEREST AND WILLINGNESS TO EXPEND SPECIAL EFFORT. Our accountant could be challenged, but not easily. The cost of continual surveillance is too high, taking time away from the professional or the image-managing aspects of the managerial position. And these are crucial to continued success. Therefore the lower participant may exert a considerable amount of influence over what may in fact, if not appearance, be policy decisions (31). For these reasons the astute boss will learn to form alliances with crucial lower participants by allowing minor infractions of organizational rules and by special indulgence. More to the point, the astute manager will never needlessly anger the lower participant.

POSITION IN THE COMMUNICATION NETWORK. Lower participants may have easier access to sensitive information than people considerably higher in organizational rank. Since lower participants are not in competition for high-status positions, they have access to "secrets" that superiors would *not* share with potential competitors. Secretaries read all correspondence, so they know the particulars of their bosses' evaluations of and plans for others, particulars that are guarded jealously from subordinates. And lower participants are allowed to attend high-level meetings from which subordinates ordinarily are barred. Therefore, they know the details of conversations among high-status people. As we have said, they also know where the skeletons are buried. The more central the lower participant's position, the greater the potential for the use of informal power. Marsh's secretary or the top sergeant in the office of the commanding general therefore have a great deal of power. Though it must be used judiciously, the information one gathers may be exchanged for favors or for complementary information in the keeping of still other privileged lower participants.

COALITIONS. This last point suggests the potential power of networks or coalitions of cooperating lower participants. These coalitions form on the basis of mutual ability to supply favors and to make others' jobs easier by circumventing the formal rules of the organization. Coalitions also constitute the underlife of the organization, and provide means of dealing with the myriad and troublesome details of the day-to-day business of the organization. Generally these details go unnoticed, except when a superior is being "punished" by such coalitions for his or her bad behavior.

BUREAUPATHIC ADHERENCE TO RULES. If the lower participants' strength is the circumvention of rules, then their strategy for punishing wayward superiors is the adherence to the letter of the rules. Few organizations could function effectively if operated precisely in adherence to the formal rules of the organization. Therefore, complete and apathetic compliance with the rules presents a handy way of disciplining superiors. For example, the first sergeant or the chief petty officer in the military will find going by the book a handy way of putting things in perspective for the eager young commissioned officer. This procedure should demonstrate to even the least astute the consequences of not allowing the lower participant to exercise independent discretion.

Some Organizational Adaptations to Deadend Careers

Occasionally the independence of lower participants may become troublesome to superiors in the organization. The problem, of course, is that of finding incentives for compliance. These incentives may take the form of punishment, negative reinforcement, or positive reinforcement. Punishment generally does not work. First of all, infractions of the rules are relatively minor, and threats are not effective since the lower participant already is in a deadend career. Negative reinforcement, strangely enough, is usually applied by instructing the lower participant that he or she will have to obey organizational rules explicitly until things shape up. One problem with this strategy is that lower participants know this is a game they also can play. Therefore a stalemate will usually result. Far better is a strategy that provides positive incentives for compliance.

Generally these incentives are organizational adaptations that recognize the right of lower participants to exercise discretion and thus restore the status motivations of their positions. For example, *participative management* is a strategy that formally recognizes that lower participants *do* exercise discretion and may have considerable informal power. One effect of participative management is to delimit formally the bounds of this informal power, thus bringing lower participants' discretion more readily under the surveillance of superiors. Job enrichment can also expand the decision making of lower participants.

To summarize, people pursuing deadend careers in organizations are sometimes assumed to possess abilities, and attitudes, values, and motives consonant with those careers. But this assumption is not always correct. In fact, lower participants, the occupants of deadend careers, may seek to exercise considerable discretion and can use considerable informal power in the organization. Although this can work to the advantage of the astute superior, lower participants can sometimes be nettlesome to the compliance structure of the organization. The problem is one of finding substitute motivations to replace those denied by the blocked structure of opportunity.

Ascribed Careers: Roles for Women and Minorities

Let us follow Claude Gilliam's career for a short while after he left HYPO. Claude's next stop was a corporate staff position; assistant to the corporate staff director for engineering and systems technical manpower development. Why he wound up there still is a mystery. However, what evolved gradually was an assignment to develop a strategy for recruiting minority professionals.

You might think that Claude would be happy with this, but he was not. Claude wanted to be thought of as just another guy, not a "minority person." He did not think that he had any special responsibility for other people just because they also happened to be black. In fact, he resented it when other people—however well intentioned—pressed him to act on what they presumed to be his special responsibility. No, he thought, he had enough responsibility just making it on his own.

Characteristically, when he got the assignment he dug into it with determination to do the best that could be done. And the more he learned about his job the more involved he became. The Company had a goal of about 10 percent black and minority employment, which corresponded roughly to the percentage in the population generally. And The Company was doing pretty well. However, Claude discovered, examining the figures in detail, that The Company was near its goal for blue-collar and clerical people, but had few professional and technical employees.

Therefore, Claude started asking some questions. Patiently he was told that it was very difficult to find qualified young black people in these specialties. Typically he asked, "What do you mean by that?" The stock answer was, All you have to do is take a look at the number of blacks in technical specialties graduating from The University and the other places where we recruit, and you will see that there are only a handful in each graduating class. Furthermore, the competition to recruit these people is enormous."

Undaunted, Claude next would ask, "Why not look elsewhere? Why not look to places where we *don't* usually recruit? How about some of the Negro colleges in the South?" The answer was, "We've tried that, but those people just aren't getting the quality education that we are looking for. How do we know? We know because they can't get an acceptable score on our standard recruiting tests."

Perhaps a word of explanation is needed here. The Company gave tests to all professional recruits interested in a career in "systems." Since, at least at the time, most colleges and universities did not have a systems curriculum, The Company felt it had to do its own selection. Also, Company recruiters had learned that even people with backgrounds in such unrelated fields as English and history might have considerable aptitude for systems specialties. Hence, they used the battery of tests.

Claude might have countered this explanation by claiming that such tests are invalid for minorities. He did not, and he did not think the tests necessarily invalid. After all, they are basically numerical reasoning. If that is the kind of aptitude systems requires, there is no reason, thought Claude, why black people shouldn't have it, too. The last thing he wanted was to hold to different standards for black systems trainees. Life had taught him that when a white failed, he or she was just another person who didn't have what it took. But when a black trainee failed, it was yet another piece of evidence that *blacks* couldn't cut it.

Still, there *was* a problem with the recruiting procedure and it did not take Claude long to find it. It had to do with *how* the testing was done. First of all, the testing took place at regional headquarters located in major metropolitan centers. These, especially in the South, were newer imposing structures appointed in the decor favored by The Company: crisp and businesslike. (Also, some felt, cold and impersonal.) Into this environment The Company brought potential recruits from the small Negro colleges of the South, putting them through several hours of rigorous testing. And by and large they failed. They failed, that is, until Claude modified the arrangement.

Claude argued that the situation was made for failure. These were not sophisticated urban kids, he said, and yes, it probably *was* true that their education was lacking in some respects. But the tests were designed to get at *aptitude*, not education. In fact, the tests did not require much knowledge, just a certain kind of ability. So Claude finally won the opportunity to have the testing sessions held at the young people's home college, and conducted by him. Certainly the procedure was not as efficient and was more time-consuming than the previous method, but it made a world of difference. Quite a few of the young recruits started passing the tests, some even with top scores.

Skeptics at corporate personnel suspected Claude of coaching his applicants in advance, or worse. They did not know Claude very well. Claude would not have done that, simply because it would have been stupid. He knew that misrepresenting ability *now* would only mean later failure, failure in a far more visible, damaging context. It would have been more unfair to the young recruits than to The Company. All Claude wanted for others, just as for himself, was equal opportunity. Falsifying credentials was not the way. What did happen, then?

Look at it this way. Suppose you have grown up black in the rural South. There are two things, at least, that you have to fight: one is your belief (often correct) that white people in positions of power and influence will not give you a fair shake, that opportunity will be denied you. The other one is the half-hidden, insidious fear that maybe you are not as capable as the next person.

Now you are informed that The Company wants to hire you—maybe. First you say to yourself, "To hell with it. Why bother just to be turned down again?" But you go. Off you go to a place you may never have seen before. And you sit in a cold, impersonal place, with a knot in your stomach and a lump in your throat. You are just another scared black kid waiting to be told once again that you are not wanted.

We do not want to overdramatize the situation, but who among us has *not* at some time suffered from *test anxiety*, a crisis of confidence so crippling that we were completely unable to perform. That was Claude's diagnosis of the problem and the key to his solution. He provided a familiar, warm, and supportive environment, and testing by an official representative of The Company who, by appearances as well as by word believed in your ability and wanted you to succeed.

Ascribed Careers and Attribution

What is to be learned from Claude's story, or from Mac's? Social organizations—societies and work organizations—are made up of interrelated positions and social roles. These roles, as we know, include expectations about appropriate behavior. So, for example, the roles of people in subordinated positions include expectations about proper deference to authority. But there is more to social organization than this. As we said earlier, each of us has a strong motivation to "tidy up" our observations of the world, to want to believe that, by and large, things are as they should be in *our* organization. Therefore we *attribute* to people in those subordinated positions *personal characteristics* that justify their assignments. And, as attribution theory tells us, observers are likely to explain the conditions of others on the basis of personal characteristics rather than the situation, especially when the situation is one of *failure* rather than success (30:100).

Minorities and women by the fact of race and sex have lower *ascribed statuses* in our society generally. Why this is so is a topic of countless volumes. Our point here is only that for centuries the positions, and consequently the social roles, allocated to women and minorities generally have been those of lower participants. Attribution theory (as well as casual conversation and reading of the newspapers) instructs us that characteristics that account for our direct observation that women and blacks overpopulate these positions then will be attributed to the black and female occupants of these roles; that is, to *people* rather than to the social *situation*. Perceptual distortion, differential treatment, and to some extent actual behavior follow. That behavior is influenced is the issue we tried to illustrate in both Mac's and Claude's stories; role expectations *do* influence social behavior.

Figure 12.4 depicts the cycle of attribution. It begins with people of lower

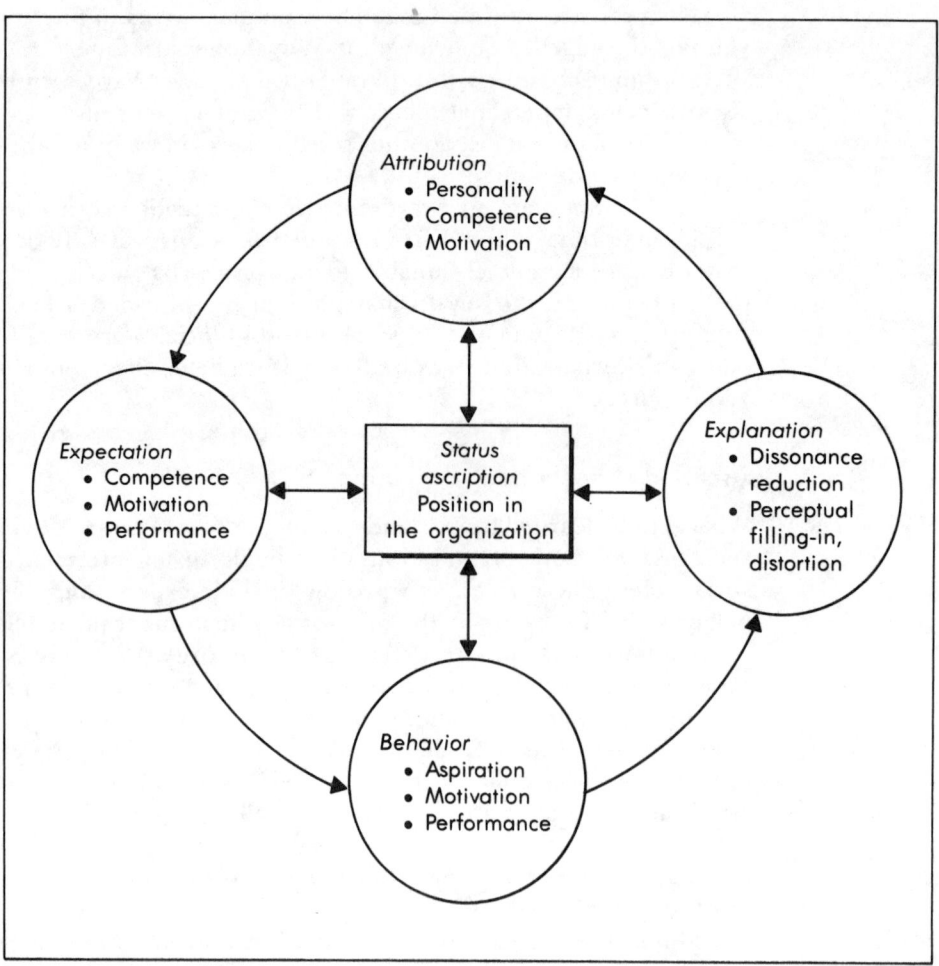

FIGURE 12.4   The Cycle of Attribution

ascribed status being limited to lower level positions in organizations. This fact—that few females or minorities are found in management positions—calls for an *explanation,* and that explanation is based on the perceptual mechanisms of filling-in and distortion. Members then *attribute* to people of lower ascribed status those personal characteristics that will account for and support these explanations—characteristics such as lack of motivation, lack of ability, and the like. Believing women and minorities to be incapable of more, members of organizations then adjust their *expectations* for the level of performance required. Expecting less, they ask for less. As a result, *behavior* tends to fall into line with those expectations. Thus, to close the loop, organizational members can then observe in fact what originally they sought to explain: that is, people denied entry into the ranks of management by reason of their ascribed status finally come to perform in ways that apparently justify their restriction to lower level assignments.

We need some perspective here. Our discussion of ascribed careers rests primarily on this assumption: within whatever ascriptive category you choose—men, women, blacks, whites—the *range* of abilities is very great. Observation tells us this assumption is true beyond question. As a consequence, we find a great many people in any of these ascriptive categories who possess above average ability (whatever that might signify). Therefore, the absence of, or token representation of, women and minorities in middle and upper management levels must necessarily be explained in terms of *social organization*.

Our point in distinguishing a special class of deadend careers as *ascribed careers* is that the structure of opportunity is blocked, not by the inevitable limitation of organizational structure and considerations of equity and human capital, but by statuses ascribed in the larger society that carry over into organizational life. The problem of ascribed careers for minorities and especially for women is one of breaking free from the shackles of unthinking attribution.

The Social Roots of Ascribed Careers

Though the situation for minorities is different in key respects from that of women, many of the consequences are similar. Therefore let us discuss the somewhat different roots of the similar ascribed statuses of women and blacks in particular.

The problem for the black person is easy to pinpoint. Until mid-century blacks systematically were excluded from every legitimate opportunity offered by American society. The military organized all-black combat units. There was hardly a black manager in local, state, or federal government. In sports there were the Globetrotters and the "negro leagues." IBM, GE, AT&T, and the others never thought of blacks as likely managerial candidates. Those positions and roles that *were* open to blacks in legitimate enterprises, in mixed racial contexts, were all subordinated roles, those of lower participants. This omnipresent exclusion of blacks required explanation in everyday life. And this was done by attributing characteristics to black people *as a group* that justified their social situation.

The contemporary scene has changed, yet those explanations persist. And this is the root of the organizational problem for blacks. Studies of white managers' opinions of blacks as potential managerial candidates find lingering traces of these sentiments. There is the continuing belief by some that black people lack the "ambition, initiative, and dependability" for success in the business world, that "Blacks' lifestyles make them unable to fit well into corporate life" (9:79). Then there are the subcultural differences that are invoked in evidence of the validity of these stereotypes. Styles of dress, speech, and personal mannerisms tend to emphasize black-white differences (9:82). The situation seems to be changing, and we are not suggesting that these beliefs persist in the majority of white managers. The evidence seems to be to the contrary. The point is that to some extent blacks still find the structure of opportunity blocked by lingering suspicions that suggest, "Why take a chance?"

The positions and roles reserved for women in organizations have been little different, except that segregation is not the issue. We can understand the situation best by looking at the roles allocated to women in organizations and the assumptions that underlie this allocation. To begin with, unlike racial minorities, women never systematically have been denied membership in work organizations. The history of the women's labor movement attests to the fact that women long have been employed in certain kinds of "light" manufacturing operations. In some professions—the helping professions, for example—women have been predominant. The term *secretary* virtually has been synonymous with *female*, and the vast army of clerical and "inside" sales people are largely female. Then why not women in management?

The underlying rule is derived from the social norm that "women's place is in the home," that sooner or later family duties will interrupt employment, and that this is how it *should* be. From this premise the reasoning follows that women must be employed in jobs where they are quickly replaceable, where experience and long-term career development are not factors affecting performance. Such jobs, in the management view, are typically lower-participant positions (1). Similarly, women reentering the work force after raising a family are virtually disqualified from managerial careers because it is believed that they have lost too much time and valuable experience.

Once again a full description of the origins of such norms and values is beyond our purpose. Nor are we arguing for the rightness of this posture. We just are describing the situation as it exists.

The facts that must be understood are those of *sex role differentiation*, and its corollary norms and beliefs. Our predominant social values and norms are based on the female position of wife and mother and the role expectations attached to that position. These expectations are different from and complementary to those for the roles of husband and father. The female role includes nurturing, providing emotional support, being submissive as opposed to dominant, being emotional as opposed to analytic. In these last two characteristics we find the convergence between the roles allocated to women and to blacks.

Now what happens is predictable again through attribution theory: personal characteristics are attributed to females *as a gender* to account for the situation. Research shows us that women are *perceived* as *not* ambitious, *not* competitive, *not* independent or aggressive. They have difficulty in making decisions. On the other hand, females *are* tactful and quiet, sensitive to the feelings of others, and capable of expressing emotional warmth (36: 464). Such beliefs account in part for the predominance of women in the helping professions. It is true also, however, that these traditionally female professions—social work, for example—are lower-status professions (36: 471).

The point once again is that role expectations, perceptions, and behavior become linked through the self-fulfilling prophecy. Where less is expected performance tends to be lower (20). If women are expected to be less assertive they will be given less opportunity to assert themselves.

Barriers to Opportunity in the Social Structure

These are the historical facts. Until relatively recently women and blacks have been limited to the kinds of position that we have described as those of lower participants. This is a direct result of the lower ascribed status of these people in the larger society, and the roles they traditionally have occupied. One visible consequence is that the managerial stratum of most organizations, especially business organizations, almost exclusively has been white and male.

However, things are changing, and changing quite rapidly. Females and blacks are being admitted to the ranks of the management, though somewhat grudgingly perhaps. Even more aspire to high-level management careers. Still, former norms and beliefs persist (18, 22, 24). Though equal opportunity may be the law, some subtle and not so subtle barriers persist within the social structure of organizations. Let us look at a few of these barriers encountered in the climb to the top of the organizational pyramid, as they are depicted in Figure 12.5.

VISIBILITY. The female or black who is *not* in a lower-participant position is highly visible, an obvious exception to expectations. Others must try to make sense of a situation contrary to persistent beliefs. And so the black or female manager is burdened continually by the symbolic consequences of his or her behavior, of being a representative of a category (9, 15, 16). Successes are "explained" as exceptions to the general rule. Blacks are a "credit to their race"; female managers are given the ultimate compliment of "thinking like a man." Yet being regarded as exceptional in itself constitutes reaffirmation of the persistent belief in the unsuitability of blacks or females for managerial

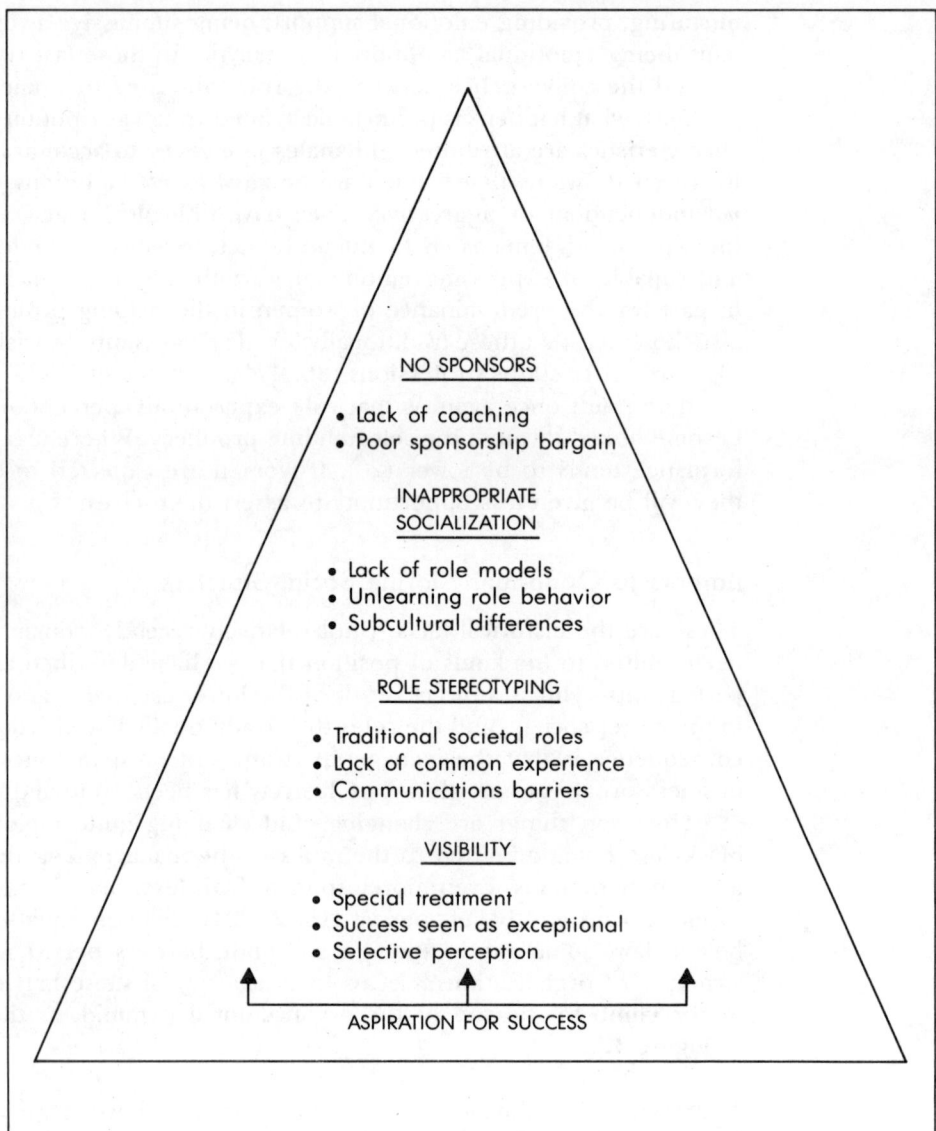

FIGURE 12.5 Barriers to Success in the Structure of Opportunity

positions. Add to this selective perception, the perceptual mechanism whereby we "see" predominantly those things agreeing with our belief, and we have the tendency to recall selectively instances of failure linked to categories of race and sex.

By way of contrast, the white male manager (who is invisible against his common background) is judged as an individual, succeeding or failing *as an individual.*

ROLE STEREOTYPING. Role expectations facilitate communication and social interaction. We know where to defer and comply. We know where to be assertive and directive. We know where to find common backgrounds of experience and we rely on unspoken understandings that result from such common experience. Therefore, when people do not behave in accordance with our role expectations, when their behavior is unpredictable and our unspoken communications misunderstood, we become confused. The situation is uncomfortable. White male managers have been socialized into a world that expects lower-participant behavior from blacks and females. "Doing what comes naturally" with black and female counterparts, however, can produce awkward and uncomfortable situations. The male manager unthinkingly sees Penny—"a female"—as occupying a role that justifies his expectations of her behavior. The point we are driving at is that the often cited male resistance to female managers lies not so much in the inability of men in general to get along with women in general, as it does in the confusion and uncertainty attendant on the unlearning of traditional role expectations. This also accounts for the alleged unpopularity of female managers with other women. (See Box 16 for another explanation.)

Box 16

Sex and Power in the Office

The traditional exclusion of women from positions of authority in organizations has been well documented. Research studies suggest that the policies and attitudes of employers provides a better explanation for this observation than the qualities and attitudes of female employees. Most prominently, there is the belief that females make poor supervisors because they tend to be overcontrolling, capricious, and bureaucratic.

The research conducted by South and colleagues at once offers a structural explanation for this behavior and illustrates the difficulties presented by the use of variables such as sex or age. Since so many aspects of social life are sex patterned, it becomes almost impossible to sort out those behaviors which are sex linked in some fundamental way (in the genes) from those which are related only superficially to sex differences.

In this case the argument is that it is a structurally related lack of power

continued

that leads to the stereotypical female supervisory style. Because women are less well integrated into the management network of sponsorship and exchange, they have less access to the means to get things done, and hence, less power. Since they are thus less able to help subordinates reach their goals they also have less power over subordinates. One consequence of this is that female supervisors may try to compensate through the use of close, controlling supervisory styles and by "playing favorites," that is, breaking the rules for those who comply and rigidly adhering to the rules to punish those who do not.

The validity of these ideas was tested in a questionnaire survey of supervisors and employees at six offices of a government agency. Both male and female supervisors were included, though only female employees were used since, of a sample of almost 900, only twenty males with female supervisors could be found. Supervisory power was measured by three factors: amount of influence on their supervisors' decisions, autonomy from supervisor, and status in the organization as indicated by government service (G.S.) rating.

The major findings were these:

- There was a strong relationship between female sex and powerlessness.
- Female supervisors generally were perceived less favorably than their male counterparts by employees.
- However, when supervisory power was controlled for, all of the significant relationships between female sex and unfavorable supervisory attributes disappeared.

From these results the authors conclude that it is power rather than some female attribute that explains the observed behavior. In further discussion of their results, however, the authors point to some other possibilities. Female supervisors generally were less educated and were assigned work groups with lower-level and less challenging tasks. Still, these conditions in themselves constitute a reaffirmation of the lower organizational status assigned female supervisors. Consequently, power, or lack of it, provides the most theoretically sound explanation of the observed data.

From S. J. South et al. "Sex and Power in the Federal Bureaucracy." *Work and Occupations* 9 (1982): 233–254.

INAPPROPRIATE SOCIALIZATION. Unfortunately, role stereotyping cuts both ways. If the white male manager has expectations inappropriate for blacks and females, it is true also that blacks and females carry the burden of learning role behaviors for which their socialization in the larger society generally has been inappropriate (9, 16). In particular, both groups see few *role models*.

Why not use white male role models? There are some problems with that. There are problems of behavior to *unlearn* as well as behavior to learn. More important, the female or minority manager, *because* of female or minority status, is in a different social situation—transitional perhaps, but no less real. Black managers thus face the problem of how to appear competent and dominant despite the tendency to see them as pushy, aggressive, and loud (9). Females aspiring to managerial positions may need coaching on how to avoid continual pressures to accept more familiar roles of mother, daughter, or girlfriend (13, 16). Specifically, women may need the opportunity to observe how successful females deal with a superordinate-subordinate relationship to males.

SPONSORSHIP. As we saw in the preceding chapter, sponsorship by a superior manager can be the cornerstone of a successful career. Yet all the factors we have cited work against the chances of females and blacks finding sponsors. For one thing, sponsoring managers want their protegés to be successful and to be effective in carrying out their part of the sponsorship bargain. For another, white male managers may be unsure of how to coach someone whose career must be different in some ways from their own. Thus, the ring of visibility, role stereotyping, and inappropriate socialization is closed through the unavailability of sponsors who might help to change the situation.

Still, change *is* taking place and undoubtedly will continue. We believe that equal opportunity will inevitably be the result. In the meantime, it is important for all to understand the existence of these barriers to opportunity.

Individual and Organizational Adaptations

Organizations and individuals are adaptive systems. Through adaptation organizations resist change. So we look for adaptations that, in effect, resist the movement of women and minorities into the role of superior. In this final section we will look at some of these organizational adaptations, and then at how individuals assigned to ascribed careers can use impression management to counter their organizational situation.

TOKENISM. The dominant managerial group and the female or minority managerial candidate may reach an implicit agreement that promotion to the higher managerial and even executive ranks is possible *if* the candidate accepts the token role. Although the understanding is implicit, the role of token is clear enough. It involves the following characteristics.

1. The token is guaranteed special treatment. The token will not be allowed to fail and will not be criticized or made an example of. A direct consequence of this, of course, is that the token will also not receive useful feedback on performance. Thus, the role of token guarantees an eventual result of what it presupposes initially: lack of ability to do the job.

2. Tokens are assigned to "safe" positions. These are not positions, say, in finance, marketing, or manufacturing; they are in personnel, public relations, or whatever function the organization feels is not problematic to achieving success. Certain positions become identified as female or minority positions. They are positions in which failure is difficult to define.[4]
3. The acceptance of the role of token means that at some point your career line will be such that, having missed certain crucial kinds of experience, you are no longer qualified for higher-level responsibility. So once again the self-fulfilling prophecy comes true.

Why then would someone accept the role of token? An obvious answer is that the person did not fully understand the implicit bargain when it first was made. Yet perhaps more to the point there is *fear of failure* (17, 23). For both blacks and females there is inevitably a residue of self-doubt planted by attitudes in the larger society. Since even token positions may represent achievement greater than hoped for, the temptation exists to accept the token role. For women there are still other reasons. There is the fear that to accept the managerial role may mean to abandon the feminine role (18). Put another way, the inevitable role conflict that develops may seem too great a price. There also are rewards for playing the traditional female role within the organizational context (18). Thus, certain lower-participant roles may be highly rewarding in terms of traditional female roles; for example, combining the roles of mother, wife, and girlfriend as an executive secretary, a position where there also is opportunity to wield considerable lower-participant power.

But what of the people who wish to resist tokenism? How do they as individuals adapt to the organizational situation? The chief answer must be impression management.

IMPRESSION MANAGEMENT. The key to successful impression management is the awareness of how others' role expectations distort perceptions of behavior. The problem faced by female or minority managerial hopefuls is that of providing cues about themselves that will ease problems inherent in interaction and communication. In this regard the problem for women is different from the problem faced by blacks, but the purpose is the same. So, for example, the female must be aware when she is being placed in the mother/wife role by a male counterpart or superior. One indication of this is when the male starts unburdening himself of his personal problems in the expectation of finding emotional support (16, 18). The female must tactfully close off such conversation, perhaps with a bit of camaraderie indicating that she has similar problems.

The parallel problem for blacks is the tendency for white managers to talk about "black issues" rather than issues of the organization. As with women, the problem is that of building the impression of *person* as opposed to *black* person or *female* person.

It also will be important to demand honest feedback about performance. Asking for critical evaluations of your own work is one way of doing this.

Summary

In this chapter we have continued our discussion of the structure of opportunity. The management hierarchy, although it serves as a system of command and coordination, also represents a series of graded career opportunities that can be used to reward superior performance. In this chapter we have given particular consideration to those structural problems which lead to blocked opportunity for advancement and consequently to potential problems of motivation.

Although we have ranged over many topics, there are two ideas that are basic to understanding the problems of blocked opportunity. The first is the idea of career plateaus, and the second is the effect of the twin processes of status ascription and attribution.

Plateaus

Sooner or later every professional person in the management hierarchy hits a plateau. As the management pyramid narrows, limiting opportunities for further advancement, almost everyone must lose out in the mobility tournament and remain at the current level until retirement or perhaps a move to another organization. Yet most people have a number of potentially productive years to spend with their organization. There are several reasons for hitting the career plateau. The primary one is being unable to meet the increasingly stiff competition and being judged as not having the "right stuff" for further advancement. This judgment on the part of superior management might be based on the observation that ability or motivation is lacking. But it might also be the result of having followed an earlier career path that left out some career experience felt to be crucial to all top executives.

Another reason for reaching the plateau might be that the number of candidates for the available positions is far too great to allow most of these people conventional advancement into management; engineers are a case in point. In such situations being advanced upward may be almost a chance event; one may simply be in the right place at the right time. Others are hopelessly plateaued.

Third, individual managers may have decided that further advancement is undesirable. Perhaps their present positions offer everything to which they aspire. In consequence, opportunities for further promotion are turned down. Typically in most organizations, refusing two such opportunities signals the end to further advancement.

Finally, the individual may not be considered as an entrant into the mobility tournament in the first place. We have called such people lower participants.

Each instance poses potentially serious problems of motivation, and consequently serious problems in the development of commitment and compliance with organizational goals. That is because advancement in position and status constitutes perhaps the primary incentive available to promote superior performance and compliance. Without this incentive the management task becomes considerably more difficult.

Ascription and Attribution

Sociologists have found that females and minorities are generally ascribed lower social status in our society, and lower-status people generally are not considered suitable for advancement into management. This happens, first, because members of organizations try to explain the fact that people of lower ascribed status are seldom found in management positions. Through the mechanisms of perceptual filling-in and distortion they construct explanations for the facts that they observe. Then, as attribution theory instructs, they tend to attribute personal characteristics to females and minorities that accord with their earlier explanations. Armed with these beliefs about personality, competence, and motivation they adjust their expectations of females and minorities; that is, they expect less and consequently ask for less. Again, as the research literature shows, behavior tends to follow those expectations. Finally, the original expectation is verified in part as fact. So it is that people who are denied entry into the mobility tournament because of lower ascribed status overpopulate the lower-participant positions in organizations and tend to be perceived in ways that justify that assignment.

Things Are Changing

As we look to the future there is some good news, and some bad. First, women and minorities are cracking the barriers to admission to the ranks of management. And certainly they are obtaining the educational credentials necessary even to enter the mobility tournament. Therefore, although the ranks of middle management are still only thinly populated by women and minorities, things are changing. Second, organizations are devising new management arrangements that provide alternative opportunities for career advancement—dual ladders of management, for example. Although these arrangements sacrifice the organizational influence of traditional management, they provide potentially greater opportunities for interesting work and self-actualization. Furthermore, this comes at a time when new research suggests that an increasing number of the "new wave" of professional people prefer such opportunities.

The bad news is the baby boom generation. Soon the traditional career in management is just not going to be available to most college-educated professionals.

Notes

1. A discussion of this is found in Kanter (18). Experimental evidence for behavior becoming consonant with ascribed status, in this case experimentally induced, can be found in Cohen (6). Subjects placed in nonmobile positions started to behave as expected for the lower participant roles in which they were randomly cast.
2. We have observed this dual hierarchy directly and at length in two corporations employing large numbers of professional engineers and scientists. In each case supervisory management actively urged acceptance of the "staff management" side of the hierarchy, and promoted belief in its equality. Despite such exhortation, skepticism as to actual equality remained, though most accepted "half a loaf as better than none."
3. The following discussion is adapted from Mechanic (21). See also Blackburn (3).
4. In support of this view, Pfeffer finds that ascriptive characteristics are correlated more strongly with advancement in the organization in jobs where performance is difficult to evaluate objectively (26). This suggests that higher-level jobs in important functions employing administrative technologies will be given disproportionately to white males from higher socioeconomic backgrounds. Hall and Hall support this view in finding that female managers are given performance ratings equal to males when objective performance data are available (14).

References

1. ACKER, J., and D. R. VAN HOUTEN. "Differential Recruitment and Control: the Sex Structuring of Organizations." *Administrative Science Quarterly* 19 (1974): 152–163.
2. BARCLAY, L. "Social Learning Theory: A Framework for Discrimination Research." *The Academy of Management Review* 7 (October 1982): 547–594.
3. BLACKBURN, R. "Lower Participant Power: Toward a Conceptual Integration." *The Academy of Management Review* 6 (January 1981): 127–132.
4. BRICKMAN, P., and D. T. CAMPBELL. "Hedonic Relativism and Planning the Good Society." In *Adaptation-Level Theory,* edited by M. H. Appley. New York: Academic Press, 1971. Pp. 287–302.
5. CLARK, B. "The 'Cooling-out' Function in Higher Education." *American Journal of Sociology* 65 (1960): 569–576.
6. COHEN, A. R. "Upward Communication in Experimentally Created Hierarchies." *Human Relations* 11 (1958): 41–53.
7. ETZIONI, A. *A Comparative Analysis of Complex Organizations.* Glencoe, Ill.: Free Press (1961).

8. FERENCE, T. P., J. A. F. STONER, and E. K. WARREN. "Managing the Career Plateau." *Academy of Management Review* 2 (1977): 602–612.
9. FERNANDEZ, J. P. *Black Managers in White Corporations.* New York: Wiley, 1975.
10. FRIEDMAN, T. "The Baby Boom Comes of Age." *New York Times,* January 10, 1982: Section 12, p. 18.
11. GOFFMAN, E. "On Cooling the Mark Out: Some Aspects of Adaptation to Failure." *Psychiatry* 15 (1952): 451–463.
12. GOLDNER, F. H. "Demotion in Industrial Management." *American Sociological Review* 30 (1965): 714–724.
13. GOLDNER, F. H., and R. R. RITTI. "Professionalization as Career Immobility," *American Journal of Sociology* 72 (1967): 489–502.
14. HALL, F. S., and D. T. HALL. "Effects of Job Incumbents' Race and Sex on Evaluations of Managerial Performance." *Academy of Management Journal* 19 (1976): 476–481.
15. HARRAGAN, B. L. *Games Mother Never Taught You: Corporate Gamesmanship for Women.* New York: Rawson Associates, 1977.
16. HENNIG, M., and A. JARDIN. *The Managerial Woman.* Garden City, N.Y.: Doubleday Anchor, 1977.
17. HORNER, M. "Toward Understanding Achievement Related Conflicts in Women." *Journal of Social Issues* 28 (1972): 157–175.
18. KANTER, R. M. *Men and Women of the Corporation.* New York: Basic Books, 1977.
19. ———. "Where You Stand in the Power Play." *Working Woman* 1977: 26ff.
20. LIVINGSTON, J. S. "Pygmalion in Management." *Harvard Business Review* 47 (1969): 81–89.
21. MECHANIC, D. "Sources of Power of Lower Participants in Complex Organizations." *Administrative Science Quarterly* 7 (1962): 349–364.
22. NIEVA, V., and B. GUTEK. "Sex Effects on Evaluation." *The Academy of Management Review* 5 (April 1980): 267–276.
23. O'LEARY, V. E. "Some Attitudinal Barriers to Occupational Aspirations in Women." *Psychological Bulletin* 81 (1974): 809–826.
24. OSBORN, R. N., and W. M. VICARS. "Sex Stereotypes: An Artifact in Leader Behavior and Subordinate Satisfaction Analysis." *Academy of Management Journal* 19 (1976): 439–449.
25. PETER, L., and R. HULL. *The Peter Principle.* New York: Morrow, 1969.
26. PFEFFER, J. "Toward an Examination of Stratification in Organizations." *Administrative Science Quarterly* 22 (1977): 553–567.
27. RITTI, R. R. "Work Goals of Scientists and Engineers." *Industrial Relations* 7 (1968): 118–131.
28. ———. *The Engineer in the Industrial Corporation.* New York: Columbia University Press, 1971.
29. RITTI, R. R., and F. H. GOLDNER. "Professional Pluralism in an Industrial Organization." *Management Science* 16 (1969): B233–246.

30. ROSENFELD, R. A. "Women's Occupational Careers: Individual and Structural Explanations." *Sociology of Work and Occupations* 6 (August 1979): 283–311.
31. SCHEFF, T. J. "Control Over Policy by Attendants in a Mental Hospital." *Journal of Health and Human Behavior* 2 (1961): 93–105.
32. SOUTH, S., C. BONJEAN, J. CORDER, and S. MARKHAM. "Sex and Power in the Federal Bureaucracy: A Comparative Analysis of Male and Female Supervisors." *Work and Occupations* 9 (May 1982): 233–254.
33. STRAUSS, G. "Tactics of Lateral Relationship: the Purchasing Agent." *Administrative Science Quarterly* 7 (1962): 161–186.
34. THOMPSON, V. *Modern Organization.* New York: Knopf, 1961.
35. WEST, C. "Why Can't a Woman Be More Like a Man? An Interactional Note on Organizational Game-Playing for Managerial Women." *Work and Occupations* 9 (February 1982): 5–29.
36. WRIGHTSMAN, L. S. *Social Psychology,* 2nd ed. Belmont, Calif.: Wadsworth, 1977.

Discussion Questions

1. In this chapter we have used the concept of ascribed status. How is ascribed status different from earned status? Can you think of some people with especially high ascribed status? In what kinds of jobs do you think this ascribed status will foster career success?
2. Attribution theory tells us that observers are more likely to attribute the actions of others to personal characteristics rather than to the situation, and that this is especially true in situations of failure. Why is this idea especially important for understanding the motivational effect on people whose careers are plateaued?
3. In a much publicized experiment in social psychology, college students were randomly assigned to act out the roles of inmate and guard in a mock prison situation. The experimenter, Philip Zimbardo had to terminate the experiment after one week because, "What we saw was frightening. It was no longer apparent to most . . . where reality ended and their roles began." What concepts have we developed concerning ascription, attribution, expectation, explanation, and behavior in this chapter that might account for this situation?
4. We have briefly described an organizational arrangement whereby an alternative or parallel management hierarchy is provided for nonsupervisory professionals as a solution to the "pyramidal squeeze" in the structure of opportunity. The essential difference between the supervisory and professional hierarchies is that the supervisory one has authority whereas the professional does not. In your own words, what is the function of such a dual ladder of advancement? Under what conditions would you expect it to be effective in maintaining motivation? When would you expect it not to be?
5. We quoted one writer as saying "Organizations . . . are continuously at the mercy of their lower participants" (p. 338). Having read this chapter, what do you think he means? What are the key sources of power of lower participants?

6. Until quite recently women and minority members have been excluded systematically from the top management (or any level, for that matter) of business corporations. This practice was questioned by few people. How do you think "corporate citizens" explained this situation to themselves? Do you think they believed such a situation to be justified? Why?
7. Consider three types of organization: The Company, a large state department of public welfare, and the Catholic Church. Each is pressed to promote equal opportunity for females. Using what you know about the basis of authority, the technology, and the environment of each, predict the response in each case.
8. What is the function of organizational socialization in contributing to the persistence of unequal opportunity for females and minorities in organizations? How might you go about changing things if you were responsible for an equal opportunity program?

Section Three
Modifying Personal Goals: The Interaction System

So far we have analyzed the underlying structure of social organizations, the motivation system, and the mobility system. We have argued that each limits and guides organizational behavior. The social structure shapes behavior into regular patterns, making it more predictable. The motivation system directs behavior toward organizationally sanctioned ends. And the mobility system provides a structure of opportunity and of continued motivation for those whose careers may have peaked.

In our analysis of the social organization we distinguished two underlying sources of structure:

1. The formal organization: designated positions and the relationships among these positions, together with the rights and duties attendant to those positions that constitute the structure of formal authority.
2. Patterns of social behavior: the structure of social expectations appropriate for given positions and for the organization as a whole. These patterns are learned and acted out through the processes of socialization and impression management.

Now we will examine the first concrete stage of human organization—the human group. The basic concern here is the interaction of individuals in a group. Therefore, we call this building block of the organizational system the interaction system; it is illustrated in Figure III.1.

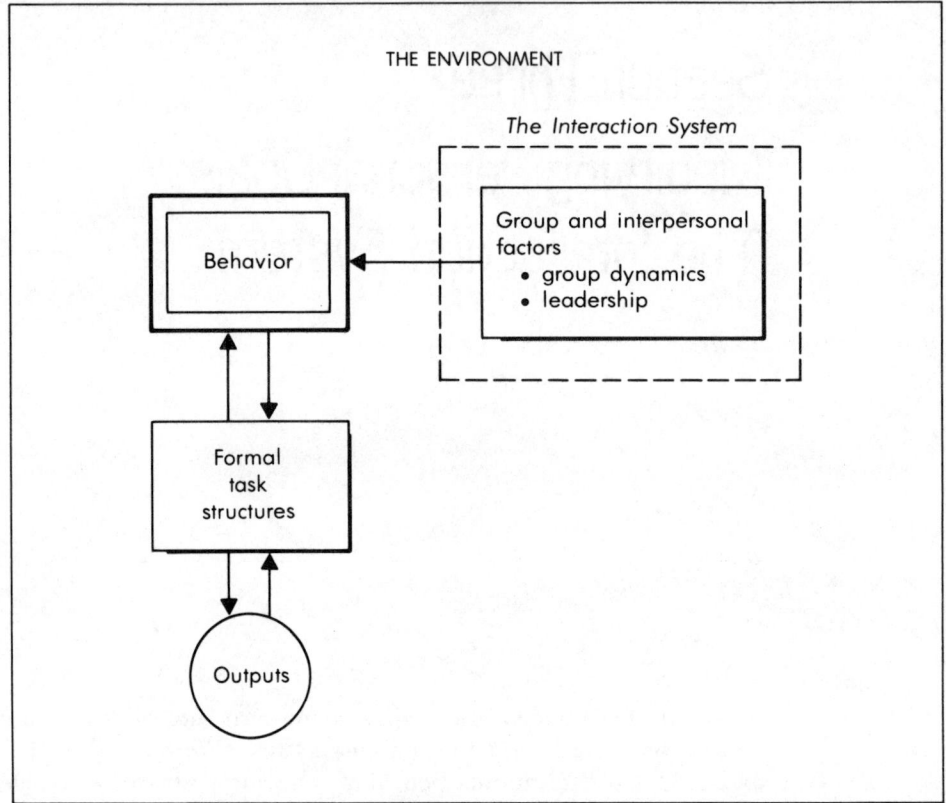

FIGURE III.1 Modifying Personal Goals: Individuals in Groups—The Interaction System

Groups are more than just simple collectivities of individuals. They are the standard bearers for organizational norms generally, and for group norms in particular.

Groups exhibit cohesiveness, a "we" feeling and a resistance to being broken apart. Since individuals attach importance to group membership, they are motivated to remain in the group and abide by its norms. Thus, groups are a key factor in modifying individual behavior.

Historically, work groups have been regarded as essential to understanding behavior in organizations. Indeed, much of the work done in organizational development and organizational change uses the primary work group as the tool for such change. One reason for this is the power of the group to facilitate modifying individual goals.

Leadership is another important characteristic of groups. Successful leaders make the achievement of both individual and group goals easier. Evidence of successful leadership, like evidence of authority, is demonstrated through behavior—through group members accepting the influence of the leader. This influence is rooted in a number of factors: the characteristics of successful leaders, their behavior, the situation in which they operate.

In this section of the text, then, we will discuss how individual behavior is modified by the existence of groups in organizations. Certainly not all of what we see in the regularities of organizational behavior can be explained by what we have analyzed already. So this is our task for Section Three: to examine the organization in action in order to build an understanding of individual interaction in groups and to see how such group process modifies individual behavior in support of, or perhaps in opposition to, forces in the systems structure of the organization.

Chapter 13
Groups and Their Dynamics

In Unity, Strength

As the two-engined commuter droned its way to Pawtucket, Stanley's thoughts drifted back over the past two years and how eventful they had been. How different New York had been from Pawtucket.

Ted Shelby had been in Pawtucket, too. Why, hardly more than a year ago Stanley had been walking down the mill floor deep in discussion with Ted. Ted had been trying to explain to Stanley how difficult it was to get "the workers" to produce at some reasonable percentage of standard, that is, the standard production rate determined by the industrial engineers.

"It's a difficult thing to put your finger on personnel-wise," Ted had said in his puzzled, concerned tone, "but it just seems they do as little as they can if we don't keep checking on them. Why, you'd think The Company owed them a paycheck instead of the other way around." Then, philosophically, "I suppose that's why they're where they are and we're where we are."

That had ended the conversation, and Stanley had gone off to continue his task of checking asset numbers on the mill equipment. Stanley remembered only one good feature of that job—he had gotten to know an awful lot of people at Pawtucket, managers and millhands both. Of the two groups the millhands were the more interesting. They came from different worlds and were headed in even more different directions. In the beginning their relationship had been a little awkward, but when they found out he wasn't connected with the industrial engineers, and that, in fact, he had little sympathy with that function, some warm friendships developed. Some of the millhands saw Stanley's presence as an opportunity to explain their situation to a member of "management."

Take the instance of the flat shear. That was one of Ted's failures. The flat shear was running about 60 percent of standard—far too low. Ted's way of learning what was going on was to put someone with a stopwatch on the job to uncover where the cheating was taking place. Stanley's approach was different.

"Hi, Jimmy. How's it going?"

"Oh, pretty good, Stan. Another day, another dollar, like they say."

"Say, Jimmy, Ted's been telling me there's been some trouble with this machine. Seems to break down a lot. I don't know an awful lot about it but . . . well, Mr. Franklyn told me to keep my eyes

362

open to figure out new ways of doing things around here, so I guess. . . ."

"You ain't got a union card so you're not supposed to work this machine. But here, I think I can teach you something pretty quick." With that, Jimmy got a new piece of flat sheet steel hooked onto the magnetic crane, put a pair of gloves on Stanley, and showed him what to do. Now, it wasn't so much that Stanley wasn't strong enough (which he wasn't) as it was that you really had to know what you were doing (which he didn't). So after a few awkward passes at the shear, and after coming uncomfortably close to being dismembered, Stanley's learning experience was terminated.

"Geez, that thing's heavier than it looks."

"Naw, it ain't so bad after you get the hang of it, but you do get pretty tired. So we figure if the machine breaks down every now and then, we get to rest for a while."

"Well, I can certainly see why," said Stanley earnestly. "I'm not sure I could do it at all. But listen, why do it this way? I mean, wouldn't they understand if you told them? I mean, you could get the standard set again."

The look that Jimmy gave Stanley was one of pure astonishment. Then he chuckled.

"Yeah, sure they would. Ah, you tell 'em for us, will you, Stan? That'd help us. Yeah, that'd help us a lot."

"O.K., I see your point. You're sure that The Company is out to get whatever it can from you, and so for your part you're out to get away with whatever you can from them."

"But why does it have to be that way? It seems to me that the union goes out of its way to make trouble for The Company. Every little job change. Why, you guys won't even switch to a lower rated job at the same pay, even just for an afternoon." Stanley noticed that Jimmy was starting to eye him suspiciously. "O.K., O.K., I'm not trying to blame anybody. It's just that I don't understand. Why make everything so hard? I mean, Ted's to blame too, I know that. Don't get me wrong. He's always out there checking up on everyone trying to get a little more out of you guys."

Jimmy's look softened. "Stan, I know you're O.K., but you just don't understand. I don't know how you could. Look, how long you gonna be with us—another year, maybe?"

Stanley shrugged. He didn't know.

"Yeah, maybe a year. You'll move on to something better. That's the way they do it around here with you guys.

"But me and the other guys, where're we going to go? Maybe only back to the graveyard shift if things get tough. About all we look for is not to get screwed too bad.

"Now don't look that way. You don't know. All you can try to do is to keep from busting your back too bad. That's where the other guys help, and the union. You know there's someone backing you, standing up for you. That's a good feeling. Anyway, we just try to do to them (the industrial engineers) what they're doing to us. That's the way it is. We give 'em a fair day's work, but they're always trying to get more. That's why we got to stick together."

With that the lunch whistle blew and Jimmy went over by the forge to join the others just opening their lunch boxes.

Jimmy had been right. In fact, Stanley had stayed at Pawtucket for less than a year before going to New York to take on a new job. But how different it had been! The new job in New York had been with the production systems group. The Company had decided to expand the group with a number of young people who would be charged with the responsibility of bringing all the plants up to date on current practice in manufacturing systems. It seemed like a big order. Stanley had been a bit afraid that it might be too much for him. In fact, he never did understand why he had been chosen.

Kerry Drake was heading the group at the time, and he made a deep impression on Stanley. Stanley never forgot that first day with Kerry.

"I guess you all know why you are here," Kerry began. "Each of you was chosen personally by your plant manager because he thought you were the best one to help The Company bring this thing off. We've got a mighty important responsibility here, I want to make sure you know that. There's no room here for people who don't want to give a little more than their share. So if any of you have second thoughts about this, now's the time to say so. I described this assignment to the plants as a temporary one, so there won't be any problem for you if you decide you want to go back. Think about it."

Now Kerry's tone changed a bit. Just a shading of pride mellowed his matter-of-fact delivery.

"I expect to be very proud of you in the next few years. Each of you is the best this Company's got to offer, so we very much expect that within the next five years each of you will be heading up your own shop at one of our plants, running the show you're helping to set up here." This really brought a thrill of excitement to the group. Naturally, they had all hoped to become Company managers some day. But so soon! And with such an important responsibility!

At that point, Kerry probably could have asked any one of them to do anything Kerry wished. (And it wouldn't be too long before he did.) But just then, within each of those young technicians stirred the beginnings of a pride and loyalty that would not soon die. As the days passed it became evident that when you worked for Kerry you ate, slept, inhaled and exhaled *work*. Even play was centered about work. Almost every evening there was something that had to be done—now. These evenings usually concluded with a gathering for a post mortem at a local pub. Saturday work was taken for granted. But it wasn't so bad. Usually they'd knock off about 1:30 or 2 for a long lunch and beer at the local hofbrau. And, of course, the inevitable shop talk.

The result was that each became convinced that nothing was more important than what he was doing, and that probably no one else was quite so capable of doing it as well. This feeling was reinforced by Kerry in a number of ways. First, it hadn't been more than three or four weeks before one of their number was "sent home." The reasons weren't altogether clear, but for one thing this one hadn't shown the fondness for evening and weekend work that the others had. That was quite noticeable. Then one day Kerry had found an error in a job the man was about to send off. It wasn't a big thing, an error of omission, of carelessness.

But few ever forgot that day. Kerry was furious. He broke every rule of the managerial book, "reaming out" the offender tactlessly and mercilessly in front of all. Yet the message was clear.

"You are the best. And the best don't make careless errors. No, no one is perfect, and from time to time we're going to make errors of judgment, errors of commission. But *don't* let me ever catch you in a mistake resulting from lack of effort. If I do, that's the last mistake you'll ever make for me."

The group was unhappy with the way the matter had been handled. Kerry had no right to do it that way. But then, their work was terribly important and the schedule was tight. So, perhaps oddly, their solidarity was greater than ever.

Another thing, no task was too small or insignificant for Kerry's personal attention. And he drummed this into the group. Many of those evenings and weekends were spent in nothing more glamorous than packaging drawings and specifications to be sent to new installations. Kerry's motto was: If you want it done right, do it yourself. Kerry often lectured the group on the necessity of personally checking the work of others in The Company. These people didn't have the same dedication as the group did, and couldn't be counted on to turn out the kind of job the group expected. Yes, there was a kind of *noblesse oblige* that fell on the shoulders of the elect.

Our vignette presents two instances of *cohesiveness*, its *origins* and its *consequences*. In the opening sequence Stanley comes to understand the strength of the solidarity of the millhands uniting against the outside threat of the industrial engineers. He also sees the function of the union in fostering group solidarity. In the second sequence a highly cohesive group forms, with Stanley as a member. The cohesiveness this time, however, is built on an entirely different basis. Group members anticipate exceptional rewards from their participation, and the manager of the group has done a number of things to create group solidarity.

The theme in each of these quite different instances is that the group is *instrumental* in achieving important individual goals for group members and that cohesiveness develops together with group norms and pressure for uniformity. The instrumentality concept, we will see, is the unifying theme of this chapter. But first, what is a group?

What Is a Group?

A group is a collection of people who are bound together in some way. The group must have value for its membership. Without value a group has less power to influence individual behavior. Groups also have a normative structure; that is, members share expectations about acceptable behavior. Thus, people behave according to the broader social context of an organization, as well as according to the group's expectations about role behavior within and outside of the group (1, 40, 64). Finally, members of the group see themselves as part of the group, and those not in it view members similarly (19).

If these conditions are met, we expect individual members to be substantially affected by what others in the group say, think, and do. As individuals try to remain members in good standing, they must be sensitive to the consequences of their behavior for such membership. They might, therefore, behave differently than they would otherwise. This is where the power of the group lies in influencing behavior.

How Groups Get Started

Figure 13.1 displays the causes of group formation. Foremost is proximity. In organizations people are often placed together randomly. Being close is one big reason why people first link up with each other (71, 86). For example, a classic study on the effect of physical proximity on group formation suggested that friendship patterns are closely related to housing locations. People who live near each other, in adjacent apartments as an example, tend to form groups more often than people in the same housing project but in more distant locations. Further, this same study showed that the people who live near the common pathways interact more frequently with others and have a wider circle of friendships (27, 86).

The study concluded that the more people interact, the more likely they are to become friends; and the more people interact within a group, the more each is likely to be included as a group member. And interactions are determined

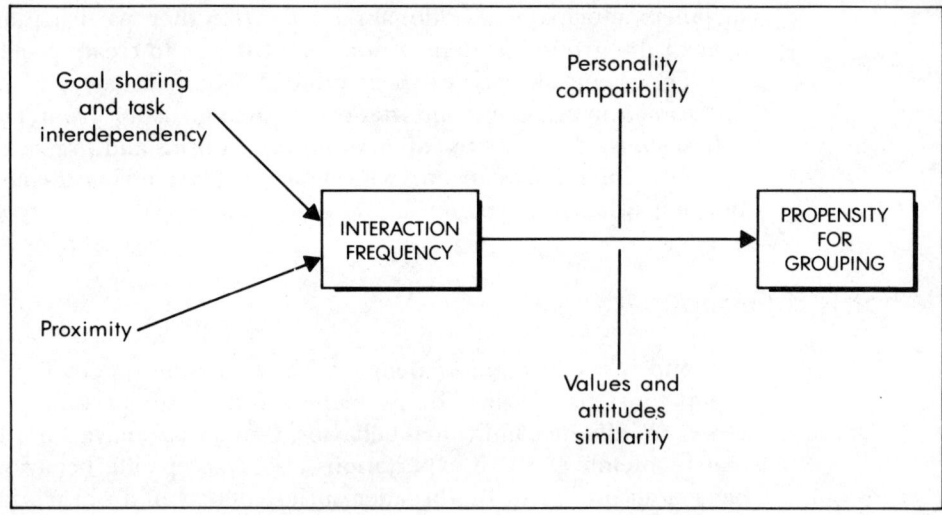

FIGURE 13.1 Causes of Group Formation

in large measure by proximity. These relationships, of course, are subject to the great variety of interpersonal needs that may exist, as well as to the rewarding qualities of the interaction itself (42).

A second condition for forming friendships is the sharing of goals and interdependency for reaching those goals (2, 73). People who share tasks or who depend on others to finish a task tend to form a group. And people have a propensity to interact when the task needs manifest themselves. In short, they may need each other to operate well in a group environment which promotes interaction. Jimmy Szekely could not have restricted productivity without others doing the same and without the support and understanding of the union.

Physical closeness and common task interests, then, are the two major reasons that people get together to form "rudimentary work groups." Each promotes interaction. Interaction then seems to be the major lead variable associated with group formation. But interaction is not the whole story, for often people interact without ever meeting the conditions of our definition of group. Two other factors seem necessary before interacting people become a group as we have defined it. One is attitude and value similarity. That is, people with similar attitudes and values tend to form a group once they have identified each other. Of course, they have to be in contact for such identification to occur. And people who share common goals often develop attitudes and value similarity (38, 106).

It is well known that people who share important values and attitudes tend to become friends. Perhaps the most detailed study of this fact involved a student housing situation where strangers were brought together and observed over two years. At the beginning each student was tested for attitudes, values, and personality. After the two years, research showed that people who had similar values were indeed attracted to one another more than those who did not share values. Also, the importance of attitude similarity for friendship was greater after acquaintanceship developed than at the initial stages of interaction. That is, the more people who shared attitudes interacted, the more they liked each other and the more they grouped (63).

The second facilitating factor is personality compatibility. It seems as though compatible personalities work more effectively together than incompatible ones and that the sense of effectiveness is positively reinforcing (12, 60, 67). Hence, compatible people will want to interact with each other whereas incompatible people will not (14).

To summarize, interaction is necessary for groups to form, and lots of interaction increases that probability. Being physically proximate and psychologically compatible increases the propensity for interaction. Finally, people who need each other by reason of task interdependence are also likely to interact frequently.

What happens to transform loosely bound groups into tightly knit relationships that exert a unique power over the behavior of their members? In order to answer this question, we must understand how groups develop beyond the rudimentary work group (46).

Stages of Group Development

Several stages of group development have been identified (79, 93).[1] These stages, are depicted in Figure 13.2. First, group members try to discover the behavior that is acceptable to other group members, test out the consequences of their own behavior, and observe the rest of the group membership, anticipating how they will interrelate. Each individual is trying to find guidelines and support. People tend to both ask for and provide orientation to others in the process of defining appropriate behavioral boundaries. They also test each other. In other words, people are *forming* bona fide groups (51).

Because people feel uncertain about their role in this stage of group development, they are anxious. A common goal, therefore, is to reduce anxiety. Hostility, which in this case is most likely a product of anxiety, may also be found. It is often directed at two targets: those who try to assume leadership and those who are inactive or disassociated members of the group. The first are targets because others resent those who seek positions of power; the second, because passivity is perceived as counterproductive (32). Interaction tends to be unpredictable and there is frequent in-fighting. People are dealing with problems of control involving struggle or, at least, an attempt to establish an individual's place in the group hierarchy (30).

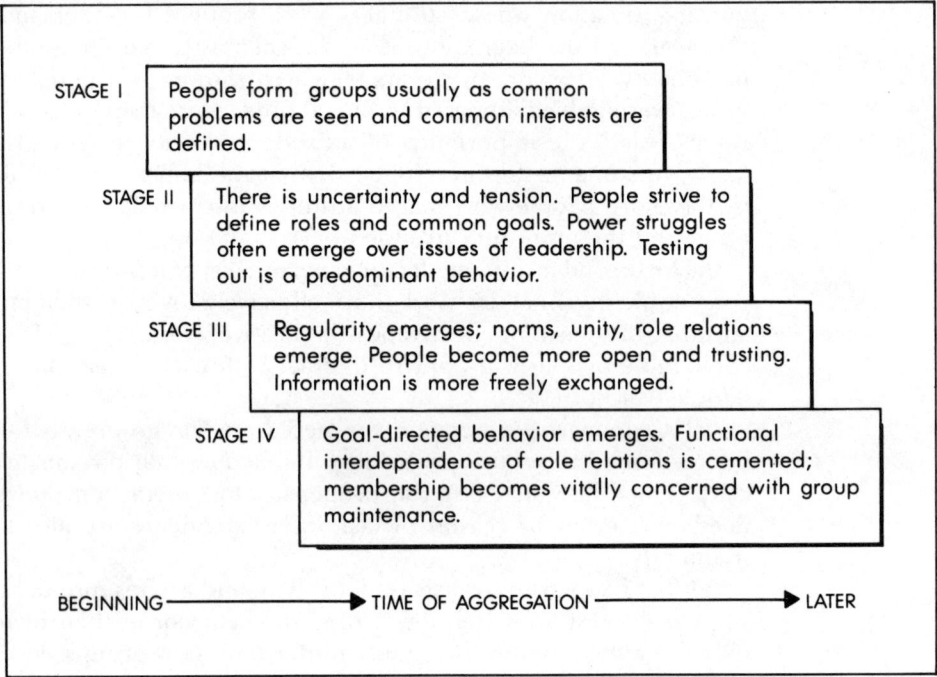

FIGURE 13.2 Stages of Group Development

Because conflict is unsettling, there is a strong tendency to move to some kind of resolution. Unity develops both in resolving social problems and in developing procedures for pursuing the goals of the group. Group members become concerned about developing and maintaining mutually satisfying interpersonal relationships. Interlocking networks of friendships tend to develop and a sense of solidarity emerges (69). During this stage, people become more task oriented. They exchange information, ask for and offer opinions, and tend to evaluate these opinions in terms of their usefulness in pursuing group goals. And group norms and role definitions emerge.

During the next stage individuals interact functionally to maintain and enhance task activities and reach group goals with a minimum of interpersonal conflict. The focus is on constructive action, and individual roles in the group structure are defined (71, 73).

As a few researchers have pointed out, groups actually develop quite unevenly. During later stages, when there is maximum group unity and task activity, people feel more secure about criticizing individuals and the group in general. That may be disruptive, and can erode the group's solidarity and its effectiveness (6, 87). These rough spots, however, are usually overcome, and groups then move ahead to get the job done. Figure 13.2 shows that although groups tend to go through stages of development, the stages overlap and hence are not mutually exclusive.

Group Structure and Role Behavior

As the group goes through the stages of development, certain structures emerge. Members begin to get a realistic assessment of what each person can do individually and how each fits into the group effort. People begin to take roles according to the contribution they make in the group (51). Consequently, leadership and "followership" roles and patterns are established. People typically assume two general types of roles: a task role and a social maintenance role (4), shown in Figure 13.3. In the task role one performs activities that are primarily goal related. For example, in every group some people constantly keep the group on track, or try to. The task leader will emerge from these task-oriented people.

The social leaders will emerge from those whose interpersonal skills help others feel good about being a member of the group. To do this these social

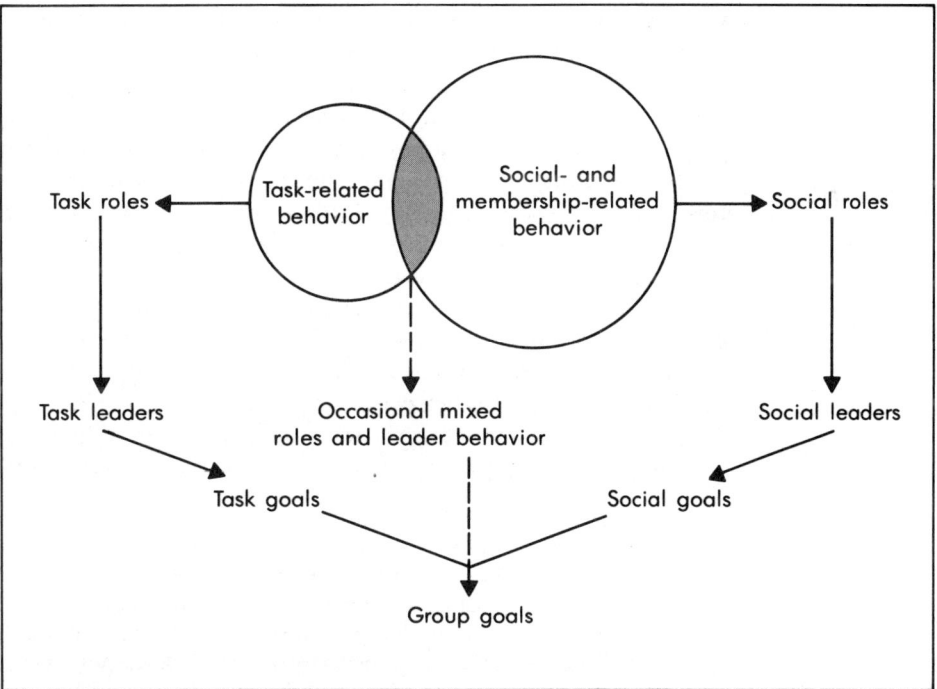

FIGURE 13.3 Task and Social Role Emergence

leaders mediate differences, make sure everyone has a say, resolve interpersonal conflicts, enforce equity considerations, and so on. Research indicates that the task leaders and the social leaders are rarely the same individuals (4). Figure 13.3 shows the two roles and how the behavior exhibited for each of the roles has only a small overlap.

Two separate leaders emerge because the areas of concern are different. Task behavior involves issues of power and competency (5). If group members are not contributing to the goals of the group, those concerned with goal accomplishment may become impatient to bring the others in line. At this point those who are more socially oriented will try to smooth over interpersonal conflict so the group can continue to function.

Thus, the group structure, in terms of emerging leadership, the roles that individuals are likely to assume, and the patterns of interrelationships, is a function of the developmental processes a group must go through as it matures into a fully functioning social entity.

Importance of Group Structure

Group structure is important in determining the roles we play (48). The roles we assume in a group are, in turn, important in determining our subsequent attitudes and behavior. One study describes the attitude change of workers who are promoted to foremen and elected union stewards (50). Each group perceived management and the union in a similar way before promotion. However, after promotion, those moving into management felt far more favorably toward management and less so toward unions, and those who moved into stewardship positions demonstrated a reverse pattern. If these groups moved back into the ranks of the workers, however, both would revert to their original attitudes. Although the study has major design flaws it does show that role taking has an important influence on attitudes.

Another study describes an experiment that vividly illustrates the effect of role assumption on behavior (107). The purpose of the study was to determine the effects of prison social order on the behavior of prisoners and guards. The investigators created a mock prison with cells and bars. The subjects were normal college students, half of whom were assigned randomly to be prisoners, and the other half to be guards. Each was to carry out the prescribed role. The author states:

> We witnessed a sample of normal, healthy American college students fractionate into a group of prison guards who seemed to derive pleasure from insulting, threatening, humiliating, and dehumanizing their peers—those who by chance selection had been assigned to the prisoner role. The typical prisoner syndrome was one of passivity, dependency, depression, helplessness, and self-depreciation. As the prisoners became resigned to their treatment over time, many acted in ways

to justify their fate in the hands of the guards—adopting attitudes and behaviors which helped to sanction their victimization. Most dramatic and distressing to us was the observation of the ease with which sadistic behavior could be elicited in individuals who were not the sadistic types. (107: 38)

A major determinant of behavior, then, is the role or roles any given individual assumes in the group. Remember, though, that roles are played out in a normative context; this is another constraint and, consequently, a determinant of behavior (85, 98).

Let us see what happens if group structure is not maintained. Schein, Schneier, and Barker describe such a situation in a book entitled *Coercive Persuasion* (78). It concerns the Korean War and Chinese prisoner-of-war camps in which American soldiers were interred. Schein et al. describe the systematic destruction of the formal-informal group structure that, in the end, resulted in widespread mutual distrust among the American prisoners and the necessity for each man to withdraw increasingly into his own shell.

The Chinese first destroyed the formal authority structure of each group by segregating all officers and noncommissioned officers, thereby eliminating the leadership. Squads were then formed and commanded by prisoners, but the appointed leaders were the lowest-ranking enlisted men or those who were willing to cooperate with the Chinese. The leadership structure of the group, therefore, was destroyed, and if by chance the newly appointed leader emerged as fairly strong, he was quickly removed and replaced by a weaker person.

The Chinese then destroyed the informal social structure of the group. Any form of organized activity was prohibited unless it was sponsored by the Chinese themselves. No emerging leaders were allowed to remain long within the group. Extensive use of spies and informers made the POWs suspect any kind of conversation with their fellows. And the Chinese constantly passed information into the group suggesting that group members were informers and collaborators. In this way mutual mistrust was created. The consequence of all these actions was to undermine the group as a group. What remained was simply an aggregation of individuals who had no mutual bonds except those of mistrust, and who could not rely on each other for support or for the development of a normative structure that would help them resist various Chinese attempts at brainwashing.

The situation resulted in collaborative behavior not motivated by disloyalty or opportunism, but rather by the will to survive. The Chinese knew that the absence of group structure and the consequent normlessness would make controlling the POWs easier. Had groups been allowed to form and develop normative supports, with an internal structure to reinforce those norms, POW behavior would have been much different (78).

Group structures also may affect performance by the way the group is organized to get a job done. An example is given in Box 17.

> **Box 17**
>
> ## The Leader-Group Match: Does It Make a Difference?
>
> O'Brien and Kabanoff designed a study to see whether agreement between leadership style and group structure might affect group performance (24, 65). The first type of leader wanted to control the structure and did not necessarily enjoy participating in group activities. The second type had a low need for control and a high need for participation. Each group was assigned to a situation where control possibilities were high and participation opportunities low, or the opposite. High control and low participation meant that only the leader had the information necessary to complete the task. Here, the leader was instructed to allocate tasks and assign responsibilities and avoid two-way participation. Each person was to complete part of the task and pass it on to another group member. In the low-control, high-participation task all members received task information and the leader was instructed to involve the group in completing the task.
>
> The researchers' basic hypothesis was that where the group structure and the leader's characteristics were similar (e.g., a low control–high participation leader with a high-participation group structure) there would be higher performance (68). The hypothesis was tested using a 2 × 2 factorial design, which enables the experimenters to measure the effects of each independent variable separately and in interaction. In this case the only variable that had an effect was *group structure*. The high-structure group produced better results in every case.
>
> The O'Brien-Kabanoff research article reports other research findings in support of their own. They conclude that in a high-structure situation it is easier to allocate tasks according to competence and to need. Group structure, then, is important to people; norms are transmitted through it, leaders develop, and tasks get done.
>
> O'Brien, G. E., and B. Kabanoff. "The Effects of Leadership Style and Group Structure upon Small Group Productivity: A Test of a Discrepancy Theory of Leader Effectiveness." *Australian Journal of Psychology* 33 (1981): 152–168.

Group Norms: A Force Toward Behavioral Regularities

Once groups are developed enough to begin focusing on a task, certain regularities in their patterns of interaction begin to emerge (61). These regularities in member behavior are a product of both role expectations and group norms. We talked about norms before. Recall that they are group-defined rules of conduct, developed through interaction among the members that produces a consensus as to behavior and attitudes. A range of acceptable deviations from these norms is also established. If behavior or attitudes are central to group goals, little deviation is permitted (20). If the issue is not important, or the deviation does not threaten group integrity, greater deviation is permitted (16, 29, 35). But how do norms develop?

A classic experiment describing the process of norm formation was conducted by Muzafir Sherif in 1948. Sherif brought people into a darkened room and flashed a point of light against the wall. A phenomenon occurs in such a situation that makes the light appear to move when it is actually stationary. This phenomenon is called the *autokinetic effect*. Each individual in the darkened room was asked to give the number of inches and the direction that they thought the light moved. These perceptions differed considerably, sometimes by as much as a foot—each individual had developed his or her own standard. When the people were brought together, however, these standards changed because of the influence of the others. That is, estimates of how the light moved began to converge. Since the participants had no real basis for judging the amount of movement, they apparently looked to each other for guidance. Ultimately, after a series of trials, the range of perceived movement had narrowed considerably. That agreed-on range was the norm. Once the norm was established, individuals tested by themselves most often responded within the narrow range. When asked, however, participants rarely acknowledged they had been influenced by others. This is usual with norm development; as people begin to internalize the norm, they govern their behavior accordingly. Also, once established, the norm holds as long as the group is intact (22, 27, 82).

Norm development is closely associated with group development (35, 36, 37). At their outset groups have no norms. Members are uncertain how to behave within the group context though they bring individual standards of behavior to the group. However, people may set aside some of these standards as they look to others in the group for direction. Norm development probably starts at this point. Group members feel uncomfortable with the ambiguity of normlessness, and use the information they can get from others in the group to begin to redefine the appropriate behavior. As they interact, they provide information, judge behavior, and develop goals or group purpose—and the norms begin to take shape. Gradually they emerge as standards of behavior against which members are judged (77). Most significantly, those who are accepted by the rest of the group usually conform to the general norms of the group, as well as to the specific norms that pertain to the role or roles they assume in the group (81).

To summarize, norms are central to the behavior of groups and their members. The development of norms is a function of the development of the group itself, the values the membership brings to the group, the goals or purposes of the group, and the values of the larger context within which the group exists. Norms almost always develop in groups and are enforced by the group membership; this is why we can see behavioral regularities among group members. Norms are the basis for uniform behavior, and as such play an important part in organizational behavior.

Conformity to group norms can generally be predicted according to the importance the group has for its individual members. This phenomenon is known as group cohesion.

Group Cohesion: A Force Toward Behavioral Uniformity

To this point we have argued that groups form and develop according to certain predictable causes and patterns; that the consequent role and normative structure have important meanings for individual behavior, primarily because the group itself provides value for its membership; and that the value is related to the group's utility for the membership. Figure 13.4 depicts the process and will serve to guide the next sections of our discussion. We now address the concept of group value—we call it *cohesion*—and some of its major causes.

Group Cohesion Defined

The influence people have over others is related to the attractiveness of those others. This attractiveness reflects the rewards or reinforcing properties that individuals have for each other—their mutual instrumentality (42, 90). Cartwright states:

> Although different theorists attribute somewhat different conceptual properties to the term, most agree that group cohesiveness refers to the degree to which the members of a group desire to remain in the group. Thus, the members of the highly cohesive group in contrast to one with a low level of cohesiveness are more concerned with their membership, and are therefore more strongly motivated to contribute to the group's welfare, to advance its objectives, and to participate in its activities. Cohesiveness contributes to a group's potency and vitality; it increases the significance of membership for those who belong to the group. (13: 91)

Cohesiveness, or cohesion, refers to the tightness of the group; it involves the total forces acting on members to remain in the group compared to those directing people away from the group (18, 27). Group cohesion can be defined, then, in terms of both the positive rewards you derive from being in the group and the expectancy that your outcomes would be lower if you did not belong to the group. The definition proposed by Cartwright is mostly satisfactory. He states, "Group cohesiveness is the resultant of all forces acting on members to remain in a group; component forces arise from (a) attractiveness of the group, and (b) attractiveness of alternative memberships" (13: 91). We would

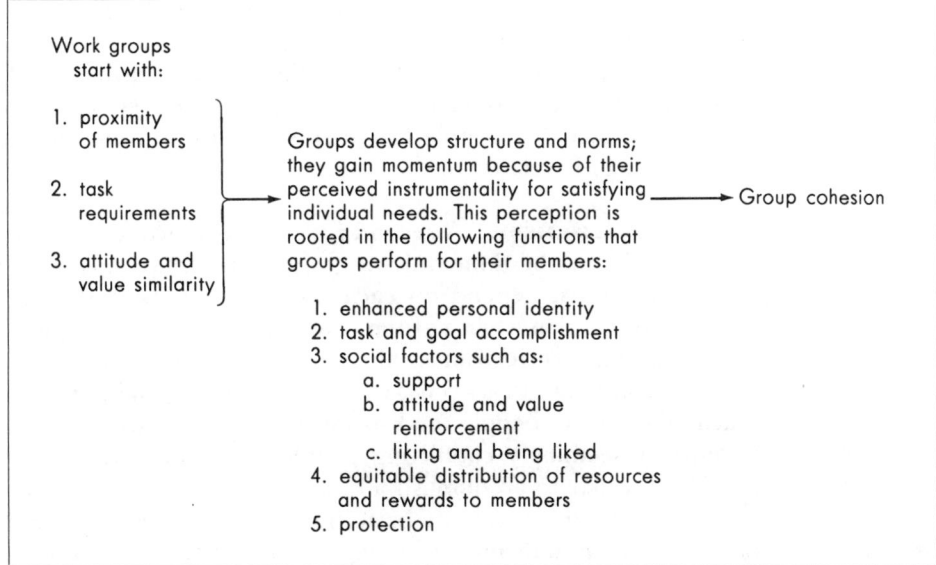

FIGURE 13.4 Development of Group Cohesion

add (c) the attractiveness of independence from the group, and (d) options for alternative membership and independent behavior. The strength of group cohesion thus depends on how instrumental members perceive the group to be in advancing their individual goals as compared to how instrumental they perceive giving up their membership would be and what options they have in fact for doing so.

Group Functions and Group Instrumentality

One way of perceiving a group's instrumentality is by examining the functions that groups provide for people. Let us look at some of these functions.

IDENTITY. First, a group can provide an identity that extends beyond members' sense of themselves. The Lords of Flatbush, Hell's Angels, Rotarians, Daughters of the American Revolution, or any of thousands of other organizations have distinct group identities. Its members perceive themselves as having greater personal value simply because they belong to the group. The black leather jacket, the ring, or the pin identify you as a member of a group, and you wear such symbols with pride. Associated with identity is *status*. That point was illustrated in our opening story in Kerry's attempt to foster elitism in his group. Although the ultimate payoffs for each individual were substantial, it was their performance as a group that concerned Kerry. He knew that if the people perceived themselves collectively as "the best," this would add power to the collective performance. They would find it difficult to face each other if their individual performance did not conform to the group's self-perception. Kerry, then, capitalized on the fact that people link themselves to a group and that the strength of this linkage is related to the group's cohesion.

TASK ACCOMPLISHMENT. A second function of a group is task accomplishment. Certain tasks can be done only in groups, and frequently work is organized so that people must depend on each other to get the task done. Furthermore, evidence shows that when a group contains a number of people with complementary skills that are instrumental for getting a job done, then there is a high degree of mutual attractiveness (33). That is, you value people who help you reach goals. Also, people tend to form a group to accomplish a common task. Groups of seemingly conflicting people can cooperate when they know they need each other to accomplish a task (82, 83).

For example, in military basic training, a company is comprised of several barracks that are individually organized into squads. Each subgrouping competes with the others for certain rewards. Squads, the smallest unit, compete on the rifle range; the best "shooters" get a weekend pass. Barracks, each comprising several squads, may compete during inspection time, with the cleanest getting relief from bad duty, whereas the "dirtiest" may have double duty. Each subunit in the company is thus pitted against each other.

However, the intense competition among squads on the rifle range turns into cooperative behavior among them in cleaning the barracks to avoid bad duty. Notice that a different grouping is involved in cleaning the barracks. That is, in each grouping people need each other to get *that* group task done. And they will work diligently with previous competitors in order to serve current mutual interests.

Kerry Drake acknowledged this at the outset to Stanley and the others. He made it clear that they were to work hard or face danger (be sent home), and that *if the group succeeded,* the members would succeed as well (become plant managers).

Another aspect of the task function that groups perform for their members concerns *successful task accomplishment.* Groups that have been successful usually have members who are more attracted to each other than unsuccessful groups. Successful athletic teams, for example, often extol their collective virtues one season and then are riddled with dissension the next—when they are no longer successful. We are familiar with the dynamics: winning or success is rewarding; losing or less success is not. In any event, it seems clear that members of successful groups are more attracted to each other than members of less successful groups (53).

SOCIAL SUPPORTIVENESS. Third, groups are instrumental in providing *social supportiveness*. Friendship patterns emerge based on mutual liking, similar attitudes and values, and the implicit understanding that we will be liked and supported as individuals. The comfort provided by such an arrangement fills a powerful and common human need to be liked by others (12, 53, 76).

Furthermore, when a group offers us values and attitudes similar to our own, the values and attitudes are validated and we tend to feel good about it (3, 57). The opposite is true if someone rejects our values. We may even feel badly if the disagreement raises serious doubts about our sense of judgment (49, 63). Some even maintain that an important function of groups is to validate our own view of the world within a socially supportive climate (25). Indeed, in two studies of small religious sects, both of which prophesied the end of the world, the common beliefs of members about the sects themselves and the rest of humanity seemed a major factor in holding the groups together after the prophecy failed (26, 38).

ENSURING EQUITY. Less obvious, though still an important social function of groups, is to ensure that all members share the rewards and costs equitably (68, 84). Groups often develop internal allocation systems whereby group resources are equitably distributed. For example, all machinists have equal access to the tool crib; all staff to a secretary; and all professors to graduate students. Further, groups induce members to adhere to these systems by rewarding those who treat others equitably and punishing those who do not. All are expected to pull their weight. Individuals who find themselves in an inequitable relationship will strive to restore equity; if they cannot, they will terminate the relationship if possible. Continued inequity, then, endangers relationships among group members and thus the group itself (15, 62).

PROTECTION. Finally, groups protect their members (21, 23). Work groups often form to protect their members against intrusions from outsiders. In fact, the norms that limit productivity have a primarily protective function. They protect members against rate changes, fatigue, and possible layoffs if workers are seen as redundant because of high productivity. Until the group perceives that higher productivity will mean a big payoff and a reduction of layoff threats, productivity norms will not be adjusted upward (74, 99).

The protective function is particularly strong when the group thinks that a threat can be met only through group behavior and not by individual effort alone (54). In fact, unionization often starts on this premise (21). Jimmy Szekely spoke eloquently to this point in our vignette. To account for the united front that he and his fellow workers presented to management concerning rates, a threatening force had to be perceived commonly. Management had unwittingly provided this perception, which strengthened both the group's cohesion and its resolve to set rates informally according to how it saw a fair day's work for a fair day's pay.

Group cohesion then is a composite of forces holding the membership together. A group may provide any or all of the functions described, though there is a common thread: if group membership can satisfy an individual's needs better than the person can apart from the group, then he or she will want to join or continue his or her membership.

Leader Behavior as an Influence On Group Cohesion

The group leader can foster group cohesion by facilitating the group instrumentality for the membership goals. The leader's task-related behavior seems particularly important in the early phases of the group's development (17, 89). Leaders who help the group to establish goals and work toward those goals, and who clarify roles and in general enable the group to function effectively also ease the progress toward group cohesion (31, 101, 103). Presumably nascent groups, lacking in structure and purpose, gain in attractiveness as they become more competent.

Well-established groups, however, appear to benefit more from supportive leaders—those who pay more attention to the social needs of the membership (79). Such leaders make groups more attractive to their members by increasing social satisfaction and making participation more pleasurable. Apparently, well-established groups have less need for structure than new groups, but the need for good social relations is still there. In either case the leader's behavior increases the instrumentality of the group for its membership. In the next chapter we will explain in detail how that is so.

Organizational Consequences of Group Cohesion

We will now examine the effect of small cohesive work groups on organizational behavior, and give two examples of this effect.

THE SEASHORE STUDY. Stanley Seashore conducted a study in a company that manufactured heavy machinery. Seashore's data were obtained from a questionnaire administered to 5871 skilled and semiskilled employees who were members of 228 work groups. Although Seashore was interested in both the causes and consequences of group cohesion, the hypothesis that concerns us suggested that a group's cohesiveness determines its power to create uniformity of behavior among its members. Variation in productivity within the work group was used as the measurement of uniformity. In other words, within each work group how much did the output of each member resemble that of the others?

Seashore first separated the work groups according to whether they were high or low on group cohesiveness. Then, within each of these two groupings, using the standard deviation of production as his measure, he determined the average variation of productivity for all the work groups. Seashore found that in high-cohesion groups productivity was fairly uniform, whereas in the low-cohesion groups, production was more varied. However, the *level* of productivity was not necessarily related to cohesiveness, for that seemed to depend on other things. Hence, highly cohesive groups may have had high or low performance, but the variation around the productivity norm within those groups was minimal. The low-cohesion groups may have fallen into the high, middle, or low production categories, but in each case there was greater variation in productivity among the membership. Figure 13.5 illustrates the results of Seashore's study. Highly cohesive groups have a very tight distribution about the group's average

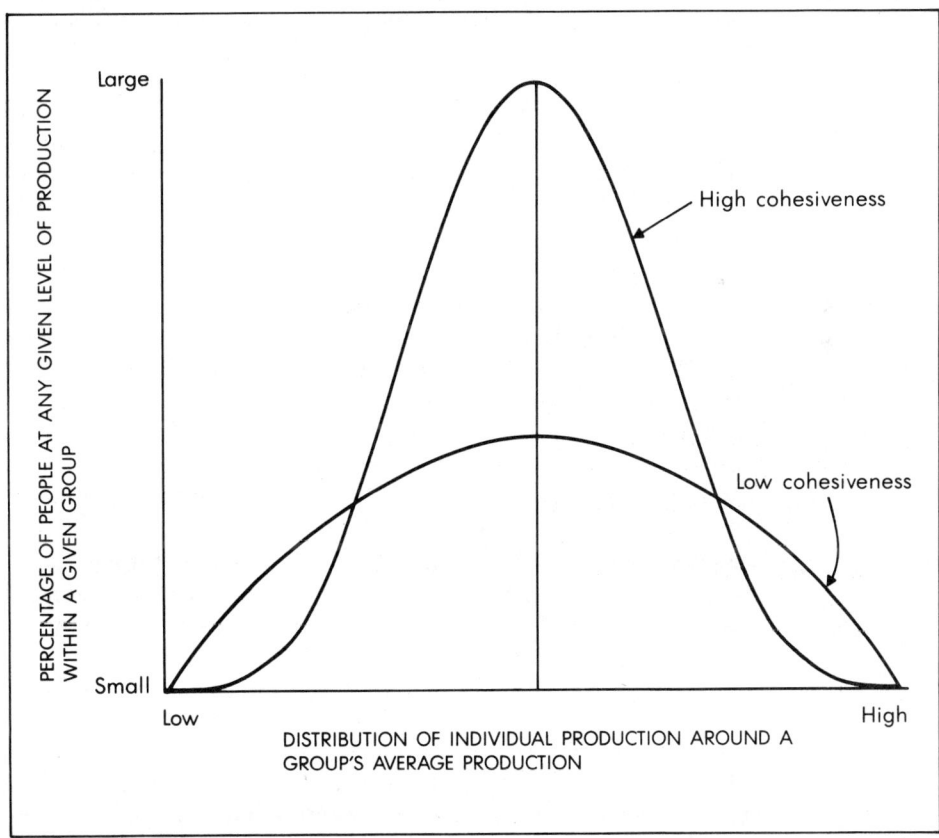

FIGURE 13.5 Variation in Production Within High- and Low-Cohesiveness Groupings

production level. Less cohesive groups do not. Hence almost everybody in highly cohesive groups produce at about the same level according to the findings of this and other studies (47, 80, 103).

THE TAVISTOCK STUDIES. The second illustration comes from a series of studies conducted by the Tavistock Institute in Great Britain. Particularly notable are studies of British coal mines in the late 1940s (91, 92). One of the major tasks of the coal miners at this time was constructing tunnels to get at the coal and extending conveyors to the point of operation in order to get the coal out. A second task was the actual gleaning of the coal from the coal face, the exposed wall of coal. This was done by hand with pick and shovel, or by a more mechanized means, sometimes including explosives. A third major activity was loading and moving the coal from the point of operation back to the surface or entrance of the pit.

The Tavistock studies compared two basic technologies incorporating these operations. The first technology, called the traditional method, centered on small work groups wherein each member performed all these operations. The group decided who did what and when. That is, at one time a member might be getting coal from the face; at another, loading or moving the coal; and at still another, constructing tunnels. Thus, each coal miner performed according to the needs of the group at that particular time, and each miner was functionally dependent on the others. Furthermore, each member of the group was paid the same and consequently there were no apparent status differences within a group. Rewards were tied to group performance, and the norms of productivity for a day's work emerged by group consensus. As you might imagine, the traditional method of technology produced highly cohesive work groups.

The second technology, called the long-wall method, was organized like an assembly line. This technology was introduced because new types of equipment could gain the coal from the face more quickly and effectively. This method, therefore, was supposed to result in greater production than the traditional method. With this technology each worker, positioned along the wall at a work station, was responsible for doing a single operation. Since these operations required different kinds of skill and each was further fractionated into subspecialties, an elaborate pay structure was developed that clearly differentiated one job from another. Consequently, a status structure emerged based on the task ordinarily performed.

Absenteeism and production from the traditional technology were compared to those from the long-wall technology.[2] The traditional technology proved superior in every aspect. Although some of the differences can be ascribed to other variables, such as the intrinsic job interest, many were due to the primary group factors. The groups in the traditional technology were highly cohesive and supportive of each other; they encouraged high performance. For all practical purposes, there were no primary work groups in the long-wall production method.

The results of the Seashore and Tavistock studies illustrate the effect of the small, primary, cohesive work group on organizational behavior. In the first instance, cohesiveness was associated with *variations* of performance within the work group, and in the second, *levels* of performance were associated with the internal dynamics of primary work groups. In each case group norms affected performance (51).

Group Goal Setting

The fact that groups choose goals is indisputable. The fact that those chosen goals are not always in the best interests of the organization is likewise indisputable. Since we will examine goals in great detail in Chapter 15 we will limit ourselves here to a look at how the level of group work goals is determined. Are they high, low, or somewhere between, and why?

Let us return to the vignette at the start of this chapter. Kerry understood well enough that the group needed to identify itself as a successful group to aid him in his efforts and so he created this identity by emphasizing the group's quality. That is the first principle: self-concepts of quality are associated with setting tough goals (28, 104, 105). Kerry also created the perception of successful work in progress. He knew that success breeds success (104).

Two things seem important here: (1) the reinforcing properties associated with motivated behavior are directed toward exceptional results; and (2) success encourages groups to set ever higher goals so long as they are seen as *achievable* through group effort (28, 103, 104).

A third principle invoked by Kerry Drake summarizes much of this chapter: the group achievement was attached to expected rewards (34, 39). In other words, the group members viewed their individual success as contingent on their collective achievement (59).

A fourth principle that Drake seemed to understand was that the expectations of others are an important determinant of goal setting (58, 66, 72). That the group was selected according to criteria of excellence was evident to others and to the group itself. People expected more and group goals were set accordingly. Had they failed it would have been far more devastating to them than if they had been an ordinary group doing ordinary things (103). Implicit in that is a sense of competition, another factor known to affect group goal-setting (104).

Szekely's group set goals at a level lower than they could achieve, but the dynamics were not opposite to those of Drake's group. Szekely and his people simply felt that their personal goals were substantially different from those of The Company and that to advance those goals it would be wise to keep production at a reasonable but certainly not high level.

In Figure 13.6 we have listed the major factors determined by research that seem related to goal selection by any given group. Of course, another way of describing those factors is to say that what a group sees as its best

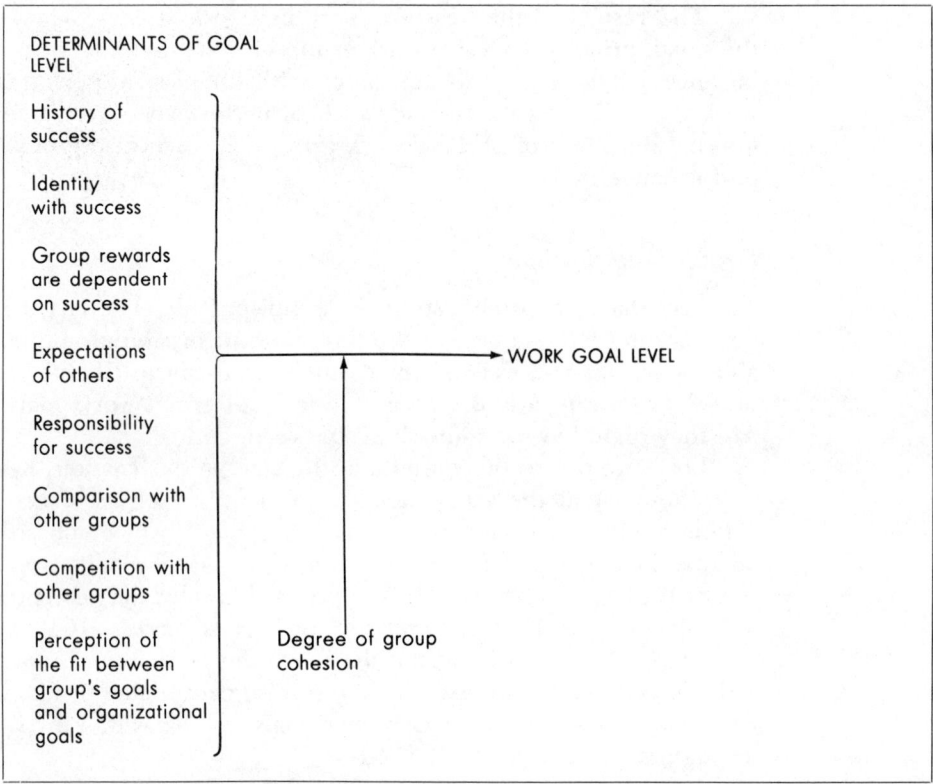

FIGURE 13.6 Group Goal Setting

interests it will do. The list provides the key elements that need to be considered when describing what the group sees as its best interests. Notice too that the relationship between the determinants of work goal level are affected by group cohesion. Although cohesion may not affect goal level itself, it will certainly affect its important determinants. That is, the condition that we have called group cohesion will have no bearing on goal level per se but will have a substantial impact in conjunction with one or more of the listed determinants (55, 97). We will amplify that important idea below.

Group Cohesiveness and Productivity

Group-directed motives have different effects from individual motives, and the two sets of motives may conflict. For example, workers under *individual* pressure to raise productivity levels, who are rewarded for doing so and punished for not, *can* erode group cohesion, but at the same time increase productivity (26). We cannot expect people to set aside their self-interest. Remember that groups become cohesive *because* their members are united to best serve their collective individual interests. After that, cohesion itself becomes a goal if the membership continues to gain satisfaction because of cohesiveness. High productivity may be a by-product of cohesion only if it serves the membership's collective interests, in which case group pressures will encourage it. If, however, cohesion is rooted in reasons antithetical to high productivity—protection against undue work pressure, for example—then we can expect lower productivity. We can only speculate what Jimmy Szekely's group might have done had management provided sufficiently large incentives for higher levels of production. The group would probably have redefined its goals and gone after the payoff. As it stood, however, the major payoff lay in protection, and this is what the group was trying to maintain.

Hence, the individual motives within a group and the motives determined by the group may match and amplify each other, or they may conflict. Evidence suggests, however, that when conflict occurs, the motives triggered by group involvement, particularly in highly cohesive groups, tend to prevail. Under certain circumstances group responsibility and *esprit de corps* seem to override the effects of personal motives (101, 102, 103, 104).

The fact that group motives can amplify individual motives and prevail when there is a conflict makes the focus on groups all the more important. We have shown that when the group goals have not been well defined or the means toward the goals fully structured, the organizational reward pattern can emphasize individual achievement and splinter otherwise cohesive groups. However, since group-oriented motives are so powerful, it would seem to be to management's advantage to develop high levels of cohesiveness under conditions where organizational goals and group goals are complementary (80). The evidence to date suggests that productivity and cohesiveness tend to be correlated positively when high productivity serves the collective interests of the group members and consequently is part of the group's goal structure (52). Harnessing the energies of group cohesiveness to support the broader goals increases the probability of the success of any organization (52). But remember, the goals will be defined within the group and the members must see these goals as serving their interests, because the sources of the cohesiveness itself are related to these goals (13).

We must look at one more point with respect to the moderating effects of group cohesion. We know that under some conditions a leader can affect group performance (8, 89). One of those conditions appears to be group cohesiveness. In other words, much as with the relationship between the determinants of goal setting and the level of the actual goal, group cohesion moderates the relationship between leader behavior and performance. Box 18 describes an example.

> **Box 18**
>
> ### Different Groups, Different Leaders
>
> Schriesheim was interested in how social contexts, in this case group cohesion, affected the relationship between leader behavior and performance. Noting that group cohesion, associated with the final stage of group development as described earlier in this chapter, was also associated with clarity of roles and of task orientation, she hypothesized that structuring behavior for already cohesive work groups would be redundant and lead to lower individual subordinate productivity. Further, she hypothesized that since considerate leaders were more likely to have subordinates accept work goals, considerate leaders were likely to get more production from highly cohesive groups than from groups low in cohesion. Using data gathered from questionnaires from 308 managerial and clerical people in a public utility and the statistical techniques of moderated regression, plus an analysis of correlation within subgroups arranged by level of cohesion, the researcher found substantial support for her hypotheses.
>
> That is, leaders who provided structure because of their task orientation were effective when the group was low in cohesion and consequently lacked structure. On the other hand, leaders who were people-oriented (considerate) were effective when groups were high in cohesion and were consequently thoroughly structured.
>
> Schriesheim, J. F. "The Social Context of Leader-Subordinate Relations: An Investigation of the Effects of Group Cohesion." *Journal of Applied Psychology* 16 (1980): 183–194.

Consensual Validation, Group Illusion, and Irrationality

Irving Janis, in a book entitled *Victims of Groupthink* (43), describes irrational decision processes caused partly by group cohesion. He takes examples from the decision-making processes of the highest levels of United States government. Janis's book underlines the consequences of too much group cohesiveness, wherein critical thinking is replaced by "groupthinking." According to Janis, when loyalty to the group and its norms is more powerful than realistic considerations, then poor decisions may follow.

This dynamic is not necessarily due to group pressures to conform (55). Pressures to conform in cohesive groups are frequently a consequence of the availability of punishments to the group, which may administer them to members with deviant views. But, according to Janis, one of the consequences of too much cohesiveness is that group members seldom have deviant views in the first place. Such an emphasis is placed on harmony and loyalty that the careful weighing of alternatives is discouraged.

Janis states:

> The central theme of my analysis can be summarized in this generalization, which I offer in the spirit of Parkinson's laws: the more amiability and esprit de corps among the members of a policy-making "in-group," the greater is the danger that independent, critical thinking will be replaced by "group think," which is likely to result in irrational, and dehumanizing actions directed against out-groups. (43:13)[3]

Janis provides an interpretation using some symptoms of groupthink. The first symptom he termed the *illusion of invulnerability*, which leads to overoptimism, that is, the feeling that "we cannot lose." Second, information that goes against groupthink can be *rationalized* in various ways; for example, religious groups who predict the end of the world feel they have simply misinterpreted the Word of God after the world has not ended at the specified time. Third, the members of the cohesive group feel they are inherently *moral*, and therefore the morality of their decisions never comes into question. Fourth, the out-group is perceived in terms of stereotypes—for example, "they" are all ignorant of the Word of God, or "they" are weak, stupid, or immoral. Therefore, the in-group will prevail in any conflict, ideological or otherwise. Fifth, the groups engage in *self-censorship*. Members do not question the wisdom of the group's policies. They do not express doubts or question the assumptions that underlie the beliefs. In order to protect the membership from disconfirming information, various members in the group assume the role of *mind guards*.

The Bay of Pigs decision in 1961 is a good example of a bad decision that may have been, as Janis points out, a product of the groupthink phenomenon. Essentially the decision was to place a small group of Cuban exiles on a beachhead in Cuba, their aim being to overthrow the Fidel Castro government. Janis states:

> On April 17, 1961, the brigade of about 1400 Cuban exiles aided by the United States Navy, Air Force, and the CIA, invaded the swampy coast of Cuba at the Bay of Pigs. Nothing went as planned. On the first day not one of the four ships containing reserve ammunition and supplies arrived: the first two were sunk by a few planes in Castro's air force, the other two promptly fled. On the second day the brigade was completely surrounded by 20,000 troops of Castro's well-equipped army. By the third day about 1200 members of the brigade, comprising almost all of those who had not been killed, were captured and ignominiously led off to prison camps. (43:15)[4]

The following are the dynamics that led to this situation. The members of President Kennedy's inner circle of advisors included all of his cabinet and several others who were widely respected and exceptionally competent; three joint chiefs of staff; and a director and deputy director of the CIA. According to Janis, this committee of presidential advisors was a cohesive group and subject to all the manifestations of groupthink. Many real experts were excluded from the decision-making process (mindguarding); thus, important information was not brought in as part of the deliberation, such as: the Cuban military outnumbered the invaders 140 to 1, and the underground resisters to Castro, who were relied on for important insurgency, were not correctly identified, were not coordinated with the invasion, and were located far from the point of the initial incursion.

The general mood of the advisory committee in moving toward the decision to invade Cuba was euphoric, with a strong sense of invulnerability. Everyone seemed biased toward attending only to the information that supported the members' shared feelings of optimism.

Castro was regarded as a weak leader whose army was ready to defect. He and his government were perceived as immoral. The out-group, the enemy—in this case Castro and his government—was perceived as devoid of any of the elements of humanity that were possessed by the president's committee of advisors.

In addition, members felt that a strong consensus existed in the advisory group. That this was not true was testified to by the fact that both Arthur Schlesinger and Robert Hillsman, the director of intelligence and research in the State Department, had strong reservations about the invasion, but did not bring these arguments to the group, partly through a fear of destroying the apparent consensus. Finally, both Robert Kennedy and the Secretary of State Dean Rusk acted as mind guards and discouraged people who had gotten wind of the invasion plans and who strongly opposed such efforts, from speaking their minds.

The upshot was that no alternatives to the Bay of Pigs invasion were seriously considered by the advisory committee, although there were numerous reasons to question the assumptions underlying the wisdom of the invasion and its ultimate effectiveness. Questioning the assumptions and rationale behind the decision to invade was never seriously considered or allowed to penetrate this inner circle. The consequences of this invasion are well known and a matter of history.

Groupthink: A Perspective

How does a cohesive group combat the problems of groupthink? Janis, using a successful decision—the Cuban missile crisis—as a vehicle of analysis, suggests that decisions not be made without considering a range of alternatives, some of which may be extreme. In addition the decision-making process should *encourage open information* and, at times, serious debate among members of the group. All pertinent information should be solicited, and advisors outside of the inner council should be brought into the deliberation. Members of the group could be assigned the role of the *devil's advocate.* The essential point is to encourage information and to evaluate it carefully so the group will not be victimized by the groupthink phenomenon (100).

Cohesiveness unleashes powerful forces that can govern behavior for ill or for good (56). The fact that Kennedy's team was highly cohesive may have contributed to the Bay of Pigs fiasco, but it also prevented them from becoming demoralized after the disaster—they supported each other, and together they analyzed what went wrong and resolved to avoid previous errors. Other important decisions that were made that ultimately were judged sound were as much a consequence of competency of the men who comprised the advisory committee as they were a favorable consequence of group cohesiveness after the defeat at the Bay of Pigs. The problem, then, is always one of balancing the morale gains of high cohesiveness and managing the forces that contribute to effective decisions against the losses incurred by groupthink. As research has suggested, group cohesiveness, if properly managed, can encourage discussion, dissension, and internal group conflict as long as the aims of the group are agreed on by consensus (17, 34, 94). Group cohesiveness should encourage the members to feel free to dissent. Accepting yourself as a valued member of the group should allay any fears of punitive action by the group when you disagree with the group consensus. Evidence of this phenomenon permeates the literature on group dynamics, though once the cohesive group sets its goals, behavior that interferes with those goals is not cheerfully accepted (11, 27, 59, 70).

Summary

In this chapter we described the essence of group dynamics and the power of the group as an explanation for much of the behavior that occurs in organizations. We examined group cohesiveness, the instrumentality of groups to achieve individual and collective goals, the power of norms as originators and moderators of behavior, and the functional and dysfunctional consequences of conformity to norms within small groups.

We viewed group cohesiveness as a function of the instrumentality of the group to satisfy individual needs and to move the group toward goals. These goals are often derived by consensus from within the group itself. Furthermore, the instrumentality of groups and the goals that ultimately emerge are rooted in the functions of the groups. Thus, when a group serves a protective function, its goals are likely to involve warding off a threat; when it functions to accomplish a task, its goals are likely to be task oriented.

We noted too that groups, once formed and cohesive, develop goals that solely concern group maintenance and continuance; that is, it becomes important for group members to behave in ways that maintain solidarity, and many of the group's efforts are directed to this end. Groupthink is an example. Indeed, groupthink is an extreme manifestation of the group's desire to maintain its solidarity and consequently can lead to ineffective decisions and behavior.

By understanding the importance of group functions for the individual, the processes of group development, and the manner in which a group structures itself with its allocation of roles, we can better understand the development of group norms. We examined how norms emerge from groups, how they relate to group goals, and what their functional relationship is to the values of both the immediate group and the overall organization. Norms were described as central forces around which drives toward uniformity were created and unleashed. However, to help you understand norms as a central organizing concept, we also described the power of normlessness.

Groups are sources of powerful forces that govern behavior for good or for ill. The group is a mechanism by which motives are triggered over and beyond individual motives. The fact that groups can energize motives to behave, we view as both comforting and discomforting for the organization. If organizational processes can harness the forces contained within the various groups comprising the larger organization, then organizational goals can be well served. Conversely, if the organization loses control of most of its groups, it is in trouble.

We suggested that the process of developing superordinate goals would serve the needs of individuals, and the purposes of the immediate work group and the larger organization. Where this occurs there is a higher probability of organizational success, and to understand organizational process, one must at least grasp this basic phenomenon. We shall see later that developing goals toward which several or more groups strive is difficult to do and in some cases improbable. The reasons concern the way groups develop goals and the basic incompatibility of some of these goals. We deal with goal development later.

Notes

1. Berkowitz (7) identifies five stages, which he calls (a) dependence/counterdependence, (b) individuation, (c) internal rivalry, (d) cohesion, and (e) true teamwork. The first three are similar to Tuckman's first stage while the other two are analogous to the rest of Tuckman's model (93).
2. The most scientifically respectable comparison was between the long-wall method and a so-called composite long wall, which, because the coal faces were too short, could not incorporate the long-wall method in its totality. Rather much of the traditional method was used, most particularly the small group organization and production means. For simplicity's sake, we describe only the basic features of the studies.
3. Irving L. Janis, *Victims of Groupthink,* Copyright © 1972 by Houghton Mifflin Company. Reprinted by permission.
4. Irving L. Janis, *Victims of Groupthink,* Copyright © 1972 by Houghton Mifflin Company. Reprinted by permission.

References

1. ALDERFER, CLAYTON P., and KEN K. SMITH. "Studying Intergroup Relations Embedded in Organizations." *Administrative Science Quarterly* 27 (March 1982): 35–65.
2. ANDERSON, A. "Combined Effects of Interpersonal Attraction and Goal-Path Clar-

ity on Cohesiveness of Task-Oriented Groups." *Journal of Personality and Social Psychology* 31 (January 1975): 68–75.

3. AWAL, DEEPA, and STEPHEN A. STUMPH. "Differentiating Between Perceived Organization and Work Group Climates." *Journal of Management* 7 (1981): 33–42.

4. BALES, R. F. "Task Roles and Social Roles in Problem-Solving Groups." In *Readings in Social Psychology,* 3rd ed. Edited by E. Maccoby, T. M. Newcomb and E. L. Hartley. New York: Holt, Rinehart and Winston, 1968. Pp. 437–447.

5. BASS, BERNARD M. "From Leaderless Group Discussions to the Cross-National Assessment of Managers." *Journal of Management* 7 (Fall 1981): 67–76.

6. BENNIS, W. G., and H. A. SHEPHARD. "A Theory of Group Development." In *Small Groups: Some Sociological Perspectives,* edited by C. Sheperd. San Francisco: Chandler Publishing, 1964. Pp. 43–53.

7. BERKOWITZ, B. "Stages of Group Development in a Mental Health Team." *Psychiatric Quarterly* 48 (1974): 309–319.

8. BIGGART, NICOLE W. "Management Style as Strategic Interaction: The Case of Governor Ronald Reagan." *Journal of Applied Behavioral Science* 17 (July–September 1981): 291–308.

9. BLAKE, R. R., and J. S. MOUTON. "Reactions to Intergroup Competition Under Win-Lose Conditions." *Management Science* 7 (July 1961): 420–435.

10. BONACICH, P. "Norms and Cohesion as Adaptive Response to Potential Conflict: An Experimental Study." *Sociometry* 35 (September 1972): 357–375.

11. BOSS, R. WAYNE, and MARK L. MCCONKIE. "The Destructive Impact of a Positive Team-Building Intervention." *Group and Organization Studies* 6 (March 1981): 45–56.

12. BYRNE, D. "Interpersonal Attraction and Attitude Similarity." *Journal of Abnormal and Social Psychology* 62 (1961): 713–715.

13. CARTWRIGHT, D. "The Nature of Group Cohesiveness." In *Group Dynamics,* 3rd ed. Edited by D. Cartwright and A. Zander. New York: Harper and Row, 1968. Pp. 91–109.

14. COMPAS, BRUCE E. "Psychological Sense of Community Among Treatment Analogous Group Members." *Journal of Applied Social Psychology* 11 (March–April 1981): 151–165.

15. COSIER, RICHARD A., and THOMAS L. RUBLE. "Research on Conflict-Handling Behavior: An Experimental Approach." *Academy of Management Journal* 24 (December 1981): 816–831.

16. CROSBIE, R. V. *Interaction in Small Groups.* New York: Macmillan, 1975.

17. DE MEUSE, KENNETH P., and S. JAY LIEBOWITZ. "An Empirical Analysis of Team-Building Research." *Group and Organization Studies* 6 (September 1981): 357–578.

18. DEUTSCH, M. A Theory of Cooperation and Competition." *Human Relations* 2 (1949): 196–231.

19. DION, K. L. "Cohesiveness as a Determinant of Ingroup-Outgroup Bias." *Journal of Personality and Social Change* 28 (November 1973): 163–171.

20. DITTES, J. E., and H. H. KELLEY. "Effects of Different Conditions of Acceptance Upon Conformity to Group Norms." *Journal of Abnormal and Social Psychology* 53 (1956): 100–107.

21. DRISCOLL, JAMES W. "Problem Solving between Adversaries: Predicting Behavior in Labor-Management Committees." *International Review of Applied Psychology* 30 (April 1981): 277–291.
22. ETZIONI, A. "A Model of Significant Research." *International Journal of Psychiatry* 6 (1968): 279–280.
23. FALK, GIDEON, and SHOSAHAN FALK. "The Impact of Decision Rules on the Distribution of Power in Problem-Solving Teams of Unequal Power." *Group and Organization Studies* 6 (1981): 211–223.
24. FERRIS, GERALD R., and M. ROWLAND KENDRITH. "Leadership, Job Perceptions, and Influence: A Conceptual Integration." *Human Relations* 34 (1981): 1069–1077.
25. FESTINGER, L. *A Theory of Cognitive Dissonance.* Stanford, Calif.: Stanford University Press, 1957.
26. FESTINGER, L., H. RIECKEN, and S. SCHACTER. *When Prophecy Fails.* Minneapolis: University of Minnesota Press, 1956.
27. FESTINGER, L., S. SCHACTER, and K. BACK. *Social Pressures in Informal Groups: A Study in Human Factors in Housing.* New York: Harper, 1950.
28. FORWARD, J., and A. ZANDER. "Choice of Unattainable Group Goals and Effects on Performance." *Organizational Behavior and Human Performance* 6 (1971): 184–199.
29. GOLEMBIEWSKI, R. T. "Small Groups and Large Organizations." In *Handbook of Organizations,* 3rd ed. Edited by J. March. Chicago: Rand McNally, 1970.
30. GOODSTEIN, LEONARD D. "Getting Your Way: A Training Activity in Understanding Power and Influence." *Group and Organization Studies* 6 (September 1981): 283–290.
31. GREENE, CHARLES N., and CHESTER A. SCHRIESHEIM. "Leader-Group Interactions: A Longitudinal Field Investigation." *Journal of Applied Psychology* 65 (1980): 50–59.
32. GRICAR, BARBARA G., and L. DAVE BROWN. "Conflict, Power and Organization in a Changing Community." *Human Relations* 34 (October 1981): 877–893.
33. GROSS, A. E., and L. G. LATANE. "Receiving Help, Reciprocation and Interpersonal Attraction." *Journal of Applied Social Psychology* 4 (1974): 210–223.
34. GUZZO, RICHARD, and JAMES A. WATERS. "The Expression of Affect and the Performance of Decision-Making Groups." *Journal of Applied Psychology* 67 (February 1982): 67–74.
35. HACKMAN, J. R., and C. G. MORRIS. "Group Tasks, Group Interaction Process and Group Performance Effectiveness: A Review and Proposed Integration." In *Advances in Experimental Social Psychology,* Vol. 8. Edited by L. Berkowitz. New York: Academic Press, 1975.
36. HACKMAN, J. R., K. BRONSSEAU, and J. A. WEISS. "The Interaction of Task Design and Group Performance Strategies in Determining Group Effectiveness." *Organizational Behavior and Human Performance* 16 (1976): 250–279.
37. HACKMAN, R., and N. VITMAR. "Effects of Size and Task Type on Group Performance and Member Reactions." In *Basic Topics in Social Psychology,* edited by L. Marlowe. Boston: Holbrook Press, 1972. Pp. 244–258.
38. HARDYK, J. A., and M. BRADEN. "Prophecy Fails Again: A Report of a Failure to Replicate." *Journal of Abnormal Psychology* 65 (1962): 136–141.
39. HILL, GAYLE W. "Groups vs. Individual Performance: Are N + 1 Heads Better Than One?" *Psychological Bulletin* 91 (May 1982): 517–539.

40. HOFMAN, JOGN E. "Social Identity and the Readiness for Social Relations Between Jews and Arabs in Israel." *Human Relations* 35 (September 1982): 727–741.
41. HOLTMAN, KENNETH E. "The Trainer as 'Scapegoat'." *Training and Development Journal* 36 (July 1982): 44–53.
42. HOMANS, C. G. "Social Behavior as Exchange." *American Journal of Sociology* 63 (1958): 579–606.
43. JANIS, I. L. *Victims of Group-Think: A Psychological Study of Foreign Policy Decisions and Fiascos.* Boston: Houghton Mifflin, 1972.
44. KABANOFF, BORIS. "A Critique of Leader Match and Its Implications for Leadership Research." *Personnel Psychology* 34 (1981): 749–764.
45. KABANOFF, BORIS, and GORDON E. O'BRIEN. "The Effects of Task Type and Cooperation upon Group Products and Performance." *Organizational Behavior and Human Performance* 23 (1979): 163–181.
46. KATZ, RALPH. "The Effects of Group Longevity on Project Communication and Performance." *Administrative Science Quarterly* 27 (March 1982): 81–104.
47. KLEIN, S. M. *Workers Under Stress.* Lexington, Ky.: The University Press of Kentucky, 1971.
48. KOLODNY, HARVEY F., and MOSES N. KIGGUNDU. "Towards the Development of a Sociotechnical Systems Model in Woodlands Mechanical Harvesting." *Human Relations* 33 (1980): 623–645.
49. LEVINGER, G. "Little Sand Box and Big Quarry: Comment on Byrne's Paradigmatic Spode for Research on Interpersonal Attraction." *Representative Research in Social Psychology* 3 (1972): 3–19.
50. LIEBERMAN, S. "The Effects of Changes in Roles on the Attitudes of Role Occupants." *Human Relations* 9 (1956): 385–402.
51. LIEBOWITZ, S. JAY, and KENNETH P. DE MEUSE. "The Application of Team Building." *Human Relations* 35 (January 1982): 1–18.
52. LIKERT, R. *The Human Organization.* New York: McGraw-Hill, 1967.
53. LOTT, A. J., and B. E. LOTT. "Group Cohesiveness, Communication Level and Conformity." *Journal of Abnormal and Social Psychology* 62 (1961): 408–412.
54. LOVE, KEVIN G., and TERRY A. BEEHR. "Social Stressors on the Job: Recommendations for a Broadened Perspective." *Group and Organization Studies* 6 (June 1981): 190–200.
55. MANZ, CHARLES C., and HENRY P. SIMS. "The Potential for 'Groupthink' in Autonomous Work Groups." *Human Relations* 35 (September 1982): 773–784.
56. MAOZ, ZEER. "The Decision to Raid Entebbe: Decision Analysis Applied to Crisis Behavior." *Journal of Conflict Resolution* 25 (December 1981): 677–707.
57. MARTIN, THOMAS N., and J. G. HUNT. "Social Influence and Intent to Leave: A Path-Analytic Process Model." *Personnel Psychology* 33 (1980): 505–528.
58. MIDDLEMAN, RUTH R. "Some Thoughts on 'The Learning Potential of the Dominant Personality with Small Intensive Training Groups'." *Group and Organization Studies* 6 (December 1981): 469–471.
59. MILSTEIN, MIKE M., and PAUL A. LAFORNARA. "Internal Change Teams in Urban School Districts: The Buffalo Experience," *Group and Organization Studies* 6 (March 1981): 96–113.

60. MOCH, MICHAEL K. "Job Involvement, Internal Motivation, and Employees' Integration into Networks of Work Relationships." *Organizational Behavior and Human Performance* 25 (1980): 15–31.

61. MORROW, PAUL C. "Work Related Communication, Environmental Uncertainty, and Subunit Effectiveness: A Second Look at the Information Processing Approach to Subunit Communication." *Academy of Management Journal* 24 (December 1981): 851–858.

62. MURNIGHAN, J. KEITH. "Defectors, Vulnerability, and Relative Power: Some Causes and Effects of Leaving a Stable Coalition." *Human Relations* 34 (1981): 589–609.

63. NEWCOMB, T. M. *The Acquaintancy Process.* New York: Holt, Rinehart and Winston, 1961.

64. NEWTON, P., and D. J. LEVINSON. "The Work Group Within the Organization: A Sociopsychological Approach." *Psychiatry* 36 (May 1973): 115–142.

65. NIGHTINGALE, DONALD V. "Participation in Decision-Making: An Examination of Style and Structure and Their Effects on Member Outcomes." *Human Relations* 34 (1981): 1119–1133.

66. O'BRIEN, GORDON E., and BORIS KABANOFF. "The Effects of Leadership Style and Group Structure upon Small Group Productivity: A Test of a Discrepancy Theory of Leader Effectiveness." *Australian Journal of Psychology* 33 (November 1981): 157–168.

67. PEARSON, JUDY C. "The Effects of Setting and Gender of Self-Disclosure." *Group and Organization Studies* 6 (September 1981): 334–340.

68. PRICE, KENNETH H., and HOWARD GARLAND. "Compliance with a Leader's Suggestions as a Function of Perceived Leader/Member Competence and Potential Reciprocity." *Journal of Applied Psychology* 66 (June 1981): 329–336.

69. RANDOLPH, W. ALAN, and BARRY Z. POSNER. "Explaining Role Conflict and Role Ambiguity via Individual and Interpersonal Variables in Different Job Categories." *Personnel Psychology* 34 (1981): 89–102.

70. ———. "The Effects of an Intergroup Development O.D. Intervention as Conditioned by the Life Cycle State of Organizations: A Laboratory Experiment." *Group and Organization Studies* 7 (September 1982): 335–352.

71. REDDY, DIANE M., ANDREW BAUM, RAYMOND FLEMING, and JOHN R. AIELLO. "Mediation of Social Density by Coalition Formation." *Journal of Applied Social Psychology* 11 (November–December 1981): 529–537.

72. ROHRBAUGH, JOHN. "Improving the Quality of Group Judgment: Social Judgment Analysis and the Nominal Group Technique." *Organizational Behavior and Human Performance* 28 (October 1981): 272–288.

73. ROSENFIELD, DAVID, WALTER G. STEPHEN, and G. WILLIAM ZUZKER. "Attraction to Competent and Incompetent Members of Cooperative and Competitive Groups." *Journal of Applied Social Psychology* 11 (September–October 1981): 416–433.

74. ROTHE, H. F. "Does Higher Pay Bring Higher Productivity?" *Personnel* 37 (1960): 20–27.

75. ROTHERMAN, MARY, JEAN LA COUR, and ALFRED JACOBS. "Variations in Group Pro-

cess Due to Valence Response Mode and Directness of Feedback." *Group and Organization Studies* 7 (March 1982): 67–75.

76. SCHACHTER, S. *The Psychology of Affiliation.* Stanford, Calif.: Stanford University Press, 1959.

77. SCHEIN, E. H., and W. C. BENNIS. *Personal and Organizational Change Through Group Methods.* New York: Wiley, 1967.

78. SCHEIN, E. P., with J. SCHNEIER and G. H. BARKER. *Coercive Persuasion: A Socio-Psychological Analysis of the Brainwashing of American Prisoners by the Chinese Communists.* New York: Norton, 1961.

79. SCHRIESHEIM, JANET FULK. "The Social Context of Leader-Subordinate Relations: An Investigation of the Effects of Group Cohesiveness." *Journal of Applied Psychology* 65 (1980): 183–194.

80. SEASHORE, S. *Group Cohesiveness in the Industrial Workgroup.* Ann Arbor, Mich.: Institute for Social Research, 1954.

81. SECORD, P. F., and C. W. BACKMAN. *Social Psychology.* New York: McGraw-Hill, 1974.

82. SHERIF, M., and C. SHERIF. *Groups in Harmony and Tension.* New York: Harper and Brothers, 1953.

83. SHERIF, S. "A Study of Some Social Factors in Perception." *Archives of Psychology* 27 (1936): 1–60.

84. STAGNER, ROSS, and BOAZ EFLAL. "Internal Union Dynamics During a Strike: A Quasi Experimental Study." *Journal of Applied Psychology* 67 (February 1982): 37–44.

85. STAW, BARRY M., LANCE E. SANDELANDS, and JANE E. DUTTON. "Threat-Rigidity Effects in Multilevel Behavior: A Multilevel Analysis." *Administrative Science Quarterly* 26 (December 1981): 501–524.

86. STEELE, F. I. *Physical Settings and Organizational Development.* Menlo Park, Calif.: Addison-Wesley, 1973.

87. STEINER, I. *Group Processes and Productivity.* New York: Academic Press, 1972.

88. STEPHENSON, BLAIR Y., LARRY K. MICHAELSON, and STEPHEN G. FRANKLIN. "An Empirical Test of the Nominal Group Technique in State Solar Energy Planning." *Group and Organization Studies* 7 (September 1982): 320–334.

89. STOGDILL, R. M. *Handbook of Leadership.* New York: Free Press, 1974.

90. THIEBAUT, J. W., and H. H. KELLEY. *The Social Psychology of Groups.* New York: Wiley, 1959.

91. TRIST, E. L. "Towards a Post-industrial Culture." In *Handbook of Work, Organization and Society*, edited by R. Dubin. Chicago: Rand McNally, 1976. Pp. 1011–1033.

92. TRIST, E. L., and K. W. BAMFORTH. "Some Social and Psychological Consequences of the Long-Wall Method of Coal-Getting." *Human Relations* 4 (1951): 3–38.

93. TUCKMAN, B. "Developmental Sequence in Small Groups." *Psychological Bulletin* 63 (1965): 384–399.

94. VAN DE VEN, ANDREW. "Problem Solving, Planning, and Innovation. Part I. Test of the Program Planning Model." *Human Relations* 33 (November 1980): 711–740.

95. ———. "Problem Solving, Planning, and Innovation. Part II. Speculations for Theory and Practice," *Human Relations* 33 (November 1980): 757–779.
96. WALDIE, K. F. "The Learning Potential of the Dominant Personality with Small Intensive-Training Groups." *Group and Organization Studies* 6 (December 1981): 456–468.
97. WHITE, SAM E., JOHN E. DITTRICH, and JAMES R. LANG. "The Effects of Group Decision Making Process and Problem-Situation Complexity on Implementation Attempts." *Administrative Science Quarterly* 25 (1980): 128–440.
98. WHYTE, W. F. *Street Corner Society.* Chicago: University of Chicago Press, 1943.
99. ———., ED. *Money and Motivation.* New York: Harper, 1955.
100. YETTON, PHILIP W., and PRESTON C. BOTTGER. "Individual Versus Group Problem Solving: An Empirical Test of a Best-Member Strategy." *Organizational Behavior and Human Performance* 29 (June 1982): 307–321.
101. ZANDER, A. *Groups at Work.* San Francisco: Jossey-Bass, 1977.
102. ———. *Motives and Goals in Groups.* New York: Academic Press, 1971.
103. ———. "Team Spirit Versus the Individual Achiever: Productivity and Group Success." *Psychology Today* 8 (November 1974): 64–68.
104. ZANDER, A., and W. ARMSTRONG. "Working for Group Pride in a Slipper Factory," *Journal of Applied Social Psychology* 2 (1972): 193–207.
105. ZANDER, A., and C. ULBERG. "The Group Level of Aspiration and External Social Pressures." *Organizational Behavior and Human Performances* 6 (1971): 362–378.
106. ZIMBARDO, P. G. "Involvement and Communication Discrepancy as Determinants of Opinion Conformity." *Journal of Abnormal and Social Psychology* 60 (1960): 86–94.
107. ZIMBARDO, P. G., W. C. BANKS, C. HANEY, and D. JAFFE. "A Pirandellian Prison." *New York Times Sunday Magazine*, April 8, 1973.

Discussion Questions

1. What sources of cohesion were contained in our opening vignette? What were the consequences of each?
2. Think of a group of which you now are or have been a part. Describe that group's development, using the stages of development we described as your framework. Describe the consequence of group structure and role relationship.
3. What is the effect of group structure on membership behavior?
4. Describe the role of group norms as behavioral determinants. How and why do they develop? Are group norms good for organizations?
5. Given the powerful forces for conformity, explain nonconformity.
6. How is the notion of the instrumentality of groups useful for the purpose of understanding organizational behavior?
7. Why do groups become cohesive? Why not? Explain the consequences of cohesiveness in terms of organizational behavior.

Discussion Questions

8. If you were a manager, would you encourage your work group to become cohesive? Why and under what conditions? Why not and under what conditions?
9. Motivation is determined by goals, incentives, organizational norms and individual factors. In what ways do groups modify motivation and amplify or suppress those other factors?

Chapter 14
Leadership

Rank Has Its Privilege

Stanley, Penny, and Claude were full of questions when Kerry announced to them that he would be departing for a new assignment. For two years now, Kerry had been program manager for PIPER (Procedures Improvement Program Evaluation Research), and he was ready to move on. The structure of PIPER, at least the group's part of PIPER, was a bit unusual for The Company. The group hadn't had a project manager for over a year. Instead, Kerry had let the group operate independently, and they liked it. For his part, Kerry had been much too busy traveling around The Company, visiting various production facilities and collecting, in Ted's words, "our best thinking, systems-wise." But now the planning phase was over. And with the program settling down into the more routine implementation phase, Kerry was moving on to "new responsibility."

And what was the Procedures Improvement Program? It was a large-scale work procedures improvement program for blue-collar workers. Top people had been pulled in from all over The Company to get it started. And because the potential effect on The Company was so great, results were to be monitored carefully. And yes, you guessed it, Dr. Faust had been called in as consultant for the multifaceted evaluation effort, with Kerry responsible for organizing the initial stages from within.

Stanley, Claude, and Penny constituted one part of the evaluation team charged with developing the "systems implications." Stanley, as Faust's former student, had been suggested as the systems person; Claude had been selected for his knowledge of production engineering methods; and Penny had been brought from communications because of suspicions that two engineers might find it difficult to turn out a readable document.

But now Kerry was leaving, to be succeeded by someone the group had never met. Kerry had suggested that the new person would be able to provide the "leadership" they had never really had. Thus, they now also wondered about this "leadership" they had never felt they *needed* while working for Kerry. Who would the new person be? What would his qualifications be? How would he provide leadership? Unfortunately, it didn't take long to get the answers.

"I've had it. I've had it with him. That's the third, no the fourth time I've been in there today about this stupid report." Penny was not happy. "This time he wants to know why the 'implications for action' section is first, not last, where *he* says logically it ought to be. But he doesn't really want to know. He just wants me to do it.

"Then he says that this paragraph ought to be changed here and there. So I tell him, 'O.K., here, change it to read the way you want.' But oh no! He says that's what *I'm* being paid for. Rewrite it and he'll look at it tomorrow. What'll he want next?"

The "he" was Warren Gray, Kerry's replacement, and the scene was taking place within a month of his arrival. Gray, it seems, had come to Company headquarters directly from an assignment as a second-level supervisor of production engineering in the Portsmouth plant. As was common practice in these things, he had been brought into the program at the request of a third-level manager with whom he had worked on a number of previous assignments.

But back to the group. Penny wasn't alone in her experience with Mr. Gray. Stanley was having his problems, as well. "So then I said, here, why don't you read this, it'll save both of us some time. But he says, 'No, I want to hear it from you. You say in here that the factors you are describing are correlated .81, which—in your own words—means they are virtually one and the same. What exactly do you mean by that?'

"Well, Jesus, how can I explain that?" Claude, listening, nodded as Stanley continued. "I mean, either he knows what a correlation is, or he doesn't. If he does, then the meaning is obvious, and if he doesn't well. . . .

"So then he says, 'I'm sure that you understand one of the main reasons this group was put together is to provide a clear, crisp presentation of the systems aspect of this thing for management. Now if you can't communicate this to *me*, then it is difficult for me to understand how . . .'" Stanley spoke the words with exaggerated emphasis to underscore his own feelings.

Claude too spent a lot of hours the same way—accounting for what he had done and receiving direct, though somewhat obscure, instructions as to how to "improve" his work. And, in addition, Claude was irked at the quite obvious, though implicit, assumption by Warren Gray that Stanley was the leader of the group—which wasn't true. Claude was offended by Gray's unwitting assumption, as Claude saw it, that the leader of the group naturally would be a white male. And even then it wasn't the prejudicial overtones that bothered him so much as that it was just so unsophisticated. Research managers ought to have more on the ball than that.

This was how the situation stood with the PIPER group when Dr. Faust made a visit. Faust noticed that all was not well, and when the opportunity arose, he asked Stanley about it privately.

"I have the feeling that all is not well here. Am I correct in assuming that it has something to do with the recent change in, ah—leadership?"

"If that's what you want to call it, then yes. That's the problem, no question." Stanley then went on to describe what had been taking place. He gave detailed examples of Gray's apparent ignorance of the project, together with Gray's insistence that things be done his own way. "What I want to know is how in the hell did they come to pick a turkey like that for this job! And he's supposed to be one of The Company's real comers. If *that's* true, God save us from the rest!"

"Yes, I think I *do* see what you mean," was Faust's unenlightening reply. And with that Faust reached for the nearest ashtray. He said nothing for several minutes as he completed the ritual process of cleaning, refilling, and lighting his pipe.

Then, leaning back amid a freshly generated cloud of acrid smoke, he asked, "You don't understand why this man Gray is doing this? Is that it?" Stanley was about to say yes, but Faust continued directly, "Then you cannot have given much thought to how his assignment here is different from his previous position. Tell me about it."

"Uh, you mean where Gray came from?"

Faust nodded.

"I'm not completely certain, but I'm pretty sure he was a second-level supervisor at our new manufacturing plant at Portsmouth. Yeah, that's it, because that's where one of the big PIP programs is going to be and, well, he'd be familiar with the background there. So. . . ."

"And what was his responsibility?"

"Didn't I say? I think he was in charge of a group of production engineering departments. But I'm not sure."

At this point Faust cut in, hoping to accelerate Stanley's mental processes a bit. "No matter. So Mr. Gray was in charge of, I suppose, some six or seven production engineering departments, for that is how The Company is arranged. Now, do you have any idea of how many people that might be?"

"I thought you said you knew. . . ."

"I *do* know. That was not my question. Do *you* know?"

"Well, I, uh . . . I never thought about it that way—but probably 50 or 60 anyway."

"Wrong by half. More than likely there would be 120 or more. And what does that suggest to you about his relationship to these people?"

"What relationship? If what you say is true—," at which Faust gave Stanley a quick, sharp look—"I mean, since it's like you say, I'd guess he hardly ever talked to these people—worked with his department supervisors instead." And after a moment's reflection, "Sure, but then, why does he spend so much time with us?"

"Yes, why then? What else might he be doing?" Faust pressed ahead with his questions.

"But that's just it. He . . . sure! He doesn't *know* what *else* to do. And he's probably not too happy about it either—with the way we treat him either, I'll bet. No sir. He's used to those—how many—100 or so guys saying, 'Morning, Mr. Gray,' and 'Evening, Mr. Gray,' and acting as though he's some kind of big shot. Which I guess Gray was—or is?"

"Is," Faust confirmed.

"So maybe I *am* beginning to see. Out there he had a big position, a lot of power, and a pretty cut-and-dried kind of job to do in production engineering. And since he came up by that route he's got that job down pretty pat.

"I suppose that suits him just fine, too, 'cause I've noticed that he's the kind that likes to tell people what to do. Even Bonnie finds it pretty hard to take. But then why . . . ?"

"Yes, why bring him here, into a research environment where the tasks continually evolve, and where ah—if you will pardon my saying so—deference to authority is not quite, ah—a way of life." Stanley chuckled and even Faust smiled a bit.

"That likely *was* a mistake, though I understand the reasons well enough. But you do see now, don't you? Successful leadership is a function of many factors beyond the leader's control. And I dare say that if Mr. Gray were willing to speak his mind on this you would find that he is even *more* confused and concerned by this situation than you." With that pronouncement Faust felt the lesson was complete.

Was Warren Gray a poor leader? Certainly if the group were to decide, the answer would be yes. And yet Gray had been tapped by higher management as a "comer." Of course, as Faust points out, it is precisely the fact of where Gray came from together with his own inclinations that make him ineffective in the current setting. He is jealous of his authority, whereas Kerry Drake had delegated authority to the point that the group was mostly free to set their own goals and establish their own procedures. Drake operated that way because under his leadership the group had been successful before, and he had confidence in them. Yet their performance was partly due to Kerry's ability to get the most out of people.

Gray, on the other hand, came from a situation where he could hardly function as Drake did. The technology required that the operations be arranged in a fairly structured hierarchy where formal authority was more in evidence. Furthermore, the norms supported a hierarchical approach to decision making and to interpersonal relations.

Could Drake's leadership style have been successful had he been transferred to Gray's old job? It is hard to say, but probably not. He too would have to address both the way the people were used to operating and the constraints that are forced on any leadership position by the formal authority, the technology, and the people. Effective leadership, then, depends on a lot of things, many of which may be beyond the leader's control. Behavior that is successful in one set of circumstances may not be in another. These circumstances involve the nature of the leader, the kinds of people with whom he or she interacts, the group that is being led and its normative systems and goals, the technology that is used to get the job done, and the larger system's values, norms, and organizational arrangements.

Leadership Defined

Before we tell you what leadership is, let us tell you what it is not. Leadership is not:

1. Performing only the routine function of the role requirements such as allocating work, issuing directives, assigning responsibility, and controlling behavior, although these jobs have to be done and done well (107).
2. Using authority and the sanctions that go with positions of authority as the primary way of ensuring control of behavior (84).
3. Relying primarily on formal organizational structure, rules, and procedures to justify gaining compliance (29, 47, 102, 103).
4. Interacting almost exclusively with the group over which one presides, although such interactions are an important leader behavior (49, 65, 70, 85, 105).

Formally designated heads of organizational units may be effective if they do these things, but leaders usually do more. So what then is leadership?

Leadership has been defined in many ways, although most include the notion of social influence (1, 47, 61). That is, leaders must be able to influence those they lead, peers with whom they interact, and those above them to whom they are accountable. As we have noted, organizational behavior occurs within the broad context of a social organization.

Mintzberg (65) and others have shown that less than half a manager's time is spent with subordinates, the rest being divided first with peers and then with people higher up in the organization. And since many of these role relationships are ill-defined, leaders must be concerned with creating role relationships that work to their group's advantage (30). Consequently, leaders create and modify structure, work around existing structural constraints, and piece together aspects of the existing structure that can serve the group (30, 47). Leadership, then, must be viewed in broad organizational terms: existing in a social network and constrained by formal structures leaders must deal with in order to advance their own and their groups' position.

There is substantial evidence that leaders are preoccupied with power (10, 36, 58, 59). However, it is the way power is used that is of interest here, for if power is viewed simply as personal dominance, it has little organizational untility and consequently is not organizationally legitimate. If, however, it is used for organizational purposes and to achieve sanctioned ends, it does have legitimacy, and like it or not, it is used frequently by effective leaders (10, 59). Hence, leaders need to understand power and its organizational usage; that is the context in which organizational leadership must be seen. It is political, and it involves power and social influence.

Basically, however, leaders are defined by their followership. Without that followership and the power base it can provide, there can be no leader. Most leadership studies note an elemental aspect of the leader phenomenon that reflects this—namely, the ability to mobilize a group to advance group goals. The effectiveness with which a unit head can first help a group define its goals, and then enable it to reach those goals, is central to our view of leadership in an organization (16, 40). Leadership is also—partly at least—the ability to motivate people beyond the normal job requirements (32, 40, 47, 87, 89).

We define organizational leadership, then, as social influence that occurs in a complex political context involving lateral and vertical relationships. It has motivational and power components, and its general purpose is to enable the followers to define and reach their collective goals.

We will now begin to explore the particulars of what a leader is or what a leader does to fulfill the motivational and political parts of our definition. Our organization will follow generally the historical development of the field. For a synopsis of the chronological development of leadership theory, see Box 19. We will examine first the traits that have been associated with effective leadership.

Leadership Traits and Charisma

> I'm in a lousy situation. In Pawtucket I could get things done. Ben [the plant manager] listened, and the others—they respected me. I could talk to them and they didn't give a damn when I used bad grammar or when I cussed, because I was usually right and they knew it. Up here they drink Chivas Regal with their little pinkies sticking out. I'm still right; I still know my manufacturing—more than the rest of them put together—but they make me feel dumb [A successful manager who was promoted to corporate headquarters].

Like Warren Gray in our vignette, this man, Linc, was a fish out of water in his new environment. His behavior, highly successful with the shirtsleeve crowd, was viewed as uncouth in his new milieu. He was indeed competent, and yet the face he presented to his current peers impeded his effectiveness in his new

Box 19

On the Road to Understanding Leadership

The study of leadership has a long and varied history. A chronology of this history is set forth below (74).

The Traits of Leadership

The systematic examination of leadership traits began in the very beginning of the twentieth century and continued through the 1950s. The contention was that there were a limited number of personal traits that could distinguish effective from ineffective leaders. According to this view, leaders were born with certain innate characteristics, or at the very least, had developed these characteristics so early in life that they had become dominant features of the individuals' personalities. According to this view then, people could be selected for leadership positions according to the traits that were associated with effective leadership behavior. However, after more than seventy years of research only three traits ranked consistently high on most lists: intelligence, initiative, and responsibility. Furthermore, by 1950 it became clear that it was almost impossible to identify the appropriate traits for good leader selection (1).

Leadership Behavior

Although many people were unable to relinquish the rationale underlying trait theory of leadership, it became increasing clear that a finite list of traits that predicted leadership effectiveness was not going to appear. Consequently, those interested in leadership research turned their attention to leadership behavior. Behaviors could be observed and objectively measured, and hence, this new interest had greater scientific validity.

The first programmatic research of leadership behavior occurred in two large midwestern universities, almost concurrently. The first, the Ohio State Leadership Studies, identified about 150 behaviors that ultimately were reduced to two primary dimensions: *initiating structure* and *consideration* (25). Initiating structure included such leader behavior as clearly stating goals, work assignments, and the expectations for each subordinate. Stated somewhat differently, people working for leaders who were high on initiating structure knew what they had to do, how they were to do it, and precisely where they stood. The second dimension, consideration, comprised behaviors that showed concern for people and their welfare.

The Michigan studies uncovered similar dimensions that denoted similar leader behaviors. However, the Michigan studies noted that two other factors seemed to be part of the total leadership pattern in any group: (1) interaction facilitation (the extent to which the leader encouraged people to become involved in the group) and (2) the extent to which group members took an active leadership role (5). This latter work culminated in Rensis Likert's continuum of leadership, which

continued

ranged from high leader authority behavior, where the leader behaved in an authoritarian fashion issuing directives and goals unilaterally, to a highly participative style, where the leader involves the group, democratically in all manners of decisions, and seeks consensus on all important work-related matters. According to Likert and his colleagues, the latter style is associated with effectiveness *if* high goals are set (54).

The behavior theories of leadership produced far more insights concerning effective leadership than the trait theory. Nevertheless, the research results produced mixed findings (1). These findings will be discussed more thoroughly in this text. However, the somewhat disappointing outcome of the research on leader behavior led to further theory development.

Contingency Theories

The basic proposition of the contingency theories is that leadership behavior will be effective depending on the circumstances. Fred Fiedler was the first major researcher of contingency leadership, and his is one of the two major programmatic research efforts on contingency theory (17–19). Fiedler identified two basic dimensions analogous to those in the Ohio State and the Michigan studies, which he called task orientation and employee orientation. His findings indicated that depending on the situation one or the other of the orientations seemed to be most effective (18–20). The major situations that Fiedler identified were: (1) leader-member relations (trusting and supportive versus antagonistic); (2) task-structure (a clear-cut, routine, and easily measured job versus a job that was ambiguous, variable, and not easily measured); and (3) position power of the leader, particularly with respect to authority as we have defined it. Fiedler's results indicated that, depending on the situation, the task-oriented leader or the employee-oriented leader would be most effective. For example, where the leader-member relations were good, and the task highly structured, a task-oriented leader seemed more effective. Employee-oriented leaders were more successful when the job provided moderate amounts of task structure and moderately good leader-member relations. These findings, along with the recent developments in motivation theory that we have already discussed, led to another major contingency research program, generally called the path-goal theory of leadership (16, 40, 42). Since we deal with that theory in detail elsewhere, we will not deal with it here.

To summarize, the concern with leadership theory dates back to the early 1900s and has shown a steady transition from orientation to orientation. Each of the theories contributes something to our knowledge of leadership. However, it seems clear that contingency orientations predominate today and will continue to produce numerous research studies.

The above discussion is based on an excellent article entitled "A Reappraisal of Leadership Theory and Training" by James Owens appearing in *Personnel Administrator*, November 1981, pp. 75–99.

job. Before his promotion, the people in manufacturing were in awe of his prodigious grasp of issues, his forthrightness, and the fact that he was almost always right. His name alone terrified those who felt they might be confronted by him. His physical attributes added to his substantial presence, for he was huge. He was nicknamed "Big Foot" because of his size 14 shoes, and when he stomped down the halls pounding his feet everything seemed to shake. Adding to his image were the myths that had grown around him. In his younger days, it was said, he singlehandedly wiped out a bar of local rowdies who had spoken disparagingly of The Company—after, we might add, supposedly having consumed a half case of the local brew.

Linc said that some of the myths could be true, but that, by and large, they were blown out of proportion. But these myths were enthusiastically perpetuated by the people in the plant. He was one of them—though he had risen through his efforts and abilities to become their leader—and they basked in his reflected glory.

But now, none of that seemed to matter. He was with a group of sophisticated men, educated in eastern universities, none of whom valued prodigious fighting or beer-drinking qualities. Instead, they enjoyed wit and subtlety in their interpersonal relations—and all of this was beyond poor Linc. In short, the charisma that Linc had exuded in Pawtucket became its opposite in New York. Linc had not changed, but the people and the situation had. Thus, if we had had to describe Linc's traits, or Warren Gray's for that matter, we could have been lulled into thinking that we had identified the key characteristics of a leader or those of a nonleader, depending on the time of our analysis. Personal attributes that trigger a sense of charisma in one situation may not in another.

There is no universal set of traits that characterize the charismatic leader—other than the general ability to trigger a charismatic response at a given time and among a particular group of people. Thus, devising a list would be neither useful nor effective. The folly of doing so is illustrated by two articles that appeared in the *Wall Street Journal,* each trying to capture President Jimmy Carter's leadership traits.

The first, dated July 12, 1976, lists: determined, disciplined, self-confident, combative, shrewd, humorless, vindictive, relentless, brassy, brilliant, moralistic, obsessed with punctuality, iron-willed, doggedly meticulous, stormy, humanitarian, expedient, and enormously ambitious. The second, dated September 23, 1977, considered Carter to be bright, confident, cool, prudish, hard-working, not terribly funny, fair, loyal, poised, aloof, princely, soft, assured, and arrogant, a man who hugs women but who is not one of the boys, a person who soaks up detail but lacks vision—and so on. Can one be arrogant, humanitarian, vindictive, loyal, soft, combative, stormy, and cool all at the same time? Probably not, though it may be possible to be all these things at different times. However, in this case, which traits are associated with Carter the leader and which with Carter the husband, friend, and father?

Even carefully constructed studies have not identified a consistent body of traits associated with effective leadership, charismatic or not. Filley, House, and Kerr point out that "the weight of the evidence does not lend strong support" to the proposition that there are a finite number of identifiable traits linked with leadership (22: 218–219). Furthermore, if such traits can be associated with effective leadership, are they all necessary, and if not, which are most important and under what conditions? Can one individual possess all or most of the traits? The answer to each of these questions is simple: we don't know.

Many of us seem to have implicit theories of what makes an effective leader. That is, we have beliefs of what a leader should be. Consequently, we attribute these traits to successful leaders to explain their success. Hence, it is logical to assume that the traits ascribed to any given leader will change according to the leader's performance.

Where are we then? To be a charismatic leader one has to be perceived as such by the group he or she leads (15). This recognition by the followers creates the charismatic leader. Of course, such leaders must furnish proof of their exceptional abilities or qualities so it will be easy for followers to be personally devoted (78). If the charismatic leader fails to do this, the charismatic authority disappears and the proofs are not contained in a compendium of traits.

Organizations implicitly realize that although they may not be able to squeeze leadership traits into a manager, they can construct situations that will increase the probability of the sense of charisma appearing. They do this by designing structures that ensure continuity of a leadership position and by sending managers to leadership training courses where elitism and the will to lead are hammered into their self-concepts—a further element of the socialization process (57). Such structures and processes are the trait levelers that help to ensure that people promoted to leadership positions will be effective, even though they possess different traits. We will deal with those organizational factors next.

Organizational Supports for Leader Behavior

We define organizational supports as those factors, apart from the person, that the organization provides to increase the probability of influencing followership behavior. The authority of the hierarchy is one; the control over rewards and punishment is another (48).

Symbols of Rank

Most organizations develop structures to separate leaders physically and symbolically from followers and enhance the leaders' ability to gain compliance and minimize costs, as well as to encourage them to exercise the leadership role.

The symbols of rank and status are evident in most instances. Wh[en we] walk into the corporate offices of any large organization, you can easily [distin]guish people in higher ranks by the kind of offices they occupy, the location of those offices, the furniture within them, and so forth. The purpose is clear. Status symbols embellish the leadership position and delineate the leader's freedom of action for those of lesser status. Also, each rank has its own symbolic charisma that is added to that of the person—an extension, in a sense, of the way in which people present themselves.

Allocation of Power

Other ways that organizations try to embellish leadership positions involve granting the leader the power to distribute organizational rewards, to facilitate task-related resource acquisition, and to develop enough policies and rules to become clearly perceived as one who has the legitimacy to command. The leader must then capitalize on the organizational support systems so that this legitimacy to lead is perceived by the group.

The leader is instrumental in providing rewards and must be perceived as such by the followership. Hence, organizations often provide the leader not only with control over rewards, but also with guidelines for their distribution. These guidelines tell the leader how to dispense rewards (for example, according to work) and also provide measurements of performance. Thus the leader, by referring to system standards, is able partially to depersonalize the manner in which he or she uses the power to punish while at the same time reserving for him- or herself the chance to praise that usually goes with offering rewards.

Since the cost of inaction when the situation clearly demands action is great, the leader must be perceived as a person who creates appropriate activity (58). Thus, in addition to everything else, leadership is a process of action (65), and the leader is empowered to initiate action. The extent to which the followership responds to this initiation of action is due in part to its own views of the rewards that will follow the action. Consequently, organizational support systems must be constructed with the followership in mind, and the rewards of following must be sufficiently clear to them.

For example, let us contrast two organizations, academic and business, that have very different leader support systems. In an academic institution, the prevailing notion of governance is collegial. That is, decisions are made among colleagues of nearly equal rank. The faculty are typically empowered to provide significant input into a wide range of decisions, including those involving promotions, scheduling, and even the policies and by-laws under which the organization is governed. Further, faculty, once tenured, cannot be fired except under severe financial exigencies or gross and willful neglect of duties. The department chairperson acts as the first among equals; providing input for promotion and tenure decisions, making recommendations on salary decisions, scheduling courses, and allocating faculty resources. However, in most cases, chairpersons are selected by the faculty, serve at their pleasure, and have little discretion in distributing money sanctions, because such resources tend to be limited. The support systems, too, are limited hierarchically and, in fact, rest to a large extent in the hands of the faculty itself. The task of leadership is primarily an interpersonal process embedded in relations with the faculty. Leadership, in this case, relies on charisma, the power of expertise, and the politics of establishing coalitions among the membership in support of a decision.

Most business organizations have very different leadership support systems. They are clearly hierarchical. Job continuance is not in the hands of the followership, and decisions to promote are made by management. There are clear organizational distinctions between those led and those who lead; enough resources are ordinarily made available for task accomplishment and for differentially distributing rewards and punishments and, as a consequence, the leadership position allows greater latitude of choice in determining the methods by which the leader may choose to relate to the group. Moving into management is normally perceived as an attractive means of satisfying power and achievement needs, not to mention career and financial mobility considerations.

Thus, the problems of leadership in these two organizations are quite different and depend to a large extent on the organizational support systems. Where strong support systems exist, the leader has more behavioral discretion (43), being less dependent on the good graces of the group. Where support systems are minimal, leaders must exercise great caution in their leadership attempts and in exercising power, for their continued incumbency is related directly to how the group views them.

Power, Influence, and Leadership: Some Nonobvious Implications

Using the power inherent in the formal structure of authority in an appropriate and equitable way may be part of the leadership process. However, our argument has been that a leader must derive some power from sources other than the formal authority structure. For example, the ability to grant or withhold personal favors is a source of informal power. We should examine leadership in the context of these other power sources, for much additional influence stems from them (30).

Reward Equity

A leader at any level in the hierarchy has the legitimate right to distribute sanctions to the followers depending on their behavior. Thus, the very important aspect of the leadership role that should increase one's legitimacy both up and down the hierarchy—but particularly with the group that one manages—is equitable distribution of the rewards and punishments among the group. This is not an inconsequential act and, indeed, is a very difficult one (11, 66). There is a dual problem in the distribution of rewards: the accurate measurement of performance, and the employee's tendency to perceive that his or her performance is more substantial than objective observers might perceive it to be (62). This problem is further compounded by the fact that other rewards and sanctions exist within an organization than those typically thought of. For example, leaders can choose to support people or not as they see fit. They can influence others in the organization to withhold or give support. And they can place people in positions of visibility or nonvisibility that can have a significant effect on the individuals' careers. Each of these acts involves the informal distribution of sanctions and does not necessarily derive from the formal authority structure or the power embedded in this structure. But they are, nevertheless, important acts of power, and where they are exercised, they create perceptions of power that reinforce the probability of influencing the behavior of the followership.

When rewards are distributed inequitably within a group, the use of power may backfire and coalitions may form against the leader (36). Here, power may diminish and the probability of influence diminishes as well. Thus, exercising a duly recognized power source, namely, the power to distribute sanctions, has significant implications for other informal power bases residing in the group. The ability of the group to withhold its consent for action is an example.

The Authority of Expertise

The use of the authority of expertise to influence decisions is leadership behavior, even though it is exercised outside the structure of formal authority. Furthermore, once exercised and successful, the "expert" can move into positions of formally designated leadership and thereby combine the authority of expertise with formal authority. This combination is difficult to resist.

Let us look at an example. The Company employed an industrial engineering consulting firm to implement a work-measurement program for the blue-collar employees. No expertise in the organization could challenge and discredit the data that this firm generated.

The work-measurement system was implemented, productivity increased, and the program was considered successful. The industrial engineers from the consulting firm who were subsequently hired in staff positions were seen as the experts and the driving force behind the efficiencies. Some of these industrial engineers were moved into line positions. As they became able to exercise power through the line hierarchy, their power grew and as a result, more of the manufacturing units were covered by the work-measurement system. And so it went. Thus, a rather significant organizational change occurred. In fact, not only was the work-measurement system implemented extensively, but a new orientation was being developed among other line management that placed an ever-increasing emphasis on production efficiency. That this occurred in the face of decreasing morale, as documented by attitude surveys, was a tribute to the power exercised by the new breed—influence that accrued originally to the authority of expertise, and then later, to that combined with formal authority. The men who enjoyed such authority were, for a time, unchallenged leaders in organizational change.

To summarize, leadership is a function of at least four important things: the *person,* the *group,* the *situation,* and the *organizational context* in which acts of leadership occur. However, because leadership involves social influence, people must respond to those who are engaging in acts of influence according to the intents of these acts—and the features that encourage such a response include the leader's charisma. Since charisma, however, is based on many intangibles, often ephemeral, organizations must provide support systems that encourage compliance regardless of the personal characteristics of the leader. These systems may be designed to increase charisma, such as symbols of rank, status, and social distance, or they may include the granting of formal authority and the power to distribute rewards. Typically, they are a combination of such things. But the intent is clear: namely, to enhance the ability of those in leadership positions to gain compliance from the followership.[1] Thus, we will turn our attention next to the things that leaders *do* to be effective.

Leader Behavior: Building a Power Base in the Group

Leaders must build on their personal attributes and the organizational supports offered to their position. They do so by behaving in ways that help the group reach its goals; satisfy important needs of the membership, individually and collectively; and develop wide networks of contacts in order to gain information and develop influence laterally and upward. In other words, leaders have to establish themselves with the group by satisfying the group's needs and by aiding its effectiveness. At the same time they must establish themselves as people to be reckoned with in the organizational context (16, 68).

Now let us refresh your memory concerning the nature of formal organizations. Remember that formal organizations are really a series of specified roles linked to each other by hierarchy and function. Each role incumbent, down to the nonsupervision level, is in a leadership position organizationally speaking. Furthermore, each is also a subordinate to the person he or she reports to, and at the same time, is a member of a peer group. In this way, most organizational supervisors occupy a "link pin" role; that is, they link the group they supervise with the group immediately above it (11, 30, 31, 32). Figure 14.1 illustrates the link pin concept.

Several relationships thus become important for those who are link pins. They must relate to their superior, to their peers, and to their subordinates.

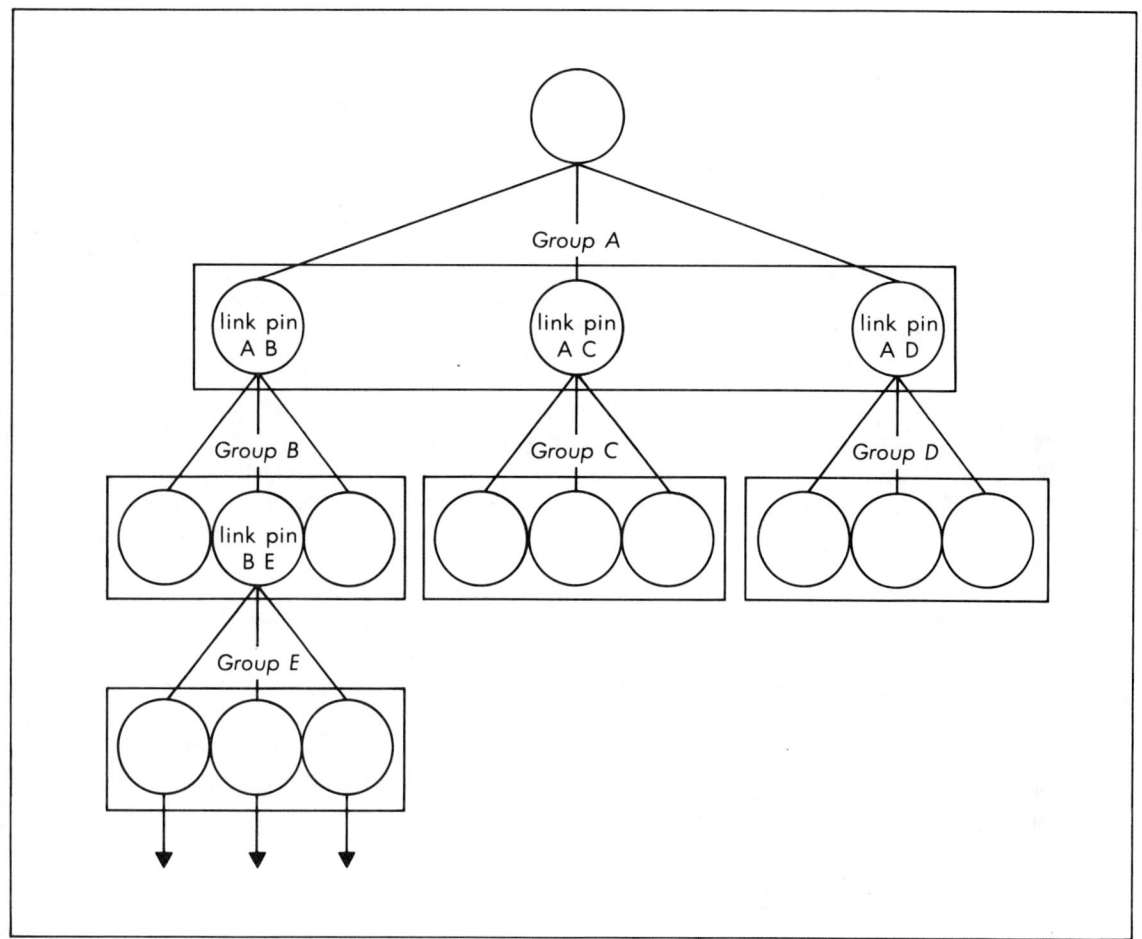

FIGURE 14.1 The Linking Function of the Leadership Role

And if they are to take the group in which they are the designated leaders to that group's goals, the quality of those relationships must be good. That is, the leader must be able to influence all those from whom the necessary goal-related resources can be gathered.

Let us first consider how leaders can build their power base within the group they lead, for with a committed and supportive group standing behind the leader, influence at other levels is more probable. We begin by examining leader behavior as a series of one-to-one relationships and then move to the leader's relationship to the group as a whole. In each case, the leadership role is constrained by how the leader facilitates reaching the goal.

Leader-Follower Dyad

As you assume the role of group leader, one of the first things that requires attention is your relationship with subordinates as individuals (49, 53). Indeed, the leader's initial activity often involves establishing role relations with each subordinate. This role-making activity is fundamental to the later relationship with the subordinates as a group and includes important goal-setting behavior (79, 80). Recent research has disclosed that the quality of the leader-follower dyadic relationship relates to several variables including job problems that subordinates face, and the leader's ability to exercise influence and "make things happen" outside the work unit (7, 11).

What is the quality of the dyadic relationship? Graen et al. state:

> Interdependencies have been found to vary in quality from something approaching a "partnership" (i.e., reciprocal influence, extracontractual behavior exchange, mutual trust, respect and liking, and common fate) at the high pole to something approaching an "overseer" (i.e., unidirectional downward influence, only contractual behavior exchange, role-defined relations, and loosely coupled fates) (32: 206).

More specifically, a vertical linkage comprises three elements: (1) a superior role, (2) a subordinate role, and (3) a series of exchange relationships between the two roles. When the leader is flexible and amenable to influence, goes beyond normal contractual relations that exist between boss and subordinate, and exhibits trust and respect, then the quality of the exchange is said to be good. And the extent to which it is seen as good is the extent to which lower participants view their situation as good. Such relationships are the infrastructure of leader-group relationships (31, 32).

Leader-Group Relations

From a historical perspective, the interest in the behavior of leaders overlapped and then supplanted the interest in traits as a research focus. The question, "What do leaders actually do to establish quality relations with subordinates and to gain high productivity from the group?" became the predominant research focus. The newer focus seemed potentially more productive as a way of understanding leadership and then providing a means of doing something to increase the leadership competency of an organization. In trait theory, the assumption was always that people are born with the traits or learn them at a very early age. That assumption places emphasis on selecting the right people. An important assumption underlying the behavior approach was that behavior could be learned. Hence, training supplanted selection as the prime means of increasing the organization's leadership competency.

Historically, three dimensions of behavior have been identified as important leader behaviors toward the group. These are task-oriented or goal-seeking behavior, people-oriented or group-supportive behavior, and participativeness (1). Task-oriented behavior includes specifying roles, issuing directives, supervising closely, emphasizing behavioral control, focusing on high performance, and setting and facilitating goals. Many of these behaviors have been associated with high productivity, although some, such as close supervision and behavioral control, have also been associated with lower levels of satisfaction (25).

People-oriented behavior includes supporting the followership, being genuinely concerned about their needs, and treating individuals as individuals within a general pattern of even-handedness. Leaders concerned with such things usually seem to have satisfied groups and sometimes higher-performing groups (4, 47, 54).

There is some evidence that task and people orientation can occur together in the same leader (2, 34, 54) or at least in the same group, if leadership is extended to include group members as well as the formally designated head (5, 54). When both orientations occur within the same group, most of the evidence so far suggests that the groups are effective or that leaders are judged as effective by their superiors.

For example, Fleishman and Harris (23) found that task orientation is associated with grievances and employee turnover. If, however, the superiors are both task-oriented and people-oriented, the grievance and turnover rates are low. They concluded that considerate supervisors can place production demands on their people without many negative consequences. There is also evidence that performance is associated with task orientation when, in addition, the leader is supportive, but not when the leader is nonsupportive (9, 24).

The idea that there are two basic dimensions to leader behavior is an attractive one for several reasons: (1) it follows closely the discovery that there are two general categories of group needs as we discussed in the previous chapter; (2) the idea emanated separately from two distinct research programs at Ohio State University and at the University of Michigan; and (3) the idea is simple and logical.

Still the research to date is inconclusive (13, 69). There seems little doubt that outcome variables correlate with both people orientations and task orientations but it is not altogether clear that the dimensions have been properly measured or that the direction of causality has been adequately determined (33).[2] As an example, we know now that follower behavior influences leader behavior and that there are significant problems with the use of the major instrument for measuring leader behavior (1, 87). Yet it seems incontrovertible that the two dimensions are important. Further, it seems intuitively sound to assume that effective leaders need to gain an *esprit de corps* from the groups they lead, which seems best done by addressing both task and social needs of the membership (1, 91).

In summary, the quality of the relationship in any superior-subordinate dyad, being related to other organizational outcomes, may be necessary for effective leader behavior. Since a leader-group relationship is made up of several such dyads, the sum quality of dyadic relations should partially determine the general relationship that the leader has to the group. Furthermore, quality seems partially a function of the variable we have previously described as a people orientation. Hence, in general, and despite some evidence to the contrary (52), people orientation is an important ingredient of leader behavior. It may even limit the negative effect of task-oriented behavior, for when the quality of the leader-group relationship is good, the leader can make more rigorous task demands (17, 18, 19, 20, 23, 87).

Participative Leadership: Increasing the Link Pin Quality

Participative leadership involves the followers directly in decision making. Leaders solicit and share information, provide opportunities for all group members to voice their opinions, encourage members to exercise influence laterally and hierarchically, and make decisions using the memberships' joint input. Decisions under participative leadership are usually consensual, and although the leader is not passive, he or she acts as the first among peers rather than as a unilateral decision maker. The leader's role is first to ensure that the democratic process is used for decision making and then to aid in decision implementation (92).

The benefits of such leadership are embedded in the process since gaining consensus implies developing norms of commitment to group goals. Furthermore, under participative leadership, the full use of the human resources existing in the group is more probable; this helps develop *esprit de corps*. Other evidence shows participative leadership increasing role clarity and subordinate knowledge about the relationship between performance and rewards (93).

The evidence suggests that participative leadership can be effective. For example, in a review of thirty-eight studies, Filley, House, and Kerr showed that participative management almost always relates positively to satisfaction, productivity, or both (22). The only negative findings occurred when (1) the people in the group were engaged in tasks that required independent work, (2) the tasks were highly structured, or (3) the tasks were routine. In the last two instances, participation is less relevant because the goals are typically defined by mechanistic standards and there is little room for discretionary behavior. However, if a change is to take place, it seems useful to involve people in determining the shape and direction of the change (8, 60).

Since participation requires not only the group's input and involvement in decision making but group consensus as well, the participative leader must deal with the group as a unit. By doing so, the leader enhances the prospects of developing group cohesion (54, 95). Notice that if a leader is instrumental creating group cohesion, the consequences of cohesion are more likely to be in line with the leader's goal than if cohesion results from other forces, particularly those motivated by a need for protection.

Kerry Drake understood this well. In Chapter 13 we saw how he initiated the force for cohesion by creating a sense of elitism, common purpose, and uncommon rewards. In this chapter we saw the group at a later stage—still cohesive, used to exercising influence, and making their own decisions. And then Warren Gray became the group manager. Notice the responses as Gray picks at the group members' individually, while guarding his authority. Gray is demanding, but on small matters; he is not supportive; and he did not grasp the fundamental properties of leading that group. Kerry Drake, on the other hand, was demanding in a larger sense. He demanded high performance as befitting the capabilities of the elite and the importance of the group effort. But, having set the stage, he left much of the execution up to the group. Under Drake, in fact, the members of the group felt that they did not *need* leadership: they could do the job well themselves. Yet it was precisely Drake's leadership style that produced this climate.

Participative leadership may seem attractive, but such a style must be used with care for there are two major, nonobvious pitfalls. First, as Pelz (76) and others have shown, participative decision making, to be fully effective, must be done in an organizational context in which the leader has enough influence or commitment of resources to execute the group's decision. Otherwise, the expectations created among the group members that they are indeed influencing decision making may not be fulfilled and the participative approach can backfire (54, 95, 99, 104).

Second, and related to the first, many managers mistake the form for the substance of the participative approach—a deadly mistake if one's credibility is to be valued. For example, a plant manager we know thought he liked the participative approach but he misunderstood it. He would use his group to bless decisions he had already made by bringing the members together and carefully manipulating the discussion, rejecting all ideas except those which reflected his inclinations. It did not take long before the man's subordinates realized what a farce the group meetings were.

When properly used, participative leadership can help the group reach a goal—the goal of developing better decisions toward organizationally sanctioned ends. However it is not always a style that will lead to higher productivity. In a recent review of all of the well-controlled studies of participative leadership, Locke et al. disclosed no consistent relationship between the use of participation and performance (56). Slightly more than half of the studies showed a positive relationship. Participation seemed to work best when the subordinates had needed skills or information and when a change was introduced that required lower participants to have a stake in the process in order to minimize resistance to change.

The Vroom and Yetton Normative Model of Participative Leadership

The Vroom and Yetton model identifies some conditions that can guide a manager in deciding whether or not to involve subordinates in decision making and, if so, how much (104). The model suggests several feasible decision styles:

Authoritative

A1. The manager makes the decision unilaterally with the information he or she has.
A2. The manager makes the decision unilaterally after getting information from other sources.

Consultative

C1. The manager makes the decision after consulting with relevant subordinates.
C2. The manager makes the decision after consulting with subordinates in a group.

Group

G1. The superior and a given subordinate make the decisions together in an intensive, one-on-one mode of decision making. As a decision mode this does not fall into the general framework of decision rules applicable to the other five modes. Rather it is more relevant to the role-making theory of Graen et al. discussed before (32).
G2. The group makes the decision together with the manager; the manager acts as a chairperson rather than as an advocate.

Vroom and Yetton suggest that three things need to be considered before engaging in participative decision making. They are: (1) the quality or rationality of the decision, (2) acceptance or commitment on the part of the subordinates to execute the decision effectively, and (3) the number of man-hours required to make the decision. Accordingly, they suggest seven decision rules. The first three rules protect the quality of decisions and the last four their acceptance.

- *The information rule.* If the leader does not possess enough information to decide and the quality is important, A1 behavior is not possible.
- *The goal congruence rule.* If the subordinates do not share the organizational goals served by the decision, G2 behavior is not feasible.
- *The unstructured problem rule.* If the quality of the decision is important,

and the leader lacks the needed information, but the problem is vague and ambiguous, A1, A2, and C1 behaviors are not appropriate.
- *The acceptance rule.* If acceptance of the decision by subordinates is important, and if a unilateral decision made by the leader would not receive acceptance, A1 and A2 behaviors are not feasible.
- *The conflict rule.* If acceptance of the decision is important, unilateral decision would not receive acceptance, and subordinates are likely to be in conflict or disagreement, A1, A2, and C1 behaviors are eliminated.
- *The fairness rule.* If the quality of the decision is unimportant and if acceptance is important and not certain to result from an autocratic decision, all except G2 behaviors are eliminated.
- *The acceptance priority rule.* If acceptance is crucial, but not ensured by an autocratic decision, and if subordinates accept the goals, all but G2 are eliminated.

According to this model, then, if the manager can meet the quality and rationality requirements of the decision, and if it is highly probable that the group will accept his decision and commit themselves to execute it effectively, then the number of man-hours required to make the decision is of the utmost importance. That is, even when full participation would lead to an effective decision, if more authoritative or consultative procedures would use fewer man-hours, then one of these would be preferable. Only when the subordinates' acceptance of the decision is important and problematic, and when the group shares organizational goals to be served by that decision is full participation clearly prescribed by the model.

More important, the model suggests when participative decision making may be inappropriate: primarily when the group does not share the organizational goals served by the decision or when there is much conflict among subordinates concerning the wisdom of the decisions. In all other cases, the so-called feasible set of options for decision making may include full participation.

Other developments in this contingency approach recognize the advantages of group participation beyond the requirements specified by the man-hour decision rule. And two additional models are proposed. The first is the time-efficient model; here, one would select a process on the basis of time required. The second is the time-investment model; here, one recognizes that participation contributes to personal and team development and will result in more informed responsible behavior by subordinates (21, 44, 45, 104). Figure 14.2 depicts our discussion of the normative model. Notice that, in all of the prescribed cases, the decision to use or not to use participation is related to the utility of that participation. When participation is neither prescribed nor proscribed, its use is a judgment call.

Vroom notes that in the research done to test the model, managers seem to conform, with training, to its constraints. However, he also says that these

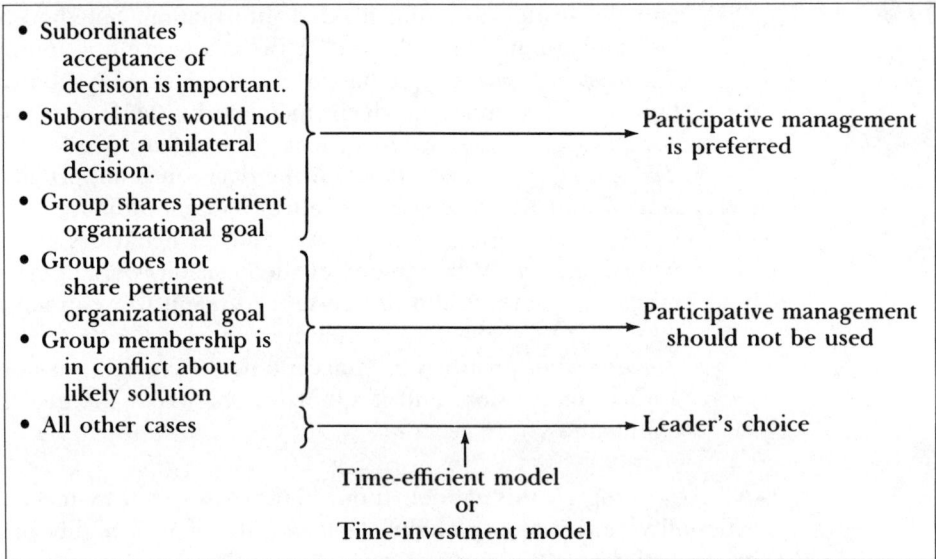

FIGURE 14.2 Prescriptions and Proscriptions of the Normative Model for Decision Making

managers seem to use the time-efficient model—most often a finding that seems perfectly logical to us since time efficiency best conforms to the organizational constraints under which most managers labor and to the values they hold (21).

Furthermore, Vroom's research and that of Heller who offers a similar model (37, 38), indicates that there is considerable variation in style within one leader depending on the circumstance. Leaders will change from authoritarian to consultative to participative according to how they view the situation (92). However, Heller's work suggests that superiors tend to perceive subordinates as less competent with less influence, and they see more of a gap between their own skills and the subordinates' skills than the subordinates do. This situation is hardly conducive to participative leadership.

Heller notes other constraints on the use of participation that are embedded more in the organizational and social requirements of the situation than in the individual leader's propensity to choose one mode of behavior over another. Some of the important constraints identified by Heller are (1) large spans of control, (2) the superior's own lack of freedom, (3) the importance of any given decision to the organization, and (4) the subordinates' lack of experience (38).

Consequently, and despite the obvious trends toward employee involvement in many of the largest and best-managed organizations, there are important organizational limitations on the use of participative management. Still it is a leadership tool that at the least ought to be considered seriously since almost all of the pertinent research evidence indicates that participative leadership provides satisfaction among most of the group and can be valuable in gaining commitment and *esprit de corps*.

We have now described the major dimensions of leader behavior as disclosed by decades of research on leadership. These behaviors include task-oriented and people-oriented behavior and the use of participative techniques to extend influence downward, gain commitment, and establish *esprit de corps* or group cohesion. We also noted that such behavior does not always work, for important situational factors may render these behaviors ineffective. Successful behavior, then, depends on the situation and on how the leader orchestrates this behavior to fit the situation. Figure 14.3 summarizes and elaborates our discussion of the behavioral approach to leadership. It shows most of the relationships and moderating variables so far supported by research evidence.

A careful examination of Figure 14.3 discloses a common feature of the suggested relationships. Either the direct relationships or the conditions under which they occur involve the way that leader behavior may help in goal attainment. For example, Figure 14.4 shows how participation can gain essential elements of effective decisions. After that, task-oriented behavior can facilitate execution of the decision, and ensure group goal reaching and effective leader behavior. In other words, the extent to which the leader behaviors are associated with group goals partly describes the leader's effectiveness.

The Leader as Instrumental to Group Goal Attainment

Evans (16), House (40), and House and Mitchell (42) have developed a model commonly called a path-goal theory, which links the leader's behavior to satisfaction of group members' needs.

The path-goal theory holds that a leadership style is effective to the extent that it clarifies and then facilitates the relationship between the subordinates' behavior and goal reaching. Furthermore, according to the theory, the leader is able to establish performance-payoff linkages. For example, in the Chapter 13 vignette, Kerry Drake established the payoff for his group: promotion to plant manager. But he made this payoff contingent on effort and performance. According to the path-goal view of leadership, the leader has an important motivational function and it is best described by:

> increasing the number and kinds of personal payoffs to subordinates for work goal attainment and making [the] paths to these payoffs easier to travel by clarifying the paths . . . and increasing the opportunities for personal satisfaction. (42: 85)

House and his co-workers feel that the path-goal behaviors are essentially those which we have previously described, i.e., task orientations or directiveness and people orientation or supportiveness and participatory leadership. To those are added goal setting as an emphasis on achievement much as we have described in our chapters on motivation.

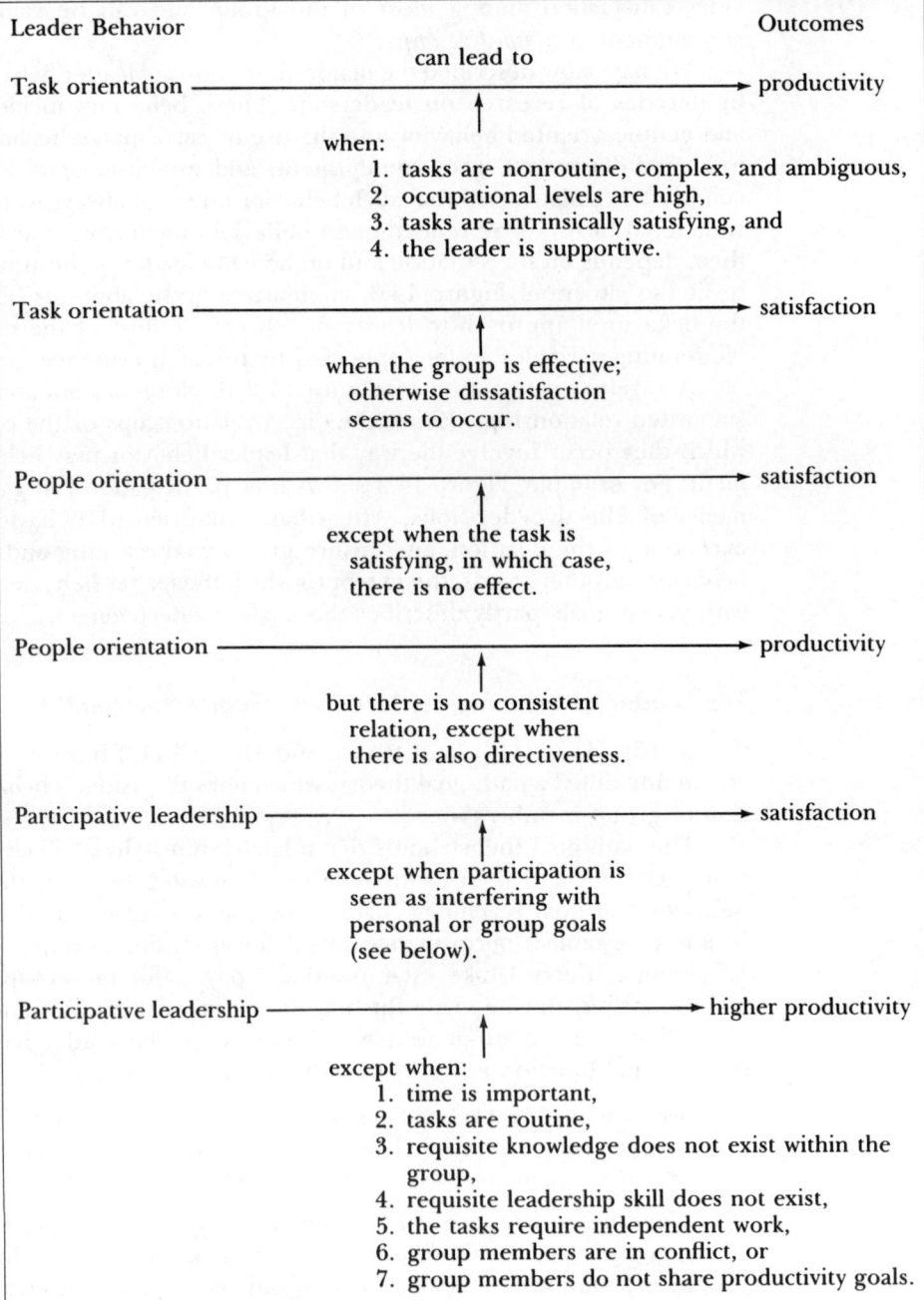

FIGURE 14.3 Some Leader Behavior: Circumstances and Outcomes[3]

A Normative Model of Participative Leadership

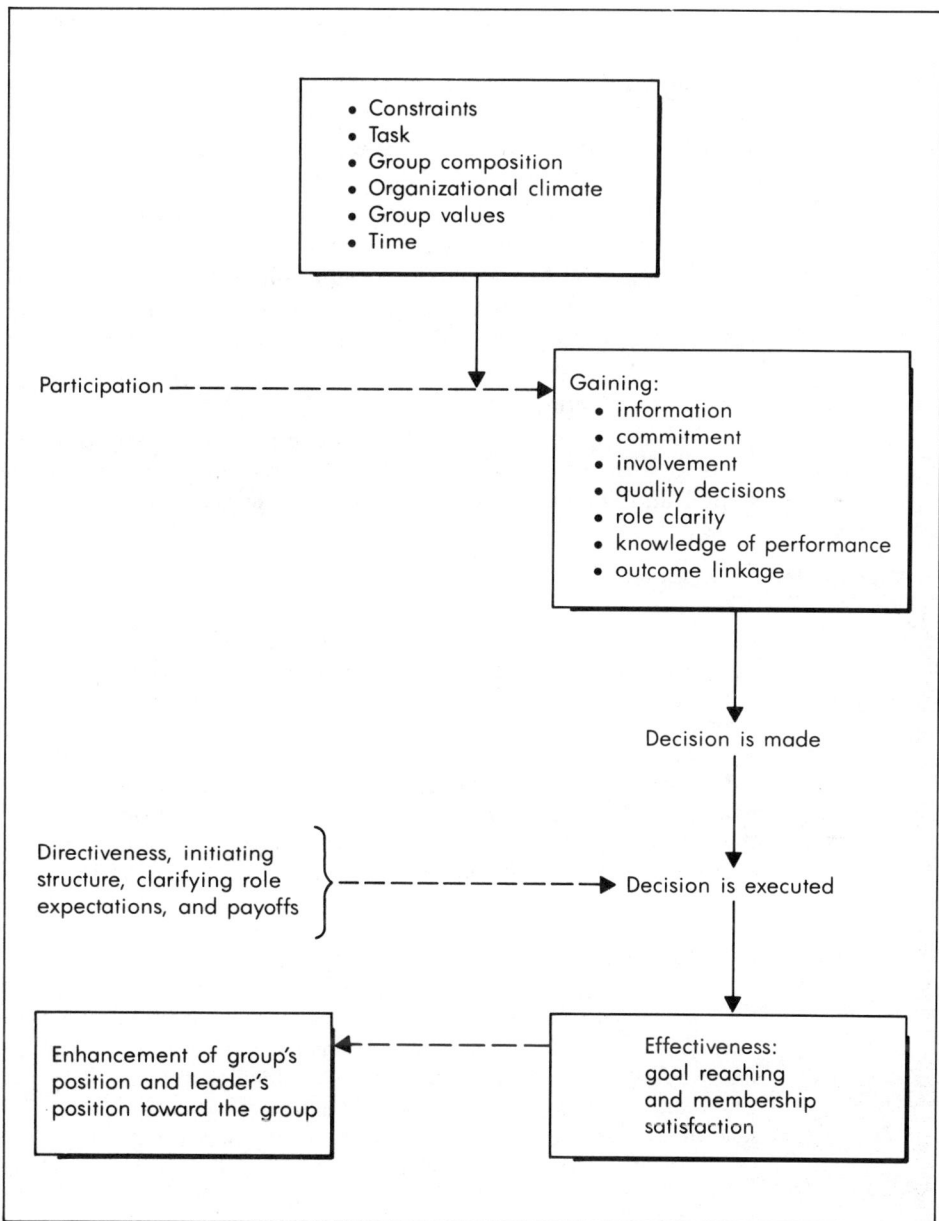

FIGURE 14.4 Goal Reaching and Leader Behavior: An Example Using Participative and Directive or Task-Oriented Behavior as Explanatory Lead Variables

Path-goal theory offers some opportunities to further specify contingencies or moderators. For example, initiating structure leads to satisfaction when the job is ambiguous (86), and when the leader has upward influence (71). In each case, structuring behavior is clearly a means by which subordinates could better reach their goals. A study by O'Reilly and Roberts, showing the effect of several moderators, is presented in Box 20.

Another study designed explicitly to test the path-goal theory as an explanation of nonobvious relationships found that initiating structure was moderated by task variety. When variety was high, initiating structure predicted high levels of satisfaction. But when variety was low the relationship between the variables was negative (34). These and other studies support the path-goal theory particularly well because they demonstrate relationships that are not obvious from other theories and research (26, 67, 88, 90, 100).

Path-goal theory is particularly compelling as a follow-up of our view of motivation in organizations. Remember that we presented motivation in instrumental and rational terms. That is, people could be motivated to the extent

---

Box 20 — When Leaders Are Viewed as Instrumental

Charles O'Reilly and Karlene Roberts set out to test certain moderators of the relationships of consideration and initiation of structure to satisfaction, commitment, and performance. The moderators included subordinate mobility, aspirations, and the amount of the leader's influence. They surveyed 562 naval high-tech personnel of all ranks using a variety of questionnaire indices for all variables except performance. Performance was measured by superior ratings on four dimensions: professional performance, military behavior, military appearance, and adaptability. These traits were combined in a single measure of performance.

The data were analyzed using a four-factor, two-level, nonorthogonal analysis of variance which enabled the investigators to determine the effect of each of the independent variables separately and then in all combinations of interactions. Most noteworthy were the findings that high initiation of structure (task orientation, directiveness) was positively associated with attitudes and behavior when subordinates had high mobility aspirations and the superior was high in influence. Put somewhat differently, when subordinates view their superior's initiating structure as instrumental to their own goal achievement, the effects were positive.

O'Reilly, C. A., and K. H. Roberts. "Supervisor Influence and Subordinate Mobility Aspirations as Moderators of Consideration and Initiating Structure." *Journal of Applied Psychology* 63 (1978): 96–102.

that they saw their action resulting in favorable payoffs. Path-goal theory posits similar outcomes but in addition places the leader within the motivational context as a facilitator or mediator of organizational needs and subordinate outcomes. That is, the leader responds to organizational needs by establishing and clarifying objectives, channeling behavior toward those objectives, and then distributing organizational payoffs according to subordinates' behavior and needs. The same view may be generalized from leaders' behavior toward subordinates to their behavior toward groups.

Notice what leaders must do under such a model. First, they must have a fairly explicit set of work goals and clearly communicate these to their group. Second, they must know and communicate what behavior is most likely going to be instrumental in achieving such goals. Third, they must be able to gain the necessary resources from the organization so that the rewards for goal attainment can be distributed to the members. Finally, they must be able to measure goal accomplishment so that inequities do not arise.

Those things are difficult to do. Furthermore, and this point is made by House and Dessler (41), the leader's role is largely supplemental and subordinate to other organizational or task constraints. For example, if the situation were highly structured, the outcome of individual efforts easily counted, and the payoffs in direct proportion to the input as with a piece-rate system, the leader's role would hardly be necessary. And there is some evidence that group performance determines leader behavior regardless of task structure (33).

Because of these and other factors, the data so far are not conclusive as to the validity of the path-goal model (68, 90). Recent research has even indicated that where the leader's freedom of action is limited, the path-goal model does not help us define "good" leader behavior (87). And we already know that organizations try to limit freedom of action in order to predict outcomes better. Nevertheless, as a means of observing leadership behavior, the model is useful, and most of the studies conducted so far support its basic propositions (63). Furthermore, the theory is consistent with our previous discussion of groups, for it is the extent to which leaders actively pursue their instrumental role in goal reaching that affects their relationship with the group. Figure 14.5 summarizes this discussion.

As we see in that figure, the extent to which leaders are instrumental in helping the group membership reach their collective goals, then, is the extent to which they have satisfactorily performed their leadership function toward the group. However, since goals of various groups may conflict and because there are finite resources within an organization, the leader may be placed in a difficult position and have to negotiate, ingratiate, and at the very least, persuade people who are empowered to decide who gets what and how. Also, another demand is placed on the group leader by those empowered to give and take away in any organization—namely, satisfactory performance.

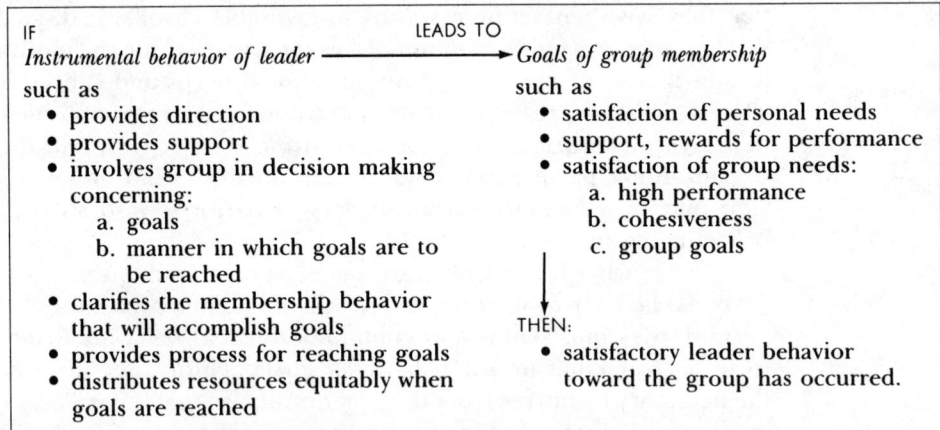

FIGURE 14.5 Leader Behavior: Goal Reaching and Leader Effectiveness

Political Behavior as Leadership

Long-term research by Fiedler revealed the importance of placing the leadership variable in an organizational context, (although this was not the research focus (17–20). Fiedler's work, the first and most extensive of several so-called contingency theories of leadership, examines the relationship between the leader's motivational orientation and group performance. That research suggests that the relationship between motivational orientation—toward people or toward task—and performance is affected by the leader's hierarchical position, the nature of the task, and the leader's relationship with the group. For example, if the leader has solid relationships with the group and is granted power because of position, and if the task is structured and unambiguous, that leader will be most effective if motivated by task (83). That is, under conditions where leaders could exercise a directive style because their hierarchical relationships both up and down were sound, and they did so, they seemed to get higher performance than when they were not directive. Fiedler calls such a condition "high situational control" (20). Fiedler's research highlights for us the political context of the leader's behavior, even though that was not the intent of the studies.[4]

An example of what we mean by political is provided by Martin and Sims (61). Using many interviews with corporation officers, they specify behaviors that earmark the successful executive. These include:

1. Taking counsel, but cautiously and only when the executive desires it and feels it necessary for his or her own purposes.
2. Forming alliances with those above and below, for in the struggles for influence, one needs devoted followers and close alliances with other

executives. Such relationships protect and provide ready communication channels.
3. Maintaining flexibility by not becoming identified with a controversial point of view. Such a person can bend with the wind when faced with forces beyond his or her control.
4. Controlling the flow of information—determining who gets what information and when—but always to suit the executive's purposes.
5. Compromising with "tongue in cheek"—giving ground on small matters while pressing forward on larger ones.
6. Applying negative timing, that is, refraining from making a decision that seems inadvisable while appearing to take action. The executive studies and plans and seems to be in the process of moving ahead until the whole thing blows over.
7. Self-dramatizing and displaying confidence, issues we dealt with earlier.
8. Always being the boss, therefore never sufficiently committed to a subordinate friend to seem uneven in handling subordinates or unduly affected by subordinate problems.

The positions drawn by Martin and Sims, as we see them, reflect organizational reality and describe accurately the behavior of many executives who have been considered leaders (10, 65). And they underline the political aspect of the social organization. Indeed, much of the research to date, although not designed with politics in mind, nevertheless demonstrates quite clearly that influence through social networks is associated with leader effectiveness. Even more than in the Fiedler work, this is true of studies from the Institute of Social Research of the University of Michigan. One of the studies from the institute showed the unhappy lot of participative leaders who had no organizational influence (76). Moreover, the most systematic program of studying organizations as social systems conducted at the institute shows that organizations operate as integrated networks of social contracts, power, and influence. That is how they get their work done; hence, the effectiveness of the system is related to the effectiveness of the political behavior. The link pin function we described before shows that each leader is a member of several groups, influencing and being influenced (54).

Lateral Relations as Leader Behavior

If we assume that effective leadership is a consequence of how the individual relates to the group in executing organizationally legitimate goals, then we must focus on how the leader can accrue resources that will enable him or her to satisfy the needs of the members. Frequently, these resources are held by others in the organization not directly under the control of the leader. It is up to the leader, then, to ferret out these resources and develop exchange relationships with those in control of the resources so that the group can advance toward its goals.

Remember that people who occupy comparable hierarchical positions are granted comparable formal authority. However, the formal organizational structure does not account for all social relationships, and it cannot take care of all the problems that occur as the various subunits move toward their part of the general organizational goals. Katz and Kahn point out, consequently, that "the formal structure of the organization must be continuously and creatively embellished or pieced out" (47:308). Furthermore, the use of existing structures may vary from one unit head to another. It is the effective use of such structures, together with the "piecing out," that distinguishes headship from leadership.

For example, a unit head who relies solely on formal authority—who goes by the book—may fulfill the formal requirements of the organization but may not be an effective leader. We have seen how Kerry Drake operated after he established his credibility with the group. He traveled around making contacts and selling his product, while his group was alone, doing what they had to do. In other words, Drake understood that he had to operate within a system that was incompletely spelled out by any formal structure or procedures.

In complex organizations there is, along with the formal structure, an informal organization that relies almost solely on social relationships. Bargaining that can add to or detract from effective leadership behavior goes on constantly within this informal organization. This is particularly true as one moves up the hierarchy and an increasing number of different functions become dependent on each other (5). For example, staff people who have no line authority must cooperate with line management in order for both to do their jobs effectively. Because staff people exercise their influence as experts, they have an implicit bargaining strength that lower-level leaders must reckon with. When staff people use the authority of expertise to advance their group's goals, they are acting as leaders.

Industrial engineers (IEs) in manufacturing organizations are a good example of this. These people are responsible for the design and setup of manufacturing processes and, in many cases, for establishing work standards by which lower-level leaders are governed. Because this staff input is typically fed into the decision-making process at higher levels in the organization, the expert knowledge that comes from this group may be used either for or against lower-level leaders through the direct hierarchy authority relationship. In this sense, the staff IEs exercise considerable influence. As a consequence, the organizationally savvy manager establishes relationships with them that are mutually beneficial, and equally savvy IEs reciprocate.

Certain trade-offs may be made. For example, the line manager may encourage the IE to accept less rigorous standards by guaranteeing performance approximating 100 percent of standard. Thus, meeting standard is not backbreaking and, therefore, undue pressure does not need to be exerted to ensure acceptable performance. But standards cannot be too loose, for this may be easily detected by higher management.

A delicate balance, therefore, needs to be struck between rigor and reason, and the chief actors in such a bargain are typically lower-level management and the IEs. Such trade-offs work to the advantage of each individual, but, more importantly for the direct line manager, the bargain is perceived by the group as effective leader behavior. The IEs are kept off the group's backs and higher-level management is reasonably well satisfied with the production level. Goals are perceived as reasonable and achievable (96).

Since the managers and the industrial engineers are not part of the same chain of command and neither has direct control over the other, the relationship can be described as negotiation, persuasion, and the exchange of favors. Three excellent studies of managers' behavior emphasize the importance of the manager's information exchange network (10, 65, 85). The better managers (leaders) seem to acknowledge the importance of establishing complex systems of information sharing that include a wide variety of informal contacts and exchange relationships. And in terms of effective leader behavior, a good deal of data suggests that those people who either position themselves in a central communication network, or who are so positioned, develop control and influence through contacts that are denied to people in more peripheral positions (35). Remember, many of the contacts a leader makes are in nonauthority relationships, and it is in this context that the social and political aspects of the leader's role are played out (77).

Relations Upward

Accumulating evidence suggests that leader behavior must be placed in a hierarchical context, for the hierarchy places greater restrictions on the latitude of the leader's behavior. That is, you have to please your boss, and in many cases your boss's boss, in order to gain latitude of action and the resources necessary to pursue the group's goals. Hence, although the hierarchy places constraints on freedom of action, compliance with these constraints paradoxically increases freedom of action in other spheres. In other words, as a leader gains the confidence of those higher up, it is likely that he or she will be less closely supervised, less subject to the demands of the formal structure, and thus freer to act according to his or her own perceptions of what is appropriate. It is necessary, then, to establish the "right" relationship up the line in order to better integrate the group's goals with broad organizational goals.

The most successful leaders are those who can bridge the gap between the organizational goals as defined hierarchically and the group's goals (28, 47, 54, 94, 97, 105). Recent research on the quality of the link-pin relationship upward, for example, discloses how that quality affected the working life of lower participants. That is, a group leader's relationship with his or her own manager affected the group that he or she headed. Leaders in high-quality linking pins with strong ties to their managers were in a better position to advance group goals (30–32).

Finally, by virtue of their position in management, leaders must focus on high levels of task accomplishment, whereas followers may not. This is typically a role requirement of leaders, and they are evaluated on how well they execute it. Clearly, the task activity has full legitimacy within the hierarchy and, under most conditions, is perceived as legitimate by the group (26). Thus, those leaders who can best help the group accomplish their task should be perceived as effective by their superiors. If effectiveness is recognized, influence should increase. Effective leaders are then given the opportunity to exercise this influence on behalf of their group. If they choose to do so, their relations with their groups would be enhanced. The consolidation and development of organizational power bases upward, downward, and laterally are key aspects of leader behavior. Effective execution of such leader strategy also enables leaders to be more directive in their relations with the group—a logical conclusion drawn from numerous leadership studies (18, 20).

Summary

Leadership is a complex set of behaviors that involves one's followers, peers, and superiors. It is a process of social influence that has motivational, political, and power components. And most of all it includes the leader's responsibility for satisfactorily moving the group toward its goals. The extent to which the leader is instrumental in legitimizing and then achieving such goals is the extent to which he or she may be judged a leader.

We described general categories of leader behavior toward the group. These are directiveness, supportiveness, and participativeness. Each has been related to measures of group effectiveness, although the extent and direction of the relationship depend largely on the circumstances. Participativeness particularly captures our attention because it has often been associated with important organizational outcomes. We specified the known conditions under which the association usually occurs. Further, participation is directly associated with power, and we noted that many organizations are currently, though tentatively, engaged in some power equalization efforts.

Further, each leader behavior described is successful to the extent that it pertains to the goals of the group members and the extent to which it cements the path-goal relationship. If the behaviors have little relevancy for goal attainment, they may have minimal motivational properties and consequently will be ineffective.

We placed leadership in the broader organizational context, for it is within this context that leadership roles are played out. We suggested that organizations provide support systems that increase the probability of compliance, enhance personal charisma, and thus better ensure that the leader can be successful as he or she strives to gain compliance and commitment from the group.

A major point in this chapter was that political and power considerations, often ignored in leadership studies, are central to leader behavior. The few studies that address actual leader behavior in organizations uniformly show that leaders spend more than half of their time in relationships apart from the group itself. This is because, to be effective, exchange relationships must be cultivated with those over whom leaders have no direct control. By establishing such relationships, leaders broaden their power base laterally and hierarchically, and increase the chances of reaching group goals. If the group successfully reaches organizationally sanctioned goals, then the leader's power is further enhanced. Leaders who attend primarily to the group, without considering the issues of politics and power, lose their effectiveness in the long run and thus fail in their leadership role.

The importance of the group has been noted. It is at the will of the group that the leader leads. There can be no continuation in power if the group itself does not recognize the legitimacy of such power. Thus, the leader must establish exchange relationships with the group that typically involve a choice of exercising or not exercising the power inherent in the formal authority relationship. Leaders who understand that (1) not exercising control, (2) not enforcing rules and regulations, and (3) going out of their way to support the group's position all involve an exchange that puts others in a position of owing them favors are leaders who understand their role. Thus, leadership is, among other things, a process of reciprocal influence based on an exchange relationship upward, sideways, and downward.

In addition, leadership is an important means of gaining visibility in organizations. Leaders who are perceived as successful by others in the organization increase their visibility and therefore their probability of being promoted. Most important, however, in the process of gaining visibility leaders can gain greater power in the organization; this has a direct effect on their ability to exchange favors in a ratio favorable to themselves and their groups. Both of these advantages increase leaders' legitimacy among group members. In addition, such visibility can add to charisma, which further embellishes the support systems the organization offers a leader for successfully executing responsibilities.

Further, leaders are often preoccupied with power, for the acquisition of power greatly facilitates the leader's ability to activate the group drive toward goal accomplishment. A major point in this chapter has been that the charisma that a leader either has or gains through actions within the organization stems from that leader's ability to get the job done. The perception of such expertise bolsters the position power of the formal authority structure. A leader who is able to capitalize on a variety of power bases increases his or her freedom to use power appropriate to a given situation.

In the final analysis, it is up to leaders—in fact, it is their responsibility—to execute decisions, and they may have to employ unilateral and autocratic behavior to do so. The success of leadership hinges on relationships upward and laterally—for participation, to be effective, must be perceived by others more powerful in the hierarchy as instrumental in getting the job done. Consequently, participative leadership as effective leadership behavior needs to be placed squarely within the hierarchy and its inherent authority. Of course, our argument has been that the skilled leader moves well beyond the limits and prescriptions of this hierarchy.

We also noted that as groups form, they develop goals that are part of and yet apart from organizationally defined goals. Furthermore, we noted that it is part of the leader's role to originate and participate in the process of goal definition. After that, the leader, in order to maintain that position, facilitates group goal getting. But we have not yet described how goals really come about in organizations. We will do that in the next chapter.

Notes

1. Of course, such structures can limit leader discretions just as well as ensure compliance (43, 72, 73, 81, 82). The discretion-limiting function of structures is probably a major reason for many of the disappointing results from studies designed to test the effectiveness of leader behavior (14, 89, 100).
2. There is substantial evidence that task orientation and people orientation are negatively related (87). Further, a major theory of leadership behavior polarizes these dimensions and considers leaders to be primarily motivated by a concern toward people or a concern toward task (19) and that successful leader behavior is firmly rooted in the situation. If, for example, the leader has established good relations with the group, is able to influence key people including his own supervisor, and the task is highly structured, then task-oriented rather than people-oriented leaders are more effective as measured by group productivity. The reasons for this probably have to do with a clearly established goal orientation and an unambiguous drive toward that goal (18, 20). Also, Larson, Hunt, and Osborn (52) provide compelling evidence that the combination of the two variables does not lend much more predictive power to extra satisfaction or performance than the use of one variable by itself. In other words, being high on both variables is unlikely but, if it does occur, it may not be necessary to establish appropriate relationships with the group. It is our view that social and task needs exist within a group, and the extent to which a leader is instrumental in satisfying needs simultaneously may be related to the extent to which he or she has a firm power base in that group. Beyond that, there is little to be said at this time.
3. The behavior-outcome relationships and the modifiers of these relationships are culled from several excellent reviews of leadership research (1, 22, 87).
4. There are significant and extensive criticisms of Fiedler's theory and his methods that we cannot describe here. The interested reader can refer to Schriesheim and Kerr (87), Hosking and Schriesheim (39), or Kabanoff (46).

References

1. BASS, B. M., and R. M. STOGDILL. *Handbook of Leadership,* revised ed. New York, Free Press, 1981.
2. BLAKE, ROBERT R., and JANE S. MOUTON. "Management by Grid Principles or Situationalism: Which?" *Group and Organization Studies* 6 (December 1981): 439–455.
3. ———. *The Managerial Grid,* Houston: Gulf Publishing, 1964.
4. ———. "Theory and Research for Developing a Science of Leadership." *Journal of Applied Behavioral Science* 18 (1982): 275–291.
5. BOWERS, D. G., and S. E. SEASHORE. "Predicting Organizational Effectiveness of a Four-Factor Theory of Leadership." In *Readings in Organizational Behavior and Human Performance,* edited by W. E. Scott and L. L. Cummings. Homewood, Ill.: Irwin, 1973.
6. BUTTERFIELD, D. ANTHONY, and GARY N. POWELL. "Effect of Group Performance, Leader Sex, and Rater Sex on Ratings of Leader Behavior." *Organizational Behavior and Human Performance* 28 (August 1981): 129–141.
7. CASHMAN, J., F. DANSEREAU, JR., G. GRAEN, and W. J. HAGA. "Organizational Understructure and Leadership: A Longitudinal Investigation of the Managerial Role-Making Process." *Organizational Behavior and Human Performance* 15 (1976): 278–296.
8. COCH, L., and J. R. FRENCH, JR. "Overcoming Resistance to Change." *Human Relations* 1 (1948): 512–523.
9. CUMMINS, R. C. "Leader-Member Relations as a Moderator of the Effects of Leader Behavior and Attitude." *Personnel Psychology* 25 (1972): 655–660.
10. DALTON, M. *Men Who Manage.* New York: Wiley, 1959.
11. DANSEREAU, F., JR., J. CASHMAN, and G. GRAEN. "Instrumentality Theory and Equity Theory as Complementary Approaches in Predicting the Relationship of Leadership and Turnover Among Managers." *Organizational Behavior and Human Performance* 10 (1973): 184–200.
12. DAVIS, KING E. "The Status of Black Leadership: Implications for Black Followers in the 1980s." *Journal of Applied Behavioral Science* 18 (1982): 309–322.
13. DREILINGER, CRAIG, RICHARD McELHENY, BRUCE ROBINSON, and DON RICE. "Beyond the Myth of Leadership Style Training: Planned Organizational Change." *Training and Development Journal* 36 (October 1982): 70–74.
14. DUBIN, R. "Supervision and Productivity: Empirical Findings and Theoretical Considerations." In *Leadership and Productivity,* edited by R. Dubin, G. D. Homans, F. C. Mann, and D. C. Miller. San Francisco: Chandler Publishing, 1965.
15. EDEN, DON, and ABRAHAM B. AHANI. "Pygmalion Goes to Boot Camp: Expectancy, Leadership, and Trainee Performance." *Journal of Applied Psychology* 67 (April 1982): 194–199.
16. EVANS, M. G. "The Effects of Supervisory Behavior on the Path-Goal Relationship." *Organizational Behavior and Human Performance* 5 (1970): 277–298.
17. FIEDLER, F. E. *Personality and Situational Determinants of Leader Behavior.* Seattle: University of Washington, Dept. of Psychology Technical Report, 1971.

18. ———. *A Theory of Leadership Effectiveness.* New York: McGraw-Hill, 1967.
19. FIEDLER, F. E., and M. M. CHEMERS. *Leadership and Effective Management.* Glenview, Ill.: Scott, Foresman, 1974.
20. FIEDLER, F. E., M. M. CHEMERS, and L. MAHER. *Improving Leadership Effectiveness: The Leader Match Concept.* New York: Wiley, 1976.
21. FIELD, R. GEORGE. "A Test of the Vroom-Yetton Normative Model of Leadership." *Journal of Applied Psychology* 67 (October 1982): 523–532.
22. FILLEY, A. C., R. J. HOUSE, AND S. KERR. *Managerial Process and Organizational Behavior,* 2nd ed. Glenview, Ill.: Scott, Foresman, 1976.
23. FLEISHMAN, E. A., and E. F. HARRIS. "Patterns of Leadership Behavior Related to Employee Grievances and Turnover." *Personnel Psychology,* 15 (1962): 43–56.
24. FLEISHMAN, E. A., and J. SIMMONS. "Relationship Between Leadership Patterns and Effectiveness Ratings Among Israeli Foreman." *Personnel Psychology* 23 (1970): 169–172.
25. FLEISHMAN, E. A., E. HARRIS, and H. E. BURIT. *Leadership and Supervision in Industry.* Columbus: Ohio State University, Bureau of Educational Research, 1955.
26. FULK, JANET, and ERIC R. WENDLER. "Dimensionality of Leader-Subordinate Interactions: A Path-Goal Investigation." *Organizational Behavior and Human Performance* 30 (October 1982): 241–264.
27. GHISELLI, E. E. "Traits Differentiate Management Personnel." *Personnel Psychology* 12 (1959): 535–544.
28. GIBB, PETER. "The Facilitative Trainer." *Training and Development Journal* 36 (July 1982): 14–19.
29. GILMORE, THOMAS N. "Leadership and Boundary Management." *Journal of Applied Behavioral Science* 18 (1982): 343–356.
30. GRAEN, G. "Role-Making Processes Within Complex Organizations." In *Handbook of Industrial and Organizational Psychology,* edited by M. D. Dunnette. Chicago: Rand McNally, 1976.
31. GRAEN, G., and W. SHIEMANN. "Leader-Member Agreement: A Vertical Dyad Linkage Approach." *Journal of Applied Psychology* 63 (April 1978): 206–212.
32. GRAEN, G., J. CASHMAN, S. GINSBURG, and W. SHIEMANN. "Effects of Linking-Pin Quality on the Quality of Working Life of Lower Participants." *Administrative Science Quarterly* 12 (September 1977): 491–504.
33. GREEN, CHARLES N. "Questions of Causation in the Path-Goal Theory of Leadership." *Academy of Management Journal* 22 (1979): 22–41.
34. GRIFFIN, R. "Relationship Among Individual, Task Design and Leader Behavior Variables." *Academy of Management Journal* 23 (1980): 665–683.
35. GUETZKOW, H. "Communications in Organizations." In *Handbook of Organizations,* edited by J. March. Chicago: Rand McNally, 1965. Pp. 534–573.
36. HALBERSTAM, D. *The Best and the Brightest.* New York: Random House, 1969.
37. HELLER, FRANK A. "Decision Processes; An Analysis of Power-Sharing at Senior Organizational Levels." In *Handbook of Work, Organization and Society,* edited by Robert Dubin. Chicago: Rand McNally, 1976. Pp. 687–745.

38. ———. "Leadership, Decision Making and Contingency Theory." *Industrial Relations* 12 (1973): 183–199.
39. HOSKING, D., and C. SCHRIESHEIM. "Review Essay of Fiedler, Chemers and Maher's 'Improving Leadership Effectiveness: The Leader Match Concept.'" *Administrative Science Quarterly* 23 (September 1978): 496–506.
40. HOUSE, R. J. "A Path Goal Theory of Leader Effectiveness." *Administrative Science Quarterly* 16 (1971): 321–338.
41. HOUSE, R. J., and G. DESSLER. "The Path Goal Theory of Leadership: Some Post-Hoc and A Priori Tests." In *Contingency Approaches to Leadership,* edited by J. G. Hunt and L. Larson. Carbondale, Ill.: Southern Illinois University Press, 1974.
42. HOUSE, R. J., and T. R. MITCHELL. "Path Goal Theory of Leadership." *Journal of Contemporary Business* 3 (1974): 81–97.
43. HUNT, J. G., R. N. OSBORN, and R. S. SCHULER. "Relations of Discretionary and Nondiscretionary Leadership to Performance and Satisfaction in a Complex Organization." *Working Paper Series,* College of Administrative Science, Ohio State University, December 1977.
44. JAGO, ARTHUR G. "A Test of Spuriousness in Descriptive Models of Participative Leader Behavior." *Journal of Applied Psychology* 63 (1978): 383–387.
45. JAGO, A. G., and VROOM, V. H. "An Evaluation of Two Alternatives to the Vroom-Yetton Normative Model." *Academy of Management Journal* 23 (1980): 347–355.
46. KABANOFF, BORIS. "A Critique of Leader Match and Its Implications for Leadership Research." *Personnel Psychology* 34 (1981): 749–764.
47. KATZ, D., and R. L. KAHN. *The Social Psychology of Organizations,* 2nd ed. New York: Wiley, 1978.
48. KERR, S., and J. M. JERMIER. "Substitutes for Leadership: Their Meaning and Measurement." *Organizational Behavior and Human Performance* 22 (1978): 375–403.
49. KIM, KEN. I., and DENNIS W. ORGAN. "Determinants of Leader-Subordinate Exchange Relationships." *Groups and Organization Studies* 7 (March 1982): 77–89.
50. KIPNIS, DAVID, STUART SCHMIDT, KARL PRICE, and CHRISTOPHER STITT. "Why Do I Like Thee: Is It Your Performance or My Orders?" *Journal of Applied Psychology* 66 (June 1981): 324–328.
51. KOCH, J. L. "Effects of Goal Specificity and Performance Feedback to Work Groups on Peer Leadership, Performance and Attitudes." *Human Relations* 32 (October 1979): 819–840.
52. LARSON, L. L., J. G. HUNT, and R. N. OSBORN. "The Great (Hi-Hi) Leader Behavior Myth: A Lesson from Occam's Razor." *Academy of Management Journal* 19 (1976): 628–641.
53. LIDEN, R. C., and G. GRAEN. "The Generalizability of the Vertical Dyad Linkage Model of Leadership," *Academy of Management Journal* 23 (1980): 451–465.
54. LIKERT, R. *The Human Organization,* New York: McGraw-Hill, 1967.
55. LIPPITT, RONALD. "The Changing Leader-Follower Relationships of the 1980's." *Journal of Applied Behavioral Science* 18 (1982): 395–403.
56. LOCKE, E. A., D. B. FEREN, V. M. MCCALEB, K. H. SHAW, and A. T. DENNY. "The

Relative Effectiveness of Four Methods of Motivating Employee Performance." In *Changes in Working Life,* edited by K. D. Duncan, M. M. Greenberg, and D. Wallis. New York: Wiley and Sons, Inc., 1980. Pp. 363–387.

57. LUNDBERG, C. C. "The Effect of Self-Expectations on Perceived Leadership: An Experimental Inquiry." Working Paper, School of Business, Oregon State University, 1978.

58. MCCALL, M. W., JR. "Leaders and Leadership of Substance and Shadow." In *Perspectives on Behavior in Organizations,* edited by J. R. Hackman, E. Lawler, III, and J. W. Porter. New York: McGraw-Hill, 1977. Pp. 375–385.

59. MCCLELLAND, D. C. *The Achieving Society.* Princeton, N.J.: Van Nostrand, 1961.

60. MARROW, A. J., D. G. BOWERS, and S. E. SEASHORE. *Management by Participation.* New York: Harper and Row, 1967.

61. MARTIN, N. H., and J. H. SIMS. "Power Tactics." In *Organizational Psychology, A Book of Readings,* edited by D. A. Kolb, I. M. Rubin, and J. M. McIntyre. Englewood Cliffs, N.J.: Prentice-Hall, 1974.

62. MEYERS, H. H. "The Pay-For-Performance Dilemma." *Organizational Dynamics* (Winter 1975): 39–50.

63. MINER, JOHN B. *Theories of Organizational Behavior.* Hinsdale Ill.: The Dryden Press, 1980.

64. ———. "The Uncertain Future of the Leadership Concept: Revisions and Clarifications." *Journal of Applied Behavioral Science* 18 (1982): 293–307.

64. MINTZBERG, H. *The Nature of Managerial Work.* New York: Harper and Row, 1973.

65. MITCHELL, TERENCE R., and LAURA S. KALB. "Effects of Job Experience on Supervisor Attributions for a Subordinate Poor Performance." *Journal of Applied Psychology* 67 (April 1982): 181–188.

67. MITCHELL, TERENCE R., JAMES R. LARSON, and STEPHEN G. GREEN. "Leader Behavior, Situational Moderators, and Group Performance: An Attributional Analysis," *Organizational Behavior and Human Performance* 18 (1977): 254–268.

68. MITCHELL, TERENCE R., and ROBERT C. LIDEN. "The Effects of the Social Context on Performance Evaluations." *Organizational Behavior and Human Performance* 29 (April 1982): 241–256.

69. NYSTROM, PAUL C. "Managers and the Hi-Hi Leader Myth." *Academy of Management Journal* 21 (1978): 325–331.

70. OBERT, STEVEN L. "Where, Then, Shall I Dump My Garbage? A Case Study of Trainer Development." *Group and Organization Studies* 6 (March 1981): 34–44.

71. O'REILLY, C. A., and K. H. ROBERTS. "Supervisor Influence and Subordinate Mobility Aspirations as Moderators of Consideration and Initiating Structure. *Journal of Applied Psychology* 63 (1978): 96–102.

72. OSBORN, R. N., and J. G. HUNT. "An Adaptive-Reactive Theory of Leadership: The Role of Macro Variables in Leadership Research." In *Leadership Frontiers,* edited by J. G. Hunt and L. Larson. Kent, Ohio: Kent State University Press, 1975.

73. ———. "Design Implications for Mechanistically Structured Systems in Complex Environments: Alterations in Contextual Variables." In *The Management of Organizational Design: Research and Methodology,* Vol. 2. Edited by R. H. Kilmann, L. R. Rondy and D. P. Slevins. New York: American Elsevier, 1978.

74. OWENS, JAMES. "A Reappraisal of Leadership Theory and Training." *Personnel Administrator* 27 (November 1981): 75–99.

75. PEARCE, JANE L. "Leading and Following Volunteers: Implications for a Changing Society." *Journal of Applied Behavioral Science* 18 (1982): 385–394.

76. PELZ, D. C. "Leadership Within a Hierarchical Organization." *Journal of Social Issues* 7 (1951): 49–55.

77. PETTIGREW, A. M. *The Politics of Organizational Decision Making.* London: Tavistock, 1973.

78. PHILLIPS, JAMES S., and ROBERT G. LORD. "Causal Attributions and Perceptions of Leadership," *Organizational Behavior and Human Performance* 28 (October 1981): 143–163.

79. QUICK, JAMES C. "Dyadic Goal Setting and Role Stress: A Field Study." *Academy of Management Journal* 22 (1979): 241–252.

80. ———. "Dyadic Goal Setting Within Organizations: Role Making and Motivational Considerations." *The Academy of Management Review* 4 (1979): 369–380.

81. REIMANN, B. C. "Dimensions of Structure in Effective Organizations: Some Empirical Evidence." *Academy of Management Journal* 17 (1974): 693–708.

82. REIMANN, B. C. "On the Dimensions of Bureaucratic Structure: An Empirical Reappraisal." *Administrative Science Quarterly* 18 (1973): 464–476.

83. RICE, ROBERT W. "Leader LPC and Follower Satisfaction: A Review." *Organizational Behavior and Human Performance* 28 (August 1981): 1–25.

84. RITTI, R., and F. H. GOLDNER. "Professional Pluralism in an Industrial Organization," *Management Science* 16 (December 1969): 233–246.

85. SAYLES, L. R. *Managerial Behavioral.* New York: McGraw-Hill, 1964.

86. SCHRIESHEIM, C., and A. S. DI NISI. "Task Dimensions as Moderators of the Instrumental Effects of Instrumental Leadership. A Two-Sample Replicated Test of the Path-Goal Leadership Theory." *Journal of Applied Psychology* 66 (1981): 589–597.

87. SCHRIESHEIM, C., and S. KERR. "Theories and Measures of Leadership: A Critical Appraisal of Current and Future Directions." In *Leadership: The Cutting Edge,* edited by J. G. Hunt and L. Larson. Carbondale, Ill.: Southern Illinois University Press, 1977.

88. SCHRIESHEIM, C., and C. J. MURPHY. "Relationships Between Leader Behavior and Subordinate Satisfaction and Performance: A Test of Some Situational Moderators." *Journal of Applied Psychology* 61 (1976): 634–641.

89. SCHRIESHEIM, C., and R. M. STOGDILL. "Crucial Dimension of Leader-Group Inter-Actions." In *Leadership: New and Developing Directions,* edited by J. G. Hunt and L. Larson. Carbondale, Ill.: Southern Illinois University Press, 1980.

90. SCHRIESHEIM, C., and MARY ANN VON GLINOW. "The Path-Goal Theory of Leadership: A Theoretical and Empirical Analysis." *Academy of Management Journal* 20 (1977): 398–405.

91. SCHRIESHEIM, J. F. "The Social Context of Leader-Subordinate Relations: An Investigation of the Effects of Group Cohesiveness." *Journal of Applied Psychology* 65 (1980): 183–194.

92. SCHULER, R. S. "Participation with Supervisor and Subordinate Authoritarianism." *Administrative Science Quarterly* 21 (1976): 320–325.
93. SCHULER, R. S. "A Role and Expectancy Perception Model of Participation in Decision Making." *Academy of Management Journal* 23 (1980): 331–340.
94. SGRO, J. A., P. WORCHEL, E. C. PENCE, and J. A. ORBON. "Perceived Leader Behavior as a Function of the Leader's Interpersonal Trust Orientation." *Academy of Management Journal* 23 (1980): 161–165.
95. SHASKIN, M. "Changing Toward Participative Management Approaches: A Model and Methods." *The Academy of Management Review* 1 (1976): 75–85.
96. SIROTA, D., and A. D. WOLFSON. "Pragmatic Approach to People Problems." *Harvard Business Review* 51 (January–February 1973): 120–128.
97. SMIRCICH, LINDA, and GARETH MORGAN. "Leadership: The Management of Meaning." *Journal of Applied Behavioral Science* 18 (1982): 257–273.
98. STOGDILL, R. M. "Interactions Among Superiors and Subordinates." *Sociometry* 18 (1955): 552–557.
99. STRAUSS, G. "Participative Management, A Critique." *Industrial Relations Research Proceedings, Cornell University* 12 (1966): 3–6.
100. VAN DE VEN, A. H. "A Framework for Organizational Assessment." *Academy of Management Review* 1 (1976): 64–78.
101. VECCHIO, ROBERT P. "Situational and Behavioral Moderators of Subordinate Satisfaction with Supervision." *Human Relations* 34 (1981): 947–963.
102. VERGA, S. *Small Groups and Political Behavior: A Study of Leadership.* Princeton, N.J.: Princeton University Press, 1961.
103. VROOM, V. H. *Some Personality Determinants of the Effects of Participation.* Englewood Cliffs, N.J.: Prentice-Hall, 1960.
104. VROOM, V. H., and P. W. YETTON. *Leadership and Decision Making.* Pittsburgh: University of Pittsburgh Press, 1973.
105. WOFFORD, J. C. "An Integrative Theory of Leadership." *Journal of Management* 8 (Spring 1982): 27–47.
106. WORTMAN, MAX S. "Strategic Management and Changing Leader-Follower Roles." *Journal of Applied Behavioral Science* 18 (1982): 371–383.
107. ZALEZNIK, A. "Managers and Leaders: Are They Different?" *Harvard Business Review* 55 (May–June, 1977): 67–78.

Discussion Questions

1. How and under what conditions might Warren Gray's leadership style be effective? What about Kerry Drake's style?
2. Why is leadership closely related to gaining compliance in organizations? How and when would a leader use power, authority, or influence to gain compliance?
3. Discuss the use of organizational supports for leader behavior? Why are such supports necessary?

4. Discuss the ways in which a leader may build a power base in the group. Why should it be important to build such a base?
5. In what ways does the instrumental theory of leadership help to summarize effective leader behavior toward the group? How does it relate to motivation?
6. The link pin concept helps to integrate leader behavior and the role of leadership in the overall organizational context. In what way?
7. Discuss the pros and cons of participative management. When might participative management be effective?
8. Discuss in detail the normative model of participative decision making. According to the model when should you and when should you not use participative leadership?

PART IV
Achieving Management Goals: Organizations in Action

Introduction to Part IV
Achieving Management Goals—The Feedback and Control System

The function of the motivation system in organizations is to energize human activity and direct this activity toward the achievement of organizational goals. Productive behavior is directed by providing individual incentives that are linked to the achievement of the outcomes desired by organization management. These incentives are in the form of material and normative rewards and punishments at the disposal of the management.

Two key axioms of reinforcement theory must hold if the motivation system is to function as expected:

- Incentives must be provided for the desired behavior.
- Individuals—consciously or subconsciously—must be able to associate the provision of the incentive with the desired behavior.

Fulfilling this second axiom is the function of our final systems building block: the feedback and control system. This means that the people responsible for promoting directed behavior—management at all levels of the organization—must be able to tell to what extent organizational goals are being achieved by individuals and subunits. Figure IV.1 illustrates schematically what is required for this.

First, goals must be *specified* at the task level for all levels of organization. This requires a sequence of breaking down or factoring higher-level goals into appropriate action-oriented subgoals at each level.

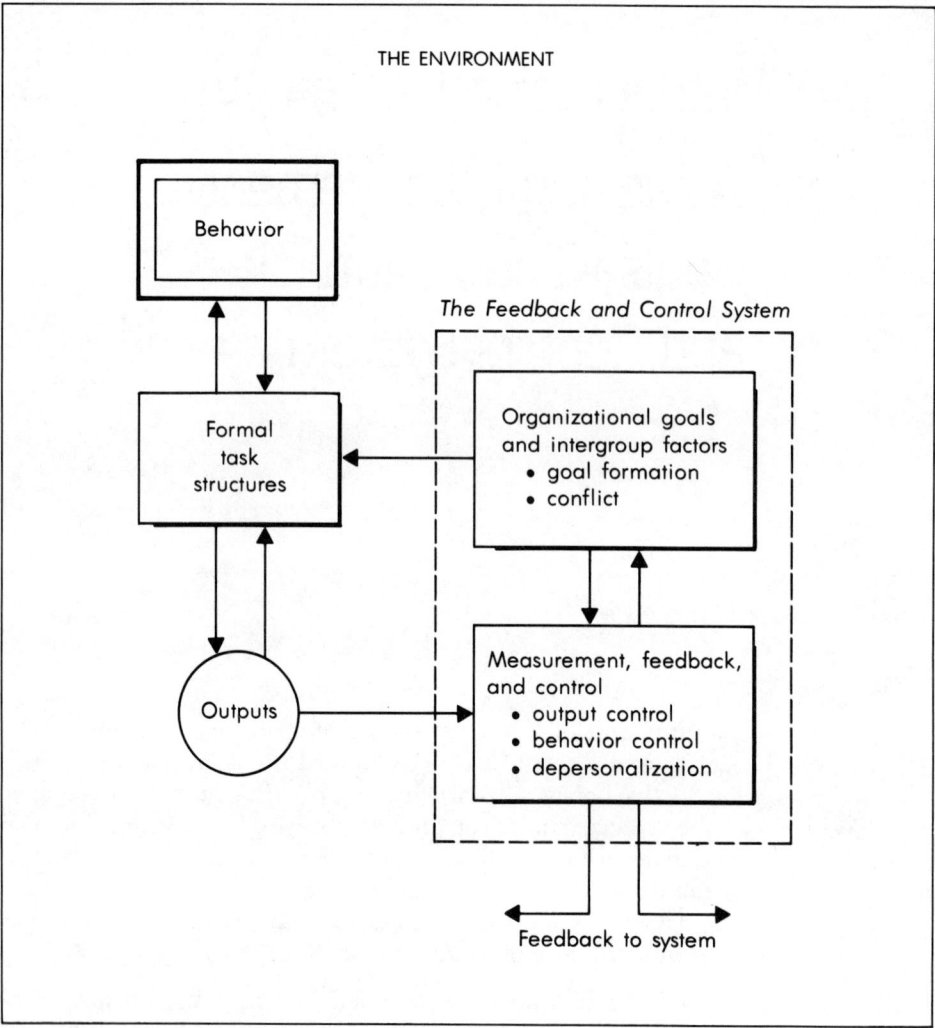

FIGURE IV.1 Achieving Management Goals—The Feedback and Control System

Next, outputs must be *measured;* an assessment must be made of the extent to which organizational goals are being achieved. If the extent of goal attainment is unknown, then obviously it is impossible to establish the link between behavior and organizational goal attainment.

This formulation requires that some means of *feedback* be available in order to inform individuals and groups of the outcomes of their behavior—to provide "knowledge of results."

Finally, *feedback* must also be provided to those in charge, the controllers of the organizational system, who may want to adjust goals, the motivation system, or the task structure in order to modify behavior.

Following this logic we have broken this part into four chapters covering the processes by which goals are developed, the consequences of systems used to measure goal achievement, the feedback and control systems used to modify behavior in light of these results, and finally, how intergroup conflict results from these processes of goal formation and goal achievement.

More than in other chapters we focus on the *systems consequences* of these organizational arrangements. And nowhere do we find Murphy's law—"If something can go wrong it will"—more in evidence. First, the process of factoring higher-level goals into action-oriented, task-level goals is imperfect. Translations warp the intent of the higher-order goal, often in the direction of promoting subunit goals of maintenance and growth. Next, because measures often do not bear a perfect relationship to the outcomes they are presumed to represent, and because control systems can handle only limited observations, feedback and control systems often produce results quite different from those desired by the management. It is this tendency and the reasons for it that constitute the major themes of the next chapters. As we have said before, ours is a problem orientation; we believe more can be learned from what goes wrong than from what goes right.

Organizational Behavior and Organizational Effectiveness: A Point of View

In this part of our text we will talk about those organizational processes for "achieving management goals." We do this from a viewpoint consistent with the perspective we have taken throughout this text: that of preparing the student to understand organizational behavior as a future professional participant in an organization. The difference between our perspective and a perspective aimed at preparing future organizational scientists will be apparent.

Here we will not be concerned with organizational design—with best ways for achieving goals, for measuring outcomes, for information feedback and control, for dealing with conflict. We will take it for granted that members of all organizations understand themselves as continually being engaged in these activities, and that they are attempting to carry them through as best they can from the standpoint of their own particular positions within those organizations. Our objective here is to understand how the principles of organizational behavior shape these processes and lead to one set of outcomes rather than another. We want to know, for example, how organizational goals come into being and what role goal formation plays in increasing or reducing intergroup conflict.

Still, the idea of being able to increase the effectiveness of our activities in organizations is a compelling one, for both members of organizations and students of organizational behavior. All of us believe that we know how we might act to increase the effectiveness of our activities. The idea of effectiveness makes sense to us. We think we would know it if we were to see it. Indeed, a casual reading of the business section of newspapers and magazines will yield numerous stories of exemplary effectiveness or ineffectiveness.

It is therefore perhaps surprising that researchers have had so much difficulty in arriving at satisfactory ways of defining and of measuring organizational effectiveness. The concept itself is poorly understood, leading to many and occasionally conflicting ways of measuring it. A recent text on organizational design notes that "the assessment of effectiveness has proven to be one of the more intractable problems in organization theory. There has been no simple solution" (5:93). Others have either concluded that the concept has so many definitions that it is virtually undefinable, or have questioned even the utility of studying the concept (3, 9, 10, 11).[1] Despite this state of affairs the idea of organizational effectiveness is a useful one for understanding why people do what they do in organizations. Therefore, to serve as a background for this part of the text we will now review some of the main approaches to the study of organizational effectiveness.

Organizational Effectiveness as a Concept

As we have said, how members of an organization make judgments about the effectiveness of activities is crucial to understanding organizational behavior. Researchers interested in organizational design have made some important distinctions between different ways of determining the effectiveness of organizations, and between the concepts of effectiveness and efficiency.

EFFECTIVENESS AND EFFICIENCY. Put briefly, the difference between effectiveness and efficiency is the difference between doing the right thing and doing a thing right (6:5). Effectiveness is a measure of the extent to which an organization achieves the purposes for which it exists. However, since organizations have multiple purposes, assessing effectiveness is a complicated matter. Still, we would say that a business that consistently turns out a better product than competitors is a more effective organization. A sales force that captures an ever-increasing market share is an effective one. Efficiency, on the other hand, is a technical concept. An efficient organization could produce the same output with fewer resources than an inefficient organization. Thus, efficiency is the ratio of output produced to input resources required. Efficiency is the narrower concept, since it is related to a limited aspect of effectiveness. An organization that is effective in other ways will be more effective if it also is efficient. However, an ineffective organization could pursue its way out of business quite efficiently. Dollars saved in the name of efficiency on a new plant and equipment, on product innovation, on marketing, and so on, eventually may bring on a serious loss of market share and perhaps the organization's demise.

Approaches to Measuring Effectiveness

Organizational researchers have proposed three primary means of assessing organizational effectiveness.

- Goal effectiveness, focusing on the extent to which stated goals of the organization are being fulfilled by output products or services (7).
- System resource effectiveness, focusing on the extent to which the organization is successful in acquiring needed input resources from its environment (4, 13).
- Internal process effectiveness, focusing on the extent to which the organization uses its human resources in ways that researchers have identified as characteristic of effective organizations (12).

Since the last two means have been proposed largely because of the observed shortcomings of the goal effectiveness approach, we will briefly investigate them before considering goal effectiveness.[2]

The *system resource* approach has been proposed primarily to handle the study of public organizations such as social services agencies or other state and municipal organizations. The goals of such organizations are often stated in terms of a public good and not in terms of tangible output. There is no "bottom line" for these organizations, and the number of units of service rendered depends directly on the resources available to generate these services. For these reasons it does make some sense to view effectiveness essentially as the ability of the organization in competition with sister organizations to acquire resources from the environment. This idea is made more compelling by the fact that success in acquiring these resources depends largely on the good opinion of that organization held by its public constituencies, on the belief that the organization indeed is doing an effective job and will use its resource allotment well.

The *internal process* approach has been most fully proposed by Rensis Likert in his "system 4" management approach (12). For many years Likert had been concerned that an organization might appear to be effective over a period of years, but that this appearance was maintained only at the price of liquidating its human assets. The use of authoritarian, pressure-tactic management, Likert argued, might increase productivity over the short term but only at the expense of increased internal conflict and breakdown of working relationships. This short-term increase in productivity, or seeming effectiveness, was being achieved through a process akin to the liquidation of capital assets. Therefore, a truer measure of effectiveness might be achieved through the assessment of internal processes such as open communications up and down the line, group processes in decision making, and the like.

Although these two approaches have been used by organizational researchers to assess effectiveness as part of research studies, it is doubtful that many professionals and managers in organizations think of the day-to-day effectiveness of their organizations in these ways. It is much more likely that they see resource acquisition and internal process as means to ends, rather than as ends in themselves. They will talk about the activities of their organizations and what they hope to achieve by those activities. In short, they will talk in terms of a goal achievement model of effectiveness.

Goal Achievement as Effectiveness

The most logically satisfying way to talk about organizational effectiveness is the way that experienced managers talk about it: in terms of specific results to be achieved and the actions intended to achieve those results. The more obvious part of effectiveness is the extent to which those actions in fact do bring about the desired results—doing the thing right. But the other part—doing the right thing—is more elusive. Just how do people in organizations develop a plan—goals—for doing the right thing? And then how do they determine that their actions indeed are following the plan, achieving the intended goals? These are the questions we intend to take up in this part of our text. We are going to analyze, from a behavioral perspective, just what goes on in an organization as professionals and managers arrive at goals and at action plans to achieve those goals.

However, we are *not* going to address the issue of organization design, of how rationally to construct organizations to be more effective. We have already pointed to some of the complexities of these issues, and, from our point of view, it is quite enough to try to cope with the complexities of understanding what goes on in organizations as professionals and managers try to program their own actions for greater effectiveness, as *they* understand the idea. We want you to understand why things take place as they do, where problems are likely to develop. As you will see, there are good reasons why not everyone can agree on a given course of action, why goals and actions are products of the "political" activities surrounding conflict and compromise. We want you to understand the problem of measuring effectiveness from the perspective of the day-to-day operations of a complex organization, and to understand why this measurement process is commonly distorted by practical problems and by the needs of participants. We want you to understand why the feedback and control process involves a great deal more than the construction of an effective management information system—to understand that the complexities of the control process involve an entire organizational system, and, finally, to understand why systems designed to produce a planned outcome in fact often produce something considerably different.

Notes

1. A good description of the complexities involved in the definition and measurement of organizational effectiveness is given by Ford and Schellenberg (8).
2. A more general framework combining aspects of all three of the listed approaches has been proposed in Connolly (2).

References

1. CAMERON, K., and D. WHETTON (eds.). *Organizational Effectiveness: A Comparison of Multiple Models.* New York: Academic Press, 1982.
2. CONNOLLY, T., E. CONLON, and S. DEUTSCH. "Organizational Effectiveness: A Multiple Constituency Approach." *Academy of Management Review* 5 (1980): 211–217.
3. CUNNINGHAM, J. B. "Approaches to the Evaluation of Organizational Effectiveness." *Academy of Management Review* 2 (1977): 463–474.
4. ———. "A Systems Resource Approach for Evaluating Organizational Effectiveness." *Human Relations* 31 (1978): 631–656.
5. DAFT, R. *Organization Theory and Design.* St. Paul, Minn.: West, 1983.
6. DRUCKER, P. *Managing For Results.* New York: Harper & Row, 1964.
7. ETZIONI, A. *Modern Organizations.* Englewood Cliffs, N.J.: Prentice-Hall, 1964.
8. FORD, J., AND D. SCHELLENBERG. "Conceptual Issues of Linkage in the Assessment of Organizational Performance." *Academy of Management Review* 7 (1982): 49–58.
9. HANNAN, M., AND J. FREEMAN. "Obstacles to Comparative Studies." In *New Perspectives on Organizational Effectiveness,* edited by P. Goodman and J. Pennings. San Francisco, Calif.: Jossey-Bass, 1977.
10. KALLMAN, E., L. REINHARTH, AND M. WAHBA. "Organizational Effectiveness: A Review of Theory and Research." *Eastern Academy of Management Proceedings* (April 1976): 44–48.
11. KIRCHHOFF, B. "Organization Effectiveness Measurement and Policy Research." *Academy of Management Review* 2 (1977): 347–355.
12. LIKERT, R. *The Human Organization.* New York: McGraw-Hill, 1967.
13. YUCHTMAN, E., AND S. SEASHORE. "A System Resource Approach To Organizational Effectiveness." *American Sociological Review* 32 (1967): 891–903.

Chapter 15
What Is an Organizational Goal?

Plan, Organize . . . (Part 1)

"I think you'll find everything you'll need here, Stanley." The voice was Dr. Faust's. The "everything" was a tape recorder, a set of tape cassettes, a note pad, and a dictating machine. Stanley's assignment was to listen to the tapes, take notes, and condense the "critical" material for Dr. Faust. If questions arose during the process, Stanley was to consult Dr. Faust, Faust being ensconced temporarily in the adjoining office.

Dr. Faust had been called in as consultant to The Company to provide some "perspective" for the executive management on what appears to be a growing problem—maintaining "crispness" and "responsiveness" in top management decision making. The Company had been growing rapidly. And, especially in its high technology business, it had lately witnessed a few outstanding fiascoes. For this reason, Faust had been instructed to turn his attention to the research and development segment of The Company. But he had also been given explicit instructions to inform the participants in his study that this most definitely was *not* another corporate "witch-hunt," contrived to ferret out, to "put the finger on," the guilty parties. This was strictly a constructive effort. Top management technical people would be interviewed in a group situation. Dr. Faust would do most of these himself. Other interviews with lower-level managers would be handled appropriately by lower-level interviewers.

Stanley was "on loan" to Dr. Faust to help him in whatever way possible in preparing his report. Right now he's sitting down to listen to his first batch of tape-recorded interviews—those done by Faust himself. The first interview started slowly as the participants warmed to the task. Stanley thought he recognized some of the voices, but this next one was Kerry, for sure. The group was talking about the difficulties of assessing future technical outcomes, and consequently the risk involved in top management decision making.

Kerry, in particular, seemed adamant. "This is something I think is eating us alive, something I do blame the management of this Company for. Major technical advances are made by taking all kinds of technical risk, not by being able to quantify the dollar amount of the risk being taken. We've had a lot of disasters in the last two or three years, I know. And as a result we've instituted a lot of formal rules. We ask engineering management to work up all the technical alternatives, and we have their technical alternatives quantified. Then we demand that technical people present these alternatives together with their associated dollar values at every one of the check points we have set up.[1]

"The problem is that the decisions [on these alternatives] are made by 'professional' managers who don't have judgment born of their own experience. They discount your technical judgment if you can't back it up with figures. This has been personally frustrating to me and I know goddamned frustrating to others. The 'professional' manager won't accept anything on faith."

"Ah—professional manager? I'm not certain that I understand your meaning here, Kerry." The question was Faust's.

"They're the New York corporate staff guys. Marsh has two assistants who have not a smattering of technical background. Don't get me wrong, they're good men, but he has nobody who can read between the lines and see the same things we do. They have worked up all kinds of controls. They *should* be a help, but they've become an end in themselves. You know what we do? We list *every* program with a dollar value and a priority. And all the programs are ranked. When things get tight, and you're looking for resources to keep another program going, you just knock off the bottom. Why it's absurd. How can you rank-order them? They all have different merits. Look, I do think something of this kind has to be done, and if the guys affected have the belief that management knows and understands what's going on, why then it's tolerable. But if they *don't* believe it, if they see it's done by machine, then you're dead.

"The problem is we don't run our own division. Mason [R and D division president] doesn't run it. In fact I've got a group of guys below me whose life blood is direct negotiation with the financial and forecasting guys in New York. Mason can't run this division because these New York guys get the figures before *he* has them."

"I think Kerry's on target, Doc." This next voice was unknown to Stanley. "The way things have been set up now it's almost impossible to make risky decisions because it's out of our hands. So it's not risk taking that bothers me so much now. What really scares me is that we've gone to wearing the belt *and* suspenders. We have demands for 100 percent guarantees to deliver; to guarantee that what you promise *is* going to happen. Anything you say you're going to do, I want a 100 percent guarantee.

"Now all you have to do [in this kind of situation] is remove a couple of guys when they couldn't keep that promise, and you're going to see the schedules start to fatten. What happens is that people make sure there is enough fat in the schedule so they can't possibly miss. But then that's *not* a schedule, not a target. What good is a target with a bull's-eye so big you can't miss?"

Once again Dr. Faust broke in. He was getting confused, he said. Perhaps a concrete example would help; an example of the kind of failure that had caused the situation they were talking about.

"No problem there," said the next speaker. "Take our manufacturing automation project. It was *created* on the basis of failure. The Company got into automation as a reaction, on a panic basis. No time, effort, or deep technical thought went into it. When New York couldn't get a commitment from one group, they changed their approach and went to another group to get a commitment. They created a mass of people and presented them with a commitment.

"But you also have to remember that it wasn't the *most* crucial project at the time. The Company also had our new expandrium process to bring on line, and this had priority when it came to key people or resources. So those people on the automation project had the feeling they were on a loser, on a panic."

Then another voice—yes, Kerry again.

"That's why the thing caused such a stink when it collapsed. When the boys walked out of the hole and said, 'We are not going to make it,' they were up against the gun of having missed their commitments. They were receiving a lot of grinding management attention. But it wasn't fair. The commitments they were trying to meet were made by others who met top management pressures and promised things that the guys who had to do the work felt could not be met. Those guys were left holding the bag."

"I see," said Faust. "But how, ah—in what way does such a promise get made, when all see it is impossible to begin with?"

"Oh! I wouldn't say all. You've got to remember that there were a lot of pressures on The Company to get into plant automation. So, regardless of the warnings, perhaps it was something that couldn't have been avoided. Total automation sounded like the next thing if you listened to The University people. But our people didn't like it. They said it was impossible, that *economically* it could never work. Franklyn said that two years from now, when the world wakes up, you're going to be in a hole you don't know how to get out of.

"[It was because] Another Company made a lot of okay promises, got a lot of good publicity by saying the right things, saying that they could whip the total automation problem. So when our people were so negative, corporate management said, 'You guys have lost your vision. Another Company is going to take the whole market.'

"I think New York felt we were going to lose the customers we already had; they lost confidence in the ability of the people handling the program to do the job and appointed a new man. They appointed a guy to go out and get the business. Well, he got the business. He promised *everything* they wanted to *anyone* who wanted it. Remember there are always some people who say that they *can* do the job. And there were also guys in research who said that we can do it. There are always conflicting opinions.

"The net result is that today Another Company is completely out of the ball game. They couldn't implement it any more than we could. It was liar's poker and they got out. But we're stuck with it."

"I would like to underscore Kerry's last point, Professor Faust." Stanley recognized that voice; it was the division vice president, and the tone carried authority.

"The difficulty was that the technical problem had been grossly underestimated. At the time, we hadn't realized that big technology breakthroughs would be required. And this problem was amplified because we had initial success with customers. Knowledgeable customers felt that what we were doing was right. The problem was that we didn't have the technical base to do the job. We still hadn't built the technical base in systems that we have in engineering.

"You see, even though a number of people were saying 'don't do it,' the people fighting against the automation program were *not* saying to avoid it because of *technical* reasons, they were saying, 'don't do it for *business* reasons.' Unfortunately, the key New York people who made the decisions were not qualified technically."

"Interesting," said Faust, noncommittally. "But I am still curious about a point Kerry made earlier, about those paying the penalty *not* being the ones who made the commitment in the first place. Why should that be?"

In answer to this question Stanley heard a new, unrecognized voice. "There are a number of top guys who had some skin in this thing. There were a number of violent arguments about it. But the guys who said yes, it would be done, mostly went on to other things. The net result is that the guys who remained on this thing lost the confidence of top management."

"But why should the ones who *committed* you to this project *not* remain to follow through? I still fail to see. . . ." Dr. Faust was interrupted before he completed his question.

"You've got to understand, Doc, that there have got to be the 'shakers and the movers' in any organization. These are the bright and successful guys who get things done in The Company. They're needed elsewhere to start new programs. So when a project gets into the implementation phase, it's usually felt that their talents are no longer being used to best advantage.

"And you've got to remember that we were developing a whole new system with this thing, in a company that encourages competition. So there are always going to be a lot of different ideas about how it should be done. You've got to let those people with different ideas fight it out among themselves, then pick one out and dry him off."

With this Stanley turned off the recorder. He sat for a minute or two, jotting down a few words on his note pad; then he strode with conviction into Dr. Faust's office.

"I think I have some answers for you, Dr. Faust. Why, I think anyone with an ounce of brains could see what the problem is here."

"So you're telling me that you have found the problem, is that it?" said Faust, with just the slightest hint of humor in his tone.

"Why, yes. At least I *think* so. Why it's clear even from just the way these people talk. How can you have effective decision making when you don't even know where you're going? You should hear them . . . !"

"I *have*," interjected Faust to remind Stanley that he had been the one who had conducted those interviews.

"Well, then you know what I mean. I mean all this talk about personal disagreement, and 'unsympathetic interpretation' of facts, about finding someone who's willing to say you can do it, even when everyone knows you can't. Why, even someone who had taken only Management 200 would know better than that."

"He would?" Dr. Faust's eyebrows arched a bit in disbelief.

"Sure. The key to effective decision making is. . . ." Stanley proceeded to set down the steps involved in setting clear, unambiguous objectives, gathering all the available facts, and then arriving at the best action alternatives—the management decision.

"Ah, yes, Management 200. Yes, I suppose you could look at it that way, though I daresay your instructor might object. But your problem, Stanley, continues to be that you make many unwarranted assumptions. You are saying to yourself, 'If *I* were making the decisions, this is how *I* should proceed. And possibly you are right. But you are making some assumptions about the process of decision making; most prominently about the origin and nature of the goals of an organization."

Faust continued, "Now I *do* recall these discussions very well. I think you will find they illustrate several important points. What were they?" This last obviously was a rhetorical question. Consequently, Stanley waited while Faust knocked the spent contents from his pipe, leaned back in his chair, and prepared to deliver his analysis.

"First, we see an illustration of the relationship of organizational goals to past experience. We had an executive talking about 'reading between the lines' and seeing the same things that he does. He talked about 'judgment born of experience.' The point, of course, is that people from different functions of the organization will interpret the objectives of the organization differently.

"Next, another of our executives talked about the measurement of projects against schedules, and how one would see the, ah—'fattening' of schedules in response to pressures to guarantee performance. Now this illustrates another aspect of goals, the tendency to concentrate on measurable aspects of organizational goals rather than on what is actually wanted. We call it *goal displacement."*

Stanley was about to ask what "goal displacement" might possibly mean, but Faust was not to be interrupted.

"We also saw a number of instances of disagreement and conflict over the direction that projects should take. Some of our executives were pushing for the use of technical criteria; others emphasized business criteria. Once again these differences are rooted in the inability of various groups to comprehend fully criteria other than those with which experience in their own function has made them comfortable.

"The business environment also plays a role. What Another Company was doing—or even more to the point—what Another Company was *suspected* of doing, what it *might* do, was a key consideration. Another aspect of the organization's goal.

"To complicate matters, the personal goals of individual executives must be factored into the equation. The personal goals of the professional advocate, for example. Recall the total plant automation project. That particular, ah—'disaster' was launched on the basis of this person's belief that his role in this project would be beneficial to his career in The Company. And so, of course, he made the implementation of that project an important objective for The Company.

"Now, unless I am quite wrong, Stanley, what you interpret as indecisiveness, lack of planning, and disorganization is, in fact, the very heart of the goal-setting process in this kind of organization, with this kind of technology. Disagreement in good faith over the probable outcomes of particular organizational actions, and hence over goals, is not only likely—it is *inevitable*. And perhaps . . . yes, perhaps, it is even desirable."

Organizational Goals and Organizational Behavior

At first, the question, "What is the goal of the organization?" seems simple enough. For business organizations, most people will reply, "To make a profit, of course." When pressed, some will concede that considerations of survival and growth must be weighed against the goal of profit maximization. For public organizations, things are somewhat less clear. The goal of profit maximization is not applicable, yet similar single goals can be found—"provide a decent and humane environment for the elderly," for example.

Despite the seeming simplicity of the question, deeper analysis provides more questions than answers. In fact, perhaps the only thing on which there is widespread agreement is that defining and identifying the goals of an organization is not easy (9, 20, 26). Nevertheless, we believe that understanding the nature of organizational goals—how they evolve from organizational processes and how they influence the behavior of members of the organization—is crucial in understanding organizational behavior.

Our purpose in this chapter is to provide a behavioral view of how organizational goals come into being, how they are modified, and how they are acted on. We try to explain that organizational goals are the outcomes of complex organizational processes involving a blending of goal statements by executives, together with the personal goals of management and the consensual goals of organizational subunits. We describe why using "the good of the organization" as a guiding principle for goal setting is next to useless, for what is thought best for the organization at the operational level is a matter of considerable informed disagreement.

Products of Conflict, Compromise, and Negotiation

Let us return for a minute to Dr. Faust's interviews with top R and D management. Through these interviews several things should have been evident about the goal formation process. The comments of each speaker revealed a great deal of dispute and disagreement concerning:

- what "the facts" actually were,
- what would be the basis for judging the relevance of "the facts"—business or technical criteria, and
- what course of action was implied by "the facts"—in effect, the choice of which goals to pursue.

The key point to understanding the message of this chapter is that the process of goal formation is much more akin to a behavioral model involving conflict, compromise, and negotiation, than to a "management" model in which goals are handed down from above, graven in stone, for action to be taken by lower levels. One of the major reasons for this is that goal statements formulated at various levels of the organizational hierarchy call for different degrees of specificity; higher-level goals are more general, perhaps even ambiguous. Therefore, since organizations constitute systems of coordinated activity, what actually is to be done and who is to do it necessarily are matters of compromise and negotiation among subunits at all levels of the organization.

In pursuing this analysis we will question first the nature of an organizational goal, and find that, in reality, it is a complex set of goal statements that must be considered when choosing among possible actions. We will find also that these goal statements vary both vertically and horizontally; by organizational level and by function. Goals stated broadly at executive levels must be translated by lower levels into operational, measurable objectives for the approval of the executive management. Similarly, at any given level of the organization these goal statements differ among subunit functions, primarily in terms of which of the statements will be chosen as the key opportunities for action. The fact that different subunits of the organization—for example, engineering and production—may choose to emphasize different aspects of the goal set accounts for the possibility of intergroup conflict. And it seems to us that at least some conflict is inevitable if that the stated goals of organizational subunits become a blueprint for the allocation of resources among those subunits.

Finally, much of what we will learn is explainable by the fact that organizations as such do not have goals; only people occupying positions in organizations do (20:134). The result is that the interpretation and modification of organizational goals are strongly related to the personal goals of organizational members in particular positions. Thus, organizational goals are the products of organizational processes that have both technical-rational and behavioral elements. To emphasize one at the expense of the other would be to misunderstand the nature of human organization.

In sum, we have two objectives for you in reading this chapter. First, we want you to understand that "organizational goal" is a far more complicated concept than it might appear at first, and why this is so. Second, we want to illustrate that this complexity derives from the fact that goal formation is at the heart of the "political" activity of the organization, and that this is so not only because goals direct choices among alternative organizational actions, but because they also embody resource allocation decisions.

Goals Embody Resource Allocation Decisions

We need to clarify why goals and resources are tied together. A nice example is the manufacturing automation project alluded to in Dr. Faust's interviews. To adopt manufacturing automation as a goal of The Company requires the equipment, space, and personnel to support the effort. These can be found either by reallocating existing resources from other uses to the new project, or by otherwise creating new equipment, space, and positions. An increased marketing effort would have the same consequences, though perhaps this is less obvious. It might be possible to put pressure on the sales force for a period of time, but this is not likely to produce long-term results of any magnitude. More than likely what will be required is an increased sales force, a larger investment in advertising, and the like. Any important effort that involves adopting a new goal or shifting the expected level of goal attainment will require additional resources.

In almost any organizational situation these resources are limited. Consequently the decision to pursue one particular goal is in fact a decision to reallocate resources away from some other goal. So to understand why conflict, compromise, and negotiation are essential features of goal formation, we must realize that resource allocation decisions represent trade-offs among vested interests of organizational subunits. If management allocates increased resources to Subunit A, then B and C must be reduced. If the choice is to go with the program proposed by Subunit A, then Subunit B's proposed program is in jeopardy, and so on. What makes these choices fraught with conflict is that personal ambitions, careers, and even the survival of entire subunits may be at stake.

What Is an Organizational Goal?

In this discussion of goals we assume that behind any organizational action there lies some explicit (or perhaps implicit) purpose that this action is supposed to achieve. This purpose commonly is called the *goal* of that action. Organizations are systems of such goal-directed activity. However, if we go beyond this common sense view and inquire at a deeper level just what we mean by goal, things become more complicated.[2]

Goals Have Different Time Horizons

Many large organizations prepare one-, two-, and five-year plans each year. These plans embody goals at differing levels of specificity. For example, a five-year goal might be to build market share to 25 percent, or perhaps to make a successful entry into the copier market. Corresponding one-year goals might be to expand the sales force by 10 percent, or to build a copier product development team headed up by Kerry Drake.

The further the objective is removed from immediate and specific action, the more difficult it will be to predict the outcome. Setting up a copier product team this year is certainly a logical step toward entering the market in five years, but it is no guarantee of success. The point is this: Very often the value of specific short-term goals depends on presumed links between these goals and their more remote outcomes. The more difficult it is for specific actors in organizations to see the effects of their actions on remote outcomes, the more likely it is that they will base their opinions about the desirability of a given action solely on the achievement of a short-term outcome—the condition we have called goal displacement (18).

Consider the soul searching that American management has been going through in the 1980s. The competitive success of Japanese industry has raised some questions; the unprofitability of some of our most basic industrial sectors has raised others. One explanation for these setbacks that has been offered by business policy strategists is that American industry has neglected the fundamentals of production and product development (13, 14). American management has increasingly been turned over to financial and legal experts who, in Kerry's words, "can't read between the lines and see the same things that technical people do." In particular, the financial management criterion of "discounted cash flow" is taken to task. The question asked is, X years from now will this project yield a greater cash flow than we can realize by investing the resources elsewhere? Technical people see such questions as engaging in long-term guesswork; this is Kerry's complaint again. In addition, these resource allocation decisions are likely to be judged against fairly predictable short-term returns—year-end returns on investment, a favorable price/earnings ratio on stock.

As a result, existing stocks of plant and equipment go unreplaced and become obsolete, and at a decided competitive disadvantage. Uncertain, long-term product development projects are foregone for the immediate benefits derived from mergers, tax write-offs, and the like. The point is that organizational goals are complex, embodying longer- as well as shorter-range objectives. Not all are easily quantified. The people who have been winning the resource allocation battles have been those with modern management training, people basing resource allocation decisions on quantifiable financial criteria that overemphasize short-term return to the neglect of qualitative long-term goals.

Goal Sets

To further illustrate the complex character of organizational goals we will need a model of the goal formation process.[3] The model is seriously oversimplified, but it serves our purpose here. To start, the goal formation process gets under way when all levels of management submit one-, two-, and five-year plans. The overall management task is to achieve the greatest *utility* possible within the restrictions of limited knowledge and limited search for alternatives. By utility we mean the *overall well-being* of the organization. This sounds terribly subjective, of course. But it is inevitably a subjective quality because utility represents inherently incomparable outcomes. Examples are needed. At the most concrete level the goal of obtaining favorable price/earnings ratios for stock has obvious utility. It is the key to maintaining sound fiscal condition. It is also high quantifiable. Considerably less concrete are the so-called image considerations. Large American corporations allocate considerable resources to what might best be described as attempting to ensure a favorable climate for business generally. Campaign contributions—often to *both* major political parties—are one means to this end.

But isn't it true, one might say, that in the long run all these things are just ways of attempting to ensure the greatest possible return on investment? When all is said and done, isn't increasing profits really the *only* goal of the business organization?

The difficulty with that line of reasoning is that it is very similar to Ted's notion that the only motives are selfish motives. If the only goal of the organization is to increase profits in the long run, then such a concept of goal cannot explain why a given short-run action was taken or not taken. For example, let us say that The Company's Management Committee (its top executive group) is considering whether to enter the copier market or to refurbish their plant in Petaluma. A number of positions, pro and con, will be taken, but each executive will argue that the course of action he or she advocates is the best to ensure long-term profitability. Therefore, since the long-term goal can account for *any* rational action, it serves no purpose here in helping us to understand organizational behavior.

Opportunities and Constraints

The goal set to be arrived at through the process we are describing consists of many statements representing the domain of various activities of the organization—design, manufacturing, sales, personnel—in various aspects—legal, financial, scientific. These statements can be thought of in two distinct ways. First, goal statements may serve as *constraints*. These are statements that limit the range of permissible actions by the organization. For example, "avoid any action that may invite antitrust proceedings," "maintain average salary levels at 115 percent of industry standard." Second, statements may serve as *opportunities*. These statements set forth *preferred means* of increasing the utility of the actions to be taken. For example, "enter the copier market." Constraints can also affect utility directly by ruling out some actions that would otherwise increase utility but are not permissible under that constraint (25).

To complicate matters, note that one person's opportunity is another person's constraint. Goals embody resource allocation decisions. The Company's decision to enter the copier market may mean that Kerry will not get his automation project. This, of course, is why conflict, compromise, and negotiation are such common features of the goal formation process.

In Figure 15.1 we present a few of the many goal statements representing the entire domain of activities of The Company. Each statement represents a contribution to the overall utility of the coordinated set of actions to be taken by The Company this year. Both Kerry, as a representative of development engineering, and Ted, as a representative of finance, agree completely that all of these are valuable activities. This is why in disputes over goals you frequently

What Is an Organizational Goal? 455

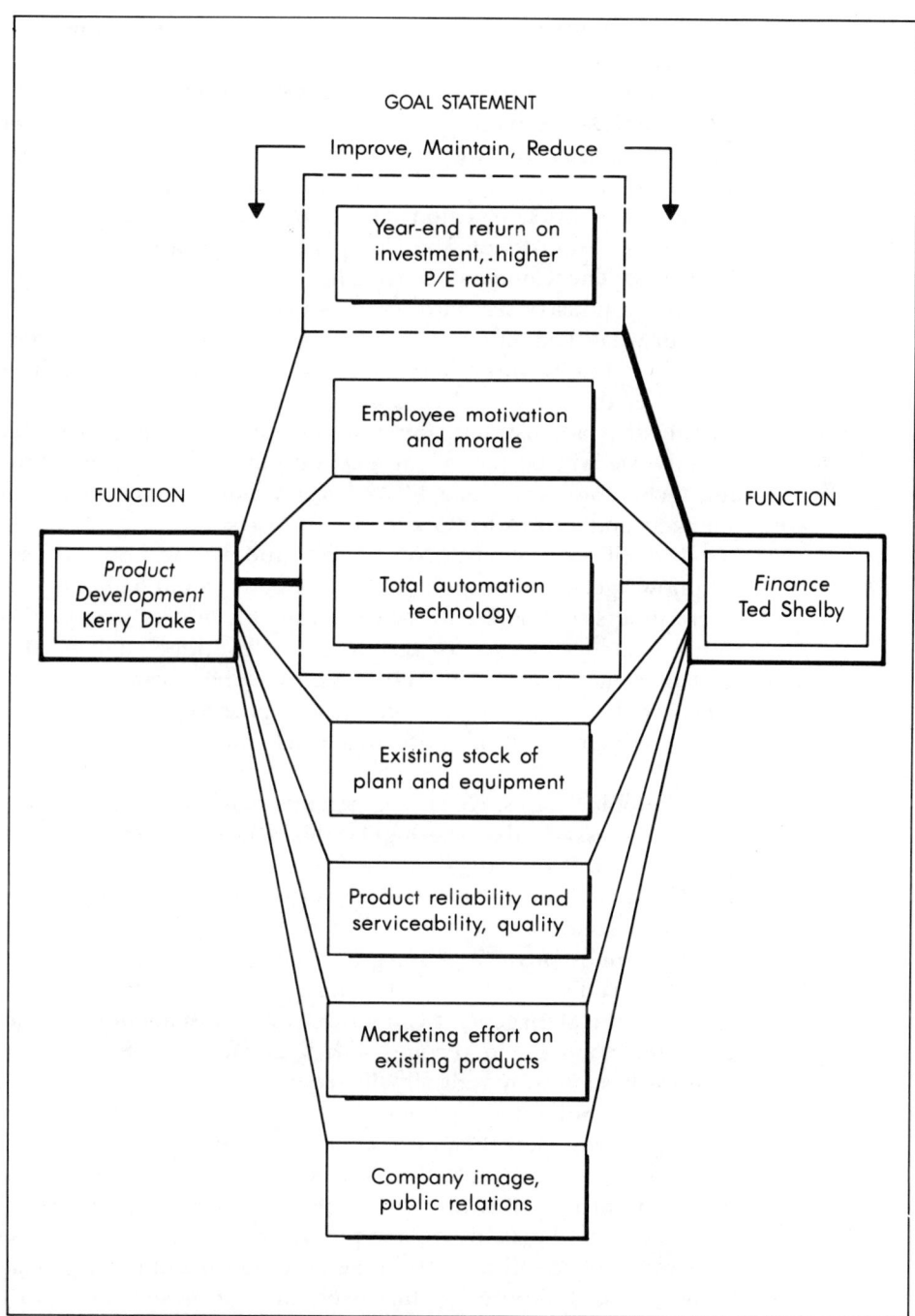

FIGURE 15.1 Goals as Opportunities or Constraints

hear, "What are we fighting about? We all want the same things don't we?" And that is true.

In each case there is a resource allocation choice involving whether or not to increase, maintain, or reduce the level of activity representing the goal. To put it another way, there is the choice of whether to treat the goal statement as an *opportunity to increase utility,* or as a *constraint that must be followed* to allow a permissible course of action. Thus, both Ted and Kerry agree that maintaining the human resources of The Company is necessary. Therefore, they can both agree that The Company must continue to follow the policy of paying 115 percent of industry standard wages—a constraint.

But what Ted and Kerry and others like them do not agree on, and what they will fight out with others on the battlefield of the executive meeting room, is whether that new total automation technology project is an opportunity or whether it is a constraint. Kerry will argue vigorously, that, "Ten years down the pike we will be out of the expandrium business if we don't get into this new technology now, today!" And Kerry will produce some trends, facts, and semifacts and figures to "prove" it.

Ted will say politely, "Nonsense." And Ted will produce some discounted cash flow figures showing that The Company would be better off investing elsewhere unless, of course, Kerry can prove his figures wrong. Ted will go along with a limited allocation of resources to "continue studying the feasibility" of total plant automation; he knows The Company cannot just drop that effort. However, Ted treats automation technology as a constraint. The Company needs some minimum level of effort, that is all. But that is not at all what Kerry has in mind.

The point is this: Kerry understands that the financial health of The Company is necessary, that the higher this year's price/earnings ratio, the better off they all will be. However, he knows also that five to ten years from now The Company will be better off, with perhaps a lower price/earnings ratio this year but a solid basis in automation technology for the future. His problem is that he cannot prove it. His figures are really guesses. They do not look as factual as Ted's. Therefore, Ted and Kerry will fight it out, trying to convince others on the Management Committee and consequently to establish goals and attendant resources in keeping with their views. Such conflict, then, does not necessarily stem from radically different goals, but rather from different choices of which to look on as opportunities and which to look on as constraints. For, typically, if you view the entire complex set that constitutes the organizational goal, you would conclude that indeed there is great commonality of purpose. It is only through this distinction between opportunities and constraints that we come to understand why people in organizations who perceive themselves to be pursuing identical goals in the best interests of the organization frequently become locked in bitter conflict over some proposed course of action (25).

Horizontal and Vertical Goal Differentiation

We use a typology of organizational goals that differentiates among political goals, planning goals, and action goals.[4] The distinctions are these: *Political goals* are statements generally made at the executive level for the purposes of maintaining resources of sentiment and power both within and outside the organization. Such statements may or may not coincide with the *planning goals* of the organization, for often political goals are stated in terms of ideals. The publicly proclaimed goals of many public sector and "service" organizations fall into this category, as do the statements of some corporations with regard to issues of environment and conservation. The public proclamation of these goals alerts the entire organization that these values are important, but specific planning goals are not given.

Planning goals are actually intended for use in guiding choices. In some instances these may even be contrary to public statements of political goals (19). Planning goals are general statements of organizational intent that provide the basis for comparisons among alternative planned strategies. They are most often voiced by middle and upper management.

Action goals are the goal statements that can be acted on directly without further specification. The distinction between action and planning goals is necessary because the planning goals set forth by middle management may not imply direct action steps by first-level management. In fact, most often it is the task of first-level management to report back to superiors to seek approval for goals phrased in action terms.

This is a descriptive typology setting forth expected states of affairs in the organization. But, in fact, there is no reason why the first-level manager may not set political goals for his or her subunit, or why an executive may not specify an action goal.

Let us turn now to the distinction between planning and action goals, and how these relate to the horizontal and vertical dimensions of the organization. Recall that in earlier chapters we saw that tasks are broken down or "factored" into subtasks—the division of labor—as one proceeds down the organizational hierarchy. The same holds true of organizational goals. For example, at the top of the organization, the vice president for manufacturing, noting that plant productivity has fallen over the past several years, may set the planning goal of increasing plant productivity over the coming year. Several levels below, at one plant location, this may translate into the action goal for first-line managers of sacrificing quality of production in order to increase quantity. Goals vary in specificity by level in the organization, with first-level managers attending to very different kinds of things than vice presidents. To first-level managers the planning goal of increasing profit is too remote to act on directly; they need more specific action goals; these action goals are presumably linked later to the profit objective. Conversely, attending to the specific details whereby action goals for increasing profit are developed explicitly is not the business of a corporate vice president.

In principle there is a link between level in the organization, level of specificity of goal statements, and the time horizons noted earlier. Executive management states general objectives. Lower-level management attends to specific outcomes. That is, goals are stated by executive management as diffuse value statements, perhaps with a political orientation; whereas goals at lower levels of the organization are specific action statements representing a "measurement" orientation.

Differentiation by Function

Just as the functional specialization of tasks occurs at lower levels of the organization, so also does a functional differentiation in goals. Functional specialization of tasks means that different subunits are equipped to serve different organizational purposes. Thus, subunits will likely choose as opportunities for action

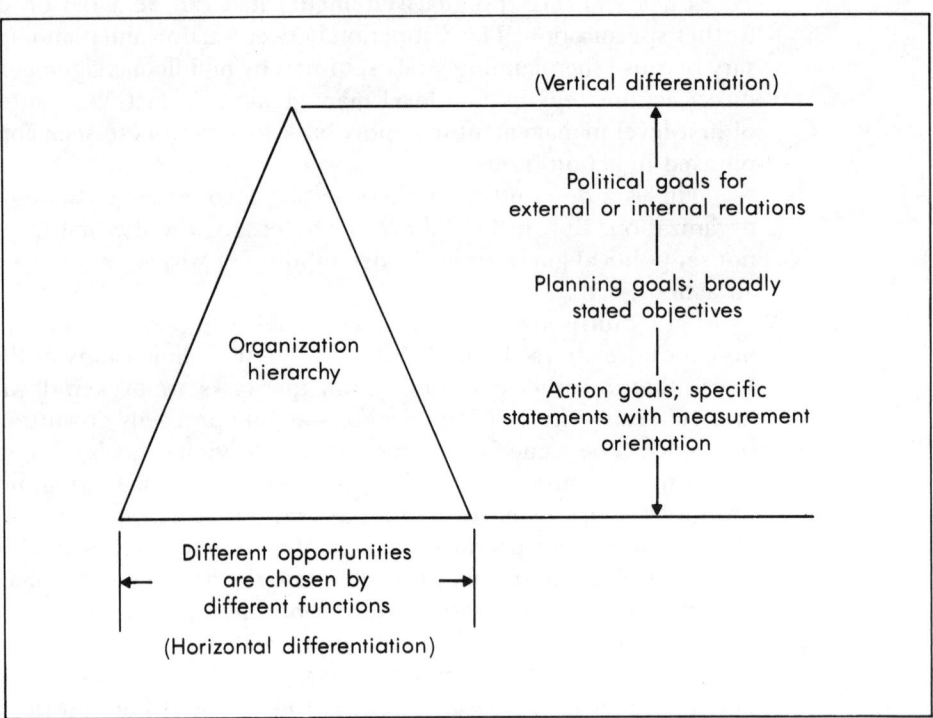

FIGURE 15.2 Schematic Relationship of Organizational Goals to Horizontal and Vertical Dimensions of Organization

those parts of the complex goal set that correspond to their particular purpose. Other parts of the goal set will be treated as constraints. The reasons for this, of course, flow directly from our earlier observations about resource allocation. Choices of opportunities for action therefore will differ widely among lower-level functions. These relationships are summarized in Figure 15.2.

To summarize thus far, goals must be understood as complex sets of statements that guide the actions of organizational members. Goal statements exist at all levels of the organization, but vary with respect to specificity, that is, with the extent to which they can be acted on directly by lower-level management without further elaboration. We can identify three dimensions along which goals vary in terms of specificity: time horizon, organizational level, and functional specialization.

Two major consequences flow from these observations. The first is that the chosen opportunities for action differ according to the function of the organizational subunits involved. Different units emphasize different opportunities, and hence, there is a potential for real disagreement as to actions to be taken. Second, as we saw earlier, the *process* of goal setting is one in which upper

TABLE 15.1 A Typology of Organizational Goals
Definition: Organizational goals are complex sets of statements that guide actions.

Goal Type	Dimension		
	Organizational Level	*Time Horizon*	*Language Used*
Political	Executive management	Organizational states perhaps never fully achievable	Diffuse and vague; possibly ambiguous
Planning	Middle management	Conditions to be achieved within some specified time, but not now	General statements of organizational intent that allow value comparisons among strategies; stated in terms of desired policy
Action	First-level management	Consequences of actions to be achieved now	Specific statements expressing preferences among action alternatives with measurable consequences

and middle management present diffuse planning goals to lower-level management, together with the charge to translate these into suitable action goals. Because the concerns at each lower level of the organization are with increasingly concrete and *measurement-oriented* goals, it is often left to lower-level management to specify how action goals are to be achieved. This situation is depicted in Table 15.1 (see the preceding page).

These facts about goal setting are important in telling us how action goals come into being. Unfortunately, depicting the process of goal setting as passing tasks from the top to successively lower levels suggests that the process itself evolves this way. But this is not true. When lower levels supply action goals they not only are responding to upper-level requests, but are also initiating the development of action goal statements. Such action goals initiated from below are justified within the more diffuse statements generally acknowledged by executive management to constitute the standing goals of the organization—planning or perhaps political. But because these action goals tend to reflect particular subunit goals linked to the survival, development, and growth of the subunit(s) involved, this process of subgoal formation—known as *suboptimization*—is regarded as potentially dysfunctional (8, 28).

Plan, Organize . . . (Part 2)

These were the things Dr. Faust told Stanley in response to his questions about the interviews he had been listening to. But Faust knew the lesson was not complete. In particular, Stanley should understand the *process* of goal setting. So it was with "new eyes," as it were, that Stanley returned to the tapes; this time he listened to interviews with directors of R and D laboratories in order to get their perspective.

These lab directors proved to be just as outspoken as the executives. Stanley was fascinated by the vivid language and the deep personal involvement that that language displayed. He was so fascinated, in fact, that it wasn't until the first few speakers had told their stories that Stanley remembered what he was supposed to be doing.

"I think you may be getting a one-sided picture of this corporate interference thing," the next speaker was saying. "There are times when *only* New York can see the big picture that local people tend to forget. Take our manufacturing automation project. New York gave them the green light to go ahead and buy systems components on a completely independent basis. And what did they do? They got a lower bid from Another Company and went ahead and bought from *them*.

"The effect on us was never considered. It was as though our laboratory wasn't considered an appropriately important part of The Company. Ours isn't like the rest of the business. The competition in systems components is far more undisciplined. Everyone's advertising new components, and most of it's misleading as hell. They're measuring these things on such different bases that the speeds and capabilities reported are just plain fictitious.

"But let me get back to my point. The basic effect of what happened to us was to generate fear in New York. The New York people started to doubt we could do the job. So we were merged with another division and our advanced components development capability has practically been destroyed."

The next voice was that of the interviewer. "I take it, then, that you think New York should have come in right in the beginning and forced the automation project to buy our own systems components?" But before the speaker could reply, yet another laboratory director impatiently disagreed.

"I can't buy that. Remember when the decision came down to take expandrium processing development out of the laboratory at Portland. It was just the same kind of thing you're talking about. Management was ready to lie down and let it happen. But Jim Johnson [laboratory director] came right back and said 'Are you all going to lie down and quit, or are you going to fight? If you want to keep your projects here, get to work. Get out some product proposals and tell me what you can do for us.'

"And that's just what Bud and I did after that machine automation fiasco. Here we had forty-five people with nothing to do. But we weren't going to give them up. Bud and I got together and dreamed up a list of products we could develop that would keep those people going. And we sold New York on them—just to keep the people going. And you know, some of them *were* dogs, but others were better than we expected."

"You hit it right on the button, Tom. Listen, nobody wanted the Techmatic System when we first came here with it, either. But we went back again and again. We went through a bloodbath with New York to get that program accepted. And look how successful it's been!

"That's our strength. Every technical decision is made right here in the laboratory. That's the problem at Paducah; it's run by a guy who's not a strong technical guy and that program is in trouble. Technical competence is the key to engineering management; and you've got to beat New York to the punch. Look, here's Marsh and some of our corporate sales planners who want to take away part of our lab, part of Jim's, and some other pieces, and pull together a new group. But it won't work that way. Here's a bunch of greenhorn salespeople going to Marsh and making recommendations about product development. But they just don't understand the relationship between manufacturing and development.

"So to keep those projects here where they belong you've got to be more aggressive than they are; you've got to be farther down the road than the New York bunch; you've got to convince Marsh and his staff that you're the best goddamn engineers to do the job. You've got to fight every step of the way."

Once again it was the voice of the interviewer, asking for clarification, "One point keeps coming up time and again and it kind of puzzles me. Maybe one of you can clarify it for me. Most of your comments seem to center around problems you have had with the New York corporate staff concerning technical issues. Is that usual procedure?"

"It was, but it isn't any more." The voice carried the authority of a senior man. "You've got to understand that engineering and manufacturing in The Company are the profit divisions; but sales . . . why, in the past the marketing people have been able to demand anything whether it was profitable or not. All they're interested in is in making their sales quota.

"So the problem was that before, the only place where technical problems as opposed to marketing ones could be ironed out was at the very highest level of the organization; the dirty linen was washed out at the highest level. It was only natural for Marsh and his staff to lose faith in engineering when all these problems were being aired daily before them, and all they saw was the conflict and uncertainty of top engineering management.

"But now that's changed. Now the battles are being fought at the divisional level. No, it's not the kind of day-to-day clawing that used to take place: it's not the pitting of the lions in the den. It's a different kind of battling and a different relationship between the top of The Company and the laboratory. It's got to be better this way."

This was enough for Stanley. Now the problem was pinpointed with certainty. Once again he roused Faust from his deliberations and presented him with the analysis: "These guys are thinking only of their *own* well-being, *not* of The Company. I mean, sometimes you've got to take a bath for the good of The Company, they should know that. So I can see where I was wrong before, it's not the executives who are to blame. It's just too much to expect them to corral that herd of wild bulls out there in the laboratories. Marsh has got to take a stronger hand in this thing—make sure that everyone is pulling together." Stanley was about to elaborate on his analysis further, but Faust simply produced another tape. Puffing slowly on his pipe, saying nothing, he took it into Stanley's room and threaded the tape into the machine. Then he gestured for Stanley to listen.

The new tape had a preface announcing that these were interviews of engineers and first-level managers in Company engineering laboratories. The content seemed more rambling than before, but several sequences bore a remarkable similarity to the previous tapes.

"In order to keep our group alive and active we need design problems," an engineer was saying. "You have to understand that we use three basic technologies in our automated systems, and our group, from the beginning, has been tied to the thin film technology. But it looks to all of us now that we're headed up a blind alley working on that, and that's a point of concern to us. So, if you take a look around, you see that Jim Brown's group is working on solid-state stuff and that they are going to do their own systems design. Why, it looks like our group will just disappear."

"So you think that will happen, do you?" interjected the interviewer.

"No, not if I have anything to say about it. Every engineer has to do some selling—spend a certain amount of his time doing it. People are continually fighting for their beliefs. For what, in their opinion, is best for The Company. So if there's going to be a switch to solid-state technology then we are going to have to convince people that we can do the job; no question, thin film will die."

With the topic established, another engineer joined in to voice his own concern, "We had the same thing with our group. Just a few months ago we got involved in a hassle of our own. We had developed a super new system for air cooling lightweight machines, but the people from Pawtucket had their own system. They weren't willing to accept ours. So finally it came down to the systems people having to make the decision.

"Some days you have to get out there and wage political warfare, you have to battle for your convictions. If you don't—if you're not willing to battle for your beliefs—then the other guy is just going to take all the money and go home."

"But why should that be so important to you? Isn't it enough to know that you've done the best job possible?" Again the interviewer.

Then it was another's turn, "Maybe so, maybe not. The problem comes if your approach *isn't* chosen. Then they cancel the project and that's just time wasted. You put in all that effort only to have the thing cancelled before it comes to fruition.

"And when your *project* gets killed, more often than not your *group* gets split up. You haven't proven yourself and you have to start all over again. You can't go back and point to what you've accomplished. That only hurts your career. But when your group *expands,* it creates the opportunity for advancement."

"Advancement?"

"Sure, career advancement. That's important, too, because it gives you the ability to choose your jobs—to get more involved in making decisions. You don't always want to come in at the bottom doing detail drawings."

Again it was the interviewer's turn. "Well then, I guess I do understand why the survival of your group is important, but you make it sound so arbitrary. So . . . so *political*. What I'm trying to say is that engineers have right or wrong answers, don't they? Isn't it just a question of which solution is technically better than another?" This obviously was *not* a good interviewing technique, but the interviewer truly was confused.

"Son, you've got to understand that decisions often have to be made by edict because you just can't make a good engineering judgment." This speaker seemed older than the others. "You can't know how things may change two years from now, so you'll never know whether you did the right or wrong thing at any given time. We make a lot of assumptions that are good to about plus or minus 50 percent. You have to include all the dimensions, all the variables, and you have to guess three to five years early in the game. You get a lot of overlap in your alternatives because of this; you can't make a solid engineering judgment. You need an edicted answer, an arbitrary answer. And, you know, if you get that arbitrary answer made fairly early in the game it perpetuates itself: it stands up because now they say, 'That's the way it's being done.'"

With that, the tape was over and Stanley was perplexed. It wasn't just the laboratory managers who seemed to be more interested in feathering their own nests than in the good of The Company. The engineers were no different. And this was disturbing. Somehow Stanley had expected better things of the engineers. Where was the rationality, the technical, information-based approach to problem solving? Stanley had the distinct feeling that he knew less than he did when it all had started.

Stanley told Dr. Faust about his perplexity, and Faust seemed unusually sympathetic. He admitted that for once the situation was so complex that there weren't many helpful actions he could suggest. Perhaps this was the way things had to be. But he did volunteer to provide a framework within which Stanley could at least understand what had been taking place for, he said, there were several major points that might help clarify why the things Stanley had observed would almost inevitably take place in this kind of organization.

Organizational Goals and Personal Goals

Professional people in organizations have a great personal involvement in the activities of their organization. And this is true not only of engineers, but of people in finance, marketing, and production—and, for that matter, of people in mental health, social services, and criminal justice. Professionals all seem to have deep personal beliefs about what people in their organization should be doing, and how they should be doing it. Interestingly, these suggestions or beliefs are almost never stated in terms of what is good for the individuals involved, but in terms of what is "best for the organization."

And, as Stanley observed, what apparently is best for the organization is seen in different and contradictory ways by people in different parts of the organization, who judge "what is best" not as *individuals,* but as people who are part of *different subunits.* That is, what Stanley noticed was not so much that different individuals hold different views—obviously that happens—but that these views of what is "best for The Company" are closely related to what seems best for their own subunit (8).

Resource Allocation: One More Time

This close relationship between "best for the Company" and "best for the subunit" impressed Stanley most in the interviews of laboratory directors and engineers. Both groups saw themselves fighting for what was best for The Company, and what was best for The Company was invariably what would ensure the continued growth and survival of their own organizational subunit. Engineers were fighting for projects to keep their project group going; laboratory directors were fighting to keep their laboratories intact by adopting new functions or new products.

The basis of the situation is simple: organizations have only limited resources—dollars and people—to allocate to various activities. Inevitably, the demands on these resources are greater than their supply. Consequently, decisions must be made about which activities to support and which not to support; about additional resources to be given to some groups and taken away from others. Thus, we saw laboratory managers dreaming up new products to stay alive; exhorting their people not to take this lying down; fighting to keep functions from being taken away from their laboratories and consolidated elsewhere. What we were seeing was the process of developing new goals for the laboratories and departments that would justify continued allocation of resources to them and hence continued survival of these organizational subunits.

PERSONAL GOALS AND SUBUNIT GOALS. Aren't these people misrepresenting their position when they say they are fighting for "what is best for The Company"? No. Why they are not is the outcome of three principles developed earlier. The first is *functional socialization*. Members of organizations are socialized into values, attitudes, and motives appropriate not only to the larger organization, but to their functional subunit as well. A point of view is developed in which the activities of that subunit are overvalued compared to the activities of competing subunits (26). Second, such motives and group norms are reinforced and supported by the development of *group cohesiveness* within the subunit, and the consequent desire to maintain the subunit's existence. Third, there is the conceptual distinction between goals that serve as opportunities for action and those which serve as constraints. Emphasis on the particular activities of the subunit as preferred opportunities and action, as opposed to constraints is a logical means for expressing such beliefs. And especially in work like research and development, where the relationship between future outcomes and current activities is relatively uncertain, the emphasis by different subunits on different opportunities is predictable.

Consequently, the link between personal goals and subunit goals is to be expected. In fact, it would be strange if personal goals and subunit goals were *not* related. As our engineers noted, career development is tied to the growth and integrity of the subunit, and the failure of the subunit means "coming in at the bottom and starting all over again."

SUBUNIT GOALS AND ORGANIZATIONAL GOALS: GRASSROOTS GOAL DEVELOPMENT. A major task of subunit leadership is finding the resources necessary to continue the existence of the subunit. This necessity leads directly to "grassroots" goal development—the development of higher-level organizational goals through the activities of lower-level subunit leadership (24, 30). In order to describe this process we use the distinction between *planning* and *action* goals. Using this distinction, we can outline two processes by which goals come into being.

The first process has executive management setting a planning goal—a "program"—and calling for lower levels of the organization to carry out the program. In response, lower levels present programs stated in terms of action goals for approval by executive management. The larger and more complex the organization, the more levels of management involved. Each successively lower level presents for approval goals stated in increasingly specific and measurement-oriented terms—increasingly in *action* terms. As these goals evolve downward, they are increasingly keyed to the subunit goals of survival and growth, and increasingly they reflect subunit preferences in the choice of opportunities for action rooted in functional viewpoints.

For example, Company executive management wanted a share of the manufacturing automation market, and started the project mentioned in Stanley's interviews. Another Company was obviously actively pursuing a project of its own. Action was necessary. It took only one person to say, "We can do it," but the details of the actual project were subject to a great deal of bitter dispute and lower-level controversy. At the executive level, then, all that was necessary was for someone to come forward and say "we can do it," and to present a general plan of attack. The details were left to the lower levels of the organization, subject to approval from above.

The second process by which goals evolve begins with the lower levels of the organization trying to convince executive management that a given program, a program that involves the future action goals of the subunit, is necessary for the achievement of a standing planning goal of The Company. In this process, lower-level management carefully tailors its presentation to higher management in terms of the goals of that next level—and so on *up* the line. The number of organizational levels involved depends on the size of the proposed program, its implications for the organization, and the resources it will need. If the program is ambitious enough and relates to a planning goal recognized by executive management as problematic for the organization, then a goal statement reflecting an opportunity for the program may be incorporated into the goal set of the entire organization.

For example, both of us participated in the personnel research function at IBM. Our objective was to do behavioral research within that company's plant and laboratory operations, and one vehicle we used to carry out that research was the questionnaire survey. Because plant and laboratory management invariably resisted these surveys, we tried to make surveys acceptable by establishing the procedure as part of the routine business of the organization. Each of us in the personnel research subunit did a great deal of "selling" to communicate to upper levels of management that the action goal of periodic "morale surveys" was the surest way to meet executive management's planning (political?) goal of maintaining high employee morale.

Probably the farthest thing from the collective mind of executive management was the need for a unit to conduct periodic surveys; we can attest to that personally. Yet because of our efforts to develop grassroots support for such surveys within lower levels of management, the notion of a periodic assessment of morale finally became established as a planning goal of the company. (For an analysis of grassroots goal development see Box 21.)

> **Box 21** **The Role of Idea Champions in Organizational Growth**
>
> The horizontal differentiation of organizations into distinct and specialized functional subunits is known to be related to the size of the organization. As organizations grow, new subunits are formed. But little is known of the internal processes by which decisions are made to allocate resources to the formation of these new subunits. In particular, how does the goal of establishing a new subunit come into being?
>
> This process of goal formation was examined in an exploratory study by Daft and Bradshaw. The authors collected historical data on the formation of thirty new departments in a sample of five universities. Their findings reveal that two separate processes are necessary to account for the birth of new departments: one to account for new administrative subunits, the other to account for new academic subunits. The major differences of interest between the two are in the location of the "idea champion" responsible for the initial proposal and nurturing of the idea for a new department, and the stimulus for the idea as coming either from a need internal to or outside of the organization.
>
> Idea champions for administrative departments typically are members of the university administration, whereas those for academic departments are faculty members or deans. New administrative departments are adopted rather quickly and easily, but the gestation period for academic departments often is long and difficult. Thus, this research supports the idea that organizational goals may be developed and implemented from the top down—the administrative process—or from the bottom up—the grassroots process—depending on the idea and the idea champion.
>
> A further conclusion of the study is that the decision to adopt the goal is really a sequence of two decisions—the more visible being the second, the formal decision to create the new subunit.
>
>> The first decision, however, occurs before the formal organization choice. Someone senses a problem and decides to propose and champion an idea as a solution. . . . Thus a very important decision that leads to structural change may be outside the dominant coalition and occur before the visible, formal choice made by the organization.
>>
>> The idea champion provides energy to move the system, energy to gain acceptance for a change; and if the work is done well, the later, visible organization decision may be a formality (455).
>
> Daft, R. L. and P. J. Bradshaw. "The Process of Horizontal Differentiation: Two Models." *Administrative Science Quarterly,* 25 (1980): 441–456.

Goals, Decisions, and Organizational Process

What we have been describing may seem to you to be *decisions*—the *consequences of goals*—and not the goals themselves. You are right. Particularly in the interviews that Stanley listened to, the executives and managers were talking explicitly about decisions that were made on the basis of goals that were not stated explicitly, but had to be *inferred* from the speaker's intentions. For example, recall the engineer who said that the switch from thin film technology to solid-state technology posed a threat to the existence of his subunit. Unquestionably the directive to proceed with the new technology was a *decision* by upper-level management. But also unquestionably it *is* an action goal for lower-level subunits. The use of different terms, then, becomes confusing only if we fail to see goal setting as an organizational process proceeding both up and down the organizational hierarchy. Planning goals at upper levels of the organization are translated into action terms (decisions) at the next level; in multilevel organizations these decisions are then passed down once again as planning goals to be translated into action terms at the next lower level.

The reverse process also takes place. Programs are "sold" from below, and justified in terms of goals appropriate at higher levels. If these programs are "bought," then this *decision* ratifies the program as an explicit *goal* of the lower organizational subunit. (Figure 15.3 illustrates the goal formation process.)

The process of organizational goal development that we have described thus far is both complicated and "political." Furthermore, the connection between immediate outcomes and sought after longer range objectives is often rather obscure. This condition within the organization often leads to the state of affairs called *goal displacement* (18).

Goal Displacement

Goal displacement is the process by which lower levels of the organization substitute or displace "claimed goals in favor of means as ends in themselves" (31:541). The most common underlying cause of goal displacement is that the initial charter of the organization is embodied in political goals stated so vaguely or diffusely that only at the level of action goals, of concrete *organizational means and procedures*, can desired outcomes and objectives be agreed upon. Such "intangible" political goals have been described as

> unanalyzable abstractions [which are] expressions of intended states of affairs that do not adequately describe the desired states or the activities that would constitute their achievement. Such intangible goals do not provide adequate guidance for group action, and as a consequence, more tangible substitutes are developed. (31:540)

Although such statements of political goals are more likely found in public organizations than in profit-making ones, the principle applies equally to all.

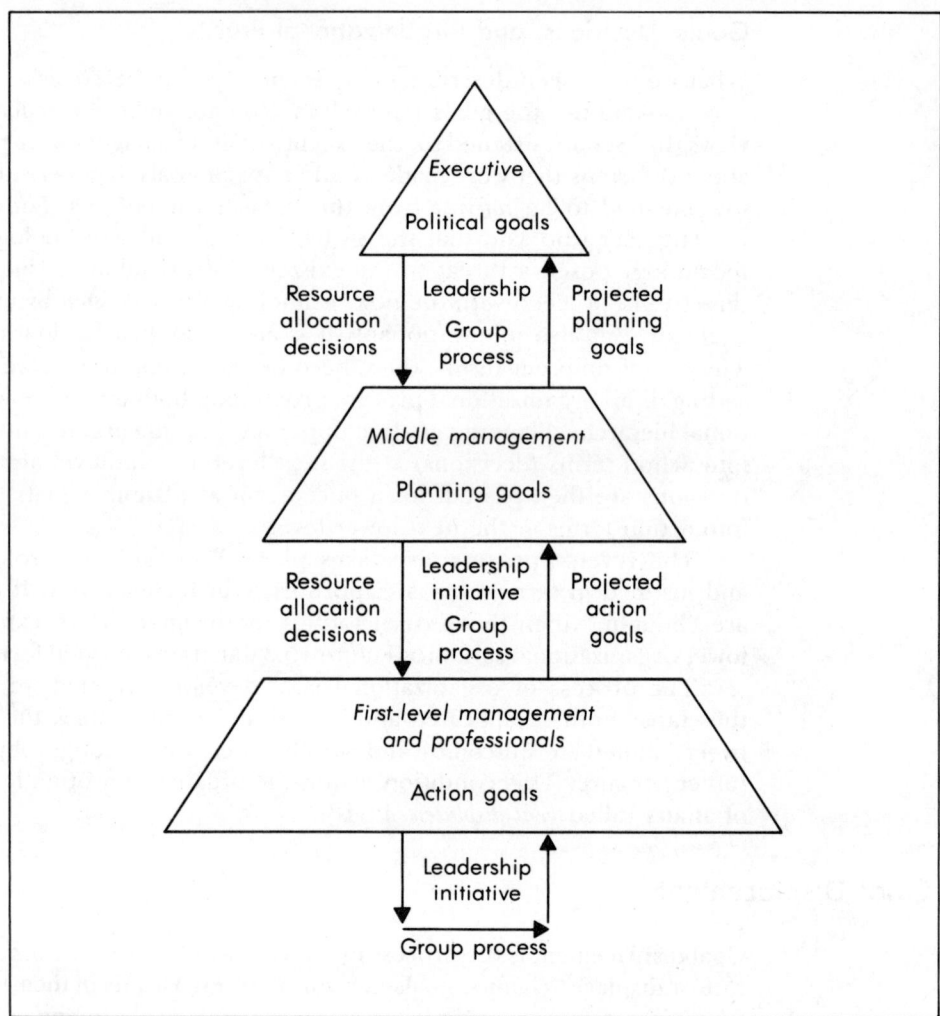

FIGURE 15.3 A Schematic of the Goal Formation Process

Four reasons can be identified as to why political goals are stated like this:

1. To accommodate diverse and even inconsistent subgoals. Programs or projects whose goals are stated in such a form can be "all things to all people," consequently allowing different suborganizations or people to feel that their interests are being served.
2. To facilitate flexibility and adaptation. Since it is impossible to state clearly which action goals can, and which cannot, be subsumed under political goals, actual organizational procedures can thus be changed

without going through the frustrating process of trying to gain agreement from diverse organizational factions.
3. To permit dramatization of organizational purposes as a spur to action. Goals stated in extravagant terms can help move people to action. Yet, goals stated in such terms, since they are idealized, seldom in themselves point directly to concrete actions.
4. To make it possible to accept the assumption that the organization is effective. If political goals are stated in such a way that it is not clear how action goals relate directly to the achievement of those political statements, then effectiveness can be claimed because certain operational procedures, practices, and processes are being followed as prescribed. Similarly, *impression management* becomes important: "Effectiveness tends to be imputed to those organizations whose personnel seem enthusiastic, sincere, hard-working, and the like." (31:545.)

If these are the reasons for the statement of goals in such a way that goal displacement is likely, then what are the likely consequences?[5] The first consequence is that organizational achievements are likely to be judged in terms of readily available, concrete statistics, records, and reports that, it is argued, are linked to the political goals. Since these are the "public" data against which the achievements of the organization are to be judged, it follows that individuals and subunit managers will tend to concentrate their efforts on "looking good" on these measures rather than directing their activities toward the organization's claimed goals.[6]

A second consequence is that program planning and rule making within the organization will be keyed to past experience and administrative expediency rather than to logical means–ends chains. Thus, actions that presumably reflect the pursuit of organizational goals actually serve the more immediate ends of system maintenance and conservation of traditional practices (31:547).

Finally, where are we likely to find goal displacement activities within organizations? The more vaguely and ambiguously stated the goal, the more likely it is to be met by displacement activity. At the action level "social responsibility," even under the best of intentions, may be acted on through speeches to civic organizations and reports of industry surveys of environmental practices rather than by real changes in possibly harmful organizational practices. At the action level, service to the customer and quality of production are displaced by more readily measurable quantitative aspects of activity.[7]

Summary

This chapter has been devoted to understanding the nature of organizational goals. We feel this topic is especially difficult—and important—for at least two reasons:

1. On the face of it, the meaning of *organizational goal* seems exceedingly simple. The goal of any organization is to make a profit, or to cure the sick, or some similar statement.
2. We usually accept the idea that the goals of the organization are those set forth by executive management, with the lower levels being responsible only for elaboration and execution.

It follows from this that conflict among factions within the organization must be the result of either "poor communications" or willful wrong-headedness.

Our contention is that all of these ideas are seriously wrong. They are wrong largely because they are based on far too simple a picture of the process of goal formation and, hence, of the nature of an organizational goal.

It is important to understand this because understanding organizational goal formation is a major part of understanding organizational behavior. Organizational goals are the keys to *resource allocation* and therefore to the *development of organizational conflict.* How is this?

A major task of management is the allocation of limited resources of dollars and manpower among subunits of the organization. As we pointed out in Chapter 13, each subunit seeks to expand, or at least to maintain, its functions and existence. Therefore, in addition to establishing cooperative relations with other subunits, each subunit is also in competition with the others for resources. And these resources are allocated largely on the basis of judgments by higher management of the extent to which the specialized functions of the subunit are crucial to the overall functioning of the organization. Note that such judgments are made among organizational units at all levels of the organization and are a key part of the management responsibility.

Disagreements arise over resource allocation even though everyone is working together for the good of The Company. The reasons why this is so lie largely in the following characteristics of an organizational goal.

Goals are complex. At any time the goal of a given action of the organization can best be understood as a complex set of guides to action, a series of tests that the action must pass to be acceptable. To single out any one of these as *the* goal is misleading. Goals take on additional complexity on the time horizon. There may be several hoped for ends of the action, some relating to immediate outcomes, some to more remote objectives, and some to quite distant ends or ideals, ends that may be unattainable in practical terms. Thus the question arises as to which of these hoped for end results is said to be *the* goal of the action to be taken. Do we emphasize the immediate and specific, or the remote? Note that there may be far less agreement on whether the action will attain the remote objective than on whether it will attain the immediate outcome.

Goals have an organizational structure. Organizational goals are understood differently both at various vertical levels of the organization and among the functions within each level *horizontally.* How is this a source of potential disagreement?

Vertically, it means that goals are stated in relatively vague and ambiguous terms at executive levels: vague, because exactly what must be done at the subunit level to achieve the stated objective is not specified; ambiguous, because goals most likely *do* relate to longer term objectives and the link between possible immediate outcomes and these objectives might be pursued in a number of different ways. Also, goals set forth at executive levels may be political statements, designed for both internal and external consumption, to bolster support so that few can object to the proposed course. The result is that translating these *political* goals into *action* goals is left to middle and subunit management.

Within a horizontal level not all elements of the goal set are of equal importance to all functional subunits in the level; that is, different subunits inevitably focus on different opportunities for action. They do this because some subunits are better able to deal with some actions than with others. Engineers know product design, not accounting; marketing people know how to sell, not produce. So they focus on action opportunities centered in their own functions that usually entail allocating additional resources for their subunit. Engineers need manpower or new laboratories; production people see the need for advanced production technologies. And so it goes.

Thus, our second source of disagreement is that lower levels must translate political or planning goals into action goals, together with differences in choice of action opportunities among these subunits.

Goals develop through group process. Personal and subunit goals of growth and maintenance become involved. Given the situation already depicted and the need for unified subunit action, we can observe at least two things.

First, organizational goals are generated at the grassroots level by subunits seeking to expand their function and, with it, the careers of people in the subunits. This process occurs by developing action goals for the subunit that are justified through their *explicit relationship* to the achievement of higher-level planning goals and thus the longer-range objectives of the organization. This process of goal formation is one employed primarily within staff subunits that continually need to justify their existence.

Second, where higher-level goals are ambiguous, action goals developed through group process may be designed explicitly, though not exclusively, to foster the ends of individual and group development. To the extent that the outcomes associated with these actions serve no real organizational purpose in the growth and survival of the larger organization, we call this condition *goal displacement.* That is, to the extent that action goals and attendant outcomes serve primarily the purposes of *resource allocation to the subunit,* we call these goals *displacement goals.*

What all this means to you in your first position with an organization depends to a large extent on the technology and environment within which the organization operates, as well as to the type of function you are assigned to—staff or line. We suggest there are differences between growth environments and no-growth environments, that there are differences between well-understood, stable technologies and those that are poorly understood and developmental. In each case the nature of goal statements within the organization will be affected. In line organizations as compared to staff there will be less need to justify the function of the subunit and consequently less goal development activity, but there might be greater disagreement horizontally over the choices of action opportunities.

The stage is now set for understanding the measurement of goal achievement in organizations. We will turn to that topic in our next chapter.

Notes

1. Statements made by participants in these interviews are actual verbatim quotes from engineering executives; they were taken in an individual rather than a group context, however. Quotes are excerpted and edited from lengthier interviews. For a published partial account of this research see Ritti and Goldner (21).
2. Some writers have suggested that goals are invoked by participants simply to account for actions already taken. See Brown (4).
3. The following analysis is based on Simon (25).
4. Several writers have made distinctions similar to these using the terms *official, operative,* and *operational* (8, 19, 28). We have changed the language to make the terms easier to remember.
5. Examples of the process of goal setting and consequent suboptimization are given by Cyert and March (8).
6. Chapter 16 covers the organizational processes of measurement and their consequences.
7. Goal displacement, in which concrete, measurable, and quantitative production goals displace the maintenance of "human capital" has been a major concern of the work of Rensis Likert (15, 16).

References

1. ACKOFF, RUSSELL L. "Towards a System of Systems Concepts." *Management Science* 17 (July 1971): 661–671.
2. BERK, BERNARD. "Organizational Goals and Inmate Organization." *American Journal of Sociology* 71 (1966): 522–534.
3. BLAU, PETER M., and W. RICHARD SCOTT. *Formal Organizations: A Comparative Approach.* San Francisco: Chandler, 1962.
4. BROWN, R. H. "Bureaucracy as Praxis: Toward a Political Phenomenology of Formal Organizations." *Administrative Science Quarterly* 23 (1978): 365–382.
5. BUCK, VERNON. "A Model for Viewing an Organization as a System of Constraints." In *Approaches to Organization Design,* edited by James D. Thompson. Pittsburgh: University of Pittsburgh Press, 1966.

6. CRESSEY, DONALD R. "Contradictory Directives in Complex Organizations: The Case of a Prison." *Administrative Science Quarterly* 4 (1959): 1–19.
7. CROZIER, MICHEL. *The Bureaucratic Phenomenon.* Chicago: University of Chicago Press, 1964.
8. CYERT, RICHARD M., and JAMES G. MARCH. *A Behavioral Theory of the Firm.* Englewood Cliffs, N.J.: Prentice-Hall, 1963.
9. DAFT, R., and P. BRADSHAW. "The Process of Horizontal Differentiation: Two Models." *Administrative Science Quarterly* 25 (1980): 441–456.
10. ETZIONI, AMITAI. "Two Approaches to Organizational Analysis: A Critique and a Suggestion." *Administrative Science Quarterly* 5 (September 1960): 257–278.
11. GROSS, EDWARD. "The Definition of Organizational Goals." *British Journal of Sociology* 20 (1969): 277–294.
12. HALL, FRANCINE S. "Organizational Goals: The Status of Theory and Research." In *Managerial Accounting: the Behavioral Foundations,* edited by J. Leslie Livingstone. Columbus, Ohio: Grid, 1975.
13. HAYES, R., and W. ABERNATHY. "Managing Our Way to Economic Decline." *Harvard Business Review* 58 (July–August 1980): 67–77.
14. HAYES, R., and D. GARVIN. "Managing as if Tomorrow Mattered." *Harvard Business Review* 60 (May–June 1982): 70–79.
15. LIKERT, RENSIS. *The Human Organization: Its Management and Value.* New York: McGraw-Hill, 1967.
16. ———. *New Patterns of Management.* New York: McGraw-Hill, 1961.
17. MANIHA, JOHN, and CHARLES PERROW. "The Reluctant Organization and the Aggressive Environment." *Administrative Science Quarterly* 10 (1965): 238–257.
18. MERTON, ROBERT K. *Social Theory and Social Structure,* revised ed. Glencoe, Ill.: Free Press, 1957.
19. PERROW, CHARLES. "The Analysis of Goals in Complex Organizations." *American Sociological Review* 26 (December 1961): 854–866.
20. ———. *Organizational Analysis: A Sociological View.* Belmont, Calif.: Wadsworth, 1970.
21. RITTI, R. RICHARD, and FRED H. GOLDNER. "Professional Pluralism in an Industrial Organization." *Management Science* 16 (December 1969): B233–B246.
22. SCHEFF, THOMAS. "Differential Displacement of Treatment Goals in a Mental Hospital." *Administrative Science Quarterly* 7 (1962): 208–217.
23. SCOTT, ROBERT A. "The Factory as a Social Service Organization: Goal Displacement in Workshops for the Blind." *Social Problems* 15 (1967): 208–217.
24. SELZNICK, PHILIP. *TVA and the Grass Roots.* Berkeley and Los Angeles: University of California Press, 1949.
25. SIMON, HERBERT A. "On the Concept of Organizational Goal." *Administrative Science Quarterly* 9 (June 1964): 1–22.
26. SIMON, H. A. "Rational Decision Making in Business Organizations." *American Economic Review* 69 (1979): 493–513.
27. SIMPSON, RICHARD L., and W. H. GULLEY. "Goals, Environmental Pressures, and Organizational Characteristics." *American Sociological Review* 27 (1962): 344–350.

28. STEERS, RICHARD M. *Organizational Effectiveness: A Behavioral View.* Santa Monica, Calif.: Goodyear, 1977.
29. TERREBERRY, SHIRLEY. "The Evolution of Organizational Environments." *Administrative Science Quarterly* 12 (1968): 590–613.
30. THOMPSON, JAMES, and WILLIAM MCEWEN. "Organizational Goals and Environment." *American Sociological Review* 23 (1958): 23–31.
31. WARNER, W. KEITH, and EUGENE A. HAVENS. "Goal Displacement and the Intangibility of Organizational Goals." *Administrative Science Quarterly* 12 (March 1968): 539–555.
32. WARRINER, CHARLES K. "The Problem of Organizational Purpose." *Sociological Quarterly* 6 (1965): 139–146.
33. WIELAND, GEORGE F. "The Determinants of Clarity in Organizational Goals." *Human Relations* 22 (1969): 161–172.
34. ZALD, MEYER N. "From Evangelism to General Service: The Transformation of the YMCA." *Administrative Science Quarterly* 8 (1963): 214–234.

Discussion Questions

1. What is the distinction between those parts of the goal set called action opportunities and those called action constraints? Recall your own behavior during the last school term. List as many factors in your goal set as you can. Which of these served as opportunities and which as constraints? How does this help to explain your own choices?
2. List as many factors as you can from the opening case of this chapter that were discussed by executives as part of the organization goal set. Identify the action opportunities and constraints among these factors.
3. How does the definition of an organizational goal as a multiple set of opportunities and constraints help you to understand the disagreement that develops in complex organizations over which courses of action to pursue?
4. In this chapter we outlined a typology of organizational goals by level of organization. Define each type. How does this differentiation help you to understand how disagreement over organizational goals may arise?
5. Based on the concepts and ideas from previous chapters on groups and leadership, explain how the process of organizational goal setting is related to the interaction system. What group concepts help explain the development of disagreement over goals? What is there in the role of group leader that may ease or aggravate this disagreement?
6. In his 1962 McKinsey lectures at Columbia University, T. J. Watson, Jr., chairman of IBM, outlined three beliefs he felt to be the basis for the success of the IBM company: respect for the individual, service to the customer, and superior effort in everything we do. Are these goals? Why? If so, what kind? Try to derive planning and action goals from these "beliefs."
7. In this chapter we made the point that organizational goals and personal goals are related. Why is this the case? Think of ways in which these are related at the organiza-

tional levels of executive, middle manager, and first-level manager or professional. What bearing does the process of resource allocation have on the relationship between personal and organizational goals?

8. What do we mean by goal displacement? Under what conditions is it likely to occur? Consider the goal set of a university. How are organizational goals stated at the political level? The planning level? How do you think the action goals of the teaching departments may differ from these? Why? Give some examples of academic goal displacement.

Chapter 16
Measuring Performance: Consequences of the Process

Outstanding

Ted felt a knot growing in his stomach as the appointed time drew near. This was the one thing he hated most. Yes, hated! Every year, The Company said, *every* year *every* manager must sit down with his employees and discuss his appraisal of their performance. In this appraisal the manager should point out aspects of performance that needed improvement, and suggest ways to improve. A recent innovation required the employee to indicate that he had seen the appraisal (something that always hadn't happened in the past) by signing the form and saying whether or not he agreed.

If that doesn't sound too bad, you've probably never had to go through the process. Ted has. And today is the day for his "appraisal interview" with Stanley. Now keep in mind that Stanley isn't all that difficult to get along with, and that he is usually reasonable enough when it comes to his opinion of himself. So where is the problem? Well, let's hear what Ted tells Stan.

"Morning, Ted. How was the trip to Portland?"

"Interesting. We've got some real innovations up there that might be the wave of the future. Talk to you about it later.

"Right now, I guess you know that this is your annual appraisal. We're supposed to do this every year, and I think it's a good idea. Gives us a chance to get it all down. In our case, though, I don't suppose we have to be so formal. It's not as though we don't get to see each other very often."

"Yeah, I guess that's right, isn't it." Stanley's manner was casual. He agreed with Ted that this would be largely a ritual performance, deemed necessary by Company regulations.

"Let me start off by saying I'm very satisfied with your performance over the past year." Ted had some notes in front of him and he actually read that first line. From there he went on to praise Stanley generally for his effort, and for his interest in the department. Then, with this first or favorable slice of the appraisal sandwich complete, he went on to the less tasty meat of the interview.

Pointing to the appraisal form, "I've rated you 'exceeds requirements' for the past year. And that's very good you know. So really, I'm not sure we have all that much to go over." Ted hoped, *prayed,* that Stanley would say, "Yeah, I guess so." That would then lead into a brief, but positive discussion of possible points of improvement where Stanley might take "still further initiative" in departmental projects. The interview would then terminate amicably with a discussion of future plans—the remaining positive slice of the sandwich. Yet the growing knot in his stomach told him that this was not to be.

"Exceeds requirements?" Stanley's tone was one of shocked disbelief. He stated the words slowly with agonized precision. "I thought you said you were *very* satisfied? Why, an 'exceeds requirements' rating is just what everybody gets. Listen, I want to know why you downrated me. I want some reasons."

Now the fact of the matter is that Stanley was right, in part. The Company's rating scheme was based on five points: *outstanding, exceeds requirements, meets requirements,* the ominous sounding *meets minimum requirements,* and the terminal *inadequate.* The manager's manual described all in "behavioral" terms. For example, the definition of *outstanding* was:

> Performs at a level rarely achieved by employees with similar experience and training in that position. Demonstrates creativity and special initiative in seeking out responsibility . . .

And so on. Finally,

> The Company expects that perhaps 5% of all employees may achieve outstanding performance.

There was a similar description for *exceeds requirements,* with the stricture that 20 percent might achieve that level of performance. *Meets requirements* should account for another 50 percent, *meets minimum requirements* for 20 percent, and *inadequate* for 5 percent. However, that was theory; in practice perhaps 15 percent were rated *outstanding,* 40 percent *exceeds requirements,* 40 percent *meets requirements,* with the remaining 5 percent in the doomed *meets minimum requirements* or *inadequate* categories. Ted knew it; so did Stanley.

"Tell me *specifically* . . . I mean I want to know just *exactly* what your reasons are for downrating me!" Now Stanley was irate.

"Now, just a minute, Stanley. I think you've got this all wrong. Why that's. . . . Why, I *am* giving you a superior rating." The knot grew larger. "Very few of our people can be rated outstanding you know. Listen, here it says. . . ." Ted recited the litany from his manager's manual.

"Oh, yeah? Then how come you gave Claude an outstanding rating?" was Stanley's reply.

Ted was tempted to lie, but thought better of it. Why did these damn guys persist in talking to one another about ratings and salaries? It was against Company policy anyway. "I don't see that this has any relevance for our discussion, Stan."

"Baloney it doesn't! You tell me what Claude has done that's better than what I've done. That's the point. If you can't—and I don't see how you can—then I should be rated outstanding, too!"

The knot in Ted's stomach grew tighter. He knew he couldn't get away with rating everyone outstanding and, well, he knew that Claude would be difficult. There was a question of possible prejudice there. So he took the easier way. Actually, both were pretty good employees. But Stanley had to have his answer. Well, then, so be it.

"All right. If you insist." Ted mustered up his best angered/aggrieved manner. Then, "Remember that presentation you made to the automation people—the one about changing requirements at the man-machine interface? Well, you really blew it in the discussion that followed. Recall, you kept talking about. . . ." Ted went on from there to present a catalogue of Stanley's past errors, great and small. In fact, in his zeal to make his case as convincing as possible, Ted resurrected some pretty petty stuff.

"Oh, Jesus, Ted, you've got a memory like an elephant." Stanley was stunned. "Half that stuff didn't even happen last year. And another thing. About that automation session. At the time you told me to forget it, not to get upset 'cause it wasn't all that important anyway. And now, why now you're throwing it up at me as a reason for downrating me. That's just not fair!"

And, you know, Ted didn't think it was fair either. But what was he to do? He felt he was giving Stanley an honest rating, yet how could he justify the difference between an *exceeds requirements* and an *outstanding*—or a *meets requirements,* for that matter? It was all so subjective. So what he did, inadvertently, was to dredge up every incident, of whatever moment, that could justify his conclusion. The net result was to picture Stanley in a much more negative light than he had wished, placing Stanley's genuine achievements in question, and hurting both Stanley and himself in the process.

There are several points to this story. The first is that The Company wants to get feedback to its employees. How can you improve your performance without knowing what that performance has been? But the measuring tools are crude indeed. This leads to the second point. The appraisal process assumes that a superior reports the facts and an accompanying judgment to a subordinate who recognizes the authenticity of those facts and the validity of the judgment. Officially, the process cannot recognize that there may be no facts, in the usual sense of the word, or that group process is involved. And it does not recognize that the superior may have other important, though officially inadmissible, reasons for giving particular ratings (28).

Assessing effectiveness—*measuring* performance and *evaluating* that measured performance—is a key process in the feedback and control system of organizations. This process also is extremely complex and as yet poorly understood in large, complex organizations. The problems responsible for this lack of understanding are compounded by the multiple levels on which the measurement process is focused: on individuals, on subunits, and on entire organizations.[1]

In this chapter, therefore, we focus on the motivational effect of the measurement process itself, and take as given the organizational intent supporting the definition of effectiveness that underlies that process. We focus as well on the visible blemishes on that process—where the *intent goes awry*. We do this because we feel that the best way to understand the effect of the measurement process is to examine cases where the intended purpose of the organization failed to be achieved.

The Process of Measurement in Organizations

All organizations measure performance, yet they probably would not state it just that way. The usual definition of measurement is rather narrower than the one we use. So let us define our terms once again.

Defining Measurement

The most general definition of measurement, and the one that suits our purposes best, is: *measurement* is a set of rules for assigning numbers to events or things (31). Consequently, even the most subjective attempt by management to differentiate the performance of one employee from another, or of one organizational unit from another, is measurement. The rating scale that Ted used to assign a value to Stanley's performance is a form of measurement; *outstanding* being assigned a value of 5, *inadequate* a value of 1. Similarly, engineering top management is measuring the worthwhileness of its current product development projects when it ranks all 253 of them from 1, highest priority, all the way to 253, lowest priority.

The measurement process includes more than developing rules for *assigning* numbers; it also includes developing standards for *evaluating* those numbers. The facts, in other words, do not necessarily speak for themselves. In an appraisal interview, for example, assume that the appraisal form has a number of subscales on it with labels such as *shows initiative, is responsible, shows creativity, is punctual,* and the like. And assume that three people—A, B, and C—are all rated on one of these scales: *responsibility.* We can learn from our rating scales that A is more "responsible" than C, and we can even hope that we know how much more responsible. But we still do not know how much better in overall performance A is than C for having been so. That is a matter of *evaluation.* We can do the same with organizational units: of departments A, B, and C, we know that A is higher than C on some measure of output. But how much better is A than C for being higher?

One solution to this problem is to settle on a single measure and say that evaluation will be based solely on standings on that measure. This procedure has the advantage of avoiding subjective evaluations. We might also set up a weighting scheme for the rated attributes, which would automatically combine them into one composite measure. As we will see shortly, however, all such schemes have drawbacks accompanying their positive functions. They also have different effects on organizational behavior.

Measurement, then, is the complete process by which outcomes are labeled, ordered, or otherwise quantified *and* by which those outcomes are evaluated. Remember, the facts speak for themselves only under very special circumstances.

The Search for the Perfect Measure and Why

The perfect measure would be quantitative and unambiguous, yet capture the subtleties of performance; it would reflect the contribution of the "whole person." Everyone would be able to relate the measure directly to the stated objectives of the tasks assigned, and the measure would reflect directly the priorities among these objectives (17). In other words, the perfect measure would be specific yet comprehensive, unambiguous yet flexible, precise yet fair.

The attributes of the perfect measure can be learned directly from everyone's gripes about what is wrong with existing measurement systems. As a well-known management theorist has pointed out, neither superiors nor subordinates are satisfied with current appraisal systems (18). They all believe that judgments are subjective and impressionistic, hence debatable and to some extent invalid.

Managers feel guilty and uncomfortable when faced with the task of making judgments based on limited facts. This, of course, is the situation depicted in our opening story.

Both superiors and subordinates, therefore, yearn for the perfect measure. From the subordinates' point of view, it would remove the problem of ambiguity, of not knowing exactly what contributes to high performance. It would be fair, allowing direct comparison of achievement to objectives. And such a perfect measure would also guarantee a fair shake in the dispensation of the organizational rewards of dollars and promotions.

From the superiors' point of view, the perfect measure is highly desirable as well. Obviously, it gives the superior a direct means for control of subordinates' behavior. Furthermore, it turns the subjective and anxiety-provoking process of performance appraisal into a matter-of-fact event. More accurately, no appraisal at all would be required since the perfect measure would speak for itself. And finally, the perfect measure would link directly the behavior of subordinates to departmental goals. From the management point of view, the perfect measure would be the key to the motivation system, allowing accurate feedback and flawless management control.

Unfortunately, the perfect measure is probably impossible to attain. The basic problem is interrelating the different measurement attributes—we can achieve one characteristic only at the expense of another. Single, objective, and quantitative measures are unambiguous and speak for themselves, yet, by definition, they cannot recognize multiple objectives or capture subtleties in the performance of the "whole person." The difference can be seen in the comparison between a machine-scored multiple-choice examination and a term paper essay.

Faust's First Law

"The long and short of it is, Dr. Faust, that we think we've got the problem whipped. Still, we'd like to hear what you've got to say before we go 'on line' with the system." Kerry had invited Dr. Faust to the laboratory to consult on a new performance appraisal system developed by laboratory management. The problem they were working on was an old one—that of getting accurate and unbiased appraisals of research engineers. Most rating schemes were subjective, and they wanted to develop a better system. Being technical people, numbers and using the computer seemed to be the way to do it.

Faust and Kerry are old friends. Faust knows that Kerry understands how to take care of his consultants; that is, he knows how to protect a consultant's most precious asset, his reputation. For his part, Dr. Faust repays the favor by being exceptionally honest. And he tells Kerry, "It is not going to work, you know. I would not waste my time with it were I you."

"How in the hell can you know that? I haven't even told you what we are planning to do yet!" Kerry's tone was one of astonishment rather than anger.

"Yes, of course," was Faust's reply, "but such systems never do work. And this one will be no exception. Rest assured of that."

"I still don't see how you can be so damned sure," said Kerry. "Tell you what, since you *are* so sure, bet you ten bucks you *can't* tell me what's wrong with it."

"Oh, that bet I would never take," returned Dr. Faust. "No, I am not at all sure that I could tell you how it will fail, only that fail it must. I, ah—just consider it part of my consulting fee."

"Thanks. Look, here's how the system works. First we identify our raters, all laboratory management who have worked with our guy during the last ten years. Everyone who knows this guy is asked to rate him on an 11-point scale running from 0 to 10. Now we develop the weighting factors. The first thing we want to know is, how long ago has the manager worked with the guy. We figure that the raters who know him best ought to count more. So we weight the scores inversely by the number of years it's been. If the guy works for that manager now, we give the full rating; if he worked for him two years ago we divide by two, ten years ago by ten. You get the idea."

But immediately Faust had a question. "No, I am not certain that I do. Simply because one has known an individual recently is not to say that one has known him well."

"Aha! We thought of that. We also get a factor for how well the rater knew this guy. If he worked for the rater directly we give that a weight of 1, if he worked with him closely on another project that's a 2, if he worked with him but not closely on a different project that's a 3, and if he knew of his work indirectly, well that's only a 4. So we've thought of that problem."

Once again Faust seemed uncertain. "I must say that I still don't see how that handles the problem of rater bias. You know as well as I do that some raters are more lenient and some more strict."

"Oh, yes indeed." Kerry was now smiling broadly because he had anticipated Dr. Faust's objection. "For just that reason we standardize all ratings. So if a rater gives, say, an *average* rating of 1 we divide all his ratings by 1. If his average is 3, then we divide by 3. That way each rater has no more influence than any other on the overall ratings. See, I told you it would work."

"So that solves the problem of rater bias, does it? It certainly sounds complicated. Still. . . ."

Kerry cut in, "But it's not complicated at all. The computer handles it. All we do is feed in the numbers—even those we have on mark-sensing forms."

Faust paused. For a minute or two he said nothing, apparently deep in thought. Then, "What would I do if I were one of your managers? How would I beat this system—so to speak?" Another pause.

"Let us say that I want my own people to come out high in the ratings, but that I'm conscientious about my responsibilities to the laboratory as well. I would not want to penalize others unjustly, of course." Another pause. Then with a look indicating that he found the answer, Faust pointed his pipe stem at Kerry. "Yes. What would *you* do under those circumstances?"

Kerry looked a bit taken aback, then replied haltingly, "Well, ah, I suppose that I might try to give my own people the better ratings and give lower ones to people on other projects. I'd have to protect myself because I'd figure that's what the other managers would be doing. But that wouldn't be fair. And besides, it would be too obvious. I can't believe the system would work that way."

"Oh, come, come my friend. You can do better than that. Think of the weights. You have two sets of them to work with."

Kerry's face dropped showing he'd solved the problem. "Yeah. I'd take those guys I knew not very well and a long time ago and I'd give them 0 ratings or something like that. That's a combined weighting factor of a tenth (ten years ago) times a fourth (knows indirectly)—only one-fortieth of the weighting that goes with a ''works for now'' weighting factor. Sure. Giving that guy a zero rating is not going to hurt him at all, but it sure brings down my average rating. That way I can really bump up my own guys." And then after a moment's thought, "But what if I averaged the whole business—ratings times years times. . . ."

Dr. Faust held up his hands in mock dismay. "Enough. Enough. Cease. You are flying in the face of—ah, let us call it Faust's First Law. Yes, that has a ring to it. To wit: when people providing management information have something to gain by modifying that information to suit their purposes, and where such modification is essentially judgmental and hence, not easily detectable, then said modification will take place."

Faust looked pleased.[2]

The Fox and Henhouse Principle

Occasionally, when a large industry threatens to become too large or too powerful, the federal government appoints an investigatory or regulatory committee to safeguard the "public interest." And occasionally the chairman of this committee is drawn from the industry to be regulated—say, an oil company executive for the petroleum industry, a financier for banking. And admirals and generals are occasionally appointed to keep our defense industry honest.

The reasoning behind this is that it is desirable to appoint, as chairman, someone who knows the industry, or knows the defense business. But country folks have a saying that expresses this kind of situation well; they call it *setting the fox to watch the henhouse.* The implication should be clear. Not that industrial and military foxes are dishonest. But once you have developed a taste for chicken, well. . . . After all, there *are* lots of facts and lots of different points of view, and by being a bit selective you can help ensure the "right" outcome.

This, of course, is Faust's First Law applied more broadly to the organization. Thus far our examples have dealt with individual measurement because this is the least complicated case, but the selective manipulation of statistics and measures in the name of enlightened self-interest takes place at all levels of organization, from the production floor to the executive suite (1, 10, 11, 19, 20, 24, 32, 33). In most cases these manipulations are harmless enough, serving the purpose of impression management as much as anything else. But occasionally such selective representation of the facts is the basis for major problems.

To illustrate some general principles—including the Fox and Henhouse Principle—in applying measurement in organizations, let us look at some examples from The Agency, The University, and other organizations.

Some Consequences of Different Approaches to Measurement

These examples deal with the nature of the measurement process and the characteristics of the measures. In each case we will try to highlight both the advantages and drawbacks of the measurement system illustrated. By looking at different kinds of organizations we will also illustrate the generality of the processes involved. See Box 22 for a recent example.

Measurement in The Agency

Peter Blau, in his *Dynamics of Bureaucracy,* was perhaps the first to state explicitly that the characteristics of performance measures have a variety of consequences for human behavior in organizations (5). A state employment agency is the site of Blau's study. The basic operation of the agency is finding suitable jobs

> **Box 22**
>
> ## Creating Crime by Measurement
>
> The Uniform Crime Reports (UCR) of the FBI constitute a record of the official crime rates for eight index crimes, the most serious categories of crime. Thus, when officials comment that crime rates are up or down, this invariably means that the UCR for a given crime is up or down. Since true crime rates cannot be known, only those which are reported, it is of interest to criminologists to locate the sources of error at various stages in compiling the UCR.
>
> McCleary's research covers three "natural experiments" (of which we report two) which identify organizational structural factors that produce considerable variation in the measurement of crime rates.
>
> ### Errors by UCR Coding Clerks in Jurisdictions
>
> In most jurisdictions coding clerks are employed to classify the crime reported by the investigating officer into one of the eight index categories, or to decide that this is not an index crime. In one "experiment" the detectives of a major city were assigned for twenty-one months to investigate all burglary complaints. This action resulted not only in a major decrease in burglary but also in a systematic reduction in month-to-month variability of the burglary rate. However, when this practice was terminated, burglary rates soared (see Figure 16.1). What happened was this. First, coding clerks depend on the reports of the investigating officer to indicate what type of crime has been committed, if any. Ambiguous, incomplete reports cause errors. Next, the uniformed officers who usually make these investigations very often file pro-forma reports with no call for follow-up investigation. During the period in question, however, all burglaries were investigated by detectives, specialists who appreciate the nuances of the UCR classification system, who understand the fine definitional distinctions among burglary, theft, and vandalism. Furthermore, since the detectives are a smaller group, there are fewer individuals filing the reports on which the coding clerks depend. Since errors tend to inflate the burglary rate, the net effect was a sharp drop in crime as well as an apparent stabilization of the rate during the experimental period.
>
> ### Protection of Personnel
>
> A major source of unreported crimes are those crimes reported to police which, for one reason or another, police refuse to treat as "real" crimes. For example,

continued

police often suspect that reports of stolen vehicles coming from poverty areas are really "repos"—repossessions by credit companies. In such instances police dispatchers will refer the call to a different agency and not dispatch an officer with a "call for service." Since any official crime must begin with such a call, it is evident that an increase in calls for service can potentially affect crime rates. And this is just what happens in our second "experiment."

In this case, the supervising sergeants usually present in the dispatch bureau were removed from most shifts. Normally, these sergeants make the usual police distinctions between "real" crimes and complaints. And they discourage dispatchers from issuing calls for service for the complaints. If the dispatchers cannot deflect the complaint, customarily they rely on the higher authority of the sergeant, either to handle the call or to decide what should be done. In this way the dispatchers are protected in the case of an error from civil suits or an internal investigation. With the removal of the sergeants, however, this protection also is removed. The result is that the dispatchers now refer even questionable complaints, complying with the letter of the regulations in order to protect themselves. The net effect in this case was an increase in the measured crime rate, an apparent incipient crime wave.

R. McCleary et al. "Uniform Crime Reports as Organizational Outcomes: Three Time Series Experiments." *Social Problems* 29 (1982): 361–372.

for unemployed clients. The basic raw material of the agency is a list of job openings received daily and a list of clients and their qualifications. The task is to refer a qualified client to a suitable job opportunity. The ultimate aim is to place a client in a permanent position. This process seems simple enough, and, in fact, seems to offer little opportunity for creative effort. Yet considerable creative activity was taking place—though not necessarily that anticipated by management.

In this agency quantitative records had been used widely in operations to facilitate administration control. However, in one department a new system of performance records was instituted, and reports were issued monthly and made available to all employment interviewers. Eight basic measures were used. These were based on *interviews held, job referrals made,* and *job placements obtained,* or some combination of these factors. For example, one measure was the proportion of referrals that resulted in a job placement. This measure provided a check on the quality of work, for it was possible to make a large number of referrals by simply referring a lot of clients—qualified or not—to a large number of jobs where placement was not likely to result. One feature of the measurement

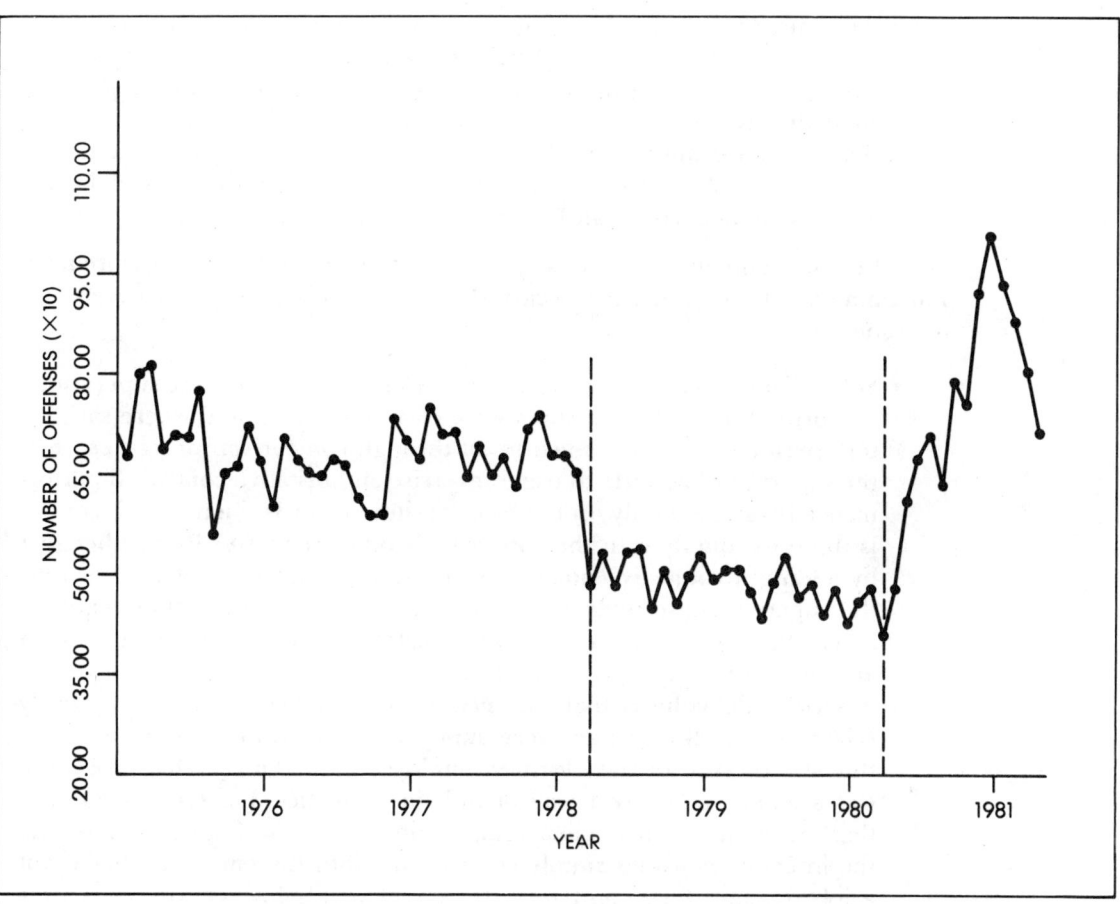

FIGURE 16.1 Monthly UCR Burglaries for City A from January, 1975, to May, 1981. (The vertical dotted lines indicate onset and termination of an experimental program.) Reprinted with the permission of the Society for the Study of Social Problems and the author.

system used in this department, then, was multiple objective measures but subjective *evaluation* of those measures. Evaluation depended on the priorities or weights assigned to the various measures by the supervisor.

Four positive results of this measurement system were noted.

- Productivity generally was increased through better feedback to individual employees.
- Hierarchical control was made more effective through selective use of one or more of the measures involved. By emphasizing the importance of the proportion of referrals to placements, the department head could effectively enforce a policy of quality work on his or her supervisors.

- The measures enabled superiors to introduce change quickly and effectively. Once again, by differential emphasis on one of the eight measures, pressures could be brought to bear to introduce changes in work practices immediately.
- The measures improved relations between section supervisors and their interviewers. As one supervisor put it, ". . . I just let [the records] speak for themselves. That's all I want" (5:40).

These were the intended consequences of the new system of measurement. But unintended consequences occurred as well, consequences that were not desirable.

- Sole reliance on these performance measures undermined the supervisor's authority. Where the measures were clear and direct, and where satisfactory performance was known to all through comparison of figures, then the supervisor had little to use to exercise authoritative control. If performance is assessed only on the basis of these records, then what incentive is there to comply with the supervisor's other requests? Remember that by adding a subjective quality to the overall evaluation of the records, the supervisor also adds an incentive for compliance to other requests. After all, how is one to know what factors will come into play in such an evaluation?
- A second difficulty is that the measurement indices were not perfectly related to the things they were supposed to measure. One example of this was the use of the "former employee procedure." This procedure was a simple and direct way of inflating statistics. On receiving notice that an employee had been temporarily laid off with intent to rehire, the interviewer would simply confirm this with the employer, make out a job opening form, and refer the client to his former job. In a later study of this same agency the level of this activity was estimated at one-half the total activity of the agency (7).
- Another drawback of the new system was the workers' general dislike of having to mold their activities to satisfy a set of impersonal statistics. As one employee put it, it was "like working in a factory."
- Finally, under certain conditions the use of these measures generated interpersonal conflict and competition among the workers.

This last point needs somewhat greater elaboration. The study contrasts two sections of the department; the supervisors in these sections used the measures in different ways. In one section, characterized by competitiveness and interpersonal stress, the supervisor relied heavily on the direct use of the measures for performance rating. In the other section, characterized by cooperation and better interpersonal relations, the supervisor relied less on the measures than on a subjective overall judgment.

In the first section competition developed over the supply of job openings. Since the effective placement of a client can be made only when an appropriate job opening is available, interviewers in the competitive section worked out various schemes for hoarding openings and keeping them from co-workers. This occurred despite instructions that openings were to be pooled and shared by all. What evolved was an atmosphere of distrust and competitiveness. However, though personal productivity was highly related to the degree of personal competitiveness—the more competitive interviewers had higher performance ratings—the opposite was true when entire sections were compared. The group advantage in the less competitive section resulted because the entire pool of job openings was available to all—consequently, a better match could be made between individual clients and available job openings.

Measurement in The University

Anyone who has been associated with the academic world for some length of time has heard the phrase "publish or perish." It signifies that academics laboring at major university centers have most of their rewards and security tied to a simple, quantitative system of measurement: number of articles and books published. Similarly, there is no academic who at some time in his or her career has not commented wryly on some absurd aspect of that system. Complaints include the open secret that occasionally these "publications" are useless and banal, that a long list is better than a short one, whatever the quality, and that in any event the time would be better devoted to the "real" business of the academic—excellence in teaching. It is rumored also that some of the most productive scholars occasionally neglect their classroom assignments.

These criticisms may or may not be valid, but no one would deny that reliance on this single, largely quantitative measure shifts the productive behavior of academics to some extent away from the classroom and toward the typewriter. The suggestion is usually made, then, to achieve a better balance between teaching and research.

Such balance is difficult to attain, however. One basic reason seems to be the inherent differences in the measurability of different kinds of performance. Teaching performance, for example, is extremely difficult to evaluate, even with the somewhat suspect innovation of student evaluations of classroom performance. But evaluating publication performance is simply the act of counting articles in journals, or something similar.[3] This leads to another principle: *Indicators of performance that are easy to measure are more likely to be used than indicators of performance that are difficult to measure.* These easy-to-measure indicators will be used even when their connection to the goals and objectives of the organization is more remote than that of less measurable indicators.

Also, a given indicator of performance is more valid at certain times than at others. For example, a highly successful coach and general manager in professional basketball describes certain periods of a professional game as "garbage time." He means by this that when a game is safely won (or, less frequently, when it is hopelessly lost) the players on the floor are simply working to build their personal performance records. From his point of view, a basket or an assist or a rebound during garbage time is meaningless. These statistics serve only to build performance records. We suggest that the concept of "garbage time" is applicable to almost all organizations.

Measurement in Business and Industry

Dependence on a single objective indicator of performance is often undesirable because a single indicator usually cannot reflect accurately the multiple goals of organizations. The academic necessity to publish is an example of this. However, multiple indicators have dynamics of their own. We will now examine, therefore, two instances of the use of multiple indicators of performance, paying special attention to the relationship among these indicators.

A simple instance is the use of both quantity and quality of production in manufacturing work. Since quality often suffers when quantity is emphasized, using quantity of production as a single indicator of manufacturing performance may lead to problems (2, 4, 12). Yet the use of both quantity and quality leads to other difficulties. Since the indicators are related, one suffers when the other is emphasized. Obviously, then, it is necessary for someone to define the trade-off between the two—for example, to set a minimum acceptable quality level. This is possible but can become complicated.

Another solution is to add a third indicator—scrap. To some extent the problem of achieving both high quantity and high quality might be resolved through producing excessive scrap. By not accepting marginal raw materials, or by scrapping pieces that are not working out well, a worker can increase quantity while maintaining a quality standard. Thus, scrap rates may have to be introduced as a third, and balancing indicator of performance. But now the relationship between all three must be specified, and so on. As you can imagine, it very quickly becomes impossible to specify—in reasonable and quantitative terms—not only what the indicators will be, but what the priorities among them should be.

In our second instance of the use of multiple indicators of performance, we will examine two examples at the managerial level. The first of these comes from a description of the Soviet managerial system (9). The characteristics of this system are as follows:

- Multiple and necessarily conflicting standards of performance are set by superiors for subordinate managers. (The fact that one Soviet industrial system is organized into multiple managerial hierarchies makes this kind of conflict all the more possible.)

- Subordinates may be held accountable for failure to meet any of the standards. However, the importance of the standards is not completely defined and the priority among them is ambiguous.
- Superiors modify the set of standards to comply with their changing objectives, and they enforce these standards in accordance with their changing priorities.

The next result is that subordinates are faced with a system of formal standards that are clear and quantitative, but that, in practical terms, are impossible to satisfy completely. Both superiors and subordinates recognize this. As a result, greater flexibility ensues for the system as a whole. Subordinates pick and choose among standards that seem to have highest priority at the time and ignore those which do not. "Maintenance of conflicting standards, in short, is a way of decentralizing decision-making" (9:12). Another result is that the superior's authority is enhanced in the same way it was in the employment agency. "Conflict among standards ensures that subordinates have always failed to meet *some* standard, and selective enforcement, actual and potential, keeps ever present the threat of being taken to task therefore" (9:12). Thus, the use of multiple and quantitative, yet conflicting and ambiguous standards allows the superior to employ justified subjectivity in making evaluations of subordinates.

This situation is very similar to that of the sales managers in The Company who found themselves confronted with ever-increasing numbers of performance standards against which their sales offices were to be evaluated. As The Company's business grew larger, more complex, and diversified, The Company found that its few, simple standards such as *percentage of quota* and *accounts receivable* were insufficient to exercise the control needed to achieve some of its long-range plans. As the planned objectives multiplied, then, so did the standards and controls embodied in an increasing number of measures. Finally, the situation became such that managers could no longer achieve all their planned objectives. Several of them complained bitterly about the new system, and about how they never knew when a call was coming from regional headquarters threatening action because one or another of the indicators had not been met. What had happened was that the managers had gone from a situation where they were relatively free from the authority of superiors—where they could run their local office "like my own business"—to a situation where they were more subject to the judgments of their superordinate managers.

Discretionary Control and Control by Standards

Let us summarize the principles demonstrated in all of our examples. First, the examples have presented instances both of *individual measurement* and *organizational measurement*. Measures applied to individuals affect outcomes for the organization, and vice versa. Yet the outcomes are not necessarily equivalent. For example, systems of measurement that stimulate individual competitiveness may increase the performance of the more capable or competitive individuals but decrease organizational performance as measured by the aggregate of individual efforts.

Next, different outcomes accrue to the use of single as opposed to multiple indicators of performance. Single indicators can unambiguously direct behavior toward the desired outcomes, but may fail to reflect the complexity of the organizational goal set. Multiple indicators can reflect goals more accurately, but may introduce ambiguity by requiring the achievement of conflicting outcomes while not stating the trade-off relationship, that is, the balance desired among the various outcomes.

Finally, the distinction can be made between qualitative and quantitative measures of outcomes. Quantitative measures support hierarchical control and make possible the direction of organizational subunits toward specific outcomes desired by higher levels of management. But in doing so these quantitative measures undermine the authority, the discretionary influence, of lower-level management.

In this regard we must distinguish between the *discretionary* control that can be exercised by a first-line superior over a subordinate—control over behavior—and control by the enforcement of *quantitative standards*—control over output. To illustrate, the first-line supervisors in our employment agency example lost discretionary control over the behavior of workers when higher-level management enforced the use of only a few quantitative measures. Workers who met those standards were performing satisfactorily; consequently, first-line supervisors had no other incentives available to shape other behavior. Still, they did have control over output. There were clear standards as to what constituted satisfactory performance. Similarly, if higher-level management holds subunit supervisors responsible for only a few quantitative measures of performance, then the management has little discretionary control over these supervisors. This was the earlier situation of our sales managers.

To rephrase our preceding discussion of this example, we see that discretionary control, control over behavior, can be restored in the quantitative standards case by the introduction of many and conflicting standards. Since subordinates will be unable to satisfy all standards, supervisors will now be able to render "judgment calls" as to the satisfactoriness of performance. Knowing this, subordinates will be more willing to comply with superiors' discretionary requests, thus returning a measure of control over behavior while continuing to maintain a large measure of output control through enforcement of the multiple quantitative standards.

How, then, do we choose one form of measurement over another—qualitative over quantitative, single over multiple, and the like? There may be no real answers to these questions, but in order to understand what is involved we must examine more closely the relationship between measures of outcome and the organizational goals toward which the outcomes are directed.

Organizational Goals and the Process of Measurement

Measures are the motivational tools of organizations. Individuals and organizational subunits are directed toward the achievement of organizational goals through the measurement of outcomes of activity believed to serve those goals. In the simple, concrete situations typical of many small organizations there is no apparent problem in establishing the linkage between measures and goals. However, as organizations grow in size and complexity, this apparent simplicity is lost. This, of course, was a major point in Chapter 15. Let us restate briefly some of the points in that chapter that are important for our current discussion.

First, organizational goals are multiple and complex; the goal statement itself is a value premise that may serve as input for a decision. Second, although goals are stated in general terms at higher levels of the organization, they must be operationalized for use at lower levels. Hence, at the level of the lowest organizational subunit, goals must be translated into terms of specific behaviors and outcomes that are observable; that is, goals must become *measurement oriented*.

Third, the problem of goal displacement occurs when the value premises enunciated at higher levels of the organization have intangible referents, consisting of "unanalyzable abstractions." In other words, lower levels of the organization cannot act directly on these intangible goals since it is impossible to ascertain specifically what behaviors and consequent outcomes would fulfill them.

Finally, displacement activity results when individuals and organizational subunits try to ensure their own goal satisfaction or survival even though lower-level operational goals and derived measures bear little relation to the value premises enunciated at higher levels and even though the measures themselves capture only part of the more important elements of the organizational goal set. The unanticipated and largely dysfunctional consequences of the measurement process that we have observed flow, then, from the nature of organizational goals themselves and from the extent to which measures are capable of capturing the full complexity of the goal set. Figure 16.2 suggests schematically some relationships among these concepts.

Characteristics of Measures: a Summary

We have presented examples of different attributes of measures in different organizational contexts to illustrate the process of measurement and its consequences. Let us summarize those characteristics as shown in Figure 16.3.

Relation to Source

By source we mean the individual or agency who *provides* the information. In the typical performance rating interview, for example, the superior provides the information to be used in appraisal. The subordinate has no direct control

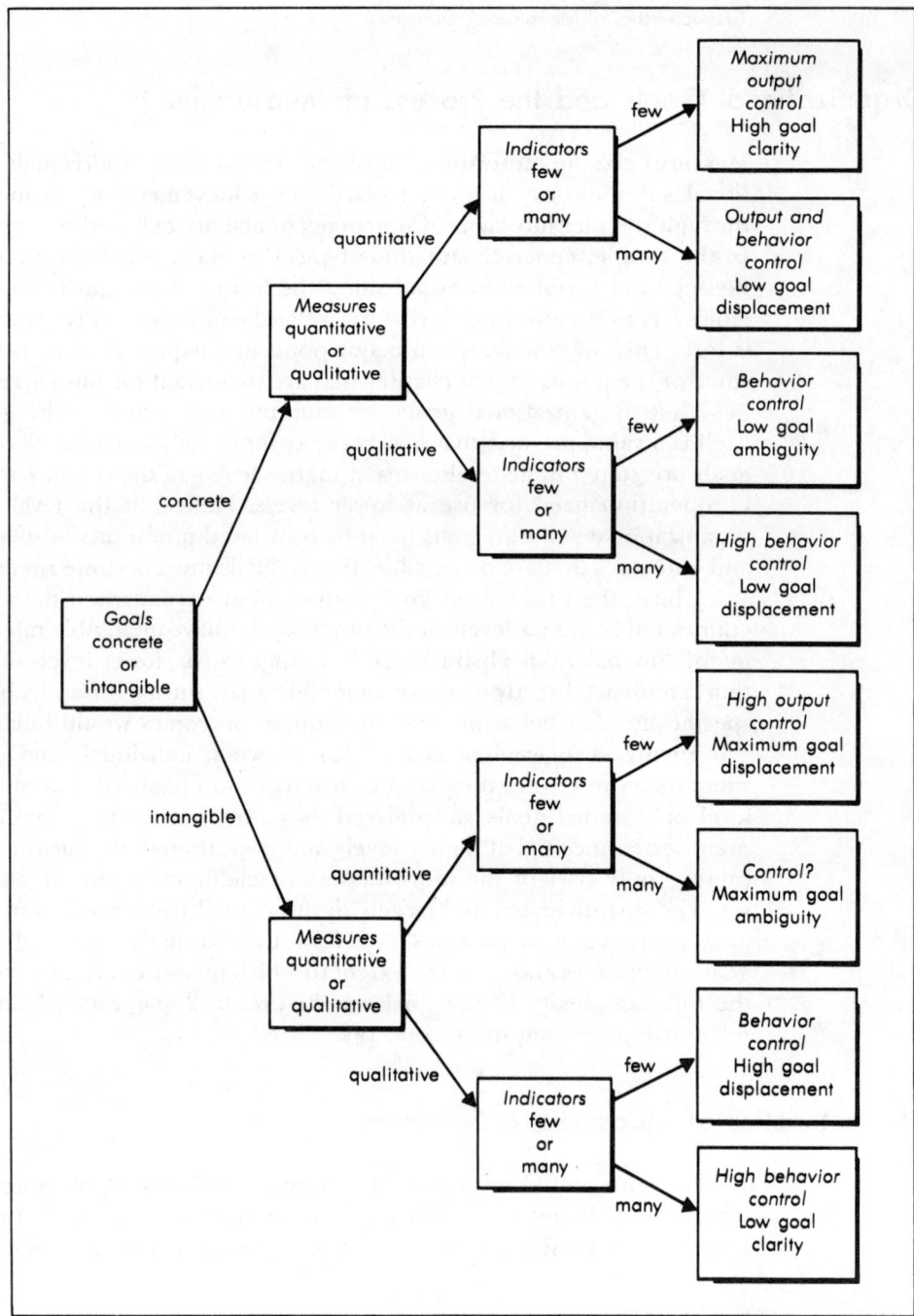

FIGURE 16.2 Suggested Relationships Among Goals, Characteristics of Measures and Control, Goal Ambiguity, and Displacement

Characteristics of Measures: A Summary

- Relation to source — Measure is based on information provided by source unaffected by outcome *vs.* source directly affected by outcome.

- Relation to outcome desired — Measure is identical with outcome desired *vs.* remotely related but easier to obtain outcome.

- Formality of procedures — Procedures specifying measurement process and indicators are completely specified and objective *vs.* unspecified and subjective.

- Number of indicators — Single indicator is to be used *vs.* multiple indicators.

- Clarity — Indicators used are ranked in importance and independent of each other *vs.* those that are ambiguous and conflicting.

- Level of aggregation — Measure reflects directly performance of individual or organizational unit *vs.* aggregated from performance of lower-level units or individual tasks.

FIGURE 16.3 Characteristics of Measures Referred to Organizational Behavior

over the choice of information, and hence cannot directly influence or otherwise distort (or correct) the resulting picture. However, the superior also has an interest in the outcome, and *can* select or distort information. This was observed by both Stanley and Kerry Drake. In our employment agency case, the source was personal statistical records. Interviewers, though affected by the measures, did not provide the information from which the measures were computed.

Relation to Desired Outcome

When the measure is identical with the desired outcome it follows that an increase in the measure reflects directly an increase in goal attainment. Yet this relationship can be difficult to achieve. In their haste to make referrals, interviewers at the employment agency, for example, made poor use of the job openings available by referring poorly qualified clients. There is also a tendency for measurability—ease of measurement—to replace validity or accuracy of representation. Measurability is also a factor in the academic "publish or perish" principle. The difficulty seems to be that the desired outcome is more complex than a single measure can reflect, or that the outcome is otherwise qualified by additional constraints. For example, quantity of production alone seems to be identical with the outcome desired. Yet there are additional constraints: quality must be sufficient, scrap reasonable, machine wear not excessive, and the like.

Formality of Procedures

To achieve complete formality the system of measurement must specify not only the indicators involved, but also the process of evaluation to be used. An approximation of complete formality was found in the employment agency with the supervisor who "let the figures speak for themselves." If the measures used had been ranked by priority, the system would have approached complete formality, with predictable consequences for authority, productivity, interpersonal relations, and the like. The opposite is the completely informal personnel system used in the church. Priests have no idea what criteria, if any, are being used to select pastors. Nor are they apprised formally of their own performance.

Number of Indicators

Seldom will an organization admit that a single indicator is being used to the exclusion of all others, yet at times this is the case. For example, quantity of production, or meeting the time schedule, may become such an overriding concern that supervisors will ignore all else. Academic use of number of publications in critical evaluations of performance is another example. Professors are told that teaching, service to the university, and the like are all taken into account, but the fact is that publications are the overriding concern. Multiple indicators of performance present a different dynamic as we illustrated in our industrial examples. Notice that "overall performance" is not a single indicator from our point of view. Rather, it is an *unspecified combination* of indicators—and thus leads to consequences for organizational behavior similar to those for multiple indicators.

Clarity

It is difficult to imagine a situation where the relationship among multiple indicators of performance can be completely specified. Furthermore, it seems undesirable to do so, for priorities can change. Our Soviet industrial example (pp. 448–489) showed some of the functions of ambiguity in the relationships among multiple measures. In fact, a major reason for the use of multiple indicators may be the very existence of mutual dependence and conflict among the indicators; indicators serve as checks and balances among themselves. The employment agency people used both referrals *and* placements, and, in addition, used the ratio of the two because placements suffered when referrals were overemphasized (leading to poor matches between clients and openings).

Level of Aggregation

Aggregated individual performance may not be an accurate measure of unit performance. For example, individual production workers are allowed to make allowances for poor materials, downtime on machines, and the like because these factors are beyond their control. Yet such allowances may not be appropriate at the departmental level. Where there is less "claiming" of scrap and downtime allowances, it is possible that aggregated individual performance figures may be lower and departmental production higher than in a similar department where greater "claiming" has boosted individual performance records.

Measurement and Technology

The relationship between types of management control and work technology was noted in Chapter 5. In process technologies, recall, the control system is part of the production process itself. Consequently, highly formal control procedures are possible. And the same has been said for measurement. The outcomes of mass production technology are inherently more measurable than, say, the outcomes of development engineering activities. But there are further consequences of technology for measurement, as Mr. Marsh has observed.

Agony[4]

"And I think that each of you is entitled to take some personal pride in the progress that our new expandrium products are making in the marketplace." The voice was that of Mr. Marsh, addressing The Company's yearly technical conference. Since The Company had become quite diversified, these conferences were necessary to bring technical people together, an added help to make sure that each knew what the other was doing. The gathering itself had the flavor of a combination pep rally and religious service, as Kerry described it.

At a table near the rear of the auditorium sat Ted, Dr. Faust, Kerry Drake, and Stanley. Each was listening in a somewhat different way as Marsh continued. "So I would like to make the point specifically here, that this is a tribute to the fine technical job that you all have done." Then, with a shift in tone and emphasis, Marsh began a new theme. "Still, looking ahead, I sometimes wonder if we're getting all we can from our technical potential."

With that phrase, Kerry leaned over to Dr. Faust and chortled, "Look out, here it comes. Now we're into the meat of the sandwich."

"As you know, I've always felt that we have the best sales force in the country" (Marsh had come up through sales). "And I can't help but believe that one incentive to this excellence has been our bonus system based on performance. Now, I realize that this might not be an easy thing to do in engineering, but we ought to be thinking about it.

"You won't find complacency in any sales office. I'll attest to that. And we don't win every time, there, either. But when you visit a sales office that's just lost a big one, well, you can feel the *agony*. It's real." Then, after a pregnant pause, "You know, I can't help wondering if we wouldn't be more effective in engineering if we didn't *agonize* a little more when programs were not meeting objectives.

"Let me continue on that point. Recently I visited one of our laboratories—we've been having problems on a particular project. So I asked the laboratory manager about it. And do you know what he told me? He said, 'I don't know. We've been thinking about whether or not to kill it, but we haven't been able to decide.'"

Again the significant pause. "We *haven't* been able to *decide!* Gentlemen, that is a symptom of the kind of decision making we can't tolerate in The Company. That is *not* leadership. So it seems to me that the key to crisp, hard-hitting leadership—the kind that has achieved excellence in sales—is better measurement of programs and of people. I am confident that this is the key to better decision-making performance, to overcoming what seems at times to be a feeling of complacency." Marsh continued in this vein for a few more minutes, then put the final positive slice on the sandwich and the speech was over.

Ted, as usual, was the first to comment, "Well, Mr. Marsh was right on target again. I've seen it myself. Engineering people just can't bring themselves to decide. After all, it's no skin off their tails. But our sales people, that agony Mr. Marsh talks about—that's real! Five thousand bucks out of your pocket, just like that! That's *agony!*"

"And what would you do, Ted?" The voice was Faust's.

"Why, what Mr. Marsh suggested. Let's measure programs and people, and tie their pay to it." Ted was right there with the answer.

"You think it would be that simple, do you?" Faust's voice had a slight edge of disdain.

But Ted was quick to reply, "I didn't say that. Mr. Marsh didn't say that. He said, I believe, that it would *not* be an easy thing to do. But we ought to be *thinking* about it." You had to hand it to Ted. He knew what Mr. Marsh had said, all right.

Now Kerry spoke up, "I think what Dr. Faust is getting at, Ted, is that things that work in sales don't necessarily work in engineering. You've got a different kind of beast to deal with in engineering. Technical people think in different ways and work for different reasons. And listen, don't be so hasty to draw the conclusion that there isn't any agony there. I'll bet you that laboratory manager and his project managers have burned plenty of midnight oil trying to bail that project out. Listen, there's a piece of them in that thing. That's their baby. And, well, maybe this is putting it crudely, but you don't kill your baby without some indecision.

"No, I think Marsh has got it all wrong. Hell, he's a salesman. How can he know? Listen, the worst thing you could do would be to try to measure our technical people like you do our salespeople and tie their pay to it. I'm not sure I can tell you why, but it just wouldn't work."

There is more to this story but you have the main points. The productive process, the work technology involved, has a lot to do with whether or not a given measurement system will work. The Company has a very sophisticated, quantitative system of measurement against which it evaluates the sales performance of both people and organizational units. As Marsh says (and he should know) it has been highly successful. And that is because the work technology of marketing lends itself to that kind of thing. Also, the point Kerry made about engineers being different from salespeople is true—if only because their organizational socialization has been different (27). Success or failure is marked by a very specific event in sales. The agony is real, but it does not last. Every day is a new day. That is not how it is in research and engineering. Successes seldom work out as well as they might, and failures commonly hold the hint of future success—if only more effort could be expended in solving the problem.

Finally, we see a failure of impression management by the engineering organization. That shows again how important impression management is when judgments are being made of success and failure and other information is nonexistent or ambiguous.[5]

Summary

What You Will Face, How You Might Act

Once again we have tried to provide you with some perspective about things you will see or do at the beginning of your career. Here we suggest some things you will do in response to the measurement system. These will be rather common, of course, and will vary with your particular assignment. We organize them by major categories.

THE TECHNOLOGY AND ENVIRONMENT. First, remember that what you do depends on the kind of job you have. Sales is different from engineering, and different still from production or personnel. You will be measured in different ways. The economic environment also makes a difference. In difficult times the measures may loom larger than in easy times.

SYSTEMS STRUCTURE. Nevertheless, the time will come when you wonder if anyone in management really knows what you are doing or really cares. Then, as you come to learn what counts and what does not, as you learn more of the "right" attitudes and values, you will find yourself starting to practice impression management. You may, for example, start staying a little after hours, occasionally coming in on Saturdays, and carrying a loaded briefcase as seems advisable. You will suspect that these things reflect more on your performance than anything else you can do at the moment. You may get the chance to read a job description for your position. It will seem highly inflated. If you ask, your boss will tell you that this is the basis for the evaluation of your work. Probably it is not. Its major function is to justify your salary to accounting.

THE INTERACTION SYSTEM. One day your boss will come to you and tell you to write a memo to so and so in Another Department. This memo is to lay out carefully the reasons why some piece of work is not on time or in some other way up to expectation. The reasons to be stated in the memo will place the responsibility for the problem squarely on the shoulders of the people in Another Department. This will annoy you because you have been trying to work things out in a comradely fashion. But your boss will insist you do it this way. And this will be your introduction to the crucial CYA (cover your ass) memo.

THE MOTIVATION SYSTEM. As you develop an appreciation of what counts and what does not you will become more selective in your work activity, and although you may not agree with the system, you will find yourself inevitably paying more attention to what counts than to what does not. You will have your first performance appraisal, and in all probability it will be a favorable one. Nothing concrete can be said yet, of course, because you are new. Your first pay raise will come at this time and it will be linked directly to the good words said about you. You will feel good. Sooner or later you will also receive your first promotion. It will also make you feel good. That is what it is for. For a while you will try harder to do well.

THE FEEDBACK AND CONTROL SYSTEM. Eventually, the occasion will arise when you will comment, "Why are we writing this report? No one ever reads them anyway." You will be told by your boss that these reports are necessary. They document the work of the department and of yourself (23). You will start writing the reports from a slightly different viewpoint. Also on occasion you will be asked to supply information about your own work and that of your department in terms of a number of different things. You will supply this information on questionnaires, in statistical reports, in oral presentations, and in other ways. Usually you will have little idea about the use to which this information will ultimately be put. You will find yourself being selective. Occasions will also arise when you, and others in your group, will be called on to justify some project or practice of your department. In this exercise you will be something more than selective. And when you have gained enough experience you may be asked to help prepare a budget. You will estimate time and costs for things about which you have absolutely no knowledge. You will produce the numbers. Those numbers will be added to the numbers produced by your co-workers and totaled. Your manager will add a 10 percent safety factor to the total, making appropriate adjustments as required. When all this is typed up and printed it will have a marvelous aura of precision. This is especially true if dollar amounts are uneven and carried down to the last $10 or so (or hundreds, depending on the total).

This is our attempt at a preview of your response to the measurement system of your new job. We realize that it is sketchy and incomplete, but it is accurate. Wait and see.

Notes

1. One critical review concludes that "there is no conceptual framework to study effectiveness, nor is there a common yardstick to measure it. No generally accepted criteria of effectiveness were found" (13:44). Another finds "evidence that no global measure of effectiveness exists, not even *among divisions of the same organization*" (16:353; emphasis added). For further discussion of this, see Cunningham (8), Meyer and Rowan (22), and Steers (30).
2. This experimental performance rating system was actually tried by an engineering laboratory, although Dr. Faust's role, of course, is invented. Although the distortion of information that is the basis of "Faust's First Law" is commonplace, studies suggest that strong socialization into a normative system that frowns on such practices can lead to accurate self-reporting. See Kaufman (14). For further details of the performance rating problem see Smith (29).
3. Evidence of the use of such criteria in the academic world can be found in publications that attempt to rank university departments by "academic productivity." Indicators of productivity include not only numbers of publications, but quality rankings of journals in which those articles are published, together with frequency of citation by other authors.
4. Mr. Marsh's speech is recorded in notes we took some years ago at a research and engineering conference in The Company.
5. Support for this statement can be found in Pfeffer (25). When performance is difficult to evaluate objectively, characteristics acquired in socialization (associated with ascribed statuses such as socioeconomic status) seem to weigh heavier in performance evaluations.

References

1. ARGYRIS, C. *The Impacts of Budgets on People.* New York: Controllership Foundation, 1951.

2. Babchuck, N., and W. Goode. "Work Incentives in a Self-determined Group." *American Sociological Review* 16 (1951): 679–687.
3. Baumler, J. "Defined Criteria of Performance in Organizational Control." *Administrative Science Quarterly* 16 (1971): 340–351.
4. Beyer, R. *Profitability Accounting for Planning and Control.* New York: Ronald, 1963.
5. Blau, P. *The Dynamics of Bureaucracy.* Chicago: University of Chicago Press, 1955.
6. Clark, B. "Organizational Adaptation and Precarious Values." *American Sociological Review* 21 (1956): 327–336.
7. Cohen, H. *The Demonics of Bureaucracy.* Ames: Iowa State University Press, 1965.
8. Cunningham, J. "Approaches to the Evaluation of Organizational Effectiveness." *Academy of Management Review* 2 (July 1977): 347–355.
9. Frank, A. "Goal Ambiguity and Conflicting Standards: An Approach to the Study of Organization." *Human Organization* 17 (1959): 8–13.
10. Garfinkel, H., and E. Bittner. " 'Good' Organizational Reasons for 'Bad' Clinical Records." In *Studies in Ethnomethodology,* edited by Harold Garfinkel. New York: Basic Books, 1967. Pp. 186–207.
11. Hofstede, H. *The Game of Budget Control.* Assen, Netherlands: Van Gorcum, 1967.
12. Jasinski, F. J. "Use and Misuse of Efficiency Controls." *Harvard Business Review* 34 (1956): 105–112.
13. Kallman, E., L. Reinharth, and M. Wahba. "Organizational Effectiveness: A Review of Theory and Research." *Eastern Academy of Management Proceedings,* April 1976, pp. 44–48.
14. Kaufman, H. *The Forest Ranger: A Study in Administrative Behavior.* Baltimore: Johns Hopkins Press, 1960.
15. Kerr, S. "On the Folly of Rewarding A, While Hoping for B." *Academy of Management Journal* 18 (December 1975): 769–783.
16. Kirchhoff, B. "Organization Effectiveness Measurement and Policy Research." *Academy of Management Review* 2 (July 1977): 347–355.
17. Lawler, E., III, and J. Rhode. *Information and Control in Organizations.* Pacific Palisades, Calif.: Goodyear, 1976.
18. Levinson, H. "Appraisal of *What* Performance?" *Harvard Business Review* 54 (1976): 30ff.
19. Lowe, E., and R. Shaw. "An Analysis of Managerial Biasing: Evidence from a Company's Budgeting Process." *Journal of Management Studies* 5 (1968): 304–315.
20. March, J., and H. Simon. *Organizations.* New York: Wiley, 1958.
21. McCleary, R., B. Nienstedt, and J. Erven. "Uniform Crime Reports as Organizational Outcomes: Three Time Series Experiments." *Social Problems* 29 (April 1982): 361–371.
22. Meyer, J., and B. Rowan. "Institutionalized Organizations: Formal Structure as Myth and Ceremony." *American Journal of Sociology* 83 (September 1977): 340–363.
23. Ouchi, W., and M. Maguire. "Organizational Control: Two Functions." *Administrative Science Quarterly* 20 (1975): 559–569.
24. Pettigrew, A. *The Politics of Organizational Decision Making.* London: Tavistock, 1973.

25. PFEFFER, J. "Toward an Examination of Stratification in Organizations." *Administrative Science Quarterly* 22 (December 1977): 553–567.
26. RIDGWAY, F. "Dysfunctional Consequences of Performance Measurements." *Administrative Science Quarterly* 1 (September 1956): 240–247.
27. RITTI, R. *The Engineer in the Industrial Corporation.* New York: Columbia University Press, 1971.
28. SMIRCICH, L., and R. CHESSER. "Superiors' and Subordinates' Perceptions of Performance: Beyond Disagreement." *Academy of Management Journal* 24 (March 1981): 198–205.
29. SMITH, P. Behaviors, Results, and Organizational Effectiveness: The Problem of Criteria." In *Handbook of Industrial and Organizational Psychology,* edited by Marvin D. Dunnette. Chicago: Rand McNally, 1976.
30. STEERS, R. *Organizational Effectiveness: A Behavioral View.* Santa Monica, Calif.: Goodyear, 1977.
31. STEVENS, S. "Measurement." In *Scaling: A Sourcebook for Behavioral Scientists,* edited by G. Maranell. Chicago: Aldine, 1974.
32. WILENSKY, H. *Organizational Intelligence.* New York: Basic Books, 1967.
33. WOLFGANG, M. "Limitations in the Use of Official Statistics." In *Criminal Behavior and Social Systems: Contributions of American Sociology,* edited by Anthony L. Guenther. Chicago: Rand McNally, 1970.

Discussion Questions

1. In our opening story, Ted was having some difficulty in his performance appraisal of Stanley. In this case, Stanley held a professional job in the personnel function. Do you think Ted's problems would have been the same if Stanley had been a commissioned salesperson? How about a research scientist? An accountant? A production engineer? What differences do you see? Why?
2. State in your own words why a "perfect" measure of performance—one that captures all the important aspects of a situation—is impossible to obtain in practice.
3. Using the terms and concepts developed in this chapter, compare the various methods you know for evaluating student performance (multiple choice, essay exams, term papers, classroom participation, and so on). What are the strengths and weaknesses of each? From your point of view, what would be the ideal approach to measuring student performance? Is this commonly done? Why? Why not?
4. In question 3, what is the role of work technology in determining different methods of student performance evaluation? (*Hint:* For example, think of doing mathematics as a work technology.) Are different methods appropriate for different technologies? Why?
5. Assume a professor is interested in promoting active and informed classroom participation. Describe a measurement system that would be most likely to promote this. What problems do you think are likely to arise from this system? What measurement system would be least likely to achieve this goal? What benefits might be associated with this second system?

6. The owner of a small engineering firm wants to promote "creativity" among design engineers in the firm. Therefore, the owner develops a plan whereby each year the engineer with the most patents receives a three-week, expenses paid, winter vacation. What will be the overall effect of this plan? What are some likely undesirable consequences of this approach? How might the owner avoid these?

Chapter 17
Systems for Feedback and Control: The Depersonalization of Management

Breakthrough[1]

Ted Shelby and Pat Jones were on their way to a meeting with B. Wismer Evans, general manager of The Company's Research Division. The Research Division was not a large division by Company standards, but it was important. Its mission was stated as that of keeping The Company in "the forefront of systems technology."

As they strolled down the corridor toward their appointment, Ted recapped their purpose. "There's no question about it, Pat. We're on the edge of a real organizational breakthrough." Ted was employing his best eager/sincere manner. "Look, you're a psychologist, that's why I want you to talk to Whiz." [The shortening of Wismer had been modified to fit his meteoric career.] "We would like to have your input on this. After all, there is just so much you can do in research. You've got people, ideas, and the motivators of dollars and promotion. There are only so many ways you can put those things together. So when you get a dynamite new management system—well, that's a *breakthrough*. And another thing. If this goes the way we think it will, why there's no reason we can't convince Mr. Marsh of the feasibility of this thing for the *whole* Company." (With this last, Ted's eyes glazed over with the thought of where that might leave him.) "Now I'm not trying to tell you your business, but I think you'll see. . . . "

At least Ted was sold.

They walked into Evans's office. "Pat, I'd like you to meet Mr. Evans, our general manager. Most folks call him Whiz." Whiz was a former technical salesperson, who did his best to maintain a "common touch."

"Nice to meet you, Dr. Jones."

"Pat," was the terse reply aimed at restoring interpersonal equity.

"Ted and I have been batting this thing around quite a bit lately and we thought we should get some professional input. I really appreciate your doing this, Pat. Actually, I originally got this idea from our assistant VP who brought it over with him from The Agency. They used the system a little differently there in letting technical contracts to bidders. But we have adapted the idea here for our own use internally.

"First, let's talk about the way we used to do things and see what's wrong with that. You know the picture. Projects are funded for a year at a time. But most projects last for *more* than a year. And it seems that when you've got a year invested in something, you've got the tendency to wait until you're 95 percent sure that it *won't* work before you're willing to kill it. Even *then* most of our project managers aren't willing to admit that their idea wouldn't have worked if we'd just held on a little longer. It's just the nature of the beast, I guess.

"Well, in that mode we have only a limited number of dollars each year, of course, to fund new ideas with. So we have to live with never-ending gripes about how 'unresponsive' we are to creative new ideas. Got the picture?"

"But the new system changes all that." Pat stated the unspoken conclusion.

"It certainly does," Ted chimed in. "Listen to the way Whiz has got this thing worked out. You won't believe it, Pat. Every angle is covered."

An impatient glance from Whiz Evans effectively conveyed the notion to Ted that this was *not* the time for sycophant chatter. Then he moved to his flipcharts.

"We call our system *Cumulative Merit Funding*. And here's how it works. Instead of funding for the entire year, with CMF we fund an initial stage of three months. This allows us to fund initially many more ideas than we could under the old system. Now at the end of the initial stage we review the project thoroughly. We keep only the most promising ideas. The survivors will be funded for an additional six months or so through a second stage, where the project people will take a closer look at the technical and economic feasibility of the idea. Again a review. Those that get through *this* stage—now maybe we're down to one in three of the original group—will get anywhere from another six months to perhaps two years, if warranted.

"See the beauty of it? With *just the same number* of dollars we get to see two, three, or four times the number of ideas researched through at least the initial stage. And we know that's about all the time it takes to get a pretty good feel for whether or not an idea is worthwhile. We also know that if you give the project managers a year they'll take a year whether they need it or not. But this way it's survival of the fittest, a kind of technological natural selection. We get *more* ideas and *better* ideas for the same money. More bang for the buck.

"What do you think of it, Pat? I mean, from the psychologist's point of view."

Pat, reflecting to herself that this last most definitely was *not* couched as a question, began somewhat tentatively. "Certainly sounds interesting. But I've still got some questions.

"You say that you can tell in three months whether an idea is worthwhile or not. But you also say that your project managers don't feel sure even after a year. Why is that?"

Whiz thought for a moment, then replied, "Two things, I guess. First of all, I suppose I *should* say that we can tell pretty well within three months that an idea is *not* going to work. There are some things that come out right away that are sure signs. So those projects we can kill right on the spot. But we still don't know if a survivor will be a really *good* idea, so that's where the second and third stages come in.

"Second, I think you can appreciate that there's got to be a difference between the viewpoint of top management and the project manager. We think we'll be right 80 percent of the time after three months. Sure, we don't have all the facts. We never will. Now you've got to understand the project managers' mentality. When it's a question of their *own* idea, these people won't be willing to give it up until they're absolutely certain it won't work. From what I've seen, that never happens with some of them. In all fairness, every now and then one of them does turn out to be right. But for us it's got to be a question of probabilities. Dollarwise we just can't afford to operate the way they'd like."

"What happens to a project manager when his idea is dropped after the initial stage?" was Pat's next question.

"Oh, they go on to become part of another project team—at least until they have the next fundable idea. Don't you see, that's the beauty of it."

"How do they like that?" Again Pat's question.

"Oh, they don't mind. Sure they'd rather be working on their own ideas, but they know they'll get another chance. You see, we don't have the usual manager-employee status distinctions here."

"You don't." The flat tone of the statement conveyed Pat's lack of conviction.

Now it was Ted's turn in his area of expertise—personnel. "No, we don't. We've arranged it so that our individual contributors are valued just as highly as our managers. We've stressed the point in our laboratories that management is just an assignment here, not a career."

The slogan formed in Pat's mind: *Just an Assignment, Not a Career.* Ted probably thought in slogans, she mused. Then the next question, "Who makes the decision as to whether projects survive or not?"

"Well, right now that decision will be made by the general manager. But when we get experience with the system we expect the laboratory managers to handle those decisions. Still, for big projects. . . . "

"Then you are going to make the decisions."

"Well, yes."

"Is that the way it's done now?" Pat thought she knew the answer to this, however.

"Well, no. Under the old system it was done in the laboratory as part of our funding procedure."

"I see." Pat was about to continue but Whiz anticipated the next question.

"Yes, I think I understand that this *is* a possible source of trouble. And I'm glad you've seen it, too. But this is only temporary, you understand, until we get this thing geared up."

There's no need to draw our story out further. You have all the elements. As for Pat, she could tell from the trend of their discussion that Ted and Whiz were looking primarily for confirmation, not criticism, and so she diplomatically turned the conversation toward the structural details of the new system. Finally, Whiz felt it appropriate to ask her opinion. "So what do you think, Pat, now that you've seen the whole picture?"

"I'm not sure I understand completely, Whiz. I have the feeling that your system is more complicated than it might just appear on the surface. But you do have a new motivational tool for sure."

What Pat *didn't* say was more significant. There was no question that they had a new motivational tool. The real question was, motivation for *what?* And it wasn't until two years later that they had the answer. That answer was motivation for things that had never occurred to them. In the wake of that "management disaster" (as it was termed by Mr. Marsh himself), Whiz Evans was no longer with The Company, and his vice president was put out to pasture where he could do no further damage. It wasn't that technological Darwinism was a false principle. It had worked and worked well. It was just that the fittest, the survivors of the process, didn't resemble one bit the beasts that top management had in mind.

The episode with CMF ultimately comes to an unhappy conclusion. But why, then, had it ever been expected to become a management breakthrough? And why was this expectation held by intelligent and experienced technical management?

One answer is that CMF brought some measure of control to a situation in which management felt insecure. The new order of the day was *planned innovation.* The Company was becoming interested only in certain kinds of technical breakthroughs, that is, in breakthroughs that fit the long-term thrust of the business. And that brought new problems. It is one thing to turn your technical development people loose with the general order to come up with the best products they can, but quite another to control the process. What the Company wanted of its engineers was innovation that reliably would yield a system ready to replace its obsolete predecessor every five years, *and* be compatible with other Company products on the marketplace at that future time.

All of this suggests another reason for CMF: as a control system CMF provided a means of stating some rather "fuzzy" planning goals in a direct, tangible fashion—or so it seemed.

Finally, CMF provided *output control*. That is, by dealing with estimates of anticipated costs and anticipated revenues, and putting these in a specific time sequence, CMF reduced the subjectivity of the resource allocation process. Now management wanted to be shown objectively. Depersonalizing the control process also simplified evaluation—the exercise of authority. Cumulative merit funding was a system of control, rather than a procedure for measurement. CMF was intended to affect the following:

1. *Motivation.* By presenting scientists with expanded opportunities for the development of their own ideas, management was attempting to bring about greater motivation through the work itself. And more ideas tried meant more ideas fitting the requirements of planned innovation.
2. *Organizational goals.* Even under earlier procedures managers had to justify proposed products under an "anticipated revenue/anticipated cost" format. However, with the longer period of time allotted previously, ideas seldom were discarded early, for scientists continued their work if only to satisfy their own curiosity. The new system, by forcing comparisons among competing ideas after a short period of time, forced managers to state their action goals early and in quantitative terms.
3. *Measurement.* Technical feasibility is an economic concept. The key question for product development is not "can it be done?" but "can it be done *within the price constraints of the marketplace?*" By setting down explicitly the quantitative terms to be used in comparisons, the measurement process was reduced to few objective and quantitative terms.
4. *Feedback.* Every three months management would get objective output data against which to evaluate the project.
5. *Control.* With control now residing in the office of the division general manager, and with the comparisons based on relatively few quantified facts, it would now be possible to monitor more closely and, hence, to control an entire program of planned innovation.

These are the things management hoped to achieve from CMF. Unfortunately, other, unanticipated consequences resulted from the interplay of these factors. Understanding why these changes took place is our topic in this chapter. During our discussion we will use two major cases, both of which we have researched personally over several years. You have seen the first installment of one of the cases. The second case describes a work methods improvement program installed in a multiplant manufacturing organization. In this case we will show you the effect of introducing motion and time measurement in a system of planning, forecasting, and production control. The purpose, as always, is to develop a set of principles and a perspective for understanding the behavioral consequences of such systems.

A Point of View

Trying to control behavior through the use of impersonal systems of feedback and control is risky in complex organizations. This is due to the adaptive and purposeful nature of organizations, of the people and the subunits that constitute them. Why this should be so is the concern of this chapter.

Most important for understanding organizational behavior is the human response to control systems, and how and why that response is often different from what management expects. We are not saying that information feedback and control systems are worthless, and we are not saying that information feedback systems in themselves present problems. What we *are* saying is that information used for control becomes increasingly subject to purposeful distortion; and, as a corollary, that when information is available, sooner or later it *will* be used for control (25, 26, 28). We believe that feedback and control systems can work to good effect under the proper circumstances, if the necessary conditions of technology and environment are met. In complex organizations they often are not. Still there is an understandable push from higher levels of management to regain the direct control they lost as a consequence of organizational size and complexity (7, 23).

This is our point of view. You need not accept it fully to benefit from the analysis presented in this chapter. The question is one of emphasis, and of how commonly the things we describe take place.

Measurement and Feedback for Control

Purposeful managerial control can be exercised only when managers have some knowledge of the results of the productive process in which their subunits are engaged. How else will managers know whether or not their instructions are helping their subunits to achieve their goals (17)? In turn, knowledge of results depends on accurate assessment or measurement of the outcomes of that purposeful activity, together with undistorted feedback to the manager exercising control. If the information fed back is no better than random noise, then attempts to control can produce no better than random results.

Using this as a basic statement of the organizational problem of control faced by the manager, let us examine what happens as the organization grows in size and complexity. To provide a concrete example, let us look first at how Ben Franklyn would run a small machine shop. Assume he has ten to fifteen employees. He is the boss, the only one. His business is mainly subcontracting jobs from larger manufacturing plants. He knows from experience which jobs will be profitable and which not, and how much he can expect to make on each. Ben's shop is pretty much a one-man show. He hires and fires, though he depends on a core group of eight people who have been with him since the early days of the shop. The rest come and go according to the variations in the business cycle.

Ben personally knows every one of these people. He knows what they are good at, and what they are not so good at. One or two are not particularly good at anything, but they have been with him a long time and are thoroughly dependable. Ben knows, at least, that he can trust them to put in a fair day's work, as he sees it. Another is a superb craftsman—when he wants to be, that is. But he has a little drinking problem and sometimes he does not show up for a few days.

Ben's in control—mostly. He knows his business inside out and his people just about as well. And they know him. They know what he will put up with and what he will not.

Let us move Ben up a notch or two to the level of plant manager and see what are the differences. One thing is obvious: now Ben does not know everyone personally. As plant manager he must depend on one or two levels of middle management for information about what is going on. He still gets detailed data on the costs and output of jobs—because he demands it—but it is not as real. Ben no longer has that "hands on" feel for how a job is going. In fact, he does not have any firsthand experience at all with some of the jobs they do. Still, he can stroll through the plant to get some sense of how things are going, and he has some friends, foremen and department managers, he trusts to tell him the truth. Yet he cannot help being uneasy when trouble develops for he does not know the situation in depth and has to depend on the judgments of others. Ben has always been uneasy with that.

Let us move Ben up a few more levels. Now he is the corporate director of manufacturing in a multiplant organization like The Company. (Of course, this is just for example. Actually, Ben would never take such a position.) His day-to-day diet has become one of problems and crises, major and minor. That is because he never hears about things *unless* they're that important. So he is getting a somewhat distorted view, one that suggests to him that nothing ever goes right. Furthermore, in this position, he no longer knows personally any of his production people and few of his managers. His personal knowledge extends only to his plant managers, probably twenty or so, both great and small, and a reasonable representation of functional managers.

Ben is conscious now more than ever that in this position he receives mostly "revised" versions of the facts (19, 37). So, for example, taking an inspection tour of a plant manufacturing floor is next to useless as a method for gathering information because everyone there will be on their best behavior, alerted a day or so in advance that "Franklyn will be through here about noon tomorrow, so look sharp."

Depersonalization of Control

Ben's response, and that of other executives like him, is to try to regain some measure of lost control (16, 23). The method that suggests itself most readily is that of developing formal rules and procedures that provide the feedback necessary to exercise day-to-day control. This can be done by requiring that these steps be taken:

1. Stating subunit goals in action terms and translating them into specific, *quantifiable, and measurable* outcomes.
2. Providing a system whereby those outcomes can be aggregated, organized, and fed back to various levels of management *directly* and *impersonally*. The obvious vehicle for this is some kind of management information system. Note that the requirements of the information system itself put constraints on the kinds of outcomes that can be reported.
3. Comparing these outcomes with stated action goals in the process of *evaluating* organizational performance and planning future performance objectives.
4. Using these evaluations of individual and unit performance to *control* behavior through authoritative use of rewards and punishments.

And what are the envisioned benefits resulting from this process? From our executive's point of view, they are:

1. The system is more objective and accurate; it provides information at whatever level of detail is desired, and provides it with little delay.
2. It provides a check on and consequently lessens total dependence on direct subordinate reports and evaluations.
3. It helps reduce anxiety about the control of subordinates and lower participants by providing, if necessary, detailed information on the results of their activities.
4. By permitting objective, impersonal comparisons among organizational units, it reduces the potential for interpersonal conflict based on disagreements about performance.
5. It restores direct control to higher organizational levels.
6. It provides ready answers to difficult questions posed from time to time by executive management.

In other words, since the process of evaluation undergirds superior power, and since control rests at least in part on the exercise of superior power, the impersonal feedback system supports higher-level superior control by making the process of direct evaluation once again possible (8, 31). But the impersonal feedback system does other things as well. First, it places greater emphasis on *output* control, and second, in so doing, it removes some measure of *behavior* control from lower-level management (5, 6).

Output Control and Behavior Control

One tendency of feedback systems used for higher-level management control is to focus on output control rather than behavior control. Having just said this, we hasten to add that all control is aimed at behavior, but that the means for getting at that behavior through the motivation system may be evaluations either of *behavior* directly—behavior control—or of the *output* of that behavior—output control (23). Let us define what we mean by output and behavior.

Output describes the outcomes of behavior that are objectively available for evaluation. These outcomes may be related to any part of the goal set of the organizational subunit observed. In manufacturing, for example, output might be the number of pieces produced, or it might be quality or scrap loss. Somewhat differently, output might also be the cleanliness of the work place, an outcome related to the goal of safety. In retail sales we have the output of dollar volume, but we also have the accuracy of sales reports or perhaps the attractiveness of sales displays (23). In product development output indicators include patents received, papers published, and the like. Our story "Breakthrough" gives some additional examples of possible output indicators. The point is that all these indicators are based on *outcomes of behavior* that can be assessed without knowledge of the behavior taking place. Even in the *least quantifiable* of our examples, evaluations of goal-related outcomes can be made directly without reference to behavior: the cleanliness of the work place, the attractiveness of sales displays, and the like.

Behavior refers to the ongoing activities of the individuals being evaluated without consideration of the end result of these activities. In manufacturing we observe employees "goofing off," taking extra work breaks, or refusing orders. The *work methods* used by a manufacturing employee are behavior. *Evaluations* of behavior might include subjective evidence of effort, such as pace. *Control* over behavior might be exercised by close supervision—ascertaining that specified procedures are being followed explicitly. In sales we might observe the manner in which the salesperson deals with customers. Dress and manner are important. In research and development more subtle aspects of behavior—such as attitude, hours spent, and the like—may be evaluated.

This distinction between output and behavior can at times become blurred. So, for example, it is difficult to know whether the behavior of a counselor or social worker is behavior or output. But in general the distinction should be clear.

Technology, Evaluation, and Control

At the close of Chapter 16 we talked about the relationship between measurement and work technology. One conclusion we came to is that some work activities are inherently more measurable than others. Let us analyze this idea in terms of the distinction between behavior and output control. We have to consider the type of work technology involved, the types of measures available, and the way in which those measures are evaluated—personally or impersonally.

WORK TECHNOLOGY. In Chapter 5 we identified several dimensions of work technology, one of which we termed the "predictability of outcomes." This dimension reflects the completeness of knowledge about means-ends relationships in the transformation process. In the context of our present discussion you might protest that to the extent these means-ends relationships are unknown, that is, to the extent that the behavior/output relationship is unknown, it is irrational to exercise control. What would be the purpose of it? Yet we know from experience this is not always the case. Control may be exercised simply to ensure that proper impression management is taking place (22, 23, 34).

TYPE OF MEASUREMENT USED. In Chapter 16 we named several characteristics of organizational measures in "either-or" fashion. Four characteristics reflect the strength or weakness of the measure used. Strong measures, we said, show these characteristics: they are *identical to the outcome desired,* the measurement process is *completely specified and objective,* single or relatively *few indicators are used,* and indicators (if multiple) are *ranked in importance and independent of one another.* The fewer of these that characterize the measure, the weaker it is in the sense of being more subjective and hence open to dispute.

MODE OF EVALUATION. In Chapter 16 we also said that *measurement* and the *evaluation* of the resulting measures constitute separate organizational processes. The evaluation of the measured outcome may be personal or impersonal, regardless of the nature of the measure itself (27). For example, though organizational subunits generally have multiple goals, the formal measures used to reflect the performance of the unit may reflect but a single goal. However, *evaluation* of the measured outcome may be based on the personal judgment of the responsible manager, and may reflect consideration of multiple goals or of environmental conditions. "Mitigating circumstances" such as changes in the marketplace or unforeseen problems may be taken into account in a *personal* evaluation. *Impersonal* evaluation, on the other hand, implies a simple comparison of outcomes to stated goals. In such an impersonal evaluation the facts speak for themselves.

These then, are the factors: *knowledge of means-ends relationships* in the productive process, *strength of the measures* available, and *mode of evaluation.* Let's examine now how these factors work to suggest the use of either output or behavior control. Figure 17.1 should aid in this task.²

For the situation labeled *case 1,* strong measures are available and the knowledge of means-ends (or behavior/output) relationships are known completely. Evaluation is done impersonally. This situation will fit well with output control. It is much the same as that in the employment agency described in Chapter 16. It is also typical of simple manufacturing, or retail sales. In these circumstances impersonal feedback and control systems may work well since relatively few measures capture the important goals of the organization (33).

The situation labeled *case 2* is just the opposite. Here there is little or no understanding of the means-ends relationship and measures are weak. Personal evaluation is the mode chosen. This is a situation for pure behavior control. An example might be some sort of political action organization. Or perhaps an institution of higher learning where teaching was the key activity—a community college, for example.

Now what would happen in the same situation if instead *impersonal* evaluation were used? For example, the manager might stress punctuality and other objectively observable behaviors. Generally, there would need to be agreement within the normative structure as to the *meaning* of such behavior. Research suggests that this situation exists in some rehabilitative programs for the mentally ill, and for criminal offenders, drug addicts and the like where, because means-ends relationships are ill understood, and because measures of improvement are weak, certain behaviors come to be agreed on as impersonal indicators of satisfactory performance (9, 22, 30).

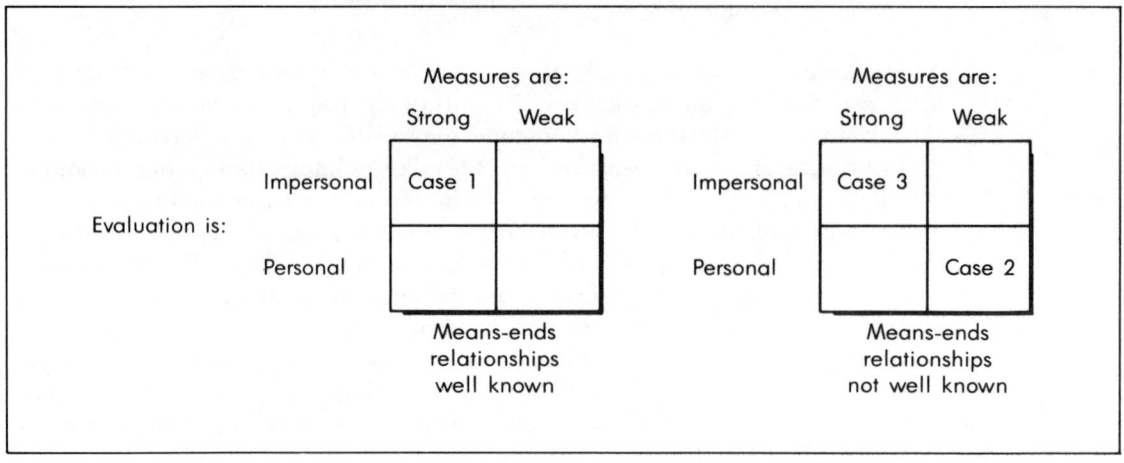

FIGURE 17.1 Diagram of Possible Relationships Among Technology, Measurement, and Mode of Evaluation with Type of Control Exercised

In *case 3* there is again little knowledge of the means-ends relationship. But in this case strong measures are available and evaluation is carried out impersonally. So output control seems likely. How can strong measures be available when there is little or no knowledge of means-ends relationships in the productive process? There are really two answers to this question.

The first is that the nature of the enterprise may make understanding the behavior/outcome relationship *unnecessary*. An example might be the life insurance business, where the goals of the organization are captured by few strong measures, although *how* the agent achieves this is another matter (23). Second, even though the measures used are strong, they are *inappropriate;* that is, the measures fail in important ways to capture the full range and complexity of the organizational goal set. Such a situation can result when the desire for output control leads to the development of measurement procedures that can make such control possible. Cumulative merit funding is a good example of case 3.

Let us summarize with a principle that relates this distinction between behavior control and output control to our more general theme of feedback and control systems. The principle is: to the extent that higher-level management wishes to exercise *direct* control over lower-level personnel and subunits, that control *necessarily* will depend on feedback systems relying increasingly on the evaluation of output. Under some conditions such as those in case 1, such a system may work well, even though employees—both blue collar and professional—seem universally to dislike such systems. But under other circumstances, such as those in case 3, output control seems unwarranted. The work technology supports neither strong measures nor the impersonal evaluation required by a feedback system that can capture only a limited amount of information.

Finally, the use of output control does not necessarily preclude the use of behavior control, and vice versa (24). Each may be addressed to different factors in the organization's goal set. We have simply explored the characteristics of each independently of the other.

These ideas have implications both for subunits and individuals. Feedback systems used for higher-level control focus more on organizational subunits. Yet such systems directly imply output control for individuals as well, focusing as they do on the aggregated output of individuals within the subunits.

With this background let us return to Pat, Ted, and Whiz as they talk with Kerry and view the effect that CMF has had on Kerry's laboratory. Almost two years have passed since their earlier conversation.

The Invisible Hand

"In all my years with The Company, Pat, I've never seen things worse in the laboratory," said Kerry. "Something's completely wrong. But I'm not sure I can put my finger on it."

Pat Jones had been called in to do a personal audit by the task force reviewing the laboratory program. It was true. Something was wrong in the laboratory. There was no question about it. In fact, several letters calling for change had been received by Marsh's office. One in particular was most forceful and articulate.

> Through both words and deeds I see now that to establish or continue any project in our laboratory we must provide definite proof of the existence of a significant market for our proposed developments.
>
> Inevitably this must mean that we must prove that our solution has a greater value than its cost before we may be permitted even to begin to invest time and money in trying to solve the problem. Because of this we invest so much time trying to justify our actions that we are left with little time and money to *take the action*.

The letter concluded, almost lyrically,

> To rely totally on the test of predicted expense to predicted revenue with a management reluctant to trust its own judgment, must lead and has led to the sterilization of the creative, the frustration of the productive, the stultification of the enterprising, and the loss of the competent. For prediction of the solution's value when we are just beginning to comprehend the problem is no better than random selection.

Yes, the task force was looking into it. Pat had compiled some data comparing the results of an attitude survey just completed with one done three years ago. Today was her day to make the presentation. Ted, Whiz, and the responsible vice president were all there, together with the task force. Following the usual preliminaries, Pat was on.

"I'll begin first with what I *know* from the data, then add what I *think* I know, and then I'll give you my *interpretation*.

"There's no question that overall morale in the laboratory is lower than I've ever seen it before." Pat produced some flip-charts with slanting lines shooting downward to the right. "Over the last three years confidence in top management has dropped off precipitously; not only in the view of your professionals, but even more so for your *first-line managers*—your research leaders."

A murmur of dismay.

"So there is no question in my mind that something is seriously wrong." Pat went on to show similar declines in other key indicators. Then, after building this suitable introduction, "So I want to show you some facts that I think point to the heart of the problem. Here, I asked our research people to tell me how much of their creative potential is required in their work. Now look at this." Pat flipped to the next chart, one showing a tall green bar reading 60 percent, alongside a very short red one reading 15 percent. "This, gentlemen, is what has happened over the period of time in question. The *job itself* has changed in important ways." Pat went on to describe how it was that the opportunity for creative expression had been destroyed by the requirements of Cumulative Merit Funding.

But with this Ted could no longer restrain himself. In his best concerned tone, but with the addition of just a hint of scorn, "Pat, I think that you would be more convincing to *most* of us here if we knew just what this 'creative potential' you're talking about really means." Ted was looking about the room in such a way as to suggest that all concurred in his opinion. Then continuing, "Why, it's a loaded question. We all know these people. Have you ever talked to one who thinks he's using his *full* creative potential? Of course not. And that's just the way we *want* it to be. You know, I think that we would be in *real* trouble if they all were satisfied. We don't want 'contented cows' here. No, I don't think that you've shown us anything at all."

This speech, of course, was greeted with murmurs of approval from the laboratory management under indictment. But Pat had been around a while. And she knew how to handle the Ted Shelbys. She was waiting for something, and it didn't take long.

"I think that's a bunch of crap, Ted." Now it was Kerry's turn, speaking, in a way, for the task force. "*I* know what creative potential is even if you don't, and *I* know when I'm using it even if *you* don't. And *I* don't think I'm using very much of it when I brush off Pat's suggestions because I'm afraid to look at the truth."

Pat judged the time to be right to add quietly but forcefully, "Actually, Ted, I'm not much concerned about exactly what the term means. I know from experience that it does mean something to our professionals because it's precisely the term *they* use when they try to describe for me what has happened here.

"Now concerning your 'contented cow' theory, I also know that *whatever* creative potential means, these people are *four times* less likely to see it in their jobs today than they were three years ago. So I have to ask myself, what happened? What might have happened here to change the job so much in three years? And my answer is Cumulative Merit Funding. Here's what one of our people said during an interview." Pat flipped to the next chart and read,

> We work our ass off just to gain the privilege of being allowed to do something.

This last, of course, was in reference to the necessity of justifying all projects before funding would be forthcoming.

Still, the task force was not convinced. They had been talking to laboratory management, and most of the gripes there were about lack of advancement and pay in the small research laboratory as compared to the bigger company locations. They had the feeling that these were the heart of the problem. So the discussion went back and forth for a while. Finally it became evident that as convinced as Pat was, the division managers and Ted were reluctant to accept what could only be termed a stunning indictment of their managerial capabilities.

Sensing this, Pat tried a conciliatory tactic. "I'll have to admit," she said, "that not all of my data are completely in line with my explanation. One thing I asked both our professionals and managers was who—what level of management—they felt had the most influence on technical decisions concerning their work. I was sure that part of our problem was that CMF had taken responsibility for these decisions away from lower management and placed them in the hands of the division general manager. Now when this happens you get an influence chart that looks something like this." Pat went to the flip-chart easel and showed this diagram.

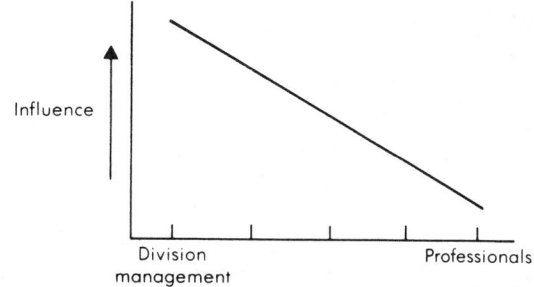

"In this case the locus of control in the organization should be right at the level of top division management. But what I found *doesn't* look *at all* like that. Frankly, I don't understand why. Here's what your laboratory looks like." With that Pat took a red felt tipped marker and drew in another line.

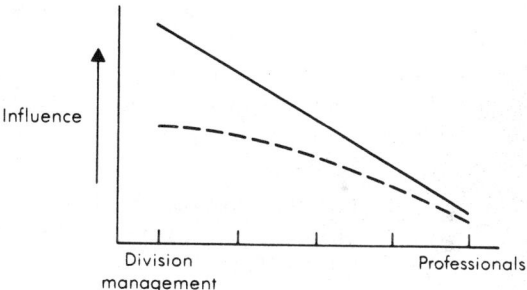

"I've never seen anything like it before," continued Pat. "I can't explain it."

Only a moment passed, then Kerry boomed out, "You can't? I can! I'll tell you what that says. It says to me that nobody's got any influence—this thing is running itself!"

Pat didn't need to say it; her look said so for her: Kerry was absolutely right! That was the missing piece of the puzzle.

Well, CMF was dead. That was certain. But in its wake, laboratory management still had more questions than answers. What had gone wrong and why? And why did such bright and energetic people fail to see it coming?

What Went Wrong?

At this point you must be asking yourself why management did not see the situation as it was. Why didn't they do something before the problem became so evident? Might some things have been changed that would have achieved the original objectives?

These are good questions, and not easy ones to answer—even in retrospect—but we will try. First, you must realize that there is no such thing as certain success in management innovation. As the division general manager told Pat, he was aware of some problems inherent in the new approach. But significant achievements are not made without taking some risks.

Next, keep in mind what management was trying to bring about. Most fundamentally, the aim of CMF was to encourage project managers to make the decision to terminate a project earlier in the project cycle in order to free funds for competing ideas. Division management understood only too well that project managers would not do this willingly. Clearly there was a need for more control at higher levels of the organization if they were to have "more bang for the buck." And there also was the trend toward planned innovation. Some projects fit management's plans better than others regardless of their inherent technical worth.

One direct consequence of CMF, then, was that decisions to terminate projects were made earlier and at a higher level than before. And since these decisions were made earlier, inherently they were more questionable than decisions made under the previous system. Furthermore, since reallocation of funds inevitably meant comparisons among all divisional projects, not just those within a given product area, project decisions had to be made at a higher level of authority, but a level that could not have intimate personal knowledge of the details of competing projects. Of necessity, then, management had to introduce a feedback and control system that employed strong measurement and output control. In this situation it was also natural enough to move in the direction of impersonal evaluation. Why? For one thing simply *because* the detailed personal knowledge was not there. But also because increased competititon among projects means increased interpersonal strife ahead for the manager making the evaluations. Letting the facts speak for themselves can ease this source of tension (5).

Our point is that the final shape of CMF as a management tool flowed directly from the dictates of the system itself rather than from some independent managerial logic. This is important. Once the objectives and the process of the feedback and control system were established, the form of management was nearly inevitable: The problems we observe are the result mostly of the poor fit of the core work technology of the organization with the administrative technology of CMF.

One difficulty with the whole CMF program came from the fact that the goals of the research division are many and difficult to state in action terms.

Take creativity, for example. Research and development managers know instances of creativity when they see them, and they can tell you that such and such a design is a good example. But they cannot tell you in so many words what creativity is, and they cannot tell you how to do it. So R and D managers ultimately rely on some form of output control (23). But the evaluation uses weak measures and it is done in the personal mode. CMF, by necessitating a feedback and control system fundamentally inappropriate to the task—yet still being something which the scientists *had* to respond to if their projects were to survive—almost guaranteed that many aspects of the organization's goal set would be sacrificed to a few.

Let us apply the system we have been developing for understanding organizational behavior to an analysis, system by system, of the effect of Cumulative Merit Funding on Kerry's research and development laboratory.

Feedback and Control System

THE LOCUS OF CONTROL. People who have studied the distribution of perceived control in organizations have arrived at two solid conclusions.[3] The first is that the *total amount* of perceived control varies from organization to organization; that is, in some organizations all levels of the organization—management and workers—see themselves as having greater control than do people in other organizations. In other words, the fact that laboratory management shares decision making with technical professionals does not of itself mean that laboratory management will be perceived as having less control (32).

The second conclusion is that the shape of the characteristic "control curve" differs among organizations—those charts of Pat's showed examples. Some of these characteristic control curves peak at top management levels; others are "humped," peaking somewhere at lower levels of management. Also, the slopes of the curves differ, some being steeper than others. (See Figure 17.2). The location of this peak in the characteristic control curve is what we mean by *locus of control* (13).

Some important effects are associated with these factors. Higher employee satisfaction seems to result where total control is greater rather than smaller, and where the locus of control is shifted toward lower levels of management. We have oversimplified, but that is the essence of it (13, 32). However, our interest here is in using the locus of control idea to describe an organizational situation rather than to establish a point of organizational design.

What did CMF do to the locus of control? One effect of CMF was to take the decision making out of the hands of lower-level management and set up instead an impersonal system of quantitative criteria such as projected revenue compared to projected expense. Projects were reviewed on this basis by the division general manager and his staff, using these specific and detailed criteria.

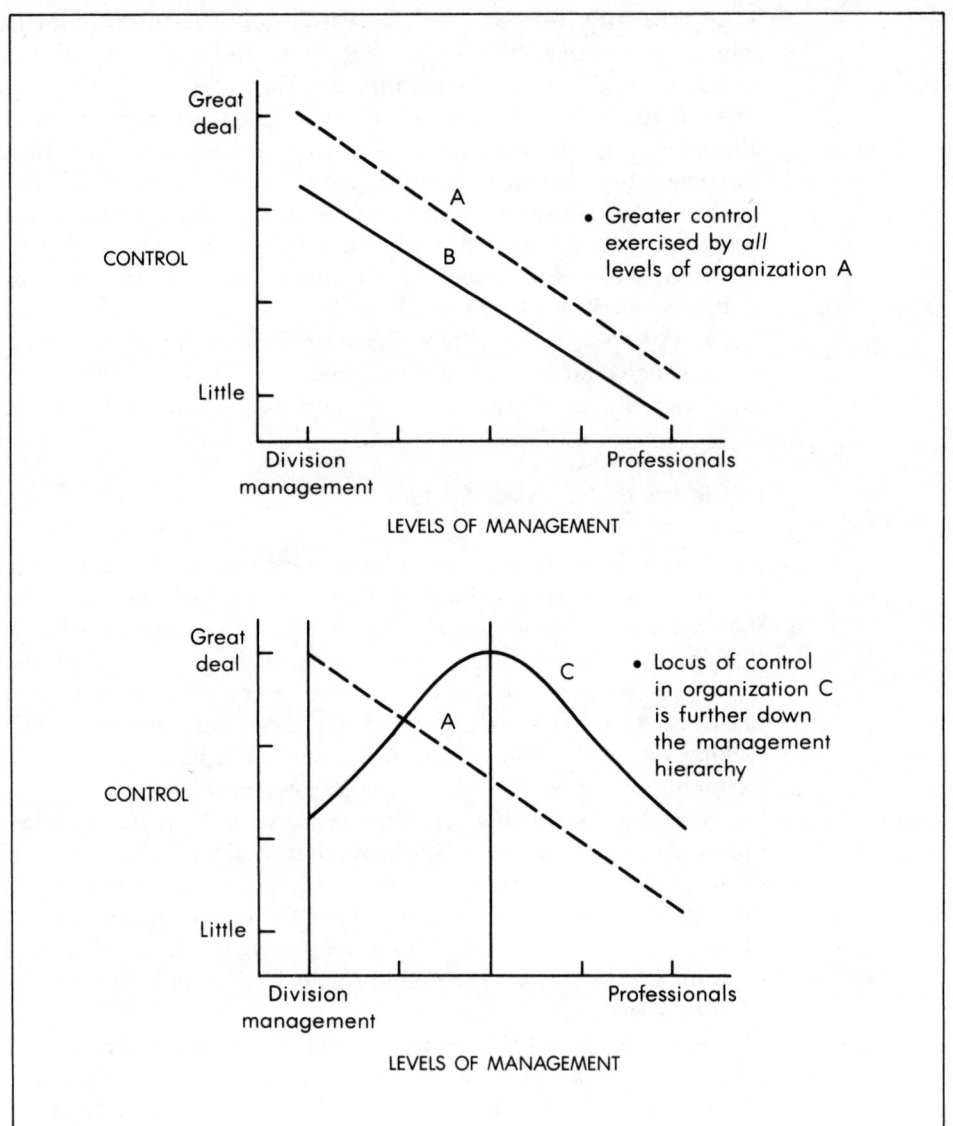

FIGURE 17.2 Amount of Control Exercised by Various Levels of Management as Perceived by Laboratory Professionals

The result, as Kerry pointed out, was not so much that control had been shifted to higher levels of the organization as it was that personal control had been removed from *all* levels of the organization. Thus, under CMF there was no avenue of appeal for personal evaluation by knowledgeable people at lower levels. The situation was similar to that of the manager in Chapter 15 who complained, "He has nobody who can read between the lines and see the same things we do."

FEEDBACK AND CONTROL. In his earlier discussions with Pat the division general manager had said there was a "world of difference" in the two approaches to project funding. And he was right. He correctly described CMF as requiring "continuous planning" on the part of project managers and as encouraging "vigorous competition" among projects. Describing the requirement of a formal report at the end of each project phase he said, "We had to put teeth into it to make it work." The direct result was that before CMF, management action from the organizational subunit involved was necessary before the project *could be killed*. With CMF management action was required in order to *continue* the project. Since the initial phase of any project might be as short as three months, the result of these requirements was that project management spent most of the time allocated to the initial project phase in preparing the presentation for feedback to top management.

MEASUREMENT. Under CMF, projects were measured earlier in the research cycle, with emphasis on demonstrable indicators of potential success. This meant formal, quantitative measures rather than subjective judgment. Since reviews came early, there was little time to arrive at valid quantitative measures, especially where the project bordered on the frontiers of technology—the so-called "blue sky" projects.

ORGANIZATIONAL GOALS. CMF inevitably warped research objectives toward those which were compatible with the feedback and control system; that is, those which were less "blue sky," more immediately measurable, and more in line with known and tested technologies. Faced with continual review, project managers quickly realized that the more speculative and the more imaginative the project, the more it bordered on the frontiers of known technology, then the *less* likely it was that they would be able to produce in a short period of time those quantitative indicators that guaranteed survival. Consequently, research objectives that ran counter to the research mission of the division and counter to the key personal goals of individual professionals were set.

Motivation System

PERSONAL GOALS. A common goal of the technical professionals in the division was the desire to work on such "blue sky" development projects. Yet it is equally important for the professional to be able to carry a project through to its final resolution—successful or otherwise. Not only are achievement needs unsatisfied in a project that is cut off prematurely, but other needs are involved as well.

First, little is learned from an idea that has not been tested. Therefore, there is little opportunity for personal development, for broadening the knowledge base. Second, it is difficult to build a professional reputation on incomplete projects. There is nothing on which to build a professional identity. As we shall see, CMF procedures developed a conflict between personal goals centered on the "work itself," and the desire to work on projects that would survive phase cutoffs.

Mobility System

THE STRUCTURE OF OPPORTUNITY. When a project is terminated, the project manager generally loses managerial status. The basic dynamic of CMF was one of initiating more projects but also terminating more projects. This made steady career progress uncertain, and the threat of failure more imminent. However, the motivational element to remain in the managerial position remained unchanged, as did the normative definitions of success and failure. This situation, then, had a direct effect on organizational goal setting.

Interaction System

LEADERSHIP. One consequence for group leadership stemmed directly from the immediate necessity of preparing feedback presentations for management review. The project manager, ordinarily a research leader, had to start preparing early in the project cycle for the crucial first project review. Thus, leader behavior became more structured and more oriented toward output control and impersonal evaluation. In some ways the project managers became extensions of the system—and they did not like it.

Systems Structure

AUTHORITY. Another direct result of a formal, quantitative system of feedback and control is the erosion of managerial authority. If rewards and punishments accrue directly and impersonally to formal, quantitative criteria, then what is the point of managerial judgments? Pat Jones noticed this effect in her research concerning perceptions of control within the division as well as in low managerial morale.

RECRUITMENT AND SOCIALIZATION. Recruitment into the laboratory, as is usual in such cases, was done on the basis of both ability and values. Laboratory management wanted technical professionals capable of working on the frontiers of new technology and highly motivated to do so. Socialization within the laboratory organization also emphasized these values. However, CMF set up pressures that worked counter to these motivations. As a consequence, several things could be observed: professionals became less committed to the organization and some key people left to go elsewhere; the informal recruiting network ceased to function as it had; and new professionals were no longer socialized into the same set of values that had prevailed earlier.

IMPRESSION MANAGEMENT. Because of the short lead time available to justify a project, impression management became a key factor in project success. Since early figures estimating project success often were speculative at best, the polish of the management presentation and the skill in presenting an image of competence became more important than ever. Numbers not only had to be *presented*, they had to be *defended* as well. Interestingly enough, problems of impression management also developed for the division general manager. He had been scheduled to make a management presentation to Mr. Marsh and his top aides. But he was unwilling to reveal his own early apprehensions for fear of appearing indecisive before them. As he said, "If I don't paint a black-and-white, for-it or against-it picture, I am going to run into trouble. It will look as though I can't make up my own mind on this thing."

COMMUNICATION. And so a full-scale communications problem had evolved up and down the line. What was being communicated symbolically through rule and procedure, and through top management action was in direct conflict with what was being said. Thus, top management, paying heed only to its own rhetoric, was unaware of the scope and severity of the problem until it was far too late to be corrected easily. As a result some not so symbolic heads rolled.

And so the systems cycle proceeded. With each turn, all the forces tended to push the system more out of line with its original goal—which was to produce higher-quality, more creative projects through survival of the fittest. We will turn now to another case example of a feedback and control system. In its particulars it is very different from the first; in its consequences, very similar. Comparing these two detailed examples will help us develop a better understanding of the behavioral consequences of such complex systems.

The One Best Way[4]

"This is *my* plant, and as *long* as it is *my* plant there's going to be none of your goddamned engineers in here holding stopwatches on the men." Ben was being "difficult" as only Ben could be. He was convinced, absolutely and completely convinced that what was going on today was absolutely the worst possible thing for The Company to do.

"Why Mr. Marsh [Sr.] would turn over in his grave if he knew what we were planning to do. He built this company on faith in our working guys" (which was true). "And now you come along and tell me that you're going to have this, this damned *gestapo* out there checking up on them" (which wasn't true).

"Now wait a minute, Ben. I don't think you've really listened to what Bill's been saying." (Bill Banfield from the consulting firm.) The voice was that of Marshall Mason, vice president for manufacturing. He and Banfield were sitting together opposite Ben. "No one is going to do any of the things you're so worried about. This is a work *measurement* program, a *planning* tool, not some sort of, of—well. . . ." Words failed Mason because Ben's protest had been more emotional than logical, and certainly "gestapo" didn't relate at all to what Mason had in mind.

But Ted, sitting on Mason's right, was quite ready to fill in. Ted's job was to be the internal educational liaison for the consulting firm. "Mr. Mason is right on target there. There'll be no one looking over a worker's shoulder. Why, just as you say, there's no need for it. This is *still* The Company that Mr. Marsh, Sr., founded on faith in his employees. That's why we call it a *Procedures Improvement Program*. And that's the meaning of our slogan—"Work Smarter, Not Harder." We *know* our people are giving 100 percent, maybe 110 percent. It's just that . . . well, it's just that they are not giving it in the best way." Ted, smiling, looked about him to observe the effect of this obviously lucid exegesis of the fat PIP document.

Now it was Bill Banfield's turn, trying to cut Ted off before he finally put his foot in it. "Ben, I think we need to keep this program in perspective. We're just a *piece,* just one part of a comprehensive planning and forecasting system that Mr. Marsh feels is necessary to keep The Company competitive in today's marketplace. That's the basic game, to make it possible to plan production schedules and forecast delivery dates. This means it is absolutely necessary for us to have comparable production standards throughout The Company. Frankly, it was just incidental to our feasibility studies that we found your plants are operating at perhaps only 65 to 70 percent of industry standards."

Now it was Ben's turn, crimson spreading from the collar up. "WHAT? Whose numbers are those? Not mine! I don't know what the hell 'industry standard' is, but my men don't work at 70 percent of it. I *do* know that."

"Now hold on Ben," Banfield again, "that's just the point we've been trying to make. I don't think you really have been listening. No one said that your *people* aren't working, just that our *plants* are operating under 70 percent. There's a difference. The fact is that we all agree that our people are giving 100 percent. The problem is that we're not getting 100 percent results. What we're talking about is reeducation, methods-wise, so that we *do* get 100 percent results. That's the message of our slogan, 'Work Smarter, Not Harder.' "

"Gentlemen." Mason saw the need to introduce some order. "I think we had better get back to our purpose here today. We are here because Ben wanted to be filled in, in detail, on our approach to PIP. That's why I've asked Bill Banfield to go over the philosophy of the program for all of us so that we understand Ben's objections. Frankly, Ben, I think that once you get the *complete* picture you are going to feel quite differently."

With this Banfield moved to the head of the table, pulling down a projection screen. "Would you turn on the projector, Stanley."

Well, you've already been briefed by Bill Banfield back in Chapter 8. We'll spare you the second round. But since Banfield has his pitch down pat, if you want to you can go back and review it. Here we move ahead a bit and find Mason anxious to learn Ben's reaction. "Well, Ben, that's the sum and essence of what we are proposing. How does it strike you now?"

Ben gave no indication that he heard. He was deep in thought.

"Ben?"

"Oh, yeah. How does it strike me, you wanted to know." Another pause, then, "I guess I'm not too good at figuring out these new schemes for running my plant that everybody wants me to try. And maybe that's why I usually don't try them. But it strikes me that we don't give the men enough credit for knowing how to do their work. Listen, you can't do a job for two, three, five years and not know *something* about it, can you?

"But you wanted to know, how does it strike me." Ben paused for dramatic effect. "One thing that strikes me is what about scrap and what about quality when all this, this PIP program cares about is numbers? Our guys are proud of their work. The

Old Man [Marsh, Sr.] made 'em proud of themselves and their work. Now it seems to me you're telling 'em we don't care anymore."

"You're right on target there, Ben, and that's just why this is first an *educational* program." Ted, seeing his chance, broke in eagerly. "We're still doing things in the old, wasteful ways. The major source of scrap is faulty raw material, right? So first we've got to educate our people not to *accept* substandard materials, and second, not to spend precious time trying to rework them. Systems-wise, this actually gives us better control over the production process as a whole.

"The quality thing is another educational problem. I know how you feel, Ben. But in today's competitive situation we've got to take the view that quality actually may be wasteful. Our message is 'good enough is best.'" Ted looked especially pleased. "Get the idea? We just can't have our folks spending precious time polishing off burrs and aligning wires just for appearances' sake. Why, that's far more costly than they possibly can imagine. No, *good enough is best.*"

Ben had no immediate reaction. Slowly he gathered his thoughts, "Well now, that's the way you see it, is it?" Ben was looking Banfield right in the eye. "I guess I see a few more things, too. And mostly what I see I *don't* like.

"I see at the bottom of this, regardless of what you say, that you figure my guys will do as little as they possibly can unless somebody's checking on 'em.

"I see that you also figure that my guys aren't very smart either, and they've got to be told how to do a good job. Or maybe they just don't care.

"And I also see you've got the idea that they don't give a damn one way or the other about what The Company wants; that all they *do* care about is themselves, that even if they could figure out a better way they wouldn't do it 'cause it'd be too much trouble.

"And finally, what I see most of all, yeah, *most of all,* is that from where you guys sit my millhands are no different from the machines they run, that they don't need to have any pride in what they're doing or . . ."[5]

"Oh *no,* Ben, that's just not true." Ted was genuinely aghast at Ben's irreverent soliloquy.

Ben didn't so much as glance at Ted. But he did pause. Then he resumed in a steely tone, "Now I'll tell you something that you *don't* know: I'm *not going to do it.*"

Several months passed. Yet Ben and Marshall Mason still were at an impasse. For his part, Mason was getting all kinds of "heat" from Marsh's office. But his hands were tied. Franklyn wouldn't budge.

What could Mason do? Fire Ben? Out of the question. Marsh wouldn't hear of it. As we've said, top-drawer plant managers are harder to get than corporate vice presidents. So Ben wasn't going anywhere. No, it was up to Mason to "bring him around," in Marsh's words. Poor Mason, he'd wake up at three o'clock in the morning and engage in phantom conversations with Ben; wheedling, cajoling, pleading, threatening, promising. All to no avail. Because Mason knew the reply: "I'm *not going to do it.*"

What followed now will strain our credibility. But it's true. Honestly. Word came through corporate communications that Ben had suffered a heart attack. Though it had been relatively severe, he was now out of danger, resting easily at a local hospital.

Thus it was that the idea formed in Mason's mind. In defense of Mason, only a man under extreme duress would have carried through with it. But that's exactly how he felt: hounded by corporate watchdogs from behind, facing an immovable obstacle in Ben, daily losing his own credibility as a corporate executive. So next day he hopped the first plane to Pawtucket. He was going to visit Ben— at the hospital. Mason reasoned that it wouldn't do any good to order PIP installed in Ben's absence. Local management knew how Ben felt so they'd hold out for the OK from him. And even if Mason could start things going on PIP, why, Ben would scrap it all anyway six months later.

But this might be a chance to get Ben's OK. Even *his* will to resist must have its bounds. So that afternoon Mason started explaining his predicament to Ben, painting a grim portrait of the risks he was taking by standing up for Ben to Marsh's people.

At the time Ben was under an oxygen tent as part of his regular therapy. But they could see and speak to one another.

"So the way I see this thing, Ben, our best bet is to go ahead and try PIP in a few trial departments at first, just to get our procedures shaken down. And you don't have to give it even a thought yet; your job now is just to get well as fast as you possibly. . . ."

Suddenly Mason broke off. A thrill of fear shot through his body, for before him, under the oxygen tent, lay Ben, making not a sound but showing that characteristic flush of crimson rising up the neck.

My God, what have I done, thought Mason. He panicked. He lost his composure completely and promised Ben on the spot that there'd be no more talk of PIP from him while he remained vice president, manufacturing.

Ben smiled.

So Ben won his case. Actually, what happened was that Ben promised to deliver higher productivity from Pawtucket but *in his own way.* The essential difference between Ben's way and PIP was that Ben insisted that his production workers be allowed to *decide for themselves* which work procedures to use. Ben's way assumed that his people were willing and able to increase production *if* The Company made it worth their while to do so, and trained them to study their own jobs to discover for themselves ways to improve procedures.

We will get to that story in Chapter 21. For now, let us review the basic elements of PIP to see how that control system compares with CMF, our previous example.

The most obvious difference between the two is in the core work technology, that is, manufacturing compared to research and development. Equally obvious is that the workers, their educational background and expectations of the job, are different. Not quite so obvious is that the PIP system applied control directly to both individuals and organizational subunits. Under CMF, control was applied directly only to projects, not to individuals. Still, the two situations are similar in many ways. Referring back to Figure 17.1, we see that the difference is primarily that PIP is a case 1 situation whereas CMF is case 3.

There are also important differences that cannot be captured completely by crude distinctions such as personal-impersonal, strong-weak. Under PIP not only are organizational subunits evaluated impersonally, so are individual workers. Output control is accompanied by behavior control. Workers must perform the task in "the one best way." Incidentally, this is a good example of *impersonal* evaluation applied to *behavior* control.

Why not take some time now to see how many similarities and differences you can find between the situations. Do not try to analyze the case fully as yet, for we have more to tell you.

Now we will examine some underlying principles for understanding the organizational consequences of feedback and control systems.

Some Principles of Control Systems

The problem of control can be stated in terms of two overall strategies available to the controller (management): (1) the controller can expand the number of actions management can take to regulate the existing variety of organizational behavior; and (2) the controller can limit or constrain the varieties of behavior of subunits and individuals thus making behavior more predictable. The formal statement of this principle is called *Ashby's law of requisite variety*.[6] Ashby's law, by virtue of the law's own mathematical logic, is universally true for all systems. The extent to which it applies to real organizational systems is a function only of the extent to which organizations conform to our assumptions about systems. We think Ashby's law has important implications for understanding organizational control. The formal statement is this: *The minimum variety of actions available to the controller must be at least equal to the minimum variety of actions characterizing the system.* This a necessary condition, but not sufficient. The systems controller must have at least one countermeasure that checks any given action by the organizational system. This principle also is part of Ashby's law.

To this point we have talked of control exercised by *increasing* variety. But since Ashby's law speaks only of the relationship between the variety of actions and variety of countermeasures, there is another way to maintain control: reducing the variety available to the organizational system by *introducing rules or constraints*. Finally, Ashby's law applies in the same way to the requisite *rate of variety*. If the system can vary actions faster than the controller can produce countermeasures, then the system is out of control.

To conclude, Ashby's law, a mathematically derived principle, sets some fundamental conditions for the operation of control systems. In fact, Ashby's law helps us to explain many of the activities that we observe taking place in organizations.

Examples from Organizational and Social Systems

Ashby's law says something about why feedback and control systems employed by higher levels of management inevitably come to rely on detailed and quantitative reporting systems: These increase the variety of *direct* actions available to the controller and increase the *rate* of response. Such systems make possible the evaluation of organizational performance through the impersonal comparison of outcomes to goals, and make these comparisons possible at almost any level of organization desired. The controller, of course, needs to employ a staff to make these detailed comparisons.

However, such systems almost inevitably mean additional constraints on operating units simply to make the control system feasible. Because impersonal, quantitative systems inherently have more limitations than control through lower-level managerial judgment, behavior must be constrained to limit the variety of possible outcomes. Generally this means focusing the motivation system on a few outcomes and ignoring others. Consequently, the outcomes fed back through the system are limited to those countermeasures available to the controller through the feedback and control system. The important point here is that these systems are shaped not necessarily by management preference, but by the inexorable logic of Ashby's law. The organizational system must be constrained to make direct control feasible.

Looking back at our examples we can see that this is precisely what management was attempting to do. In the CMF example management wanted *planned* innovation, and that required control. Variety of behavior in the research division was reduced in several important ways to make this possible. First a corporate instruction was issued specifying how and how often projects would be evaluated. Specific, quantitative measures replaced the customary "seat of the pants" judgments. Second, top management evaluated projects three to four times more often than previously. As a result engineers had no place to hide pet projects within larger, long-term efforts. Finally, the use of standardized, quantitative measures permitted the objective comparison of competing projects, with unambigous decision rules for picking those which would be allowed to continue. Consequently, engineers could pretty well rule out in advance high-risk projects that would not be able to meet the new, impersonal standards. This is another reduction in variety.

The PIP example is most obvious. Objective measurement, together with the prediction and control of costs, required both workers and organizational subunits to use standard procedures. This meant the use of the "one best way" by manufacturing workers, and a uniform system for applying standard times to the measurement of production. Thus, in both these examples we see the shifting upward of the locus of control, together with lower overall levels of control. That is just what we would predict from Ashby's law.

However, this depersonalization—this loss of control at lower levels, together with additional formal constraints—brings with it unanticipated and often dysfunctional consequences. Thus, *because* human beings are adaptive systems in themselves, and because organizational subunits are adaptive systems, we often observe that the organization as a system adapts in ways to achieve the accustomed goals of people and subunits. Ironically, the ways in which variety is reintroduced into the organizational system are often based on the characteristics of the control system itself. The following are examples of two such principles describing how this takes place.[7]

THE PRINCIPLE OF OPPORTUNITY *New opportunities occur for action to meet personal goals; these opportunities are direct adaptations to features of the control system.*

In PIP, for example, provisions for "claiming" time against faulty materials and machine downtime presented opportunities to build production figures to a higher "percentage of standard" without necessarily increasing production. Where money incentives are paid, workers have opportunities, at the expense of the system, to make relatively high wages on jobs with relatively loose standards (29, 35). On jobs with tight standards, they choose not to attempt to make additional wage incentives. The net result is that workers achieve perhaps 70 percent of standard on tight jobs and 130 percent on loose jobs. From their point of view it is more money for less effort.

A second example occurred a number of years ago when The Company tried to stimulate patent activity by offering cash awards for filing patent "proposals." The immediate response was very gratifying. Large numbers of patent proposals were received by the patent officer. This continued for several months until suddenly activity dropped off precipitously. This happened for the following reason. Each development engineer, at the request of The Company, had for years kept an "ideas notebook" that served as a legal record in case of patent suits. Previously, only the genuinely good ideas had resulted in patent applications. However, with the new award program, engineers ransacked their notebooks for even the least promising ideas. After all, now they were worth money. The award program had not stimulated creative activity, just the unearthing of what, until then, had been considered worthless.

THE PRINCIPLE OF CONSISTENCY. *Feedback through the control system tends to be consistent with the structure of the system and the theory of behavior that structure supports.*

Generally a great deal of time and expense goes into constructing the system and collecting data, so there is some resistance to changing the format. Thus, data continue to be collected to conform with system requirements. Oddly enough, as time passes this tendency becomes stronger since the developing trends and historical comparisons become increasingly valuable tools for higher-level control. Thus, the system itself comes to define what are and what are not important problems (2).

For these reasons and also because the initial goals against which performance is compared may have been distorted or unrealistic, lower-level management and professionals are likely to supply data that are *consistent* with the expectations implicit within the system, though not necessarily *accurate* (19, 26). Thus, if auditors are allocated fixed times to complete a job, then times that are consistent with the expectations embedded in the system will be reported at the conclusion of the job. As experience with the system grows, so does the assumed truth of the historical record, and honest reports deviating from the standard become more damning.

An excellent example of this is the "faculty activity cards" filled out at Pennsylvania State University. By legislative mandate the average weekly hours per term put in by each faculty member must be accounted for in terms of eight major categories. Since department heads (supervisors) cannot know what these hours are, faculty members supply the figures, and they are then attested to by the department head. One difficulty is that these reports of time spent must agree to the percentage point with the officially budgeted allocation of time (that is, to the time allocated to research, administration and teaching, and so on). If they do not, the computer rejects them and they must be filled out again, this time "properly." Total times reported are themselves of interest, averaging 50+ hours! But then, who can know?

Apparently other universities are subject to this procedure as well. During a recent legislative budget debate the faculty was told that Pennsylvania State faculty spent an average of 17 percent *fewer* hours per week than the faculty of a comparable institution of higher learning.

Summary

We think that many of you will have found this chapter to be a difficult one to digest fully. This is because we have tried to bring together many elements of the organizational system to explain the effect of feedback and control systems on human behavior. Yet the underlying theme is direct enough: what appears at first to be a straightforward technological task of providing feedback and control is in fact an enormously complicated enterprise. These complications are rooted in the adaptability of human systems in pursuing the same goals under varying conditions, and in the inability of technological systems to capture fully and accurately all the aspects of the situation to be controlled. We have devoted much of this chapter to illustrating some of the likely consequences of this state of affairs.

In reviewing a manuscript version of this chapter one student put his finger on what he felt to be the crucial question. It seems, he said, that what you really are saying is that the problem here is a lack of trust in lower-level management by higher levels. Is that what you are getting at?

We thought about that question a while and the answer is, partly yes and partly no. It does seem that the kinds of feedback and control systems we describe are used to constrain the activities of lower-level management. Cumulative merit funding was one such example. And we must suppose that a completely trusting upper management would not have seen the need for such a system. But it also is true that the mistrust is not so much in the ability and motivation of lower-level management as it is in their presumed lack of perspective. Our observation is that upper-level management mistrusts the ability of lower levels to see the implications of the larger picture; that is, it feels they are unable to see where a course of action is leading until the problem develops. Let us see how this comes about.

We start with one basic assumption: that organizational environments are becoming increasingly turbulent, are becoming more and more difficult to predict. Partly because of this, organizations themselves are becoming increasingly complex. In response to these trends organizations have attempted to regain some measure of control over their circumstances by adapting through long-range planning, planned innovation, and planned change. Thus, reasons for actions taken today may be rooted in objectives desired, say, five years from now. The result is that the management of such a program inherently is more complex than one attempting to bring about short-range outcomes.

We must also reckon on the typical personality of executive management. Executives are action-oriented doers and problem solvers. That is how they got where they are. As we illustrated earlier in the chapter, as managers reach higher levels, they become more likely to see only crises. That is because lower-level problems are not likely to reach them until the problems are obviously out of hand. Generally, subordinates feel they can handle a problem until it grows to such magnitude that it becomes clear they cannot. In addition, subordinates attempt to manage the impression of competence. Creating this impression means that the fewer problems brought to the attention of executive management the better.

A typical executive reaction in the wake of a major crisis is to arrange things so that this cannot happen again. Two major ways of doing this are: (1) to issue new corporate rules and corporate instructions, or possibly to arrange new budget constraints; and (2) to arrange for systems of direct feedback that will allow the executive staff to ferret out problems *as they develop* rather than after they have become full-blown. Both of these functions now become components of a feedback and control system. But because of the nature of feedback and control systems, the elements of information tend to be quantitative and aimed at the outcomes of actions (outputs) rather than at the actions themselves (behavior). The net result, thus, is what we have described throughout this chapter: depersonalized, quantitative feedback and control systems focused on output control that replace the more subjective methods of control appraising both output *and* behavior.

This is not to say that all such systems will be counterproductive. The question is whether or not there is a fit between the core work technology of the organization and the administrative technology of the feedback and control system. Where the work technology is routine, where means-ends relationships are well known, and where measures capture all important aspects of the goal set, such systems may work well (36). Furthermore, the requirements of the economic environment in some industries may require that the locus of control in the organization be at higher levels than it is in other industries if the organization is to be effective (18).

Even under the best of circumstances, however, it is apparent that employees dislike such depersonalized feedback and control systems. And it appears that the likely alternative to such systems is, as suggested by our student, the development of mutual trust among various levels of the organization.

Notes

1. The following is a brief synopsis of an actual case we researched over five years. Conclusions are based on survey data, personal interviews, observation, and Company documents.
2. Figure 17.1 is adapted from Ouchi (23). We have added the "mode of evaluation" variable.
3. "Perceived control" is usually measured by asking members of the organization—in this case nonsupervisory professionals—how much influence they feel they have over policies that directly affect them. Response categories range from *a very great deal* to *none*. See Tannenbaum (32) for details.
4. The following is an actual case we researched over several years. For published partial accounts see Klein (13, 14) and Klein and Ritti (15).
5. Unquestionably Ben never heard of McGregor's Theory X and Theory Y assumptions about workers, but he summarized the gist of them pretty well here.
6. A good discussion of Ashby's law of requisite variety can be found in Hare (10).
7. These principles of control systems have been adapted directly from Wilkins (38). Although Wilkins's discussion concerns crime control, his principles still have general applicability.

References

1. Ackoff, R. "Management Misinformation Systems." *Management Science* 14 (December 1967): 147–156.
2. Argyris, C. *The Impact of Budgets on People.* New York: Controllership Foundation, 1951.
3. ———. "Management Information Systems: The Challenge to Rationality and Emotionality." *Management Science* 17 (February 1971): B275–B292.
4. Becker, S., and D. Green, Jr. "Budgeting and Employee Behavior." *Journal of Business* 35 (1962): 390–402.
5. Blau, P. *The Dynamics of Bureaucracy.* Chicago: University of Chicago Press, 1955.
6. ———. "Formal Organization." *American Journal of Sociology* 63 (1957): 58–69.
7. Burns, T., and G. Stalker. *The Management of Innovation.* London: Tavistock, 1961.
8. Dornbusch, S., and W. Scott. *Evaluation and the Exercise of Authority.* San Francisco: Jossey-Bass, 1975.
9. Goffman, E. *Asylums: Essays on the Social Situation of Mental Patients and Other Inmates.* New York: Doubleday, Anchor Books, 1961.
10. Hare, V., Jr. *Systems Analysis: A Diagnostic Approach.* New York: Harcourt, Brace and World, 1967.
11. Helfgot, J. "Professional Reform Organizations and the Symbolic Representation of the Poor." *American Sociological Review* 39 (1974): 475–491.
12. Jelinek, M. "Technology, Organizations, and Contingency." *Academy of Management Review* 2 (January 1977): 17–26.

13. KLEIN, S. "Two Systems of Management: A Comparison that Produced Organizational Change." *Industrial Relations Research Association Proceedings* (December 1963): 17–26.
14. ———. *Workers Under Stress.* Lexington: University of Kentucky Press, 1971.
15. KLEIN, S., and R. RITTI. "Work Pressure, Supervisory Behavior and Employee Attitudes: A Factor Analysis." *Personnel Psychology* 23 (1970): 153–167.
16. LAWLER, E., III. "Control Systems in Organizations." In *Handbook of Industrial and Organizational Psychology,* edited by Marvin D. Dunnette. Chicago: Rand McNally, 1976.
17. LAWLER, E., III, and J. RHODE. *Information and Control in Organizations.* Pacific Palisades, Calif.: Goodyear, 1976.
18. LAWRENCE, P., and J. LORSCH. *Organization and Environment: Managing Differentiation and Integration.* Homewood, Ill.: Irwin, 1969.
19. LOWE, E., and R. SHAW. "An Analysis of Managerial Biasing: Evidence from a Company's Budgeting Process." *Journal of Management Studies* 5 (1968): 304–315.
20. MCCLEARY, R. "How Structural Variables Constrain the Parole Officer's Use of Discretionary Powers." *Social Problems* 23 (December 1975): 209–225.
21. MCGREGOR, D. *The Human Side of Enterprise.* New York: McGraw-Hill, 1960.
22. MEYER, J., and B. ROWAN. "Institutionalized Organizations: Formal Structure as Myth and Ceremony." *American Journal of Sociology* 83 (September 1977): 340–363.
23. OUCHI, W. "The Relationship Between Organizational Structure and Organizational Control." *Administrative Science Quarterly* 22 (March 1977): 95–113.
24. OUCHI, W., and M. MAGUIRE. "Organizational Control: Two Functions." *Administrative Science Quarterly* 20 (1975): 559–569.
25. PETTIGREW, A. "Information Control As a Power Resource." *Sociology* 6 (1972): 187–204.
26. ———. *The Politics of Organizational Decision Making.* London: Tavistock, 1973.
27. REEVES, T., and J. WOODWARD. "The Study of Managerial Control." In *Industrial Organization: Behavior and Control,* edited by Joan Woodward. London: Oxford University Press, 1970.
28. RONEN, J. "Budgets As Tools of Control and Motivation." In *Managerial Accounting: The Behavioral Foundations,* edited by J. Leslie Livingstone. Columbus, Ohio: Grid, 1975.
29. ROY, D. "Quota Restriction and Goldbricking in a Machine Shop." *American Journal of Sociology* 57 (1952): 427–442.
30. SCHEFF, T. "Control over Policy by Attendants in a Mental Hospital." *Journal of Health and Human Behavior* 2 (1961): 93–105.
31. SCOTT, W., S. DORNBUSCH, B. BUSCHING, and J. LAING. "Organizational Evaluation and Authority." *Administrative Science Quarterly* 12 (1967): 93–117.
32. TANNENBAUM, A. "Control in Organizations: Individual Adjustment and Organizational Performance." *Administrative Science Quarterly* 1 (1962): 236–257.
33. TURCOTTE, W. "Control Systems, Performance and Satisfaction in Two State Agencies." *Administrative Science Quarterly* 19 (March 1974): 60–73.

34. WARNER, W., and E. HAVENS. "Goal Displacement and the Intangibility of Organizational Goals." *Administrative Science Quarterly* 12 (1968): 539–555.
35. WHYTE, W. *Money and Motivation: An Analysis of Incentives in Industry.* New York: Harper and Row, 1955.
36. WILDAVSKY, A., and A. HAMMOND. "Comprehensive vs. Incremental Budgeting in the Department of Agriculture." *Administrative Science Quarterly* 10 (December 1965): 321–346.
37. WILENSKY, H. *Organizational Intelligence.* New York: Basic Books, 1967.
38. WILKINS, L. "Crime and Crime Prevention Measures of 1990." Paper delivered to American Association for the Advancement of Science, February 1974.

Discussion Questions

1. In his position as president and chairman of the board of The Company, Mr. Marsh has been described as being responsible for everything, yet directly in control of nothing. Some of Marsh's feelings along this line were expressed in the last case of Chapter 16, "Agony," where he expressed his concern about The Company's product development engineers. In terms of the discussion in this chapter, what is there about the CMF system that would appeal to Mr. Marsh?
2. At the outset of this chapter we set forth a "point of view." Restate this in your own words. From your reading of this chapter, what are some of the key considerations in determining whether a management information and control system will perform as expected?
3. Why is depersonalized control a likely tendency in large, complex organizations? Think of a large university and ask what kinds of classroom information and control systems are likely in the following two cases: Professor A is responsible for 600 students in Management 100. His job responsibilities are to prepare course objectives and materials, and to supervise ten graduate assistant instructors who do the actual teaching. Professor B has an advanced seminar of five doctoral students. What are the differences in the kinds of information and control systems they are likely to use? Why?
4. State in your own words the definitions of *behavior control* and *output control.* For each of the following occupations and work technologies, which seems most appropriate: consumer survey interviewer, accountant, priest, office equipment salesperson, public relations specialist, symphony orchestra violinist, infantry squad leader?
5. In our case "The Invisible Hand," the title refers to Kerry's observation that no one is running the laboratory; it is running itself. What do you think he meant by that? Why was this situation a direct result of CMF? Is this an example of the depersonalization of control? Why? Why not? What steps might be taken to change this situation?
6. This chapter uses two key cases of information and control systems: CMF and PIP. Try to construct the key management motives behind each of these systems. Are these motives similar or different? If we assume that there are differences in the work technologies involved, do you think that the production workers under PIP will react to the new system in the same way the research engineers did under CMF? Why? Why not?

7. State in your own words the basic idea of Ashby's law of requisite variety. How does this principle explain the popularity of comprehensive information and control systems? How does it explain the tendency for such systems to be accompanied by additional constraints on lower-level personnel? How do technology and measurement systems affect the necessity for such constraints?
8. State our four principles of organizational adaptation to the constraints of information and control systems. Can you apply these to your own university or college situation? Think of the classroom grading system as an information and control system. Does this seem to be a sound analogy? Why? Why not? Can you give an example from grading systems of each of our four principles of adaptation?

Chapter 18
Intergroup Relations: Conflict and Cooperation

What's Best for the Company

". . . So let me do the talking. They're dead set against this project, don't forget. They'll be looking for any excuse they can dream up to keep us out of Pawtucket."

Kerry was talking directly to Stanley, though his eyes were on the road ahead. This was the final briefing before they were to meet with the "Pawtucket folks" to hammer out some sort of agreement on the new inventory and production control system Kerry's group had developed. Also in the car on their way to Pawtucket were Penny and Claude, members of the corporate team who had developed the new system.

Kerry went on, "It's not so much Franklyn who's the stumbling block. I don't think Ben gives much of a damn one way or another. It's his plant administration guy—Shelby. As near as I can make it out, Shelby figures that as long as they've got their own system, he's got complete control over manpower ratios, inventory, and that kind of thing; and he can build cushions into each that he can use to keep him from looking bad. But it's just because he's got his own system that it's so tough to compare Pawtucket cost ratios to Portland's, or Paducah's for that matter."

"So that's when we show 'em how *our* system will make all the plants perfectly comparable, right?" Kerry couldn't look, but he was sure that Stanley was wearing his bright "gee whiz" look to accompany that statement properly.

"Wrong. Dead wrong! And that's why I want you to keep your mouth shut unless I ask." If Kerry hadn't always been right, most of his people wouldn't have put up with him. As it was, though, you could learn a lot from Kerry by listening; that is, *if* you listened.

"But, I mean, isn't it plain that this is what's best for The Company—isn't it? How can they fight it?" Stanley truly was puzzled.

Kerry's tone was softer this time, "Look, Stan, we're just about there. And I wouldn't have time to answer that question if we had the whole day. Just promise me—let me do the talking, O.K.? I'll try to explain later."

Actually, Stanley's query was not based so much in innocence—he knew there would be objections—he'd seen them before. What he could not understand was how, in good conscience, people could reject their system when so obviously it was in the best interest of The Company. Because he felt this way he suggested to Kerry that they let Mr. Marsh "use the hammer" to bring people into line. Kerry had said, yes, that might work, but it would be the last time that anyone at any of the plant locations would cooperate with anyone from the project. And you just can't keep going back to Mr. Marsh time and again. Marsh's "handlers" would see to that. Their conclusion would be that Kerry and his crew were just incapable of doing the job. No, the Marsh "hammer" was out.

So this was the situation: Kerry and his group had top corporate approval to *develop* a unified inventory and production control system, and to *try to sell* it to the plant locations. The reasoning was that if the system was good, the plants would buy it. If not, well, it must be flawed in some way. And Kerry's group did have the support of top corporate management. Top management saw in their system an opportunity to develop a uniform basis for comparison of the cost effectiveness of the various plants—labor costs in particular. Up till now it had been difficult to do this because The Company's various product lines were so different. It was difficult to tell which operations were inherently more cost effective than others.

Then why the problem? Ted Shelby had an answer.

"But that's exactly the problem, systems-wise, Kerry. You're telling us that we're supposed to be comparing our apples to, oh . . . Portland's oranges. There's no *validity* to it. How does it help us? What you're asking us to do is to replace a system tailored to our needs, a system that gives us vital operating information, with a . . ." (words failed Ted for the moment)" . . . with a *gerrymandered* setup whose only benefit, near as I can tell, is to ease corporate anxiety about the effectiveness of local operations.

"Don't get me wrong, we're in sympathy with the idea behind your system, but there are still too many bugs to be ironed out of it. Our feeling here is that it's not in the best interest of The Company to go along."

Kerry didn't say much, and Claude, Penny, and Stanley had been assigned to take detailed notes.

But Kerry did ask for some of the facts behind Ted's statements. And he got them. Plenty of them. Ted had brought along his own "systems person" to detail why it was that Kerry's system couldn't meet Pawtucket's requirements.

When the meeting was over, Ted seemed quite pleased. It seemed he had made his point, that nothing would be changed. Then . . .

"Say, Ted, I don't suppose you'd have any objection to my meeting with Ben about this, would you? You're welcome, too, of course. But I'd just like to get Ben's personal point of view on it." In fact, Ben Franklyn and Kerry Drake respected each other's views in most matters, and Kerry had a hunch that he could get Ben to go along—as an experiment at least. There wasn't much Ted could do, for Kerry's request was appropriate within Company standard operating procedure. So the meeting took place.

Later, on the way back to New York, Kerry detailed what had turned out to be his successful strategy. "I knew Ted would never change his mind, no matter what facts we had, because he's looking at this only from his own point of view. He *is* right, you know. In fact, his systems guy is pretty sharp. I've got to hand it to him. In some ways our system won't do the things for him that their old system can. And the new things we can do for them really aren't of all that much benefit to them.

"But from a Company-wide systems point of view, why it makes some things possible that we've dreamed of for years. Well, you know that. But think of the data base we'll have now for the development of new optimization techniques."

Kerry ran through the litany of benefits, real and imagined, to the corporate production systems staff that had been envisioned from the beginning of the project.

Then Claude had a question. "But I still don't understand why Franklyn went along, especially if what you say about their local system is true. Is it just 'cause you're tight with Franklyn?"

Kerry laughed. "Listen, when it comes to running his plant, old Ben is tight, as you put it, with *nobody*. Oh, no, if there weren't something in this for him he wouldn't be doing it. Don't worry about *that*. But I figured that there were two things here that Ben wouldn't mind seeing come to pass. First of all, you've got to remember that he's always figured himself to be 'the best goddamned plant manager in this whole goddamned Company.'" Kerry did a pretty good imitation of Ben. "So he wouldn't mind coming up with some numbers to *prove* that. I figured he'd take the bait. Pawtucket is a tough job to run, and our system ought to help him show that.

"But even more, I don't think that Franklyn likes Shelby very much. They're completely different animals. But Ted's built quite a bit of power for himself on the basis of the control system he's rigged up. So I figured that Ben wouldn't mind undercutting him a little, and getting him back down to size, so to speak."

"And that's where Ted's objections *really* come from, right?" offered Penny. "Not only does Ted lose control, but he runs the risk of somebody looking at our data and questioning what he's been doing over the past few years. That's all he gives a damn about, I'll bet."

Kerry thought for a moment. Then, "Well, yes and no. You know, I don't like Ted a great deal either, but he's a good Company man. If he really were convinced that Pawtucket would benefit, why I think he'd go along with us. No, it's more complicated than you say.

As the months rolled by, Kerry and his group encountered every conceivable kind of objection at the local plant level. Finally, however, a major impasse developed: The entire Expandrium Products (EP) Division, a major division of The Company, rejected the system outright. Dire "industrial relations" consequences were foreseen, since the EP Division, unlike others in The Company, had been experiencing labor troubles over the past year.

"We just can't afford this additional risk. It may look to our people as though we were policing them," was the opinion of the division manufacturing vice president. "Perhaps in a few years when we've got this union thing licked, but right now, it's out of the question."

Kerry's analysis of the situation for his group was this: "That union business is pure smokescreen. They're scared to death of what our system will show. That's the *real* problem. Yeah, they've got personnel problems all right. But it's because their whole manufacturing setup is so SNAFU.

"Now, nobody's ever been able to *show* that, because of the way their part of the business is run—the same way it was before The Company acquired it." Kerry paused, thoughtful for a moment.

"We've *got* to have them in the system!" Kerry pounded his fist into his palm to underscore his determination. "That's what will *make* our system; that's what will show how our capability for cross division and plant comparisons can save money for The Company. When they see *those* figures, they'll wonder how they ever got along without us."

Thus Kerry's plan evolved: bring the "participating" plant managers together and get their collective endorsement. Then go to EP and *show* them the risks of looking bad since everyone else is going along. If that doesn't work, the corporate manufacturing brass can "put the arm" on the EP division—for the good of The Company—and EP knows it.

And it worked. With some compromises from Kerry's group to skirt possible "industrial relations consequences," the system was installed at all Company locations and the data began to pour in. Their system didn't do everything that had been promised, but neither did it bring the problems envisioned by some of The Company's doomsayers. In fact, it actually pointed the way toward some significant improvements in the embattled Expandrium Products Division.

It brought as well a wealth of previously unavailable planning data to Kerry's project staff, and, incidentally, new recognition and prestige for that little group of talented people.

"What's Best for The Company" illustrates a pervasive condition—some would say problem—in organizational life. Goals among subunits *do* clash, and conflict is probable. Indeed organizations without conflict at some time or other are so rare as to represent an unnatural condition. Therefore the problem is not how to avoid conflict but rather how to manage it effectively.

The vignette illustrates too that often conflict arises from the decent motives of people trying to do a good job but defining "good" in the particularistic terms of their own interests. Ted did that, but then to some extent, so did Kerry. Ted felt his system served his plant, and hence The Company, far better than Kerry's. His motives were partly selfish, but then he had worked hard to establish something that worked, and from the narrow view of the Pawtucket plant, Ted's system had worked.

Then along came Kerry and his corporate group with a new system. Not only did the new system provide data that compared Pawtucket with other manufacturing plants—a threat in itself—but it also supplanted Ted's system. Here was a clear incompatibility of goals. Kerry knew this would be the case, so he showed Ben Franklyn how Ben's goals could be served by using the corporate system. Had Drake not been successful with his strategy, the conflict could have been resolved only by the "hammer," a solution that would not have served Drake's long-term goals.

Over the months, similar difficulties arose with other plants for the same reasons they had at Pawtucket. The corporate system represented a threat, for it provided measurements that were incompatible with the goals of some of the plants. The ultimate process of conflict resolution, which Kerry arranged with the EP Division was a group meeting of peers, carefully structured to bring in those sympathetic with his project, so that EP could see that not to go along was significantly more dangerous than to do so. Kerry simply rearranged EP's opportunities and constraints.

However, goal incompatability, although a main cause of organizational conflict, is only part of the story. Some processes that go on in organizations provide conflict potential, and, subsequently, conflict momentum.

Conflict Defined

We define conflict in behavioral terms (15, 22, 34). Conflict can be characterized as attempts of one entity to interfere with the ongoing activities or goals of another entity in the face of resistance from that entity (10). The context of conflict involves *situations, attitudes, perceptions,* and *behavior*. The situational aspects typically involve differences in group goals and tasks, the allocation of resources that are often scarce in organizations, and the different procedures that groups use to do a task. They may also involve spatial and geographical barriers. Attitudes and perceptions are how various groups view each other; fear, anxiety, and hostility may be created in the context of conflict as a consequence of those views. The behavior is the conflict itself. Figure 18.1 describes the context of conflict.

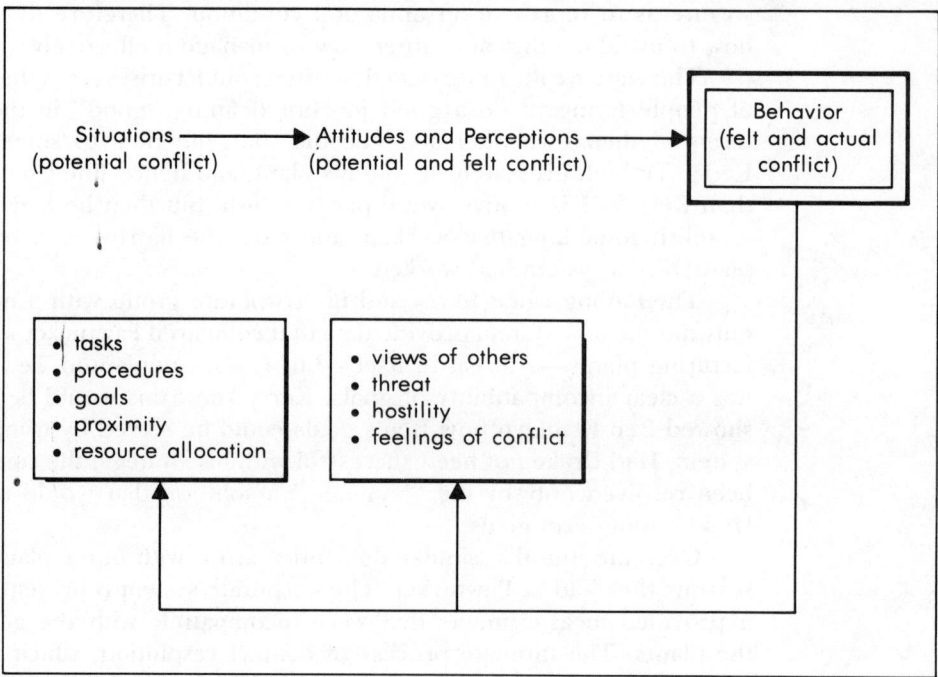

FIGURE 18.1 The Context of Conflict

Conflict as Process

We consider conflict, as depicted in Figure 18.1, to be an ongoing process. Typically, it is a sequence of events that can be characterized as goal or interest incompatibility among various groups that has its roots in the situational conditions and produces attitudes and emotions such as fear or hostility. If the conditions continue and the emotions escalate, the resulting behavior is likely to be an aggressive promotion of a group's self-interest that may block another group's attempts to promote its own self-interests.

Because most organizations are designed to promote cooperation and coordination, the atmosphere is usually one of civility (9). Therefore, one conflict episode may be excused as an isolated event that can be resolved through management action. However, as such episodes occur over a period of time, the behavior inexorably results in some kind of serious conflict (34).

Conflict, then, involves a series of behaviors and not discrete episodes that either may not occur again or will occur so infrequently that the groups cannot really be considered *in* conflict (32, 35). This latter point is demonstrated in Figure 18.2. As each act of goal interference occurs and the sum of these acts

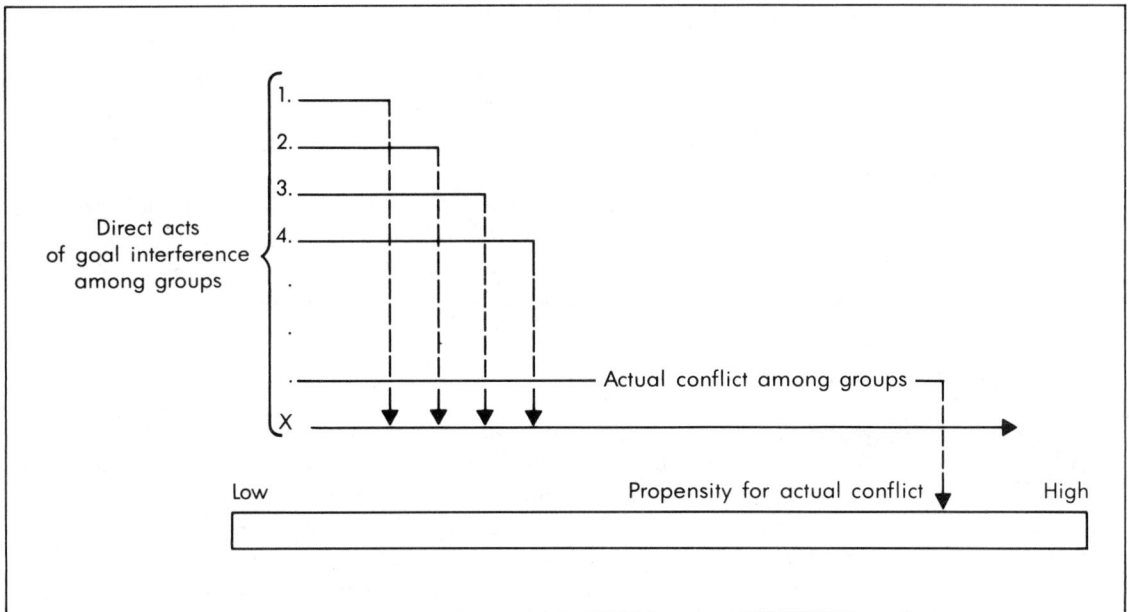

FIGURE 18.2 Conflict Episodes as Antecedents of Actual Conflict

increases, the propensity for further conflict likewise increases. In other words, acts of goal interference can be cumulative and, as they build up, more serious conflicts are likely (15). Furthermore, the aftermath of each episode contributes to the potential conflict condition.

Conflict Aftermath

Conflict episodes produce certain emotions, and these emotions have to be dealt with. If one feels hostile, anxious, or aggressive after a conflict episode has ended, this aftermath can lead to further conflict situations (27, 28). If, however, the motivations created by the conflict can be resolved by groups committing themselves to reducing that conflict or working cooperatively, then this too may be considered an aftermath. Also, occasionally if conflict is suppressed, particularly in organizations that perceive it as dysfunctional and that encourage groups, through the reward structure, to keep their differences underground, a new condition may be created, which we have already labeled *potential conflict*. As long as the conflict is suppressed, the conditions producing conflict do not go away but merely fester. And the emotions created by such festering frequently explode into more serious kinds of conflict—for example, wildcat strikes—at a later time. Wildcat strikes are often triggered by incidents that, taken alone, do not seem conducive to such extreme behavior. However, many wildcats are a product of rational goal behavior by management; such behavior acts as a trigger *after a series of grievances* has failed to be resolved through the normal and legal contractual means developed in previous bargaining situations. Each unresolved grievance produces an aftermath that contributes to the potential explosiveness of the conflict situation that is always present in a union-management adversary relationship. As the pool of grievances builds, so does the potential for a blowup (28). *Organizational conflict, then, is a process with several episodes that are characterized by one entity knowingly interfering with the ongoing goal-oriented activities of another entity in the face of resistance by that other entity.*

Competition Versus Conflict

Many people confuse competition and conflict. They are similar but not the same. It is true that people and groups normally compete for a scarce commodity—a prize, money, status, or some such thing. It is also true that if one side wins, the other does not; in that sense competition involves goal interference. However, much competition is not characterized by one's interference in the ongoing activities of another (18, 22). Runners compete, teammates compete, and organizations compete in the marketplace, but that competition is not considered conflict unless it is also associated with direct interference in the *pursuit* of the goals of the competition. Such interference is generally considered unsportsmanlike and in poor taste; therefore, there are strong sanctions against competitors engaging in conflict.

However, competition contains many of the seeds of conflict (10, 18, 22). When winning becomes the only important thing, and the stakes are large, temptation to escalate the competition to open conflict is probable. And, in organizations, the competition is often for scarce resources that are important to the well-being of the competing groups. Under such circumstances, it is not surprising that conflict emerges (2, 9, 16, 28, 29). But what are specific causes of conflict in organizations besides competition for scarce resources?

Causes of Organizational Conflict

To recap some important points made in the previous chapters and in this one, we view conflict as primarily a consequence of goal selection by groups that have different interests. The groups' leaders use these goals as they negotiate with others in the system to obtain the resources that are necessary for goal achievement (13).

The manner in which organizations are differentiated, hierarchically and laterally, also lends itself to conflict situations. In particular, when jurisdictions are ambiguous, groups must compete for resources or become mutually dependent to achieve their own goals (12).

We see conflict, too, as a natural result of the group processes and leadership actions described before. For example, goals are developed through group processes and are designed to serve the group's interests (35). Group goals, if they are based on self-interest, most likely produce some goal incompatibilities among groups (11, 24). Kerry and Ted's confrontation was an example of this. Kerry took advantage of the possible differing objectives of Ben and Ted in order to line Ben up with the new system. Kerry knew that Ben and Ted might have different action goals, even though they were members of the same plant and in a superior-subordinate relationship.

Furthermore, because most organizations are functionalized and require specialists, we expect that the way goals become operational will depend on the values and constraints existing among the various groups. Conflict, then, can arise because of organizational conditions that require specialization and competition for scarce resources. The group's value premises and choices of specific aspects of the organizational goal set creates conditions right for conflict. After the choices are made, group processes reinforce the wisdom of these choices and the group expects its leader to facilitate resource acquisition to serve group goals. Group leaders, therefore, compete with each other to gain resources for their groups (6).

Incompatible Goals

Groups that engage in conflict behavior often have incompatible goals. The idea of incompatible goals is different from the idea of competition for scarce resources and from the idea of the uniqueness of constraints or opportunities, although all these ideas are clearly related. Here we find groups that merely have different agendas, and the accomplishment of one will interfere with the accomplishment of another. An example would be quality control engineers and industrial engineers who set work standards. The former group is evaluated according to quality standards, whereas the latter often is evaluated on how "tightly" the standards are written. Quality and quantity are not often easy partners.

Goal incompatibility and the competition for scarce resources in order to gain group goals are likely to account for most organizational conflict. But some other factors are also important.

Group Factors

We have discussed how groups form around common interests, and how, by developing cohesiveness, they formulate additional common interests and intensify those already in existence. We also discussed how groups develop their own action goals, which serve these interests. Research and development labs, for example, have goals quite different from those of sales groups, though they are within the same organization. Even within subgroups, units form around common tasks or shared interests and develop their own goals.

For example in a manufacturing plant, production management is interested in efficiency, effectiveness, and increasing profitability, whereas personnel, although not necessarily uninterested in these, is primarily concerned with industrial relations, morale, and personnel problems. Thus production management may, in the rational pursuit of its own goals, induce work pressures that can be perceived as unreasonable by personnel. Further, production management may hire staff people sympathetic with their views, such as industrial or manufacturing engineers, to see that standards are maintained, controls are objectively implemented, and technologically efficient production processes are introduced. In that way, pressures between the two groups within the organization are increased.

Members of a group identify with each other and regard others as part of the out-group. In-group members talk among themselves, reiterating their own values; and they reject information not consonant with these values. Furthermore, they often perceive the out-group as unreasonable, and sometimes immoral and uninformed. In short, they see them as people you do something to rather than with (14).

Furthermore, because group cohesiveness is pleasant, members of the in-group attempt to preserve their groupiness. Thus, the very existence of the group as a cohesive entity becomes an important goal, and any challenge to this contributes to conditions encouraging conflict (3, 4, 5).

Each group, in setting its own goals, establishes a motivational pattern for its membership that often takes precedence over larger goals. As we have seen, the immediate, small, and constantly interacting work group provides powerful incentives for the individual to behave in ways defined by the normative structure of that group (1, 12, 21, 34).

Social Structure

In the last chapter and this one we have discussed at greater length the reasons why goals will be different or at least have a different cast in different parts of an organization. There are still some points that need sharpening. They have to do with the way people and groups are arranged within an organizational social structure (35).

A point that has been repeatedly made in different ways is that the division of labor—a necessity in complex organizations—has within it most of the necessary contributors to conflict. Groups are separate and distinct; they are differentiated by functions and by task; and they compete for finite resources. All of this is by design and considered to be necessary for the proper functioning of the organization. What is unanticipated is that opportunities and constraints will be so differently defined by the groups and that the group dynamics that wall off out-groups and their logic makes conflict probable (6).

There is an irony here. Specialization and division of labor require coordination among interdependent groups. Therefore, hierarchies are established just to ensure that different groupings function interdependently and cooperatively. Such hierarchies create conflict as significant as the problems that they solve. The conflict centers on two basic issues; control and resource allocation. Hierarchical conflict occurs when higher levels in the organization try to control the behavior of lower-level participants or when they allocate resources according to the planning goals as they see them. Organizations, in pursuing their goals, consider predictability and the various control mechanisms serving predictability as essential for their planning and for their allocation of resources. In order better to predict what will occur, the organization tends to expand the area in which it expects the lower-level participants to accept the orders or the rules from above—that is, to expand the workers' zone of indifference—while expanding its own formal authority. At the same time, however, an opposing force comes from the lower-level participants—namely, to increase their own autonomy. This sort of conflict occurs in virtually all organizations that are hierarchically structured and is dramatically demonstrated when supervisors try to control and then evaluate subordinate behavior (29).

Further, larger groups, which are also hierarchically arranged, are often in organizational conflict—for example, plants versus division headquarters and division headquarters versus corporate headquarters for similar reasons. Each group wants to expand its own area of autonomy, whereas the group immediately above it wants to establish control procedures that limit the potential behavior of subordinate groups. The central issue of such conflict is control.

In large multiproduct companies R and D labs are likely to be arranged according to product. The lab in Pawtucket works on expandrium products, the one in Paducah on cybernetic factory systems, and the one in Lubbock on solar energy systems. Each is functionally specialized and reasonably self-contained to avoid the problem of coordinating efforts across geographical areas. But let us see what happens within the labs.

Engineers, because of their training and expertise, may be interested in producing the best possible equipment with a reasonable degree of sophistication and elegance. However, the lab managers may be forced to focus on expediting certain projects that have already been marketed, and on developing prototypes that may be somewhat less sophisticated and elegant than the engineers would like. Further, the lab management may want to organize the work situation for easy product development. This will require that the engineers work on ever simpler tasks, divide their labor to expedite the projects, and be organized according to models developed in production facilities. There will be front-end developmental work, a middle stage in which the product is pieced together, and a final stage in which engineers clean up. The stage at which the engineer works will have a direct bearing on visibility and so on his or her career (30).

Each stage of product development has serious implications for *resource allocation*. Those at the front end are involved with planning for technical improvement. Because of this, and because planning involves uncertainty, organizations often allocate more resources to such tasks, particularly in advanced technological organizations. Management wants to ensure that the projects will work. Once the project is under way, much of the uncertainty is eliminated, and, hence, fewer resources are allocated to those at the middle stage of product development. Logically, the clean-up stages get still fewer resources. As a result of this situation, much organizational conflict in R and D labs centers on groups of people who propose projects in which they will be involved with the developmental, front-end phases. The leaders of such groups must then advance their causes in competition with each other, each hoping that higher management will decide in favor of "the cause" (7, 8, 31).

When management decides in favor of the "cause," that group will be satisfied—at least until the next budgetary go round. But what of the others? They will probably question the wisdom, or at least the values, of the decision makers. Widespread questioning of hierarchical actions provides fertile grounds for hierarchical conflict (34).

Competition Revisited

Throughout this and the previous chapters runs the common thread of competition for resources as a primary condition of organizational conflict. We took care to distinguish between competition and conflict conceptually. Still, competition seems to lead to conflict, particularly under conditions of shared, finite resources. Box 23 contains one of the best illustrations of what we mean.

The groups described in the Box were in a state of conflict resulting from a win-lose competition. The dynamics described reflect organizational reality, although organizational conflict might not be so obvious. Particularly salient is how the groups became cohesive, determined to win and susceptible to judgmental and informational distortion.

Conflict Escalation

Conflict seems to generate a dynamic of its own. The dynamic is illustrated by the aftermath when the conflict has not been resolved satisfactorily. Hostility and fear remain as part of the context and tend to distort perceptions. For example, several studies show how in-group qualities are glorified and out-group sins are magnified (6, 19, 20). Hostility and aggression directed toward the out-group are justified in this way (14).

Further, there seems to be a tit-for-tat mentality among groups engaged

> **Box 23**
>
> ## Competition, Win-Lose, and Conflict
>
> A classic description of how competition for finite resources develops into conflict is provided by a rather old study. The investigators formed two or four groups of nine to twelve people from a larger group of executives going through a management development program. The first twelve or fourteen hours of a ten-day to two-week program was devoted to group building. In these initial hours the groups would be brought together from time to time to discuss what was happening within the group and how the dynamics might pertain to organizational life. Each group showed a healthy interest in the affairs of the other groups and demonstrated a willingness to learn from the others' experience.
>
> After the fourteen hours, each group was given the same problem to solve as a group and was told that the group with the best solution would win and the others would lose. The problem was given to the groups at 7:00 P.M. and they were told they had until 8 A.M. to come up with the group solution. Altogether, some 150 groups participated. Many worked until 4:00 or 5:00 in the morning. The spirit of competition was clearly evident, but the normal poise associated with executives began to give way in the heat of the battle. Conflict was emerging. Here are some of the other consequences of the competition.
>
> Everyone accepted the win-lose situation as a natural event, and each group placed a great emphasis on winning. Cohesion increased markedly, deviant ideas within the group were suppressed, and almost all of the groups closed ranks, became tighter. The representative to present the group's solution was the task leader—aggressive, hard driving, incisive. Groupthink was beginning to emerge.
>
> Once the groups got back together for the competitive judging, some interesting intergroup behavior was observed. First of all, the group representatives showed no inclination to comply with the other groups' judgment and selected their own solution as the best. Thus, the competition accelerated. There was a significant distortion of judgment. Each group judged its solution to be the best even when it clearly was not. Each group also distorted information coming from the other groups. Even though there often was substantial overlap among the solutions of the various groups, the commonalities were ignored. Adversaries were attacked and discredited. Conflict was clearly evident.
>
> Blake, R., and J. S. Mouton. "Reactions to Intergroup Competition Under Win-Lose Conditions." *Management Science* 7 (1961): 420–435.

in serious conflict with each other. A hostile or aggressive response is answered in kind and generates a similar response in return. Once such a cycle has begun the most probable outcome is that the issues of conflict will broaden. Such outcomes become wasteful. Therefore, how can we manage conflict to avoid the vicious cycle?

Conflict Management

The issue of conflict management is most complex. Because our analysis of conflict is largely structural—the antecedents of conflict being embedded in the situation—we will deal with its management in similar terms. When reduction of conflict would help each party, communications of that fact tend to reduce conflict. One extensive series of experiments that support that contention is reported in Box 24.

Box 24

Knocking 'Em Off the Road

A series of experiments examined the effects of competition, cooperation, and individualism on conflict behavior. Two subjects participated at a time. Each was to move a truck from a starting point to a finish point over either a common one-lane road or an alternative but much "longer" route. Each subject controlled a gate near his or her starting point and the other subject's finish point at either end of the one-lane road. Therefore in transversing the road the subject had to encounter either direct conflict with the other party or permission and cooperation from the other. The payoff to each subject was the number of completed trips.

The researchers gave the subjects the following instructions: (1) Maximize your joint payoffs; (2) maximize individual payoffs; or (3) maximize the difference between your payoff and your opponent's. The percentage of cooperative choices was then calculated for each condition (1) when the subjects could communicate before acting and (2) when they could not.

The results were based on the number of cooperative choices made individually and by both members of the party. As you might expect, when the directions encouraged cooperation it was extremely high with or without communication. When the subjects were instructed to maximize their own situation but not at the expense of the other (true for much organizational life) the number of cooperative choices by individuals went from 27 percent in the no-communication situation to 63 percent when communication was encouraged. However, when it was not to the players' advantage to cooperate—in the competitive situation—communications, although helpful, did not result in much cooperation. Similar results were disclosed when percentage of cooperative choices by the pair was used as the measure of cooperation. Figures 18.3 and 18.4 show the results.

Deutsch, Morton. *The Resolution of Conflict.* New Haven, Conn.: Yale University Press, 1973.

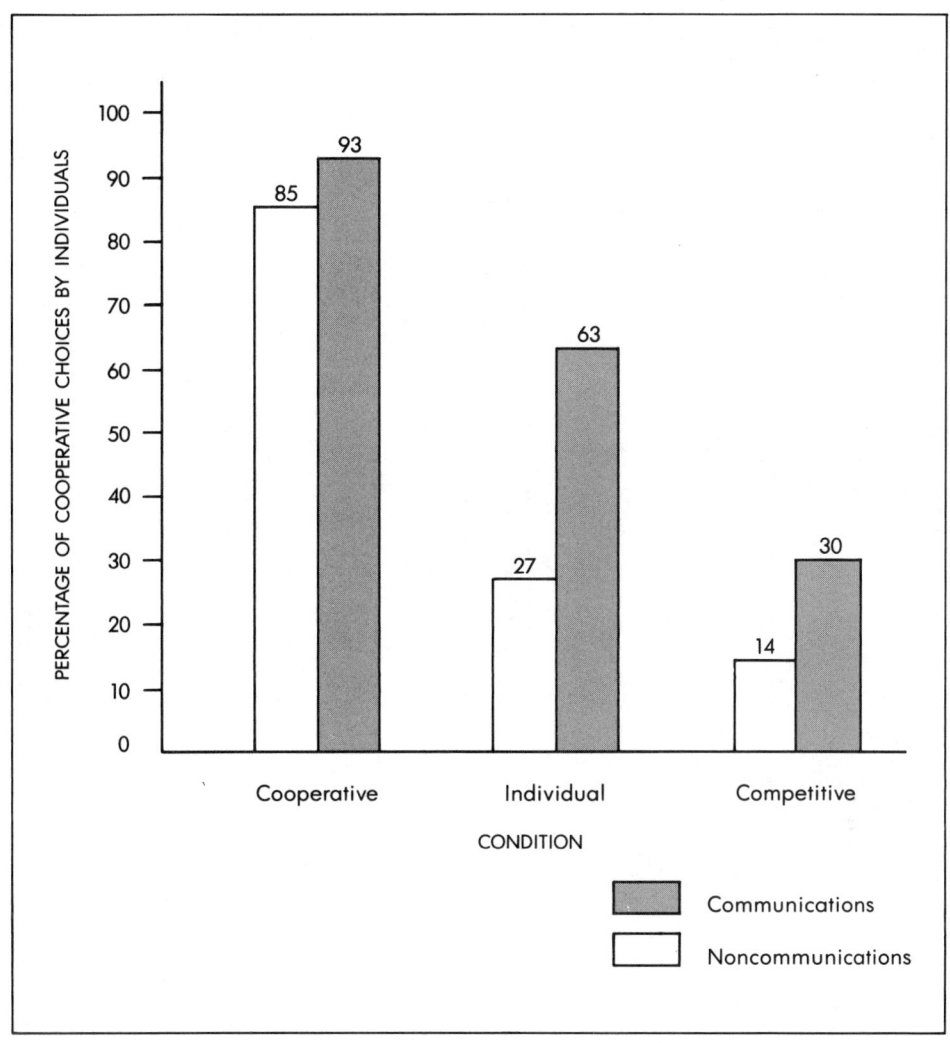

FIGURE 18.3 The Effect of Individual Communications on Cooperation Under Three Payoff Conditions

Notice from the data shown in Figures 18.3 and 18.4 that the instructions concerning the conditions of payoff were extremely powerful. They placed significant limits on the probable behaviors. Further communications seemed to help in all conditions, but they helped most when the subject was given instructions to maximize his or her own position regardless of how the other pair member did. Under that condition common interests involved cooperation and when

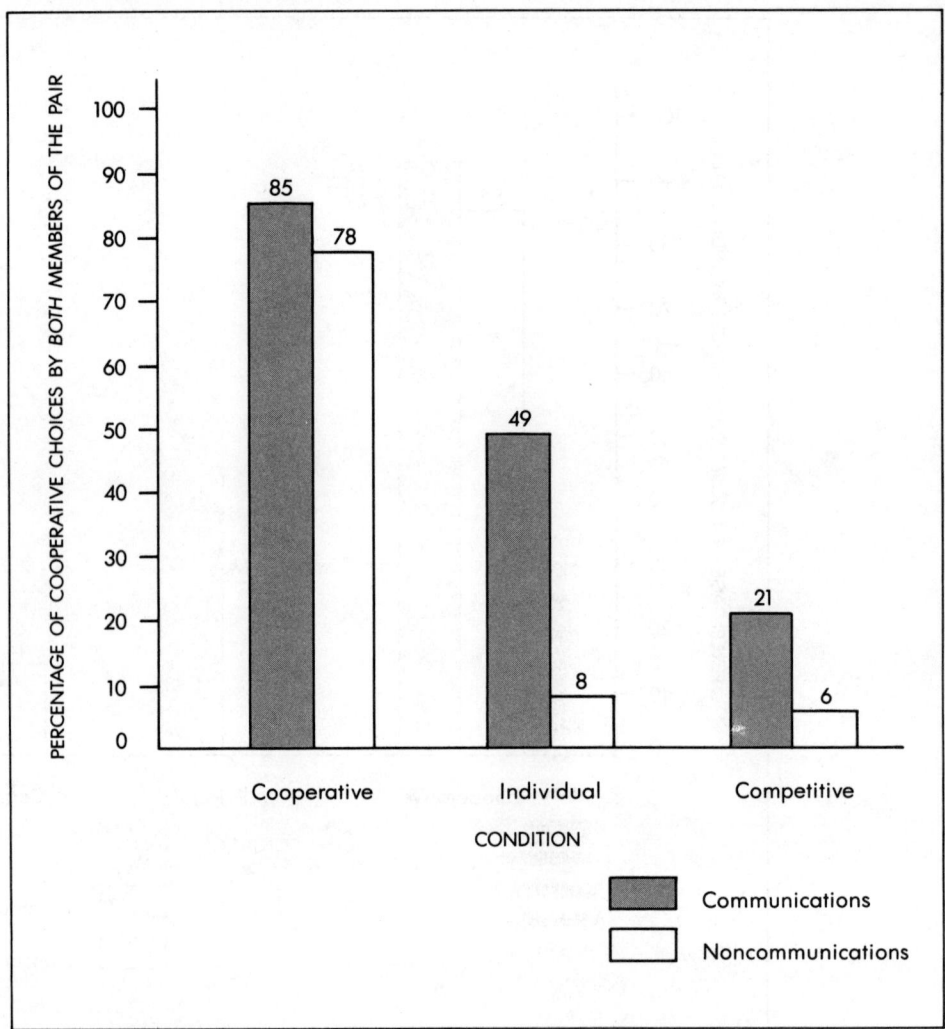

FIGURE 18.4 The Effect of Group Communications on Cooperation Under Three Payoff Conditions

allowed to communicate with each other, the subjects showed a marked tendency to behave cooperatively. When the individuals' interests were to behave competitively, that is what they did regardless of the communications level. And so, although a lot of communication is obviously useful and in many cases necessary for conflict reduction, it is not sufficient, particularly when the goals of the competing parties are in conflict.

Another point needs to be stressed with respect to communications. A skilled third party can bring conflicting groups together to exchange perceptions and in this way get to know and understand the assumptions and rationale underlying each other's actions. We will deal with such techniques later in the book, but let us briefly state a typical process.

The conflicting groups are usually in some important interface, and thus the problems created by the conflict are readily apparent. That provides motivation for getting the groups together. The neutral third party is then responsible for preparing the groups for a joint meeting. Typically, this involves interviewing the members of each group in order to begin delineating the problems that each group is having with the other (6). It also involves setting the stage for a productive confrontation in a nonthreatening context, normally away from the work site and in a problem-solving mode.

Once the groups are convened together, the third party provides an introduction, emphasizes the benefits of working together, and highlights the problems that each group is having with the other. The problem-solving orientation is again emphasized. After that, some means of getting the problems out in the open is employed. One typical means is to have each of the groups separately develop at least two lists. One will include that group's perceptions of the other group, and another would include how the group thinks the other group views them. The groups are then brought together and the lists are displayed and discussed. The misperceptions become readily apparent under such circumstances and provide a point of intense discussion. Through this process misperceptions and consequent misunderstandings can be cleared up. The clarification can lead to a final activity that centers on joint problem solving (6, 34).

Although there are a variety of similar mechanisms, their primary feature is intensive communication that centers on the problems that the groups are having with each other, and their primary purpose is resolving the difficulty in favor of a more collaborative mode of interacting. Under such conditions communications appear to be most helpful (12).

Deescalation and Reciprocal Strategies for Conflict Resolution

Since conflict contains a dynamic that seems to lead to escalation, it would seem logical that a reversal of the dynamic might lead to deescalation. That is precisely the rationale underlying the strategy, put forth several years ago, for resolving international conflicts (26). According to that strategy, if an act of conflict (or aggression) produced hostility, fear, misperceptions of intent and character, and a response in kind, then a conciliatory, cooperative, or helpful response would produce a response in kind as well (26). The initial research in the area produced mixed results, and two important elements were introduced to the paradigm (22). First, the initiators of the deescalation process were to announce that they intended to employ a conciliatory strategy. Then they were to take some unilateral conciliatory steps, each preceded by an announcement and an explanation. Reciprocation is not expected immediately because the initiators understand that the other party is distrustful.

A second element is the intolerance of exploitation, or of additional escalation on the part of the other party. Exploitation will result in a response in kind from the initiators of the strategy. That retaliatory response should be carefully measured in order not to resume escalation in conflict and, once made, should be followed promptly by another conciliatory act designed to reestablish the deescalation process. The strategy is called Graduated and Reciprocated Initiatives In Tension-Reduction, or GRIT (56). An example of the efficacy of GRIT is contained in Box 25.

Box 25

An Eye for an Eye . . .

Thirty-two three-person groups participated in these experiments. Each group could make a competitive response or a cooperative response in a win-lose game. The idea behind the game was to accumulate as many points as possible, but each group's points depended on what it did together with what the other group did. Ostensibly, each group was to work with another group in another room, but in reality that other group was simulated and their responses programmed by the experimenters. The simulated group took the initiative in conveying messages, which were posted on a game board. The messages could be:

M-1. "I will make choice 1 (a cooperative response) next trial," or
M-2. "I will make choice 2 (a competitive choice) next trial," or
M-3. "I want to send a note." That note always read, "I will always make choice 1. That is the way we can make the most points."

If both teams cooperated (choice 1) each would receive four points. If both competed (choice 2) then each would lose four points. If one cooperated and the other competed then the cooperative group lost five points and the competitive group won five points. Note that the worst case for cooperation is when one group cooperated and the other competed, a situation that most people avoid. Hence, in the absence of certain knowledge of what the other group would do, the "safest" or the least-risk response is the competitive one because the most that would be lost is four points. Furthermore, should the other group make a cooperative choice, the least-risk competitive response also had the advantage of winning five points for the group making the competitive choice.

continued

Each experimental session had thirty trials. The first ten trials for all groups had a 50 percent random cooperative response coming from the simulated group. The experimental difference occurred in the second block of ten trials. The GRIT strategy had simulated players sending M-3 on the eleventh trial, but just prior to that, the simulator chose the cooperative response. Thereafter, that group always sent M-1 unless the experimental subject competed on the preceding trial, in which case it sent M-2. However, after making the competitive response and a retaliation, the simulated subjects always returned to the cooperative mode, sending M-1 and following through. In other words, the simulated group began by making a cooperative response, then told the experimental subjects that they would make the cooperative response because it was to their mutual benefit. When betrayed it responded with a competitive response but then *always* returned to a cooperative mode regardless of what the experimental subjects did on the preceding trial.

In the competitive situation, the simulators lied on the eleventh trial—making choice 2, after sending M-1. Thereafter, they always sent M-1 unless the subjects made a competitive choice on the preceding trial choice. However, the simulated group was 50 percent truthful when they sent an M-1 message, and 100 percent truthful when they sent an M-2 message.

The tit-for-tat strategy had the simulated groups always responding in kind with no sent messages. For all groups the last ten trials had 100 percent cooperative responses coming from the simulated group.

The analysis of the results indicated that:

1. the GRIT strategy produced significantly more total cooperation than the other strategies,
2. the least cooperation occurred in the competitive situation,
3. the GRIT and the tit-for-tat groups felt there was significantly more credibility, confidence, trustworthiness, and predictability in their sessions than did the competitive group, and
4. oh yes, women displayed considerably more cooperation than men.

From Svenn Lindskold and Michael G. Collins. "Inducing Cooperation by Groups and Individuals: Applying Osgood's Grit Strategy." *Journal of Conflict Resolution* 22 (December 1978): 679–690.

A variation of GRIT—actually a process bearing similarities to both the tit-for-tat strategy and GRIT—is the reciprocal cooperation strategy: a cooperative action is taken by one party and simultaneously a reciprocation is requested. If compliance is gained and another cooperative act is made under the same condition, then the process of deescalation has begun. If the cooperative act is met with aggression or competition, that is reciprocated; but after the reciprocation another announcement of cooperative intent and requested reciprocal cooperation is made.

An important assumption underlying the effects of reciprocal deescalation is that both parties in a reciprocal relationship have more to gain from cooperation than from competition. The concept of a net gain by cooperation must also cover the risk of maximum loss (20, 33, 34).

The Superordinate Goal Idea

The reciprocal deescalation strategy brings us to a major point: if conflict is often the product of goal incompatibility, then cooperation should be the product of goal compatibility. The implication of that statement is that common ground needs to be sought and then enlarged. Once the common interests are identified, they serve as *superordinate* goals, that is, the goals that the groups would share and that take precedence over the parochial interests. As the groups work together to reach that shared goal, they often discover other common ground. Further, many of the stereotypes and misperceptions that accrue to conflicting parties wash away as the parties come together in meaningful cooperative efforts.

The Federal Mediation and Conciliation Service understands the dynamics well. A major means of its conflict management strategy is to identify any common grounds between the parties' bargaining positions and then to get unions and management working on these common grounds; the common grounds are then expanded, and finally driven toward the common goal of conflict resolution. Another example is the union-management committees that are becoming increasingly popular as means of avoiding the last-minute hard bargaining over seemingly unresolvable issues. Such committees work together continuously to address differences as they come up and to resolve them before they accumulate and escalate to hardened positions certain to bring the ultimate industrial conflict: a strike. The superordinate goal here is to maintain labor peace, or at least to avoid a costly strike.

Let us pick up our chapter opening story and examine another facet of the situation. Things had not gone exactly the way Kerry had hoped. Although most of the divisions were easy enough to bring on board with the new system, Ted Shelby of EP's Pawtucket plant still presented a bit of a problem. Pawtucket had been the only other group in the company to develop an inventory and production control system and Ted, responsible for Pawtucket's system design, did not let it go easily. He had raised enough questions with Ben and with the corporate staff to warrant an integration with Kerry's system. We pick up the events at an impass between Kerry and Ted.

What's Best for The Company (II)

Company vice presidents have arrived at that station in life at least in part through their impressive stature. Marshall Mason, vice president manufacturing, was no exception. Today, at the head of the long, oval table in the Expandrium Product Headquarters, he was laying down the law to the assembled group.

"I believe that I am correct in stating that fully three months ago I requested that you, Kerry, and your staff, and you, Ted, and the EP operations staff, sit down and develop a plan that would reflect the best in each of your proposals." Mason's granite-colored eyes bore steadily on the two principals. "Yet, what I have heard here today reflects a total lack of progress. Three months. Nothing.

"Well, gentlemen, you are going to get off the dime. I do not want to hear from you, Mr. Shelby, that the two systems are, as you put it, hopelessly incompatible. And neither do I want to hear from you, Mr. Drake, that respecting the local problems of the Expandrium Products Division will, as you put it, so seriously degrade the overall system as to render it cost ineffective. What I *do* want to hear, gentlemen, is exactly how you propose to work out a compromise system that indeed reflects what is best for The Company.

"I expect to find your initial proposal on my desk Friday next. Your detailed system will be on my desk exactly one month from today." Mason might have added, and if you can't do it, I'll find someone who can. He didn't need to. Everyone in the company had memorized *that* line.

What was the problem? Why didn't Kerry's corporate staff group just install their system over plant objections? The answer is that they couldn't. As corporate staff, Kerry had no line authority to do so. Then why didn't Mason order it, since he did have the authority? The answer here is that in corporate life as in politics, you cannot afford to squander political capital. You must carefully choose when, and over which issues to take a stand. And this was not one of them. So he did the next best thing. He said, "Give me a compromise and give it to me now."

The next week was a hectic one for Ted, Kerry, and their representatives. They understood the technical dimensions of the problem well, but giving up a feature you cherish isn't easy. In the end it was Kerry who broke the ice.

"See here, Ted. I think that I do understand why you don't want to share this particular group of data with other locations. I do see that the divisions really are different, and if they start looking at one another's numbers that could lead to serious problems of misinterpretation. So why don't we do this? Why don't we build a secure module that will serve the needs of all the locations? Now we have a common system, but this stuff is accessible only to the parent location."

Ted brightened, "What do you think, Sherm?" This to Sherman March, Ted's systems person. March nodded that it looked okay.

Next they tackled the thorny dual coding problem. Ted had maintained all along that Kerry's system would force him either to scrap his entire system, specialized as it was to EP's needs, or to code and enter all EP data twice, at an estimated annual cost of several hundred thousand dollars. But now Claude had come up with the perfect solution, one requiring a slight modification of both systems but actually upgrading the capabilities of both.

Well, there's no need to continue the story. Working with the combined expertise of both groups, and for the first time honoring the motives of each, Ted and Kerry found that the "systems problem" melted away. Working together actually turned out to be a rewarding experience for both groups. In fact, the final systems design, superior to either of the initial ones, landed on Mason's desk a week early. No, Kerry didn't get everything *he* wanted, and Ted had to give up some control over *his* system, but Mason's forced compromise was indeed what was "best for the company."

Depicted in the vignette is a superordinate goal in action. Of course, it did not become a superordinate goal until Mason made it clear enough that careers were on the line. Still, once Kerry's group and Ted's had adopted the same

goal, the conflict melted away and together the two groups produced a resolution satisfactory to each and better than each of the groups' systems separately.

Our last point in the examination of conflict is this: often when groups have to work together but have different interests and often conflicting goals, organizations can resolve the differences by creating temporary task forces or teams made up of representatives from conflicting groups. The groups are convened for a special mission, usually with a target date for completion, and the team members are evaluated on how well the mission is accomplished. In fact, as with our vignette, two groups previously in conflict but later working toward a superordinate goal are often effective, establish relationships that prove helpful even after the task force is dissolved, and demonstrate that conflict often has beneficial results (6).

To recap our section on conflict management the following things need to be considered:

- Does the conflict divert enough of the productive energies away from the conflicting groups to obviate the benefits of conflict such as a heightened focus on problems, the divulging of new information, and the releasing of energies not available under more tranquil environments?
- Does the conflict interfere with the goals of the larger units?

If the answer to either of the above questions is yes, then these questions need to be considered:

- Should the hierarchy of authority be involved to reduce the conflict?
- Can common ground among the groups be identified?
- Can a superordinate goal be established, and does it make sense to do so?
- Are there structural means of reducing conflict and increasing collaboration?
- Can different patterns of communication be explored that will create greater understanding among the conflicting groups?
- Can patterns of reciprocated cooperation be established to reduce conflict?
- Do the groups need to be convened on neutral ground with a third party as mediator?

The answers to such questions can direct attention to the appropriate conflict reduction strategy. We will be dealing with several more of these strategies in Chapter 21.

Summary

As we defined it, conflict is the behavior of one group that interferes with the goal seeking of another group. Groups in conflict are usually interdependent and have different action goals, and at least one of the groups has the power to interfere with the goals of others. Conflict has several components, beginning with situational factors that are conducive to this goal interference. These factors may include differences in tasks, values, attitudes, and goal priorities as groups try to gain scarce organizational resources. These factors become what we have called the *context* of conflict.

Furthermore, because organizations often comprise many functions and hierarchies, groups can select many action generators or action goals, from the set of constraints, even though they agree on the planning goals of the organization. They choose these partly because of their different tasks, values, and attitudes—all of which are reinforced within their own grouping. Hence, they see "what's good for the company" in terms of what serves their own interests. The pursuit of group goals, defined by criteria different from those defining other groups' goals, provides a breeding ground for conflict.

We also suggested that conflict consists of episodes, each with aftermath. When an episode is resolved to the conflicting parties' mutual satisfaction, its aftermath tends not to contribute to the potential for conflict. It may even reduce such potential, since the groups may now understand each other better or have developed superordinate goals. If, however, there is a series of conflict episodes, the aftermath of each will increase the potential for conflict. Attitudes toward the other party can be expected to become less favorable, any voluntary interaction between the parties may be expected to decrease, and conflict will tend to escalate.

The roots of conflict, which contribute to goal and value differences, may be found in several areas. These include group cohesiveness and the process by which norms, which center on maintaining cohesiveness, pursuing group goals, and accomplishing group-defined tasks, are developed. The value premises and logic created within an in-group tend to shut off these groups from the arguments of outsiders. This creates firmer boundaries between competing and conflicting groups, which further contributes to latent conflict. The boundaries tend to create a sense of territoriality that escalates the process of conflict still further.

Conflict in organizations is inevitable and not necessarily bad. Consequently, we focused on conflict management strategies. Since group conflict is often the product of different group goals, virtually all the conflict management techniques include a search for common territory among the conflicting groups. This territory is then exploited as a baseline to extend the common ground and to develop superordinate goals. In the process, many of the by-products of conflict such as distrust, hostility, stereotyping, and misperceptions are likely to be altered, and hence provide a new context that reduces the probability of frequent dysfunctional conflict. Indeed, conflict examined in this light has some benefits for the organization because it often brings new information to light and produces new ways of looking at issues.

References

1. ARGYRIS, C. *Integrating the Individual and the Organization.* New York: Wiley, 1964.
2. BEER, M. *Organizational Changes and Development: A Systems View.* Santa Monica, Calif.: Goodyear, 1980.
3. BLAKE, R. R., and J. S. MOUTON. "Reactions to Intergroup Competition Under Win-Lose Conditions." *Management Science* 7 (1961): 420–435.
4. ———. *Group Dynamics—Key to Decision Making.* Houston: Gulf, 1961.
5. BLAKE, R. R., H. A. SHEPARD, and J. S. MOUTON. *Intergroup Conflict in Organizations.* Ann Arbor, Mich.: *Foundation for Research on Human Behavior,* 1964.
6. BROWN, L. DAVID. *Managing Conflict at Organizational Interfaces.* Reading, Mass.: Addison-Wesley, 1983.
7. CROZIER, M. *The Bureaucratic Phenomenon.* London: Tavistock, 1964.
8. ———. "The Relationship Between Micro and Macro-Sociology." *Human Relations* 25 (1972): 239–251.
9. DALTON, M. *Men Who Manage.* New York: Wiley, 1959.
10. DEUTSCH, M. *The Resolution of Conflict.* New Haven, Conn.: Yale University Press, 1973.
11. ETZIONI, A. "Dual Leadership in Complex Organizations." *American Sociological Review* 30 (1965): 688–698.
12. FILLEY, A. C. *Interpersonal Conflict Resolution.* Glenview, Ill.: Scott, Foresman, 1976.
13. GRIMES, A. J., and S. KLEIN. "Empirical Investigations of the MBO Process in Disparate Organizations." Proceedings of the Midwest Academy of Management Meetings, 1975.
14. JANIS, J. L. *Victims of Groupthink: A Psychological Study of Foreign Policy Decisions and Groupthink.* New York: Houghton Mifflin, 1972.
15. KATZ, D., and R. L. KAHN. *The Social Psychology of Organizations,* 2nd ed. New York: Wiley, 1978.
16. KELLEY, H. H. "Salience of Membership and Resistance to Change of Group-Anchored Attitudes." *Human Relations* 8 (1955): 275–290.
17. KERR, S. "On the Folly of Rewarding A, While Hoping for B." *Academy of Management Journal* 18 (1975): 769–783.
18. KLEIN, S. M. *Workers Under Stress: The Impact of Work Pressure on Group Cohesion.* Lexington: University Press of Kentucky, 1971.
19. KOCHAN, T. A. "Determinants of the Power of Boundary Units in an Interorganizational Bargaining Relation." *Administrative Science Quarterly* 20 (1975): 434–452.
20. KOCHAN, T. A., G. P. HUBER, and L. L. CUMMINGS. "Determinants of Intraorganizational Conflict in Collective Bargaining in the Public Sector." *Administrative Science Quarterly* 20 (1975): 10–23.
21. LIKERT, R. L., and J. G. LIKERT. *New Ways of Management Conflict.* New York: McGraw-Hill, 1976.
22. LINDSKOLD, S., D. MCELWAIN, and M. WAYNER. "Cooperation and the Use of Coercion by Groups and Individuals." *Journal of Conflict and Resolution* 21 (1977): 531–550.

23. LINDSKOLD, SVENN, and MICHAEL G. COLLINS. "Inducing Cooperation by Groups and Individuals: Applying Osgood's Grit Strategy." *Journal of Conflict Resolution* 22 (December 1978): 679–690.
24. MERTON, R. K. *Social Theory and Social Structure.* New York: Free Press, 1957.
25. MYERS, D. G., and H. LAMM. "The Group Polarization Phenomenon." *Psychological Bulletin* 83 (1976): 602–627.
26. OSGOOD, C. *An Alternative to War or Surrender.* Urbana: University of Illinois Press (1962).
27. PONDY, L. R. "Organizational Conflict: Concepts and Models." *Administrative Science Quarterly* 12 (September 1967): 296–320.
28. ———. "A Systems Theory of Organizational Conflict." *Academy of Management Journal* 9 (1966): 246–256.
29. RENWICK, P. A. "Perception and Management of Superior-Subordinate Conflict." *Organizational Behavior and Human Performance* 13 (June 1975): 446–456.
30. RITTI, R. *The Engineer in the Industrial Corporation.* New York: Columbia University Press, 1971.
31. RITTI, R., and F. H. GOLDNER. "Professional Pluralism in an Industrial Organization." *Management Science* 16 (1969): 233–246.
32. SCHEIN, E. H. *Process Consultation: Its Role in Organizational Development.* Reading, Mass.: Addison-Wesley, 1969.
33. SCHMIDT, S. M., and T. A. KOCHAN. "Interorganizational Relationships: Patterns and Motivations." *Administrative Science Quarterly* 22 (1977): 220–235.
34. THOMAS, K. "Conflict and Conflict Management." In *Handbook of Industrial and Organizational Psychology,* edited by M. Dunnette. Chicago: Rand McNally, 1976. Pp. 889–931.
35. WALTON, R. E., J. M. DUTTON, and T. P. CAFFERTY. "Organizational Context and Interdepartmental Conflict." Administrative Science Quarterly 14 (1969): 522–543.

Discussion Questions

1. How does our discussion of goal development help us to understand what happened in our case at the beginning of this chapter?
2. Why is conflict inevitable in complex organizations?
3. What are the key elements in our definition of conflict?
4. Describe the roots of conflict. Explain why they cause conflict.
5. Describe the actual process of conflict. Why is conflict a process and not a single occurrence of conflictual behavior?
6. Discuss conflict as a product of group dynamics and leadership behavior.
7. Discuss conflict as a function of the formal task structure of the organization.
8. What is the idea of the superordinate goal? How does the superordinate goal help us understand the management of conflict?
9. In what ways does communication help to manage conflict? In what ways does it not?

PART V
Processes for Organizational Improvement

Our discussion in Part IV of the feedback and control system completes our description and analysis of our basic "building blocks" of the organizational system. We hope that through this description and analysis you have developed an understanding of the forces shaping organizational behavior and of how they are interrelated. In the course of our analysis we have frequently focused on the problems encountered in the management of human organizations. More often than not these problems arose just because such interrelationships exist and because these interrelationships have not been perceived accurately by the management.

Inevitably, then, the question must arise: Can't we *do* something to improve organizations, to shape or change human behavior for the purpose of correcting these problems? The answer is yes, and many people have. However, these attempts at improvement are often ineffective. And often when they have been effective, they are so only temporarily.

Why should this be the case? We feel the answer is that to the extent that the systems model is an approximately correct model of human organization, then organizations *as systems* will resist change. We are aware that this is only a model, that human organizations do not exist apart from the individuals that constitute them. But that is what we mean by a model: that the organization appears to behave in ways that can be usefully described in systems terms.

Our task of this final part is to develop an understanding of processes for organizational improvement, to try to understand how and when attempts at organizational improvement work or fail to work. In doing this we call directly on the framework we developed earlier, for the processes for improving human organization primarily affect three systems: the interaction system, the motivation system, and the feedback and control system.

Our focus on these three systems does not mean that the *systems structure* has no relation to organizational improvement. Quite the contrary. The rearrangement of technology, that is, work tasks, of authority relationships, and of formal structure are key ways in which practitioners try to bring about beneficial effects in the interaction, motivation, and feedback and control systems. Examples that come to mind are job enrichment, the development of "autonomous" work groups, the flattening of organizational hierarchies, and the like. These changes in the systems structure are effective, however, not for themselves but rather for the changes that they bring about in other systems.

Processes for Organizational Improvement

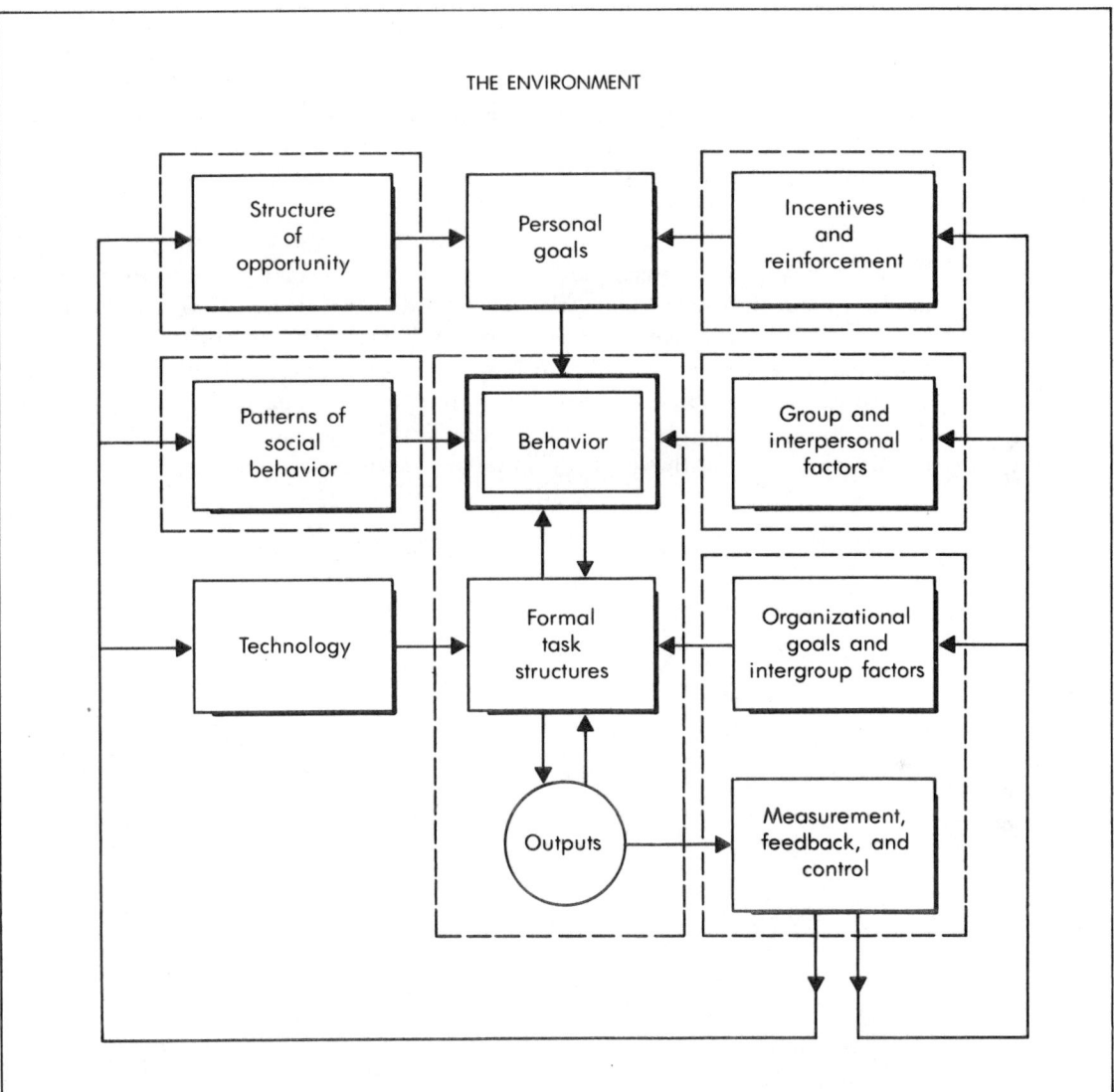

FIGURE V.1 The Organization as a System

Change for organizational improvement may also be brought about by *direct* intervention in these three systems: direct intervention in group process through organization development techniques or participative management; modification of the motivation system through production incentives or rearrangement of the structure of opportunity; change in the control system through management by objectives or work measurement. We urge you to maintain throughout an awareness of the systems interrelatedness that characterizes the change process (see Figure V.1 on the previous page). We urge you to be alert to the fact that a change brought about in one system often has a substantial, though unplanned effect on other systems, and that these unplanned effects may neutralize the planned ones. In other words, organizational improvement is no game for amateurs.

Finally, to understand *planned* change also requires the understanding of the *action research* process. That is, changes are often adaptations to problems disclosed through data. Thus, the data need to be clear, compelling, and not subject to interpretative error. Furthermore, changes that reflect assumptions about cause and effect should be based on solid research evidence including evaluations of previous changes. To show you how behavioral research is conducted in organizations and what problems are associated with those changes, we have included in this part a chapter on research.

Chapter 19
Understanding Organizational Change

Friendly Persuasion

"They just won't listen to reason, Dr. Faust. They're so involved in this thing that there's just no way now that we're going to get them to back down." The voice was Stanley's. Though he was talking to Dr. Faust, seated beside him in the two-engine commuter, the "conversation" was more like a monologue, for Faust was off in another world.

"The IEs [industrial engineers] have got a big stake in this thing. Why, before PIP what were they? Just a bunch of guys who made recommendations on materials, standards, and manufacturing procedures and . . . and now look at 'em. Why they're running the whole show near as I can see. Everybody's scared of 'em.

"Wow! They come in and say you're doing 60 percent of standard and—zap!," Stanley pounded fist into palm just as he had seen Kerry do many a time, "the manager had better shape up or ship out."

Faust stirred, brought out of his reverie by Stanley's gesture, in time to hear Stanley conclude, "So the thing is, they just aren't going to pay any attention no matter what we show them."

"Um," mused Faust. "I venture to say that you are probably correct as you've stated it. No, if left to their own inclination I doubt that our industrial engineers would pay the slightest attention to our findings. And that is precisely why we must make sure that they are not left to their own inclinations."

Stanley and Dr. Faust were returning to New York following a visit to Portland. There they had presented some disconcerting facts about PIP to a meeting of plant management, industrial engineers, and personnel people. Mason, vice president of manufacturing, was present as well.

The facts? Dr. Faust in his role as consultant to the Company had, during the past year, conducted an attitude survey on "quality of working life" at the Portland plant. If the original purpose of the survey had been relatively obscure, what had been uncovered was not. Let's return to that meeting for a moment and listen. Dr. Faust is summarizing the conclusions of his presentation.

"And so, ladies and gentlemen, the evidence is abundantly clear. Work groups operating under our Procedures Improvement Program for the past year show systematically lower work satisfaction—lower quality of working life—than do those not so covered. The facts suggest that we reexamine our Company-wide commitment to PIP."

563

"Most interesting, Dr. Faust." Mason was the first to speak. "Your survey certainly suggests that we should be doing some additional thinking about our Procedures Improvement Program."

The assembled personnel people murmured and nodded their approval. Then Drew Bolt, Portland's head of industrial engineering, rose from the table and walked over to Dr. Faust's flipcharts. "I think we are all in agreement that Dr. Faust's findings are *suggestive,* Mr. Mason. We've seen them earlier as you know. But what they suggest, well, that's another question.

"Here, I think I have to call on the experience that we as industrial engineers have with industrial data. Let me make three points. Fundamentally, we have committed here a most common error or misinterpretation—that of confusing association with causality. Why, there are all kinds of reasons why we would expect these departments to be lower in work satisfaction. First of all, and most likely, is that they are different in the first place. Look," said Bolt, tapping the charts with his fist, "these are all *low-skill* departments. That's why we introduced PIP first in these departments. Second, because of their positions, these people have been with The Company a shorter period of time. They're newer people, not really Company people yet. Finally . . ."

As Bolt continued it became quite clear that the industrial engineers had dredged up every possible reason why the departments so indicated *should* be lower in "morale," and even that it was probably a good thing. Even Ted, in his role as representative of the corporate industrial engineering staff, joined in to explain that some loss in morale might possibly accompany marked gains in productivity. Certainly, he said, The Company was interested in maintaining high morale. But then, perhaps they had been too interested in the past—that is, the price paid, in lost productivity, for happy workers may have been too great.

In the end what it all boiled down to was the inconclusiveness of the data Faust had presented. There just were too many alternative explanations. Still Faust had not come away empty-handed. Mason indicated that he indeed was concerned. Although he was unprepared to take any action, he believed that it shouldn't cost a great deal to learn a bit more about the effect of PIP on quality of working life. So he capped off the meeting by saying, "Gentlemen, I think we should proceed in the following way. Within the next two weeks, Dr. Faust should make a proposal as to what he might do in order to get a better fix on this problem. New York will provide what resources it can to support this study, but the final decision as to its conduct must rest, as always, with local plant managers."

This was the problem with which Stanley and Dr. Faust were wrestling on their flight back to New York. Let's return to their conversation.

"Now, then," Faust was saying, "what do we do to ensure that they are *not* left to their own inclinations? Umm . . . ah, yes. Stanley, you know the schedule for implementing the PIP program, do you not?"

Stanley nodded yes.

"This May, one year will have passed since the first survey. Ah, how many additional work groups will be covered by PIP by that time?"

"Er, well, that's kind of tough to say, Dr. Faust. But let's see. At the time of your first survey, only about a third of Portland's direct manufacturing groups were covered. And, oh, I seem to recall that the PIP program was supposed to be fully implemented at Portland by January 1 of this year. Of course, they'd never make that schedule. So I'd say it's a pretty sound guess that maybe 80 percent of the direct manufacturing work groups would have about six months experience with PIP by this May."

"Splendid." Faust was visibly pleased.

"Ah, I don't see . . ."

"And how many other plants will have experience with PIP by then?"

"Well, everyone in the Expandrium Products Division ought to be covered, partially at least. And the Consumer Products Division, almost all of them. That's like eight plants, Dr. Faust, except that some of them are pretty small."

"No matter. But what about Pawtucket? Have they brought Franklyn around yet?" Faust asked.

"No, Ben's doing his own thing. What does he call it? . . ." Stanley paused. "Yeah, that's it, *task simplification.*"

"And how is that working, would you say?" queried Faust.

"Working? Beats me. But you know Ben. If

his guys were really against it he wouldn't be doing it. But honestly, Dr. Faust, I just don't see what all this . . ."

"Certainly you do," interrupted Faust. "You just haven't had time to piece it all together." With this Faust symbolically knocked out his pipe—there was no smoking on the commuter—in preparation for one of his Socratic tutorials.

"Now then, let's say that you and I, and the personnel people, believe that we have good reason to fear what PIP has done to the quality of working life in The Company. On the other hand, let's say that the industrial engineering group sees nothing but good coming out of this program. Why the difference?"

"Er, well, I guess that we are looking at different things mostly."

"True. But why?"

"Why, like I said before, because this program really makes them important people in The Company and . . . oh, it's more than that. They really believe in PIP. And why not? It's their thing. And it certainly does look like productivity goes up."

"Yes. And the personnel people?"

"Us, you mean? Oh, pretty much the same thing, I guess. Our thing isn't productivity so much as maintaining good employee relations. Yeah, and I guess we believe—I know I do—that there doesn't really have to be a trade-off between productivity and work satisfaction. You don't necessarily have to give up one to get the other."

"Very good." Faust's tone indicated that he was pleasantly surprised by the answer. "Now then, the engineers' primary voiced objection to our argument has been what? Simply that work satisfaction doesn't count?"

"No, although I think that's what they *really* believe. No, near as I can tell they figure it's just no sense getting into that when it's easier just to say that our data are no damn good."

"And why not?" Faust pressed on.

"Why, mainly because there are just so many other explanations for . . . oh, I see what you're going to try, Dr. Faust. What you want to do is to come back this May and survey the people at Portland again. Now you've got your old data and some new data and . . . and some of those departments in our new data will have gone over to PIP during the year. And if *they* look bad, well . . ."

"Exactly. If they show a marked decline in work satisfaction that will be difficult to explain, won't it? Especially if those work groups still not covered by PIP remain unchanged."

"But do you think that's what we'll find?" Stanley was excited at the prospect of the new study.

"One never can be sure. But if our analysis of the problem is correct—and I think it is—that is what we will find."

"But why then do you want the other plants? You won't have the first batch of data with them so you can't do the same thing."

"We won't have to. Possibly you can tell me why?" Faust seemed to be enjoying himself.

"Er, I'm not so sure that I can. I mean won't we be in just the same position we are here? Can't they just discount the data from these other plants in the same way?"

"Can they? Think a minute," said Faust.

"Why sure they can. They'll just say . . ." Stanley paused in thought for a bit. Then it came to him. "No, of course they can't," he announced triumphantly. "Of course they can't because we've already shown in Portland that the cause is PIP. So it becomes pretty absurd for them to say, yes, it is this way in Portland but it's totally different in these other plants."

"That's the idea. Correct. But do not for a minute believe that they cannot or will not say that. They probably will attempt to say that Portland is special, or possibly that our survey itself was responsible. One can never know. The fundamental problem, you see, is that our industrial engineers really do not *believe* in work satisfaction as an idea. They do not believe in the *reality* of it. For them it does not have the same level of existence as do twenty expandrium forgings. And yet, neither can they ignore it." Faust lapsed into deep thought.

"But I guess that's what I really mean, Dr. Faust, about them not being *inclined* to do anything about it. I mean that when push comes to shove, I can just hear Shelby saying, 'Yes, gentlemen, it's a sad fact that there are no free rides in this world today. We've paid a price in order to remain competitive productivity-wise, but it's a necessary price.' "

Faust responded with a rare chuckle. "I fear that you have been around Ted too long, Stanley.

Yes, that's exactly what he will say. And that is where Ben and Pawtucket come in."

"Ben?" Stanley's tone was one of disbelief. "You're going to survey *Ben's* plant? Good luck!"

"And why not?" countered Faust. "Remember, Ben Franklyn has problems of his own with PIP. What better way to show the rest of The Company that his approach is the correct one? We shall have to make concessions to be sure, for Ben is a wary sort. But he will go along, wait and see. He will go along."

"If you say so," Stanley was dubious. "But I see how this fits the plan. Here's Pawtucket, a plant that everybody agrees is a high-productivity plant. In fact, it even seems to be getting better with this, this 'task simplification' approach. So if your quality of working life data look good there, why, that's your case." Stanley looked pleased.

So there you have a firsthand account of the birth of the ideas that eventually led to the demise of PIP as it was known in The Company. Dr. Faust did do his survey in the other divisions, with the help of pressure applied from the corporate staff. And Ben did go along with his role in the survey, just as Faust had predicted, although he was enormously troublesome during the process. Ben, it seemed, always wanted a stacked deck when dealing with corporate staff. And why not?

What did their new data show? By and large, they showed just about what Faust and personnel people had thought they would—together with some interesting exceptions that suggested ways in which PIP might be modified. In the process, the engineers were finally stripped to their ultimate argument: that high productivity is more important than high morale. Yet even this was questioned by the fact that Ben's Pawtucket plant stood head and shoulders above the others in both satisfaction and productivity.

The key to the change process, however, proved to be the "disaster" at Portsmouth, a new plant where the apparent reaction to the introduction of PIP had been so negative that the top corporate people feared dire "industrial relations consequences." The goal of higher productivity, declared Mr. Marsh himself, is not best achieved through industrial strife.

The upshot of it all was that Dr. Faust, the industrial engineers, and the Portsmouth plant management team cooperated in designing a field experiment to test some of the ways in which PIP might be modified to preserve quality of working life while maintaining some of the management benefits of PIP. But make no mistake about it, the days of PIP were numbered.

Our story includes many of the elements required for a meaningful change effort. The key element is a potential industrial relations blow-up at Portsmouth; this major force motivates management to consider seriously doing away with PIP altogether. But even before that, PIP, as the IEs had conceived it, was for all practical purposes, dead. Why was this so? Let us go back to the beginning of our story for the answer.

Faust failed to convince anyone in the big company headquarters meeting because, although he was correct in his conclusions, he did not provide compelling enough evidence to justify a major change in PIP. His data were weak and could not stand up to the attacks of the aggressive and not disinterested Bolt. Faust had not even come close to proving that PIP caused lower morale. He knew it, Bolt knew it, and so did everyone else in the room.

Furthermore, it seemed that PIP had, in fact, done what was intended—it had raised productivity. People like Mason tend not to want to tinker with success, particularly if there are no obvious compelling reasons to do so. And remember,

Bolt and his people had a tremendous stake in PIP. They had created it, and their organizational fortunes depended on its success.

So Faust, understanding these forces and remaining firm in his belief that PIP was doing mischief, plotted with Stanley to create forces for change. What they needed were better data and some alternatives—primarily to convince Mason and other management people that a change was warranted. They got these when they were able to show that PIP "caused" lower morale and that Ben Franklyn ran a good shop without PIP. And of course, the Portsmouth situation did not hurt their case.

The point is that organizational change is a product of forces that motivate the desire to change—among those who count. These forces must be strong enough, that is, justified by enough evidence to counteract the forces against change. In the remainder of this chapter we will develop that point.

The key concepts that we deal with are: the extent to which *pressures* demand change; who and how many within the organization *feel* the pressures; the *process* by which the changes are devised and implemented; the manner in which the change programs *affect* other aspects of the organization; the *consistency* of the change with prevailing authority, social, interaction, motivation, and control systems; the extent of *involvement* of those most affected by change; the *incentives* that lead to acceptance of or resistance to the change by those most affected by it; and finally the organizational *supports* that *sustain* the changes themselves.

You will see, too, that the effects of change are often unanticipated. However, if the lessons of this section are well learned, you should have a better feel for such unanticipated effects.

The Dynamics of Change

Change as a Way of Life

Most organizations change because powerful forces—which may be social, economic, or technical—require it. Organizations must respond to these forces in order to survive. Competition, a wellspring of our economic structure, encourages us to seek an edge on our competitors; it is a potent force for change. In addition, there is evidence that people seek change—that they become bored with doing things the same way and want varied experiences (15). And career mobility is affected to some extent by the manner in which new role incumbents redefine their roles. Those who simply do what has been done before may be viewed as unimaginative—as trustworthy plodders—and not worthy of further advancement. Ted Shelby understood that point, so he helped CMF and PIP get started. Such programs may be started, then, not because of their intrinsic worth, but because someone, often a Ted Shelby, has identified a problem and come up with a "solution." In fact, the mobility patterns of many sophisticated organizations are designed to encourage new ways of looking at things—either by moving people around or by encouraging the Ted Shelbys (41). One author has even suggested that a significant organizational problem is resistance to stability—that is, change for its own sake regardless of consequences (1). But let us be more specific and describe some forces that work toward change in organizations.

Forces for Change

Generally, change is a product of some problem (see Figure 19.1), and problems are discovered when someone or some group identifies "what is" as somehow different from "what ought to be." That is, people in organizations typically have in mind a model that suggests appropriate behaviors or outcomes. When actual behaviors or outcomes differ from the model, then a problem is said to exist (40).

For example, PIP was introduced initially because of pressures to reduce costs and because the IEs had determined that the average worker was producing at only 65 percent of standard. The standard was developed by computing data from tens of thousands of workers doing jobs requiring similar operations. These

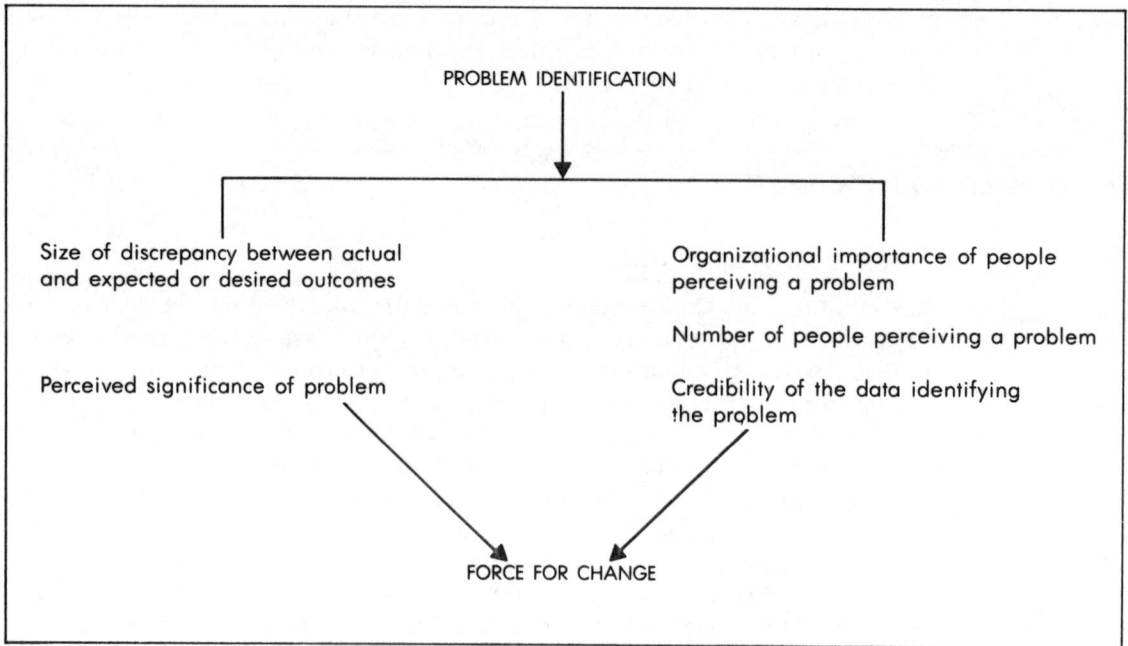

FIGURE 19.1 Forces for Change

standards then became the data for a normative model that stated how people *should be* doing. Clearly, the workers in The Company did not measure up, and consequently management saw a problem. Later, Faust disclosed that morale had dropped because of PIP. The original morale level was the standard against which morale was measured after PIP had been put in operation. This was another problem that motivated a change.

Resistance to Change

Where there are few compelling reasons to change, the comfort of the status quo can be a strong force for resisting it. People and groups can get locked into stable social patterns—into predictable and therefore comforting environments—and incursions into such tranquility can be threatening (7, 29).

Furthermore, change is constrained by existing system forces and system structures. Whenever the process of change substantially alters what exists, there is likely to be trouble implementing the change. Too many complex system relationships and vested interests are threatened when change comes too quickly and too radically.

As systems develop, the patterns of behavior, expectations of future behavior, values, and norms that sustain such systems are created. When these patterns are shown to work, they become institutionalized and hence stable. Then as more and more sustaining patterns are created and reinforced, the defenses against change become almost impenetrable.

For example, certain types of people tend to be recruited for certain roles. Once these people enter an organization, they are further socialized according to the norms and values of those with whom they associate—who, in fact, are not much different from the recruits themselves. Training programs that are designed to reinforce the norms and values, as well as to train the recruits, may follow. After that, the reinforcement pattern for the "right" behavior becomes a matter of organizational reality. Customary ways of doing things are built up over time, and the justification for each custom is rooted in past needs and the response to those needs (13).

Such customs in any organization have a priori and post hoc justifications. These justifications constitute the "value" of traditional ways to members of that organization; they are supported by norms, attitudes, and so forth. The patterns are difficult to change even when it is clear that a change is required. As Katz and Kahn state, "enduring systems are 'overdetermined' . . . and when it comes to change, organizations show defenses in depth" (24:715).

Further, remember that after a time people develop a vested interest in the status quo. They profit from the way rewards are distributed, from the various power relationships, and from the roles they have made for themselves (23). For example, take the IEs and PIP. Clearly, Bolt and his people would have profited had PIP continued.

Another force for stability is the interrelationships among the systems we have described. If change would occur discreetly, there might be less resistance. But, of course, most important changes touch areas beyond those targeted. Changes rationally motivated by problems discovered in one area may create problems in another (35, 45).

So, the forces for change often are cancelled by the forces against change. Figure 19.2 lists the major forces for and against change. It also shows that the forces tend to work against each other, which results in a probability that some change will occur (38). The probability of course depends on the strength of the forces in operation.

One important factor in organizational change is called "organizational readiness" (16, 17). It can be described partly in terms of the total strength of the forces for and against change. That is, if the forces for change are substantially stronger than those against, then the organization can be considered ready for change (6). However, something else is involved in readiness. If the changes are designed to increase desirable behavior and decrease undesirable behavior, then those groups within the organization which already tend toward a favorable

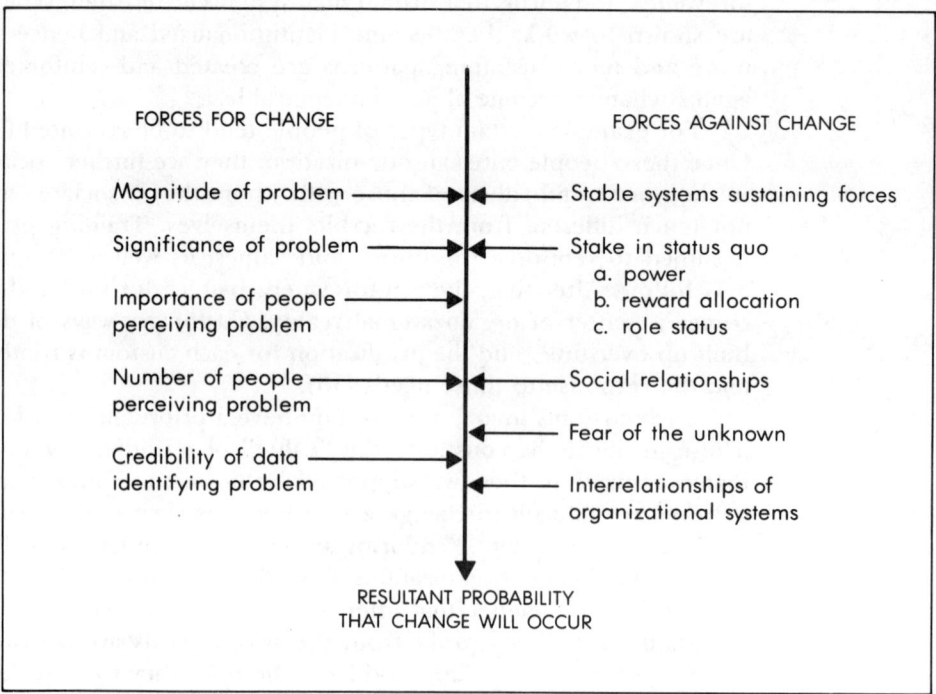

FIGURE 19.2 Forces For and Against Change

balance in behavior will improve the most. They have already adopted behavioral patterns consonant with the projected change and will therefore continue in that direction.

For example, Friedlander (16, 17) reports that in a comparison of groups that benefited most and least from organizational development training designed to increase group effectiveness and teamwork, those groups which initially showed the most effectiveness and teamwork were also the ones that improved the most. According to Friedlander, the members of the most improved groups had already decided that the proposed changes were right, and the change efforts simply reinforced and then supported the wisdom of those decisions. Hence, they were ready.

We have stated that on the organizational level people tend to respond to "what is" by conforming to cues provided by the organization; also, they are socialized according to the values, norms, and customs of the organization, are responsive to the power of authority, and develop motivational patterns consonant with the reward structure and are reinforced accordingly. It is then a logical extension of these ideas that readiness to change be related to the manner in which the proposed change is consonant with these factors (1, 22, 52). Traditional behavioral patterns always have some justification, although sometimes the justification is difficult to identify or is no longer appropriate. Furthermore, once people are accustomed to behaving in certain ways, post hoc justifications may be concocted. Consequently, if behavioral patterns are to be changed, the new patterns must either have similar, perhaps more powerful, justification or be seen as extensions of the old patterns (49–51). Thus, organizational readiness for change depends not only on the composite of forces for or against change, but also on the degree to which the change is consonant with tradition.

At this point we can make some interim conclusions. Often, a change is carried through due to the resolve of top management. However, in order for that change to be effective, some of the following things need attention. First, the change should accommodate the *prevailing system structure*. Second, the change should accommodate *prevailing attitudes and common norms and values* unless the change deals with these factors themselves. Third, the change should accommodate the people affected by giving them the *opportunity* and the *incentive* to develop a stake in the new way. Fourth, the change should address itself to ramifications that are *not specific* to the change itself, but that, nevertheless, are possible consequences of it. The following questions would be useful to ask when a change is contemplated:

1. Is the pressure for change significant? (It ought to be if change is to be initiated.)
2. Is the pressure felt by important members of the organization? (This helps considerably.)

3. Is the pressure felt by significant numbers of people affected by the change? (The more the merrier.)
4. Is the proposed change consistent with prevailing practices? (This helps considerably.)
5. Is the proposed change consistent with prevailing ideology? Mores? Values? (This helps considerably.)
6. Will the proposed change substantially affect systems outside the target system? (This is an essential question if contingencies are to be a part of the planning process.) And if so, what are the answers to questions 4 and 5 above as they pertain to the nontargeted system?
7. Have provisions been made for the people most affected by the proposed change to become involved in the substance and execution of the change? (This is most helpful.)
8. Are the incentives such that those affected will be induced to "buy in" rather than to resist or subvert the proposed changes? (This is essential for maximum success.)

If the answers to the first three questions are yes, you can assume that a change will take place. The extent of success, however, depends on the answers to the other five questions. And if the change is successful, the probability of wider applications is increased (18, 34).[1]

Strategies for Change

Empirical-Rational Strategies

Chin and Benne have identified three types of strategies for change (9). The first is the so-called *empirical-rational strategy*. The underlying assumption of this strategy is that most people are rational and will follow their best interests. This strategy involves building a body of basic knowledge that supports the need for change, then diffusing this knowledge to the targets of change. People so informed would then (naturally enough, according to the assumptions of this strategy) be motivated to adopt the change.

Such strategies, based on creating knowledge through research and then disseminating it through staff specialists, seem to work well when technical innovations are involved (21). That is, people are likely to accept technical innovations if those innovations are seen as improving their performance and subsequent payoffs. However, the strategy does not seem to work so well with changes in the social or interaction systems—primarily because attitudes, values, and customs often interfere. One person's rationality may not be another person's, and one group's may not be another group's. As we have seen, this is particularly true with regard to organizational goals. In short, the empirical-rational strategy for introducing change has a great deal of merit and appeals to those who value rationality.

Normative-Reeducative Strategies

The empirical-rational strategy does not take into account the different attitudes, values, and goals that exist within any social system. Consequently it requires supplementation. One possible supplement involves what Chin and Benne call the *normative-reeducative strategy*. The assumptions underlying this strategy are significantly different from those of the empirical-rational strategy. Under the normative-reeducative strategy people are seen as active, impulsive, and in quest of immediate need satisfaction. Furthermore, they are seen as guided by perceptions, norms, and cultural requirements. If change is to occur, it must be preceded by alterations in the normative structure, which guides behavior, and in the organizational roles that define such behavior. Under this strategy, people must participate in the process so the change becomes normative and, subsequently, institutionalized. In short, such strategies take into account the social and psychological features of individuals and groups as they play out their roles in organizations. The focus, therefore, is on the clarification and reconstruction of values and norms, and on the individual's active participation in such changes.

The normative-reeducative strategy is not an irrational strategy. It involves collecting data, identifying problems, and using feedback to determine the consequences of action. It goes beyond the empirical-rational strategy, however, in that it requires the active involvement of those associated with the change. In a sense, then, the people create their own data and generate their own changes; thus, they develop a commitment to the change itself.

The normative-reeducative strategy also emphasizes *experience-based* learning as an ingredient of all enduring changes in human systems. It assumes that people learn from their experience and that, in this way, changes are sustained. Indeed, a combination of empirical-rational strategies and normative-reeducative strategies would probably be warranted in that information supporting "a better way" can be infused into an organization or one of its subsystems by means that go beyond simply transmitting information. As Chin and Benne state:

> [Under the normative-reeducative strategy] the rationality and intelligence of men are not denied. Standards of action and practice are supported by social and cultural norms and by commitments on the part of individuals to these norms. Social cultural norms are supported by the attitude and value systems of individuals—normative outlooks which undergird their commitments. Change in a pattern of practice or action according to this view will occur only as the persons involved are brought to change their normative orientations to old patterns and develop commitments to new ones. (11:98)

Power-Coercive Strategies

Power-coercive strategies use organizational sanctions, hierarchically enforced, to gain compliance for change. In general, these strategies use political and/or economic power within the organization to coerce organizational members to do things they might not otherwise do.

Although they can undeniably produce change quickly and effectively, they have several problems. The use of power implies that the people subject to the change do not want to change and may be divisive and cause resistance to the change. Such strategies, therefore, although they are frequently used, can be effective mainly when the changers have extensive control over economic and political resources and the means of measuring behavior and output (36).

We feel that power-coercive strategies should be used cautiously. Because of the hierarchical nature of organizations and the manner in which people tend to respond to the power of authority, those in power can use strategies based on their position most effectively when the justifications for change are clear to the majority of the organization's participants. Consequently, power-coercive strategies are better used in combination with the other strategies (7, 37).

Depth of Change

Another issue in organizational change strategy is the depth of organizational intervention for planned change (20). Depth here means the extent to which information is private or inaccessible. For example, data on productivity, absenteeism, the means of production, or organizational structures may be fairly public. However, information about personalities, feelings, and interpersonal or intergroup conflict are more likely to be private and hence less accessible. Changes targeted toward these deeper levels, therefore, may be more wrenching, more threatening, and possibly more dangerous, and are more likely to be resisted by the organization. Consequently, if change is anticipated two basic factors should be kept in mind: (1) the requirements to produce enduring changes and (2) the level at which the organization is willing to commit itself (18). Incorporated in the overall strategy should be the requirement that, regardless of the specific strategy used, it should go no deeper than required to produce lasting change or than is willingly accepted by those in the organization.

Creating Expectations

Finally, part of the overall strategy for change may acknowledge the importance of expectations about the consequences of the change. Social psychological literature suggests that expectation often determines outcomes of even controlled experimental studies. That is, if you expect a person to do well, then that person is likely to do better than someone for whom you have lower expectations, *even though their abilities may be the same* (42).

A recent study suggests the same sort of phenomenon may be acting in organizational change experiments. According to the study, four change treatments were created. Two plants were changed using job enrichment and two using job rotation. One plant in each set was told that production would increase as a consequence of the change and the other was not. The results showed that where plants were told that production would increase, it did *regardless* of the change. The other two plants showed no such increases, again regardless of the treatment (25).

The Process of Change

There is no single process of organizational change, though several requirements are common to the processes in the change literature. The first is that *information is required*—that is, an organization has to have information that identifies a problem. Although this may seem obvious, deficiencies of information gathering are well known in most organizations. It is the nature and quality of information that is at question.

For example, it is well known that people tend not to report information that might harm them; thus, they may not disclose problems in the first place. And it is well known that information tends to become distorted as it moves up, down, and across organizational levels (19, 39). Enough timely and reliable information about key organizational issues seems a requirement of any change model.

Another common thread is that *pressure* beyond what the information provides must be brought to bear on those empowered to make change. In other words, once a problem is disclosed, the magnitude of that problem has to be demonstrated to the right people so that they become motivated to begin the change process. As with the information requirement, this one is deceptively simple. For as Argyris has proclaimed, the bulk of the evidence suggests that executives are:

> So busy controlling others in order to win, to advocate their position, and to do so in a way that cannot be disproved or publicly tested, that they create self-sealing processes. (4:411)

Such behavior suggests that executives are immune to problem disclosure unless the problem is great enough to create a significant threat.

Most change models have a *diagnosis* requirement. That is, it is not enough to identify the problem. Its dimensions and sources need to be identified as well. Typically, diagnosis requires additional data gathering and analysis so that causal relationships are demonstrated with some reasonable certainty.

After diagnosis, most models include *action planning*. At this time, those responsible for implementing the change make hypotheses concerning the source of the problem and how it might be changed. As hypotheses are generated, some are discarded and others are accepted. The accepted hypotheses then constitute the basis for action.

The models seem to include a preparatory stage during which the targeted areas are "readied" for the change. Typically, such preparatory activity involves either communicating the rationality of the change to the people or involving the people themselves in the process of change.

The next step is *action*. That is, the change is tried out, or in some cases, because of either a theoretical or organizational justification, it is spread from the first throughout the organization. Typically, however, it is more desirable to try out the change first.

Feedback is a requirement. That is, the consequences of change must be recorded and evaluated. Because of this evaluation, the change will be continued and diffused, or modified, or the change effort will be terminated.

Finally, we must consider the use of power. There are several ways of looking at power as a variable in organizational change. One is to view it as part of one of the overall strategies—the power-coercive strategy—that we just discussed. Another way to view it as a necessary part of *any* change strategy, and to deal with it in process. For example, Greiner (18) classified organizational change along a power dimension. At one extreme he placed strategies that rely on unilateral authority; that is, one powerful person or a group unilaterally decrees change. In the middle he put the shared approaches; that is, all those touched by the change are involved in developing the actions and, in some cases, identifying the dimensions of the problem as well. At the other extreme he put the "delegated approaches." With these, "almost complete responsibility for defining and acting on problems [is] turned over to subordinates" (18:217).

Greiner found that neither extreme was associated with his criteria of success. Rather, he found that power is represented hierarchically by pressure felt at and then extended downward from the top of the organization, although diagnosing and developing solutions is left to lower participants. Further, the data generated through action are then introduced to all levels as part of the continuing change process. In other words, power is unilateral at the outset of the successful change process, but is later shared.

To summarize, as depicted in the model in Figure 19.3, the change process seems to incorporate:

1. an *information requirement*, so problems are identified,
2. *pressure* enough to warrant motivation to change,
3. *a diagnosis* that identifies the source of problems and hypothesizes causal linkages—that is, that "readies" the organization for change,
4. *action planning*,
5. *action taking*, wherein the hypotheses are acted on, usually in an experimental situation,
6. *feedback* concerning the consequences of action, and
7. the manipulation of *power* to ensure maximum commitment and minimum resentment.

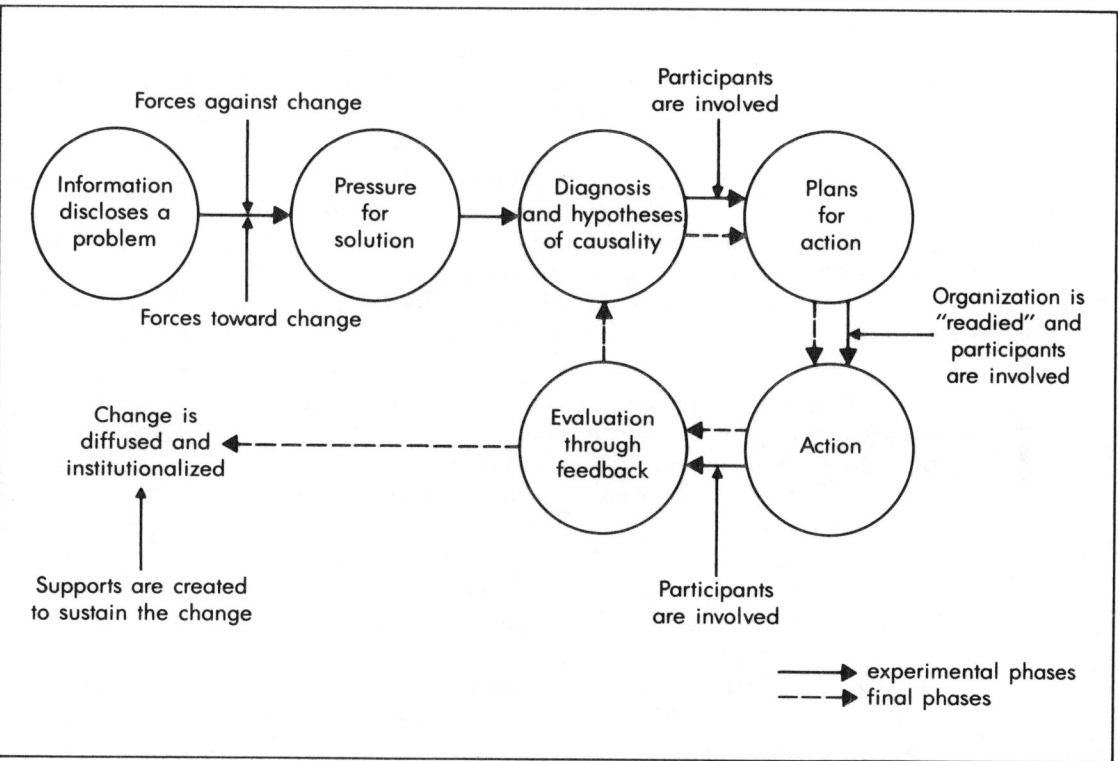

FIGURE 19.3 The Process of Change

This process involves all three of the strategies previously described. According to Greiner's description, the major force for change comes from the top of the organization and represents the power-coercive strategy. The involvement of those affected by the change represents the normative-reeducative strategy, and the spirit of experimentation and the data requirements represent the empirical-rational strategy. The negative effects of the use of power alone may be diffused by a redistribution of power by the top echelons as they share it with those below them. Such power redistribution occurs incrementally through a sequential process of collaboration and involvement. [See especially (31) and (32).]

Change from the Bottom Up

Virtually all the models and most of the organizational literature suggest that changes must come from the top down. This, however, has not been our experience, for indeed many changes are changes of practice motivated by the fact that past practices no longer work or do not work as well as they ought to. Then lower participants will make a change. If the change proves successful, others will emulate it. If this emulation process diffuses through the organization, then a major organizational change can be said to have taken place (46).

Let us give you an example. We talked previously about the use of attitude surveys in organizations as a way of monitoring the psychological health and job satisfaction of lower-level participants. How did such surveys get started in The Company? The opponents of PIP wanted systematic data that could "prove" that the program would have a negative effect on the workers. The personnel manager of one of the divisions affected by work measurement hired a social scientist to conduct an attitude survey in one of the plants as a means of showing that effect. The survey was sold as a good way of finding out how people felt about several issues—a selling point completely consonant with the prevailing company ideology. The survey worked. Therefore, the surveys were used throughout the entire production system.

As the surveys were defined and the feedback to all employees was seen to be useful, the process was expanded to all parts of the company—engineering, sales, headquarters, and so on—until everyone in The Company was surveyed periodically. Not only did the surveys help identify and solve problems, but they served two other purposes as well: they gave employees an opportunity to state their thoughts, and they allowed management to take this thinking into account (3, 14, 25, 26, 27, 38, 44). They also provided management with an additional control on lower management levels by incorporating employee morale into the reward system.

All of the purposes served fit The Company's ideology. Surveys are still used extensively in The Company. All of this was started without the knowledge, much less the support, of top management. Only later, as success accumulated, did the top levels become supportive and the process become part of business as usual. Others have witnessed similar phenomena (7, 10, 12, 32).

A word of caution: although we know of several important instances of successful change beginning at the lower organizational levels and then spreading, it does not always work that way. In fact, sometimes it can backfire. For example, one report described a change in the whole organizational orientation of a group of low-level supervisors with the result that many became frustrated by the traditional ways and quit (2). Another report described an effort to build a strongly cohesive team out of a previously diverse group of low-level supervisors. The change occurred successfully but the organizational context impeded its spreading. Consequently, there was no effect felt anywhere else in the organization (5).

The lesson is that changes, if consonant with the prevailing systems, if accepted on lower levels, and if demonstrably "rational," can begin anywhere. Changes from the bottom up occur all the time in organizations; if they are perceived as providing payoffs, then others buy in. Thus, a momentum may be created that ultimately produces far-reaching changes—and the ultimate support of top management.

Organizational Change and the Norwegian Experience

During the 1960s substantial changes were taking place in the means of production across several key industries in Norway. These changes focused on democratizing the workplace by providing decision-making powers on production pace, methods, and human resource allocation to members of work groups. Before these changes, the jobs were fractionated, simple to perform, and routine. The means of controlling production were typically machine-paced; that is, they employed assembly lines or similar technologies whereby raw materials were inputted, processed, and completed in sequential fashion. Each individual had a small task in the production process; when one person was finished, he or she passed the materials on to another station for another routine operation. This technology was thought to lead to worker alienation and withdrawal measured by absenteeism and turnover rates. In order to change, the Norwegians set up an "industrial democracy program." As Thorsrud, Sorensen, and Gustavsen report:

> The industrial democracy program aimed primarily at the development and testing of alternative organizational forms and their impacts upon employee participation on different job levels. Major emphasis was placed upon the concrete conditions for personal participation, including technological factors, structuring of tasks, the work goals and the wider organizational environment of workers. A project within the program could not be limited only to the level of the workers since major changes in any work system cannot be sustained without qualitative changes eventually at all levels of the organization. . . . Well within the Norwegian cultural framework, it was possible in the 1960s to establish a set of starting conditions for large scale social change over a period of at least 10 years. The strategy of change was based on leadership and support from key unions and employers associations and eventually from government. (48:422)

Thus, the Norwegian experiments included the people and institutions that were touched by the change. The strategy that was ultimately devised had its roots in decades of systematic research on organizational change that disclosed the relationship between the social system and the means of production (49).

The Norwegians adopted a stepwise strategy of change. It included:

1. The establishment of the joint national committee that was organized to represent *labor* and *management.*
2. *A systematic analysis of the target company.*
3. The establishment of *local action committees* representing operators, supervisors, and higher-level management.
4. The *drafting of the changes in cooperation with all the personnel in the experimental departments* and with company specialists. The action committees played

a major role in formulating and presenting the programs. Typically, the change programs included changes in task structure, information and control systems, reward systems, and means by which materials were moved from one group to another.
5. *The institutionalization of the change programs* in the sense that the process and the responsibility for the process was switched from the action committees to management and the shop stewards.
6. *The diffusion of the results of the change* throughout the industry in which they took place. [Paraphrased from Thorsrud, Sorensen, and Gustavsen.(48)]

Thorsrud, Sorensen, and Gustavsen report four experiments that were based on the above strategy. Each illustrates the necessity of looking at the interrelationships among the subsystems of the total organization whenever an organizational change is contemplated.

The results of the studies indicated that productivity and quality increased after the changes were made. However, attitudes toward the new systems were divided. For example:

> A polarization occurred when further integration of processing and services dragged out and when the foreman turned against the new system. A new role for the foreman in the emerging situation was not developed early enough. After nearly a year of preparation and six months of rapid development and change, a year long stagnation set in until new projects were begun in a neighboring department. (48:433)

The Norwegian experiments are among the best organizational change efforts ever reported. They were well planned, they proceeded according to the suggestions coming from years of empirical research and theoretical development, and they had the backing of the key groups required to ensure a successful change effort. Yet each reported experience ran into some sort of unanticipated problem, and the problems typically had to do with how the change touched an untargeted area.

The success and failure of any particular change, then, is often not a consequence of the merits of the change itself, but rather of the manner in which the change proceeds throughout the organization.[2]

Sustaining Change

If a change were introduced using the best procedures, and if it were shown to be effective, then all might be well. The change would be institutionalized because of its merits, and the organizations would benefit. However, things are not that simple (33). If organizational change is to be sustained, system supports need to be established that clearly reinforce the intent of the change and thus provide incentives for behavior consonant with it. And remember, the establishment of such supports is one of the factors that lead to resistance to subsequent change. In other words, sustaining forces in a sense lock in the change so that it becomes standard operating procedure. As an example, Bowers and Seashore (10) identified three general sustaining factors.

First, they discussed organizational readiness, although they did not use that term. They wrote:

> A continuation of the intended change might lie in the earlier legitimation of concern about organizational processes . . . , the habit of deliberate and self-conscious examination of the potential side effects of the many policy and operating decisions. . . . [The organization was] habituated at all levels to think about, discuss openly, and to weigh properly the full range of elements in the organizational system [that contributed to] unusual capacities for self-maintenance. (10:233.)

Second, they identified the lock-in devices that we mentioned earlier:

> A central idea was to make structural changes in the organization that matched the work system and that did not violate reasonable assumptions about the values and motives of the individual members. For example, the revitalized piece rate pay system was viewed to be viable only if sustained by . . . allowed higher earnings, . . . information flow that assured instant supervisory response to low earnings, . . . and prior job assignment systems so that a production employee could become skilled in the work assigned. (10:233.)

Third, Bowers and Seashore feel that the change itself shows sufficient merit so that people who experience it like it, want to lend it their support, and hence maintain it.

Summary

Although we have been discussing organizational improvement, changes are initiated for other purposes as well. The likelihood of permanent change, however, depends on whether or not the change results in some kind of improvement and therefore retains the interest of management (2). Sustained change requires *support systems*. When interest wanes, people turn to other things. Even the best-intentioned changes often have a faddishness about them, and like all fads disappear after a time. Busy managers do not have the time to play in theoretical sandboxes and thus they will look to other more productive ways of spending their time.

Some changes are easy to make or are mandated by others. These sorts are likely to occur. Further, some changes are completely consonant with past practices and require tinkering rather than significant breaches from the past. These too are likely to occur. Finally, some changes are consonant with traditional values and ways of thinking and are thus likely to be embraced by management when changes are perceived as required (20).

Changes most likely to occur would be technical innovations that ostensibly *improve ongoing* practices. Recruiting strategies, selection procedures, training programs, work measurement, or other control and planning procedures are areas where such changes are likely. Each corresponds with past practices and traditional values, mind sets, and norms. In fact, such changes are often made not only in keeping with convention, but to reinforce convention as well.

There are other changes that are not as well received by management. Typically, they focus on process: decision making, the distribution of power, interpersonal or intergroup transactions, and the like. Although process changes can affect the way organizations conduct their business, there is some ambiguity as to precisely what the effect may be. It is perhaps this ambiguity that creates the greatest discomfort among managers and scholars alike (5). It is for that reason that process changes require either strong incentives or an eloquent selling job before management agrees. Introducing the T-group and its variants, team building, and intergroup intervention fall into this category.

Midrange changes for improvement fall between the above extremes. Each of these has some face validity but is not completely consonant with tradition. Job enrichment, the use of attitude surveys, and variants of incentive systems are examples.

Several common points run through most of the changes described in the literature. First, the impetus for change typically comes from two sources: (1) problems are perceived by the initiator of the change, and these problems can be documented usually by showing that organizational expectations are not being met or some aspect of performance is falling short: (2) the initiation may have political undertones. A manager or group of people sees the implementation of change as a vehicle for gaining organizational mobility or for ax grinding and push their program, either through the political process or by bootlegging. Our attitude survey is an example of that sort of thing. Often such change occurs from the bottom up: it illustrates the manner in which far-reaching change programs can get started with only tacit approval from the upper levels. In any event, there is usually a reason for change that provides justification within some organizational grouping.

Second, there has to be some organizational support before a change can be initiated. At the very least, some of the people affected by the change have to be united at the outset though the level of involvement and the organizational level of the participants can vary depending on the nature of the change. Further, if the change is to remain permanent or gather momentum, additional support needs to be developed. This may or may not be a political process that goes beyond the substance of the change. If the norms of the organization are such that change is welcomed, data indicating the effectiveness of the change may be all that is required. However, if the norms do not encourage change or data are inconclusive, support from others in the system is necessary. Remember in our discussion of leadership that exchange of chits, mutual back-scratching, and agreements not to block pet programs so that one's own program may be carried out are all part of the change process as well—because of the need for organizational support.

Third, changes beyond the minor procedural sort will affect aspects of organizational functioning which are not anticipated. This is what is referred to over and over again as the *systems* nature of changes. Extensive documentation has been built up to show the far-reaching consequences of seemingly small changes (5, 43, 50). Refer back to Chapter 2 if this point is not yet clear.

Fourth, change for improvement should be data-based and evaluated against criteria developed from these data. It does not matter what sort of change is being considered, because the justification may be embedded in the data and a good manager will note progress through the data. Data can take many forms. They can be a hard productivity measure or a subjective attitude measure, but, regardless, they should be systematically developed with an eye toward long-term measurement.

Fifth, most changes involve values, attitudes, and assumptions about people—about their motivations to work. This area is perhaps the most controversial, since a wide range of values, assumptions, and motivations exists within and between organizations. But these values and so on determine the types of changes initiated, as well as expectations of possible consequences. Clues as to what changes are likely to be encouraged can be obtained from examining the organization's structure, the distribution of authority and power, the decision-making process, the emphasis on human resource goals as opposed to capital and hardware resource goals, the kinds of control systems used, and the manner in which controls are executed and rewards distributed.

For example, if the organization is highly centralized, with decisions held closely within the formal authority structure: and if the control systems are evident and elaborately executed and the reward system is primarily if not exclusively financial, then we might expect the normative structure to accept more easily mechanistic changes incorporating technology, work measurement, or management by objectives—changes completely consonant with the values and assumptions typically embedded in such organizations. Team building or other human process change techniques are likely to be viewed suspiciously.

Sixth, the process of change, although possibly employing several strategies meaningfully, will be most successful if—at the diagnosis, planning, and implementation stages—it involves those who are affected by the change. After a change takes place, many of the significant problems that occur in nontargeted areas touched by the change, apparently were not involved in the process itself.

Finally, there is the matter of *reinforcement* and the development of supporting structures for the change. Virtually all of the current change literature emphasizes reinforcement, and thus requires follow up with some evaluation built in. As you keep tabs on what is happening, the good should be reinforced, expanded, and institutionalized; and the not-so-good, either changed or dropped.

Notes

1. What we have described is a relatively rational process by which the need for change is identified. But changes in organizations sometimes take place on irrational grounds. If, for example, a Ted Shelby, in his headlong rush for promotion, identified an area where a little creativity might be helpful, it is entirely possible that he would devise some change program where no change really was required. Shelby would have to create a "perception" of a problem by gathering data that "proved" to his supervisors that a problem existed or was about to exist and that his program would take care of that problem. If the program was "judged successful" (and you can bet that evidence would be generated to ensure such a judgment), then the progress might be expanded to various other systems within the total organization.
2. Many changes were made in the Norwegian study described. Standards, measurements, and pay structures were all changed along with the sociotechnical system. Consequently, it is impossible to determine the predominant causal linkage. That is, the determinants of increased productivity and quality might as easily have been the new standards or the new bonus system, or both. What does seem clear, however, is that the success of the change was at least partly due to the process and yet, despite that process, the foreman, and manufacturing, management, and contiguous work groups felt threatened.

References

1. ALBANESE, R. "Overcoming Resistance to Stability." *Business Horizons* 13 (April 1970): 35–42.
2. ALDERFER, C. P. "Change Processes in Organizations." In *Handbook of Work, Organization and Society,* edited by R. Dubin. Chicago: Rand McNally, 1976.
3. ALPER, W., and S. M. KLEIN. "Impact of Feedback on Employee Attitude Surveys." *Personnel Administration* 33 (1970): 54–57.
4. ARGYRIS, C. "Leadership, Learning and Changing the Status Quo." In *Perspectives on Behavior in Organizations,* edited by J. Hackman, E. Lawler, III, and L. Porter. New York: McGraw-Hill, 1977. Pp. 409–434.
5. BEER, M. "The Technology of Organizational Development." In *Handbook of Industrial and Organizational Psychology,* edited by M. Dunnette. Chicago: Rand McNally, 1976.
6. BENNIS, W., K. BENNE, and R. CHIN. *The Planning of Change.* New York: Holt, Rinehart and Winston, 1961.
7. BOSS, R. WAYNE. "It Doesn't Matter If You Win or Lose, Unless You're Losing: Organizational Change in a Law Enforcement Agency." *The Journal of Applied Behavioral Science* 15 (1979): 198–220.
8. BOSS, R. WAYNE, and MARK L. MCCONKIE. "The Destructive Impact of a Positive Team-Building Intervention." *Group and Organization Studies* 6 (1981): 45–56.
9. BOWERS, D. G. "O. D. Techniques and Their Results in 23 Organizations." *Journal of Applied Behavioral Science* 9 (1973): 21–43.

10. BOWERS, D. G., and S. E. SEASHORE. "Durability of Organizational Change." *American Psychologist* 25 (March 1970): 227–233.
11. CHIN, R., and K. D. BENNE. "General Strategies for Effecting Changes in Human Systems." In *Organizational Development*, edited by W. French, C. Bell, and R. Zawacki. Dallas: Business Publications, 1978. Pp. 94–111.
12. DAFT, R. L. "System Influence on Organizational Decision Making: The Case of Resource Allocation." *Academy of Management Journal* 21 (March 1978): 6–22.
13. DUNLOP, J. T. *Industrial Relations Systems.* New York: Holt, Rinehart and Winston, 1958.
14. DUNNINGTON, R. A. "Research for Organization Theory and Management Action, Introduction and Conclusion." In *Proceedings of the 16th Annual Meeting, Boston, December 27–28, 1963,* edited by G. Somers. Madison, Wis.: Industrial Relations Research Association, 1963. Pp. 150–154, 176–179.
15. FISKE, D. W., and S. R. MADDI, EDS. *Functions of Varied Experience.* Homewood, Ill.: Dorsey Press, 1961.
16. FRIEDLANDER, F. "A Comparative Study of Consulting Processes and Group Development." *Journal of Applied Behavioral Science* 4 (1968): 377–399.
17. ———. "The Impact of Organizational Training Labor upon Effectiveness and Intervention of Ongoing Work Groups." *Personnel Psychology* 20 (1967): 289–308.
18. GREINER, L. E. "Patterns of Organization Change." In *Organizational Change and Development.* Edited by G. Dalton, P. Lawrence, and L. Greiner. Homewood, Ill.: Irwin and Dorsey Press, 1970. Pp. 213–229.
19. GUETZKOW, H. "Communications in Organizations." In *Handbook of Organizations,* edited by J. G. March. Chicago: Rand McNally, 1965.
20. HARRISON, R. "Choosing the Depth of Organizational Intervention." *Journal of Applied Behavioral Science* 6 (April 1970): 182–202.
21. HAVELOCK, R. G., and K. D. BENNE. "An Exploratory Study of Knowledge Utilization." In *The Planning of Change,* 2nd ed. Edited by W. G. Bennis, K. D. Benne, and R. Chin. New York: Holt, Rinehart and Winston, 1969.
22. JACQUES, E. "Executive Organization and Individual Adjustment." *Journal of Psychosomatic Research* 10 (1966): 77–82.
23. JAY, ANTHONY. *Management and Machiavelli.* New York: Holt, Rinehart and Winston, 1967.
24. KATZ, D., and R. L. KAHN. *The Social Psychology of Organizations.* New York: Wiley, 1978.
25. KING, A. S. "Expectation Effects in Organizational Change." *Administrative Science Quarterly* 19 (1974): 221–230.
26. KLEIN, S. M. "Two Systems of Management: A Comparison That Produced Organizational Change." In *Proceedings of the 16th Annual Meeting, Boston, December 27–28, 1963,* edited by G. Somers. Madison, Wis.: Industrial Relations Research Association, 1963. Pp. 155–165.
27. KLEIN, S., A. KRAUT, and A. WOLFSON. "Employee Reactions to Attitude Survey Feedback: Study of the Impact of Structure and Process." *Administrative Science Quarterly* 16 (1971): 497–514.

28. KOMACKI, JUDI, ARLENE T. HEINZMANN, and LAMSON LAROALIE. "Effect of Training and Feedback: Component Analysis of a Behavioral Safety Program." *Journal of Applied Psychology* 65 (1980); 261–270.

29. LAWRENCE, P. "How to Deal with Resistance to Change." In *Organizational Change and Development,* edited by G. Dalton, P. Lawrence, and L. Greiner. Homewood: Ill.: Irwin and Dorsey Press, 1970. Pp. 181–197.

30. LEAVITT, H. J. "Applied Organizational Change in Industry: Structural Technological and Humanistic Approaches." In *Handbook of Organizations,* edited by J. G. March. Chicago: Rand McNally, 1965.

31. LIKERT, R. *The Human Organization.* New York: McGraw-Hill, 1967.

32. MANN, F. C. "Studying and Creating Change: A Means to Understanding Social Organization." *Research in Industrial Human Relations* 17 (1957): 146–167.

33. MARROW, A. J., D. G. BOWERS, and S. E. SEASHORE. *Management by Participation: Creating a Climate for Personal and Organizational Development.* New York: Harper and Row, 1967.

34. NADLER, DAVID A. "Managing Organizational Change: An Integrative Perspective." *The Journal of Applied Behavioral Science* 17 (1981): 191–211.

35. NAYLOR, JAMES C., ROBERT D. PRITCHARD, and DANIEL R. ILGEN. *A Theory of Behavior in Organizations.* New York: Academic Press, 1980.

36. OUCHI, W. G. "The Relationship Between Organizational Structure and Organizational Control." *Administrative Science Quarterly* 22 (March 1977): 95–113.

37. PORRAS, J., and P. BERG. "The Impact of Organization Development." *The Academy of Management Review* 3 (April 1978): 249–266.

38. PORRAS, JERRY I., and ALAN WILKINS. "Organization Development in a Large System: An Empirical Assessment." *The Journal of Applied Behavioral Science* 16 (1980): 506–534.

39. PORTER, L. W., and K. H. ROBERTS. "Communication in Organizations." In *Handbook of Industrial and Organizational Psychology,* edited by M. D. Dunnette. Chicago: Rand McNally, 1976.

40. POUNDS, W. "The Process of Problem Finding." In *Organizational Psychology: A Book of Readings,* edited by D. Kolb, I. Rubin, and J. McIntyre. Englewood Cliffs, N.J.: Prentice-Hall, 1971.

41. RITTI, R., and G. FUNKHOUSER. *The Ropes to Skip and the Ropes to Know: Studies in Organizational Behavior.* Columbus, Ohio: Grid, 1983.

42. ROSENTHAL, R. "Interpersonal Expectations: Effects of the Experimenter's Hypothesis." In *Artifact in Behavioral Research,* edited by R. Rosenthal and R. L. Rosnow. New York: Academic Press, 1969. Pp. 181–277.

43. SCHEIN, E. H. *Organizational Psychology.* Englewood Cliffs, N.J.: Prentice-Hall, 1965.

44. SIROTA, D. "A Study of Work Measurement." In *Proceedings of the 16th Annual Meeting, Boston, December 27–28, 1963,* edited by G. Somers. Madison, Wis.: Industrial Relations Research Association, 1963. Pp. 155–165.

45. SOLDOW, GARY F. "Change in the Organization: The Detriment and Benefit of the Double Bind." *Group and Organization Studies* 6 (December 1981): 500–513.

46. STEIN, BARRY A., and ROSEBETH MOSS KANTER. "Building the Parallel Organization: Creating Mechanisms for Permanent Quality of Work Life." *The Journal of Applied Behavioral Science* 16 (1980): 371–388.
47. TANNENBAUM, A. S. *Hierarchy in Organizations,* San Francisco: Jossey-Bass 1974.
48. THORSRUD, E., B. S. SORENSEN, and B. GUSTAVSEN. "Sociotechnical Approach to Industrial Democracy in Norway." In *Handbook of Work, Organization, and Society,* edited by R. Dubin. Chicago: Rand McNally, 1976.
49. TRIST, E. "The Professional Facilitation of Planned Change in Organizations." In *Management and Motivations.* Harmonsworth, Eng.: Penguin, 1968.
50. ———. "Toward a Post Industrial Culture." In *Handbook of Work, Organization, and Society,* edited by R. Dubin. Chicago: Rand McNally, 1976. Pp. 1011–1033.
51. TRIST, E. L., and K. W. BANFORTH. "Some Social and Psychological Consequences of the Long-Wall Method of Coal Getting." *Human Relations* 4 (1951): 3–38.
52. WHYTE, W. F. *Organizational Behavior: Theory and Application.* Homewood, Ill.: Irwin and Dorsey Press, 1969.

Discussion Questions

1. Describe the forces for and against change in organizations.
2. What is the meaning of organizational readiness? How does it relate to previous materials in the book?
3. How does the Norwegian experience illustrate the change process and its likely outcomes?
4. Describe the key elements of a successful organizational change. Why are they so important?
5. Discuss the process of change.
6. Discuss the strategies of change. What are the strengths and weaknesses of each? What might be a good overall strategy?
7. How would you analyze the case at the beginning of the chapter in terms of strategy and power?
8. Discuss sustaining change and resistance to change as stemming from the same organizational dynamics.

Chapter 20
The Research Foundations of Organizational Change

Work Smarter, Not Harder

Off in a small vacant office on the executive floor Faust was busily preparing his flip charts. As usual in these things Dr. Faust had prepared the charts himself. In this way they had what he felt to be the necessary look of economy. Assisting him in preparing a "communications package" on this latest study was Penny Scribner. Present as well was Stanley who had been invited to help assist in the "dry run" of the presentation.

"But I guess I still don't get the full meaning of your use of the term *claiming,* Dr. Faust, and why that *doesn't* affect 'standard' production but *does* affect total production. Actually, I *think* I understand but I'm not so sure that I will be able to put it in words that others will understand." The voice was Penny's.

"Then let us go over it again, shall we? Here [pointer tapping] we show standard production in 1976 as estimated by our friends, Banfield Associates. And here is our current 1979 production. Again as a percentage of standard. The difference is about 20 percent, to the good, of course. Now what do we mean by standard production? We mean the number of units produced compared to the number of units calculated to constitute 100 percent of standard—*after* [pointer aimed at Penny] the standard allowances made for claims for machine downtime, substandard materials, and various other allowances."

Faust uncovered the next flip chart. "And here is a quarterly chart of progress." Dr. Faust traced a red line progressing steadily upward from left to right. "According to our records progress has been steady, improving quarter by quarter, so that to date we are at very nearly 90 percent of standard production.

"Now what might account for this progress?

"The most obvious answer is increased production as a result of improved procedures. As they say, ah . . ."

"Work smarter not harder," Penny supplied the slogan.

"Yes, exactly. And this, of course, is what we should like to believe. Yet unfortunately there are other plausible explanations. There are data indicating that the number of hours *claimed* is going up as well. In itself this is reasonable enough. Both workers and department managers are learning the PIP system and taking advantage of the opportunities it offers for legitimate claims to time allowances. Ah, but once the game is learned well. . . ." Faust paused in thought.

"So just possibly our people *are* learning to work smarter not harder," laughed Penny.

"Well then, Dr. Faust, are you saying that production itself has not gone up? Is that the thrust of your presentation?" Stanley, in his simulated role as critic tried his best to mimic the crisp manner of a Company executive.

"Not necessarily. Although it *is* possible to draw that conclusion, yes. But my point is that we cannot be sure that the *total* production, unlike *productivity*, is up from three years ago."

"Now you've just got me confused again, Dr. Faust," said Penny. "Why *can't* we just look at the production figures? Why won't they tell us?"

"I suppose there is every reason to believe that production figures would tell the story. But such is not the case. You see it is the nature of The Company's business that many different departments make many different products and that these change fairly rapidly over time. So one really can never know, for example, whether fifteen a day of Model X three years ago is more or less than ten a day of Model Y in current production. I realize that it seems to you that these comparisons ought to be possible nonetheless; but the margin of error is sufficiently large as to make the conclusion highly ambiguous. Recall that the inability to make just such comparisons was one of the primary selling points for PIP to begin with."

"But surely, Dr. Faust, from your experience you must have *some* idea of what is taking place here." Acting in his executive role Stanley felt that he had handed out the challenge as Mason might.

With an uncharacteristic chuckle, Faust replied, "Why yes, Mr. Mason, I do. My best guess would be that production has in fact gone up, but not nearly to the extent that the standard productivity figures indicate. Here I am putting my faith in what our department managers have said. Most of them will grudgingly admit that output has increased, though they themselves detest the system."

"Is that really so?" asked Penny. "Why I should think that the PIP system would make things easier for them."

"In some ways yes, but mostly no. You must recognize that quite a price has been paid for this increased productivity. Make no mistake about that." With this Faust flipped to his next chart.

Work departments having PIP in time period

Dr. Faust paused as the group took in the full meaning of the chart. Then, pointer in hand, "From these data it is true beyond question that the PIP program itself has been a major factor in the precipitous decline of work satisfaction in The Company. Comparing our morale measurements taken in 1980 shortly after the inception of the PIP program in some departments, and in 1982 when PIP coverage had been increased considerably, there can be no question about the facts.

"The reasons seem to be several. First of all, contrary to our slogan, the workers report that they are working harder. Second, our people feel that the old emphasis on quality has been abandoned completely. And this, of course, is true to great extent. Part of our educational program is that indeed Good Enough is Best.

"Finally, our people complain that they can no longer get a fair hearing from the department manager. And this also is a direct consequence of PIP. For what can the manager say?"

As Faust talked on, Stanley thought back to one of his first conversations with Jimmy Szekely back at Ben Franklyn's mill. Stanley remembered the conversation well because he had been surprised by Szekely's attitude.

"But don't get me wrong, Stan, it's really pretty good here. Yeah, we do a lot of bitching about management—still, it's not all that bad. After all, you've got to have something to talk about.

"But there are good things, too. This is no assembly line. See, The Company really wants us to do a first-class job. That's what old man Marsh always talked about. He said people in The Company were here because they were the best, that The Company wouldn't hire just anybody, and that he expected the best from us. And he told us that he wasn't disappointed very often and that he was proud of us.

"You know something? I think he really was, 'cause we'd make sure that things looked just right before we sent them on. Look, look here." Jimmy showed Stanley a small machine of unknown function. "Isn't that beautiful? We don't *have* to do that, you know. We could leave them wires all which ways, but it would look terrible. So we won't send it out that way. When she goes out of here you can say to yourself that you're proud of your work." What impressed Stanley was that Jimmy sincerely believed what he was saying.

Stanley was snapped out of his reverie by a sharp question from an irritated Penny, "Right, right, fine. But you *still* haven't answered my first question, Dr. Faust. You said the department *managers* didn't like PIP. Why? You still haven't told me."

"Oh, yes, I did say that. Yes, it is true. Actually there are several reasons. First, it certainly must be evident from what I've shown you that department managers have lost a great deal of their control over the situation. They are presented with new work standards and rules about which they have nothing to say. Then they are held responsible for achieving those standards and enforcing those rules, as well as for the absenteeism that results when the men react badly to them.

"But what can they do? Their role has been changed from one of manager to one of rule enforcer. Their workers know that too. So they've lost control, and with it, status."

"I'm sorry. I still don't see it," said Penny. "How have they lost control? And if they have, who's got it now?"

"Perhaps I should say that they have lost 'discretionary' control. For that's actually what 'management' means. But who has it now?" Faust paused, "No *one* I think.

"As the workers see it the industrial engineer is in control. But we know that such is not the case. For theirs is simply a technical responsibility; set the work standards and determine the method and that is that." Stanley envisioned the spirits of industrial engineers hovering over the jobs on which they set standards.

"So what happens, as I see it," Penny concluded, "is that once that standard is set, the manager can't change it and the industrial engineers won't, so that everything important about the job is covered by the procedures and standards of PIP. And *that's* the problem, isn't it?" Then, thinking to her journalistic duties, Penny posed the crucial question, "Can we say that, though? I mean, isn't that a pretty stiff indictment of the whole PIP setup?"

Here Stanley interceded, "That all depends on how you look at it, doesn't it, Doc? After all, in one sense who cares? I mean, they don't pay dividends on work satisfaction yet, do they?" Here Stanley was only half playing his role of critic and half posing his actual feelings on the subject at hand.

"Who cares? Marsh cares. I believe that Mr. Marsh cares very much, in fact," Faust replied. "I think that Mr. Marsh does not want to lose the good will of his work force, but even more I know he does not want labor trouble. Excellent employee relations has always been one of the great strengths of The Company. No, make no mistake about it, Marsh cares.

"No, Penny, we should, er—how do they say

it—tell it like it is. Marsh's people will take this seriously and they will want to know. PIP is about to bring about fundamental change in employee relations in The Company. I'm quite certain of that."

"O.K., Doc, but you can't just tell 'em that, can you?" Stanley queried. "I mean Marsh's people always want a solution along with the problem, don't they? So what's the solution here? Dump PIP? Oh boy, I want to hear you tell 'em that." Stanley was rubbing his hands together gleefully.

The tone of the question, if that's what it was, did not sit well with Faust. "I fail to see where the humor in this situation might lie, my friend. Yes, they will want a solution. And no, they will *not* want to dump PIP, as you put it. Marsh and his people are far too much committed to the idea now." Faust paused for a moment. And then added, *most* uncharacteristically, "Tell me, my young friend, what would *you* do?"

"Work Smarter, Not Harder" is actually a continuation of three previous vignettes, "His Master's Voice" (Chapter 8), "The One Best Way" (Chapter 17), and "Friendly Persuasion" (Chapter 19). The three together depict the problems associated with developing sufficiently compelling data to make the organization decide to make a substantial change. The situation was this:

- The company had to respond to the new competitive pressure of the marketplace.
- They did so by implementing a work measurement system (PIP) in manufacturing. The decision was based on data from industrial engineers that showed the millhands producing about 65 percent of the expected rate according to the best studies available ("His Master's Voice").
- Then Faust and his group presented data suggesting that PIP caused work satisfaction to go down, but these data were not compelling because they could not in any way "prove" causation. Consequently, management did nothing except sanction further studies ("Friendly Persuasion").
- Ben Franklyn resisted the implementation of PIP in his plant because he "knew" it would cause lower job satisfaction, lower quality, and increase "fudging" of production figures. Franklyn felt that employees would lose commitment because they would feel they had lost control over their job territory ("The One Best Way").
- Although Franklyn was able to resist the onslaught of PIP because of his excellent reputation and strong personality, nothing much would have changed in the plants covered by PIP had not Faust and his group come up with "better" data concerning the program's negative effect and why that was so ("Work Smarter, Not Harder").

Notice that the key elements in the whole process were the beliefs that people had about causation, values concerning appropriate plant management, the relative merits of production versus work satisfaction, and the adequacy of the data that either supported or challenged their beliefs and values. It is this last issue, the adequacy of the data, that we will deal with in this chapter. We hope you will learn two lessons: the requirements of sound causal interpretations and the necessity of research for changing organizations (3,23).

Our plan in this chapter is to introduce you to ways that behavioral scientists have gone about changing organizations, the models underlying these changes, and the technologies that reflect research. We will discuss how data are generated to identify problems, to enable the researcher to diagnose the sources of the problems, and to help the so-called change agent evaluate the consequences of the changes that he or she attempts to bring about. Most change technologies require diagnosing plans for action, and then once actions are taken, evaluating their consequences (15). To do these things one must have knowledge of some basic research concepts. Although change techniques may differ, the data requirements for problem identification, diagnosis, and evaluation are similar. That is, to know what the real problems and their causes are, we need to collect good data and to analyze those data properly. In the next section we will deal with these issues.

Research and Its Importance

Our approach to research encompasses two assumptions. The first is that good managers act in much the same way as scientists whenever a decision is to be made. That is, many decisions rest on the best available evidence, as do hypotheses. The second assumption is that it would be useful for students to understand the sources of knowledge in organizational behavior and the adequacy of such knowledge, which depends on how it was developed.

The scientific method requires empirical observation, that is, scrutinizing the environment with a hard eye on facts. Most scientists undertake this scrutiny with an implicit theory or conceptual framework in mind to avoid being overwhelmed by random data. Nevertheless, at the beginning stages of theory development and programmatic research, the scientist ought to be flexible enough to pursue research avenues suggested by the facts.

Managers behave similarly when faced with problems that require solutions through decision making. We do not claim that managers pursue decision making with the same systematic rigor that scientists pursue their research. Indeed, they base many decisions on convenience, availability of management coalitions to support decisions, impressionistic evidence, and happenstance (21). Still, most good managers, within the constraints of a dynamic environment and the press of organizational forces, try systematically to screen and then order data coming from an environmental scan (22).

The next step in a scientific method requires placing the observed facts into a more systematic framework, making order out of factual chaos as it were.

Managers do the same thing. Once the framework is established, scientists look for systematic variations among variables with an eye toward co-variation and cause-and-effect relationships. That is the beginning of theory construction (5). Managers, too, build theories, though perhaps not so neat and elegant as those of scientists, which enable them to make sense out of situations they have no direct relationship with and to make decisions with a reasonable probability of success.

Some years ago when we worked for "The Company," we observed the situation depicted in the vignette "The One Best Way." Perhaps you wonder how such a situation could occur in a well-managed company. It occurred because of what The Company's upper management believed about organizational behavior. Here were its systematic observations: management typically knew more than nonmanagement about what is best for The Company; technical people knew better than nontechnical people how to look at technical issues; employees are responsive to technical directions; technically justified procedures will be beneficial to the company and so should be implemented. In other words, The Company believed that its interests would be best served by the bureaucratic tenets of rationality, hierarchy of authority, and functional specialization. That is, bureaucratic theory augmented by the related theory of scientific management justified the decision to implement a work measurement program. That reasoning seems correct, does it not?

It did not seem so to Franklyn, for he had another theory based on these observations: people usually know their own jobs better than others know those jobs and feel demeaned when that fact is overlooked; people do not like to be closely monitored by impersonal standards over which they have no control; people find ways of circumventing controls they do not like. Ben's theory would be that programs, regardless of their technical merit and established worth, will not succeed unless the workers have a personal stake in them and feel personally enhanced by making them succeed.

Therefore, we have two views of what should be done. Each is supported by a theory, and neither is wrong or wholly right. Each is also well supported by evidence, facts derived from empirical observations. And each suggests a different course of action or decision. That is our next point. Both scientists and managers use their theories to take action. The scientist's action takes the form of a testable hypothesis; the manager's action is a decision.

Once a hypothesis or decision is made, it must be evaluated. This evaluation ought to be done systematically and empirically. Data collection and analysis are the keys here. Normally the data will determine the wisdom of the hypothesis or decision and suggest whether or not the theory requires modification. Although the processes are not strictly parallel—the scientist seems to require more rigorous proofs and is not constrained by such things as time and profitability—they are close enough that we can apply the scientific method to things apart from science.

Some Pitfalls in Attributing Causality

The attribution of causality is often confounded by errors (1, 4, 6, 10, 15, 16). Things we think to be true are often not and things we know to be false are often true. This is the case even for scientists who may take great pains in developing causal assumptions. There are three primary sources of error associated with causal assumptions: (1) direction of causality, (2) multiple causality, and (3) spurious causal assumptions (4, 5, 6, 19).

Direction of Causality

Frequently we see things in association. They seem co-variant and we assume that one thing caused another without actually witnessing the sequence of events that would allow such an assumption. And because we have not witnessed the sequence we may be wrong in our assumption.

As an example, a series of early studies on the effect of leadership on productivity noted an association between close supervision and low productivity. The researchers assumed that close supervision caused low productivity when, as disclosed some years later, it was really the other way around. Therefore, when we note related elements, we must assess directionality before we assess causality.

Multiple Causality

In social affairs it is rare that only one thing causes another. More often two, three, or more variables are combining, interacting, or acting independently to produce a consequence. Examples abound and you may select your own, but the trick always is to tease out the prime causes.

For instance, the studies of PIP disclosed that the drop in employee satisfaction was attributable to control over job factors, the responsiveness of the grievance channels, the perceptions of equitable pay for increased work expectations, and work pressures—in that order. Yet management, when asked to what they attributed the decline in satisfaction, typically mentioned one of the last two but not the others.

Spurious Causation

Spurious causation or false causation is the most difficult problem to disentangle because it is often the least obvious. It involves attributing cause to one variable because it co-varies with another variable when the only reason for the co-variation of the two is that each is influenced by still another variable. That is, X and Y are correlated and it is clear enough that X came before Y. We assume that X causes Y. On further analysis we find that Z causes the variation of both X and Y and hence when Z varies so do X and Y together, but Z is the only reason for that co-variation.

Let us be more concrete. It is commonly assumed that it can be "too cold to snow." That is, snowfall is geared in some way to the temperature, and when the temperature falls below a certain level it "causes" snow not to fall. The reason for that causal assumption is that often extremely cold weather is associated with clear weather and it is not as likely that snow causes higher temperatures as it is that higher temperatures (still below 32°) caused the snowfall. Actually, during the winter extremely high pressure systems cause clear skies and very low temperatures at the same time. So the temperature (X) co-varies with clear skies (Y) because each is associated with the barometric pressure (Z), which causes each.

Let us look at some organizational research. Some years ago we studied Ben Franklyn's plant to find what his management magic precisely was. We found that in Franklyn's plant productivity was on the rise along with job satisfaction. There was intense debate in corporate circles as to which caused the other, or even if there was a reciprocal causal relation going on—high satisfaction causing high productivity, the productivity in turn raising the levels of satisfaction, and so on. As it turned out, the primary dynamic was that Franklyn had instituted an employee involvement program and a meaningful pay-for-performance system. The two together were the primary "cause" of the increases in performance *and* job satisfaction. And so performance (X) and job satisfaction (Y) co-varied mostly because each was related to the employees' involvement and their sense that the incentives were fair (Z).

Requirements of Proof

Because of the problems we have described, we must be reasonably certain that the evidence we use to solve our problems is sound. The following are requirements for making decent causal assumptions: evidence of co-variation, evidence that one or more of the variables really did preceed the others, and evidence that other variables not under consideration are not the prime causal factors (4, 5, 9, 10). The following study designs deal with these requirements.

Major Study Designs

Although there are many variations, three study designs seem the most prevalent in organizational behavior. They are *cross-sectional, uncontrolled longitudinal,* and *experimental.*

The *cross-sectional* design includes data collected at one point in time and correlation or some variant as its primary analytical statistic. It is cross-sectional because data are collected from a cross-section of groupings that one wants to compare. We have conducted a number of one-time surveys in research and development laboratories and in plants. The units and the samples or populations are compared. Also, we usually have demographic variables such as age, length of service, education, or job classification. Such data enabled us to compare a variety of groups on their questionnaire responses. But since the data were collected at one time, in most cases it was hard to know which co-variant preceeded which.

We knew, for example, that satisfaction with pay was correlated with feelings of work pressure and we could assume in some cases that people who had to work harder would feel that they should be paid more. But we might have assumed that people who did not like their pay would feel they had to work too hard!

In the *uncontrolled longitudinal* study we take measures at two or more periods of time and observe the changes in the measures as well as changes in the situations between the time periods. This design helps to identify direction of causality because it includes at least two points in time. Therefore, if between time 1 and time 2 a work pressure program is installed and satisfaction with salary goes down, then one can assume that the work pressure came first. Furthermore, there are statistical ways of determining direction of causality if we have identical measures of the variables in each time period (4).

However, in an uncontrolled study, spuriousness and other unidentified variables as potentially causal are particularly serious problems. Many things are going on in a dynamic organization that are either unknown or relate to the variables under study in peculiar or unknown ways. The Hawthorne studies are an example of that even though these studies were reasonably well controlled experiments (2). Consequently, although we know the causal sequence better than in the cross-sectional design, the elimination of causality due to variables not under study is difficult and in many cases impossible.

The only design that can give us reasonable certainty that our requirements of proof are mostly fulfilled is the *controlled experiment*. A proper controlled experiment always has a control group that is matched either through random sampling or variable by variable with the experimental group. Without that control group, we have no good way of knowing whether changes have occurred.

Three major kinds of experiments are possible in an ongoing organization. Each has its merits and its weaknesses. They are: the before and after with the experimental group serving as its own control; the after only with one control group; and the before and after with one control group. Several other designs can help with the deficiencies of these three but they are rarely encountered in organizational field research (6). We will not deal with them.

The Before-and-After Experiment with No Separate Control Group

In the first form of the experimental design, you randomly select the experimental group in order to represent the population to which you will make inferences.

You measure the variable under consideration—job satisfaction, perhaps. You introduce your experimental variable, let us say work measurement. Then, after an appropriate period of time, you measure job satisfaction again using the same instrument and under the same conditions. The difference in job satisfaction between time 1 and time 2 is ostensibly the effect of the experimental variable.

There are two primary weaknesses to this before-and-after design; a lot of things happen between the two measurement periods besides the experimental manipulation, e.g. a reduction in workforce, a wage increase, a change in management or in organizational structure. We call these things *concurrent events*. They could have a substantial effect on job satisfaction independently or in interaction with each other or with the experimental variable. You cannot tell the extent of such an effect from the before-and-after design with the experimental group serving as its own control.

A second major problem with that design is that the measurement itself may affect the results (1, 7, 10, 11). This is called the premeasure effect. It may sensitize people to issues they had not thought important, or they might be susceptible to a Hawthorne effect independent of the experimental variable.

The After-Only Experiment with One Control Group

In the after-only design you use two randomly selected or otherwise matched groups, only one of which is given the experimental treatment. Then, after an appropriate time, you compare the two groups on the variables of interest. Since both groups have been exposed to concurrent events and since neither has been measured before on the variable of interest, you can assume that any differences are due to the experimental variable. This design is a good one, but it has one major drawback: you can be only reasonably sure, never completely, that the groups were really equivalent before you introduced the experimental variable. That problem was pointed out by Bolt when he criticized the initial data disclosing the negative effect of PIP. You also cannot be sure of the independent effects of the experiment not interacting with concurrent events or of the concurrent events by themselves (1, 10).

Before-and-After with One Control Group

The design that helps best with the problems inherent in the previous designs incorporates the best of each (6). Here we take measures before and after in both the experimental and control group. To simplify, let us use the following notations:

E^1 = the before measure in the experimental group
E^2 = the after measure in the experimental group
C^1 = the before measure in the control group
C^2 = the after measure in the control group

- The design allows us to see if the groups were comparable to begin with ($E^1 = C^1$).
- We can determine the effect of concurrent events by calculating $C^1 - C^2$ although the result may be contaminated by the premeasure effect.
- We can determine the effect of concurrent events in conjunction with the experimental effect by calculating $E^1 - E^2$, although again the premeasure effect may be present.
- We can determine the effect of the experiment with minimal contamination by concurrent events and the premeasure by subtracting ($C^1 - C^2$) from ($E^1 - E^2$). This difference provides a fairly pure measure of the effect of the experimental treatment (6).

Of course, you may expand this design to include one other postmeasure but not premeasure control group in order to get an idea of the potency of concurrent events alone (6). Or you can vary it by not premeasuring the experimental group to extract the effect of the premeasure. However, the problems associated with such variations seem to preclude their common use.

AN ILLUSTRATION. Let us go back to the vignette in the previous chapter to see the importance of proven research methods as they may apply to organizational change. The first data about PIP that Faust presented to the corporate staff was a cross-sectional design, although it had elements of an experimental after-only design. That is, it was not truly experimental because neither of the groups was randomly selected, nor were they matched. The comparison was between PIP and non-PIP departments, with the PIP departments having much lower satisfaction. But because the study was cross-sectional we could not rule out the alternative explanations suggested by Bolt, including the possible spuriousness of PIP's introduction and lower satisfaction being caused by the lower skill of those initally covered by PIP. And since we had no before measure who could really tell?

To correct that deficiency, data were collected again about ten months later. In the interim, many departments became covered by PIP, others remained covered, and still others were not covered at all. Consequently, Faust could compare the differences between the two times for the departments covered in both years (control group), those covered in neither year (control group), and those not covered in the first year but covered in the second (experimental group). The fact that satisfaction declined in the experimental group but not in the two control groups pretty well ruled out the alternative explanations as to the causal effect of PIP.

The study did not stop there. Once satisfied that PIP "caused" lower work satisfaction and that low work satisfaction is not an inevitable result of pressures for higher production (remember the comparison to Ben Franklyn's plant) management was greatly concerned about the aspect of PIP that was the major causal culprit. Consequently, additional studies were performed including a well-controlled field experiment that helped to justify a major organizational change. And without the reasonable certainty as to cause that was provided by those studies it was unlikely that management would have had that justification, particularly since PIP's effect on performance was undeniably positive.

Some Major Data Collection Techniques

There are three major classifications of data that interest us. They are behavioral, cognitive, and affective. *Behavioral* data are simply objective behaviors objectively recorded. Productivity, absenteeism, and turnover are examples of such things. In most cases such events are already part of the record, and measures of them may be taken from those records with reasonable confidence that they are accurate (20).

Cognitive and affective measures present greater difficulties for they can be recorded only through some subjective response. *Cognitive* factors are what you perceive to be true, what you know. *Affective* factors are what you feel—your values and attitudes. Both cognitive and affective factors are measured indirectly through people's responses and are consequently subject to potential ambiguity or distortion. How do you deal with those problems?

Three primary methods are used to gain information about perceptions, attitudes, and values: attitude surveys, interviews, and working with the group targeted for change. Three criteria can be used to show the strengths and weaknesses of each method. The first criterion is commonly called *reliability*. If we were to ask the same questions at a different time or use different people to gather and analyze the data, would the results be similar in similar circumstances? For example, suppose we were interested in job satisfaction, and we asked a series of questions at time 1 that we thought measured the dimensions of job satisfaction. If the measurements were reliable, we would expect to get the same responses to those questions at time 2, if nothing had changed in the interim. If the results were largely similar, we would say that our measurements were reliable. If they were not similar, then either the questions were unreliable, or the situation had changed enough to produce different results.

A second criterion concerns the extent to which the data reflect reality or measure what they are supposed to measure. This criterion is called *validity*. Suppose, for example, we were trying to measure salary levels in an organization. We might ask people to tell us what their salary is. If their responses checked out against actual salary data, then we would say that our data were valid.

It is difficult to deal with the validity question using the data-gathering techniques we have described (18). We are asking for perceptions or reflections of feelings, and frequently the responses do not match what we know is actually the case. This does not mean, however, that the measurements of perceptions are not valid—only that perceptions and reality are different. If perceptions are at the heart of whatever other problems are occurring in an organization, then we need to deal with those perceptions. Finally, data cannot be valid unless they are reliable.

The third criterion, data *richness,* concerns the complexity of the data themselves and the extent to which they reflect subtleties and nuances in meaning. Richness is difficult to measure if responses to questions are the sole means of measurement. An expression, a wave of hand, a turn of a phrase, a way of asking a question all may have important meaning for any given interaction. Yet how can such things become part of the data bank of casual observers? They can not usually, and that presents problems for the data collectors. Let us look now at the major means of data collection.

Attitude Surveys

A common way of collecting data to measure perceptions, attitudes, and values is through attitude questionnaires. These questionnaires may include items designed to measure different aspects of the work situation. Typically, several items are used to measure each dimension of interest so that the reliability of the index for that dimension is increased. For example, suppose we wanted to measure the challenge that a particular subgroup saw in its job. We might ask one question: "How challenging do you find your job?" Then later in the questionnaire we might ask, "To what extent would you agree that your job was challenging?"

Attitude surveys often cover many variables, and are administered to many people at the same time, but they should be administered under the same conditions. Consequently, well-constructed attitude surveys can be reliable and, if properly constructed by people thoroughly knowledgeable of the situation, reasonably valid as well. However, attitude surveys are usually not very rich. Questions are highly structured and specific. Consequently, the questions force people into certain responses that do not reflect contingencies, special circumstances, or fine degrees of difference. Nevertheless, because attitude surveys can cover a lot of ground quickly, cheaply, and anonymously, they are frequently used to measure attitudes, values, and perceptions. Furthermore, well-constructed attitude surveys have *face validity* to management, that is, the items can be easily understood—they make sense—and they provide objective measures to which numerical values can be ascribed—something management can deal with comfortably.

Interviews

Interviews involve one or more persons, preferably well-trained interviewers asking questions of another person, or in some cases a group of people. The interviews can be highly structured—indeed, as highly structured as an attitude questionnaire—or they can be completely unstructured. In the latter case, an interviewer might simply ask as an initial question, "Well, how are things going?" A skilled interviewer can then let the interview develop freely and come out at the end with some very rich data.

However, there are significant problems with the interview method. It is expensive and typically cannot cover as much ground as an attitude survey. At best it takes one interviewer per small group of people, and if the interviews are well conducted, each can take a great deal of time. Furthermore, interviews are not anonymous. The best you can offer is confidentiality—an offer that may or may not be acceptable to the interviewee. Finally, the data are subject to substantial error. That is, the kinds of questions asked, the rapport established, and the data extracted from the protocols can be subject to the personal idiosyncracies of the interviewers—even well-trained interviewers. Hence, a problem of reliability and validity exists.

Group-Generated Data

Group-generated data are typically used by people engaged in intergroup or intragroup change methods. Problems should have been identified already from a different data set, and the decision should have been made that the groups should get together to work through the problems. The data generated within the group, then, should elaborate problems, identify their causes, and, through periods of intensive interaction, develop solutions to them.

There are many ways of generating data in such groups. Most commonly the group leader identifies a general problem and then asks the group to "fill in." As an illustration let us examine the *nominal group technique* (8). There are six steps to this process. The first involves the "silent generation of ideas in writing," wherein group members are supposed to write key ideas "silently" and independently. The second step is "the round robin recording of ideas," wherein the leader goes around the group and requests that each member submit an idea. These ideas are then recorded on a flip chart or blackboard for all to see. The third step, "discussion for clarification," has the group discussing each idea. The list of ideas is first edited for redundancy. The fourth step involves "a preliminary vote on item importance." The group is asked to select from the entire list of ideas certain priority items. From this vote a preliminary list of these items is drawn. After that is the fifth step, wherein there is a discussion of the preliminary vote to ensure that the priority rankings really reflect group consensus. The sixth step involves a final vote.

In this way the data are generated solely from the group, and the key problem areas are identified through group consensus. A similar sequence of steps can identify solutions to the problems as well. The point, of course, is that most of the data pertinent to the group's problems are generated by the group, which can then work on the process of change.

This method of data collection can produce rich data, particularly with a skillful group leader, and data from the group will have face validity for that group since it created the data in the first place. Consequently, the reasons for change will have more substance than if an outsider gathered the data through, let us say, an attitude survey. As a general data collection technique, however, the method suffers from problems similar to those of the interview method.

Checking for Reliability and Validity

Although the professional competence of the people designing and applying the measuring instrument is the best assurance of reliability and validity, here are two questions to ask. (1) Is there a reliability coefficient of approximately 0.80 or above? That is, either through correlating items that ostensibly measure the same thing or by repeating the measurement at a later time and then correlating the results, the two sets of measurements should correlate at the 0.80 level or better. (2) Is there a validity coefficient of about 0.40 or better? That is, does the measure you are using correlate at least 0.40 with some other independent measure of that variable?

As an example, take the Scholastic Aptitude Test (SAT) or the American College Test (ACT) that you may have taken in high school. Such tests are supposed to predict collegiate achievement because they are supposed to measure your aptitude for college work. Each has gone through extensive reliability tests, and each has a reliability coefficient of 0.90 or better. Furthermore, each of the tests has been correlated with measures of collegiate success such as the grade point average, frequency of graduation, and attendance at graduate and professional schools. Normally, the validity coefficients are around fifty and sometimes better. Furthermore, each has been *cross-validated:* similar correlations have been produced across a variety of populations, such as make, female, rural, urban, public schools, private schools. Hence, despite their inperfections, we can conclude that the two tests are reliable and valid.

A Strategy for Data Collection

Because all of the methods described have strengths and weaknesses, it has been our experience that a combination of these methods produces the best total data set. For example, a strategy may include the following steps (shown in Figure 20.1):

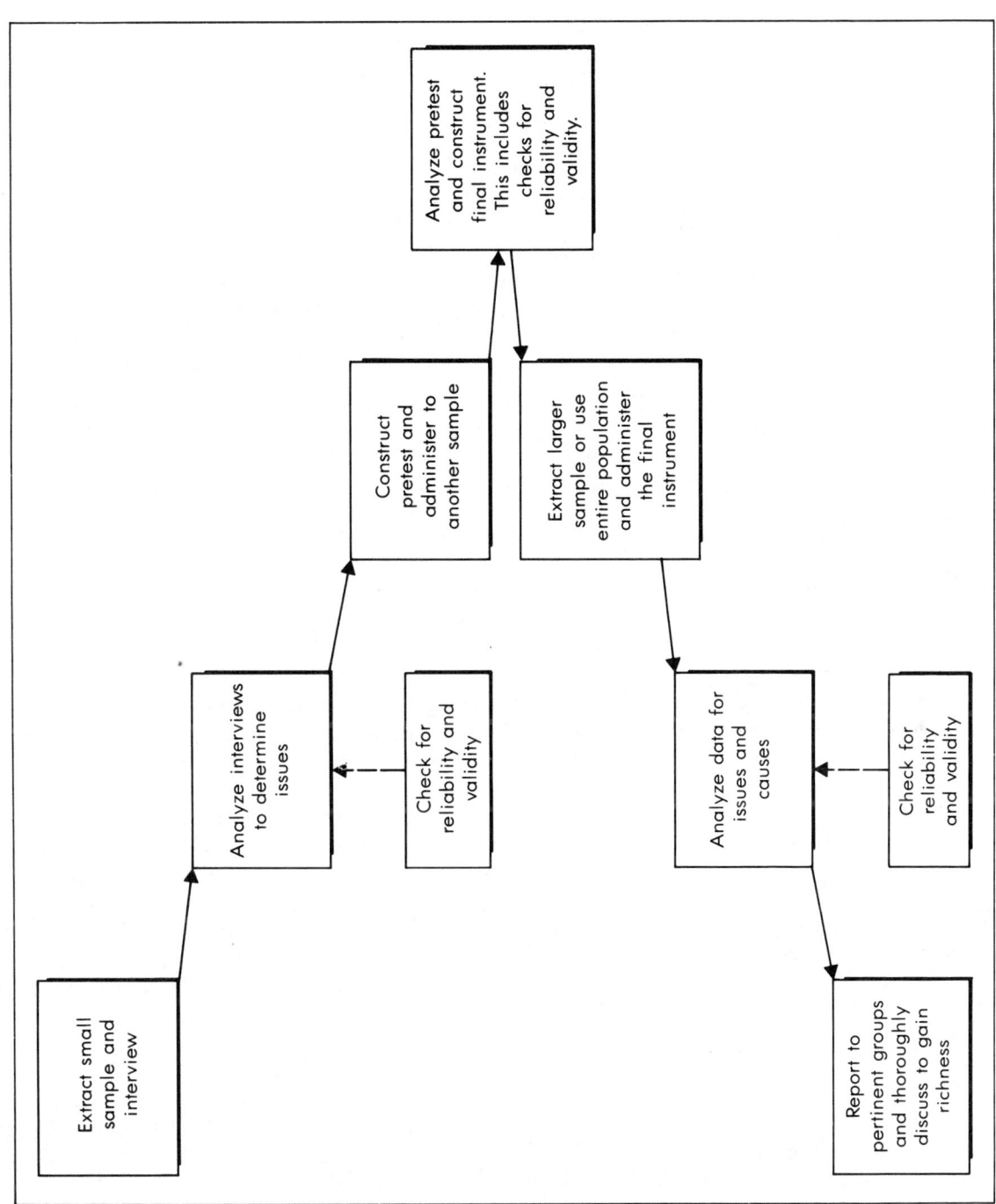

FIGURE 20.1   A Strategy for Data Collection

1. Extract a small sample from a target population.
2. Interview this sample to identify a possible array of problems. Analyze the interviews and extract common issues. Check reliability and validity.
3. For the common issues, construct question items to be used in an attitude survey.
4. Extract another small sample and pretest the instrument. The pretest itself will help determine the reliability and validity of the instrument if the appropriate analyses are conducted.
5. Administer the questionnaire and analyze the data; at this point reliability and validity of the instrumentation must be determined to meet acceptable levels; then the work groups themselves can be convened and the data discussed. At that time, the group-generated data method can be incorporated.

Action Research: Theory to Practice

Let us now apply these observations in a systematic way to organizations. Organizations are continually beset with problems or at the least the necessity of changing in response to changing environmental demands. Many of these problems are solved on an ad-hoc basis; however, many require more extensive analysis. The total process is contained in what has been called the *action research model* (13–15). The model is shown in Figure 20.2.

Notice the similarity of the action research model to the model of change in the previous chapter. Notice, too, that sound data collection and analysis, action, and then appropriate evaluation of action are requirements of the model. Furthermore, the model requires collaboration among several organizational groups; at the least, key management, those involved with the change, and those responsible for collecting the data.

Let us briefly run through the PIP experience to illustrate what we mean. PIP was a response to competitive pressures. However, a number of people in the organization felt that PIP might cause some industrial relations problems. Consequently, two behavioral scientists were hired by The Company to examine the effect of PIP on the affective variables. These two proceeded to collect data in the following manner: first they conducted several interviews in one of the two plants that initially had agreed to introduce PIP. These interviews were thoroughly analyzed and enough job dissatisfaction was disclosed to warrant broadening the studies.

The second step was to construct a pretest of a large questionnaire. The pretest was constructed to permit reliability checks and to get an idea of the face validity of the questionnaire items. The face validity was determined by asking those selected for the pretesting questions about how well the questionnaire items measured the variables of interest such as work pressures, the adequacy of the grievance procedures, and job satisfaction. Furthermore,

Some Major Data Collection Techniques

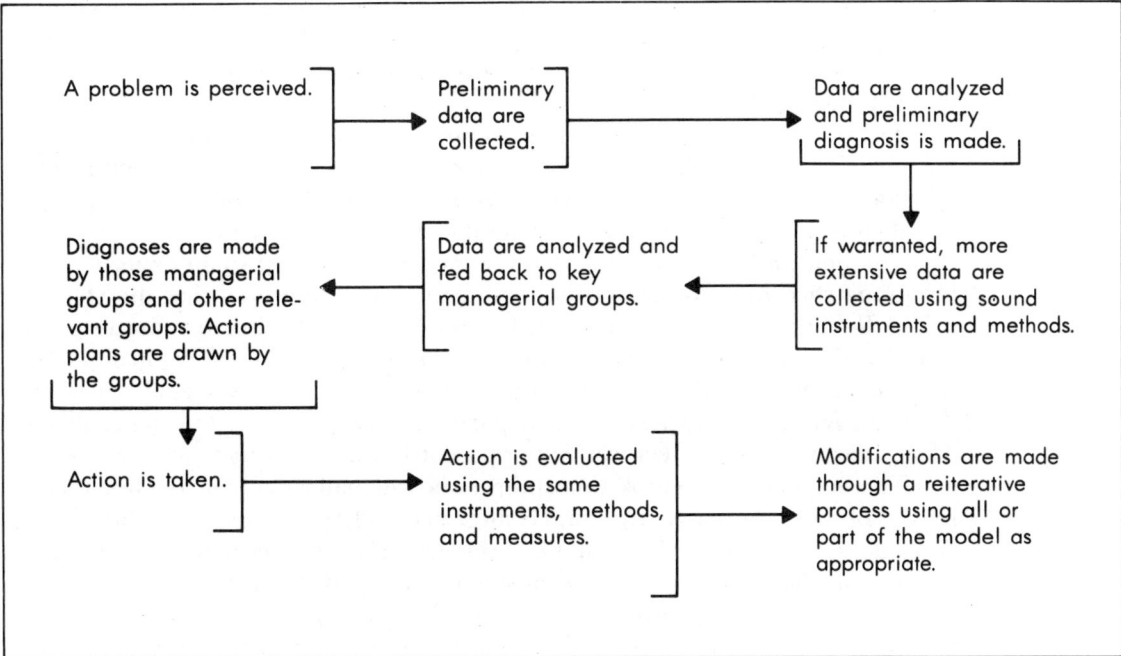

FIGURE 20.2 Action Research Model

preliminary analyses were conducted to see whether or not the departments subjected to PIP felt more work pressures and reported accurately what had happened to them under PIP.

The questionnaire was modified accordingly and administered to a stratified random sample of one third of all the departments in the manufacturing facility. These data were analyzed and the appropriate comparisons were made between the departments covered by PIP and those not covered.

As depicted in "Friendly Persuasion" the data were fed back to the appropriate management groups and the decision was made that although compelling, the data were not conclusive and that PIP should continue as originally conceived. However, everyone felt that more studies were needed to continue the evaluation process.

The next series of studies were able to incorporate a before-and-after study design with two control groups. These data were far more conclusive than the previous ones because of the superior research design and seemed to warrant changes in the PIP implementation. Some of the story was described in "Work Smarter not Harder." Still another impetus for changing PIP came from information from one of the plants that job satisfaction was so low that something needed to be done fairly quickly. Consequently, the industrial engineers and the behavioral scientists together became responsible for developing a way to change the direction of employee job satisfaction and still not lose the benefits that PIP provided.

The two groups worked together to come up with a mechanism that changed the basic structure of PIP. Supervisors were to be permitted to take employees off standard when they complained about its fairness. A thorough investigation was then to be conducted to determine the standard's fairness.

The new method (experimental treatment) was applied to an experimental group matched by a control group. The experiment indicated that the change halted the slide in employee work satisfaction. Work satisfaction increased significantly in the experimental group but only marginally in the control group. Detailed data analyses also disclosed that the results were most beneficial when the managers of the experimental departments were new to the department. That "new manager" effect was not apparent in the control group.

This action research took almost three and one-half years from the beginning to end. Because the major structural change in the PIP program proved beneficial and had no negative effect on performance, PIP was modified accordingly throughout the company and job satisfaction stopped its slide.

The sequence conforms almost point by point with our action research model. A problem was disclosed through research. The data were collected, analyzed, and fed back to key management groups throughout the process. Pertinent organizational units collaborated to produce changes, which were evaluated and modified as warranted. We conclude that by conforming to the guidelines of the model, changes are likely to proceed at an appropriate pace, provide opportunities for modifications of the change, and ultimately to produce more successful and lasting change efforts.

Summary

In this chapter we concentrated on data-based justifications for organizational change. We emphasized the need for sound data, for without it the need for change would not be well grounded. We suggested too that the process of gathering data for scientific purposes was similar to that for a lot of decision making, and hence managers often use a rudimentary scientific method before making decisions and then for evaluating the efficacy of those decisions.

We focused on the problems associated with causal inferences. To make such inferences fairly certainly one must have evidence of variable co-variation, a sequence of such variation, and the elimination of alternative explanations to the hypothesized causal relationships. Furthermore, we suggested that confidence in any causal inference depends on the means of data collection or study design; the most rigorous is some variant of a controlled experiment using means and measurements that are acceptably reliable and valid. The criterion of data richness is also important to the process of developing appropriate causal interpretations.

Incorporating those ideas as they apply to organizational change, we described a model of action research. The model emphasizes the need for front-end data collection, feedback of the data to key management groupings, joint diagnosis of the problems and of the intended actions, and evaluation of such actions using sound study designs.

Of course many organizational changes take place without the systematic and rigorous procedures we described. Yet the currently popular idea of strategic management normally encompasses much of the action research model. Data are collected, forecasts are based on those data, objectives are developed, required resources are hypothesized and plans are made, actions are taken and then evaluated, modifications emerge, additional actions are taken, and so forth. And the strategy is typically only as sound as the data and causal assumptions embedded in it. Hence, at any level in the organization it seems wise to conform to the basic scientific method and research processes that we have described.

The next two chapters incorporate many of the ideas that we have developed in the previous chapter and in this one. We will describe possible organizational changes as they pertain to interactions, motivation, and organizational control.

References

1. ARMENAKIS, A. A., and ROBERT W. ZMUD. "Interpreting the Measurement of Change in Organizational Research." *Personnel Psychology* 32 (1979): 709–723.
2. BARTLEM, CARLETON S., and EDWIN A. LOCKE. "The Coch and French Study: A Critique and Reinterpretation." *Human Relations* 34 (1981): 555–566.
3. BHATTACHARYYA, S. K. "Making Organizational Design Changes Effective: An Approach Based on Indian Experience." *Group and Organization Studies* 5 (1980): 418–437.
4. BLALOCK, HUBERT M., JR. *Causal Inferences in Nonexperimental Research.* Chapel Hill: University of North Carolina Press, 1964.
5. BROWN, R. *Explanation in Social Science.* Chicago: Aldine, 1963.
6. CAMPBELL, D. T., and J. C. STANLEY. "Experimental and Quasi-Experimental Designs for Research on Teaching." In *Handbook of Research on Teaching,* edited by N. L. Gage. Chicago: Rand McNally, 1963. Pp. 171–246.
7. CORMALL, COLIN A. "The Evaluation of Work Organization Change." *Human Relations* 33 (1980): 885–916.
8. DELBECQ, A. L., A. H. VAN DE VEN, and D. H. GUSTUFSON. *Group Techniques for Program Planning.* Glennview, Ill.: Scott, Foresman, 1975.
9. GLOCK, CHARLES Y., ed. *Survey Research in the Social Sciences.* New York: Russell Sage Foundation, 1967.

10. GOLEMBIEWSKI, R. T., K. BILLINGSLEY, and S. YEAGER. "Measuring Change and Persistance in Human Affairs." *Journal of Applied Behavior Science* 12 (1976): 133–157.
11. GOLEMBIEWSKI, ROBERT T., and KEITH R. BILLINGSLEY. "Measuring Change in OD Panel Designs: A Response to Critics." *Academy of Management Review* 5 (1980): 97–103.
12. GREENHALGH, LEONARD. "Maintaining Organizational Effectiveness During Organizational Retrenchment." *The Journal of Applied Behavioral Science* 18 (1982): 155–170.
13. MOORE, MICHAEL L. "Assessing Organizational Planning and Teamwork: An Action Research Methodology." *Journal of Applied Behavioral Science* 14 (1978): 479–491.
14. NICHOLAS, JOHN M. "Evaluation Research in Organizational Change Interventions: Considerations and Some Suggestions." *The Journal of Applied Behavioral Science* 15 (1979): 23–40.
15. RANDOLPH, W. ALAN. "Planned Organizational Change and Its Measurement," *Personnel Psychology* 35 (1982): 117–139.
16. RANDOLPH, W. A., and R. G. EDWARDS. "Assessment of Alpha, Beta, and Gamma Changes in a University-Setting OD Intervention." *Academy of Management Proceedings* (1978): 313–317.
17. ROBERTS, NANCY, and JERRY I. PORRAS. "Progress in OD Research." *Group and Organization Studies* 7 (1982): 91–116.
18. SCHMIDT, FRANK, JOHN E. HUNTER, and KENNETH PEARLMAN. "Progress in Validity Generalization: Comments on Callender and Osburn and Further Developments." *Journal of Applied Psychology* 67 (1982): 835–845.
19. SIDMAN, MURRAY. *Tactics of Scientific Research: Evaluating Experimental Data in Psychology.* New York: Basic Books, 1960.
20. WEBB, EUGENE J., DONALD T. CAMPBELL, RICHARD D. SCHWARTZ, and LEE SECHREST. *Unobtrusive Measures: Nonreactive Research in the Social Sciences.* Chicago: Rand McNally, 1966.
21. WEICK, K. *The Social Psychology of Organizing,* 2nd ed. Reading, Mass.: Addison Wesley, 1979.
22. WILLIAMS, T. A. "The Search Conference in Active Adaptive Planning." *The Journal of Applied Behavioral Science* 15 (1979): 470–483.
23. ZMUD, R. W., and A. A. ARMENAKIS. "Understanding the Measurement of Change." *Academy of Management Review* 3 (1978): 661–669.

Discussion Questions

1. Why will The Company *not* dump PIP? Use the research ideas developed in this chapter to help your answer.
2. In what ways are the scientific method and managerial decision making similar? In what ways are they not?
3. What are the most important pitfalls in attributing causality? Give an example of each along with an explanation.

4. Describe each of the major study designs. Explain the strengths and weaknesses of each.
5. What are the three major criteria against which data adequacy are measured? What means of data collection best meets each of the criteria? Why?
6. How does the action research model compare to the model of change in the previous chapter? In what ways does it not? Would you use an action research model as part of the planning of change or as part of the process, or both?

Chapter 21
Changing Interaction Patterns for Organizational Improvement

I'm Okay, You're Okay

"And *that* is the most blatant piece of self-congratulatory nonsense that I have heard in all my born years, Bo." The voice was Penny's and the Bo she was addressing was Milton Mason. As the oldest of seven children, Mason had been called simply "brother," and this had been corrupted to Bo by the remaining youngsters. Mason, at the time, was assistant plant manager.

Plant manager! Then what in the world was Penny doing addressing him that way? What she was doing was participating in a training group, or T-group, as it is called. This T-group was constituted as a "family" group—it was composed of people working in related functional "families" at Pawtucket. In addition to Penny and Mason, there were Ted, Ben, Kerry, Stanley, Pat, and a few others.

And what is a T-group? Well, perhaps the best way to find that out is to listen. Let's go back to the first day the group was in session. Sunday evening the participants had driven the four hours it took to reach an isolated estate perched atop a mountain. Actually, it wasn't an estate any longer because the owner had bequeathed it to The University. Now it was used for various kinds of executive development sessions by The Company and others. Most thought it ideal, for here they were removed completely from the day-to-day concerns of professional existence; they were inaccessible except by way of a long road that wound back and forth up the mountainside and ended just inside a large gate.

Oh yes, the T-group.

Sunday evening there had been a "kickoff" session in which Jim Leland, the "trainer," had explained their purpose. "What we have here is a situation to help each of us learn about our own behavior. I assume that we will be learning how groups behave by observing how we do as members of this group."

Following this brief introduction, Jim went on to discuss some principles of group problem solving, but added nothing more as to the procedures the group would follow. Then they adjourned for the evening.

Monday morning the group gathered at eight. "Hal and I don't have any agenda for you folks. Fact is, we're not going to say much at all," Jim began. "You'll just have to decide among yourselves how you want to use your time here." Now that was quite a bit of time. A whole workweek plus Saturday morning.

Silence.

More silence.

Then, "Look, we are all busy people here. I propose we elect a committee to work out an agenda for the group," Ted continued in his most sincere/concerned tone. "We just can't afford to sit on our hands all day.

"How does that strike you, Mr. Mason . . . uh . . . Bo?" All group members had been instructed to wear informal attire and use first names. But that practice came hard to Ted.

"Why yes, that does seem reasonable under these circumstances, Ted." Mason's reply was not especially enthusiastic.

"Notice that Ted seems to feel it necessary to get Bo's approval, people. Why is this?" The trainer posed the question for the group.

But Ted chose to ignore the question of his behavior, replying, "Jim, believe me, if you've got a better suggestion, let's have it. We're busy folks and if we're here to build an understanding of group process and not to waste time, let's get at it.

"All in favor of electing an agenda committee, so indicate by raising hands," said Ted. With some hesitation, the majority of hands went up.

"Looks like we've got outselves a committee," observed Stanley quizzically.

"Committee for what, for God's sakes," shot back Ben. "I didn't vote for any damned committee. From what I see, I'm not so sure that most of the rest of us don't want it, either. Looks like we're just going along with Bo and Ted out of force of habit. But as I get the drift of what we're doing here, that's just what we're *not* supposed to do!"

"But Mr. . . . Ben, if we don't get some structure here, how are we going to accomplish anything at all?" puzzled Stanley.

"Damned if I know and damned if I really care. Let's see what happens. Ted's got enough damnfool ideas for all of us most of the time, anyway." Ben's forthrightness was unusual for that stage of group development, but then Ben himself was unusual. Mostly, the people in the group were trying to discover what they were *supposed* to do and to arrive at an agreed-on way for doing it.

The day ended in complete confusion. Yet, as they discussed the day's events with the trainer, he seemed unconcerned, though he did have a question for them: Why were they all so jumpy? Why were they so intent on working out a structure? What was it they thought structure would help them accomplish?

The second day started out very much the same as the first. Ted now proposed that they form a committee to develop some group goals. The group had spent nearly an hour discussing the pros and cons of this suggestion when Hal, the assistant trainer, interrupted. After getting their attention he paused, silent for nearly 30 seconds—though it seemed like an eternity to the group. Then he spoke slowly and deliberately, "Do you people understand why you are spending so much time insisting on some logical, rational procedure? Is it possible that this is a way that all of us can avoid talking about *us*, of avoiding having to deal with our *feelings?*"

Nonetheless it was becoming clear that frustrations were starting to mount. With the issue of an agenda dead, what was there to take its place? In one instance, Kerry launched into a lengthy monologue about his Korean stint in the Navy. His story seemed to have no beginning, and no end, yet it did fill the vacuum created by the lack of agenda. For his part, Hal, the assistant trainer, continued to urge the group to focus on their own behavior, on their own feelings for one another.

Another result of the frustration was a mounting tension that led to sharp exchanges. It was at this point that the opening exchange between Penny and Bo Mason took place. The occasion had been Bo's casual attempt at humor concerning his belief about the appropriate role of women in the cosmic scheme of things. So the group was getting underway. By the end of the second day, they had begun to focus—for better or worse—on their reactions to one another as people.

The third day's meeting started with Hal presenting the group with a suggestion that they enter into competition with one of the other T-groups. The idea would be to see which group could work up the most creative exhibit from the everyday materials available in the conference room. At day's end, a panel would be appointed from group and staff members to pick the winner.

The group decided to take the challenge. But how to proceed was another matter. There was a great deal of discussion back and forth, with the only concrete suggestion coming from Ben. "I'm going to make myself available for whatever we decide to do," said Ben. "But I warn you, I'm not going to be much good to you. Don't think there's an artistic bone in my body."

"Why maybe this is your chance to find out, Ben," laughed Kerry. "Seems to me that you're the guy we usually count on when the going gets tough."

More small talk followed, during which it was agreed upon that Bo would be "in charge," and Penny, who "*should* know something about communications," would be responsible for execution. The group was in consensus that after their earlier exchange, perhaps working together as an executive committee would help Bo and Penny learn more about one another. Each of the remaining group members took on various tasks of planning, fabrication, or criticism.

As they set to work, it became evident that somehow Ted had counted himself in as part of the executive committee. He was full of suggestions and comments about the work of the others. Nonetheless, despite the disruptive influence, the group finished its task on schedule and felt quite pleased with the results of their efforts. Understandably then, it came as quite a blow when the panel of judges decided for the other group. In fact, the group members were surprised at how deeply disappointed they were. Especially Penny.

Then Ted spoke up, precisely at the wrong time. "The problem is that we just piddled around too long. If we'd just got going with some organization, we'd have won. I'm sure of it."

"That reminds me of something I've been meaning to ask you, Ted. Who invited you in as part of the committee, anyway?" said Kerry in an unmistakably hostile tone. "It seems to me that you're always trying to tell us what to do, but never willing to do it yourself."

"Now that's not just true, Kerry," Ted's tone was one of righteous indignation.

"Baloney, Ted. Everyone in this group sees it," Mason continued. "We're here to learn to work as a group, not as a bunch of individuals." Mason was really getting into his role as a group member. "You know, I think you might want to ask yourself why you're always doing this."

This last really shook Ted, because Bo was still *Mr.* Mason to him.

"Yeah, it seems that you're always taking advantage of what the people below you do and then sucking up to the people above you," Stanley put in. "You're always trying to put yourself in the position of telling other people how to do things I don't think you know how to do yourself. What are you trying to cover up?"

Now Ted was angry. "Who asked *you*, Stanley? What in the devil would you know about *leadership?*"

"Well, just a minute there, Ted," Kerry shot back. "That's not the question here. We're talking about your behavior as a member of this group, not what Stan knows or doesn't know about leadership. And I think Stanley's right on target about your behavior toward this group."

With that, the other group members joined in a chorus of critical observation focused directly on Ted's behavior.

Then it happened. Bo Mason had just finished a particularly incisive comment. But this time Ted did not reply in anger. Quite the contrary. He said nothing, but was visibly making an heroic effort to pull himself together—and not succeeding. Tears brimmed in his eyes and his hands trembled. When he spoke, it was in a small hollow voice. "I don't see why everyone is after me. The only thing I've ever tried to do is what I thought to be best for The Company."

"Not true, Ted. Ask anyone," Penny cut in. "It's always what's best for you."

"No, no. I don't see how you can say that. I . . . I just don't see. I've given up my weekends and evenings when I had to, just to get a job done on schedule. . . ."

"So you'd be in line for the next promotion, you mean," Penny was relentless.

"But what's wrong with that?" pleaded Ted. "Isn't that what we are all here for? To take on as much responsibility as we can?"

And now, speaking to no one in particular, "But I know that you've never liked me and that's just not fair. Have I ever hurt any one of you? Fact is that I've always tried to help when I can."

"Yes, I think you have, Ted," Ben's voice was surprisingly soft. "You know, people, I think Ted's right in a way. I admit that I've always looked at Ted's harebrained schemes as something only for himself. But maybe I haven't been completely fair in that." A long silence followed, then Ben continued. "But maybe you've been wrong, too, Ted. You know, a lot of people *do* like you and they *do* feel they can count on you. It's just . . ."

Ben stopped because Ted now was visibly sobbing, head in arms folded atop the table.

"It's just that you seem always so anxious to please, to be just perfect," Penny continued. "Like sometimes you don't seem to be very *human*. There's . . . there's no way to get through to the real you, it seems. No feelings. Just an image, a veneer. You know, I think today's the first time that we've seen that you do feel."

Later that day, Hal, the assistant trainer, and Jim Leland met to recap the day's sessions. "How'd it go today, Hal?"

"Great, just great, Jim. We had some real self-discovery. One fellow, Ted Shelby, made some real progress."

Our story describes one method of changing interaction patterns that, among other things, is supposed to alert people to the effect of interpersonal interactions on group members. As you will see later, this method has led to others, the purpose of which includes changing behavior because of increased interpersonal sensitivity. In turn, the changes in behavior are supposed to improve interpersonal effectiveness.

Our plan in this chapter is to introduce you to ways that behavioral scientists have gone about changing interaction systems, the models underlying these changes, and the technologies that reflect the knowledge disclosed by research. We want to provide you with some general models for changing interaction systems that can be applied to a wide range of techniques.[1] To do this, we will focus on changing interactions to build better work teams, to manage intergroup conflict, and to make hierarchical relationships more productive for the organization. For the most part, we will avoid describing specific techniques, since at this time little compelling evidence differentiates one from another in terms of effectiveness (45, 47). Exceptions to this statement will be given later in the chapter.

Why Interaction Patterns Should Be Changed

The fact that changing interaction patterns is a continuing interest to both researchers and practitioners raises certain questions. Why should organizations want to change interaction patterns? How do organizations go about changing these patterns? We will deal with the first of these questions in this section and the second in the next section.

There are five general problem areas that often warrant changing interaction patterns. These are listed in Table 21.1. First, remember that the organizational structure and the exercise of power through this structure creates certain problems. Subordinates learn soon enough that they must approach superiors with some caution (53)—for superior–subordinate relationships lend themselves to

TABLE 21.1 Organizational Problems Motivating Changes in the Interaction System

Sources of Problems in Interaction	Outcomes	Desired Outcomes
1. The authority structure and power relationships	Rigid and constricted relations; fear and caution predominant; low risk taking; suppression of information concerning problems; minimal use of lower-level human resources	Free-flowing information; problems disclosed; open relationships that are oriented toward problem solving
2. Incompatibility of group goals and the allocations of organizational resources	Intense intergroup competition for scarce resources; dysfunctional conflict; minimal cooperation among groups; hoarding resources	Manageable conflict; high degrees of cooperation centering around superordinate goals; sharing needed resources; enlightened self-interest
3. In-group/out-group orientations	See (2); distorted perceptions of other groups, their motives, their character, and so on; groups sit on information	See (2); accurate perception of other groups; open interchanges of information
4. Allocation of intragroup rewards	Intense intragroup competition; interpersonal conflict; low levels of group cohesion	Interpersonal cooperation; teamwork; high group cohesion
5. Existing interaction patterns that have outlived their organizational utility	Incentives to maintain patterns, despite their dysfunction; resistance to change	More flexibility and receptiveness to warranted changes

the use of power and the gaining of compliance in a variety of ways, not the least of which is implicit threat (22). The fear associated with implicit threat (or the hope of ingratiation) may discourage risk taking or problem disclosure (2, 33, 53). Further, organizational structures that carry rewards for conforming to authoritative requests, while increasing regularity and predictability, discourage hierarchical interactions that tap the creative forces lower in the organization (44). Consequently, vertical interaction patterns are frequently constrained by rules, procedures, and by fears of going beyond what is prescribed or what is perceived as appropriate (14). As we shall see, one of the ways of dealing with this problem is to change the nature of the hierarchical interaction patterns and power relationships.

A second problem concerns goals and goal conflict, which we dealt with in Chapter 18.

A third problem source is embedded in the group itself. We know that groups develop their own norms, goals, and a strong internal identification. Consequently, people in groups tend to look inward, regard their group as being better than outsiders, and then behave in ways described in our section on "groupthink."

A fourth problem source is the internal reward structure of a given group. If people respond to incentives, and if the incentives are set up so that when someone in a group gets more, someone else gets less, as in many incentive systems, then people within a group may develop perceptions of intensive intragroup competition (29).

A fifth problem source is outdated interaction patterns, that is, those which have outlived their purpose. Chapter 19 dealt with this issue.

There is one other major reason for changing interaction patterns—one that is not necessarily associated with a problem. That is, it is useful to build group cohesion or *esprit de corps*. The reasons for this are well documented in Chapter 13. Also, for example, several studies show that the most effective fighting units tend to be highly cohesive. Indeed, the major motivation for soldiers to go beyond the normal requirements of combat involves the social relations of small combat units (55, 57).

Most of the problem sources have been described before. In general, how we relate to other people in other groups reflects the way a hierarchy is organized, its consequent social system, the forces contained within the group itself, and the kinds of goals that emerge from the groups, particularly as they pertain to the goals of other groups. Interaction patterns, then, are difficult to change for the very reasons that they exist in the first place. And although the purposes they originally served may be obscure or no longer valid, the reasons for change must be more compelling than the reasons that justify the existing practices. How do we change to interaction patterns that seem more functional for organizational purposes?

Methods of Changing Interaction Patterns

The technologies of current interaction change efforts are founded in two primary methods: the *laboratory training group* and *attitude survey feedback* (19).

Laboratory Training

Laboratory training (T-groups, encounter groups, sensitivity training) deals with the feelings of the people who are members of that group. An example was presented in our opening story. The focus is the experience within the group—how people feel about themselves, others, interactions, and the effect that each member has on the others. Although the objectives of the training may differ, depending on who is being trained and who is doing the training, there are some common elements:

1. developing insight about your behavior and feelings in a social situation,
2. developing insight into others' behaviors and feelings,
3. understanding the effect of your behavior on others and their behavior on you,
4. developing insight into group processes—how groups develop, the roles people assume in groups, and so on—and
5. developing diagnostic skills concerning these points.[2]

The training group usually has ten to twelve people, who may or may not know each other. The group is unstructured. There is no agenda and there are no role allocations, such as a designated leader to lead the group discussion. There may, however, be a trainer who sets the tone of the meeting. The trainer's role is to facilitate the group process and serve as a role model and a resource. He does this by being passive, supportive, and nonevaluative so that people are free to express their feelings about themselves and about others within the group. The trainer may point out behaviors that need analysis, ask questions or probe, but he or she is not supposed to interject direction or evaluate feelings. That is, *any* feeling is seen as legitimate.

The members begin to discuss any topic they want, though they focus on the so-called here-and-now behavior that occurs within the group. In addition, they feed back information to other participants. This feedback should be nonevaluative, interpretive, and oriented toward either analysis or feelings. For example, they may ask why people behave in certain ways and how others may have felt about that behavior.

This kind of feedback is believed to create anxiety, which is the precursor of an *unfreezing* process—in which one begins to evaluate critically one's previous assumptions, attitudes, and behavior in social interaction. That marks the beginning of the change in *forces* contributing to dysfunctional behavior. Theoretically, once the unfreezing process begins people start to examine alternative behaviors, values, assumptions, and expectations about other group members.

An important norm that is developed in such groups is social supportiveness. Behaviors, attitudes, and values are examined in light of this supportiveness so that people who are feeling anxious or hostile or who question others' behaviors do so at minimal risk. However, when they do raise these questions, the questions may become the subject of discussion—although, again, in a supportive way. The norm of supportiveness has been called *psychological safety*. It is within the climate of psychological safety that the most effective self-examination ought to occur, and the self-examination behavior itself is *reinforced* within the group (3). Through the reinforcement of new behaviors, and the new insights created by the lab experience, *change* is thought to begin. People have begun to challenge their old assumptions and values and have been exposed to new ones.

After the lab experience, the members are expected to try out new behaviors "back home," where a *refreezing* process is theoretically supposed to occur, since the idea that these new behaviors are better than the old should be reinforced.

Two things are being affected by the unfreezing-change-refreezing process: (1) values and assumptions about social interaction and (2) learning itself. Thus, changes in both substance *and* process are hypothesized outcomes of the lab experience. The substance learning has to do with the role of feelings and emotions in interactions since the lab should demonstrate that such things are part of many interactions—though they are often suppressed—and that it is good to let them out for an open and honest interchange. Openness and honesty, therefore, become valued. The process outcomes of lab training have been simply labeled as "learning how to learn"—trying out new behaviors, interpreting others' behaviors, getting their reactions, and being reinforced for doing so (19, 51).

Remember our opening story? It was felt that, by convening this organizational "family" in a T-group setting (recall that the "T" is for "training"), the participants would be more sensitive to each other, more understanding of the effect of their behavior on others, and hence more effective in their subsequent interpersonal dealings back home in The Company. What happened?

At the outset, Ted, as usual, took over, trying to introduce some structure into the situation—with "Bo" Mason's approval, of course. The rest of the group, still cautious and not quite trusting, went along in a half-hearted way. The members tried to avoid a potentially threatening situation by voting for an agenda committee—not an uncommon occurrence in T-groups during the first day or so of their existence (24). But the attempt to introduce structure collapsed and tension began to mount—the beginning of the unfreezing stage.

Then, as the group began to focus on the work at hand, things began to explode. More attention was focused on behavior, and more negative feedback was introduced (41). The culmination was a strong attack by most of the members on Ted. And what they had to say was right on target. The group hoped that their comments—unmistakably hostile but at the same time honest—would produce changes in Ted's behavior. Members hoped that the confrontation would lead Ted to begin to question his assumptions about what was right and wrong, and would lead him to try out new behavior later back home and hence make life easier for the rest. Whether or not these hopes were realized, of course, remains to be seen, for we are still not altogether sure that T-groups produce anything of lasting value, organizationally speaking. Let us examine this last point for a moment.

The lab experience apparently has some effect, though it is not completely clear at this time what that effect is. The most common changes reported are more interpersonal flexibility, open communications, sensitivity, listening skills, solicitation of feedback, and more open relationships with subordinates or peers (3, 15, 20, 25, 35, 45). The durability of these changes, of course, depends on several things, including the organizational climate in which the trainee returns. If the experience creates significant learning, the learning can be translated into action in a benign or reinforcing environment. If the environment and its incentives suggest different behavior, then it is not likely that what was learned in the lab would be generalized back home.

Our experience has been that those going through lab training feel strongly about it, pro and con, though most are pro. The cons, however, should be considered. For example, the most common criticism is that the experience, although perhaps worthwhile, has no organizational utility (15, 45, 47). It does not fit the bureaucratic model of behavior to which most organizations subscribe, and it does not fit the image of how one presents oneself in an organization imbued with the values of rationality and incisive decision making. Considering these things, will Ted change later on? And will the change be permanent or will he resort to his previous behavior?

There are logical inconsistencies in the hypothesized dynamics of laboratories. For one thing it seems difficult to be supportive and critical at the same time. For another the ideas of psychological safety and anxiety seem mutually exclusive. Are we quibbling? We think not. Put yourself in Ted's shoes. Would you feel safe and supported by the group?

Then there is the problem of the tyranny of the group itself (59). The lab group's source of strength, namely, the norms and culture that it develops in these intensive interactions, creates conformity that, in the spirit of doing good, may actually pressure members to behave in ways functional only to the lab group itself. This is not unlike the groupthink dynamics described in Chapter 13. Further, the best comprehensive studies at this time suggest that lab training by itself is among the least effective methods used to change interactions in organizations (11, 12, 45, 47).

Why then do we treat lab training in such detail? Primarily, because it is an important antecedent of other forms of process-oriented organizational changes. The values of lab training, which include openness, honesty, trust, and collaboration for the purpose of problem solving, are the basis of most other technologies designed to change interactions. The basic goals of lab training are compatible with the process of developing functional interaction patterns for organizational improvement. For example, removing barriers that are erected between groups or among individuals because of misperceptions can lead to better interpersonal relations and thus to more cooperation and collaboration between otherwise conflicting groups.

Attitude Survey Feedback

We have already described attitude surveys as a means of collecting data. But what do you do with the data once they are collected? Our interest here is a feedback procedure that is designed to produce change. Let us go through this process step by step.

First, the data are collected, as we have described. After the data are analyzed and summarized, they are fed back to each identifiable unit in the organization. The feedback is usually organized to identify both the strengths and the weaknesses of those units. Feedback sessions usually include all the group members, even the group manager (30). The agenda usually focuses on problems and problem solution. The group discusses the data to better understand the dynamics at work. After several such sessions, causes are determined by consensus. Then the group members including the manager commit themselves to work on the problems.

The data are fed back, as in Figure 21.1, to each hierarchical grouping, though the process within each grouping is the same. For example, suppose that an attitude survey is conducted in a manufacturing plant whose lowest operating unit is the department. Projects are the next highest unit, then functions, and finally the total plant. The data can be grouped according to each of these units and fed back sequentially. Hence, the plant manager sees the plant data and deals with the issues at that level; the functional managers see functional level data; and so forth—with each level responsible for dealing with the problems raised by the data. The advantage here is that each manager sees the results of the attitude survey from his or her level on down through the organization. Top management would then request action.

Also, attitude survey feedback, to be an effective change vehicle, should be continuous. That is, the survey should be administered periodically so that everyone knows that progress can be checked and evaluated. Figure 21.1 summarizes the process described.

Attitude survey feedback, then, is a process by which data are fed back to *all* units within the organization. The focus of the data is on problems and problem solving—hence organizational improvement. The process is built into the hierarchy of authority, and incentives are developed that encourage problem-

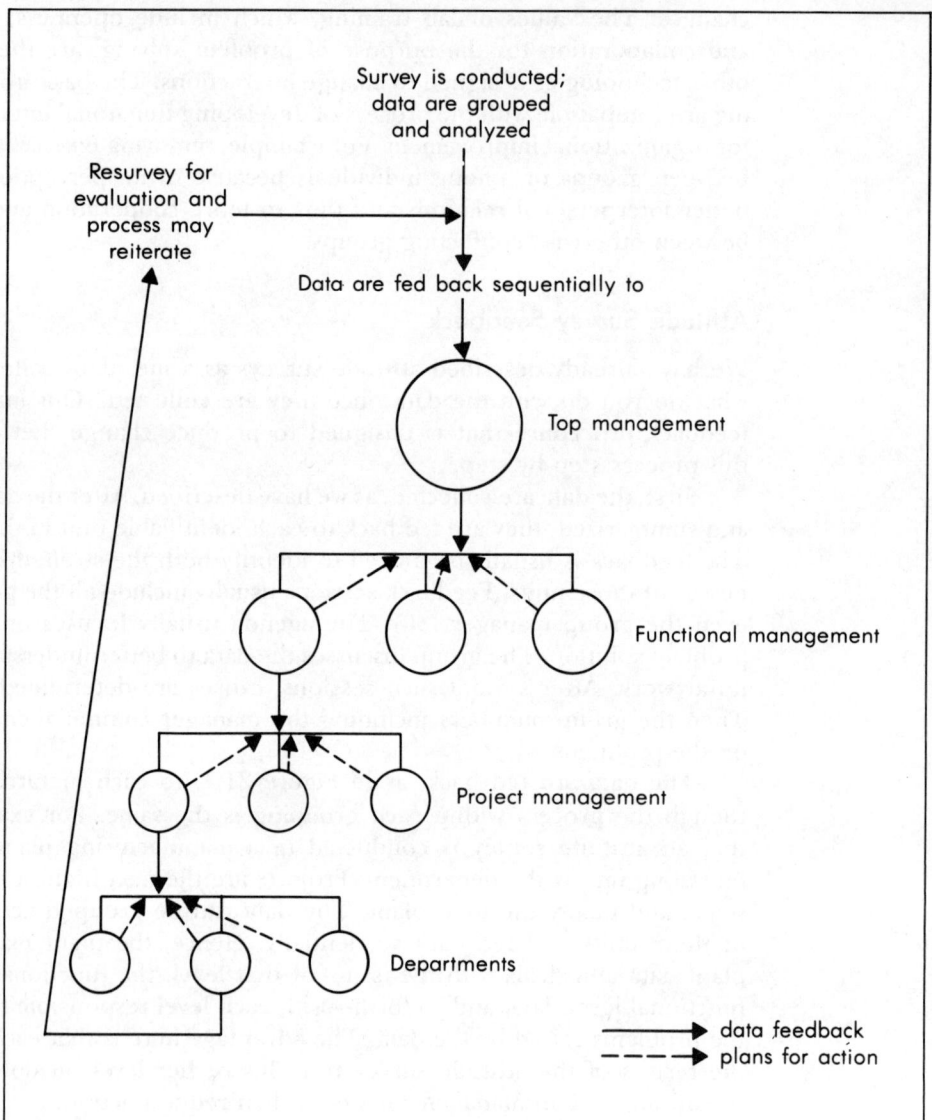

FIGURE 21.1 Survey Feedback as a Method of Change

solving activities (1, 30). This process can encapsulate a variety of problems, but it is often designed to focus on interaction patterns, particularly those that pertain to superior-subordinate relationships.

The laboratory method and attitude survey feedback can be used together. For example, in several studies questionnaire data were fed back to intact work groups and, after the groups were confronted with the data, team-building workshops using laboratory training techniques were employed (28, 45). Indeed, the fact that any change in interaction systems requires a solid evidential base of problem disclosure suggests that the two methods *ought* to be used together to maximize the effectiveness of each (19, 40, 43).

We suggest a new model, shown in Figure 21.2, that undergirds most reported change techniques (20). The basic terms of the model include the requirement for data, diagnosis, participation, planning, actions, evaluation, diffusion, and sustenance. The following discussion uses the new model as a framework.

Team Building and Conflict Management[3]

Team-building activities are designed to increase the effectiveness of intact work groups. As French and Bell state:

> [Team-building activities] may relate to task issues, the way things are done, the needed skills to accomplish tasks, the resource allocations necessary for task accomplishment; or they may relate to the nature and quality of the relationships between the team members and the leader. (19:107)

Conflict management usually focuses on intergroup relations but, even though the objectives appear to differ, the basic dynamics are similar to those of team building. Remember, the idea is to build smoother, more effective interpersonal relationships in each instance.

Most often the strategy of changing interaction systems by building teams and managing conflicts is a normative-reeducative one. This is not to say that empirical-rational and power-coercive strategies are not employed as part of the total strategic effort for change, for they often are. Since most change efforts, regardless of their target, are initiated at the higher levels of organizations, the power variable is clearly evident. Indeed, the use of normative-reeducative tactics as part of a larger power-coercive strategy is common. One author reports the use of T-groups to make demoted managers "feel good" about their new and unasked for status (21).

As for the empirical-rational component of a comprehensive change strategy, initial compliance by the groups targeted for change requires some justification, often in the form of objective data that disclose a problem. However, since many of the problems that interfere with effective group behavior or with the relationships among groups concern attitudes, beliefs, values, and norms, it is

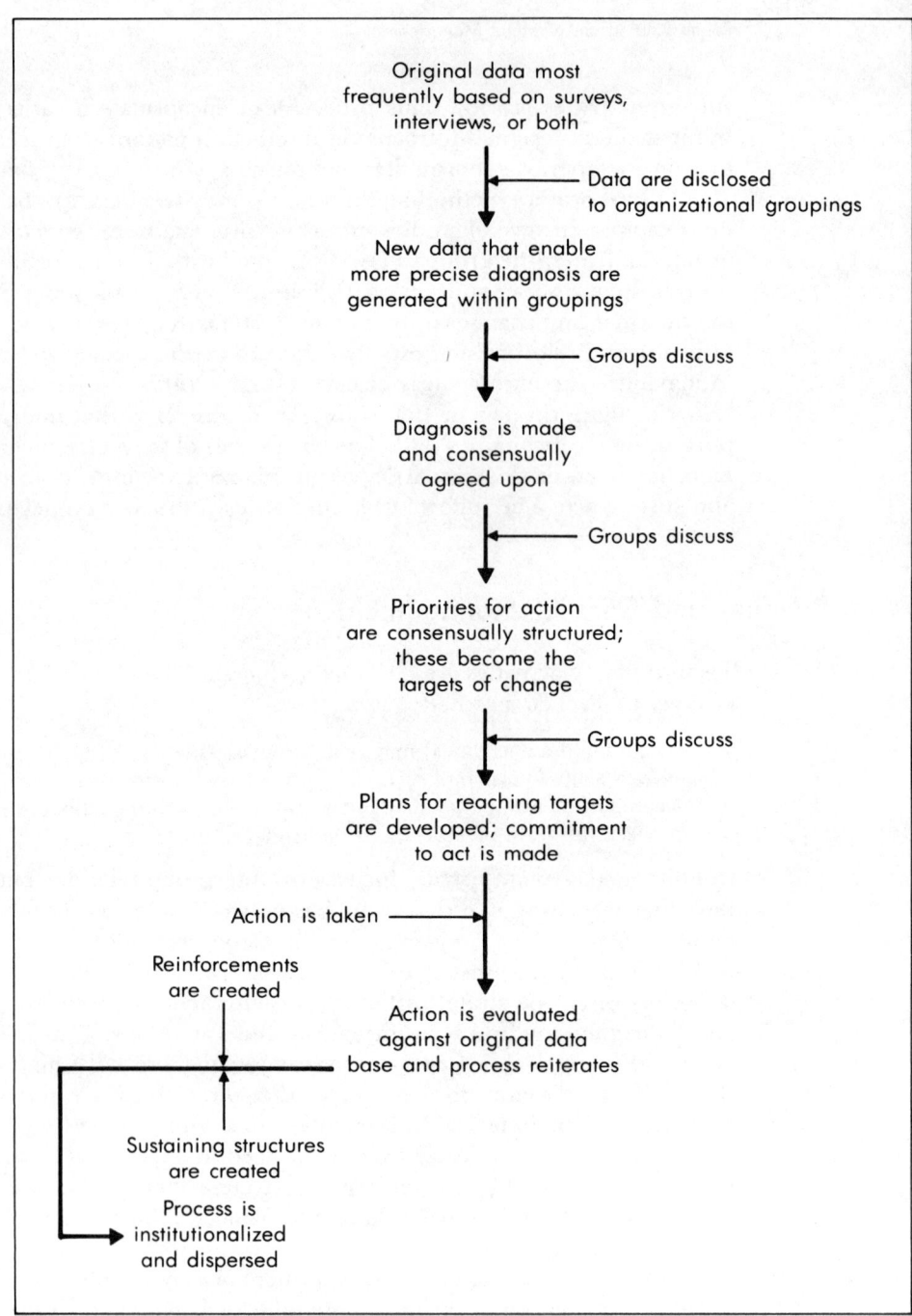

FIGURE 21.2 Suggested Process for Changing Interaction Systems

ultimately the normative-reeducative strategy that seems typically to dominate *as a process* (21).

The *focus* of change in the interaction systems is usually *intact work groups* (19). These work groups may exist at any level of the organization and often overlap. For example, if we were to begin our change efforts with a group of frequently interacting executives, our focus might be team building for *that* group, but each executive is responsible for and a member of a work group lower in the hierarchy.

Ideally, the targeted group begins to diffuse change through the organization because of that linkage. If the purpose of the change effort is to develop a "better" team, then the work group itself is the focus. If, however, the purpose is to manage conflict, the linkages or the point of interface become the focus, and two or more groups are brought together to deal with the issue (19, 40).

It is common to deal with team building and intergroup relations simultaneously (19, 45) or sequentially (5, 28).

The changes in interaction expected for any given targeted group are also expected in the groupings that are associated through the hierarchy (40).

Since the process occurs with the group, the membership itself diagnoses, plans, and consents to act. In this way, the data create the justification for action, and the norms lend support to such action. But let us examine the common factors in most of such change efforts.

First, the problems are identified, possibly through one of the methods described before and usually with the aid of a *neutral* third party, perhaps a consultant. The group or groups then convene to feed back the data or, as we shall see, to generate additional data that fill in—adding richness to the original data. The following factors seem typical of most interaction change efforts after that:

1. The meetings are almost always confronting. That is, the participants generate data that indicate problems the members are having among themselves. For example, if individuals are having difficulty working together, these difficulties are identified and discussed. Or, as in the case of intergroup relations, points of conflict or nonproductive competitions may be disclosed. Often the confrontation involves showing the members differences between what they see as common practice and what they would like to see as common practice. Frequently people or groups are asked their perceptions of others; these perceptions are then matched against self-perceptions in order to disclose perceptual differences that may be the source of interpersonal conflict. In each case, the bases of conflict are identified and attempts are made to resolve the underlying issues (40).
2. Usually some mechanism is devised to get at the source of the problem. For example, participants may be asked to list the reasons why the prob-

lems exist. The lists are then shown within the group, discussed, and edited until the group itself reaches a consensus concerning cause.
3. The group membership is almost always responsible for developing solutions to the problems, again by consensus.
4. The group is almost always required to develop a consensus to take some action designed to reduce or eliminate the problem. That is, there is a drive toward a superordinate goal that transcends the particular goals evident in groups or among individuals (54).
5. Usually the group must develop plans to execute the action with specific behaviors that are designed to change the problem interaction.
6. Often the group agrees to some kind of evaluation at a later time to check on progress or to continue momentum.
7. If intergroup conflict is the issue, several groups are often formed consisting of members of each group. These groups are responsible for resolving specific problems underlying the conflict.

But do interactions actually change as a result of such activities? And if they do, in what way? The answers to these questions are still not clear, although there is enough evidence to provide some tentative conclusions.[4]

Some Research Evidence

Porras and Berg (46) in a comprehensive review of studies dealing with changing interactions report that only thirty-five studies from 1959 through mid-1975 used the processes that we described and include concrete supporting evidence.[5] Of these studies, only 46 percent report positive changes. Friedlander and Brown are more sanguine, though their review includes, as part of their evidence, case studies with anecdotal reports (17).

A more recent review disclosed that team building can be effective if it is a continuing process, with top management commitment and a context that encourages team building (45). If team building occurs with only one unit in a largely neutral context, problems are likely. For example, one study reported a highly successful team-building effort among a group of first-level supervisors. However, the rest of the organization was uninterested and in some cases overtly hostile. The group disintegrated (10).

Furthermore, in two separate studies, one a pre- and posttreatment of almost 15,000 people in more than twenty companies, and the other a treatment using the same design but in large military organization, the effects of four programmatic efforts to change interaction patterns were investigated (12, 13). The change tactics that were used in the studies were:

1. survey feedback, much as we described previously in this chapter;
2. interpersonal process consultation, wherein an expert consultant helps

people become more aware of the effect of their behavior on others, the effect of others' behaviors on them, and the dynamics of interpersonal and intergroup relations;
3. task process consultation, in which an expert consultant helps people analyze how things get done and how objectives are set (task structural changes often occur as a consequence of this method, but in any event the purpose is to help the individual and the group carry out their work more effectively);
4. laboratory training, much as we described previously in this chapter; and
5. data handback, which is simply the distribution of the survey results to supervisors of all work groups, but with no encouragement to do anything about them.

The dependent variables of interest to us here included: (1) group processes, that is, how the various groupings work together; (2) peer leadership, how members of the group would take the initiative to support others, help members interact with each other, and get the job done; (3) managerial leadership, how managers would support the group membership, help them interact, help them develop as a team, and get the work done; and (4) organizational climate, particularly as it pertains to communication flow and the distribution of influence throughout the organization. Each of these dependent variables is thought to affect other organizational outcome variables such as performance, absenteeism, and turnover. The reasoning is that if the leadership and group processes are good, then so are the outcomes of the processes. The treatments were compared to each other on the dependent variables.

The results indicate that the survey feedback method produces substantial positive changes on all dependent variables except for managerial leadership. The only other treatment group that showed positive results was the interpersonal process consultation. That method seemed most effective in the managerial and peer leadership areas.

As for the task process consultation and the laboratory training, the changes that were produced seemed mainly negative. Indeed, the data handbook, which was considered a "no treatment" method, and which relied on the line managers themselves to do something about the data, showed more net positive changes than either of the others.

Why should the results turn out as they did? A couple of explanations fit well into the framework of our previous chapter. First, attitude surveys are fairly consistent with typical management practices. The data are fed back in groups hierarchically; they have some objectivity in the sense that each of the dimensions has numerical values placed on it that are readily identified and easily understood; and the survey feedback method is more likely to be systemwide than the other methods. Furthermore, the focus is on the same data used both for evaluation purposes and for feedback. In other words, the data that are fed back to improve interactions are the baseline data for future evaluations. Thus, because of this anticipated evaluation, there is a built-in incentive to change.[6]

According to French and Bell the interpersonal process consultation shares some of these characteristics, whereas laboratory training and task process consultation are not systemic and do not provide a clear focus on the behaviors that are likely to be measured again for evaluation. Hence, groups subjected to those two treatments may have no incentive to change. Of course, this does not explain the negative effects of each of these treatments. And, in fact, at this time it would be unwarranted to assess such treatments negatively, for, as French and Bell point out:

> It may be that the treatments are not exactly comparable in that some treatments— laboratory training and task process consultation especially—are not systemic in nature. That is, the target is usually a small part of the organization, not the total system. The questionnaire measures systemic problems of a wide range; some treatments are much more narrowly focused. (19:251)

One final review deserves particular attention, because it goes well beyond the criterion of change and looks carefully at consequences of change intervention in terms of hard measures of behavior (45). These measures included four classes of behavior. The first, called work force behavior, included absenteeism, turnover, and grievances; the second included profits, operating costs, and sales volume; the third was quality of performance; and the fourth, productivity, included quantity, efficiency, and effectiveness.

These change methods were examined:

A. Human process approaches
   1. Structured laboratory training-group training experiences that focus on interpersonal behavior and group process issues.
   2. Team building.
   3. Survey feedback.
B. Technostructural approaches
   4. Job design and job enlargement.
   5. Job enrichment—work functions from a "vertical slice" of the unit are brought together into a single job to provide greater task identity and significance, employee autonomy, and feedback.
   6. Sociotechnical systems design—directed at the fit between the technological configuration and the social structure of work units as in the Norwegian experiments described in the previous chapters.
C. Multifaceted approaches
   7. Interventions that employ multiple techniques, such as survey feedback, team building, and job enrichment.

The results of the analysis disclosed that the technostructural changes were most effective at the lowest levels of the organization—the workgroups where the actual production takes place. The human process approaches were not effective at that level although they were effective in most instances at the white-collar, professional level. Furthermore, the "winning combination" was the multifaceted approach when workers "participated in goal setting, decision making and job design . . . developed through some sort of team building effort" aimed at several organizational levels, a situation closely akin to the technostructural approach.

To summarize, the following conclusions seem warranted:

1. Change efforts directed toward interaction systems appear successful if they take place in a system context and incorporate or are consonant with the important system variables that we have been discussing throughout the book. Chief among the context facets are (a) the support of the change offered by higher management, (b) the consistency of the change with prevailing norms, and (c) the extent to which reinforcements direct behavior toward changing interactions.
2. A facilitating factor is the intensive involvement in the change process of the people affected by the change (36).
3. Successful changes seem to require a targeted and demonstrable outcome that is reasonably tangible and organizationally sanctioned, such as a change in job design, or more cooperative behavior among groups.
4. These outcomes must be measured and incorporated in the normal organizational control procedures.

Changing Hierarchical Interaction Patterns

In this section we will discuss a way of looking at interactions as part of the hierarchical system. The major intent of the change efforts we deal with is to extend influence downward through the organization. An underlying rationale is contained in our previous discussions of the "locus of control" in organizations and of participative leadership.

Participation and System 4

It seems clear at present that participative methods can be effective in gaining commitment to decisions (11, 16, 34, 37, 38, 39, 43, 49). We introduced this idea before, but to better understand it let us look more closely at the dynamics involved. There are three components. First, members come to *individual* decisions as a consequence of the group interaction. Second, they perceive that others within the group have come to similar decisions—thus, the decisions are *normative* (4). And third, because several people provide input along with evaluative discussion, there is a greater variety of options expressed, and therefore the *quality* of the decision *appears* to be *better* (23, 24).

Now remember that we offered participative management as a possible option for managers as they strove toward effective leadership. However, we dealt primarily with the leader-follower relationship, which is a small part of the total organization. Also, although individual leaders may choose to be participative, their attempts are likely to be attenuated by other system constraints. For example, Mann disclosed that those managers who chose to be participative when their own managers *were not*, were judged ineffective by the subordinates (42). One reason for this is that participative managers in an authoritarian situation created expectations among their subordinates that could not be fulfilled, for the influence upward was simply not there. Consequently, those who advocate participative management view larger systems as the appropriate target. Rensis Likert has classified management systems into four groupings: (1) exploitative-authoritative, (2) benevolent-authoritative, (3) consultative, and (4) participative-group. The first two recognize and support the complete legitimacy of the hierarchy of authority as being the system that inevitably governs human relations. The third system, the consultative, spans the authoritative and the participative styles but is still primarily a dyadic arrangement where the subordinate and the superior negotiate positions. Under this system the subordinate has some but not major influence.

System 4, the participative-group system, attempts to build highly cohesive groups, involves the groups in the decision-making processes, and then establishes high goals through those groups. System 4 is perceived by its proponents as a step toward the ideal organizational state (12, 38, 39).

Let us give you an example of each system. Assume we are examining the character of (1) the motivational forces in an organization system and the manner in which motives are used and (2) the interaction influence process. Table 21.2 describes these for each of the systems. As you can see, the process under System 4 is clearly geared toward involving people as members of a group and taking advantage of the group forces described before.[7]

There are other ways of classifying the extent of participation in decision making. Miles suggests three basic models: (1) the *traditional* model, (2) the *human relations* model, and (3) the *human resources* model (45); Vroom and Yetton speak of (1) authoritative, (2) consultative, and (3) participative methods of decision making (62). Although these are not precisely the same as the System 1 through 4 typology, there are enough similarities to consider them in the same framework.[8] However, Miles notes that there are really only two preferred states of managing: those preferred when one is *doing* the managing and those preferred when one is *being* managed. A consultative model is preferred in the first instance, and a fully participative model in the second. When they are in

TABLE 21.2 Examples of Systems 1 Through 4

	SYSTEM 1 AUTHORITATIVE EXPLOITATIVE	SYSTEM 2 AUTHORITATIVE BENEVOLENT	SYSTEM 3 CONSULTATIVE	SYSTEM 4 GROUP PARTICIPATIVE
Assumptions concerning motivational forces	primarily motives of fiscal security, economic security, and desire for upward mobility	economic and occasional ego motives, for example, the desire for upward mobility	economic, ego, and some other motives such as the desire for new experience	full use of a variety of motives such as economic, ego, social, a desire for new experiences; for example, motivational forces arising from group processes
How motives are used	fears, threats, punishment, and occasional rewards	balanced in the direction of rewards with some occasional or at least potential punishment involved	rewards, occasional punishment, and some involvement on a one-to-one participative basis	a wide variety of factors, including economic rewards based on compensation systems that are developed with and through the group, full group participation and involvement in goal setting, improving method of appraising progress and evaluating the extent to which the goals are reached
Character of interaction-influence process; amount and character of interaction	little interaction and always with fear and distrust	little interaction and usually with some condescension by superiors; fear and caution by subordinates	moderate interaction, often with fair amount of confidence and trust	extensive, friendly interaction with high degree of confidence and trust

a superior position, managers want to reserve their right to define the issues *and* the extent of participation, but when they are subordinates, they want to participate fully and in depth. Corroborating evidence is provided by those doing research with Systems 1 through 4 (38–40, 43).

This is one of the reasons there seems to be a need to change interaction patterns: if all levels of management generally want more influence upward, and yet treat their subordinates in a way that forecloses upward influence, the system is caught in a circularity that prohibits such changes from taking place.

Box 26

Faculty Voice

This study was motivated by results disclosed in an attitude survey which suggested that nursing educators placed a high value on having influence in determining nursing school policy but in fact had little voice. The Dean of one of the nursing schools determined to do something about the dissatisfaction. Here is what was done.

Change was implemented to bring about decentralization and faculty participation in decision making. Faculty were surveyed before and after the change, with controls for turnover and changes in faculty values over the six years.

Before the change the Dean made all committee appointments and important policy decisions. The change itself had the following major characteristics:

1. The Dean asked a faculty-elected committee to study faculty participation and present a plan for faculty reorganization.
2. The committee made several recommendations that were implemented, including the establishment of additional elected faculty committees that made decisions on a variety of school-related issues.
3. There was a subsequent streamlining of the committee structures. That permitted faculty input on two levels without taking unnecessary faculty time: (a) a standing committee, with the advice and consent of the faculty could change a school policy; and (b) the changes were to be ratified in special faculty meetings chaired by the Dean.

Those changes together provided a significantly greater faculty voice in all important faculty-related issues. The results of the study showed improvement in almost every measure of satisfaction over a six-year period. The only areas that showed less satisfaction were with salary, fringe benefits, and the probability of tenure—areas that were not affected by the organization change.

Bonjean, Charles, Billye J. Brown, Burke D. Grandjean, and Patrick D. Macken. "Increasing Work Satisfaction Through Organizational Change: A Longitudinal Study of Nursing Educators." *The Journal of Applied Behavioral Science* 18 (1982): 357–369.

That is, unless something intervenes to point out the circularity, demonstrate persuasively the logic of changing, and provide incentives to make the changes, such changes are unlikely. Box 26 provides an excellent example of this.

The study in Box 26 indicates that hierarchical interaction patterns can be changed to lower the locus of decision control to the operating level by decentralizing decision making. It should be noted that the Dean still had final authority in most matters but always worked through the committee structure. Of course, the study took place in a university—an organization that places great credence in in collegial authority (8). Can a similar restructuring take place in more traditional business organizations? Probably not to the extent depicted in the study, but let us examine that probability.

The Weldon Experience

Before the change described in this section was introduced, the Weldon Company was managed according to System 1 precepts; that is, management tended to be autocratic and nonparticipative, and control was clearly held by those at the top of the organization (43). The pressure for change occurred primarily because the company was unprofitable and had been purchased by another company that had been practicing System 4 management techniques for a decade and a half at the time of purchase. The actual change efforts occurred over about two years. The changes had three main objectives: (1) to conserve the human resources of the plant, (2) to improve substantially the plant facilities and methods of production, and (3) to move the hierarchical interaction patterns from the System 1 approach to System 4 in the hope that the motivation system would subsequently change.

Accordingly, the following changes were made:

1. Higher work standards were established, and different pay schedules, including an extensive incentive system, were initated. The incentives were determined on the basis of production against standard.
2. A year after those changes were made, the movement toward System 4 began. Participation in decision making was extended to all levels of management.
3. Similar products were produced within the same work units, and allowances were made for longer production runs and fewer job changes.
4. Each work group in the plant was responsible for identifying work-related problems and then solving such problems through participative techniques. In this way power was shared throughout the system.
5. Sensitivity training sessions were open to all people in supervisory positions. The sensitivity sessions were partly instructional in that all the supervisors were introduced to the benefits of System 4.

6. New training programs were established wherein employees were trained in work methods. This was particularly intensive for workers who were not doing well and consequently were not benefitting from the incentive system. The focus on the less efficient worker was called the "earnings development program"—a euphemism for developing the skills of these workers so they could produce more and subsequently earn more.
7. In order to emphasize the new focus on high productivity, workers who could not measure up to the new standards or who were judged ineffective employees in some other way were fired.

Although the researchers report a substantial increase in profits, our focus here is not on the variables that contributed to such profitability.[9] Rather, we are concerned with the movement of the production facility from System 1 to something close to System 4. The data suggest that indeed such a change took place and that it was fully substantiated and had picked up some momentum over a five-year period (52).

In addition, the researchers report substantial increases in employee morale over the period. Such increases were undoubtedly due, at least in part, to the changes in the management system. Certainly the managers and supervisory personnel themselves seemed happy with the movement from System 1 to System 4. Indeed, the results reported at the end of five years closely approximated the "ideal" that the same personnel had described before the change.

To summarize, it seems clear that when a systemwide and highly motivated effort is made to change interaction patterns, such efforts are likely to succeed. Of course, had the other changes not been made—in the incentive system, for example—and consequently no dramatic improvement in performance had been observed, we wonder if the changes in the interaction pattern could have been sustained. Nevertheless, to quote from the researchers:

> The original change program contained some notions of seeking mutually reinforcing change actions across the psychological, organizational and technological domains. A central idea was to make structural changes in the organization that matched the work system and that did not violate the reasonable assumptions about the values and motives of individual members. . . . The idea of systemic consistency is surely an elementary one, no more than common sense—a habit of thought for those who have learned to view the factory as a total system. (52:233)

Summary

Our discussion has been based on the assumption that forces exist in organizations that create problems in interactions. Many of these forces are inherent in hierarchical arrangements where power is an issue and scuffling for scarce resources is a way of life. Some are due to the precepts of division of labor—where groups are organized along functional lines, goals are established within the various groupings and then given priority according to the interests of these groupings. Consequently in-group/out-group mentalities may result—a condition that can lead to conflict.

The reason for changing interaction patterns, then, is to reduce both the hierarchical and the lateral problems created by these forces. In the first instance, the changes typically involve increasing the influence of lower participants through participative decision making—thus providing them with more incentive to buy into a system and gain greater control of their fate and personal autonomy. Such changes also allow the company to better tap the substantial reservoir of talent that is said to exist among lower participants. In the second instance, the focus is usually on resolving conflict or on team building.

Running through our commentary was an emphasis on several things. First, a data-based analysis is required that highlights problems. Second, a climate needs to be established that deals with problems in ways that will lead to problem resolution.

Third, there needs to be built into the entire process means for evaluation and reinforcement of the change. Last, institutionalization, reinforcement, and support structures are required to ensure that the changes become an organizational way of life.

The last point is perhaps the most difficult to accomplish because of the forces created by the hierarchy and by functional divisionalization. Indeed, organizations are defined in these terms. Thus, creating counterforces that encourage properly functioning interaction patterns that both fit organizational requirements of predictability and control and avoid their problems is a difficult challenge for management.

We provided several illustrations to support our major points. In each case the main objective was to increase the effectiveness of the interaction system for the purpose of organizational improvement. The research data suggest that indeed interactions can change in the desired direction, though the evidence linking interaction changes to other measures of organizational improvement is not always persuasive. But then the arguments against such linkages are no better. Our conclusion, consequently, is that improvements can be made in interaction systems if the appropriate process is employed, but that such improvements, by themselves, may or may not result in other organizational improvements. Other factors probably have to be considered—factors associated with such criteria as productivity, performance, profitability, and organizational efficiency. We will deal with two of these factors, the motivation system and the control systems, in our last chapter.

Notes

1. What we will *not* deal with in this chapter are changes that are made for other purposes but affect interaction patterns, even though such changes sometimes have a dramatic effect on interaction (18). For example, technological changes in the British coal indus-

try markedly altered the composition of the miner's workgroup and consequently the interactions patterns, but the change was for purposes other than altering interactions. The Norwegian studies described in Chapter 19 are another example, though the distinction of purposes is less clear since one of the reasons for the autonomous workgroup was to create a more benign social climate.

2. Our use of the term *lab training* is somewhat more specific than is often the case. Some definitions include varied activities, such as lectures and other structured experiences. Our view is that most lab experiences focus on group dynamics and, that, consequently, is the predominant characteristic of such training.

3. Most of the work describing team building and conflict management is commonly called organizational development (19). OD has been defined in a number of ways, but most definitions seem to include: (1) planned change; (2) a focus on interpersonal relationships, interaction patterns, perceptions of self and others, and values of the participants; (3) a purpose of *organizational* improvement; (4) use of an action-research model that is data-based; and (5) an evaluation of the consequences of such actions (see *Organizational Development Newsletter,* Academy of Management, Winter 1978). However, we do not use OD per se as a conceptual framework much as we are in sympathy with many OD practices, for as Robert Kahn states:

> OD is not a concept, at least in any scientific sense of the word; it is not precisely defined; it is not reducible to specific uniform behavior; it does not have a prescribed and verifiable place in a network of logically related concepts. (28:485)

For some excellent reviews and descriptions of OD, see Friedlander and Brown (20), French and Bell (19), and Strauss (58).

4. Many technologies address interaction patterns. They range from completely unstructured T-groups that focus on feelings as the process unfolds, to role negotiations that specifically address desired and undesired behavior between parties, and then to a bargaining process that requires reciprocal and concrete agreement to change such behavior. For two excellent reviews of technologies, see Friedlander and Brown (20) and French and Bell (19).

5. Porras and Berg (46) classify these techniques as organizational development, a point we made earlier. The studies they report include: (1) lab training focusing on interpersonal and intergroup relations and team building, (2) managerial grid, (3) survey feedback, and (4) other process techniques.

6. For detailed descriptions of eclectic and systemwide change efforts, along with supporting data concerning the effect of those efforts, see Blake et al. (6, 7) and Kimberly and Nielsen (29).

7. Using a questionnaire, we found that most organizations fall somewhere between the benevolent-authoritative and the consultative models according to the perception of the respondents. However, when the organizational participants are asked how they would *like* to be managed, they typically fall somewhere between the consultative and the participative group modes. Thus, there is a considerable discrepancy between perceptions of what actually occurs in organizations and the organizational members' ideal state. As you might imagine, this finding presents some lively discussions in the group feedback sessions (60).

8. The major difference between the System 4 and the human resource model is that the former speaks explicitly to the importance of *group* factors whereas the latter

does not. The human resources model is more flexible in that it allows the interaction patterns to proceed either in a group fashion or in a dyadic fashion, as long as the employees involved have a real influence on most of the important decisions that affect them (44).

9. To return to the results on the so-called hard measures of production against standard—absenteeism, turnover, and profitability—all changed for the better, sometimes remarkably so. For example, in a three-year period of time profitability changed from a net loss to a substantial gain. It is not our intent to infer that the changes in the interaction system produced the changes in profitability. A careful reading of the study would suggest that the main contributors to increases in productivity were the reorganization of the work process and the establishment of new work standards and the incentive system. Furthermore, any time an organization purges itself of substandard performers and either does not replace them or brings in new, more competent personnel, it can expect substantial increases in performance.

References

1. ALPER, W., and S. M. KLEIN. "Impact of Feedback on Employee Attitude Surveys." *Personnel Administration* 33 (1970): 54–57.
2. ARGYRIS, C. "Leadership Learning and Changing the Status Quo." In *Perspectives on Behavior in Organizations*, edited by J. R. Hackman, E. E. Lawler, III, and L. W. Porter. New York: McGraw-Hill, 1977. Pp. 409–420.
3. BEER, M. "The Technology of Organizational Development." In *Handbook of Industrial and Organizational Psychology*, edited by M. Dunnette. Chicago: Rand McNally, 1976. Pp. 937–994.
4. BENNETT, E. "Discussion, Decision, Commitment, and Consensus in 'Group Decision.'" In *Group Dynamics: Research and Theory*, 3rd ed. Edited by D. Cartwright and A. Zander. New York: Harper and Row, 1968.
5. BLAKE, R. R., H. A. SHEPARD, and J. S. MOUTON. *Managing Intergroup Conflict in Industry*. Houston: Gulf Publishing, 1964.
6. BLAKE, R. R., L. B. BARNES, J. S. MOUTON, and L. E. GREINER. "Breakthrough in Organizational Development." In *Organizational Development: Values, Process and Technology*, edited by N. Margulies and A. P. Raia. New York: McGraw-Hill, 1972. Pp. 556–591.
7. BLAKE, R. R., R. L. SLOMA, J. S. MOUTON, and B. P. LOFTIN. "A Second Breakthrough in Organization Development." In *Organizational Development: Values, Process and Technology*, edited by N. Margulies and A. P. Raia. New York: McGraw-Hill, 1972. Pp. 592–601.
8. BONJEAN, CHARLES, BILLYE J. BROWN, BURKE D. GRANDJEAN, and PATRICK O. MACKEN. "Increasing Work Satisfaction through Organizational Change: A Longitudinal Study of Nursing Educators." *The Journal of Applied Behavioral Science* 18 (1982): 357–369.
9. BOSS, R. WAYNE. "It Doesn't Matter If You Win or Lose, Unless You're Losing: An Organizational Change in a Law Enforcement Agency." *The Journal of Applied Behavioral Science* 15 (1979): 198–220.

10. Boss, R. Wayne, and Mark L. McConkie. "The Destructive Impact of a Positive Team Building Interaction." *Group and Organization Studies* 6 (1981): 45–56.
11. Bowers, D. G. "O.D. Techniques and Their Results in 23 Organizations: The Michigan ICL Study." *Journal of Applied Behavioral Science* 9 (1973): 21–43.
12. Bowers, D. G., and D. L. Hausser. "Work Group Types and Intervention Effects in Organizational Development." *Administrative Science Quarterly* 22 (March 1977): 76–94.
13. Bowers, D. G., J. L. Franklin, and P. A. Pecorella. "Matching Problems, Precursors, and Interventions in O.D.: A Systemic Approach." *Journal of Applied Behavioral Science* 11 (1975): 391–409.
14. Bryson, J., and G. Kelley. "Political Perspective on Leadership Emergence, Stability and Change in Organizational Networks." *The Academy of Management Review* 3
15. Campbell, J. P., and M. Dunnette. "Effectiveness of T-Group Experiences in Managerial Training and Development." In *Readings in Organizational Behavior and Human Performance*, edited by W. E. Scott, Jr., and L. L. Cummings. Homewood, Ill.: Irwin, 1973. Pp. 568–594.
16. Coch, L., and J. R. P. French, Jr. "Overcoming Resistance to Change." *Human Relations* 1 (1948): 512–533.
17. Delbecq, A. L., A. H. Van de Ven, and D. H Gustafson. *Group Techniques for Program Planning*. Glenview, Ill.: Scott, Foresman, 1975.
18. Filley, A. C. *Interpersonal Conflict Resolution*. Glenview, Ill.: Scott, Foresman, 1974.
19. French, W. L., and C. H. Bell, Jr. *Organizational Development*. Englewood Cliffs, N.J.: Prentice-Hall, 1978.
20. Friedlander, F., and L. D. Brown. "Organization Development." *Annual Review of Psychology* 25 (1974): 313–341.
21. Golembewski, R. T., S. B. Carrigan, W. R. Mead, R. Munzen-Rider, and A. Blumberg. "Toward Building New Work Relationships: An Action Design for a Critical Intervention." *Journal of Applied Behavioral Science* 8 (March 1972): 135–148.
22. Grimes, A. J. "Authority, Power, Influence and Social Control: A Theoretical Synthesis." *Academy of Management Review* 3 (October 1978): 724–734.
23. Hoffman, L. R., and N. R. F. Maier, "Quality and Acceptance of Problem Solutions by Members of Homogeneous and Heterogeneous Groups." *Journal of Abnormal and Social Psychology* 62 (March 1961): 401–407.
24. ———. "Valence in the Adoption of Solutions by Problem Solving Groups: Quality and Acceptance as Goals of Leaders and Members." *Journal of Personality and Social Psychology* 6 (1967): 175–182.
25. House, R. J. "T–Group Education and Leadership Effectiveness: A Review of the Empiric Literature and a Critical Evaluation." *Personnel Psychology* 20 (1967): 1–32.
26. Jago, A. G., and V. H. Vroom. "Hierarchical Level and Leadership Style." *Organizational Behavior and Human Performance* 18 (1977): 131–145.
27. ———. "Predicting Leader Behavior from a Measure of Behavioral Intent." *Academy of Management Journal* 21 (December 1978): 715–721.

28. KAHN, R. "Organizational Development: Some Problems and Proposals." *Journal of Applied Behavioral Science* 10 (1974): 485–502.
29. KIMBERLY, J. R., and W. R. NIELSEN. "Organization Development and Change in Organizational Performance." *Administrative Science Quarterly* 20 (June 1975): 191–206.
30. KLEIN, S. M., A. I. KRAUT, and A. WOLFSON. "Employee Reactions to Attitude Survey Feedback: Study of the Impact of Structure and Process." *Administrative Science Quarterly* 16 (1971): 497–514.
31. KOOPMAN, PAUL L., PIETER J. D. DRENTH, FRANS B. M. BUS, AGAATH J. KRUYSWIJK, and ANDRE F. M. WIERSOSMA. "Content, Process, and Effects of Participative Decision Making on the Shop Floor: Three Cases in the Netherlands." *Human Relations* 34 (1981): 657–676.
32. LAWRENCE, P. R. "How to Deal with Resistance to Change." In *Organizational Change and Development*, edited G. W. Dalton, P. R. Lawrence, and L. E. Greiner. Homewood, Ill.: Irwin and Dorsey Press, 1970. Pp. 181–197.
33. LEAVITT, H. J. "Applied Organizational Change in Industry: Structural, Technology and Humanistic Approaches." In *Handbook of Organizations*, edited by J. G. March. Chicago: Rand McNally, 1965. Pp. 1144–1170.
34. LEWIN, K. "Group Decision and Social Change." In *Readings in Social Psychology*, 3rd ed. Edited by E. Maccoby, T. M. Newcomb, and E. L. Hartley. New York: Holt, Rinehart and Winston, 1958. Pp. 197–211.
35. LIEBERMAN, M. A., I. D. YALOM, and M. B. MILES. "The Impact of Encounter Groups on Participation: Some Preliminary Findings." *Journal of Applied Behavioral Science* 8 (January 1972): 29–50.
36. LIEBOWITZ, S. JAY, and KENNETH P. DE MEUSE. "The Application of Team Building." *Human Relations* 35 (1982): 1–18.
37. LIKERT, R. *The Human Organization*. New York: McGraw-Hill, 1967.
38. ———. *New Patterns of Management*. New York: McGraw-Hill, 1961.
39. LIKERT, R., and J. G. LIKERT. *New Ways of Managing Conflict*. New York: McGraw-Hill, 1976.
40. LORSCH, J. W., and J. J. MORSE. *Organizations and Their Members: A Contingency Approach*. New York: Harper and Row, 1974.
41. LUNDGREN, D. C., and D. J. KNIGHT. "Sequential Stages of Development in Sensitivity Training Groups." *Journal of Applied Behavioral Science* 14 (1978): 204–222.
42. MANN, F. C. "Studying and Creating Change: A Means to Understanding Social Organization." *Research in Industrial Human Relations* 17 (1956): 146–167.
43. MARROW, A. J., D. G. BOWERS, and S. E. SEASHORE. *Management by Participation*. New York: Harper and Row, 1968.
44. MILES, R. E. *Theories of Management: Implications for Organizational Behavior and Development*. New York: McGraw-Hill, 1975.
45. NICHOLAS, J. M. "The Comparative Impact of Organization Development Interventions on Hard Criteria Measures." *Academy of Management Review* 7 (1982): 531–542.
46. PORRAS, JERRY I. "The Comparative Impact of Different OD Techniques and Intervention Intensities." *The Journal of Applied Behavioral Science* 15 (1979): 156–178.

47. PORRAS, J. I., and P. O. BERG. "The Impact of Organizational Development." *Academy of Management Review* 3 (April 1978): 249–268.
48. ROSEN, BENSON, and THOMAS H. JERDEE. "Effects of Decision Permanence on Managerial Willingess to Use Participation." *Academy of Management Journal* 21 (1978): 722–725.
49. SASHKIN, M. "Changing Towards Participative Management Approaches: A Model and Methods." *Academy of Management Review* 103 (July 1976): 75–87.
50. SCHEIN, E. H. *Process Consultation: Its Role in Organizational Development.* Reading, Mass: Addison-Wesley, 1969.
51. SCHEIN, E. H., and W. G. BENNIS. *Personal and Organizational Change Through Group Methods.* New York: Wiley, 1967.
52. SEASHORE, S. E., and D. G. BOWERS. "Durability of Organizational Change," *American Psychologist* 25 (March 1970): 227–233.
53. SHEPERD, H. "Changing Interpersonal and Intergroup Relationships in Organizations." In *Handbook of Organizations,* edited by J. G. March. Chicago: Rand McNally, 1965.
54. SHERIF, M., and C. SHERIF. *Groups in Harmony and Tension.* New York: Harper and Row, 1953.
55. SHIRON, A. "On Some Correlates of Combat Performance." *Administrative Science Quarterly* 21 (September 1976): 419–432.
56. SIROTA, D., and A. D. WOLFSON. "Pragmatic Approach to People Problems." *Harvard Business Review* 51 (1973): 120–128.
57. STOUFFER, SAMUEL, ET AL. *The American Soldier, Vol. 2: Combat and Its Aftermath.* Princeton, N.J.: Princeton University Press, 1949.
58. STRAUSS, G. "Organizational Development." In *Handbook of Work, Organization and Society,* edited by R. Dubin. Chicago: Rand McNally, 1976.
59. THOMAS, K. W. "A Satire: The Phenomenology of the Confirmed Thinker or Catch-22 in a T-Group." *Academy of Management Review* 2 (April 1977): 303–308.
60. TRIST, E. L., and K. W. BAMFORTH. "Some Social and Psychological Consequences of the Longwall Method of Coal Getting." *Human Relations* 41 (1951): 1–38.
61. VROOM, V. H. "Leadership." In *Handbook of Industrial and Organizational Psychology,* edited by M. D. Dunnette. Chicago. Rand McNally, 1976. Pp. 1227–1252.
62. VROOM, V. H., and P. W. YETTON. *Leadership and Decision Making.* Pittsburgh: University of Pittsburgh Press, 1973.

Discussion Questions

1. What are some of the sources that motivate actions to change interaction systems?
2. How do you feel about lab training? Do you think it might be effective in changing interaction patterns? Why? Why not?
3. Discuss the use of attitude survey feedback as a means of changing interaction patterns.
4. How would you go about designing an effective programmatic change effort to produce better teamwork?

5. Discuss a strategy that would include the use of attitude survey feedback to reduce lateral conflict. Could a similar strategy be used to reduce hierarchical conflict? Why or why not?
6. Why does the "multifaceted" strategy for change appear to be the "winning combination"?
7. Describe the Weldon Experience. How does that experience help to summarize a lot of what you have learned about motivation, the interaction system, and organizational change?

Chapter 22
Changing Motivation and Control Systems

Better Lucky Than Right?

"It can't be done. There's just *no* way to *do* it." Ted was voicing his frustration to Stanley—frustration stemming from his efforts to get the staff people representing the various personnel functions to agree on a new personnel rating scheme. They could all agree that current procedures were no good, but they just couldn't agree on an alternative. Ted continued, "It's just no use. I don't have the authority to *make* them do it. So what do they care? How in the world did I even get myself into this, anyway? You've just *got* to have the clout. The only way to get those people to act is just plain fear." And Ted's expression showed that he relished the thought.

Fear? As Ted gave vent to his frustration Stanley's thoughts drifted back to his days as student representative on The Faculty of The Department at The University. His mentor, Dr. Faust, was head of The Department at the time. Now if ever there had been a difficult group to handle, it had to be this group of "distinguished faculty." They agreed on nothing other than the right of the faculty to govern. This right applied to Dr. Faust as well, under the one man, one vote rule. But as *chairman*, Dr. Faust had the power *only* to carry out the consensus of the faculty.

Still, during that year, Dr. Faust seemed to have been exceptionally successful in getting what he wanted, and obviously *not* through fear. There was, for example, the issue of "inflated grades." In itself the problem was direct enough. During the "student unrest" in the late 1960s, the grading system, like most everything else, had come under strong attack from student activists and from certain sympathetic faculty. The rhetoric called for breaking the "oppressive system of discrimination" produced by "socially repressive forces." There were also less colorful demands for greater student freedom to elect courses for which they lacked adequate preparation, without fear of "retaliation" through the "obsolete" system of grading. One activist professor had even adopted the stance of giving straight A's to all students, the logic being that *all* students at this university were above average and grades ought to reflect this. The aftermath of this tempest could be observed in the fact that the "average" grade at this point hovered at 3.0 or B.

But with the coming of the new era of student "responsibility," with the former furor over, it was no secret that Dr. Faust believed the time was at hand to restore normality—for the faculty to reassume the responsibility of sorting the academic wheat from chaff, so to speak. Yet Faust had spoken openly to no one of his interest, or so it was thought. Consequently, events at the first faculty meeting of the new academic year were somewhat surprising. Not for what happened as much as for what *didn't* happen. At first the meeting had proceeded as usual. Old business was disposed of, and Dr. Faust made the call for new business.

"Yes, Mr. Chairman. It occurs to me that we have an issue before us at this time of *considerable* gravity, an issue which we have successfully ignored over the past years; that of faculty responsibility for providing honest appraisals of student work, both for students and for their prospective employers. As you know . . ." The speaker, a distinguished professor widely respected by the faculty, proceeded to set forth the issue of "grade inflation" in a most eloquent, forceful, and reasonable way. Following this, Dr. Faust, from the Chair, noted interest in the issue and asked if there might be further comments. There were. And so he selected a speaker, apparently at random, from the sea of hands. This commentator was one of the junior faculty, a bright young scholar, a future star, yet one who seldom spoke up on such matters. Actually, he seldom even showed up at faculty meetings. But this time, and taking a tack very different from the first speaker, he brought forth a tightly reasoned and complementary argument supporting the stand of the first speaker.

"I see," commented Faust following this last statement, "that there seems to be a great deal of faculty interest in this matter. Perhaps we had best devote more time to this issue. Are there other opinions?"

Once again Faust selected from the sea of hands. This time, however, the speaker designated was a different sort. He was known to all as a dedicated teacher, yet one who invariably seemed to misunderstand the issue. Equally invariably, he persisted in the careful and logical development of a lengthy rejoinder unrelated to whatever topic was at hand. So in this case he proceeded to point to the value of higher grades in attracting better students to the departmental major, since, as all knew, it was indeed the better students who had the higher grades. Again, as usual, his discourse drew rejoinders from several professors of no particular persuasion in the matter, who could not resist the sport of pointing out the error in his logic. Of course, in doing so they supported, if only implicitly, the position taken by the earlier speakers.

Again it was the Chair's turn to speak. "Gentlemen, I believe I detect a considerable consensus here toward developing an approach to restoring the integrity of our method of assigning grades. The Chair will entertain a motion from the floor to charge a committee with responsibility to report to this body next month on the means to carry through such a change. Do I hear such a motion?"

And so it was done. The committee was appointed mostly from the speakers advocating change, but carefully included an influential "radical" professor who almost certainly would be against such a change. Even more oddly, the suggestion to include this professor came from one of the committee members just appointed, one who most certainly knew of this professor's opinion. Come to think of it, there was something else odd about those first nominations: all were people who were extremely productive, extremely busy—the kind who usually gracefully decline to serve on such ad hoc administrative committees. But none did so in this case. Strange.

At the following month's meeting, a "declaration of the sense of the faculty" that the average overall grade for departmental courses ought to "display a central tendency" of 2.5—halfway between a B and a C—was passed, though not without some vocal dissent. Also included were statements elaborating the safeguards protecting individual faculty judgment. No, not every section needed to average 2.5. And no, it was not the intent of the system to penalize the better teachers by forcing them to assign lower grades even though their students could show above average performance. That issue might best be handled by building a more standard content into lower-level core course examinations, and then by providing each faculty member with a summary sheet displaying the average grades for each section of each course.

In the end, the system adopted dealt with almost all objections in a sensitive yet serious way, scrupulously acknowledging individual faculty rights while accepting the necessity of providing feedback to all faculty. Oh yes, one serious objection did develop. Several faculty members objected to circulating average grades for each section to the entire faculty. They felt it might be possible to misinterpret these grades if one were unfamiliar with the course content. However, this discussion was resolved surprisingly well by a faculty member previously thought to be uncommitted who convincingly argued that such detail was needed in order to provide "constructuve feedback."

As it turned out, the new system worked extremely well, though one professor took pride in refusing to change his ways. Unlike some of his colleagues, he refused to yield to the needling of other faculty members about his being a "rate buster." As for Dr. Faust, he never did, and never would, say a word to any of the faculty about their section grades, though obviously he knew the identities of the occasional offenders. After all, he had no power, had he? He was there to carry out the wishes of the faculty—no more, no less . . . was he not? And wasn't it a lucky thing that the right people had spoken up at the right time to help him bring about the change that he had thought to be absolutely essential?

We close this book with a statement about changing motivation and control systems. We do so because of the universality of such systems and because such systems often touch other organizational systems. In a sense, then, much organizational behavior is affected by the implementation of new motivational and control systems (2). In this chapter we will show you how that is so.

Remember that productive behavior is directed by providing individual incentives that are linked to the achievement of the outcome desired by organization development. Two key axioms of reinforcement theory must hold if the motivation system is to function as expected (4, 17):

Incentives must be provided for the desired behavior.

Individuals, consciously or subconsciously, must be able to associate the provision of the incentive with the desired behavior.

Our opening story describes a change in a motivation system. The change is designed to set things right—to encourage the faculty to change their grading behavior. Of course, the students objected, and that is the point, for why were grades inflated to begin with? The faculty were on the firing line. They were the ones that had to deal with the problems associated with giving low grades—student complaints, low enrollments, poor student evaluations, and so forth. And how do academic administrators judge good teaching? They use student complaints, popularity of classes, and student evaluations. Therefore, Faust, with several other faculty members concerned about academic standards and the meaning of the grading system, had to change the incentives that directed faculty behavior. They did so, not through the heavy hand of ediction, but through the subtle manipulation of the self-regulatory system, where the incentives were changed by the faculty itself. Remember, too, that one of the functions of organizational control systems is to enable that association between incentives and behavior. Such enabling is best achieved through the measurement and feedback of the outcomes of behavior and then the appropriate administration of reinforcement. You may analyze our story accordingly.

We will do several things in this chapter. First, we will describe a change of a change in a control system (PIP). Next, we will describe a change in a motivation system (SIMP). Then we will show how control systems are related to other organizational systems. You will learn, for example, that changes in control systems can have an effect on authority relationships, on interpersonal relationships, and on the structure of incentives and hence the motivation system.

We will describe some innovative attempts to deal with the problems created by mechanical or automated control systems such as assembly lines. Most of such documented efforts have taken place in the Scandinavian countries, most notably Norway and Sweden.

We will deal with a control system called MBO, which has evolved from a basic management philosophy to a well-articulated, often formalized system, the intent of which is to focus on output. As you shall see, MBO incorporates participative management as the process for establishing goals and the behavioral means for reaching goals. Further, we shall show you how, despite that commonly held philosophy, MBO often ends up like other mechanical control systems (24, 41).

Finally, you will see that the internalized motive to work and the external organizational controls designed to ensure output are often in conflict. It is as though they are the flip sides of the same coin, and when one is up the other is down (38). An attempt to deal with that bothersome issue is contained in a comprehensive system change called the Scanlon plan. We will deal with that as well.

Changing a Changed Control System: PIP Is Modified

Recall the vignette "Friendly Persuasion" in Chapter 19. There we depicted a major organizational change that was designed to control the productive output of the manufacturing facilities of The Company. It was also supposed to increase the production of the millhands who, to the consternation of management, seemed to be producing at only 65 percent of the synthetic standards derived by The Company's industrial engineers. "Work Smarter, Not Harder" in Chapter 20 picks up the story about a year later when Faust and his people were able to demonstrate to The Company management that PIP was not doing all that was intended and in fact did something quite unintended—contributed substantially to a significant decline in the millhands' work satisfaction. That unhappy occurrence resulted in a desire to make some further adjustments.

Before we deal with the change in PIP, let us first describe The Company manufacturing system before PIP. Then we will briefly describe PIP and its consequence.

There were four important characteristics of The Company before PIP. First, production standards were "past actuals"; that is, production was planned and scheduled according to what had been done in the past. Moreover, workers were evaluated against these historical records. If they met or exceeded the past actuals, then they were judged satisfactory performers. And since the standards were ones that they had already met, there were few instances when they could not meet them again.

Second, the credo "a fair day's work for a fair day's pay" represented the relationship between The Company and the workers. The assumption here was that if you treated people well, they would respond in kind. Hence, highly formalized external control systems were seen as not needed—redundant in fact—for what more could people do than provide a fair day's work?

Third, work unit managers were seen as "in control" of their own shops. That is, they could be trusted to exercise their own judgment as to what constituted a fair day's work, transmit the reasons for that judgment in a way that would be acceptable to the workers and motivate them to conform to that reasonable judgment.

Finally, everyone viewed quality to be a major element of performance (32). The norm of quality permeated the entire manufacturing system—so much so that workers spent a great deal of time in making things right. The quality was so good before PIP that the quality assurance function was confined to a small group of "final testers" in each of the plants—and then primarily as a fail-safe assurance to customers—not in any sense a behavior control. Job satisfaction in The Company was remarkably high (57).

PIP Is Introduced

Here are the specifics of PIP. First, the "one best way" for each manufacturing job was identified by industrial engineers, and then a synthetic time standard was attached to the method. The workers were then evaluated according to how well they measured up to these standards. In this way "reasonable" norms were established to provide The Company better prediction and hence better planning and scheduling capability.

With the replacement of the past actuals by synthetic standards, the workers were required to shoot at targets never before attained. A fair day's work was defined upward, implying that before PIP people were not doing a fair day's work. Also, supervisory discretion and control were extracted from the work unit and replaced by normative data and performance records. And finally, quality became subordinated to quantity as an evaluation criterion and hence important normative value.

PIP was implemented throughout The Company, except in Ben Franklyn's plant. And what were the effects? Dr. Faust explained them pretty well. The percentage of standard production went up from approximately 65 percent to about 90 percent, the number of hours claimed increased, and job satisfaction as measured by attitude surveys dropped a great deal. Further data analyses indicated that PIP seemed to be the cause of the decline in satisfaction (32). And the work unit's managers did not like the PIP program any better than the workers, even though output increased and the performance measures were better (14).

The reasons for these negative results are basic to the problems of such control procedures. As we suggested, good control procedures require measurement. Measurement in turn focuses attention on what is measurable—sometimes to the exclusion of more subjective aspects of performance, such as quality. Furthermore, as we said, measurements that are easily accessible will be used to limit discretion concerning the range of possible behaviors, primarily those related to the measured outputs. Such measurement also tends to narrow the other areas in which discretion can be exercised, because the controllers will concentrate on the measurements and not on the nonmeasured outputs or behavior. Consequently, decision makers are virtually forced to attend to measured factors and to concern themselves only with how well their groups are doing relative to those factors. That is, did the groups meet the standards? Never mind downtime, scrap and rework, absenteeism, and the like.

Data Analysis and Changes in PIP

As Faust explained, the PIP program was identified as the primary cause of a decline in satisfaction among blue-collar workers. However, Faust pointed out that there was no way The Company was going to dump PIP. PIP had, in fact, accomplished what had been intended. What then was the organizational response?

The people responsible for disclosing the problems with PIP were also given the responsibility of identifying the aspects of PIP that contributed to the decline in morale. Several things were noted: people were working harder, quality and craftsmanship had been downplayed (Remember "Good enough is best"?), and the employees felt that their complaints about work pressure and standards were not given a fair hearing. However, since "working harder" was not seen as bad by management and since significant quality problems did not seem to surface, management was reluctant to back off from their emphasis on production. So, at the outset they focused on the grievance procedure.

The primary reason the grievance channels were blocked concerned who seemed to determine methods and quantity of production. The office or unit level where methods and quantity decisions were made was called the locus of control (14, 57). Under PIP the locus of control was removed from the work units, and even from the lower levels of the line management. Instead, the workers and unit managers saw the locus residing in the industrial engineering staff function.

Neither the unit manager nor the workers had much influence over important aspects of their work. The IEs *could* change methods and standards, but they were not likely to do so. The data came directly from their "scientifically developed" data books, and anyway, they did not want to look bad. Thus the "blocked" grievance channels.

The Northland Experiment

Management was not about to lose the benefits of PIP. But they also did not want a further decline in job satisfaction. Therefore they decided to conduct an experiment in one of the plants to determine whether or not modifications of the control structure could be made without losing the benefits of PIP. This is what they did.

First, they established experimental and control groups. These groups were matched on technology and satisfaction levels. Group meetings were held to discuss the problems the workers saw in carrying forth their responsibilities. Further, the workers were encouraged to bring their work problems to the unit manager. In the experimental group *but not in the control group,* the unit managers were empowered to take an employee off a standard immediately if they found that standard to be questionable. The worker was no longer evaluated against standard once the removal decision was made. After that, the manager took the disputed standard to industrial engineering for a final determination.

Careful records were kept of the number of times employees complained about standards, the percentage of these complaints that were sustained, and the productivity records against standards. An attitude survey was conducted six months later. Here are the results of the experiment.

1. Job satisfaction increased significantly in the experimental group but not in the control group, though the difference between the two groups at the end of the experiment was not statistically significant (59).
2. Additional data analyses disclosed that employees in the experimental groups whose managers *changed* during the experimental process had the highest rate of increase in job satisfaction and that these increases were far greater than for any other group. Indeed, changes in management seemed to be the primary variable moderating the relationship between the experimental change and the subsequent changes in satisfaction. The reason for this seemed to be that changes in the structure of the control system did not have the intended results unless changes in the interaction system occurred as well. Apparently managers who had long-established interaction patterns with their work units found it difficult to change even though the previous constraints were removed.

3. Productivity remained the same. Further, only 17 percent of all of the jobs on standard were removed from standard due to the common agreement that was struck between the worker and his manager, though well over 90 percent of the challenged rates were sustained. In other words, workers complained infrequently, and when they did, it was for good reason.
4. After the experiment, job control was seen as being more substantially located within the work unit. No such finding occurred in the control groups. Further, the probability of having grievances fairly heard increased substantially in the experimental group but not at all in the control group.

What does all of this mean? First, the implementation of rigorous control procedures for one purpose can result in the use of measurement for quite another purpose. In this case, production controls for planning, scheduling, and raising production focused on the latter and ultimately served to control behavior.

Second, if controls become too demanding and are used to evaluate people, there will be a great deal of motivation to try to beat the system (38).

Third, the use of controlling measures can easily cause decisions about proper output to be made away from the actual operations. It can lead as well to depersonalization of management to the point where the measurements and the control system are actually making the decision, not management. This phenomenon leads to the common phrases "going by the book" or "by the numbers." Such a situation clearly affects managerial discretion (41).

Fourth, where managerial discretion is limited "by the book," so too is the employee's. The net result then of rigorous control systems is to reduce lower participants' ability to influence the system. And from the operating level, despite higher management's view that things are better controlled, the lower participants are likely to feel that they have less net influence (12). As we have seen, such a condition tends to be negatively associated with measures of effectiveness (45, 62).

Finally, in order to reduce these problems, two classes of action may be taken. The first is tightening the controls to ensure expected output or behavior (41). This course, however, appears to lead to similar problems. The second is shifting control downward to the operating level (1, 38). The Northland experiment is an example of that. The Northland experiment (hereafter referred to as "PIP-changed" or PIPC) guided subsequent changes in the company plants—changes that earmark those plants today.

Ben's Response

Recall Ben Franklyn's aversion to PIP and the lengths the company went to to get him "on board." The situation was described in "The One Best Way"

(Chapter 17). Let us put this experience into the proper context. The change was a response to PIP. Ben Franklyn would have nothing to do with work measurement because he anticipated the problems associated with it. He knew intuitively the difference as well as the relationship between control and motivation.

Ben's resistance to work measurement was found in two of his basic premises. The first was that employees would resist controlling procedures and, as a consequence, would be motivated only to meet standard but no more. Beyond meeting standard, the employees would then be free and, more importantly, motivated to find ways of beating the system. Second, Ben felt that the overall goal of increasing performance could best be met by attaching all of the plant's important incentives to that goal. Ben, therefore, instituted the following procedures. First, he incorporated a "work simplification" approach to changing methods. Under work simplification, employees are trained in industrial engineering principles. However, the employees themselves make the methods changes, not the industrial engineers.

Second, Ben attached all rewards to the performance objectives (3, 11). For example, the suggestions program was incorporated into the reward structure. All suggestions for improvement were given at least a nominal award. Substantial suggestions received commensurate awards. And to avoid the pitfall Whyte suggests (69), whenever a suggested methods change was incorporated into the production process, all employees who changed their methods, and hence increased their performance, were given merit increases. Finally, regardless of other qualifications, top performers were given the first shot at promotion, either to higher skill levels or to management. The program was called the Simplification, Improvement, and Motivational Program (SIMP) (32).

What were the consequences? We know that costs of production went down considerably. In fact, the costs went down so much that The Company had to maintain an artificially high product price in order to avoid antitrust problems because of too great a market penetration. Furthermore, once the training program was officially terminated, crucial elements became part of the ongoing management system. For example, methods changes were constantly being made by the employees. These changes were processed through the suggestion system, and the level of participation in that system substantially exceeded all other plants in The Company. Furthermore, in contradistinction to what went on under PIP, the employees expressed strong satisfaction with the management system, their job, and the reward system (14, 32).

Notice the similarities between this experience and that of Lincoln Electric described in Chapter 9. In each case, the incentives were largely financial, and the primary means for getting these incentives was performance improvement. Further, the expectation that such linkages were a reality seemed shared by most people. To do other than put forth one's best efforts was to violate the system requirements.

These points are not made to advocate financial incentive systems. Rather, they are made to underline the importance of clearly and unequivocally connecting desired behaviors with organizational reinforcements, whatever their nature. As we have said, there is little evidence that a change in motivational schemes without concrete incentives, objective standards or goals, or the direct accountability of people to some standard or goal actually increases performance.

Changes Compared: The Systems Effect of Three Programs

One of our main points is that, although the systems we describe are conceptually separable, they are, in actual fact, related. That is, a change in the control system may affect the motivation system, which in turn may affect the social system, and so forth. The precise direction and definition of the network of relationships is generally indeterminate, but by now you should have some ideas about what the network might look like.

Table 22.1 illustrates this system interrelationship. The table, which compares PIP, SIMP, and PIPC, discloses that the most widespread and significant changes occurred under PIP, but that each of these changes had an effect beyond its intended target.

For example, take the effect of the change programs on the authority structure. PIP and PIPC directly affected that structure by relocating power away from and then back to the work unit. Further, each had a direct bearing on the discretionary authority of the line management and the staff IEs. SIMP, however, only reinforced the old authority system. Notice too that because of the change in discretionary authority under PIP, the fundamental nature of the worker-manager relationship changed as well.

The Assembly Line and Organizational Controls

Perhaps the most common and, to some people, oppressive organizational control is the assembly line. This machine-paced method of production controls both behavior and output. The predominant characteristic of an assembly line is that the product to be assembled moves along a conveyer at a relatively fixed rate and people must accommodate to that rate in order to do their job. Such a mechanically controlled procedure allows little room for personal autonomy and provides maximum knowledge of predicted output. In this sense, then, an assembly line illustrates the quintessential organizational control.

The responses to such control are predictable and are illustrated in a quote from a student of ours who was an assembly-line operator for General Motors.

TABLE 22.1 Changes in Systems Compared

Changes	PIP	SIMP	PIPC
In control system	From "past actuals" historical standards to objectively and scientifically derived synthetic standards; external control. Shift in locus of control away from line management and toward work measurement. Control depersonalized; changes in methods and standards came from industrial engineers, not the workers.	*Internal* and *external* control; past actuals still operative but *improvement* became the standard. Locus of control shared in the department. Changes in methods and standards came from workers.	Combinations of synthetic standards and negotiations between management and employees when standards are seen as unfair; locus of control partially shifted down through line hierarchy; changes in methods and standards codetermined by workers, unit manager, and industrial engineers when a standard was questioned.
In social system	Shift in norms, values, and ideology from a familial to formal; from the value of quality to "good enough is best." Depersonalized evaluation.	Changes in the criterion for mobility; stronger emphasis on improvement, otherwise norms, values, and ideology remained intact.	Reaffirmations of value that employee *could* participate in the process of control; that unit management was compelled to use judgment concerning standards.
In power and authority systems	Discretion of unit manager for decision making reduced. Viewed by employees as having less power. Unit manager views his or her manager as having less power. Staff power increased; authority of expertise enhanced.	No change.	Unit manager provided old discretion in decision making; view by employees that manager has such discretionary power of authority partially reinstated.
In interaction systems	Changed relations between supervisor and subordinate; supervisor became enforcer and transmitter; increase in individual behavior, decrease in group cohesion.	Supervisor's role as supporter enhanced; groups were cohesive.	Reinstated negotiation process between management and employee, though primarily when unit manager was changed. No data on group cohesion.
In motivation system	Increased motivation to produce high quantity; decreased motivation to produce high quality; shift from intrinsic motive patterns to extrinsic; rewards were extrinsic but reinforcement was negative; increased motive to beat the system.	Increased motivation to produce high quantity; values of quality static; intrinsic and extrinsic motive patterns remained in same balance; rewards were extrinsic and reinforcement was positive.	Some evidence that incentives for claiming were reduced.

> Man it's terrible. Nine hundred to twelve hundred pieces an hour on the feeder machine. Choop, Choop, Choop, Choop. That's all they do man—on the fly. That's what they call it—the machine don't stop. Day after day after day. Choop, Choop, Choop—here it come, here I am, there it go. I run alongside to do my job and then I run back to catch another. Man, it's terrible. A monkey could do it.

Though some do not mind, may even like such work, our student's response is not unusual. Typical correlates of machine-paced assembly lines tend to be high turnover, absences, and other manifestations of frustration, tension, and anger (see 40, 60, 64 for additional documentation of these points).

Management is in a dilemma about assembly lines. Since such technologies have proved effective, and since much capital has been invested to establish them, management is reluctant to tinker with them very much. However, given an ever-increasing emphasis on the quality of working life (13), there appears to be a trend toward a search for alternative modes of production. The Scandinavian countries have been foremost in designing such alternatives (65). One documented case is presented in the next section along with a discussion.

The Autonomous Work Group: Experiments in Alternative Modes of Production

During the 1960s absenteeism and turnover were significant problems in many manufacturing enterprises in Sweden. The problem was particularly bad in the automotive plants of the Saab and Volvo companies. Each of these companies, with the help of an organization called the Swedish Employer's Confederation, conducted experiments wherein the assembly lines were modified to incorporate autonomous work groups empowered to control their pace of production. The success of the experiments led to the establishment of new plants without assembly lines as we have come to know them. Both the Saab and the Volvo experience deserve attention, but since the changes in production technology were similar in both and had similar results, we will report only the experience of the Saab engine plant.

Before the new engine plant was designed, Saab was experiencing high rates of unplanned work stoppages, turnover was as high as 70 percent annually, recruitment to the new plants was difficult, and absences ran as high as 25 percent on days adjacent to weekends or holidays. Furthermore, there was a problem with quality. The Saab auto had developed a reputation as a high-quality product during the late 1950s and early 1960s—a reputation diminished because of serious troubles with the autos beginning in about 1965 or 1966. These problems were the predominant factors that led Saab to search for alternatives to the traditional assembly-line process, a process they had determined was at the root of their trouble.

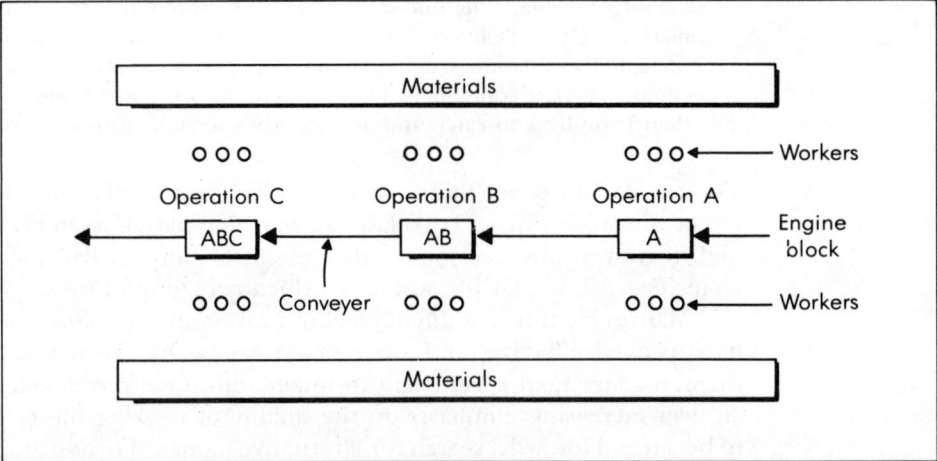

FIGURE 22.1 Traditional Assembly Line

The changes that occurred are illustrated in Figures 22.1 and 22.2. Figure 22.1 shows the traditional assembly line, wherein the engine blocks move on a conveyer along which there are numerous work stations manned by assemblers. Each assembler is expected to do a small, short-cycle job as the block passes his or her station. At the end of its line run, the block is complete.

Figure 20.2 describes the change. According to the new process, the blocks move along a conveyer, and then are channeled to a work station. At the work station is a group of assemblers who assemble a complete engine block. The completed block then is moved along to further disposition.

Several things are supposed to happen under such an arrangement. First, the groups make decisions about who works where and at what time. Job rotation is common. Each person learns to perform any operation in the assembly of the engine block. And although the conveyer to some extent still controls the speed at which people work, it is completely different from the typical assembly line. The group itself *determines the pace* of production. Consequently, group norms become a more prominent determiner of production speed.

Second, the job cycle goes up considerably. For example, depending on the decision of the group, the work cycle for a completed job may run as high as twenty-five to thirty minutes, whereas on the traditional assembly line the cycle was about two minutes.

Third, the work group is responsible and therefore accountable for quality. Accountability for variations in quality, therefore, is easily placed (63).

Fourth, the new assembly system directly affects the manager of the work group. Since the group itself controls production and quality, as well as human and material resource allocation, supervisors lose some control over internal

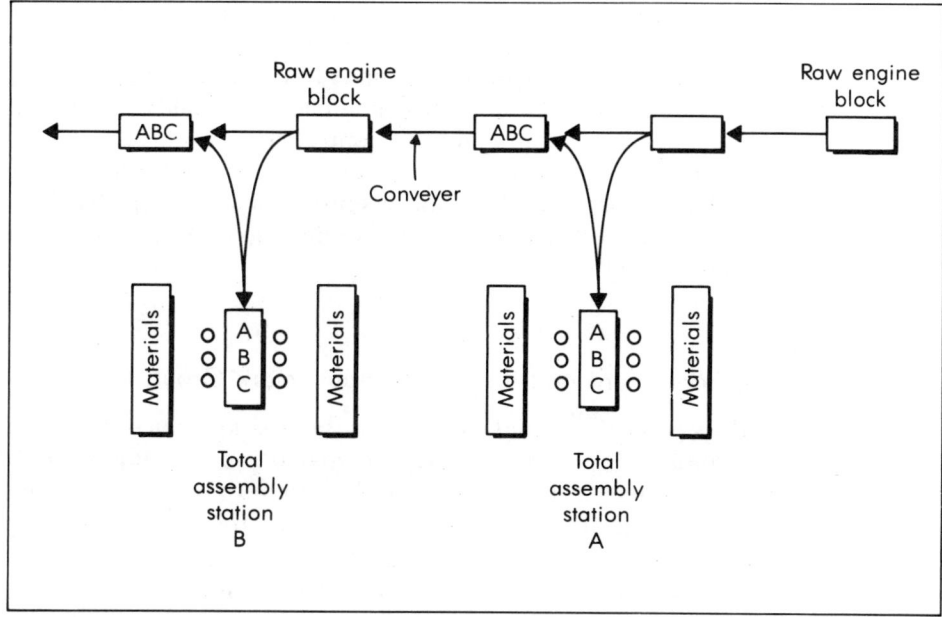

FIGURE 22.2   Autonomous Work Group Assembly Process

group matters. At the same time, however, they are freed to spend more time on intergroup relations, resource procurement, and other kinds of external boundary work.

This new arrangement, then, shifts the locus of control for most production matters (such as quantity, quality, and resource allocation) from an assembly line into the work group. The new arrangement offers the group a good opportunity to develop production norms and group cohesiveness. Perhaps most important, the group itself decides how its human resources are allocated and apparently does so according to time and circumstance.

What are the production results? Quantity of production is about the same as in traditional assembly-line operations, quality has gone up to some extent, absences and turnover have diminished considerably, and downtime as a percentage of total manufacturing time is down from 6 percent to 2 percent.

Well, then, what have we got? We know that the assembly lines of Saab and Volvo have been replaced by autonomous work groups and that this new technology has affected the control system which, in turn, seems related to the interaction system and the authority system. We know too that the jobs have been enriched to the extent that assembling a complete engine block offers workers more complexity, interest, and job challenge than the simple tasks associated with the assembly line. And we know that on several criteria of effectiveness, improvements have taken place.

What we do not know is the precise relationship between the changes in the control system and the subsequent network of relationships (15). Nevertheless, it seems to us that the predominant causal factor is that output and behavioral control shifts from a machine-paced assembly line to the work group. The assemblers became able to control their work pace. They could allocate tasks according to work needs within the work groups and pretty much by consensus. And accordingly there was a sense of shared responsibility for the quality of the final product (63, 65). These findings warrant careful consideration by manufacturing management.[1]

Job Enrichment and the Autonomous Work Group Compared

Perhaps it has occurred to you that there is not much difference between our description of the autonomous work group and that of job enrichment. Indeed, job enrichment is an essential ingredient in most reported changes to the autonomous work group. The differences between the two lie primarily in intent and scope.

As for intent, job enrichment is usually seen as a means of increasing motivation. The autonomous work group is seen as a way of reducing the restrictions of a control system and of democratizing the workplace. Make no mistake, the heart of the philosophy behind the autonomous work group effort is that imposed controls and consequent restriction of freedom and influence in the production process are at the root of the dehumanized workplace.

Job enrichment is primarily derived from psychological constructs. The intent is to focus on intrinsic job factors and hence the relationship between the worker and job. Rarely is it intended as a systemwide change, and as Sirota and Wolfson point out (58, 59) this specific targeting is job enrichment's strength as well as its weakness. Its strength is that a diagnosis can be made for a specific job category, and if job enrichment is warranted in one or two areas, these become the targets. Its weakness is that a change in job enrichment is difficult to isolate from the rest of the organizational parts. Consequently, possible resistance among those related organizational units might make it difficult to sustain. Indeed that was one of the points made by Locke et al. (43).

Neither is there evidence at present that job enrichment can sustain the job motivation of a lot of people (7, 26, 27, 67). Why this should be so is thus far unclear. The autonomous work group, on the other hand, is designed to overcome these weaknesses.

Furthermore, job enrichment ordinarily says little about group factors—group decisions to allocate human and material resources and the relationship of the change to other aspects of the plant or office.[2] In autonomous work group efforts such things are central features of the changes.

Finally, the autonomous work group concept itself is derived on one hand from democratic values and on the other from many reports on the role of work groups as an interface of the individual and the larger social and technical organization (65). Consequently, when it has been tried, other changes have been made consistent with democratic values and with the requirement that the group be allowed to establish its own control system (36-38). In some cases changes in the incentive system have occurred as well, though we view this as targeted to sustain production at high levels and not as a requirement for the primary intent of changing the locus of control (36).

Limitations of Autonomous Work Groups

There are some important limitations to the use of autonomous work groups. Box 27, which describes a study of Pennsylvania coal mines, illustrates this point.

Another study at the Volkswagon plant in Salzgitter, West Germany, provided only modest support for the efficacy of AWGs (34). That plant went about the change in much the same way as the Norwegian studies reported in Chapter 19. It was coordinated with the support of the government in collaboration with management and labor and with solid preparation and training and participation of the workers. However, problems arose between the union and management over two issues: the extent of autonomy to be enjoyed by the worker and the level of remuneration; the workers felt that they should be paid at a higher level according to the additional responsibilities. The issues were not resolved, and the union withdrew its participation. Although the experiment proceded anyway under the sponsorship of the company, the following conclusions were drawn:

1. The costs associated with complex, highly mechanized assembly are probably lower than with AWGs.
2. AWG requires more highly skilled (and presumably more costly) labor.
3. Reduced absenteeism and turnover and higher quality cannot compensate for the additional costs of AWGs. Management felt that AWG was not economically feasible in mass production.

The Pennsylvania coal mining study and the Volkswagon report signal caution. Although most evidence suggests that there are some significant benefits to AWGs, these benefits seem limited by context. It seems possible to work out some of the problems associated with the coal miner's job switching, but those inherent in large-scale mass production are troublesome. Still, the idea of moving the control over job territory to the worker motivated quite a number of very large mass production industries to take an interest in the so-called quality of work life (13, 21, 22, 23, 31, 53).

> **Box 27**
>
> ## We'd Rather Be Safe Than Switch
>
> A thirteen-month study examined the occurrence of job-switching behavior in autonomous work groups (AWGs) in a coal mine located in the soft-coal region of central Pennsylvania. A major feature of AWGs is that members of the group switch from job to job according to the work need and to their inclinations to switch. Since switching is an essential element of the AWG, if it does not occur regularly, or if it is rejected by group members, AWGs may not be successful. Indeed according to the major AWG theorists group members are "able to self-regulate and control the group task best where the members are multi-skilled all around workmen [so as to] replace co-workers when they are tired, bored or absent" (p. 289). However, the researchers noted that much less switching took place than expected during the beginning stages of the study. The question was, why?
>
> To find the answers the investigators observed the switching behavior of fifty-four miners in two AWGs. In addition each miner filled out a seventy-six-item questionnaire that measured the following variables: attitude toward switching, job satisfaction, authoritarianism, job status, job anxiety, legitimacy of participation, the job core dimensions described in Chapter 9, job ability and job involvement. Also measures of age, seniority, education, and direction of job switching (high to lower status or vice versa) were observed.
>
> Correlations were then run between job switching and all of those measures. The results of interest were: (1) the better the education, the more the job switching; (2) the less the seniority and age, the more the job switching; and (3) the higher the job status, the less the switching. Age, job satisfaction, and status were found to be among the best predictors to switching behavior. Furthermore, the switching ordinarily occurred toward higher-status jobs.
>
> The researchers conclude that age and social structure place significant limits on job switching in AWGs. Older people feel comfortable in their work routines and are threatened by change, whereas younger miners want to develop a greater breadth of job competence. Furthermore, when there are status differences within the AWGs, those in higher-status jobs want to hang on to them whereas those in lower-status jobs want experience in the higher-status ones—a source of possible conflict when the avenues to higher-status jobs are closed. Finally, a demonstrated ability of the lower-status people to handle a higher status job threatens people in two ways: (1) the myths surrounding the higher-status jobs (only old, more experienced and cleverer people can handle them) are effectively destroyed, and (2) people who have demonstrated their ability to handle the higher-status jobs do not want to go back to lower-status ones.
>
> Melvin Blumberg, "Job Switching in Autonomous Work Groups: An Exploratory Study in a Pennsylvania Coal Mine." *Academy of Management Journal* 23 (1980): 287–306.

The American Experience

One of the American responses to the productivity problems that first surfaced in the mid-1970s was to examine the role of production workers in the whole process. Many of our industrialists looked to Japan for some guidance since the Japanese had been our chief competitors in two of our major industries, autos and steel. And they were beating us. Our industrialists found that the Japanese were systematically including production workers in several plants in devising work methods and product improvement programs. Some of these programs were called *quality circles.* They were so named because the original focus was on quality and the group gathered in circles to discuss quality improvement. Ideas coming from this process were often incorporated.

Although the ideas behind the quality circles had been known in this country for many years, the combination of a productivity crisis and Japan's success produced an intense interest in incorporating the ideas here. What has been done generally is not much different from what we described under participative decision making, but two experiences bear discussion.

The first is the GM plant in Tarrytown, New York (22), and the second is the Ford transmission plant in Sharonville, Ohio (21, 23). Involving workers in changing their work environment is at the heart of both programs.

Both the Ford and GM plants had been suffering from poor labor relations for some time and both were considered by their respective corporate management as poor performers and candidates for closing. That provided a major motivation for change. In each case there was strong support for the change at the top of both the management and union hierarchies.

Although there were differences in the programs, the employee involvement effort at the Ford Sharonville plant can illustrate the major features of each. This is what they did:

- There was total union involvement in the inception, design, and implementation of the program.
- Forty problem-solving groups were created under the auspices of a National Joint Committee of union-management membership.
- A new plant manager was involved with and committed to the program.
- A union-management coordinating committee was created, co-chaired by the chairman of the state bargaining committee and a high-level line manager.
- The joint committee set forth model plans for establishing problem-solving groups at the shop-floor level.
- A group of worker volunteers were selected from a department in each of two major plant areas. These set the pattern for the subsequent establishment of the rest of the groups.
- Forty groups were made up of about six hourly people, staff support,

and supervisors, but each group also elected its own leader, usually not a supervisor.
- The groups were trained in problem solving, participation, and group processes, and communications, and in rudimentary statistical procedures as they pertained to quality and production.
- The groups had complete freedom to choose their problems and to establish their priorities. They had the authority to call on any expertise in the plant as needed.
- The program ultimately encompassed the entire plant—white- and blue-collar, management and nonmanagement alike.

The Tarrytown experience differed in three important respects. The original impetus for the total program came much more slowly with more of a push from the UAW as part of the union Quality of Work Life (QWL) emphasis. Indeed, in 1973 the UAW and GM included in their national contract a letter committing each party to QWL. The process itself was more elaborate and longer because it was subject to the natural forces that existed within the plant. Finally, the so-called big commitment came about four years after the initial commitment, with an extensive plantwide training program that sought to indoctrinate all employees, about 3800 of them, into the ways of problem solving and involvement (22).

Both programs are ongoing, institutionalized efforts that have apparently produced substantial benefits. At Sharonville, for example, the quality is considered the best in the division, up from the worst. At Tarrytown, absenteeism went from 7.25 percent to 2.5 percent and grievances "on the docket" went from about 2000 to 22 in seven years. The Ford company, having written EI (employee involvement) programs into its 1979 national contract, as of May 1983 had involved nine Ford operations in EI. More than 9000 employees are currently meeting regularly in 780 active problem-solving groups across the country, and the program is getting larger. In a recent Ford survey using before-and-after measures and comparing EI participants to nonparticipants, substantial gains in a variety of work-related attitudes, including perceptions of quality and quantity improvements, were reported by the EI participants (23). Of course we know the problems of causal interpretations but it seems clear to all involved that the programs have been successful.

These programs then are examples of how two capital-intensive industries deal with the problems inherent in mechanized control systems such as assembly lines. The assembly lines stayed intact, but the organizations found other ways of giving employees control over their job territory and hence a stake in the process. Whether such efforts will continue to generalize extensively remains to be seen.

Some useful generalizations can be drawn from these experiences.

1. Management must be competent to run the business as a profit-making enterprise and be committed to the program as a part of that effort.
2. Where there is a union, the union should be strong, trusted by its membership, and committed to the program.
3. Management ought to take the initiative.
4. Where there is a union the union-management contract should be inviolate.
5. Middle and lower management should be completely involved in the program.
6. The program should not be used to manipulate employees for management's purposes—to speed up the line or to reduce the work force.
7. The program should be voluntary, although it should be clear that the inherent desirability will increase volunteerism.
8. The program should start on a limited experimental footing and expand according to its perceived worth.
9. Problems in the program should be solved "on the spot."
10. The program must have ample opportunities for employee's participation in problem solving, and such behavior should be reinforced.
11. The program should begin an ongoing effort that will then become standard operating procedure (22).

Let us turn now to a control system that has gained the attention of a wide variety of organizations but, as we shall see, has had only variable success.

Management by Objectives as a Control System

Management by objectives (MBO) is a management philosophy. Its major intent is to systematize the planning, goal-setting, goal-seeking, and goal-reaching functions of management in order, it is said, to enhance predictability, personnel evaluations, and motivation and, thus, performance (9, 44, 51). What is not said is that it enhances control as well. Indeed, it is our contention that the potential control function of MBO is its very heart, and the major reason why it is so attractive to management.

MBO has several key elements: goal setting, participation, planning, and periodic review. Goals are set in a participatory way, plans are developed to reach these goals, and reviews are made to evaluate progress and the extent of goal reaching (35, 36). We will examine these in detail later, but first, we will look at the general process.

First, top management states its major objectives. These objectives are considered the targets toward which the rest of the organization aims. Then as

Raia (51) suggests, there is a cascading of the objectives down through the organization, with each successively lower level carving out its piece of the objectives' pie. Thus, the objectives change from general and broad-gauged to specific and measurable as they move down through the organization.

For example, assume that the chief executive officer of a telephone company has as his or her main objectives the reduction of complaints to the FCC, an increase in sales of peripheral equipment, and a reduction in callbacks for equipment servicing. These objectives are set within a time frame of eighteen to twenty-four months.

Several groups are involved in meeting these overall objectives. The marketing function is responsible for quality service and for sales; the engineering and construction function is responsible for technical facility quality; the traffic function is responsible for the transmission of calls over the various cable networks. Each function is supposed to achieve its objectives and in this way contribute to larger objectives of the company. Marketing may allocate more resources to selling peripheral equipment; engineering to ensuring top-notch quality of on-line equipment; and traffic to efficiently processing long-distance calls.

Within each of these functions further separations are possible. For example, individual salespeople can have a set of objectives toward which they work, and which has as its end a contribution to the objectives of the larger unit. As each successively lower unit develops its objectives, the objectives become more specifically tied to actual jobs and job behavior. That is, a marketing unit manager may have a unit goal of increasing the sale of peripheral equipment by 10 percent, but it is the salesperson who must do the job.

As a consequence of this process, two things happen: (1) there is an inexorable focus on the *quantitative* aspects of the lower participants' job, and (2) each supervisor must ensure that the subordinate meets the quantitative requirements of the objectives. These consequences are similar to those of any work measurement system. In fact, regardless of the level by which the objectives are set, all writers about MBO agree that the objectives have to be *defined in measurable terms,* just as in any control system. Indeed, MBO and its components coincide with what at least three writers feel is at the heart of control systems, namely, objective setting, planning, execution, and information gathering for purposes of evaluation and modification (15, 24, 41).

However, if these were the sole ingredients of MBO, it would be nothing new. Any good management system includes objectives, planning, controlling, and reviewing. However, it is claimed that MBO will do several additional things as well.

First, it is supposed to systematize the goal-setting process. All management groupings are required to engage the process at each step, formulate concrete procedures that fulfill the requirements of those steps, and then develop means of ensuring that the steps are actually taken. And all MBO theoreticians feel that the goals ought to be set with the full participation of both the superior and the subordinate in order to gain goal acceptance, though the data are not consistent on this point (28, 29, 30, 35, 36, 38).

Second, MBO forces managers to think about their activities as well as the goals, and then gauge the relationship between the two.

Third, it focuses on resources required to meet the objectives: Are the resources available, and if so, how can they be marshalled to reach the objectives? If resources are not available, MBO forces either a reevaluation of the objectives or the development of evidence to obtain such resources.

Fourth, MBO requires detailed and concrete planning—including the establishment of timetables—and evaluation points preceding the intended completion date for each objective (44, 51).

Fifth, each party is usually required to "sign off" on the objectives, a function that serves as a contract of sorts (44).

Sixth, all writers emphasize the necessity of continuous evaluation sessions, the focus being on progress toward objectives and reasons supporting the progress. Interim sessions are supposed to allow for changes in objectives or for developing corrective actions if progress does not go as planned. Final reviews are for purposes of evaluation and perhaps reinforcement (51).[3]

To summarize, MBO incorporates several important theoretical concepts: (1) *goal setting,* which has been associated with performance (28, 30, 35, 36); (2) *participation* in goal setting, which has been associated with performance, satisfaction, and goal acceptance (36, 37); (3) *feedback,* which the preponderance of data suggest is a major contributor to learning and consequently improved performance (5); and (4) *reinforcement,* which is a key element of a successful motivation system. If the processes and actions suggested by these comments were carried forth in a systematic way as suggested, for example, by Raia (51), we could predict that MBO might be an effective program. And in fact proponents of MBO, as well as the organizations that try it do make such a prediction. However, as we will show in the next section, the evidence is equivocal on that point.

MBO: The Bark and the Bite

Although the MBO process seems simple, numerous complexities are involved. For example, research concerning the impact of MBO has produced ambiguous results. There is evidence that a well-conducted management by objectives system can have beneficial results on a variety of dimensions.[4] Carroll and Tosi (9) report improvements in attitudes and perception of motivation; Raia (51), in performance; Ivancevich (28), in short-term performance; Ivancevich, Donnelly, and Lyon (27), in need deficiency reduction; and McConkey (44), in total organizational effectiveness.

However, there are also data that indicate otherwise. Muczyk (47, 48) in the *only* well-controlled field experiment on MBO finds that it has little effect on performance. One of the main reasons for Muczyk's results is that most of the managers in his study were so caught up in the day-to-day operations of the organization that they had little time to devote to making the MBO system work. Also, most thought they had been using informal management by objectives for some time and the incremental performance that they saw coming from a formalized MBO was simply not worth the effort. This was particularly true in light of the failure of top management to provide incentives for *following through* on the program.

From our view, a most significant factor undermining the potential value of MBO for organizations is that it may be viewed as another control procedure by those who are expected to use it. It is a procedure that invites voluminous record keeping, forms, and reports—things that lend themselves to the evolution of formal controls. It also creates problems associated with precious managerial time during the process and a "keeping tabs" mentality at each evaluation point (48). For example, a study that reported on the Fortune 500 firms in the United States found that where MBO was used (a scant 10 percent of the firms as approximated by the authors), it seemed to correspond with the basic hierarchy of authority and was, therefore, approached in an authoritarian manner. That is, the goals did indeed cascade from the top but there was little input from each successively lower level in the organization. The goals were handed down, signed off on, and then used as a control procedure. Furthermore, the article suggests that many more organizations tried some variant of MBO but gave it up because of the resistance by lower-level management to the limiting nature of the control procedures. And as others have pointed out, the focus on measurable results, with each manager under pressure to meet his or her objectives, knowing that he or she will be evaluated accordingly describes a work measurement system for managers complete with a reward-punishment mentality transmitted throughout the hierarchy (41).

Indeed, as Hofstede, who considers MBO as founded on a cybernetic model applied to complex social systems, states:

> MBO is . . . advocated and applied, for indirect jobs, in medical institutions, school systems and government agencies. In these cases, accomplishment is much less measurable and it is rare to find surrogates acceptable to both parties. If a commonly agreed measurement of accomplishment is lacking, the cybernetic model again does not apply, and MBO is simply bound to fail. A second reason why MBO may fail, even if the cybernetic model does apply, is that MBO is based on simplistic and mechanistic assumptions about the relationships among the people involved; it uses a reward-punishment psychology. There is more going on between people than cybernetic objective setting and feedback alone. (24:459)

It is no wonder then that even in those studies which report success, one of the chief criticisms of MBO is that it involves more work pressure, more paper work, and less flexibility in meeting exigencies not covered by the specific MBO process (9, 51, 66).

There are other problems as well. A change to MBO will of necessity reinforce two typical dysfunctions of control systems. Since MBO focuses on the dyadic relationship of manager and subordinate, it is completely consonant with the way managers typically view organizations, namely, as a series of man-boss associations in service of the hierarchy of authority. But what happens to lateral relations that require cooperation and collaboration? It appears that these are neglected and, in fact, may deteriorate (18, 20, 25), for how are they to be measured?

Also, much managerial and professional work is either unanticipated or problematic. That is, much cannot be planned for, or, if it is, time and situational pressures render the original objective inconsequential, irrelevant, or untimely.

Furthermore, the very units for which MBO can best be applied, are probably already measured in some other sense. Consequently, MBO provides an additional way of applying pressure. It is, therefore, not surprising that a major field study showing performance increases after a change to MBO also reports grievance increases among the blue-collar work force, a population that was not brought into the process of goal setting (28). This point is made by Levinson:

> The typical MBO effect perpetuates and intensifies hostility, resentment, and distrust between a manager and his subordinates. As currently practiced, it is really just industrial engineering with a new name, applied to higher managerial levels, and with the same resistance. (41:125)

Is MBO then ineffective? Considering its firm theoretical footing and voluminous research findings that report the efficacy of goal setting, feedback, reinforcement and subordinate participation in job territory decisions (36, 37), we are reluctant to say yes at this time. The ingredients are clearly there for an effective motivation system. The problem it seems to us has always been the deficiencies in implementation and the program's proclivity for ending up as an onerous control system (24, 41). If, as an example, a completely committed management implemented MBO with the same thoroughness of planning, training, and follow-through that was evident in the QWL and EI programs of GM and Ford the probability of success would be high. A recent study of engineers suggested that goal setting and feedback together are good predictors to increases in performance but that self-generated feedback was substantially more effective than supervisory feedback (30). In other words, the control features of the program were provided by the engineers' relationship to the task—what they themselves saw as their progress toward goal achievement mattered more than supervisory feedback and control. A careful implementation of MBO, using the theories on which it is based and following the well-documented principles of successful change would probably include emphasis on self-control and less on administrative control.

A final program that we will deal with seems promising. We say that because it incorporates a system view of organizations and emphasizes the interrelationships and organizational structure. Recent studies are more and more concluding that successful change programs occur in a complex context and that successes and failures of large-scale organizational changes depend on that recognition (7, 10, 16, 23, 33, 46, 54, 55). As an example, a recent study reporting a well-planned change in the motivation and feedback and control systems in branch offices of a major bank found that the implementation of change depended on the interaction system of the branches, their organizational structure, and the technologies of two separate occupational groups, tellers and financial consultants. And the effect of the changes seemed to depend on how it was implemented. Where the new procedure was used regularly to inform tellers and to solicit their ideas for procedural and goal changes a positive effect on hard criterion measures was noted. Where the procedure was treated indifferently, negative effects were seen. With the financial consultants the new procedure took on an informal character but it seemed to provide more goal and incentive structure clarity.

The system that deals with these complexities is called the Scanlon Plan. It was designed to be consistent with traditional organizational structure and yet accommodate what is known about participation and the use of financial incentives as an important part of a motivation system.

The Scanlon Plan as a Motivation System

The Scanlon Plan is designed to increase productivity and reduce costs by providing a means for management-nonmanagement cooperation and uses of monetary incentives (39, 40, 56). However, unlike the Lincoln Electric situation, it incorporates mechanisms for employee involvement in establishing both methods of production and the distribution of cost savings to employees. Ideally, the system incorporates both motivation and the change process itself.

The plans is to be carried out through ongoing, extensive, and vigorous collaboration between management and nonmanagement personnel of any given organization. The incentives are primarily financial and are equitably shared between the company and the workers, so that the workers can readily see that they will get most of the savings that are a consequence of their efforts.

There are three essential elements to the Scanlon Plan: (1) the suggestion system by which participation and cooperation of nonmanagement people is ensured; (2) the formula by which cost savings are calculated; and (3) the philosophy of industrial cooperation. Without these three elements, the plan is likely to fail.

The Suggestion System

The suggestion system is made up of two basic committees: The production committee establishes the functional working relationships between management and nonmanagement people. It contains primarily nonmanagement people, usually of a small working unit, together with the supervisor of that unit. The membership is elected by the rank and file. The purposes of this committee are to process, define, and revise any suggestion related to work that is submitted by a member of that unit, and then to feed back the data to the employees with an eye toward getting the suggestion accepted. Of course, some suggestions are not acceptable, but the idea of the committee is to establish trust among all of the nonmanagement people of that committee so they know suggestions will be thoroughly reviewed by a committee of peers. If the suggested change does not unduly involve other work units, or if the suggestion award or other attendant costs are not substantial, then this committee has the right to implement the suggestion.

The screening committee is of a higher order. It is made up of elected representatives of all the production committees in the organization. Its responsibility is to oversee and process all suggestions of greater scope that can be dealt with by the production committee. Typically, the screening committee contains 50 percent management and 50 percent nonmanagement people.

Additional responsibilities of the screening committee include reviewing the bonus calculation, which is based on the formula described in the next section. Frequently, the screening committee is used as a vehicle to exchange information and discuss organizationally pertinent problems that may go beyond the suggestions area. For example, some companies using the Scanlon Plan provide the committee with information on pricing, market conditions, governmental regulations that constrain the organization, and so forth. Disclosing such information gives nonmanagement people more detail concerning the rationale for organizational decisions. Cooperation and the acceptance of change among both rank and file and management people are directly associated with the success of the suggestion system structure.

The two committees together contribute the primary organizational structure that facilitates communication and employee involvement on a wide variety of organizational matters, not just suggestions. Consequently, such committees are called different things in different companies such as caucuses and councils but their primary purpose is similar: to institutionalize the process of participation and multilateral information flow.

The Formula

The formula is a means of calculating cost savings, and then from this calculation, distributing bonuses to the work force. Basic labor costs are determined by establishing the ratio of labor costs to sales value of the products the organization produces. Hence, the ratio is a relationship between total labor costs and the value of everything produced as a consequence of the labor. Before the plan is installed, a baseline calculation is required so that improvements can be ascertained. For example, suppose that before the Scanlon Plan is put in, every given unit of production costs $1.00 per employee. After the plan is in operation, the cost goes down to $.90 per employee. The savings are said to be $.10 per employee. How would this $.10 be distributed? According to Lesieur, an ideal and equitable distribution would be 75 percent for the employee and 25 percent for the company (19). Hence, the employees would get $.075 and the company would get $.025 of the savings from each unit produced.

The Philosophy

Basic to the Scanlon Plan is the notion that management-nonmanagement cooperation is required if significant cost reductions are to take place. Perhaps more fundamental is the belief that the nonmanagement people are the repository of great expertise and information that can lead to cost reduction, and that the only way to tap into such a resource is through collaboration and participation within the entire organizational system. Furthermore, though not explicitly stated in the Scanlon Plan literature, it seems that those who accept the plan also believe firmly that the change acceptance can occur only through a significant restructuring of the organization, as represented by the suggestion system, together with the appropriate incentives expected as a consequence of the change.

Several other components to the philosophy are understood although only occasionally stated:

- To effectively participate, employees must be thoroughly informed of business plans and goals, competition and the economic environment.
- Employees and managers alike must assume the responsibility of participation and the accountability of their job performance.
- All employers are to receive a fair return on their investment of time and effort.
- Management must be competent in and committed to their leadership functions within the company and the plan itself.

The consequences of the Scanlon Plan appear to be somewhat mixed at this writing. A publication from the National Center for Productivity and Quality of Working Life suggests that there are more successes than failures (49). In reviewing the results of the Scanlon Plan, the study concluded that in forty-four firms, thirty were judged successful; fourteen were judged failures. The successes can be attributed to the factors we have described. That is, the changes incorporate a substantial portion of the working force; management is thoroughly behind the changes; and incentives are significant and clear enough to warrant motivation to increase performance and reduce costs. Furthermore, there seems a requirement of flexibility to meet changing circumstances. For example, see Box 28.

As for the failures, they seem due to a lot of things, such as difficulties in establishing production norms in the face of complex product mixes and changes,

> **Box 28**
>
> ### Everyone Gets a Stake
>
> A report by Judith Ramquist deals with a major change in a Scanlon Plan that was losing its effectiveness because of rapid organizational growth and a substantial change in the employee mix from 90 percent production people to a little over half (52). A representative ad hoc committee was established to assess the relevance of the plan and to propose changes. It quickly decided that a new plan had to incorporate planning, measurement and control, a new participative structure, and an expanded bonus formula to more accurately reflect the company's organizational performance.
>
> A new participative structure was established to replace the old production and steering committees. It included:
>
> - A work team—the basic work unit consisting of a supervisor and his or her supervisees. The team meets monthly to resolve problems, evaluate suggestions, and evaluate plans and goals and performance.
> - A caucus—a peer group of people with similar jobs who discuss unresolved issues from the work team and share ideas and experiences.
> - A council—elected by the consensus of each major department or division chaired by a director or vice president and including all levels of that unit. Reviews and adjudicates all suggestions. Provides information and rationale to all area work teams concerning goals and progress.
>
> The ad hoc committee also recommended a restructuring of the bonus to assume equity for employees, customers, and investors. The committee's recommendations were then submitted to all employees for study and ratification; 96 percent voted to ratify.
>
> The results to date are extremely encouraging. The company's performance resulted in 15 percent bonuses averaged over three years.
>
> Ramquist, Judith. "Labor-Management Cooperation—The Scanlon Plan at Work." *Sloan Management Review* (Spring 1982): 49–55.

negative managerial attitudes at the outset, feeling of threat among first-level supervisors due to perceived loss of managerial prerogatives, change from individual incentive systems that employees see as favorable, and the lack of meaningful participation in suggestion system committee structure (49, 68). However, the overriding problem seems to be the complexity of the formula, its poorly calculated or inequitable form, and the organization's inability to distribute bonuses that are seen as substantial and fair (68).

Hence, both successes and failures in the Scanlon Plan are attributable to the variables we have discussed. The future of the Scanlon Plan seems promising. As the National Center for Productivity and Quality of Working Life suggests, there is an increasing interest among organizations to reduce labor costs through the establishment of labor-management cooperation and to establish a "fairer and more equitable" distribution of profits or of savings (49).

As to the Future

There seems little doubt that the field of organizational behavior needs to reflect rapid changes in the environment—technical, social, and economic. Still we are impressed by how slow management is to respond to behavioral and social data disclosed by our field until crises strike. An example of that point is provided by our analysis of the GM and Ford programs, which incorporated as their nexus the substantial need for better organizational effectiveness. Exemplary programs had been around a long time, but economic forces impelled change.

Motivation and control have always been issues in the workplace, and we presume they will continue to be. The reasons for the pervasiveness of control seem to be its necessity and its paradox. It is necessary because people left completely to their own devices can hardly be expected to set aside their own interests in order to work for the greater good of all—unless, that is, the appropriate guidelines for behavior are established. As long as sanctions accompany them, these guidelines will set the limits of behavior and hence controls.

The paradox of this pervasive control is that controls, by definition, restrict behavior that might otherwise occur freely. Many people do not like this and can be expected to resist it. Failing this, they may be expected to conform to the minimal requisites of the control system. And ever more ways of establishing control to ensure efficiency and/or effectiveness will continue to be established. So it goes (19).

The field of organizational behavior grew, in a sense, out of our inability to account for behavior other than that predicted by the traditional constraints—mainly financial incentives and formal control systems. Our motive, then, and that of our colleagues is to understand as much as we can about such unpredictable behavior in order to make better predictions. And, as you must have gathered by now, we have come a long way from the milestone presented by the Hawthorne studies, though we still have a long way to go.

Where are we going? The predominant forces seem to be contained in new technologies and the need to compete in a world market. These forces will affect behavior and its study in several ways (19, 61).

The new technologies will create status differences in the workplace that until recently were not imagined. Robotics are displacing assemblers, and word processors and computers are changing all clerical work—even middle managers' work. Elite groupings of development technicians and information analysts are developing, and very large groups of workers who need only understand what buttons to push and when will replace the skilled assemblers and machinists. Computers will replace hordes of skilled people such as design technicians—even programmers—as they become more and more complex and sophisticated. Ironically, the more sophisticated these machines become, the easier it will be to use them. Indeed, the current cliché, "user friendly" means easy operation with minimal training (8, 61).

Controls will become more refined as machines with great computational capacity and artificial intelligence will replace the less accurate and humanly fallible accounting and budgetary control systems. As people work in a less challenging environment under better and less personal control systems, the issues of QWL and motivation will command our interest in ways as yet undiscovered (7).

Higher management groups and development engineers and scientists will increasingly command our scientific interest, for it is these groupings—not the lower participants or rank and file—who will contribute most labor costs in many of our largest industries. We say this not because their numbers will be greater—they may be lesser—but because what they do will have the most profound effect on the financial performance of organizations.

Still, *"plus ca change, plus c'est la meme chose"*—the more things change, the more they are the same. Many of the issues will remain and the fundamental nature of interpersonal relations, although different structurally, will involve status, norms, leadership, conflict, and motivation much as they do now.

The near-term issues, however, are clearly in the direction of control over job function, a sense of involvement, and commitment among the multitude. If we add to this the construction of interaction systems that facilitate cooperation and collaboration and guide consensus, we will have both old and new problems facing the field of organizational behavior. The QWL programs at Ford and GM are representative of the momentum being developed that focuses on bringing alienated union workers into the decision-making process. Indeed, the rationale of adversariness within the collective bargaining framework will change as management and labor recognize that the problems no longer center on how to divide an increasingly expanding pie but rather how to be more productive, turn out better quality, and reduce costs to better compete in a world market for increasingly sophisticated and demanding consumers.

Yet there is enough evidence to suggest that beyond a point many workers do not want to become deeply involved in the decision-making process. Although they might want control over job territory, other decisions seem remote from their daily experience. Certainly, management is reluctant to relinquish control, and if current experience is to be our guide, will request union givebacks, not so much in the financial area, but rather in decision areas of work allocation, job assignment, overtime assignment, and the like. Consequently, if the needs of workers and management are to be satisfied, the area in which those needs overlap must be identified and means of satisfying them must be developed. Our commentary in Chapters 9 and 10 and in this one suggest already developed ways. We refer to the strong financial incentives together with job security at Lincoln Electric (42), the development of structural means to encourage employee involvement, together with a financial stake as in the Scanlon Plan and the total system commitment to employee involvement in productivity and quality issues as in the Ford and GM experiences. These and other ways not yet devised will be the subjects of intensive study in the future.

Summary

We know that organizations need controls of some sort or another, and that there are motivational problems associated with most control systems. Generally, people do not like to be controlled, and hence a basic tension between the controller and the controllees seems likely. This leads to certain problems: (1) people seek to evade controls; (2) to the extent that extrinsic controls are established, intrinsic or "self-starting" controls are less probable; (3) controls will be exercised away from the job operations as long as appropriate measures or other control devices exist; (4) as a consequence, control systems become depersonalized and are seen solely as a tool for behavioral compliance; (5) such perceptions create feelings of powerlessness, a situation susceptible to redress through absences, turnover, or other forms of resistance; (6) motives are created to look good on control system measures, which are not necessarily the most important aspects of an individual's job. Thus, the means of control become the ends, and in this way the intent of the control system is additionally subverted.

As a consequence of these problems, many students of organizations have spent a great deal of time studying ways in which control can be shifted back to the locus of operations. Participative management is one general method studied, and management by objectives (MBO) is a more specific one. We illustrate these points by providing examples of several control procedures designed to ensure output control and in so doing affect motivation as well.

The first, PIP, was a work-measurement procedure installed in a blue-collar manufacturing population. Its intent was to gain better control of production output and, in so doing, ensure appropriate levels of production and better planning and forecasting. The problems created by this control procedure had to do primarily with the workers' and their supervisors' felt loss of control over the production process. The second—PIPC or PIP changed—was an attempt to restore some control to the work unit.

PIP and PIPC were then contrasted and compared with each other and with the systems incentive and motivation program (SIMP) as to the effect of each on the authority, social, interaction, motivation, and control systems. We suggested that, as the balance of control shifted to and away from the point of operations, other major outcomes went along with these shifts. Hence, we concluded that the locus of control directly affects important behavioral outcomes—a statement completely consonant with much research, often conducted with different focal points.

The next illustration of a change in a control system concerned the substitution of so-called autonomous work groups for traditional assembly lines. The groups themselves, under such an arrangement, are empowered to control their pace and method of production, allocate manpower, and rotate jobs. Each group, too, is accountable for quality and quantity. We noted that such a change has significant implications for the formal leadership structure, the technical means of production, the interaction systems, and the motivation systems—in short, virtually all the important aspects of the production process.

Variations in the use of autonomous work groups are often designed to meet different objectives. For example, the Swedish experiments were supposed to demonstrate that humanizing the workplace could reduce costs by reducing absences and turnover and increasing quality and ease of recruitment. The Norwegian experiments, on the other hand, although not uninterested in those kinds of outcomes, had as a major objective an increase in production through the use of incentives, group decisions, and group norms. The American experience is different still. The GM and Ford QWL and EI programs were given as examples.

Then we examined a popular management control system called MBO. We stated that MBO is very attractive to management because it fits commonly held management values including the importance of authority, the necessity for planning and controlling, and an emphasis on results. Furthermore, although it fits management ideology, MBO too has components rooted in empirical behavioral sciences—the efficacy of participation, feedback, goal setting, and reinforcement as they pertain to organizational outcomes. MBO's effective execution, however, is another matter, for apparently few companies actually engage in the process even though many report that they do. The reasons for this inconsistency seem inherent in MBO's control aspects.

Despite the apparent differences among our illustrations, several important conclusions seem warranted. First, the target of all of the changes described—with PIP as the sole exception—was the change in the locus of control over the production process and the measurement of outcomes. That is to say, the remote and mechanical controls were seen as creating problems that offset their apparent benefits. And the direction of the change of the control was toward the point of operations.

Second, an important aspect of the changes is encapsulated in the description of the Norwegian experience as "democratizing" the workplace. The operators in each instance are to have more say over important work matters—indeed, they are to make decisions about quantity, pacing, quality, and resource allocation. This point is true even with MBO, though we have seen that participation can become incidental to the overall process and function of the controlling procedure itself.

Third, changes in the control system affect most other systems directly or indirectly and indeed require changes in those other systems in order to sustain themselves. When these changes in other systems do not take place—and MBO may be an example where this is so—new control procedures can be considered to have little real influence.

Further, we stated that the primary and generally available incentives that exist in most organizations are money, possibilities for advancement, and opportunities for interesting or challenging assignments. However, the opportunities for interesting or challenging assignments, translated into organizational terms, have typically been job enrichments. Job enrichment as a means of changing the motivation system has certain problems that are primarily associated with the real incentive value of intrinsic job factors and with its narrow focus. It seems, from all available evidence at this point, that the key elements of successful job enrichment are contained in more traditional concepts such as standards or goals, personal accountability, and extrinsic rewards for performance; that is, money and job advancement.

Consequently, we turned our attention to a systemwide motivation structure called the Scanlon Plan. The Scanlon Plan deals with much more than motivation just as the autonomous work group and QWL programs deal with more than control. Incorporated in the plan are changes in the structure and processes of the organization to allow meaningful participation of lower participants concerning wide-ranging issues. The chief motivational components appear to be the distribution of rewards, primarily in the form of bonuses, according to performance criteria and calculated according to a formula developed with the full participation of elected representatives from all facets of the organization. Indeed the Scanlon Plan seems to reflect recognition of the importance of the several organizational systems and their interrelatedness as we have described them throughout the book.

Notes

1. There are many anecdotal reports of similar experiences in other companies (46). For example, the Butler Manufacturing Plant of Story City, Iowa, uses autonomous work groups in one of its plants. The plant assembles grain dryers that have as many as 3,000 parts. Each assembler knows about all of the production steps necessary. The key characteristics of the plant are:
   - There are only four supervisors for 150 regular employees.
   - There are no quality inspections.
   - People decide on speed of production and allocation of human resources.
   - People participate in the design of new products, tools, and handling devices.
   - In some areas, people purchase tools and materials, with supervisory approval required only on purchases in excess of $200.

- The team can talk directly to customers.
- The ratio of individual to direct labor costs is 25/75, whereas in other company plants it is about 40/60.
- The plant is estimated to be 10 percent more profitable than other, similar plants.
2. Recall the Locke, Sirota, and Wolfson study (22) of job enrichment reported in Chapter 10. While the study ostensibly was defined as job enrichment, both its success and failures concerned reasons inherent in autonomous work groups. For example, job enrichment appeared to increase productivity, because it was associated with the group's allocation of human resources and work assignments. The major reason the experiment produced ambiguous results or worse, seemed to be because of expected payoffs that never materialized and *resistance to diffusion and continuation by management.*
3. MBO has other purposes than its control of motivational intent. For example, several writers (23, 28, 33) argue that one of MBO's advantages is as a management development tool—a point often forgotten or obfuscated as its control function becomes predominant. If MBO is used for development, then, goal evaluation sessions should focus on progress, problems, and problem solutions, and not on performance evaluation for reward (or punishment) determinations. These latter evaluations often result in defensiveness, ill will, and other responses that interfere with problem solving and associated developmental activities (26, 27). As procedures become formalized and evaluations routinized, the decision-making discretion of many managers can become limited—a situation not conducive to personal development.
4. MBO is a generic system that has many possible variants. For example, variations are possible in the extent of participation involved, the requisite paper work, the involvement of all levels in the organizations, and the allowability of personal objectives.

References

1. ALDERFER, C. P. *Human Needs in Organizational Settings.* New York: Free Press, 1972.
2. ANGLE, HAROLD L., and JAMES L. PERRY. "An Empirical Assessment of Organizational Effectiveness." *Administrative Science Quarterly* 26 (March 1981): 1–14.
3. *Assembly Engineering,* Editorial, March 1967, p. 21.
4. BANDURA, A. *Principles of Behavior Modification.* New York: Holt, Rinehart, and Winston, 1969.
5. BASS, B. M., and J. A. VAUGHN. *Training in Industry: The Management of Learning.* Belmont, Calif.: Wadsworth, 1966.
6. BIKSON, TORA K., and BARBARA A. GUTEK. "Finding the Best Fit Between People and Machines." *World of Work Report* 8 (April 1983): 27–28.
7. BRASS, DANIEL J. "Structural Relationships, Job Characteristics, and Worker Satisfaction and Performance." *Administrative Science Quarterly* 26 (September 1981): 331–348.
8. CARRELL, PAT. "More Companies Lean Toward In-House Training as an Option." *World of Work Report* 8 (April 1983): 31–32.
9. CARROLL, S. J., and H. TOSI. *Management by Objectives: Applications and Research.* New York: Macmillan, 1963.

10. CASNER-LOTTO, JILL. "Management Choices Will be the Key to Success." *World of Work Report* 8 (April 1983): 25–26, 32.
11. *The Civil Engineer.* American Society of Civil Engineering, January 1973.
12. COOPER, M. R., B. S. MORGAN, P. M. FOLEY, and L. B. KAPLAN. "Changing Employee Values: Deepening Discontent." *Harvard Business Review* 57 (January–February 1979): 117.
13. DAVIS, L. E., and A. B. CHERNS. *The Quality of Working Life.* Vols. 1 and 2. New York: Free Press, 1975.
14. DUNNINGTON, R. A., D. SIROTA, and S. M. KLEIN. "Research for Organization Theory and Management Action." In *Proceedings of the 16th Annual Meeting, Boston, December 27–28, 1963,* edited by G. Somers. Madison, Wis.: Industrial Relations Research Association, 1963. Pp. 150–159, 176–179.
15. EILON, S. "Problems in Studying Management Control." *International Journal of Production Research* 1 (1962): 59–62.
16. FARRELL, DANIEL, and CARYL E. RUSBULT. "Exchange Variables as Predictors of Job Satisfaction, Job Commitment, and Turnover: The Impact of Rewards, Costs, Alternatives and Investments." *Organizational Behavior and Human Performance* 28 (August 1981): 78–95.
17. FEIN, M. "Motivation for Work." In *Handbook of Work, Organization and Society,* edited by R. Dubin. Chicago: Rand McNally, 1976. Pp. 465–530.
18. FRENCH, W. L., and R. W. HOLLMAN. "Management by Objectives: The Team Approach." In *Organizational Development: Theory, Practice and Research,* edited by W. L. French, C. H. Bell, R. A. Zawacki. Dallas: Business Publications, 1978. Pp. 281–290.
19. GINZBERG, E. "The Mechanization of Work." *Scientific American* 247 (1983): 68–75.
20. GRIMES, A. J., and S. M. KLEIN. "Empirical Investigations of the MBO Process in Disparate Organizations." *Proceedings of the Midwest Academy of Management Meetings,* 1975.
21. GUEST, ROBERT. "Problem Solving Groups Boost Quality, Reduce Costs at Ford Sharonville," *World of Work Report* 7 (December 1982): 89, 94–95.
22. ———. "Quality of Work Life—Learning from Tarrytown." *Harvard Business Review* 57 (July–August 1979).
23. ———. "The Sharonville Story: Worker Involvement at a Ford Motor Company Plant," Reprinted from *The Innovative Organization: Productivity Programs in Action,* edited by Robert Zager and Michael P. Rosow. Work in America Institute Inc., Elmsford, N.Y.: Pergamon Press, Inc., 1982.
24. HOFSTEDE, G. "The Poverty of Management Control Philosophy." *Academy of Management Review* 3 (1978): 450–458.
25. HOWELL, R. A. "A Fresh Look at Management by Objectives." *Business Horizons* 8 (Fall 1967): 51–58.
26. HULIN, C. L. "Individual Differences and Job Enrichment—The Case Against General Treatments." In *Organizational Issues in Industrial Society,* edited by J. M. Shepard. Englewood Cliffs, N.J.: Prentice-Hall, 1972. Pp. 387–408.
27. HULIN, C. L., and M. R. BLOOD. "Job Enlargement, Individual Differences and Work Responses." *Psychological Bulletin* 69 (1968): 41–55.

28. IVANCEVICH, J. M. "Change in Performance in a Management by Objectives Program." *Administrative Science Quarterly* 19 (1974): 563–574.
29. IVANCEVICH, J. M., J. H. DONNELLY, and H. L. LYON. "A Study of the Impact of Management by Objectives on Perceived Need Satisfaction." *Personnel Psychology* 23 (1970): 340–358.
30. IVANCEVICH, JOHN, and J. TIMOTHY MCMAHON. "The Effects of Goal Setting, External Feedback, and Self-Generated Feedback on Outcome Variables: A Field Experiment." *Academy of Management Journal* 25 (1982): 359–372.
31. KANARICK, ARNOLD F. "Employee 'Task Teams' Set the Stage for New Technology at Honeywell, Inc." *World of Work Report* 8 (January 1983): 1–3.
32. KLEIN, S. M. "Two Systems of Management: A Comparison that Produced Organizational Change." In *Proceedings of the 16th Annual Meeting, Boston, December 27–28, 1963*, edited by G. Somers. Madison, Wis.: Industrial Relations Research Association, 1963. Pp. 155–165.
33. KNOKE, DAVID. "Commitment and Detachment in Voluntary Associations." *American Sociological Review* 46 (April 1981): 141–158.
34. KUGLAND, GEORGE. "Volkswagen Tries Group Assembly in Germany Work Humanization Study; Criticizes Use in Mass Production." *World of Work Report* 5 (November 1979): 82, 84.
35. LATHAM, G. P., and G. A. YUKL. "Effects of Assigned and Participative Goal Setting on Performance and Job Satisfaction." *Journal of Applied Psychology* 61 (1976): 166–171.
36. LATHAM, G. P., T. R. MITCHELL, and D. L. DOSSETT. "Importance of Participative Goal Setting and Anticipated Rewards on Goal Difficulty and Job Performance." *Journal of Applied Psychology* 63 (1978): 163–171.
37. LAWLER, E. E. *Pay and Organizational Effectiveness: A Psychological View*. New York: McGraw-Hill, 1971.
38. LAWLER, E. E. "Control Systems in Organization." In *Handbook of Industrial and Organizational Psychology*, edited by M. D. Dunnette. Chicago: Rand McNally, 1976. Pp. 1247–1287.
39. LESIEUR, F. G. *The Scanlon Plan: A Frontier in Labor-Management Cooperation*. Cambridge, Mass.: MIT Press/Wiley, 1958.
40. LESIEUR, F. G., and E. S. PUCKETT. "The Scanlon Plan Has Proved Itself." *Harvard Business Review* 47 (1969): 109–118.
41. LEVINSON, H. "Management by Whose Objectives?" *Harvard Business Review* 48 (1970): 125–134.
42. LINCOLN, J. F. *Incentive Management*. Cleveland, Ohio: Lincoln Electric, 1951.
43. LOCKE, E. A., D. SIROTA, and A. D. WOLFSON. "An Experimental Case Study of the Successes and Failures of Job Enrichment in a Government Agency." *Journal of Applied Psychology* 61 (1976): 701–712.
44. MCCONKEY, D. D. "Writing Measurable Objectives of Staff Managers." *Advanced Management Journal* 37 (1972): 10–16.
45. MCMAHON, J. T., and G. W. PERRITT. "Toward a Contingency Theory of Organizational Control." *Academy of Management Journal* 16 (December 1973): 624–635.
46. MERTON, R. K. *Social Theory and Social Structure*. New York: Free Press, 1957.

47. MUCZYK, J. P. "A Controlled Field Experiment Measuring the Impact of MBO on Performance Data." *Journal of Management Studies* 15 (October 1978): 318–329.
48. ———. "A Common Surrogate for OD: The Dynamics and Hazards of MBO Application." In *Approaches to Planned Change,* Part 2. Edited by R. T. Golembiewski. New York: Marcel Decker, 1979. Pp. 166–179.
49. NATIONAL CENTER FOR PRODUCTIVITY AND QUALITY OF WORKING LIFE. *A Plant-Wide Productivity Plan in Action! Three Years of Experience with the Scanlon Plan.* Washington, D.C.: National Center for Productivity and Quality of Working Life, May 1975.
50. OPSAHL, R. L., and M. D. DUNNETTE. "The Role of Financial Compensation in Industries Motivation." In *Readings in Organizational Behavior and Human Performance,* edited by L. L. Cummings, and W. E. Scott. Homewood, Ill.: Irwin and Dorsey Press, 1969. Pp. 499–524.
51. RAIA, A. P. *Management by Objectives.* Glenview, Ill.: Scott, Foresman, 1974.
52. RAMQUIST, JUDITH. "SMR Forum: Labor-Management Cooperation—The Scanlon Plan at Work." *Sloan Management Review* (Spring 1982): 49–55.
53. RATHBUN, BEN. "New UAW Ford Relationship Stresses 'Partnership' and Problem Solving." *World of Work Report* 7 (November 1982): 81–83.
54. RITTI, R. *The Engineer in the Industrial Corporation.* New York: Columbia University Press, 1971.
55. ROETHLISHBERGER, F. J., and W. J. DICKSON. *Management and the Worker.* Cambridge, Mass.: Harvard University Press, 1939.
56. RUH, R., R. L. WALLACE, and C. F. FROST. "Management Attitudes and the Scanlon Plan." *Industrial Relations* 12 (1973): 282–288.
57. SIROTA, D. "A Study of Work Measurement." In *Proceedings of the 16th Annual Meeting, Boston, December 27–28, 1963,* edited by G. Somers. Madison Wis.: Industrial Relations Research Association, 1963.
58. SIROTA, D., and A. D. WOLFSON. "Pragmatic Approach to People Problems." *Harvard Business Review* 51 (1973): 120–128.
59. ———. "A Structural Modification in Work Measurement: The Northland Experiment." Internal IBM Report, 1964.
60. *Special Task Force Report to the Secretary of HEW. Work in America.* Cambridge, Mass.: MIT Press, October 1974. Pp. 96–114.
61. STABLESKI, JOAN. "Is Office Automation Hazardous to Your Health?" *World of Work Report* 8 (April 1983): 29–30.
62. TANNENBAUM, A. S. *Control in Organizations.* New York: McGraw-Hill, 1968.
63. TAUSKY, C., and E. L. PARKE. "Job Enrichment, Need Theory and Reinforcement Theory." In *Handbook of Work, Organization and Society,* edited by R. Dubin. Chicago: Rand McNally, 1976. Pp. 531–561.
64. TERKEL, S. *Working.* New York: Avon Books, 1974.
65. THORSRUD, E., B. S. SORENSEN, and B. GUSTAVEN. "Sociotechnical Approach to Industrial Democracy in Norway." In *Handbook of Work, Organization and Society* edited by R. Dubin. Chicago: Rand McNally, 1976.
66. TOSI, H., and S. CARROLL. "Managerial Reactions to Management by Objectives," *Academy of Management Journal* 11 (December 1968): 415–426.

67. TURNER, A. N., and P. R. LAWRENCE. *Industrial Jobs and the Worker.* Boston: Harvard University, Graduate School of Business Administration, 1965.
68. WHITE, J. K. "The Scanlon Plan: Causes and Correlates of Success." *Academy of Management Journal* 22 (1979): 292–312.
69. WHYTE, W. F. *Money and Motivation.* New York: Harper, 1955.

Discussion Questions

1. Discuss PIP as a control system in terms of its effect on behavior, its effect on morale, and why these results are predictable.
2. Discuss the Northland Experiment as it pertains to what you have learned about motivation. Contrast it with PIP and SIMP. If you were a plant manager, which of the three systems would you prefer? Why?
3. Describe the relationship between the "locus of control" and other organizational systems (i.e., motivational, interaction, etc.).
4. How does the autonomous work group of the Saab experience affect the control system, the motivational system, the interaction system, and the authority structure?
5. Compare job enrichment and the autonomous work group as a means of gaining high levels of production.
6. Describe and critique MBO. Be sure to include in your critique the pros and the cons. Also, be sure to evaluate MBO as both a motivational and control technique.
7. What effect might MBO have on the interaction system? How might you design a management control system that would capture the important aspects of control and minimize the problems associated with MBO?
8. Professionals and managers represent special problems in constructing motivational systems. What are these problems? How may they be overcome?
9. How does the Scanlon Plan fit with the precepts of organizational change? What might be the difficulties in implementing such a plan? How are the problems similar to those of implementing an incentive system as at Lincoln Electric?
10. Construct a motivation and control system for students in a class on organizational behavior.

Index

Abrams, General 149–150
Absenteeism, study of, 220
Accomplishment, sense of, 234
Accountability
   effect of, 275
   in performance, 48
Achievement
   factor of, in Herzberg two-factor (M-H) theory, 253
   personal need for, 257
Action
   appearing to take, 423
   latitude of, 425–426
   leader initiates, 406
   terms of, 509
Action goals, 457–458, 542
Action planning in change process, 575, 576
Action research process, 562, 604–606
Action taking in change process, 576
Activities as behavior, 62
Adaptation-level theory
   definition of 298–299
   how, affects organization, 300–303
Adaptation of organization
   to environment, 111–117
   to recruits, 137–138
Adaptive systems, 28, 30–31
Advancement. *See also* Structure of Opportunity in Herzberg two-factor (M-H) theory, 254
   professionalism or, 330–331
   rate of, 292, 296, 297
Affective data, 599
Affiliation, need for, 256–257
Aftermath of conflict, 539–540
After-only experiment, 596, 597
Aggregation level, 495
Alderfer, C. P., 252, 255
Alderfer's need theory, 252–253
Alliances, forming, 422

Allocation of resources
   conflict over, 451–452
   goals influence, 463–467
Allocation of rewards, 377, 405, 406–407
Alternative goals and statuses, 330–334
Ambiguity of demotion, 310
Anticipatory socialization, 128–130, 133–134, 151
Anxiety
   in group formation, 367
   in laboratory training, 616–619
Approval of peers, 7
Aptitude tests in recruiting, 135–136
Argyris, Chris, 16, 575
Asceticism of specialist, 173–174
Ascribed careers, 327, 341–353
Ascribed status, lower, 304, 326, 343–353
Ashby's law of requisite variety, 525
Aspiration, level of, 299–300
Assembly line
   autonomous work group and 651–656
   predictability of, 109
   problems with, 649, 651
   routineness of, 108
   traditional, 652
Assimilative effect, 193
Attitude change, 191–195
Attitudes
   behavior and, 190–191
   changing, to justify actions, 191
   communication and, 189–196
   influenced by roles taken, 370–371
   information screened by, 191
   normative nature of, 193
   similar, in group formation, 366–367
Attitude survey, 578, 619–621
Attribution
   of characteristics, 325
   cycle of, 344
   of motives, 163

Attribution theory, 344
Authority. *See also* Power
  charismatic, 78
  collegial, 82, 83
  erosion of, 520
  expertise confers, 82–83
  as justified power, 72, 73, 75–83
  legal, 76–77
  traditional, 77–78
  zone of indifference and, 304
Authoritylike relationships, 82–83
Authority relationships
  compliance demonstrates, 72
  deference in, 343
  elements of, 82
  formal organization affected by, 32, 48–49
Auto industry, 117, 186–187, 265–268, 657–659
Autonomous work group, 651–656
Average
  of current outcomes, 299
  of past experiences, 298–299

Balance, cognitive, 261–265
Banking
  recruiting for, 136–137
  stage setting for, 167
Bargaining in informal organization, 424–425, 488
Barker, G.H., 371
Basketball, measurement in, 487–488
Bay of Pigs decision, 385–387
Before-and-after experiments, 596–599
Behavioral data, 599
Behavior approach to leadership, 410
Behavior, human
  activities as, 62
  collective vs. individual, 8–10
  control of, 510
  definition of, 62
  directed (*see* Directed behavior)
  displays as, 62
  emotional factor in, 209
  limiting, for control, 525
  organizational (*see* Organizational behavior)
  patterns of, 34–35
  prediction of, 8–10
  rationality model of, 5–8
  social structure affects, 11–12
  understandings of appropriate, 12
  unpredictability of, 209

verbal, 62
work methods as, 510
Behavior of group
  collective behavior is, 210
  testing out, 367
Belief and compliance, 74
Belief and perception, 116
Bell, C. H., Jr., 621, 626
Bell Laboratories, 130
Belongingness needs, 251
Benne, K. D., 572–574
Bennis, W. G., 368
Berg, P. O., 624
Bias in perception, 136–137, 161–163
Black professional, 341–353
Blau, Peter, 482, 484–487
Blocked mobility
  dual ladder to resolve, 302–303
  explanation of, 298
  types of, 326–327
Blocked opportunity, types of, 326–341
"Blue sky" projects, 519
Body language, 166–167
Boredom. *See* Assembly line; Job enrichment
Boss, always being, 423
Bottoms up change, 577–579
Boundary of organization, 111
Bowers, D. G., 581
Bridwell, L. G., 252
Broedling, L. A. 254
Brown, L. D., 624
Bryner, Gary, 266
Budget, preparation of, 498–499
Bureaucracy, 76–77, 83–90
Bureaupathology, 89–90
Busyness, 172

Capacity to increase performance, 216
Career mobility, change and, 567–568
Career planning, 305
Career process types, 294–295
Career stages, 128–152
Carroll, S. J. 661
Carter, Jimmy, 167, 403
Cartwright, D. 374
Categorization, effect of, 162
Causality, 594–595, 596
Center for the Study of Group Dynamics, 17
Challenge, 254, 304–305
Change
  career mobility tied to, 567–568

Change *(continued)*
  competition encourages, 567
  data to compel, 591, 592
  durability of, 618
  gaining compliance for, 573–574
  justifications for, 573–574
  people seek, 567
  resistance to stability and, 568
  strategies for, 572–575
Change dynamics, 567–572
Change methods, 624–626
Change, organizational
  from bottom to top, 577–580
  depth of, 574
  expectations of, 574–575
  forces for, 568–569
  Norwegian experiments in, 579–580
  process of, 575–577
  readiness for, 570–572
  resistance to, 560, 569–572
  strategies for, 572–575
  sustaining, 580–581
Charismatic basis to justify compliance, 76, 78, 80
Charismatic response to leader, 403–404
Chin, R., 572–574
Church, Roman Catholic, 57–58
  informal personnel system for, 494
  organization of, 57–58
  traditional justification for, 77–78
  training for, 140–141
Claiming, 495, 526–527, 645. *See also* Scrap
Classical management theory, 27–28, 73
Clientele, personnel tailored to, 133
Clothes, 156–158, 166, 167
Clothing and appearance. *See* Impression management
CMF. *See* Cumulative Merit Funding
Coach in socialization, 145
Coal-getting technologies (the Tavistock Studies), 380
Coalitions of lower participants, 340
Coercive power relationships, 74–75
Cognitions, managing, 229–232
Cognitive balance theory, 261–265
Cognitive data, 599
Cognitive dissonance theory, 263–265
Cognitive process, 223–228
Cohesiveness of group. *See also* Group cohesion
  appeal of, 542
  productivity and, 378–380, 382–384

  in subunit, 464
Collective behavior, 8–10
Collectivity, 8, 9
Collegial authority, 82, 83
Command, 73
Commitment
  building, 128–131, 142, 146–150, 152
  controlling threats to, 148–149
  definition of, 146
  loss of, 149–150
  in military, 128
  role of, in success, 304
Common good, 27
Common interests and goals, 366–367
Communications process, elements of, 182–189
Communications programs, 196–199
Company song, 146–148
Comparison, social, 296, 299, 300
Competence
  impression of, in medicine, 165–166
  limited, 84, 173
  of subordinate, 171–172
  of superior, 171, 302
Competition
  attitudes and, 189–196
  change encouraged by, 567
  CMF influences, 519, 521
  conflict or, 540
  intragroup, 615
  line management as source of, 196
  meeting the, 189
  multiple channels for, 198–199
  and padding, 185
  perception linked to, 158
  special staff units for, 197–198
  win-lose type of, 544, 545
Completed career, 326–327, 334–337
  cool-out for, 337
  problems presented by, 336–337
Complexity
  organizational, 306
  of technology, 100, 107–108
Compliance, 69–95
  authority grants, 72
  belief in superior effects, 148
  in lower participant, 172, 340–341
  in military, 128
  motivation for, 72
  persuasion achieves, 73, 74, 81–82
  power achieves, 72, 73–74
  relationships of, 72

Compromise
  organizational, 450–451
  personal, 423
Condensation, 186, 187
Confidence in beliefs, 193–196, 423
Conflict
  aftermath of, 539–540
  behavior as, 537
  competition or, 540
  deescalation of, 549–552
  definition of, 537–538
  division of labor produces, 542–544
  escalation of, 544–546
  in goal formulation, 450–451
  hierarchical, 543–544
  incompatibility of goals produces, 537, 541
  potential, 539
  process of, 538–540
  resolving, 368, 549–552
  resource allocation in, 541, 543, 545
  social structure leads to, 542–544
  suppressed, 539
Conflicting stimuli, 227
Conflict management 546–549, 621–624
  communications reduce, 546–549
  control as issue of, 543
  necessity for, 537
  resource allocation as issue of, 543
  strategies for, 549–554
Conformity in organizations, 137–138
Confrontation, 623
Consensual validation, 193, 384–387
Consensus development, 624
Consistency, Principle of, 527–528
Constraints
  goals as, 454–456, 464
  organizational systems have, 31
  predictability requires, 31
  system contains, 47–49
Consultants, outside, 174, 623
Contingency theories, 103, 402–426
Contrast effect, 192
Control
  discretionary, 489–490
  executives regain, 509–510
  expand variety of, 525
  of first-line manager, 490
  limit behaviors for, 525
  over behavior, 490, 510
  over output, 490, 510
  perceived, 517–519
  refinement of, 669

  span of, 27–28
  by standards, 489–490
Coolidge, Calvin, 167
Cooling out the mark, 131, 314–317, 337
Cooperation
  common interests promote, 552
  reciprocal, strategy of, 551–552
  through communication, 548
Coordination of functions, 87. *See also*
    Integration of work activities
Core technology, 102, 103–111
Corporate organization, 54–57
Cost-benefit analysis of effort, 216
Costuming, importance of, 156–158, 166, 167
Counsel, taking, 422
Courtesy requires acceptance, 160
Creativity, control over, 517
Credibility of source, 191
Crime, measurement of, 483–484
Crises, response to, 668
Critical contingency, 60–61
Critical judgment, suspension of, 76, 80–82
Cross-sectional studies, 595–596
Cultural conditioning, 161–162
Cumulative Merit Funding (CMF)
  comparison of, to PIP, 524
  expected benefits of, 516–524
  explanation of, 504
  objectives of, 505–506, 526
  problems with, 516–524

Data
  classifications of, 599
  group-generated, 601–603
  ordering of, 592
  screening of, 592
Data collection
  analysis follows, 593
  attitude survey for, 599, 600
  implementation followed by, 593
  interviews for, 599, 601–603
  observation for, 592
  strategy for, 602, 603–604
  working with target group for, 599, 601–603
Data handbook, 625
Data richness criterion, 600
Deadend career, 327, 337–341
Deci, E. L., 255
Decision
  as consequence of goal, 407
  evaluation of, 593

Decision *(continued)*
  from hypothesis to, 593
  individual, 627–628
  normative, 628
Decision styles, 414
Deescalation, 549–552. *See also* GRIT
  exploitation and, 550
  initiators of, 549
Deference of subordinate, 168–169, 171–172
Democratic supervisory style, 17
Democratizing the workplace, 579, 654. *See also* Job enrichment; Participative management
Demotion, 297
  cool-out applied to, 315–317
  disguising, 311
  stigma of, 314
  threat of, 311
  two functions of, 311
Dependability of subordinate, 171–172
Depersonalization of control, 506, 509–510
Deprivation, 299
Depth of organizational change, 574
Dessler, G., 421
Devil's advocate, need for, 386
Diagnosis, role of, in change process, 575, 576
Diagonal promotion, 306
Diagonal relationships, 87
Directed behavior. *See* Reinforcement
Discretion, 72, 90
Disengagement from job, 316–317, 329
Display as behavior, 62, 63
Dissatisfaction, job, 299
Dissonance, cognitive, 325–326
Distortions of perceptions, 325, 344–345
Division of labor, 27, 53
Donnelly, J. H., 661
Dornbusch, S., 140
Dramaturgy, 163–174
  appropriate, for role, 169
  elements of, 166–167
  of lower participant, 172–173
  principles of, 163–169
  roots of, 163–164
  of specialist, 173–174
  of subordinate, 171–172
  of superior, 170–171
  symbols in, 167–169
Dual ladder, 302, 331–334
Dynamics of Bureaucracy, 482, 484–487

Effectiveness
  definition of, 442
  measuring, 443–444
  organizational, 668
Effect, law of, 212, 214
Effects, indirect, 29
Efficiency, 442
Effort and fatigue, 24–25
Effort-performance expectancy, 229
Elitism, 132
Emotionality, rationality versus, 7–8
Empirical-rational strategies for change, 572, 621
Employment agency, measurement in, 482, 484–487
Encounter groups. *See* Laboratory training groups
Enrichment of job. *See* Job enrichment
Environment
  buffering of, 112–113
  characterizing, 112
  concentration in, 112
  definition of, 111
  effect of, on recruitment, 132–133
  effect of, on socialization, 133
  enacting the, 116
  influence of, 32–33, 47–49
  loose coupling in, 112, 113
  organizational adaptation to, 111–117, 137–138
  perceptions of, 116–117
  stable, 112
  turbulent, 112, 116
Equal opportunity recruiting, 132–133
Equity theory, 265–268, 300–303
Esprit de corps, 411, 412, 417, 615
Esteem needs, 252
Etzioni, A., 74–75
Evaluation
  mode of, 511–513
  personal or impersonal, 511–513, 516
  role of, in measurement, 479
Evans, M. G., 417
Executives
  immunity of, to problem disclosure, 575
  looking like, 162
  successful, 422–423
Exercise, law of, 212–213, 214
Expectancy theory, 228–229, 238, 239
Expectations
  of consequences of change, 574–575

data consistent with, 527–528
goal seeking and, 223–225
perceptions affect, 6
of promotion, 299
of reinforcement, 221
about social roles, 34–35
Expected behaviors, 11–12
Expediency, 469
Experimental studies, 595, 596–599
Expertise
authority of, 82–83, 89, 407–408
of lower participant, 339
of message source, 191
of specialist, 173–174
External events, influence of, 28
Extinction, 214

Face validity, 600, 604
Facial expressions, 166–167
Facts, "revised" versions of, 508
Failure. *See also* Success
adaptations to, 314–317
ambiguity surrounding, 313–314, 352
consequences of, 292
"cooling out" after, 131, 314–317, 337
definitions of, 292, 297–298
excessive fear of, 311, 351
hiding, 188, 297
motivational consequences of, 311–314
rate of, 312–313
severity of consequences of, 312–313
success defined by, 310–311
terminology of, 313–314
Fair day's work, 11, 268, 644
Family, company as, 189
Fast track upward, 296, 297, 301–302, 305
"Father of scientific management" (F.W. Taylor), 14, 221
Fatigue
avoidance of, 223
effect of, 14–15
effort and 24–25
Favors, exchange of, 88–89, 425
Fayol, Henri, 27
Fear
as basis for compliance, 74, 80
problem disclosure discouraged by, 645
risk taking discouraged by, 615
Federal Mediation and Conciliation Service, 552
Feedback
change process contains, 576
factor of, in job enrichment, 272–276
improved performance through, 351–352
need for, in organizations, 28, 31
Feedback and control process
Ashby's law in, 525
depersonalization and, 509–510
impact of CMF on, 519
in MBO, 659–664
organizational system contains, 39–41
reports in, 498–499
Feedback loop, 188–189, 196–199
Fein, Mitchell, 232–234
Fiedler, F. E., 401–402, 422–423
Filley, A. C., 404, 412
Financial incentive systems, 9, 35, 230
First impressions, 163
First-line management
control by, 106, 490
goals of, 457–458
Fixed interval reinforcement, 217–221
Fixed ratio reinforcement, 217–221
Fleishman, Edwin, 16, 411
Flexibility in leader, 423
Ford Motor Company, 117, 186–187, 657–659
Foremen, training of, 20–27
Formality of socialization, 144–145
Formal organization, 32–33
bureaucracy as, 83–90
components of, 47–49
roles linked form, 408
Forrester, Jay, 24
Fortune, 296, 297, 301–302
Fox and Henhouse Principle, 482
French, J. R. P., 78, 79
French, W. L., 621, 626
Friedlander, F., 571, 624
Functional differentiation, 72, 87. *See also* Organization chart
Functional socialization, 464
Functional specialization, 53
Function and status, 59–61
Future of organizational behavior study, 668–670

Generalization
definition of, 213
rewards and, 223
General Motors, 117, 265–268, 657–659
Goal-directed behavior, 237

Goal displacement
  causes of, 468–469
  consequences of, 469
  definition of, 467
Goal effectiveness
  definition of, 443
  goal achievement as, 444–445
Goal formation process
  elements of, 450
  model of, 453–454
  schematic of, 468
Goal incompatibility, 552
Goal interference, 538–539
Goals. *See also* Action goals; Personal goals; Planning goals; Subunit, goals of
  conflict of, 6, 236, 615
  consequences of, 467
  difficult, 237
  functional differentiation in, 458–460
  incentive properties of, 235–239
  of individual vs. management, 227
  measurement incompatible with, 537
  measurement orientation of, 491
  organizational level and, 459
  paths to, 235, 236
  setting of, 235–239
  sharing, 365
  specific, 237
  superordinate, 552
  of those in authority, 236
  valued, 238
  work, incentives attached to, 210
Goal seeking, 223
Goal sets, 453–454, 490
Goal statements, 454–456
Goffman, Erving, 160, 162, 163, 314–316
Good of the organization, 450, 463–467, 534–537
Graen, G., 410
Grass-roots goal development, 464–466
Greiner, L. E., 576–577
Grievances
  blocked channels of, 645–647
  nonresolution of, 540
GRIT, 550–552
Group. *See also* Behavior of group
  definition of, 360, 365, 372
  development of, 365–369
  equity ensured by, 377
  goal setting of, 381–382
  identity of, for members, 375–376
  members protected by, 377–378
  norms in, 371, 372–374
  primary, 9, 15–17
  structure of, 369–372, 378
  supportiveness of, 377
  task accomplishment in, 376
  tyranny of, 618
Group cohesion, 256, 374–384
  definition of, 374–375
  development of, 375
  leader influences, 378
  strength of, 375
Group cohesiveness. *See* Cohesiveness of group
Group conflict. *See* Conflict, group
Group dynamics, 16–17
Groups, primary, 15–17
Groupthink, 384–387, 615
Growth needs, 252–253
Growth rate, organizational, 307
Gustavsen, B., 579–580

Halo effect, 83, 162
Harris, E. F., 411
Hawthorne Studies, 15, 24–25, 29
Heller, Frank A., 416
Herzberg, F., 253–256, 271–272, 275
Herzberg two-factor (M-H) theory
  dynamics of, 254
  extrinsic factors in, 253
  intrinsic factors in, 253–256
  job satisfaction researched in terms of, 268, 271
Hierarchical interaction patterns, 627–631
Hierarchy, pyramid of. *See* Pyramidal squeeze; Structure of opportunity
Higher order needs, 256–258, 259
Historical records as standards, 644
Hofstede, G. 662
Homans, George, 16
Horizontal moves, interpreting, 310
House, R. J., 404, 412, 417
Human process approach to change, 626–627
Human relations in industry, 16

Ideal bureaucracy, 76–77
Ideology in organization, 132
Identity, group confers, 373–376
"Illegal" activities, masking, 173
Illusion, group, 384–387
Images, constructed, 185
Impersonality of bureaucracy, 84–85
Impression management, 156–175

for blacks and women, 352–353
CMF shapes, 521
confirmatory facts in, 160
definition of, 35, 124–125, 158
dramaturgy in, 163–173
failure of, 497
importance of, 158–160
lower participant in, 172–173
as misrepresentation, 158, 159–160, 482
organizations use, 168
overview of, 160–161
perceptions in, 161–163
specialist in, 173–174
subordinate in, 171–172
superior in, 170–171
Incentive properties of goal, 210, 235
Incentives. *See also* Motivations
advancement as, 237
definition of, 213
as motivations and goals, 235–239, 249
system preconditions of, 232–234
wage, 9, 223–228, 237, 275
Incompatibility of goals, 236, 613
Industrial engineers (IEs)
PIP and, 646
trade-offs with, 424–425
Inequities, perceptions of, 230
Influence, types of, 73–74
Informal organization
definition of, 62, 424
leadership influenced by, 424–425
Information
discrepant, 192–193
distortion of, 507, 575
need for, in change process, 575, 576
sensitive, 339–340
use of, for control, 507
Information flow restriction, 148, 171, 423
Information overload, 198
Innocence of lower participant, 172
Innovations, technical, acceptance of, 572
Institute for Applied Behavioral Science, 17
Institute for Social Research (ISR), 16–17, 423
Institutional environment, 115–116
Instrumentality
definition of, 221
of group membership, 375–378
of leader, 420
of performance, 230
theory of, 228–229
Integration of work activities, 47–48, 53–61, 72–74

Interaction patterns, changing
methods for, 616–621
reasons for, 613–615
research on, 624–627
strategies for, 621–624
Interaction system, 38–39, 359–360
Interest, inherent, of job, 7
Interface, foreman as, 26
Internal process effectiveness, 443–444
International Harvester Company, 26–27
Interpersonal process consultation, 624–625
Interrelatedness
of systems, 28, 29–30
of work activities, 100
Interview for data collection, 599, 600
Invulnerability, illusion of, 385
Irrationality in groups, 384–387
Ivancevich, J. M., 661

Janis, Irving, 384–387
Japanese industry, 453, 657
Job descriptions and compensation, 302
Job enrichment, 271–277. *See also*
Democratizing the workplace;
Participative management
autonomous work group and, 654–655
expectations of, 574–575
motivation dynamics of, 273–274
problems with, 276–277
restructuring tasks as, 110
technological constraints to, 276–277
who wants, 277
Job rotation, 574–575
Job satisfaction, 268–271, 645
Job security, 7
Job-switching in AWGs, 656
Justifications for compliance
charismatic type of, 76, 78, 80
legal type of, 76–77, 80
organizational change may require, 573–574
traditional type of, 76, 77–78, 80
Justification for customs, 569, 571

Kabanoff, B., 372
Kahn, R. L., 253, 424, 569
Kanter, Rosabeth, 329
Katz, D., 253, 424, 569
Kerr, S., 404, 412
Klein, S. M., 300
Krupp, Alfred, 83

Laboratory training groups, 616–619, 625

Lateral movement
  horizontal move as, 310
  transmotion as, 297
Lawler, E. E., 225, 252, 255
Law of effect, 212, 214
Law of exercise, 212–213, 214
Leader
  directive, 422–423
  followership defines, 400
  instrumentality of, 420
  poor, 398–399
  power use of, 400, 405–408
  resources accrued by, 423–425
Leader behavior, 383, 384, 401–402
  dimensions of, 410–411
  group goals and, 417–422
  lateral behavior as, 423–425
  organizational support for, 404–408
  power base of, 408–418
  productivity affected by, 383, 384
  relations upward in, 425–426
Leader-follower dyad, 369, 410
Leader-group relations, 410–412
Leadership
  charismatic response to, 403–404
  CMF influences, 520
  continuum of, 401–402
  definition of, 399–400, 403–404
  managerial, 625
  in organizational context, 422–426
  political behavior as, 422–426
  role of, in group, 78, 369–370
  traits of, 400, 401
Leadership theory, 400, 401–402
Legality of bureaucracy, 76–77
Legitimacy, 78
Leveling, 186, 187
Lewin, Kurt, 17
Likeability of message source, 191
Likert, Rensis, 17, 401–402, 628–631
Lincoln Electric Co., 232–234
Link pin, supervisor as, 408–409, 412–414, 423, 425–426
Litwin, G. H., 261
Locke, E. A., 413, 654
Locus of control, raising, 517–519, 627, 645
Looking good, 469
Lordstown plant case, 265–268
Loss of commitment, 149–150
Louis, Meryl, 143–144
Lower participants
  change started by, 577–580
  control over, 338
  dramaturgy of, 172–173
  power of, 338–341
  who are, 337
Loyalty
  to group, 384–387
  personal, 85
  of subordinate, 171
Lyon, H. L., 661

McClelland, D. C., 257–258
McConkey, D. D., 661
McGregor, Douglas, 251
Maintaining motivation, 291–293
Management by objectives (MBO), 659–664
Management hierarchy, 72
Management, leadership or, 78
Management systems (Likert), 628–632
Managerial role facets, 258–260
Mann, F. C., 628
March, J., 18–19
Marginal satisfaction, 216
Martin, N. H., 422–423
Maslow, Abraham, 251–261
Material rewards, 35, 148, 230
Mayo, Elton, 14–15
MBA program
  careers after, 296, 297
  functions of, 135
MBO. See Management by objectives
Means-end relationships and measures, 511–513
Measurement in organizations
  in business, 488–489
  definition of, 478–479
  different approaches to, 482–490
  in employment agency, 482, 484–487
  Fox and Henhouse Principle of, 482
  intended consequences of, 484, 486
  as motivational tools, 491
  multiple indicators for, 488–489, 490, 494
  perfect, sought, 479–480
  single indicator for, 488, 490, 494–495
  technology and, 495–497
  type of, used, 511–512
  unintended consequences of, 484–486
  in the university, 487–488
  work technology and, 511
Measurements, characteristics of, 491–495
Mechanistic system, 115–116
Mediator, 421
Messages, 183–186, 192
Metaphors, use of, 184
M-H theory. See Herzberg two-factor theory

Miles, R. E., 628
Military, the
 adaptations of, 137–138
 basic training in, 376
 change of interaction patterns in, 624–625
 material rewards in, 128
 motivation in, 615
 need for predictability in, 128
 new recruit in, 126–128
Mindguarding in groupthink, 386
Minorities
 professionals among, 345–353
 statuses of, 326, 337
Minority professional, 341–353
Minor, John B., 258–260
Mintzberg, H., 399
Misperceptions, 6, 7
Mitchell, T. R., 417
MIT, groups studied at, 17
Mobility, blocked. *See* Blocked mobility
Mobility system, 36–38
Model with different outcomes, 568
Moderates in path-goal theory, 420–421
Money, 7, 225–228
Morale, 17, 100, 150, 465, 578
Morality in groupthink, 385
Motivation. *See also* Maintaining motivation
 basic concepts of, 218–219
 misconceptions about, 210
Motivation-hygiene (M-H) theory. *See* Herzberg two-factor theory
Motivations
 complexity of, 5–7, 209
 for compliance, 73–92
 financial and material, 35
 job enrichment as, 35–36
 as part of organizational system, 35–36
Motivators–satisfiers, 268
Motives
 personal, 235
 pure, of specialist, 174
Muczyk, J. P., 661–662
Multifaceted approach to change, 626–627
Murphy's law, 441
Mystified fast track stars, 297, 303
Myths, 185–186

National Training Laboratory (NTL), 17
Need arousal in organizations, 260–261, 262
Need hierarchy (Maslow)
 comparison of, to other theories, 252–261
 explanation of, 251
 problems with, 251–252

Need theories
 of cognitive balance, 261–265
 comparison of, 252–261
 of equity, 265–268, 300–303
 Herzberg two-factor theory as a, 253–256
 of higher-order needs, 256–258, 259
 need hierarchy in, 251–252
Negative reinforcement
 compared to punishment, 211–213
 defined, 211
Negative timing, 423
Negotiation
 in goal formulation, 450–451
 lateral relations require, 425
Network of programs, 649, 650
Neutral third party, 623
Nominal group technique, 601–603
Normative power relationships, 75
Normative-reeducative strategies for change, 573, 621–622
Normative structure
 as constraint on behavior, 62
 extent of, 64
 unwritten, 64–65
Normlessness, 371, 373
Norms, 64–65
 acceptable deviations from, 373
 compared to roles, 62, 123
 as constraint on behavior, 62, 127–128
 defined, 62, 123
 rules and, 64–65
 violation of, 65
Northland experiment, 646–647
Norwegian experiments in change, 579–580

O'Brien, G. E., 372
Occupational myth, 133–134
Occupational safety behavior, study of, 220
Ohio State University studies, 16, 401
Oldham, G. R., 273–274
Open system, organization as, 28, 30, 111
Opportunity
 barriers to, 347–351
 goal statement as, 454–456, 464
 Principle of, 526–527
 structure of, 289–322
O'Reilly, Charles, 420
Organic system, 115–116
Organizational behavior
 constraints on, 62, 99–103
 history of study of, 13–19
 major study designs of, 595–599

Organizational change. *See* Change, organizational
Organizational climate, 261, 625
Organizational development (OD), 17
Organizational goals
 identifying, 452–460
 organizational level and, 450–451
 relation of, to personal goals, 451
 time horizons of, 452–453
 typology of, 459
Organizational structure
 a best design for, 100
 constraints on, 79–103
 formality of, 99
 technical core of, 102, 104–108
Organizational system, 28–41
 adaptiveness of, 28, 30–31
 constraints of, 28, 31
 control in, 39–41
 feedback in, 28, 31, 39–41
 interrelatedness of, 28, 29–30, 41
 openness of, to environment, 28, 30
 purposefulness of, 28, 30
Organization chart, 53–61
 of the Church, 57–58
 of the Company, 54–57
 of the Department of Public Welfare, 58
Outgroup, 385, 542
Output, control of, 506, 510

Pairing employees, 262
Parke, E. L., 274
Participative decision making
 advantages of, 415
 constraints on, 416
 decision rules for, 414–415
 models of, 414–417
 requirements for, 414–415
 when inappropriate, 415
Participative-group management system, 628–632
Participative leadership
 behavior of, 411, 412–414
 benefits of, 412
 change efforts that involve, 627
 normative model of, 414–422
 pitfalls of, 413
Participative management. *See also* Democratizing the workplace; Job enrichment
 compliance gained through, 340–341
 development of concept of, 17
Passivity of workers, 25, 26

Past actuals, 644
Patent activity, 527
Path-goal model, 421
Path-goal theory, 228–229, 417–422
Paths to goal, 235, 236
Patterns of social behavior, 123, 124
Peer approval, 7
Pelz, D. C., 413
Pennsylvania Public Utility Commission, 116–117
People-oriented leader behavior, 411
Perceptions, 5–7
 communication linked to, 158
 distortions and biases in, 161–163
 misperceptions and, 5–7
 of people, 161–163
Perceptual filling in, 325, 344–345
Perceptual screens, 158
Performance and incentives, 237–239
Performance-reward expectancy, 230
Personal goals
 CMF affects, 519–520
 organizational goals and, 234–239, 463–464
 subunit goals and, 235, 237
Personnel function, 305–306
Persuasion
 compliance through, 73, 74
 lateral relations require, 425
Peter Principle, 327
Physiological needs, 251–252
Piece rates, 223, 230–232
PIP. *See* Procedures Improvement Program
Planned innovation, 505, 516, 526, 562
Planning goals, 457–458
Plateaued career, 326, 327–334
Poise of superior, 171
Political behavior as leadership, 422–426
Political goals, 457, 467–469
Porras, J. I., 624
Position compared to status, 58–61
Positive reinforcement, 211
Power. *See also* Authority; Persuasion
 allocation of, 405–406
 authority as, 75–83
 coercion in, 74
 compliance effected by, 72, 73–74
 control or, 78
 legitimate use of, 75
 need for, 257–258
 over promotions, 293
Power-coercive strategies for change, 573–574, 621
Power orientation, stages of, 257–258

Power relationships, 74–75
Predictability
  of action, 128
  of environment, 112
  of outcomes, 511
Presocializing institutions, 128, 130, 134–135, 151
Pressure in change process, 575, 576
Prestige, symbols of, 75
Presumption of power, 87
Principles of management, Fayol's, 27–28
Procedures Improvement Program (PIP)
  comparison of, to CMF, 524, 526
  comparison of, to SIMP and PIPC, 650
  modification of, 643–649
  Northland experiment of, 646–647
Process approach, 26–27
Processing in socialization, 145
Production, level of, 9, 221–223
Productivity, 14–15, 17
Product line differentiation, 87
Professionalism instead of advancement, 330–331
Profit maximization, 450
Projection, 162–163
Promotion
  within categories, 293
  diagonal, 294
  expectation of, 292
  lateral, 293–294
  to manager, 294
Psychological safety, 617
"Publish or perish" measurement, 487
Punishment
  control over, 74
  definition of, 211
  negative reinforcement or, 211–213
  as purpose of demotion, 311
Purposeful systems, organizations as, 28, 30
Pyramidal squeeze, 297, 327. *See also* Structure of opportunity

Quality as indicator of performance, 488, 490
Quality circles, 657
Quality, norm of, 644
Quantitative measures of outcomes, 509
Quantity as indicator of performance, 488, 490, 509
Questionnaire in research, 465
QWL programs, 658, 669–670

Raia, A. P., 660, 661
Ramquist, Judith, 667

Rationality
  economic, 6
  limited, 84
  principles of, 5–8
Rationalization by group, 385
Raven, B., 78, 79
Reality shock, 130–131, 142, 152
Reality, social
  construction of, 185
  unique views of, 187–188
Receiver of communications, 186–187
Recognition factor, 253–254
Recruiting traps, 135–137
Recruitment, 27, 130, 151
  beginning of, 133–135
  characteristics affecting, 131–133
  CMF affects, 520–521
  of minorities, 341–343
  patterns of, 133–140
  problems with, 135–137
  tests for, 341–343
  value orientation in, 131–132
Reference groups, 296, 299
Reinforcement
  continuous or partial, 217–221
  definition of, 211
  frequency of, 216–217
  importance of, 220–221
  model of, 215
  negative, 211–213
  positive, 211
  schedules of, 217–221
  sustaining change requires, 212–213
"Reinforcements of the future," 213
Reinforcement theory, 642
Relatedness needs, 252–253
Relative deprivation, 299
Reliability criterion, 599, 603
Remunerative power relationships, 75
Requisite variety, 525
Resocialization, 130
Resource allocation
  as factor in conflict, 451–452
  leader controls, 425–426
Resources on environment, 111, 404, 463–465, 466
Responsibility in Herzberg two-factor theory, 254
Restricting production, 9
Retaliation, 449–452
Rewards
  advanced status as, 35
  allocation of, 377, 405

Rewards *(continued)*
  control over, 74
  definition of, 211
  equity in, 300–303
  incentives tied to, 210, 213
  insufficient, 148, 230
  leader distributes, 405, 406–407
  material and financial, 35
  quality of, 216
  quantity of, 214–216
Rightness of the enterprise, 148, 149–150, 326
Rights of superior, 75
Rites of passage, 131, 142–144
Roberts, Karlen, 420
Role behavior
  and complements, 63
  social structure of, 63
Role expectations, 344, 372
Role models for blacks and women, 350–351
Role motivation theory, 258–260
Roles
  assumption of, 126–153, 370–371
  definition of, 62, 63, 123
  norms compared to, 62, 63
  social, in organizations, 11–12, 34–35, 62
Role transitions, demotivating, 130, 131
Rosenbaum, James, 294–295
Rowan, Brian, 114–115
Rules
  circumvention of, 340
  definition of, 64
  formal, 64
  norms and, 64–65

Saab plant, 651–656
Safe positions, 352
Safety needs, 251–253
Salary structure, equity in, 302
Sanctions, leader distributes, 405
Satiation, 214
Sayles, Leonard, 16
Scanlon Plan, 664–668
Schein, Edgar, 128–131, 371
Schneier, I., 371
Scientific Management, 14
Scrap, 488
Screening by presocializing institutions, 135
Screen, symbols used as, 148
Seashore, Stanley, 378–380, 381
Selection as purpose of demotion, 311
Self-actualization needs, 251–253
Self-censorship in groups, 385

Self-regulation, 197
Sense making, surprise and, 143–144
Sensitivity training. *See* Laboratory training group
Sentiments, manipulation of, 75
Shaman as early specialist, 173
Sharpening, 186, 187
Shephard, H. A., 368
Sherif, Muzafir, 373
Simon, H., 18–19, 75
SIMP (Simplification, Improvement and Motivational Program)
  compared to PIP and PIPC, 649–650
  explanation of, 648
Sims, J. H., 422–423
Sincerity of superior, 171
Sirota, D., 654
Skills, 300, 376
Skills training, 133
Sloan School of Management, 128
Smigel, Erwin, 138–140
Social context of message, 187–188
Social cues, 274
Social expectations, 123
Socialization
  anticipatory, 128–130, 133–134, 151
  building commitment in, 146–150, 152
  career stages in, 128–131
  CMF affects, 520–521
  coach in, 145
  into company, 12, 128
  into first position, 140–144
  length of, 145
  mechanisms for, 128
  remedial, 133
  serial, 145
  settings, 144–145
Social maintenance role, 369
Social perceptions and rewards, 6
Social position, 11
Social relations
  in informal organization, 424–425
  in work group, 15–17
Social roles. *See* Roles
Social structure in organizations, 11–12
Society for Applied Anthropology, 16
Sociotechnical system, 24–28
"Soldiering," 221–223
Sorenson, B. S., 579–580
Source
  of communications, 182–183, 191
  relation to, 491, 494

Soviet managerial system, 488–489
Span of control, 27–28, 106, 490
Specialist, dramaturgy of, 173–174
Specialization, 53
Special relationships, 87–88
Specialties, change in, 306
Specificity, degrees of, 450–451
Sponsor, organizational, 306, 351
Stage setting, 166, 167
Standards
  conflicting, 488–489, 541
  developing, 568–569
  past actuals as, 644
  setting of, 424–425
  synthetic, 644
Status
  definition of, 61
  different, or demotion, 325–326
  identity associated with, 375–376
  of message source, 191
  in military, 126–128
  versus position, 58–61
Status leveling, 126, 140
Stereotyping, 162, 349–350, 385
Strategic position in organization, 305
Stringer, R. A., 261
Structure of opportunity, 289–322, 520
Subcultures in organization, 161–162
Suboptimization, 460
Subordinate
  accountability of, 489
  dramaturgy of, 171–172
Subunit
  finding resources for, 464
  forming new, 466
  goals of, 457–458, 463–466
  specificity of, 450–451, 465
Success. *See also* Failure
  alternative definitions of, 316
  anticipation of, 304
  commitment and, 304, 307
  definitions of, 292, 297–298
  experience of, 304
  models for, 133, 139
  motivation and, 307
  perceiving, 298–303
  rate of, 297
  unequal, 300
"Success breeds success" model, 303–304
Suggestions program, 648
Superior
  disciplining, 340
  dramaturgy of, 171–172
  standards modified by, 489
Superior-subordinate relationship, 73–92, 148–149, 614–615
Superordinate goal, 552–554
Supervision, 17
Supportiveness, social, 377, 617
Suppression of conflict, 539
Survey feedback method, 624–626. *See also* Attitude survey
Survey Research Center, 17
Sustaining change, 580–581
Suttle, J. L., 252, 255
Symbolic acts in military, 128
Symbols
  in communications, 183–186
  distance maintained by, 148
  importance of, 167–168
  learning new, 127–128
  of rank and status, 404–405
Synthetic standard, 644
System 4 management (Likert), 627–632
System, organization as, 561
System resource effectiveness, 443
Systems designer, 101–102
Systems effects, problems of, 13

Talented, advancement of, 292
Talent, limited call for, 159
Task accomplishment, 426
Task complexity, 100
Task-oriented leader behavior, 411
Task process consultation, 625–626
Task role in groups, 369
Tausky, C. 274
Tavistock studies, 380–381
Taylor, Frederick Winslow, 14, 221
Team building activities, 621–624
Technical environment, 115–116
Technical innovations, acceptance of, 572
Technological determinism, 109–110
Technology. *See also* Core technology; Work technology
  continuous-process, 104, 105
  craft, 105
  definitions of, 100–101
  as determinant of organizational structure, 32–33, 668–669
  frontiers of, 519
  as leading factor, 102, 103
  mass-production, 104
  small-batch, 104

Technology *(continued)*
  structure and, 101–102, 104–107
  zone of indifference and, 81–82
Technostructural approach to change, 626–627
Termination resulting from failure, 297
Test anxiety, 343
T-groups, 17, 616–619
Thompson, James, 90
Thompson, Victor, 89, 159, 171
Thorsrud, E., 579–580
Threats to commitment, 148–150
Time-efficient model, 415–416
Time-investment model, 415–416
Time lag and trust, 228
Timing, negative, 423
Tit-for-tat mentality, 545, 551
Tokenism, 351–352
Tosi, H., 661
Trade-offs, 424–425, 488
Traditional management theory, 103
Traditional model of classifying extent of participation, 628
Tradition in bureaucracy, 569–572
Training groups. *See* Laboratory training groups; T-groups
Training period, 134–135
Trait theory, 410
Transmotion, 297
Trust of message receiver, 183, 186, 187
Turbulent environment, 112, 116
Two-factor theory (Herzberg)
  comparison of, to other need theories, 255, 268–277
  extrinsic factors in, 253
  intrinsic factors in, 253–256

Uncertainty
  dealing with, 90
  of environment, 112–116
  organization reacts to, 115–116
  ritual ordeals of, 165–166
Uncontrolled longitudinal studies, 595, 596
Understandings, norms as, 64–65
Uniformity requirement in military, 127–128
Unit managers in control, 644
Unity of command, 27

Unity of direction, 27
University, measurement in, 487–488
Utility concept, 5–7, 209, 453–454, 618

Validity criterion, 599–600, 603
Value orientation of organization, 131–132
Values, unlearning old, 140–142
Variable reinforcement, 217–221
Victims of Groupthink, 384–386
Vietnam, war in, 149–150
Visibility of exceptions, 347–348
Voice in impression, 166
Volkswagon plant, 655
Vroom and Yetton model, 414–417

Wage incentive, 9
Wagner Act, 15
Wahba, M. A., 252
Wall Street Journal, 291–292, 403
Wall Street types, 138–140
Watergate incident, 149
Watson, Thomas J., Jr., 85
Weber, Max, 83, 85–86, 90
Web of favors, 88–89
Weldon Company management, 631–632
Western Electric Co., 15, 25
Whyte, William F., 16, 227–228
Wildcat strikes, 539–540
Wolfson, A. D., 654
Women in workforce, 303, 326, 337, 346–353
Woodward, Joan, 18–19, 103, 104–105, 111, 116
Work ethic, 82
Work goals as personal goals, 234–235
Workplace, democratizing the, 579, 654
Work satisfaction, PIP and, 643
Work technology, 99–103
  CMF and, 516
  constraints imposed by, 47–49, 110
  definition of, 100–101
  measurement system based on, 511
  recruitment based on, 132

"Zero defects" program, 266
Zone of indifference, 80–82
  definition of, 78
  extent of, 304

221276